ENTERPRISE INFORMATION SYSTEMS VI

T0191735

Enterprise Information Systems VI

Edited by

ISABEL SERUCA
Universidade Portucalense,
Porto, Portugal

JOSÉ CORDEIRO
INSTICC, Setúbal, Portugal

SLIMANE HAMMOUDI
Ecole Supérieure d'Electronique de L'Ouest,
Angers, France

and

JOAQUIM FILIPE
INSTICC, Setúbal, Portugal

 Springer

A C.I.P. Catalogue record for this book is available from the Library of Congress.

ISBN-13 978-90-481-6927-6
ISBN-10 1-4020-3675-2 (e-book)
ISBN-13 978-1-4020-3675-0 (e-book)

Published by Springer,
P.O. Box 17, 3300 AA Dordrecht, The Netherlands.

www.springeronline.com

Printed on acid-free paper

Printed in the Netherlands.

TABLE OF CONTENTS

PREFACE

This book contains the best papers of the Sixth International Conference on Enterprise Information Systems (ICEIS 2004), held in Porto (Portugal) and organized by INSTICC (*Institute for Systems and Technologies of Information, Communication and Control*) in collaboration with PORTUCALENSE UNIVERSITY, who hosted the event.

Following the route started in 1999, ICEIS has become a major point of contact between research scientists, engineers and practitioners on the area of business applications of information systems. This conference has received an increased interest every year, from especially from the international academic community, and it is now one of the world largest conferences in its area. This year, five simultaneous tracks were held, covering different aspects related to enterprise computing, including: *"Databases and Information Systems Integration"*, *"Artificial Intelligence and Decision Support Systems"*, *"Information Systems Analysis and Specification"*, *"Software Agents and Internet Computing"* and *"Human-Computer Interaction"*. The sections of this book reflect the conference tracks.

ICEIS 2004 received 609 paper submissions from 60 different countries, from all continents. 89 papers were published and orally presented as full papers, i.e. completed work, 145 position papers reflecting work-in-progress were accepted for short presentation and another 138 for poster presentation. These numbers, leading to a "full-paper" acceptance ratio below 15%, show the intention of preserving a high quality forum for the next editions of this conference. Additionally, as usual in the ICEIS conference series, a number of invited talks, including keynote lectures and technical tutorials were also held. These special presentations made by internationally recognized experts have definitely increased the overall quality of the Conference and provided a deeper understanding of the Enterprise Information Systems field. Their contributions have been included in a special section of this book.

The program for this conference required the dedicated effort of many people. Firstly, we must thank the authors, whose research and development efforts are recorded here. Secondly, we thank the members of the program committee and the additional reviewers for their diligence and expert reviewing. Thirdly, we thank the invited speakers for their invaluable contribution and for taking the time to synthesise and prepare their talks. Fourthly, we thank the workshop chairs whose collaboration with ICEIS was much appreciated. Finally, special thanks to all the members of the organising committee from INSTICC and from Portucalense University.

Isabel Seruca
Portucalense University/Porto

Joaquim Filipe
INSTICC/Setúbal

Slimane Hammoudi
ESEO/Angers

José Cordeiro
INSTICC/Setúbal

CONFERENCE COMMITTEE

Honorary President:
Jorge Reis Lima, Universidade Portucalense, Portugal

Conference Co-Chairs:
Joaquim Filipe, Escola Superior de Tecnologia de Setúbal, Portugal
Isabel Seruca, Universidade Portucalense, Portugal

Programme Co-Chairs:
José Cordeiro, Escola Superior de Tecnologia de Setúbal, Portugal
Slimane Hammoudi, École Supérieure d' Electronique de l' Ouest, France

Organising Committee:
Jorge Reis Lima, Isabel Seruca, Maria João Ferreira, Paula Morais, Filomena Lopes, José Matos Moreira, Fernando Moreira, Helena Barbosa, Abílio Cardoso, Susana Correia da Silva, Cristina Paes, Sónia Rolland, Paulo Sérgio Costa, Pedro Leão, Alexandra Baldaque, Universidade Portucalense, Portugal.

Senior Programme Committee:

Amaral, L. (PORTUGAL)
Andersen, P. (DENMARK)
Baeza-Yates, R. (CHILE)
Bézivin, J. (FRANCE)
Bonsón, E. (SPAIN)
Carvalho, J. (PORTUGAL)
Cheng, A. (USA)
Coelho, H. (PORTUGAL)
Delgado, M. (SPAIN)
Dietz, J. (THE NETHERLANDS)
Dignum, F. (THE NETHERLANDS)
Figueiredo, A. (PORTUGAL)
Fox, M. (CANADA)
Goldkuhl, G. (SWEDEN)
Greene, T. (USA)
Guimarães, N. (PORTUGAL)
Gupta, J. (USA)
Haton, J. (FRANCE)
Laender, A. (BRAZIL)
Lenzerini, M. (ITALY)
Leonard, M. (SWITZERLAND)
Liu, K. (UK)

Loucopoulos, P. (UK)
Luker, P. (UK)
Lyytinen, K. (USA)
Manolopoulos, Y. (GREECE)
Martins, J. (PORTUGAL)
Matsumoto, M. (JAPAN)
Odell, J. (USA)
Pereira, L. (PORTUGAL)
Pirotte, A. (BELGIUM)
Pohl, K. (GERMANY)
Rolland, C. (FRANCE)
Sharp, B. (UK)
Smirnov, A. (RUSSIA)
Stamper, R. (UK)
Tari, Z. (AUSTRALIA)
Toro, M. (SPAIN)
Tribolet, J. (PORTUGAL)
Vernadat, F. (LUXEMBOURG)
Warkentin, M. (USA)
Weigand, H. (THE NETHERLANDS)
Wieringa, R. (THE NETHERLANDS)

Programme Committee:

Aguilar-Ruiz, J. (SPAIN)
Albers, P. (FRANCE)
Al-Jadir, L. (LEBANON)
Al-Sharhan, S. (KUWAIT)
Anthony, C. (UK)
Antunes, P. (PORTUGAL)
Aparício, J. (PORTUGAL)
Augusto, J. (NORTHERN IRELAND)
Baranauskas, C. (BRAZIL)
Barn, B. (UK)
Barro, S. (SPAIN)
Bastide, R. (FRANCE)
Bellalem, N. (FRANCE)
Bernus, P. (AUSTRALIA)
Bertok, P. (AUSTRALIA)
Biddle, R. (CANADA)
Bittel, O. (GERMANY)
Boavida, F. (PORTUGAL)
Gouveia, L. (PORTUGAL)
Bouchaffra, D. (USA)
Boulanger, D. (FRANCE)
Vasconcelos, J. (PORTUGAL)
Bratko, I. (SLOVENIA)
Brisaboa, N. (SPAIN)
Calejo, M. (PORTUGAL)
Calero, C. (SPAIN)
Camarinha-Matos, L. (PORTUGAL)
Cardoso, J. (PORTUGAL)
Carvalho, F. (BRAZIL)
Castro-Schez, J. (SPAIN)
Cernuzzi, L. (PARAGUAY)
Lopes, M. (PORTUGAL)
Chang, E. (AUSTRALIA)
Chapelier, L. (FRANCE)
Chu, W. (TAIWAN)
Clarke, R. (UK)
Claude, C. (FRANCE)
Colace, F. (ITALY)
Corchuelo, R. (SPAIN)
Costa, E. (PORTUGAL)
Coulette, B. (FRANCE)
Cox, S. (UK)
Dahchour, M. (MOROCCO)
Cesare, S. (UK)

Lucia, A. (ITALY)
Ribeiro, N. (PORTUGAL)
Dolado, J. (SPAIN)
Dubois, G. (FRANCE)
Dubois, J. (FRANCE)
Dustdar, S. (AUSTRIA)
Eardley, A. (UK)
Emery, D. (UK)
Estay, J. (FRANCE)
Fadier, E. (FRANCE)
Favela, J. (USA)
Fernández-Medina, E. (SPAIN)
Ferneda, E. (BRAZIL)
Ferreira, M. (PORTUGAL)
Ferreira, P. (PORTUGAL)
Ferrucci, F. (ITALY)
Flory, A. (FRANCE)
Flynn, D. (UK)
Frank, U. (GERMANY)
Fred, A. (PORTUGAL)
Garbajosa, J. (SPAIN)
Genero, M. (SPAIN)
Giampapa, J. (USA)
González, P. (SPAIN)
Goodwin, R. (AUSTRALIA)
Gordillo, S. (ARGENTINA)
Gouveia, F. (PORTUGAL)
Govaere, V. (FRANCE)
Grönlund, Å. (SWEDEN)
Guerlain, S. (USA)
Gulliksen, J. (SWEDEN)
Gustavsson, R. (SWEDEN)
Schär, S. (SWITZERLAND)
Belguith, L. (TUNISIA)
Hampel, T. (GERMANY)
Hanseth, O. (NORWAY)
Heng, M. (AUSTRALIA)
Herrera, F. (SPAIN)
Higgins, P. (AUSTRALIA)
Hollnagel, E. (SWEDEN)
Hong, J. (UK)
Quang, N. (VIETNAM)
Hu, J. (AUSTRALIA)
Huang, K. (NETHERLANDS)

Hung, P. (AUSTRALIA)
Jahankhani, H. (UK)
Jaime, A. (SPAIN)
Linares, L. (SPAIN)
Joyanes, L. (SPAIN)
Karacapilidis, N. (GREECE)
Karagiannis, D. (AUSTRIA)
Karnouskos, S. (GERMANY)
Kawano, H. (JAPAN)
Kemper, N. (MEXICO)
Kolp, M. (BELGIUM)
Krogstie, J. (NORWAY)
Labidi, S. (BRAZIL)
Lallement, Y. (CANADA)
Lehner, F. (GERMANY)
Mora, C. (SPAIN)
Leung, H. (CHINA)
Libourel, T. (FRANCE)
Lim, J. (SINGAPORE)
Linna, M. (FINLAND)
Ljungberg, J. (SWEDEN)
Loiseau, S. (FRANCE)
Lopes, J. (PORTUGAL)
Lozano, M. (SPAIN)
Lu, J. (CANADA)
Lueg, C. (AUSTRALIA)
Madeira, E. (BRAZIL)
Magnin, L. (CANADA)
Malekovic, M. (CROATIA)
Mamede, N. (PORTUGAL)
Sobral, J. (BRAZIL)
Marcos, E. (SPAIN)
Marir, F. (UK)
Martins, M. (PORTUGAL)
Martin, H. (FRANCE)
Meier, A. (SWITZERLAND)
Mendes, E. (NEW ZEALAND)
Nguifo, E. (FRANCE)
Silva, M. (PORTUGA)
Moghadampour, G. (FINLAND)
Mokhtar, H. (USA)
Molli, P. (FRANCE)
Morais, P. (PORTUGAL)
Moreira, F. (PORTUGAL)
Moreira, J. (PORTUGAL)

Munoz-Avila, H. (USA)
Olivas, J. (SPAIN)
Santos, L. (ARGENTINA)
Oriogun, P. (UK)
Papadopoulos, G. (CYPRUS)
Pastor, O. (SPAIN)
Gramaje, M. (SPAIN)
Penzel, T. (GERMANY)
Lopes, G. (PORTUGAL)
Péridy, L. (FRANCE)
Peters, S. (NETHERLANDS)
Petta, P. (AUSTRIA)
Pires, J. (PORTUGAL)
Plodzien, J. (POLAND)
Poels, G. (BELGIUM)
Polo, M. (SPAIN)
Prasad, B. (USA)
Price, E. (USA)
Ramos, P. (PORTUGAL)
Reimer, U. (SWITZERLAND)
Revenu, M. (FRANCE)
Richir, S. (FRANCE)
Riquelme, J. (SPAIN)
Rito-Silva, A. (PORTUGAL)
Rivreau, D. (FRANCE)
Rodriguez, P. (SPAIN)
Rosa, A. (PORTUGAL)
Rossi, G. (ARGENTINA)
Roztocki, N. (USA)
Ruiz, F. (SPAIN)
Rumpe, B. (GERMANY)
Salem, A. (EGYPT)
Samier, H. (FRANCE)
Schang, D. (FRANCE)
Scharl, A. (AUSTRALIA)
Schoop, M. (GERMANY)
Shah, H. (UK)
Shao, J. (UK)
Shi, Z. (CHINA)
Shih, T. (TAIWAN)
Silva, A. (PORTUGAL)
Skaf-Molli, H. (FRANCE)
Soule-Dupuy, C. (FRANCE)
Stary, C. (AUSTRIA)
Sun, L. (UK)

Taniar, D. (AUSTRALIA)
Terzis, S. (UK)
Tolksdorf, R. (GERMANY)
Torkzadeh, R. (USA)
Toval, A. (SPAIN)
Uchyigit, G. (UK)
Ultsch, A. (GERMANY)
Vallecillo, A. (SPAIN)
Vasiu, L. (UK)
Verdier, C. (FRANCE)
Vila, M. (SPAIN)

Vinh, H. (VIETNAM)
Vizcaino, A. (SPAIN)
Wang, F. (UK)
Weghorn, H. (GERMANY)
Weiss, G. (GERMANY)
Winstanley, G. (UK)
Wojtkowski, W. (USA)
Wrembel, R. (POLAND)
Yang, H. (UK)
Yano, Y. (JAPAN)
ZongKai, L. (CHINA)

Invited Speakers:

Kalle Lyytinen, Case Western Reserve University, USA
Tom Gilb, Norway
Leszek A. Maciaszek, Macquarie University, Australia
Pericles Loucopoulos, University of Manchester, United Kingdom
Jim O. Coplien, Vrije Universiteit Brussel, USA
Juan Carlos Augusto, University of Southampton, United Kingdom
Balbir S. Barn, Thames Valley University, United Kingdom

Invited Papers

PROJECT FAILURES: CONTINUING CHALLENGES FOR SUSTAINABLE INFORMATION SYSTEMS

P. Loucopoulos
The University of Manchester, Manchester, UK,
pl@co.umist.ac.uk

K. Lyytinen
Case Western Reserve University Cleveland , U.S.A.
kjl13@cwru.edu

K. Liu
University of Reading, Reading, U.K.
k.liu@reading.ac.uk

T. Gilb
Gilb International Consulting and Training,
Tom@Gilb.com

L.A. Maciaszek
Macquarie University, Sydney, Australia,
leszek@ics.mq.edu.au

Abstract: Much has been written and many discussions have taken place on the causes and cures of IT projects. This introspection is not a new phenomenon. It has been going on as long as industrial size IT systems became into being. The continuing reliance of businesses, government and society on such systems coupled to the realisation that only a little progress has been made in the last 20-30 years in delivering effective and efficient systems are sufficient motivations for continuing this debate. This paper is the product of such a public debate by the authors during the 2004 International Conference on Enterprise Information System. The paper focuses on four topics: ecological complexity, product complexity, project management and education.

1 INTRODUCTION

Information technology investments have always been risky and their mortality rates have in the long term been above the average in any industry. Research into system development in general and software engineering in particular has, over the years, suggested a plethora of approaches to address this challenge (Fitzerald, 1996) and many of them have been shown to improve software development capability. Improved technological approaches in a number of fields such as requirements engineering (Bubenko, 1995; Loucopoulos et al., 1995), conceptual modelling (Doyle et al., 1993; Yu et al., 1994), and design paradigms (Carroll, 2002; Potts, 1996) represent very significant responses of researchers and practitioners in ameliorating this situation. A recent study (The-Standish-Group, 2003) revealed that when compared to a similar study carried out in 1995, the number of failed projects has decreased, as has the cost overruns but projects continue to be delivered late and over 50% of them fail to meet their initial objectives

The UK National Audit Office in its report of 19th January 2004 on Ministry of Defence Major Projects stated that "... total current forecast costs are £51.9 billion, an increase of £3.1 billion in the last year and some six per cent over approval." and that "....projects have slipped an average of 18 months beyond their expected delivery dates" (National-Audit-Office, 2004).

This report refers to projects whose complexity and dynamism far exceeds the systems of previous times. A key question therefore is that if we were unsuccessful in delivering yesterday's systems what chance is there for developing tomorrow's systems that are intended to serve a whole raft of complex requirements? Consider the following examples. GM's next generation car will involve over 100 million lines of code and must interface not only with the car control systems (brakes, emission control etc) but also with external entertainment systems, telecommunication systems, and even business applications. Boeing's new 7E7 is not only innovative in its use of material technologies which make it the lightest commercial jet in the world but deals with the challenge of deploying new software platforms that enable large scale integration of design information and production information along the supply chain. Clearly, the main roots and challenges related to overcoming system development risks of such scale are now quite different than they were 10 or 20 years ago.

Naturally, there are many issues that could be examined in a discussion paper. Whilst recognising that these are not the only issues of concern, this paper focuses its attention on four themes:

- Ecological complexity
- Product complexity
- Project management and
- Education

Ecological complexity is about poorly understood and unpredictable interactions with the system

1

I. Seruca et al. (eds.), Enterprise Information Systems VI, 1–8.

development environment and the system development task and is discussed in section 2.

Ecological complexity interacts with and influences other levels of complexity called product complexity. *Product complexity* is normally measured by LOC measures, function points or the number of interacting system components and its theme is taken up in terms of conceptual framework in section 3.

The issue of *project management* is approached from an empirical perspective and is discussed in section 4, in terms of defining the project requirements right and then establishing a set of design actions to meet these requirements.

Educating the developers and project managers of the future, who have to deal with an increasingly challenging set of demands in a complex and fast changing environment, is the topic of section 5.

2   ECOLOGICAL COMPLEXITY

The main issue in very large scale development efforts is in understanding how strategies that drive technological choices -i.e. functional requirements, data standards, platform standards, issues of interoperability- relate to organizational control strategies i.e. who has the right to decide and control such functional requirements, data definitions etc., and how the business value of such decisions will be distributed within the industrial network. In many cases the challenge that developers face is that they cannot assume a centralized control and thereby cannot have the required capability alone to coordinate technological and business development that is necessary to build up a workable business solution.   Most development situations involve stakeholders that cannot be controlled (clients in e-business, suppliers in Boeing, telecommunication companies in case of GM, etc) and who may resist specific ways to coordinate and manage system architectures and resulting solutions.

Any development effort of a large scale socio-technical system (IT investment) within any industry can be configured within two dimensions: (a) the structure of control for information technologies, and (b) the structure of control for human/organization actors.

On the information technologies dimension, the structure of control can be configured either as a centralized (centralized databases, Enterprise Resource Planning Systems) or distributed structure (web-based services).   Likewise, the human/organization actors dimension can also be configured as a centralized structure, with vertical control systems around dominant industry actors (like Boeing in aerospace industry or the Big Three in auto manufacturing) or a distributed structure without such dominant actors (like 2nd and 3rd tier suppliers of manufacturing industries).

A *doubly distributed socio-technical system* is conceived as one in which both the information technologies and the human /organizational actors are distributed, and architectural control is lax. Successful application of information technology to date has fallen outside the boundaries of this type of doubly distributed system. In all three other areas the success has been less successful than originally imagined (e.g. the difficulty in implementing and organizing market based systems in car industry like Covisint).

The original industrial application of information technology began with centralized IT architectures in vertically integrated organizational systems *inside organizations*. In recent years, organizations have developed various forms of IT systems with centralized control that support distributed organizational designs. Prominent examples of such applications include centralized knowledge repositories or ERP systems based on centralized database for the entire enterprise. As organizations have attempted to apply the centralized IT architecture beyond the traditional boundary of the firm, they have faced numerous organizational and technical challenges. For example, many of the small 2nd and 3rd tier suppliers in the aerospace and automotive industries are still not connected to the centralized ERP systems that were implemented by the dominant players in the industry.

Similarly, distributed information technology systems can effectively serve centralized organizations, as web servers and IBM's ambitious plans for 'On Demand' service attest. If organizations attempt to seek to apply this distributed computing model into distributed organizational structures, however, it will require reconfiguration of organizational systems and control around powerful players outside the organization in order to effectively integrate different IT systems and related business processes.

This presents an unprecedented challenge for innovation and organizational change, because knowledge is embedded in local work practices and professional communities, but it must be coordinated across a larger industrial system. Reconfiguring such distributed organizing forms into a centralized system is difficult and in most cases will fail as within the current power system it may be institutionally impossible.

In a doubly distributed (DD) system in particular we do not have many examples of success. Yet, this doubly distributed quadrant will arguably be the next frontier of information technology innovations spanning industrial organizations that lack central power structures. In the DD system, firms are embedded many times in traditional contracting relations, which maintain competitive and zero sum interactions among them. Normally, each professional group has its own favoured and limited set of information technology tools, which are often not easily integrated. What is needed here is a new joined socio-technical design that supports distributed organizing forms through coupling heterogeneous IT infrastructures in multiple communities of practice.

There are multiple challenges in managing and designing such systems:

1. Most of our past research and understanding related to effecting changes in large scale socio-technical systems deal with centralized architectures. There has been much more success in such attempts lately when such control can be assumed. A good example is the success of Docomo's Imode when compared with European WAP strategy in developing and coordinating broadband content delivery to mobile terminals. However, such conditions can be hard, if not impossible to achieve in many situations. Most large scale efforts are currently in one way or another closer to DD system conditions.

2. Most attempts to develop solutions within DD assume that a powerful coalition is established within the industry to provide a power base and create conditions for a bandwagon effect. Example of such powerful coalitions are Big3 in car industry in relation to Covisint, the GEC's (Freddie Mac, Manny Mae) in Mortgage industry, or Nokia, Ericsson and Motorola in mobile service platforms (OMA). These powerbases help create necessary organizational weight for the coalition so that architectural control can be retained within the coalition. Such strategy is difficult, however, if it threatens the bases for current architectural control. For example in mobile industry the current standardization initiative around open platforms for mobile phones (WIPI) is likely to fail as it will loosen the architectural control of key terminal providers (Nokia, Ericsson, Motorola, Samsung) and shift the power balance to new system integrators (e.g. new Chinese rivals, Dell etc) where their core competency is in production and system

integration rather than in product innovation.

3. There is little research in system development literature on how different technological integration mechanisms need to be integrated with alternative organizational control mechanisms (committees, market based competition, when does the control really matter) and how they relate to means to identify and balance system requirements. Emerging work on option pricing and different innovation strategies can be helpful (Fichman, 2004). There is also a need to understand how increased formalization and standardization vs. flexibility and innovation are balanced in such initiatives.

3 PRODUCT COMPLEXITY

Product complexity, has been addressed by several technological solutions that deal with abstraction (wrappers, typing, information hiding), binding mechanisms (late binding, lazy evaluation, RMI), run time control (e.g. messaging protocols), and standardized semantics (ERP, vertical messaging standards).

Traditionally, methodological efforts focused their attention on appropriate description languages, support tools, ways of working, and architectures aimed at essentially ensuring that an engineering-like approach could be followed when developing such systems (Olle et al., 1984; Olle, 1992). The debate has shifted in the past few years towards system co-development whose aim is to ensure alignment between business processes and support technical systems.

In terms of this particular set of concerns, product complexity manifests itself in knowledge components that need to be used during co-development. The term 'enterprise knowledge modelling' refers to a collection of techniques for describing different facets of the *organisational domain* e.g., goals, structures and work roles, flow of information etc, as well as the rationale behind these operations, the *operational domain* e.g., the business processes, business rules etc and the *informational domain* e.g., the database structures, the mappings between different (possibly heterogeneous databases) and the rules for and from discovered patterns of behaviour in data (Loucopoulos, 2000; Bubenko, 1994; Loucopoulos et al., 1997; Loucopoulos, 2004).

It is a natural extension to information modelling whereby the models target not just the information system requirements but also the enterprise objectives, the work processes, the customer needs and processes that create value for customers. The models take a holistic view and cut across traditional functional boundaries. Inputs and outcomes to the development process are sign-based artefacts, making it unique amongst all other types of engineering projects. It can be regarded as a semiotic engineering, or a process of *semiosis* (Liu, 2000; Liu et al., 2002).

From a semiotic perspective, an information systems project is a process of transformation from a set of signs (at the level of representation) to another set at a different level. The systems development activities are continual processes of semiosis, each involving different stakeholders. Whilst in traditional information systems development one dealt with strictly IT artefacts, in a co-development project, we deal with multifarious objects in an effort to better align the information system to the enterprise and at the same to explore the opportunities offered by IT in developing the enterprise itself.

A semiotic transformation constitutes an assembly of interrelated sign-based activities logically linked to enable the analyst, designer and others to formalise and elicit requirements using the sign-process (i.e. semiosis). This method is highly efficient in examining and representing the requirements of the different, yet closely interrelated stages and levels of the systems transformation. The key elements which make each transformation works are the norms e.g. the rules and regulations that govern the practise of users, analysts, designers and others within each semiosis process (Liu et al., 2002).

In dealing with product complexity it is important to capture requirements as early as possible and not to rely on an assumption that somehow system requirements will emerge. What distinguishes *early* requirements from *late* (or support system) requirements, is the degree of involvement of client stakeholders. Early requirements are almost exclusively driven by client stakeholders' communication and it is this communication that has to be facilitated through a semiotic process. The modelling approach to be adopted may involve a cycle of hypothesis formulation, testing, and re-formulation until stakeholders have enough confidence about the relevance of the proposed solution. Essentially, one is developing theories, externalised as conceptual models, about the Universe of Discourse and subjects these theories to tests for their validity.

4   PROJECT MANAGEMENT

Experiences have shown that for many failed projects:

- we got our requirements wrong, and
- we did not focus our design energy and project management energy on meeting a clear set of project requirements.

In this section, ten principles of good project management are put forward which have proved in practice be feasible and effective in delivering good quality systems.

> *P1: The critical few product objectives of the project need to be stated measurably.*

The major reason for project investment is always to reach certain levels of product performance. 'Performance' as used here, defines how good the system function is. It includes

- system *qualities* – how well the system performs,
- system *savings* – how cost-effective the system is compared to alternatives such as competitors or older systems. and
- work *capacity* how fast and how much the system can do of work.

In practice one is able to be concerned with about 5 to 20 'most-critical' product performance dimensions. These are the critical dimensions that determine if a project has been a success or failure, in terms of the *product produced* by that project.

> *P2: The project team must be rewarded to the degree they achieve these critical project objectives.*

Of course if we still cannot specify the performance goals quantitatively, then no amount of motivation and freedom will get a project team to move in the right direction. They don't even know what that direction is.

> *P3: There must be a top-level architecture process that focuses on finding and specifying appropriate design strategies for enabling us to meet the critical product performance levels on time.*

If there is no clear quantified set of top-level critical requirements, then an architecture process is bound to fail. The architect cannot compare their design idea's attributes with clear performance and cost requirements. Even if the requirements are perfectly quantified and clear, that is not sufficient. The architecture designs themselves must be specified in sufficient detail to guarantee a necessary level of performance and cost impacts from them.

> *P4: Project specifications should not be polluted with dozens of unclear terms per page; there needs to be a specification quality control, and an exit at less than one major defect remaining per page.*

Experience has shown that any requirement specification has between 80 and 180 'major' defects. This is normally a 'shock' for the people involved. How can there be so many? Most people immediately agree that this is far too many. It is. And it is unnecessary! One should set a limit of no more than one major defect per page remaining before the specification is released for serious uses like design or test planning.

The conclusion is that because we do not carry out even simple inexpensive sampling measures of specification pollution, and we do not set a limit to the pollution, we live in a world of engineering that is normally highly polluted. We pay for this by project delays, and product quality.

> *P5: Design Review must be based on a clean specification, and should be focused on whether designs meet their multiple requirements.*

Before we can review a design specification regarding relevance, we must review it for compliance to rules of specification that assures us about the intelligibility of the specification.

> *P6: The high-risk strategies need to be validated early, or swapped with better ones.*

Engineers have always had a number of techniques for validating risky strategies early. Trials, pilots, experiments, prototypes, etc are the tactics. One approach in IT projects is scheduling the delivery of the risky strategy in an early evolutionary delivery step, to measure what happens – and thus get rid of some of the risk. Early evolutionary delivery steps usually integrate a strategy with a real system and

real users – and are therefore more trustworthy, than for example an expert review panel.

> *P7: Adequate resources need to be allocated to deliver the design strategies.*

It is not sufficient for the adopted design strategies will meet the performance targets. The appropriate resources must be present to use the design strategies. Furthermore, the resources must not result in an unprofitable situation, even if the resources are available. The resources are both for development and operation, even decommissioning. The resources are of many types and include money, human effort and calendar time.

> *P8: The stakeholder value should be delivered early, proven, and continuously. If you run out of resource unexpectedly – then most value should be delivered already.*

Projects may fail because they run out of time or money and have delivered nothing. They can only offer hope of something at the cost of additional money and time – this estimated by people who have already demonstrated they do not know what they are promising.

The management solution to this common problem is to demand that projects are done evolutionarily. That means there will be consciously planned early (first month) and frequent (perhaps weekly or 2% of budget) attempts to deliver measurable value to real stakeholders. Although such an approach may be contrary to practices that many people are used, there are decades of practical proof in the software and systems engineering world that this works (Larman et al., 2003).

> *P9: The requirements should not put unnecessary constraints on the delivery of performance and consequent value.*

It is all too common for projects to focus on a particular technical solution or architecture, and not to focus on the actual end results they expect to get from the technical 'design'. They end up locking themselves into the technical solution – and rarely get the results they expected.

> *P10: The project should be free to give priority to value delivery, and not be constrained by*

well-intended processes and standards.

Recommended frameworks and processes should encourage focusing on the *main results* of a project rather than exclusively on the standards processes. These 10 principles have been applied successfully on many projects worldwide. Further reading can be found in (Gilb et al., 1988; GIlb et al., 1993).

5   EDUCATION

To understand the needs for educating the next generation of information systems developers and managers, it is perhaps useful to establish a set of key observations (Maciaszek et al., 2005):

- Enterprise information system is more than a software system (it includes also people, data, procedures, communications, and of course hardware).
- Software process is part of business process (the result of a software process is software; the result of a business process is business).
- Software engineering is different from traditional engineering (the immaterial and changeable nature of software are but two factors that make the difference).
- Software engineering is more than programming (software engineering applies to complex problems that cannot be solved by programming alone).
- Software engineering is about modeling (all products of software engineering, including programs, are abstractions of reality).
- Enterprise information systems are complex (the complexity of modern software is in the 'wires' – in the linkages and communication paths between components).

First and foremost, it should be clear from the key observations that a software system of EIS complexity cannot be built bottom-up by "hacking" the code before a clear and complexity-minimizing *architectural framework* for the system is defined. It is not possible to construct a building (other than a shed in the garden) without prior architectural drawings. Similarly, it is not possible to program a system (other than a student assignment) without a prior architectural design that identifies software components and shows how they need to be integrated into a system. Regrettably, the educational perspective on architectural design issues is not helpful. It is not

quite possible in an educational set-up to teach the students the magnitude of EIS development. In education we can only afford the *programming in-the-small*. We cannot offer the *software engineering in-the-large*. And unfortunately 'in-the-small' does not scale up to 'in-the-large'.

Moreover, it is not educationally sound to teach top-down, i.e. from high-level abstraction to low-level design and programming. *Abstraction* means a purposeful concealment of irrelevant details for the intended semantics of the model. This means that the details are known to, or at least realized by, the developer. It follows that in education we have to teach details before abstraction. We have no choice but to learn about EIS development in a bottom-up way, but we will eventually apply the knowledge and skills gained in a top-down way. For many the hurdle proves too high when faced with the reality of a commercial software project. Is there anything that the education system can do to alleviate the problems raised above? Well, we must try to teach abstraction in small steps, for small tasks, even if the task could be solved (coded) directly. We must teach students modelling (no matter how trivial) before programming, thinking before doing, reading instructions and manuals before hitting the keyboard.

Second, we must move away from the *building from scratch* educational principle. This is not the way complex systems can be built. Complex systems demand reuse and collaboration. Reuse must embrace all its forms – libraries, frameworks, and patterns. Telling students that collaboration is a form of plagiarism is not good enough. The necessary condition for teaching *reuse and collaboration* is to make a *team software project* an important part of the curriculum. This should be a compulsory part of any computing or IS degree and it should ideally be a course over the full academic year. An ensuing condition is that *commercial software development platforms* should be used on the project. This includes a CASE (computer-assisted software engineering) tool supporting teamwork, an IDE (integrated development environment) supporting versions and software builds, a DBMS (database management system) supporting construction of a single database shareable by all project teams (after all in an enterprise – "applications come and go, the database stays for ever").

Third, we must engrave in students' minds that the problem is complex but the *solution must be simple*. Development of EIS software is not about innovation and satisfying developers' egos and urges. Many software projects fail because of "bells and whistles" built into them.

Fortunately, at least one requirement for simple solutions is naturally met by education. That requirement is known as *time-boxing* – a project management technique that puts "time boxes" around each task so that any expected slippages for the task completion are counteracted by simplifying the solution. As the last thing that the future users of the system need is a complex solution for their problems, time-boxing has been a very successful technique. Software projects in the educational surroundings are naturally "time-boxed" by the deadlines which must be met.

Fourth, we must educate in a way commensurate with the rapid technology changes. This means that we should teach by *passing knowledge, experience, wisdom* – passing lasting values and leaving acquisition of skills to professional training and self-education. The above does not mean that university education should be void of teaching *professional skills*. The issue is more about the mode of education to be applied so that the students can acquire necessary skills. Using a lecture room to teach the syntax of a programming language or how to debug the code is a misguided effort. This can only be done in hands-on exercises in laboratories under a careful guidance of an experienced developer. Too frequently in universities "the experienced developer" is merely a senior student or inexperienced tutor.

Fifth, we must accept that an EIS is a *social system* and that most project failures have little to do with the technology. Many technologically brilliant systems fail and many technologically inferior solutions are successful. Most project failures can be attributed to "soft components" – people, processes, management, etc.

The introduction of some compulsory "ethical and societal" component in an introductory IS subject is not the answer. Too frequently the graduates of computing and IS courses are bad communicators whose social skills must not be restricted to Internet chat rooms.

Does education matter as far as the theme of this paper is concerned? It is our belief that it does matter and that if designed properly and educational programme can make the difference. Paraphrasing the well-known observation that "great designs come from great designers", we can perhaps put forward that "successful projects come from educated developers and are supported by educated maintainers".

6   CONCLUSIONS

Rapid market changes such as electronic commerce, deregulation, mergers, globalisation and increased competition have led to a business environment that is constantly evolving. The effects of integration and evolution of information technology coupled to the increasing education of people provide opportunities for organising work in ways that have never before been possible (Malone, 2003). Nowadays, more than ever, failure of IT systems cannot be tolerated. IT developers are faced with extraordinary pressures to achieve designs that result in systems of *high reliability*.

The debate about appropriate development paradigms continues and this short paper is a small contribution to this debate. Our position is that complexity at organisational and product levels demand a closer look at the way that enterprises function and products are developed accordingly. Project management needs to be driven and organised in terms of meeting a clear set of requirements with results being visible early on and in frequent stages during the project. To achieve any sustainable improvements we need to also pay attention to educational programmes in broadening the student's technical spectrum in a way that highlights the interrelated nature of developing systems, business strategies and business processes in a systemic manner.

REFERENCES

J. Bubenko (1994) *Enterprise Modelling*, Ingenierie des Systems d' Information, Vol. 2, No. 6.

J. Bubenko (1995) *Challenges in Requirements Engineering*, in proceedings of RE'95, (ed) York, England, pp. 160-162, 1995.

J. M. Carroll (2002) *Scenarios and Design Cognition*, in proceedings of IEEE Joint International Conference on Requirements Engineering (RE'02), E. Dubois and K. Pohl (ed) Essen, Germany, pp. 3-5, 2002.

K. G. Doyle, J. R. G. Wood, and A. T. Wood-Harper (1993) *Soft Systems and Systems Engineering: On the Use of Conceptual Models in Information Systems Development*, Journal of Information Systems, Vol. 3, No. 3, July, pp. 187-198.

R. Fichman (2004) *Real Options and IT Platform Adoption: Implications for Theory and Practice*, Information Systems Research, Vol. 15, No. 2, pp. 132-151.

B. Fitzerald (1996) *Formalised System Development Methodologies: A Critical Perspective*, Information Systems, Vol. 6, No. 1, pp. 3-23.

T. Gilb and S. Finzi (1988) *Principles of Software Engineering Management*: Addison-Wesley, 1988.

T. Gilb and D. Graham (1993) *Software Inspection*: Addison-Wesley, 1993.

The-Standish-Group (2003), "The CHAOS Chronicles - 2003,", http://www.costxpert.com/resource_center/chaos_compared.html, 2003.

J. Iivari (1991) *A Conceptual Metamodel for an Information System: An Object-Oriented Interpretation*, in "Advances in Information Modeling and Knowledge Bases", H. Jaakkola, H. Kangassalo, and S. Ohsuga (ed.), IOS Press, 1991, pp. 185-207.

C. Larman and V. R. Basili (2003) *Iterative and Incremental Development: A Brief History*, IEEE Computer, Vol. 36, No. 6, pp. 47-56.

K. Liu (2000) *Semiotics in Information Systems Engineering*. Cambridge, UK: Cambridge University Press, 2000.

K. Liu, R. Clarke, P. Anderson, and R. Stamper (2002), "Coordination and Communication Using Signs: Studies in Organisational Semiotics." Boston, USA: Kluwer Academic Publishers, 2002.

P. Loucopoulos and V. Karakostas (1995) *System Requirements Engineering*, 1st ed. London: McGraw Hill, 1995.

P. Loucopoulos and R. Zicari (1992), "Conceptual Modelling, Databases and CASE: An Integrated View of Information Systems Development," John Wiley, 1992.

P. Loucopoulos (2000) *From Information Modelling to Enterprise Modelling*, in "Information Systems Engineering: State of the Art and Research Themes", S. Brinkkemper, E. Lindencrona, and A. Solvberg (ed.), Springer, 2000, pp. 67-78.

P. Loucopoulos and V. Kavakli (1997) *Enterprise Knowledge Management and Conceptual Modelling*, in proceedings of International Symposium on 'Past, Present and Future of Conceptual Modeling', P. P. Chen (ed) Los Angeles, USA, pp. 123-143, 1997.

P. Loucopoulos (2004) *Engaging Stakeholders in Defining Early Requirements*, in proceedings of 6th International Conference on Enterprise Information Systems (ICEIS 2004), (ed) Porto, Portugal, 2004.

L. A. Maciaszek and B. I. Liong (2005) *Practical Software Engineering: A Case Study Approach*. Harlow, UK: Addison-Wesley, 2005.

T. W. Malone, R. Laubacher, and M. S. S. Morton (2003) *Inventing the Organizations of the 21st Century*. Cambridge, Massachusetts: MIT Press, 2003.

National-Audit-Office (2004), "Ministry of Defence: Major Projects Report 2003," http://www.nao.gov.uk/pn/03-04/0304195.htm. London, UK, 2004.

T. W. Olle, H. G. Sol, and A. A. Verrijn-Stuart (1984), "Information System Design Methodologies: A Comparative Review." Amsterdam: North Holland, 1984.

T. W. Olle (1992) *A Comparative Review of the ISO IRDS, the IBM Repository and the ECMA PCTE as a Vehicle for CASE Tools*, in "CASE: Current Practice, Future Prospects", K. Spurr and P. Layzell (ed.), John Wiley, 1992.

C. Potts (1996) *Supporting Software Design: Integrating Design Methods and Design Rationale*, in "Design Rationale", 1996.

E. Yu and J. Mylopoulos (1994) *Understanding 'Why" in Software Process Modeling, Analysis and Design*, in proceedings of 16th International Conference on Software Engineering, (ed) Sorrento, Italy, pp. 159-168, 1994.

LARGE SCALE REQUIREMENTS ANALYSIS AS HETEROGENEOUS ENGINEERING

Kalle Lyytinen
Department of Information Systems
Case Western Reserve University
kalle@po.cwru.edu

Mark Bergman
Department of Computer Science
Naval PostGraduate School, Monterey

John Leslie King
School of Information
University of Michigan

Keywords: system requirements, functional requirements, system failures, heterogeneous engineering.

Abstract: We examine how to improve our understanding in stating and managing successfully requirements for large systems, because the current concept of a system requirement is ill suited to develop true requirements for such systems. It regards requirements as goals to be discovered and solutions as separate technical elements. In consequence, current Requirements Engineering (RE) theory separates these issues and reduces RE to an activity where a technical solution is documented for a given set of goals (problems). In contrast, we advocate a view where a requirement specifies a set of mappings between problem and solution spaces, which both are socially constructed and negotiated. Requirements are emergent and need to be discovered through a contracted process, which likens to a "garbage-can" decision-making. System requirements thereby embrace an emergent functional ecology of requirements. This leads to equate requirements engineering with heterogeneous engineering. The admitted heterogeneity of technological activity avoids a commitment to social (or technological) reductionism. Requirements engineers need to be seen as "heterogeneous engineers" who must associate entities that range from people, through skills, to artifacts and natural phenomena. They are successful only, if built socio-technical networks can remain stable in spite of attempts of other entities to dissociate them.

1   INTRODUCTION

Information systems development (ISD) has remained a high-risk proposition despite huge advances in computing and telecommunications technologies. Information systems projects in general, and large information systems projects in particular continue to fail at an unacceptable rate (Abdel-Hamid and Madnick 1990; Myers 1994; Drummond 1996; Mitev 1996; Rosenwein 1997). While some portion of troubled ISD projects is turned around successfully, intensive research in the past has generated little understanding in how to avoid failures in large systems development initiatives. From the growing incidence of failed projects, we conclude that advances in technologies are not sufficient to save large projects. Instead, they remain susceptible to failure until we learn to understand how technological, organizational and institutional changes are interwoven in large systems, and how system developers should accordingly state and manage requirements for such systems.

Consider the following example. On March 11, 1993 the world was shocked by the sudden cancellation of the Taurus project, which the London Stock Exchange had been developing for more than six years. Taurus was expected to be

9

I. Seruca et al. (eds.), Enterprise Information Systems VI, 9–23.

instrumental in the radical restructuring the securities trade, widely known as the Big Bang, by forming a backbone system for the London Stock Exchange. The project cost the Stock Exchange $130 million, and securities companies invested $600 million more (Drummond 1996). After years of alternating embarrassments and heroic efforts, Taurus was cancelled before a single module was implemented because the required functionality and performance could never be delivered.

Although Taurus was a very complex project, involving novel technologies and massive organizational and institutional scale, ineffective project controls allowed requirements to change continuously throughout the project. Moreover, management ignored clear warning signs about organizational and technical risks, whilst powerful interests pushed for Taurus' development despite confusion over the system's purpose and design. Simply, there was no understanding what the systems was supposed to do and what stakeholders it should serve. In the end, advocates held an almost superstitious faith in the project, dismissing objections and proposals for modifications and clearer statement of the requirements with comments like "...we have had all those arguments. Great idea but no, we have been arguing about it for twelve years, forget it" (Drummond 1996) (p. 352).

With the benefit of hindsight, the Taurus failure could have been averted by adjusting its course based on a more delicate and politically sensitive requirements engineering. But this was not done despite a well known truism shared both in academia and industry that systematic requirements engineering is a keystone to a successful delivery of a large scale system. The failure of Taurus can be partly attributed to the dismissal of this well known fact, but we think there is more to learn. Taurus failure was also due to the fact that we poor knowledge about how to state and manage requirements for large systems that involve political and institutional elements.

Stating requirements for such systems is not just a technical exercise, but necessitates a new mind set which we call "heterogeneous engineering" after Hughes (Hughes 1979a; Hughes 1979b; Hughes 1987). Heterogeneous engineering sees all requirements specifications to be inherently heterogeneous due to the need to establish stable networks involving both social and technical elements through engineering (if the network is not stable the system fails!). As Law (Law 1987) (p. 112) puts this: "The argument is that those who build artifacts do not concern themselves with artifacts alone, but must also consider the way in which the artifacts relate to social, economic, political, and scientific factors. All of these factors

are interrelated, and all are potentially malleable." Consequently, requirements engineers need to be seen as "heterogeneous engineers" who must successfully associate entities that range from people, through skills, to artifacts and natural phenomena.

In this paper we will examine the problem of stating and managing requirements for large system development initiatives *qua* "heterogeneous engineering." Our argument is twofold. First we will argue that failures like the Taurus disaster do not happen only because existing approaches to requirements engineering have not been adopted. In contrast, we argue that current requirements engineering techniques used *alone* will not do the job. This is because they are based on a fallacious assumption that business problems and political problems can be separated from technical *requirements engineering* concerns of how to specify a consistent and complete technical solution to a business problem. In contrast, large scale system development initiatives involve a simultaneous consideration of business, institutional, political, technical and behavioral issues. Second, based on behavioral theories of decision-making we argue, that solutions and problems are intertwined and addressed simultaneously during a requirements engineering process. Thus, requirements engineering can be understood only by using theories of behavioral and institutional decision making along with applied technical understandings, but not only through the lens of rational technical "engineering."

The remainder of the paper is organized as follows. In section 2, we shortly examine the received "view" of requirements engineering as outlined by the proponents of the current requirements engineering literature. In section 3, we propose an alternative concept of requirements engineering which we call the *functional ecology of requirements*. In this view, requirements are not discovered but constructed as mappings between solution and problem spaces. The construction process involves a protracted "walk" between these spheres. Section 4 concludes the paper by drawing some consequences for requirements engineering research.

2   REQUIREMENTS ENGINEERING DEFINED

The concept of a system requirement is relatively well known in the system and software engineering literature since mid 70's. The concept was originally conceived to involve the stating *what* the system is supposed to do before stating *how* the system produces the desired functionality (Ross 1977). The earliest concepts of system requirements can be traced back to work of Langefors (Langefors 1966) and some early attempts to develop high level system description languages[1]. One reason for separating the *how* and the *what* can be attributed to the desire to achieve what we call a "responsibility push-back". By this we mean the desire to relegate the failure to develop or implement the system to the prior environment, which gave rise to the definition of the system development task. Such attempts to move the "reasons" for failure to higher level system environments has been a continuing trend in software engineering and system development since the mid 70's. This has gradually shifted the interest of the software engineering and system development communities from implementation considerations (like "structured programming", "structured design") into problems of how to define what the system is expected to do and what this involves. This is currently called fashionably "requirements engineering" (RE) (Kotonya and Sommerville 1998).

The main concept in the requirements engineering is the desire to repeatably create successful systems. The main interest in the requirements engineering literature is to explore the means to express and articulate the desire to develop the system, i.e. how to define features of the new systems, or how to change current systems that will solve an identified business need, want, or desire (Loucopoulos and Karakostas 1995; Pohl 1996; Sommerville and Sawyer 1997). Therefore, the requirements engineering literature has concentrated on developing tools and methods which answer questions like: Who's desire? How to express the desire? Who and what defines success and failure criteria for addressing the desire? For example, when doing user-centered design, the end-users of the new or changed system are expected to define success & failure criteria (Pohl 1996; Noyes and Baber 1999). At the same time, knowledge of the current state of the art of system design can influence the choice of success & failure criteria. These can be seen as system design constraints and opportunities, which can also affect, i.e. change, the identified business wants, needs, and desires. In general, requirements in the received literature are seen to establish these success & failure criteria. The "received" definition is the IEEE standard 610.12 (Loucopoulos and Karakostas 1995; Pohl 1996), which defines requirement as:

1. A condition or capability needed by a user to solve a problem or achieve an objective.

2. A condition or capability that must be met or possessed by a system or a system component to satisfy a contract, standard, specification, or other formally imposed document.

3. A documented representation of a condition or capability as in 1 or 2.

Accordingly, requirements engineering denotes a set of methodologies and procedures used to gather, analyze, and produce a requirements specification for a proposed new system, or a change in an existing system.

3   THE FUNCTIONAL ECOLOGY OF REQUIREMENTS

3.1   Need for a Conceptual Model

In this section we will create a systematic conceptual model of RE from an *emergent functional perspective*. The term functional in the term suggests that any RE analysis is done in pursuit of practical objectives for a given task domain, such as to make task accomplishment more efficient and/or effective. We use the term *emergent* to capture the evolutionary view of how organizational goals, problems and solutions are constructed during the RE, as opposed to discovered, in alignment with a behavioral view of human decision making.

We will develop the model through a set of conceptual clarifications and definitions, which define exactly[2] the content of the major components of a requirements specification situation. These include the concepts of problem, solution, requirement, principal and goals. These are derived (though not explicitly) from a careful reading and analysis of the literature in institutional decision-making in complex domains. As with any conceptual model, our main goal is to define the major analytic relationships between these concepts. Constructing this model allows us to define more exactly *what* functional emergence means and *why* such emergence is inevitable, thus making large scale RE so hard to do successfully. We highlight how the model can explain origins and sources of RE complexity. In turn, the further analysis of the model offers means to understand the challenge we face on both conceptual and practical levels for constructing and stating adequately requirements. As we will show, the model enables us to pinpoint more exactly major disagreements with the received IEEE definition. By developing rigorously such a vocabulary[3] and underlying model for discussing large scale RE in all its complexity, the conceptual model enables us later on to formulate research questions more systematically and to develop techniques that can help manage such processes.

Though, the suggested model is still in line with a dominating model of RE in which it is assumed that organizational goals are clear[4], it digresses from it in how organizations and actors approach these goals and what mechanisms they have at hand for accomplishing those objectives. A prevailing bias in the requirements engineering literature is the notion that requirements exist "out there" waiting to be captured by the systems analyst and refined then into a complete and consistent specification for the system that will be thereafter created (Davis 1993; Loucopoulos and Karakostas 1995; Macaulay 1996; Pohl 1996; Kotonya and Sommerville 1998). Consequently, the main focus has been on formalizing the *content* of the system that will deliver the solutions and how this meets the objectives of being complete and consistent. Continued disappointing experiences in large-scale system development suggest, however, that the challenge is a good deal more complicated. One point we want to make is that the content of the system may mean different things for different people, and it is dynamical due to ambiguity and uncertainty related to the goals of the stakeholders and the solutions, which can be brought to bear upon identified problems.

3.2 Requirements Analysis Framework

The crux of the ecological view is to adopt insights from the study of human decision processes and use this to inform our formulation of the RE framework. We draw on two major sources in this endeavor that digress considerably from the dominating "technical rationality" of RE. First, in any complex development initiative, including RE, we must take seriously Simon's theory of bounded rationality [Simon, 1979;Simon, 1982] in that we can never find an optimal, but at most a *satisficing* solution. Accordingly, RE processes should be analyzed and understood from the view point of heuristics, limited search spaces and the quest for increased *intelligence* during the RE process. This is what RE methods and tools seek to offer. But their problem is that they scale up poorly for large systems, and in addition they fail to recognize the type complexity inherent in large scale RE.

Second, we will draw upon the institutional and behavioral theories of decision making which have in the past decades studied complex organizational decision making processes involving complex social, business or political change (March and

Olsen 1976; Lindblom 1979). These studies have shown that complex organizational decisions are not discrete events (i.e. bets) in which pros and cons are weighed and optimal decisions are rendered. Instead, organizational decision-making forms a protracted processes of iteration in which problems search for solutions, solutions search for problems, and decision makers search for decisions to be made (March and Olsen 1976). In the organizational theory, this is coined the "Garbage-Can Model." It is so named because of the relatively permanent nature of the cans in which different solutions, problems and decisions are "thrown" within an organizational arena. Available experience from many large scale RE (e.g., software engineering) initiatives coincide with this view. The development of World Wide Military Command and Control System (WWMCCS) of the 1970's and early 1980's formed a continued process of redefining this "can" over two decades. Hence, contrary to common assumptions underlying RE, RE decisions are implicated by solutions searching for problems rather than the other way around. The behavioral study of decision-making has thus benefited from the transformation of the "problem $\rightarrow$ solution" construction underlying RE research into a more evolutionary view of RE represented as "solution $\rightarrow$ problem $\rightarrow$ solution" iteration.

We will next refine this model. We will therefore begin with an examination of what a "solution space" means in relation to requirements, followed by an examination of the mediating "problem space." This leads us to articulate the requirements analysis process as an iterative "walk" between the solution and problem spaces. The main components of the framework are depicted in Figure 1. The acronyms M and N in the figure describe how different components in the RE environment can be related to one another during a RE process (i.e. many to many).

3.3 Solution Space

The ecological view suggests that any RE process starts from an existing solution space, S_t, that will be affected by a proposed new or changed system (see Figure 1). We depict the continuous construction and movement of solutions by rotating arrows around the solution space. The "existing solution" space, that we call the *Current Solution Space*, is denoted as S_t. Fundamentally, this space embodies a history of solved social, technical and procedural problems and it constitutes the legacy (or competency) of previously solved organizational problems. This definition denies that solutions exist a-historically. Instead, they are socially constructed

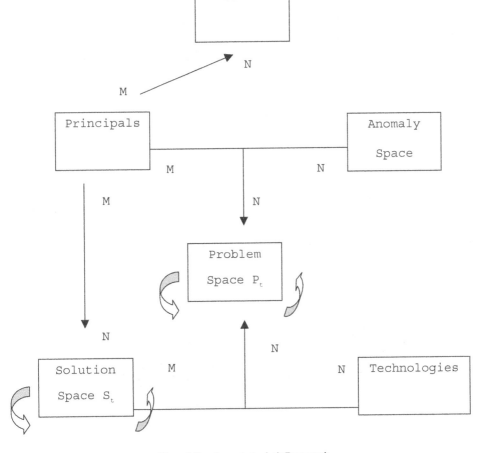

Figure 1: Requirements Analysis Framework

and legitimized. Capabilities to produce such solutions must be acquired and maintained in the surrounding socio-technical system. Therefore, the solution space is intimately related to the principals, i.e. a set of actors who have the capability to represent themselves as capable of arriving at solutions to an identified problem, or who possess specific skills that can result in specific solutions. The solutions are socially constructed also in the sense that the principals must find solutions to fit to their problems and thereby accept the legitimacy of a specific solution to their specific problem. Principals have also incentives to create their own solutions (e.g., goals) so they can influence the social system in which they reside and obtain resources.

Accordingly, many times solutions search for problems and not the other way round.

Working solutions form instantiations of one or more principals' successful attempts to adapt generic as well as custom technologies to suit to specific business, or social problems. Hence, solutions embody new and novel ways of carrying out organizational tasks often with untried configurations of social arrangements and technical artifacts. Our concept of technology is thus a heterogeneous one in the sense that it covers both social and managerial innovations, and technical innovations that draw upon properties and laws of the physical world and which demand that the final solution is a socio-technical ensemble (Law 1987).

In general there is a M:N (e.g. many to many) relationship between technologies and solutions. Hence, any given technology can be used to solve many types of problems and the same type of technology can be used to solve many problems. Moreover, any given problem can be solved or approached (in the spirit of socio-technical design) by the application of many types of technologies. This heterogeneity provides also a basis for the garbage-can model of organizational decision making: organizations can and often will throw several types of technologies into the "can" in their attempts to solve any given problem.

Organizations change over time, as do their solution spaces. A *Local Solution Space*, forms the current solution space and all locally accessible solution spaces that can be reached from the current solution space using available skills and resources offered by the principals[5]. A local solution space is a subset of a *Global Solution Space*, that can be seen to be the union of all solutions, which can in principle be reached from the current solution space if all resources and skills were available. In other words, the global solution space is the space of all feasible solution spaces, including those not currently accessible from the local solution space and which require mobilization of all principals and technologies. Reasons for not being able to reach all of them can be due to lack of resources, lack of intelligence (i.e. this solution is not known or cannot be connected effectively to any known problem), cognitive bias, shifting goals or incompatibility with organizational goal(s) or political structure.

In general, a local solution space represents the range of all locally accessible solution spaces with regard to organizational resource limitations. A local solution space is a more general form of a product space as suggested by Davis (1993), in that it contains the essential attributes and context of a product space.

3.4   Anomaly and Problem Spaces

The source of a problem is an *anomaly*, i.e. a known existing inconsistency between the current solution space and a desired solution space.[6] The set of all such inconsistencies we call an existing *Anomaly Space*. An anomaly is only a "potential" problem, because not all anomalies are attended by organizations as problems that need to be solved due to resource constraints and cognitive bias.

An anomaly becomes a *problem* only when it is observed and acted upon by a *principal with a standing to act*[7]. Standing refers here to the power to define and legitimize an anomaly as a problem to be solved by collective action, and the demonstrated

capability to mobilize means to address a defined problem[8]. This is normally defined in management statements that justify IT projects, in project goal specifications, or investment memos. A principal is thus assumed to wield organizational power, i.e. to have access to means by which she or he can influence the others and mobilize sufficient resources (Bacharach and Lawler 1980; Pfeffer 1981; Fairholm 1993). It is important to note that in large scale system development initiatives there are several or large numbers of principals who can obtain a standing in relation to problems identified. Moreover, it is important to understand that in large scale system development initiatives it is necessary to enroll a large number of principals to take a standing and agree on some level of problematization (Baier and March 1986). Standing can be later on also held by groups as well as individuals at different stages of RE process, which relate to possible rewards, incentives or side-effects of the possible system solution. Lower-level participants in organizations hold such standings due to their knowledge, or access to unique local resources that are critical in proceeding in the project[9]. A case in point here is a system analyst who is using his technical wits and unique knowledge of the situation to direct and channel the proceeding of the development project. Standing can, and often needs, to be changed later on due to learning, incentives or changed politics. Therefore standings can easily drift during a large RE process (Sauer 1994).

Due to cognitive limitations, some anomalies are not recognized by actors with a standing, and thus are not acted upon. Similarly, anomalies can be observed by principals as problems, but they choose not to act upon them due to their resource constraints, or difficulty in defining a solution space which links with the problem (e.g., goal failure). Such processes of inattention relate normally to high political, functional, technical or implementation risks of moving to a new chosen solution space (Lyytinen, Mathiassen et al., 1998b). Anomalies can also turn into problems at later stages of RE, or further down in the design process due to learning by doing. In the same vein, principals can later drop problems out of consideration and revert them to mere anomalies, or even beyond that if they change their goal sets, or observe high obstacles to move from the current solution space to the target space[10]. Thus the set of principals is not fixed even after successful RE, but instead contextually emerging and negotiated.

Although the causes of anomalies can spring from many sources, the conversion of an anomaly to a problem is a social process we call *problematization*. Problematization begins long

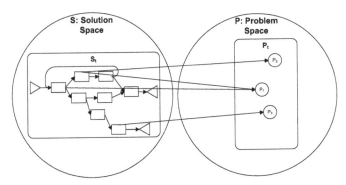

Figure 2: Solution and Problem Spaces

before a recognizable problem space has emerged. It begins with a principal's decisions standing to act or not act upon anomalies that turn them into problems. Often, these problematizations can start with the *metaproblems* of finding out what the problem is to which an existing or an emerging solution can be applied. During this activity, principals determine and apply legitimizing reasons to change an anomaly into a problem. Legitimate reasons normally relate to *goals* (see Figure 1), i.e. desirable properties of those solution spaces that can be reached from the current solution space. These goals are therefore not given or fixed, but instead are constructed and negotiated as a result of legitimizing the problematization. This process is by no means trivial exercise as any principal normally pursues several goals at the same time, and the same goal can be chosen by several principals. This results often in situations where the same problem space can relate to many different sources. Moreover, different principals can select them independently. In the same vein, these problems can be later on mapped onto alternative new solution spaces, which means that several often contradictory, or supplementary change processes may be initiated to the same problem causes.

An important capability of a principal with standing is the power to define particular characteristics of the desired problem space.[11] These relate to general value statements and rationales underlying organizational action like increased control, competitive capability, shareholder value, or employee participation. Such features can be used to dictate who has a right to address the problem space, why this is regarded as the problem space, among several competing principals who are jockeying to a mandate to address the problem space. Moreover, as Fairholm suggests, such power entails *'the ability to*

gain aims in interrelationship with others, even in the face of their opposition'[12]. Altogether, it is the principals who define the problems and their sources, and by implication, their resulting solution spaces. Thus, they must be considered the most important RE stakeholders.

The space of all problems implied by a current solution space S_t is called the *Problem Space*, denoted here as P. A problem space (e.g., the space of all selected problems) is by definition always a subset of an anomaly space. Hence, a *proposed system problem space*, denoted by P_t, contains all of the recognized and chosen problems by all of the principals at time t[13]. This does not mean that elements of this set are consistent, non-contradictory or selected by following some overarching organizational "goal" set. What we argue instead is that problems in P_t have to be contextualized into S_t[14] by some principals so that there is an observed need to change the current solution space. Accordingly, they can be later on associated with a proposed new system or system change by some principal with a standing.

Figure 2 shows a general relationship between S_t and P_t where the arcs represent connections to problems in P_t from their contextualizing source in S_t.

It is important to understand that multiple solution sources, as shown in can point to any one problem, and any one solution source can lead to multiple problems. This corresponds to the M:N relationship between the solution space and problem space as depicted in Figure 1. What this implies is that it is possible for a single problem to have multiple contextualizing sources. Also, a single solution source can contextualize multiple problems.

The process of *problematization* uncovers frequently also other anomalies that are deemed problems by principals. This can trigger an iterative reconsideration of the current solution space and its anomalies resulting in a process called *problem blossoming*[15]. This iterative process can change the contents, and hence, the structure, of the current solution space (S_t) as well as the problem space (P_t). This process may have to be iterated as long as new affected areas of S_t are being discovered and the corresponding anomalies, and resulting problems, are constructed and organized into the current problem space. Once complete, or prematurely stopped by a principal with standing due to the fear of endless search, the resulting problem set is called P_t.[16]

3.5   Proposed Solution

A Proposed Solution, denoted as S_{t+1}, forms a new subspace of the solution space. A proposed solution by definition implies the reconciliation of S_t to P_t. In other words, each part of a proposed solution must be reconciled with one or more problems in P_t until all of the problems in P_t are addressed. The process of reconciliation, changing S_t into S_{t+1}[17] by solving for P_t, is called *Solution Space Transformation*. Finding this mapping forms the heart of RE. It involves specifying a mapping from a current solution space into a future solution space that is contextualized, or warranted, by the chosen set of problems. In other words, the analyst's job is at the intersection of the two solution spaces (along with technologies embedded in them) and the problem space. During this reconciliation process, constraints are seen as limitations of current organizational resources as well as limitations concerning the future IS, including people, artifacts, rules, processes and the like.

It is a custom desire in the RE literature to find an optimum path from S_t to S_{t+1}. This is, however, seldom the case in any given requirements analysis effort, because 1) the prospect of attaining global solutions is quite remote due to changing and shifting needs and goals of the principals, problem blossoming etc, and 2) because system analysts cannot locally foresee the impact of the chosen solution spaces or the difficulty of getting there due to their cognitive and resource limits. The task of the analyst is, instead, to find a traversable path from a current solution space to a new one that meets sufficiently the requirement of removing observed problems (Haumer, Heymans et al., 1999). This needs to be accomplished also by identifying problems that will arise during the process of transformation.

A necessary outcome of the solution space transformation is to transform, and possibly expand, the local solution space, S_t. Transforming S_t means not only changing, and hence a likely expanding some principals' technical capability. It also means a changing, and presumptively by expansion, the organizational capability within the solution space. Hence, an expansion of S_t can reveal previously unavailable, but now realizable opportunities. The process can even expand a general solution space, and thus demonstrate organizational learning and innovation in the sense that new solution "frames" have been created (Lyytinen, Rose et al., 1998a) [18].

3.6   Redefining Requirements

Per our analysis, RE activity involves always a deliberate *construction* of an ecology that consists of two solution spaces and a problem space[19]. The objective of RE is to reconcile all essential aspects of the current solution space with regard to a problem space thus producing a specification for a particular solution space that can be achieved at some future time point $t+x$[20]. It is expected that this will mitigate or eliminate the identified problem space (though naturally this cannot be guaranteed). Due to the discovery of goals, problem blossoming and dynamics of the solution spaces, this is an iterative process: new information on both the solution space and the problem space is continually discovered, and consequently decisions need to be continually made to re-state both the solution space and the problem space in the direction of reconciliation. The RE specification is thus an outcome of a co-evolutionary process of discovery and decision, in which both the solution space and the problems space are iteratively constructed. This process is influenced by many constraints arising from the environment itself (e.g., physical laws, technical choices, legal considerations, institutional influences, organizational goals and capabilities, market forces). But, at the bottom, it remains a social process of negotiation and inquiry that is constrained by bounded rationality and limited organizational resources.

At this point of our treatise we can contrast this definition of RE with the "received" definition that is common to the requirements engineering literature. As previously stated a requirement as per this literature is:

1. A condition or capability needed by a user to solve a problem or achieve an objective.

2. A condition or capability that must be met or possessed by a system or a system component to satisfy a contract, standard, specification, or other formally imposed document.

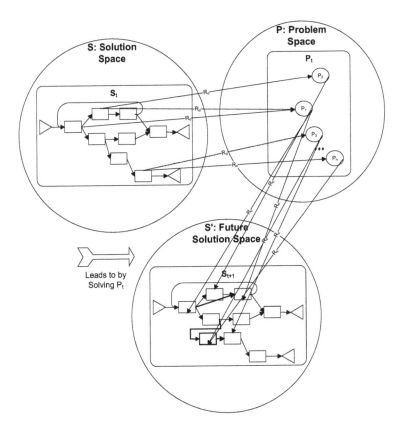

Figure 3: Solution Space Transformation – The Functional Ecology of Requirements Conceptual Model

3. A documented representation of a condition or capability as in 1 or 2.

In our terminology, item 1 focuses on meeting some expressed desire of a principal with standing, usually the client or the system's intended user. Such requirements have been called "functional" requirements (Loucopoulos and Karakostas 1995; Pohl 1996). Item 2 departs from the issue of desire and addresses compliance with conditions set by social or technical environment. Such requirements have been referred to as "nonfunctional" requirements (Loucopoulos and Karakostas 1995; Pohl 1996). Item 3 expects that a requirement needs to be represented in a document. In other words, if a requirement isn't written up, or equivalent, it is not a requirement.

A good summary of the requirements definition, accordingly, would be: *a requirement specifies a written want, need or desire that solves a problem in the context of a set of constraints or a written constraint imposed by a formal document.*[21]

We depart from this nomenclature in two ways. First, we see requirements not as solutions to problems, but as a set of *relationships* between solution spaces and a problem space. Solutions to problems are determined in design, not during requirements. As such, requirements are no more fixed than the evolving understanding of the characteristics of the two solution spaces and the problem space. Requirements in this sense cannot be *discovered*, but rather must be *constructed* by a search in the search space that covers all known mappings between the problem space and the two solution spaces[22]. Hence, requirements need to be represented by two sets of arcs, as shown in Figure 0, between the problem and two solution spaces. An analysis of the resulting requirements arcs postulates a conceivable alternative solution space for the identified problem set. More simply, once a stable set of requirements are known, one can postulate the specification for a new or changed technology, e.g. system. Still, as discussed earlier, we consider such technology heterogeneous, and thus it includes technical, social, political, economic, and alike capabilities and constraints (Hughes 1987; Law 1987). We called the whole set of possible future solution spaces a *conceivable solution space* (S_v). S_v, by definition, contains the proposed solution, S_{t+1}. Any given element in the conceivable solution space can, consequently, become the focus of the system development or enhancement project, in future. Another way of reading our definition is that requirements link desired solution spaces to their original contexts and to problems embedded therein that truly need to be addressed by a future solution. Taken together, requirements become a contextualized set of rules and constraints through which a future solution can be constructed via design. Second, we can apply insights from our definition of requirements to redefine some identified requirement types. We refer to what the literature calls a functional requirement as an *objective requirement,* denoted by R_o. An objective requirement is defined as: a want, need or desire that corresponds to a problem (e.g. P_t) as contextualized by a part or all of a current solution (e.g., S_t). A R_o is represented by an arc from a solution to a problem, as shown in Figure 0[23]. In this way, R_o can viewed as a relationship that comes from a solution looking for a problem. We refer to what the literature calls a nonfunctional requirement as *a constraint,* denoted by R_c. A *constraining requirement,* e.g., a *constraint,* is defined as: a restraining condition imposed upon a solution within S_{t+1} as contextualized by a problem within P_t[24]. A R_c is represented by an arc from a problem to a new solution, as shown in Figure 0[25]. The third part of the IEEE requirement definition remains unchanged, i.e. requirements must still be documented in some way for the principal(s).

Taken together, R_o and R_c fill in all arrows in the "solution → problem → solution" framework. Hence, it represents a model of the requirements as a functional ecology.

4 IMPLICATIONS

An implication of the new requirements definition is that since solutions and problems are heterogeneous in nature, requirements become heterogeneous in nature as well. RE should thus be conceived as heterogeneous engineering (Hughes 1987; Law 1987). This also means requirements of one type can be related to, and hence, can affect requirements of other types.

Another implication of the new requirements definition is, by transitivity, the principal(s) who own the problem(s) that are used to define an element in R_o or R_c are also the owners of that element in R_o or R_c. This point is needed to repair an ownership gap that appears between problems and requirements. Together, all of the arcs R_o and R_c form the essence of a *requirements specification.* A requirements specification is the set of statements selected for attention by the principal requirements owners. By induction, requirements owners are also the primary stakeholders of the system design. Also, by induction, since requirements are heterogeneous, the requirements specification is a heterogeneous, yet holistic, view of the future solution under consideration.

The activity of requirements analysis constructs a set of dynamic relationships between specific solution spaces and a specific problem space such that the specific principal's objectives are realized in the context of constraints. This definition is simple and clear, but its simplicity can be misleading. The challenge for researchers and practitioners alike is in the adjective *specific* that appears before the words "solution", "problem" and "principal". We argue that most requirements analyses fail first as a result of insufficient or incorrect specificity (i.e. level of detail and certainty) concerning the links between the solution and problem spaces. In fact, in many cases it can be extremely difficult to achieve such specificity due to limitations of bounded rationality, changing environmental conditions, limited resources, problem blossoming or political shifts among the stakeholders. Second, we argue that in large scale system development initiatives the requirements fail because it is difficult to stabilize the set of "specific" principals that take a common standing in relation to problems and later on to solutions due to political difficulties (see (Bergman, King et al., 2001)), or cognitive problems.

As noted earlier, multiple solution parts can point to one problem and any one solution part can lead to multiple problems. Hence, there is a M:N relationship between S_t and P_t. This suggests that there can be a nonlinear number of R_o arcs between the nodes of the two spaces. Similarly, a problem can affect multiple parts of a future solution, while multiple problems can point to (i.e. are addressed by) the same part of a future solution. Hence, similar to R_o, there is a many to many relationship between P_t and S_{t+1}. This allows for a nonlinear number of R_c arcs in relation to their sources. Altogether, requirements at any given time can be represented as the set of all of the arcs, (R_o, R_c), that reflect the contextualized connections between the problem space and the current and future solution space.

The obtained final set of requirement arcs between S_t, P_t and S_{t+1} can be seen to form a network of interrelationships, e.g., a *requirements web*. Thus, any change to even a single part of S_t can affect a large number of problems in P_t. The change is nonlinear in size. Also, due to the reflexivity of the connections via problem blossoming from P_t to S_t, any such change can show up in other parts S_t itself. Accordingly, any change in P_t can result in a nonlinear set of new or changed connections to S_t and S_{t+1}. Therefore, a small change in S_t or P_t could result in a nonlinear, i.e. potentially explosive, change in the whole requirements set (R_o, R_c).

In addition, a change in one requirement could have a non-linear change effect on other requirements. This has been observed as the "cascade effect" of requirements change, and forms the source of a phenomenon what has been called "requirements shift" and "requirements creep" (Gause and Weinberg 1989; Pohl 1996). This is a cascade effect because any requirement statement i.e. a pair of $<r_o^i, r_c^i>$ can influence or be dependent on a set of other requirements $<R_o^i, R_c^i>$ (Robinson, Pawlowski et al., 1999) and the impact may cascade recursively. Thus, in large system designs, a non-linear number of requirements connections coupled with non-linear change effects can yield a very complex, non-linear delicate requirements web.

These problems can, often in turn, lead to "requirements paralysis," i.e. the rational fear of changing requirements due to the possible devastating impacts of the change[26]. This is well supported by the observed difficulties in the Taurus project to manage shifting requirements (Drummond 1996). The combination of requirements paralysis, bounded rationality and organizational resource limitations can create the impression that any serious attempt to change requirements, or to change their sourcing problems or solutions would result in incurring spiraling costs that are simply too high for the principals. Many times this can lead into a path of escalation, e.g., increasing commitment to a failing course of action, when the project under consideration starts to falter (Keil and Montealegre 2000).

Another implication of recursive, reflexive, non-linear requirements change is the following: *determining requirements also determines stakeholders.* Thus, shifting requirements shift our perceptions of who are the principals and who are the other stakeholders. These shifts can even change who can be a stakeholder. This means that the original principals of a project may not be the final principals of the project. The implications of this can have profound affects on the process of requirements determination in ambiguous and dynamic environments. The demise of Taurus project caused by the incapability of the project management to manage the varying stakeholder set is a case in point.

5 CONCLUSIONS

The functional ecology of requirements i.e. the intricate linking and evolution of solution and problem spaces vis-à-vis a set of principals suggests that requirements are not solutions to problems. Rather, they establish links between solution spaces and a problem space in a changing environment of environmental conditions, shifting principals, and the evolution of organizational knowledge defining what is a solution, and what is a problem. Accordingly, requirements emerge through the identification of anomalies in the existing solution space that are declared by a principal with standing to be problems, followed by an effort to identify new solutions that would reconcile those problems. Any effort to identify new links between solution and problem spaces can uncover information that alters perceptions of both the problem space and the solution space and the set of principals. Under this model, requirements are not waiting to be *discovered* by an analyst, but rather they are systematically *constructed* through an iterative and evolutionary process of defining and redefining the problem and solution spaces (see also (Iivari 1990a)). This construction process is by definition imperfect and often inefficient due to bounded rationality, organizational resource limitations, uncertainty due to changing environmental conditions, and changing views of principals. Moreover, changes in the problem space can affect the solution space in nonlinear ways: with modest changes in one having the possibility of creating large changes in the other. The same holds in reverse. Thus, requirements analysis can be exceedingly difficult due to this instability, even in cases where organizational objectives are relatively clear.

We believe that an articulation of the functional ecology of requirements captures one key reason for the persistent failures in system development, when the target system operates in complex domains. The crux of the ecology is the recursive and reflexive relationship between solution spaces and problem space, and the fact that each can influence the other in nonlinear ways. This creates a situation in which "real" problems and their corresponding "real" solutions can be impossible to pin down with confidence. In such situations, the temptation is strong to abandon the analysis and shift to old, (at one time) reliable heuristics and learning by doing to implement one feasible solution without ever really pinning down its requirements and hoping that it will fit into the current ecology. Such attempts correspond to a random walk from the current solution space to an unknown new solution space. This signals a failure to state the requirements before the move and instead making the move, and then finding out the requirements for the move (i.e. the mappings between the two solution spaces). In other cases, principals can simply declare a particular problem/solution space alignment to be real and proceed to implementation. We call this the "early out strategy" and it was followed with disastrous consequences in the Taurus system. In the former case no specification is produced; in the latter it is likely that a bad specification will be produced and declared to be good by powers that be. Either can be damaging to organizational welfare, but the latter is often more destructive because resources are consumed in a futile effort to build a useful system from bad specifications and organizational confidence in system development suffers (Markus and Keil 1994; Keil 1995).

Since requirements are relationships between problems and solutions, it is very likely that there are *killer requirements* in large system development. These are accordingly, requirements that must be, but yet cannot be, adequately addressed by a current system under consideration. We argue that these are results of either improper relationships or representations of contextualized killer problems. An improper relationship is one that creates an objective or constraint, which cannot be met or makes it impossible to meet one or more separate requirements. In this case, it may be possible to either drop the requirement or rework it such that the connection between the solution and problem (objective) or problem and solution (constraint) can still be realized, and other conflicts mitigated. If such rework is not possible, this would indicate a gap that cannot be crossed between what is, and what is wanted, i.e. a killer problem. Unfortunately, such analyses are not normally done and they rarely form part of a RE exercise.

The ability to uncover additional problems by problem blossoming allows for the ability to discover killer problems, if they exist.

Unfortunately, this can lead to a search in an exponential size search space. There are at least two methods that can help deal with this problem. First, if separation of concerns and modularization are well applied, then the search space is reduced to the complex components and the combined system itself. This will help isolate such problems within these subdivisions, or at the system level, hence reducing the possible search space.

Whilst problems are often discovered by analysts, they tend to be quickly categorized according to their current understanding of how difficult it is to solve them. Most problems in new systems have therefore known solutions, otherwise the effort would be pointless. Some problems may not have obvious solutions, but usually there are known techniques to work around them. This leaves problems that are not known how to solve once they are uncovered. These are potential killer problems and they quite often relate to heterogeneous nature of the RE activity, i.e. how the resulting socio-technical system will stabilize. The list of these problems is likely to be rather small, but they are often "deadly enemies." As noted, these can also be some of the most tricky to either find, or correctly identify. Still, being able to perform problem triage to identify the most serious problems should be part of a system analyst's repertoire of RE techniques. We believe, that by applying the heterogeneous approach to system analysis would allow analysts to discover more of these potential killer problems. As such, it can be considered a risk reduction methodology.

These and other techniques needed to deal with heterogeneous RE are the subject of our future research. By improving our understanding of the complexity and uncertainty involved in RE, we should see an overall reduction in failed systems and a likely increase in the production of successful systems. In the end, this is the main goal of requirements engineering.

REFERENCES

Abdel-Hamid, T. K. and S. E. Madnick (1990). "The Elusive Silver Lining: How We Fail to Learn from Software Development Failures." Sloan Management Review 32(1): 39-48.

Bacharach, S. B. and E. J. Lawler (1980). Power and politics in organizations. San Francisco, Jossey-Bass.

Baier, V. and J. March (1986). "Implementation and Ambiguity." Scandinavian Journal of Management Studies 4(May): 197-212.

Bak, P. (1996). How nature works: the science of self-organized criticality. New York, NY, USA, Copernicus.

Berger, P. L. and T. Luckmann (1966). The social construction of reality; a treatise in the sociology of knowledge. Garden City, N.Y.,, Doubleday.

Bergman, M., J. L. King, et al. (2001). Large Scale Requirements Analysis Revisited: The need for Understanding the Political Ecology of Requirements Engineering, submitted for publication.

Bijker, W. (1987). The Social Construction of Bakelite: Toward a Theory of Invention. The Social Construction of Technological Systems. W. Bijker, T. Hughes and T. Pinch. Cambridge, MA, MIT Press: 159-190.

Boehm, B. W. (1988). "A spiral model of software development and enhancement." Computer May: 61-72.

Brooks, F. P. (1995). The mythical man-month: essays on software engineering. Reading, Mass., Addison-Wesley Pub. Co.

Checkland, P. (1981). Systems thinking, systems practice. Chichester Sussex ; New York, J. Wiley.

Checkland, P. and J. Scholes (1990). Soft systems methodology in action. Chichester, West Sussex, England ; New York, Wiley.

Couger, D. and J. Knapp (1974). Systems Analysis Techniques. London, John-Wiley & Son.

Davis, A. M. (1993). Software requirements: objects, functions, and states. Englewood Cliffs, N.J., PTR Prentice Hall.

DeTombe, D. J. (1994). Defining complex interdisciplinary societal problems: a theoretical study for constructing a co-operative problem analyzing method: the method COMPRAM. Amsterdam, Thesis Publishers.

Dowty, D. R., R. E. Wall, et al. (1981). Introduction to Montague semantics. Boston, MA, Kluwer Boston Inc.

Drummond, H. (1996). "The Politics of Risk: Trials and Tribulations of the Taurus Project." Journal of Information Technology 11: 347-357.

Fairholm, G. W. (1993). Organizational power politics: tactics in organizational leadership. Westport, Conn., Praeger.

Foucault, M. and C. Gordon (1980). Power knowledge: selected interviews and other writings, 1972-1977. New York, Pantheon Books.

Gause, D. C. and G. M. Weinberg (1989). Exploring requirements: quality before design. New York, NY, Dorset House Pub.

Graham, I. (1998). Requirements engineering and rapid development: an object-oriented approach. Harlow, England ; Reading, MA, Addison Wesley.

Haumer, P., P. Heymans, et al. (1999). Bridging the Gap Between Past and Future RE: A Scenario-Based Approach. RE'99, Limerick, Ireland, IEEE Computer Society.

Hughes, T. (1979a). "Emerging Themes in the History of Technology." Technology and Culture 20(4): 697-711.

Hughes, T. (1979b). "The Electrification of America: The system builders." Technology and Culture 20(1): 124-161.

Hughes, T. (1987). The Evolution of Large Technological Systems. The Social Construction of Technological Systems. W. Bijker, T. Hughes and T. Pinch. Cambridge, MA, MIT Press: 51-82.

Iivari, J. (1990a). "Hierarchical spiral model for information system and software development. Part 1: theoretical background." Information and Software Technology 32(6): 386-399.

Iivari, J. (1990b). "Hierarchical spiral model for information system and software development, Part 2: design process." Information and Software Technology 32(7): 450-458.

Keil, M. (1995). "Pulling the Plug: Software Project Management and the Problem of Project Escalation." MIS Quarterly 19(4): 421 - 447.

Keil, M. and R. Montealegre (2000). "Cutting your losses: Extricating Your Organization When a Big Project Goes Awry." Sloan Management Review 41(3): 55-68.

Kotonya, G. and I. Sommerville (1998). Requirements engineering: processes and techniques. Chichester; New York, J. Wiley.

Langefors, B. (1966). Theoretical Analysis of Information Systems. Lund, Sweden, Studentlitteratur.

Latour, B. (1991). Technology is society made durable. A Sociology of Monsters: Essays on Power, Technology and Domination. J. Law. London, Routledge.

Law, J. (1987). Technology and Heterogeneous Engineering: The Case of Portuguese Expansion. The Social Construction of Technological Systems. W. Bijker, T. Hughes and T. Pinch. Cambridge, MA, MIT Press: 111-134.

Lindblom, C. E. (1979). "Still Muddling Through." Public Administrative Review 39: 517-526.

Loucopoulos, P. and V. Karakostas (1995). System Requirements Engineering. London, UK, McGraw-Hill Book Co.

Lyytinen, K., L. Mathiassen, et al. (1998b). "Attention Shaping and Software Risk- A Categorical Analysis of Four Classical Approaches." Information Systems Research 9(3): 233-255.

Lyytinen, K., G. Rose, et al. (1998a). "The Brave New World of Development in the internet work computer architecture (InterNCA): or how distributed computing platforms will change systems development." Information Systems Journal 8(3): 241-253.

Macaulay, L. (1996). Requirements engineering. London; New York, Springer.

March, J. G. and J. P. Olsen (1976). Ambiguity and choice in organizations. Bergen, Universitetsforlaget.

Markus, M. L. and M. Keil (1994). "If We Build It, They Will Come: Designing Information Systems that Users Want to Use." Sloan Management Review 35(4): 22.

Mitev, N. N. (1996). "More than a Failure? The Computerized Reservation Systems at French Railways." Information Technology & People 9(4): 8-19.

Myers, M. D. (1994). "A Disaster for Everyone to See: An Interpretive Analysis of a Failed IS Project." Accounting, Management and Information Technologies 4(4): 185-201.

Noyes, J. M. and C. Baber (1999). User-centered design of systems. London; New York, Springer.

Pfeffer, J. (1981). Power in organizations. Marshfield, Mass., Pitman Pub.

Pohl, K. (1996). Process-centered requirements engineering. New York, NY, Wiley.

Robinson, W. N., S. D. Pawlowski, et al. (1999). Requirements Interaction Management, Unpublished Working Paper, Department of Computer Information Systems, Georgia State University.

Rosenwein, M. (1997). "The Optimization Engine That Couldn't." OR/MS Today 24(4): 26-29.

Ross, D. (1977). "Structured Analysis (SA): A Language for Communicating Ideas." IEEE Transactions on Software Engineering 3(1): 16-34.

Simon, H. A. (1996). The sciences of the artificial. Cambridge, Mass., MIT Press.

Sommerville, I. and P. Sawyer (1997). Requirements engineering: a good practice guide. Chichester, England ; New York, John Wiley & Sons.

Suchman, L. A. (1987). Plans and situated actions: the problem of human-machine communication. Cambridge Cambridgeshire ; New York, Cambridge University Press.

Wieringa, R. (1996). Requirements engineering: frameworks for understanding. New York, NY, Wiley.

FOOTNOTES

[1] For a good historical analysis, see Couger and Knapp (Couger and Knapp 1974).

[2] By exactness we mean here that the categories used and the nature or relationships imposed in the model are defined in an analytically exact way so that the model can be used as a basis for developing techniques and deriving systematically research questions. To this end we will use some simple set theoretic notations when introducing the concepts.

[3] [3] Some of the definitions and analyses may look somewhat complex. Therefore we have included a short glossary of terms and their definitions at the end of the paper.

[4] We have expanded later this model to cover also situations where goal congruence cannot be assumed (see Bergman et al., 2001).

[5] Those who are knowledgeable in possible world semantics (or Kripke semantics, see e.g. (Dowty, Wall, et al., 1981)) can see an immediate similarity with the set of solution spaces that can be reached from the current solution space and the concept of the accessibility relation R from any given possible world to other possible worlds. The difference is that due to organizational learning the set of possible solutions spaces accessible from the current solution space is not fixed, but changes over time.

[6] This is similar to DeTombe's simple definition of a problem (DeTombe 1994). It is also in alignment with the definition used in the Requirement Engineering literature (Kotonya and Sommerville 1998; Haumer, Heymans, et al., 1999).

[7] In the RE literature, principals are called business stakeholders (Wieringa 1996; Kotonya and Sommerville 1998).

[8] This formulation does not exclude the possibility that the principal does not have these skills and capabilities available when the time to act is in. We must, however, believe that there is some belief among actors' involved in such capabilities under the rational model, otherwise the principal should choose not to act at all. Within a political scenario, this is not necessarily the case. This suggestion is also derived from the idea that it is actors with solutions looking for problems rather than the other way round. Therefore the demonstrated capability is important in any RE process.

[9] Latour (1991) calls such contingencies or situations as passage points that are governed by "gatekeepers".

[10] These are known in the IS literature as abandoned projects or the process of de-escalation (Keil 1995; Keil and Montealegre 2000).

[11] cf. Foucault's 'those who have ability to define 'truth' are those who have power' (Foucault and Gordon 1980).

[12] *Organizational Power Politics*, pp. 22

[13] The issue of 'who gets to be a principal' is as important as 'what is the problem.' This issue is discussed throughout the rest of the treatise. A more in-depth treatment of this issue is beyond the scope of this paper.

[14] A problem is understood within the context of the socio-technical (e.g., organizational) ecology in which the

solution space resides. Each problem is constructed, legitimized, and owned by one or more principals who reside in this ecology. Hence, all problems are ecologically situated (Suchman 1987), socially constructed (Berger and Luckmann 1966; March and Olsen 1976) and owned. Contextualization includes all of these concepts.

[15] For the sake of clarity, each anomaly in figure has been defined into a problem.

[16] Problem blossoming is similar to an aspect of Checkland's Soft Systems Methodology (SSM) (Checkland 1981). However, problem blossoming is focused on problem discovery and identification of likely impacted parts of S_t. SSM, in contrast, focuses on the whole process of systems development. Problem blossoming and SSM share the basic components of iterative learning and discovery, as well as a recognition of the ability to change the current solution and problem spaces as per new insights.

[17] This space, S, is similar to Davis' *product space* defined as "the range of all possible problem solutions that meets all known constraints." *Software Requirements: Objects, Functions, and States*, pp. 42

[18] We are using here the concept of frame as defined by Bijker (Bijker 1987). Bijker uses the term frame to denote a new aggregate of concepts and techniques employed by a community of problem-solvers in its problem solving. Changes in frames embody "revolutions" and discontinuities in technology evolution. Such discontinuities are a reflected in such elements as goals of technology use, theories and concepts, problem-solving steps and tools, and organizational and managerial principles related to problem solving practices. An example of this is moving from structured programming to object-oriented programming.

[19] In theoretic terms, a solution space is the subset of the Local Solution Space (S) that is affected by as well as affecting the system change. In practical terms, a solution space can be represented as a model of this space, for instance a (richly detailed) workflow or equivalent model.

[20] For clarity purposes, $t+x$ is replaced by $t+1$ throughout the rest of the paper. This is used to indicate the time of an operational future solution space.

[21] Loucopoulos & Karakostas, as well as most of the requirements engineering literature, transforms a capability into functionality and a condition into a constraint (e.g., nonfunctionality). Functionality \ represents a want, need or desire of one or more principals in S_t for a new capability to be made available in response to one or more of their problems in P_t. This corresponds with Gause and Weinberg's view on requirements engineering: a process to discover what people desire (Gause and Weinberg 1989). It is also in line with Graham's view, which focuses on what is needed by

people (Graham 1998). A constraint represents a condition on a future solution in response to a problem.

[22] This same observation has been confirmed by researchers advocating the spiral model of software development which emphasizes the evolution and learning of requirements and the dynamic nature of mappings between requirements and implementations (see e.g. (Boehm 1988; Iivari, 1990a; Iivari 1990b)).

[23] As discussed earlier, there could be many arcs from a solution source to a single problem. Still, each arc is an individual requirement. Also, the arrow on the arc (which is informational only) indicates the node pointed to is contextualized by the node pointed from. In this case, a problem is contextualized by a solution.

[24] A constraint does not originate in a formal document. It is rooted in one or more problems that are implied in the formal document. Since, by definition, these contextualizing problems come from a formal document, they must have principal representation and, thus, are part of P_t. But, these problems are usually not clearly and specifically identified in most formal documents. This means they cannot be accurately represented within P_t. This is a source of potential requirements failure. The possibility exists of not truly solving the problems that the formal document wanted addressed by the project under consideration even if the constraints (or objectives) specified in a formal document are well met. In turn, this allows for the increased probability of an incorrect future solution, resulting in eventual deployment failure. Altogether, this highlights the importance of constraints as traceable relationships, not just stated restrictions.

[25] The lightened and bolded parts of S_{t+1} corresponds to proposed changes in the solution space S_t in response to the problems in P_t.

[26] cf. Bak's adding a grain of sand causing an avalanche in a sand pile (Bak 1996).

EVOLUTIONARY PROJECT MANAGEMENT: MULTIPLE PERFORMANCE, QUALITY AND COST METRICS FOR EARLY AND CONTINUOUS STAKEHOLDER VALUE DELIVERY - An agile approach

Tom Gilb

www.Gilb.com

Abstract: Agile methods need to include stakeholder metrics in order to ensure that projects focus better on the critical requirements, and that projects are better able to measure their achievements, and to adapt to feedback. This paper presents a short, simple defined process for evolutionary project management (Evo), and discusses its key features.

1 INTRODUCTION

In 2001, a British Computer Society Review paper indicated that only 13% of 1027 surveyed IT projects were 'successful' (Taylor 2001). In the same year, a Standish report indicated that although there has been some recent improvement, 23% of their surveyed projects were considered total failures and only 28% totally successful (that is, on time, within budget and with all the required functionality) (Johnson 2001: Extracts from Extreme Chaos 2001, a Standish Report). The US Department of Defense, a few years ago, estimated, that about half its software projects failed (Personal Communication, Norm Brown, SPMN (Software Program Managers Network)/Navy). While these figures represent an improvement on the 75% reported for failed DoD projects when the Waterfall Method dominated (Jarzombek 1999), they are still of extreme concern. We must be doing something very wrong. What can senior management and IT project management do about this situation in practice?

Some people recommend complex development process standards such as CMM (Capability Maturity Model®), CMMI (Capability Maturity Model® Integration), SPICE (Software Process Improvement and Capability dEtermination) and their like. I am not convinced that these are 'good medicine' for even very large systems engineering projects, and certainly they are overly complex for most IT projects.

Other people recommend agile methods – these are closer to my heart – but maybe, for non-trivial projects - they are currently 'too simple'?

2 STAKEHOLDER METRICS

I believe agile methods would benefit, if they included 'stakeholder metrics'. I have three main reasons for suggesting this:

- to focus on the critical requirements: All projects, even agile projects, need to identify all their stakeholders, and then identify and focus on the 'top few' critical stakeholder requirements.
- to measure progress: Critical requirements need to be quantified and measurable in practice. Quantified management is a necessary minimum to control all but the smallest upgrade efforts.
- to enable response to feed back: By responding to real experience, and modifying plans accordingly, projects can make better progress. This is something that agile projects with their short cycles, can especially utilize.

In this paper, I shall present a simple, updated 'agile', evolutionary project management process and explain the benefits of a more focused, quantified approach.

I recommend the following evolutionary project management process and policy:

24

I. Seruca et al. (eds.), Enterprise Information Systems VI, 24–29.

A Simple Evolutionary Project Management Method

Tag: Quantified Simple Evo Project. Version: July 8, 2003. Owner: Tom@Gilb.com. Status: Draft.

Project Process Description
1. Gather from all the key stakeholders the top few (5 to 20) most critical performance goals (including qualities and savings) that the project needs to deliver. Give each goal a reference name (a tag).
2. For each goal, define a scale of measure and a 'final target' goal level. For example, *Reliability: Scale: Mean Time Between Failure, Goal: >1 month.*
3. Define approximately 4 budgets for your most limited resources (for example, time, people, money, and equipment).
4. Write up these plans for the goals and budgets (*Try to ensure this is kept to only one page*).
5. Negotiate with the key stakeholders to formally agree these goals and budgets.
6. Plan to deliver some benefit (that is, progress towards the goals) in *weekly* (or shorter) cycles (Evo steps).
7. Implement the project in Evo steps. Report to project sponsors after each Evo step (weekly, or shorter) with your best available estimates or measures, for each performance goal and each resource budget.
   - On *a single page,* summarize the *progress to date* towards achieving the goals and the costs incurred.
   - Based on numeric feedback, and stakeholder feedback; *change whatever needs to be changed to reach the goals within the budgets.*
8. When all goals are reached: 'Claim success and move on" (Gerstner 2002). Free the remaining resources for more profitable ventures

Project Policy
1. The project manager, and the project, will be judged exclusively on the relationship of progress towards achieving the goals versus the amounts of the budgets used. The project team will do anything legal and ethical to deliver the goal levels within the budgets.
2. The team will be paid and rewarded for 'benefits delivered' in relation to cost.
3. The team will find their own work process, and their own design.
4. As experience dictates, the team will be free to suggest to the project sponsors (stakeholders) adjustments to the goals and budgets to 'more realistic levels.'

This simple project process and policy capture all the key features: you need read no more! However, in case any reader would like more detail, I will comment on the process and policy definition, statement by statement, in the reminder of this paper!

3 PROJECT PROCESS DESCRIPTION

1. Gather from all the key stakeholders the top few (5 to 20) most critical goals that the project needs to deliver.

Projects need to learn to focus on *all the stakeholders* that arguably can affect the success or failure. The needs of all these stakeholders must be determined –by any useful methods –and converted into project requirements. By contrast, the typical agile model focuses on a user/customer 'in the next room'. Good enough if they *were* the only stakeholder, but disastrous for most real projects, where the critical stakeholders are more varied in type and number. Agile processes, due to this dangerously narrow requirements focus, risk outright failure, even if the 'customer' gets all *their* needs fulfilled.

2. For each goal, define a scale of measure and a 'final target' goal level. For example, Reliability: Scale: Mean Time Before Failure, Goal: >1 month.

Using Evo, a project is initially defined in terms of clearly stated, quantified, critical objectives. Agile methods do not have any such quantification concept. The problem is that vague targets with no quantification and lacking in deadlines do not count as true goals: they are not measurable, and not testable ideas.

Note in Evo, the requirements are not cast in concrete, even though they are extremely specific. During a project, the requirements can be changed, and tuned, based on practical experience, insights gained, external pressures, and feedback from each Evo step (See also point 4 under 'Project Policy').

3. Define approximately 4 budgets for your most limited resources (for example, time, people, money, and equipment).

Conventional methods do set financial and staffing budgets, but usually at too macro a level. They do not seem to directly, and in detail, manage the array of limited resources we have. Admittedly there are some such mechanisms in place in agile methods, such as the incremental weekly (or so) development cycle (which handles time). However,

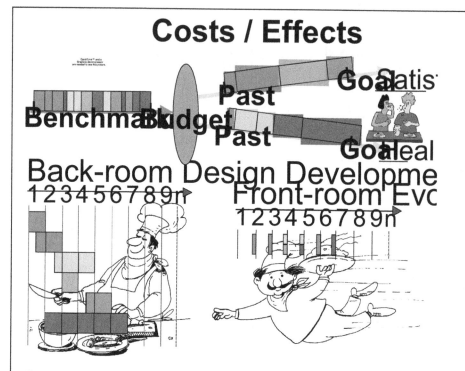

Figure 1: Evolutionary result delivery takes system components readied for integration in the 'backroom' using arbitrary acquisition duration (as in kitchens), and presents them to stakeholders in frequent short Evolutionary result delivery cycles (as in the dining room). (Illustration courtesy of Kai Gilb)

\the Evo method sets an explicit numeric budget for any useful set of limited resources. WHICH IS WHAT?

4. Write up these plans for the goals and budgets (Ensure this is kept to only one page).

All the key quantified performance targets and resource budgets, should be presented simultaneously on a single overview page. Additional detail about them can, of course, be captured in additional notes, but not on this one 'focus' page.

5. Negotiate with the key stakeholders to formally agree these goals and budgets.

Once the requirements, derived from the project's understanding of the stakeholder needs, are clearly articulated – we need to go back to the real stakeholders and check that they agree with our 'clear' (but potentially incorrect or outdated) interpretation.

It is also certainly a wise precaution to check back later, *during* the project evolution, with the stakeholders, especially the specific stakeholders who will be impacted by the next Evo step:

- as to how they feel about a particular choice of step content (that is, how they see the proposed design impacting performance and cost, and whether the original impact estimates are realistic in the real current implementation environment, and
- to check for any new insights regarding the long term requirements.

6. Plan to deliver some benefit (that is, 'progress towards the goals') in weekly (or shorter) cycles (Evo steps).

A weekly delivery cycle is adopted by agile methods; this is good. However, the notion of

Table 1: The use of an Impact Estimation table (Gilb 2004) to plan and track critical performance and cost characteristics of a system (Illustration courtesy of Kai Gilb). The pair of numbers in the three left hand columns (30, 5 etc.) are defined benchmarks (30, 99, 2500) and Goal levels (5, 200, 100,000). The '%' figures are the real scale impacts (like 20) converted to a % of the way from benchmark to the Goal levels (like 20% of the distance from benchmark to Goal).

	Step 12 Buttons.Rubber		Step 13 Buttons.Shape & Layout	
	Estimate	Actual	Estimate	Actual
Goals				
User-Friendliness.Learn 30 by one year 5	-10 33%	-5 17%	-5 20%	5 -20%
Reliability 99 by one year 200	-3 -3%	-1 -1%	20 20%	2 2%
Budgets				
Project-Budget 2500 by one year 100000	2000 2%	2500 3%	1000 1%	1000 1%

measurement each cycle, on multiple performance and resource requirements, is absent.

Using Evo, the choice of the next Evo step is based on highest stakeholder value to cost ratios. It is not simply, "What shall we do next?" It is "What is most effective to do next - of highest value to the stakeholders with consideration of resources?"

The agile methods' notion of *agreeing with a user*, about the function to be built, during that weekly cycle is healthy, but the Evo method is focused on systematic, weekly, measured delivery towards long-range higher-level objectives, within numeric, multiple, resource constraints. This means that the Evo method is more clearly focused on the wider stakeholder set values, and on total resource cost management.

The Evo method is *not focused* on simply writing code ('we are programmers, therefore we write code'). The Evo method is focused on delivering useful results to an organically whole system. We reuse, buy or exploit existing code just as happily as writing our own code. We build databases, train and motivate users, improve hardware, update telecommunications, create websites, improve the users' working environment, and/or improve motivation. So we become more like systems engineers ('any technology to deliver the results!'), than programmers ('what can we code for you today?').

7. Implement the project in Evo steps and report your progress after each Evo step.
Report to the project sponsors after each Evo step (weekly, or shorter) with your best available estimates or measures, for each performance goal and each resource budget.
- On a single page, summarize the progress to date towards achieving the goals and the costs incurred.
- Based on the numeric feedback, and stakeholder feedback, change whatever needs to be changed to reach the goals within the budgets.

All agile methods agree that the development needs to be done in short, frequent, delivery cycles. However, the Evo method specifically insists that the closed loop control of each cycle is done by:
- making numeric pre-cycle estimates,
- carrying out end-cycle measurements,
- analyzing deviation of measurements from estimates,
- making appropriate changes to the next immediate planned cycles,
- updating estimates as feedback is obtained and/or changes are made,
- managing stakeholder expectations ('this is going to late, if we don't do X').

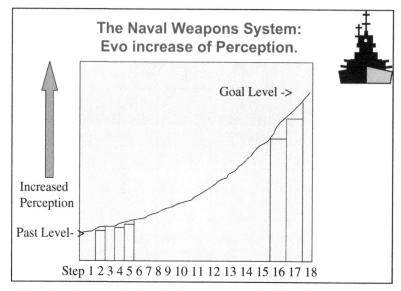

Figure 2: Results are cumulated numerically step by step until the Goal level is reached. In a UK Radar system (Author experience), the system was delivered by gradually building database info about planes and ships, tuning recognition logic, and tuning the radar hardware.

The clear intention to react to the feedback from the metrics and to react to any changes in stakeholder requirements is a major feature of Evo. It helps ensure the project is kept 'on track' and it ensures relevance. It is only by the use of stakeholder metrics that Evo is allowed to have such control.

8. When all the goals are reached: 'Claim success and move on' (Gerstner 2002). Free remaining resources for more profitable ventures.

A major advantage of using numeric goal and budget levels, compared to 'a stream of yellow stickies from users' (a reference to agile method practice), is that it is quite clear when your goals are reached within your budgets. In fact, 'success' is formally well defined in advance by the set of the required numeric goal and budget levels.

Projects need to be evaluated on 'performance delivered' in relation to 'resources used'. This is a measure of project management 'efficiency'. When goals are reached, we need to avoid misusing resources to deliver more than is required. No additional effort should be expended to improve upon a goal, unless a new improved target level is set.

4 PROJECT POLICY

1. The project manager, and the project, will be judged exclusively on the relationship of progress towards achieving the goals versus the amounts of the budgets used. The project team will do anything legal and ethical to deliver the goal levels within the budgets.

Projects need to be judged primarily on their ability to meet critical performance characteristics, in a timely and profitable way. This cannot be expected if the project team is paid 'by effort expended'.

2. The team will be paid and rewarded for benefits delivered in relation to cost.

Teams need to be paid according to their project efficiency, that is by the results they deliver with regard to the costs they incur. Even if this means that super efficient teams get terribly rich! And teams that fail go 'bankrupt'.

When only 13% of 1027 IT projects are 'successful' (Taylor 2001), we clearly need to find better mechanisms for rewarding success, and for not rewarding failure. I suggest that sharp numeric definition of success levels and consequent rewards for reaching them, is minimum appropriate behavior for any software project.

3. The team will find their own work process and their own design.

Agile methods believe we need to reduce unnecessarily cumbersome corporate mandated processes. I agree. They also believe in empowering the project team to find the processes, designs and methods that really work for them locally. I heartily agree! However, I also strongly believe that numeric definition of goals and budgets, coupled with frequent estimation and measurement of progress, are much-needed additional mechanisms for enabling this empowerment. The price to pay for this, a few estimates and measures weekly, seems small compared to the benefits of superior control over project efficiency.

4. As experience dictates, the team will be free to suggest to the project 'sponsors' (one type of stakeholder) adjustments to 'more realistic levels' of the goals and budgets.

No project team should be 'stuck' with trying to satisfy unrealistic or conflicting stakeholder dreams within constrained resources.

Further, a project team can only be charged with delivering inside the 'state of the art' performance levels at inside the 'state of the art' costs. Exceeding 'state of the art' performance is likely to incur 'exponential' costs.

5 SUMMARY

A number of agile methods have appeared, trying to simplify project management and systems implementation. They have all missed two central, fundamental points; namely *quantification* and *feedback*.

Evolutionary project management (Evo) uses *quantified* feedback about critical goals and budgets. Further, Evo also insists that early, frequent, small, high stakeholder value deliveries (Evo steps) are made to real users: this is only possible if supported by stakeholder metrics.

It is the use of stakeholder metrics that allows better focus, more measurement of progress, and more flexibility to change. It is time agile methods adopted quantified, critical stakeholder metrics.

REFERENCES

Abrahamsson, Pekka, Outi Salo, Jussi Ronkainen and Juhani Warsta, *Agile Software Development Methods. Review and Analysis*, VTT Publications, Espoo, Finland, 2002, ISBN 951-38-6009-4, URL: www.inf.vtt.fi/pdf/, 107 pp.

Gerstner, Louis V. Jr., *Who Says Elephants Can't Dance? Inside IBM's Historic Turnaround,* HarperCollins, 2002, ISBN 0007153538.

Gilb, Tom, *Principles of Software Engineering Management*, Addison-Wesley, 1988, ISBN 0201192462.

Gilb, Tom, Competitive Engineering: A Handbook for Systems & Software Engineering Management using Planguage, See www.Gilb.com for draft manuscript, 2004.

Jarzombek, S., Proceedings of the Joint Aerospace Weapons Systems Support, Sensors and Simulation Symposium, Government Printing Office Press, 1999. Source Larman & Basili 2003.

Johnson, Jim, Karen D. Boucher, Kyle Connors, and James Robinson, "Collaborating on Project Success," Software Magazine, February 2001. www.softwaremag.com/L.cfm?Doc=archive/2001feb/CollaborativeMgt.html

Johnson, Jim, "Turning Chaos into Success," Software Magazine, December 1999. www.softwaremag.com/L.cfm?Doc=archive/1999dec/Success.html

Larman, Craig, Agile and Iterative Development: A Manager's Guide, Addison Wesley, 2003.

Larman, Craig, and Victor Basili, "Iterative and Incremental Development: A Brief History," IEEE Computer, June 2003, pp 2-11.

Taylor, Andrew, "IT projects sink or swim," BCS Review, 2001. http://www.bcs.org.uk/review/2001/articles/itservices/projects.htm

MANAGING COMPLEXITY OF
ENTERPRISE INFORMATION SYSTEMS

Leszek A. Maciaszek

Macquarie University, Sydney, Australia
Email: leszek@ics.mq.edu.au

Keywords: Software complexity, software architectures, object dependency management.

Abstract: The *complexity* of modern software is not that much in the size of systems as it is in the "wires" – in the linkages and communication paths between system components. The inter-component linkages create dependencies between distributed components that are difficult to understand and manage. The difficulty is inflated by the fact that components are frequently developed and managed by separate teams and by various component providers.
                 This paper identifies main issues for successful management of complexity in large software projects. It uses the *holon* hypothesis to explain that all complex systems of a stable but evolvable character display hierarchic organization. The paper makes it clear that a complexity-aware *architectural design* paves the way for developing *supportable systems*. It makes it also clear that unless implementation is design-conformant and complexity-assured, the initial good intents may still result in an unsupportable system. Without rigorous project management, supported by tools able to compute and visualize *complexity metrics*, contemporary large software production risks delivering unsupportable systems..

1 INTRODUCTION

Complexity management and dependency management are two sides of the same coin. Dependency management is an integral part of *architectural design*. Architectural design takes a *proactive approach* to managing dependencies in software. It does so by deciding early in the process on hierarchical layers of software components and on dependency firewalls between the layers. This is a forward-engineering approach – from design to implementation. The aim is to deliver a software design that minimizes dependencies by imposing an architectural solution on programmers.

The outcomes of the proactive approach to managing dependencies must be monitored by the *reactive approach* that aims at measuring dependencies in implemented software. This is a reverse-engineering approach – from implementation to design. The implementation may or may not conform to the desired architectural design. If it does not, the aim is to compare the metric values in the software with the values that the desired architecture would have delivered. The troublesome dependencies need to be pinpointed and addressed.

This paper refers to four fundamental issues in design of enterprise information systems:

(1) component design that reduces complexity and makes component dependencies traceable in program and database structures, (2) dependency-minimizing design of the architectural layers housing application components and reaching to database and web services, (3) round-trip engineering with metrics to evaluate system complexity, and (4) identification and specification of design principles and patterns targeting minimization of complexity in enterprise information systems.

Prior to describing our approach for managing complexity in systems, the paper explains the background for it – *software holons*. The concept of *holon* (from the Greek word: *holos* = whole and with the suffix *on* suggesting a part, as in neutron or proton) was introduced by Koestler (1967) and it has since been used by various branches of science ranging from biology to communication theory, as observed by the theory originator in Koestler (1980).

I. Seruca et al. (eds.), Enterprise Information Systems VI, 30–36.
© 2006 *Springer. Printed in the Netherlands.*

2   SOFTWARE HOLONS – RATIONALE FOR LAYERED ARCHITECTURES

The complexity of living systems by far exceeds the complexity of any computer system, and yet living systems are reliable and adaptive. Therefore, it seems sensible to study the structure and behaviour of living organisms in search for paradigms to be used in the construction of software solutions. An important way of thinking in behavioural science (apart from *reductionism* and *holism*) is centered on the notion of *holon*. To quote Koestler (1980, p.447):

> "A living organism is not an aggregation of elementary parts, and its activities cannot be reduced to reeling off a chain of conditioned responses. In its bodily aspects, the organism is a whole consisting of "sub-wholes", such as the circulatory system, digestive system, etc., which in turn branch into sub-wholes of a lower order, such as organs and tissues - and so down to individual cells. In other words, the structure and behaviour of an organism ... is a multi-levelled, stratified hierarchy of sub-wholes, ... where the sub-wholes form the nodes, and the branching lines symbolise channels of communication and control. ...
>
> The point first to be emphasised is that each member of this hierarchy, on whatever level, is a sub-whole or "holon" in its own right - a stable, integrated structure, equipped with self-regulatory devices and enjoying a considerable degree of *autonomy* or self-government."

From studies of most complex systems that exist, such as biological systems, it is known that complex systems, which work well, have one thing in common – they are *hierarchies* of elements; they are not networks. Such systems exhibit layered architectures without circular dependencies within and between layers.

Holons are: "...subordinated as *parts* to the higher centres in the hierarchy, but at the same time function as quasi-autonomous *wholes*. They are Janus-faced. The face turned upward, toward the higher levels, is that of a dependent part; the face turned downward, towards its own constituents, is that of a whole of remarkable self-sufficiency." (Koestler, 1980, p.447)

Accordingly, in object-oriented system modeling, the holon abstraction can be simulated by the notion of composition. This notion has been documented and offered as a *design pattern* (Gamma et al., 1995). The *composite pattern* represents part-whole hierarchies of objects and allows treating parts and wholes in a uniform way (by narrowing the difference between the components and compositions of components). Figure 1 is a UML graphical representation of the composite pattern (Gamma et al., 1995).

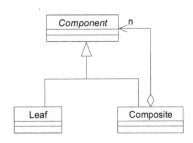

Figure 1: The structure of the composite pattern.

As stated in Gamma et al. (1995, p.163): "The key to the Composite pattern is an abstract class that represents *both* primitives and their containers." To be precise, the Component class is a partially implemented abstract class that declares an interface for objects in the composition. The behavior of primitive objects is defined (implemented) in the Leaf class and the behavior of components having children in the Composite class. Default implementations of the behaviors common to all classes in the composition can be provided in the Component class (hence, this class is "partially implemented"). Client programs use the interface of the Component class to communicate with objects in the composition. If a recipient object is a Composite, then the client's message will usually trigger requests to its child components before the requested operation can be completed.

Consistently with the holon abstraction, the composite pattern reflects the "openess" property of holons and supports "design for change". In living organisms, complex systems evolve from simple systems and there is no absolute "leaf" holon or "apex" holon. Wholes are composed of parts that can be either leaves or composites.

The composite pattern matches the holon hypothesis. Complex software systems consist of several layers of abstraction. Each one of them is a quasi-autonomous construction visible as a dependent part to the higher layer of abstraction and at the same time exerting some control over lower layers of abstraction. A layer of abstraction has its own semantics which is complete according to its specification and which is independent from the semantics of the other layers. The composite pattern determines all transitions between different layers of abstractions that make sense in such a system. The Component objects conform to the following observation by Koestler (1967) with regard to holons:

> they "...should operate as an autonomous, self-reliant unit which, though subject to control from above, must have a degree of independence and take routine contingencies in its stride, without asking higher authority for instructions. Otherwise the communication channels would become overloaded, the whole system clogged up, the higher echelons would be kept occupied with petty detail and unable to concentrate on more important factors" (Koestler, 1967, p.55)

However, there are two important differences between our view of a complex software system and the holon view of the real world. Firstly, the holon hypothesis explains the structure and behavior of an *"implemented"* system (e.g. living organism), but it does not explain the abstractions needed for the *development* of a system. Short of further analysing the evolution of living organisms, we suggest that a large system that works is always a result of an evolution of a small system that was built using a supportable hierarchical structure reminiscent of holon structures. Therefore, the development process must start with a simple architectural design that proposes a hierarchy of layers of abstractions. It is crucial then that this architectural design is obeyed in the implemented system.

Secondly, hierarchical structures found in nature tend to be relatively static. Their structure does not change much over time but behavior can moderately change. On the contrary, hierarchical structures in software must support change much more readily. Enterprise information systems and business applications change in structures and in behavior (after all company structures, product and employee classifications, plant operation specifications, and many other aspects of business are in a constant state of flux). The *design for change* demands a special attention to dependency management, which is discussed next. It also explains the principle (that undeprins the composite pattern) to „Favor object composition over class inheritance" (Gamma *et al.*, 1995, p.20). Inheritance model works poorly on dynamic structures.

3   DEPENDENCY MANAGEMENT

A *dependency* between two system objects exist if a change to the object that supplies a service may necessitate a change in client objects that demand that service.

If all dependencies in a system are identified and understood, the system is said to be *supportable*, i.e. the system is understandable, maintainable and scalable. A necessary condition for supportability is that a sheer number of dependencies is tractable. Consequently, a task of software engineer is to minimize dependencies (Maciaszek and Liong, 2004).

In software systems, dependencies can be identified for objects of varying granularity – components, packages, classes, methods. The dependencies between more specific objects at lower levels of granularity propagate up to create dependencies at higher level of granularity. Accordingly, dependency management necessitates a detailed study of the program code to identify all relationships between data structures and code invocation between software objects.

Figure 2 shows an example of quite troublesome dependencies in a simple program. The example refers to three Java classes AAA, XXX, and YYY. YYY is a subclass of XXX. AAA obtains a reference varA1 to YYY when instantiating it, but it keeps this reference as XXX type.

When operA1() is called, it invokes operX1() on the superclass XXX. However, operX1() calls operXY1(). The operation operXY1() exists in the superclass, but it is overridden in the subclass (as shown in the Class Specification window). Accordingly, the overridden method is called in a down-call to YYY (because varA1 refers to YYY).

The operation operA1() executes also operXY2() on the superclass XXX. Again, because operXY2() is overridden in YYY, the execution involves a down-call to YYY. However, the overridden method is an extension of the parent method. The parent method is invoked in an up-call to XXX.

This simple example illustrates difficulties faced by developers and maintainers when trying to understand and maintain dependencies in the code. Interestingly, the example is not demonstrating any bad programming practice. It only illustrates how one of the dominant reuse techniques, namely *implementation inheritance*, "naturally" results in unduly complex, perhaps even unsupportable, code.

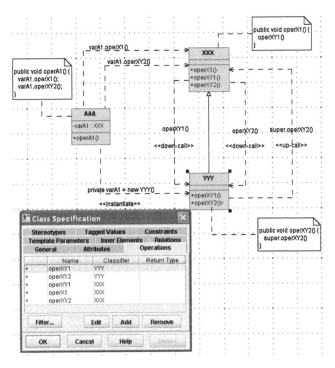

Figure 2: Dependencies in a simple program.

There are many techniques to eliminate undesirable (and circular) dependencies like in Figure 2. Some interesting techniques include replacing of inheritance by *composition* and using of *interface inheritance*. For details, the reader is invited to Maciaszek and Liong (2004).

4   SOFTWARE ARCHITECTURE

As stated, dependencies on low-level programming constructs propagate up to higher-level constructs. At the top system design level, the dependencies exist between subsystems. A *subsystem* encapsulates a high-level chunk of system's behaviour (Maciaszek, 2005). For dependency minimization, the services of the subsystem can and should be defined using *interfaces*.

The notion of a subsystem can be used, in a proactive approach, to determine the *architectural framework* for the system. The framework must introduce a hierarchy of software layers and it must result in dependency minimization. The composite pattern is an initial and dominant construct in

establishing the layers and in controlling dependencies between and within the layers. This results in a holon-like architectural design for the system.

This said, there are many specific ways to deliver *holonic* design. There is no one unique or best architectural framework that can result in a supportable system. The difficulty seems to be in picking up a framework early in the design phase and sticking to it in the implementation phase of software development. The framework, which we advocate, is called *PCMEF* (Maciaszek and Liong, 2003; Maciaszek and Liong, 2004).

The *PCMEF* framework "layers" the software into five subsystems – presentation, control, mediator, entity and foundation (Figure 3). The acquaintance subsystem is an application-specific library of interfaces. It is used to reduce dependencies between the main five subsystems.

The presentation layer contains classes that define GUI objects. The user communicates with the system via presentation classes. Accordingly, the class containing the program's main function is typically housed in the `presentation` package (alternatively it can reside in the control package).

The `control` layer handles `presentation` layer requests. It consists of classes responsible for processing user's interactions (passed to `control` from `presentation` objects). As a result, `control` is responsible for bulk of the program's logic, algorithmic solutions, main computations, and maintaining session state for each user.

The `entity` subsystem of the `domain` layer handles `control` layer requests. It contains classes representing "business objects". They store (in program's memory) objects retrieved from the database or created in order to be stored in the database. Many entity classes are container classes.

The `mediator` subsystem of the `domain` layer establishes a channel of communication that mediates between `entity` and `foundation` classes. Mediation serves two main purposes. Firstly, to isolate the two subsystems so that changes in any one of them can be introduced independently. Secondly, to eliminate a need for `control` classes to directly communicate with `foundation` classes whenever new `entity` objects need to be retrieved from the database (such requests from `control` classes are then channelled via `mediator` classes).

The `foundation` layer is responsible for all communications with database and web services, which manage persistent data required by the application program. This is where the connections to database and web servers are established, queries to persistent data are constructed, and the database transactions are instigated.

The PCMEF main dependencies are downward, as shown by arrows in Figure 3 – `presentation` depends on `control`, `control` depends on `domain` (on `mediator` and, possibly but not necessarily, on `entity`), `mediator` depends on `entity` and on `foundation`. Upward dependencies are realized through loose coupling facilitated by interfaces, event processing, acquaintance subsystem and similar techniques. Dependencies are only permitted between neighboring layers.

In the context of the holon abstraction, looking *downward* along composition dependencies, an object (method, class, component, etc.) is an independent whole. Looking *upward* along composition dependencies, an object is a subservient part. Accordingly, lower-level objects (holons) must be designed to be more stable – a change to an object at a lower layer has a more profound effect than a change to an object at a higher layer.

Acquaintance happens when within a method, a message is sent to the object that is a parameter of the method (Maciaszek and Liong, 2004). In PCMEF, acquaintance in the *downward* direction to objects in neighboring packages is not normally

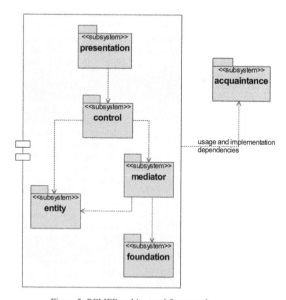

Figure 3: PCMEF architectural framework.

employed because PCMEF subsystems support such communication. Acquaintance in the *upward* direction to objects in neighboring packages can employ interfaces in the `acquaintance` subsystem to eliminate cycles. Also, acquaintance that in effect spans *non-neighboring* objects can be channelled through interfaces grouped in the `acquaintance` package.

The PCMEF dependency structure conforms to a number of important *architectural principles* (Maciaszek and Liong, 2004). Four of these principles are defined below (Maciaszek and Liong, 2003):

1. *Downward Dependency Principle* (DDP)

   The DDP states that the main dependency structure is top-down. Objects in higher layers depend on objects in lower layers. Consequently, lower layers are more stable than higher layers. They are difficult to change, but (paradoxically) not necessarily difficult to extend. Interfaces, abstract classes, dominant classes and similar devices should encapsulate stable packages so that they can be extended when needed.

2. *Upward Notification Principle* (UNP)

   The UNP promotes low coupling in bottom-up communication between layers. This can be achieved by using asynchronous communication based on event processing. Objects in higher layers act as subscribers (observers) to state changes in lower layers. When an object (publisher) in a lower layer changes its state, it sends notifications to its subscribers. In response, subscribers can communicate with the publisher (now in the downward direction) so that their states are synchronized with the state of the publisher.

3. *Neighbor Communication Principle* (NCP)

   The NCP demands that a package can only communicate directly with its neighbor package. This principle ensures that the system does not disintegrate to an incompressible network of intercommunicating objects. To enforce this principle, message passing between non-neighboring objects uses delegation. In more complex scenarios, a special "acquaintance" package can be used to group interfaces to assist in collaboration that engages distant packages.

4. *Explicit Association Principle* (EAP)

   The EAP visibly documents permitted message passing between classes. The principle demands that associations are established on all directly collaborating classes. Provided the design conforms to PCMEF, the downward dependencies between classes (as per DDP) command the associations.. Associations resulting from DDP are

unidirectional (otherwise they would create circular dependencies). It must be remembered, however, that not all associations between classes are due to message passing. For example, both-directional associations may be needed to implement referential integrity between classes in the entity package.

The architectural principles, as those explained above, define (in the holon context) "… a set of fixed, *invariant rules*, which account for the coherence, stability, and the specific structure and function of its constituent holons." (Koestler, 1980, p.454). Koestler calls such a set a holon's canon. The canon is fixed but it leaves room for *variable strategies*, which determine how rules are actually "implemented"

5 UNIFYING PROACTIVE AND REACTIVE DEPENDENCY MANAGEMENT

As stated in Introduction, the supportability of the system must be *proactively* designed into it as well as *reactively* monitored and verified. The resulting roundtrip engineering requires the support of a *dependency management tool*. This Section presents briefly how a dependency measurement tool, called DQ (*Design Quantifier*), is used for roundtrip engineering with metrics (Maciaszek and Liong, 2003). *DQ* is designed to analyze a program code and evaluate its conformance to the architectural framework (*PCMEF* or similar).

DQ calculates class, message and event dependency values for each class in a subsystem, the sum of metric values for the subsystem as well as for the whole system. It highlights any non-conformances that it discovers. The non-conformance ranges from offending fields, offending methods to offending classes as governed by the implemented framework.

DQ reverse-engineers a program and discovers all object dependencies. Class dependencies represented as associations are easily noticeable both in the system design and in the code. However, implicit dependencies such as acquaintance and local variables of methods are difficult to see. These implicit dependencies are hidden assumptions that may significantly impact the supportability features of a system. Implicit dependencies (typically in message and event dependencies) may introduce new class dependencies that need to be presented to the system designer.

DQ performs an *architectural conformance analysis* (i.e. if the code conforms to the design).

The tool accepts the *PCMEF* framework for conformance analysis but it can be easily configured to suit other frameworks. *DQ* understands and computes various complexity metrics, not discussed here (ref. Maciaszek and Liong, 2003).

DQ is configurable for other frameworks provided the definition of the framework is given to it. The information that is required includes the notion of neighboring packages, naming conventions used to identify methods or classes of significance such as event classes, weights of different association links. With these values provided, *DQ* can calculate the dependency metrics for a system and can produce detail information whether the system conforms to the architecture.

DQ supports *roundtrip engineering* by making the retrieved information available to any visual modeling tool. The tool can be used in visualization environments to provide informative details regarding the system. In particular, *DQ* can provide a trace of method calls (services) from one class to another and therefore provide an impact analysis on a system when a particular method is called (or modified).

Tools like DQ provide useful reactive metrics for a given program and assist in proactive analysis of the program design. They can be used to verify that the system conforms to an architecture framework and if the dependency minimization principles are adhered to. Without a rigorous architectural framework, supported by tools that measure the conformance of the system to the framework, managing a complexity of any large development is infeasible.

6   SUMMARY AND CONCLUSION

This paper summarizes fundamental findings of industry-based research conducted by the author over the last decade or so (Maciaszek *et al.*, 1996). The research aims at identifying necessary conditions for building *supportable systems*. The intellectual background behind the research has been provided by the *holon* abstraction for interpretation of structures and behaviour of biological systems (Koestler, 1967; Koestler, 1980).

To be able to manage *complexity* of enterprise information systems, we have to be able to measure complexity of system designs (proactively) and programs (reactively). Although not discussed in this paper, the metrics must be able to determine the *comparative level* of system's supportability (understandability, maintainability and scalability).

Object dependencies, to determine the supportability level, are initially computed from a system design. A proper architectural design, such as the *PCMEF* design, minimizes the object dependencies for a system. However, the principles of an architectural design can, and frequently are, broken by bad programming practices that allow for indiscriminate communication between objects.

Computing dependencies from the code has two main goals. Firstly, we are able to discover programming violations of an architectural design. Secondly, we are able to reverse-engineer all dependencies from code to design models and, in the process, we are able to revise the dependency metrics for the system. The ultimate outcome is, hopefully, a system with supportability characteristics.

Measuring *supportability* of designs and programs cannot be done manually. The paper referred to a tool, called *DQ* (Design Quantifier), which is able to analyze any Java program, establish its conformance with a chosen supportable architectural framework, compute complete set of dependency metrics, and visualize the computed values in UML class diagrams.

REFERENCES

GAMMA, E.   HELM, R.   JOHNSON, R. and VLISSIDES, J. (1995): *Design Patterns. Elements of Reusable Object-Oriented Software*, Addison-Wesley, 395p.

KOESTLER, A. (1967): *The Ghost in the Machine*, Hutchinson of London, 384p.

KOESTLER, A. (1980): *Bricks to Babel*, Random House, 697p.

MACIASZEK, L.A. (2005): *Requirements Analysis and System Design*, 2nd ed., Addison-Wesley

MACIASZEK, L.A. GETTA, J.R. and BOSDRIESZ, J. (1996): Restraining Complexity in Object System Development - the "AD-HOC" Approach, *Proc. 5th Int. Conf. on Information Systems Development ISD'96*, Gdansk, Poland, pp.425-435

MACIASZEK, L.A. and LIONG, B.L. (2003): Designing Measurably-Supportable   Systems,   *Advanced Information Technologies for Management, Research Papers No 986*, ed. by E. Niedzielska, H. Dudycz, M. Dyczkowski, Wroclaw University of Economics, pp.120-149.

MACIASZEK, L.A. and LIONG B.L. (2004): *Practical Software Engineering. A Case Study Approach*, Addison-Wesley, 829p.

ENGAGING STAKEHOLDERS IN DEFINING EARLY REQUIREMENTS

Pericles Loucopoulos

Department of Computation, University of Manchester Institute of Science and Technology,
P.O. Box 88, Manchester, M60 1QD, U.K.,
pl@co.umist.ac.uk, http://www.co.umist.ac.uk/~pl

1 INTRODUCTION

Dealing with organisational change and information systems development is about two sides of the same coin – *designing for the future*. Developing business strategies, designing business processes and implementing support systems are interrelated activities that need to be considered at a systemic level in order to deliver high quality results. From a Systems Engineering perspective it is no longer appropriate to focus exclusively on functional and non-functional aspects of the intended system. It is also crucially important to understand the trade-off of requirements against all stakeholders' parameters.

As a field of intellectual endeavour and industrial practice, Requirements Engineering has traditionally been concerned with goals for, functions of and constraints on software intensive systems. The need for a greater understanding of the interdependencies between enterprise functions and information systems functions challenges this view and forces us to consider a broader perspective, one that enables us to analyse alternatives to realising different strategic options available to (re)design of systems.

A key challenge in the development of systems is the engagement of domain experts in their articulation, agreement, and validation of requirements. This challenge is particularly pronounced at the so-called *early requirements* phase when multiple stakeholders from different divisions and often different organisations need to reach agreement about the intended systems. Decisions taken at this stage have a profound effect on the technical and economic feasibility of the project. It is no longer appropriate for information systems professionals to focus only on functional and non-functional aspects of the intended system and somehow assume that organisational context and needs are outside their remit.

What distinguishes *early* requirements from *late* (or support system) requirements, is the degree of involvement of client stakeholders. Early requirements are almost exclusively driven by client stakeholders' communication. Issues of early requirements include: (a) the customer profiles of a business process, (b) the likely demand for product or service made by each type of customer, (c) the level of desirable service that the business process should strive to achieve, (d) the resources that are required in order to achieve these levels of service and (e) the trade-off between levels of service and requisite resource between all client stakeholders of a business process. Only when these issues have been resolved can one then begin to develop specifications of requirements for support systems. The analyst will need to know how the support system interacts with other systems, what kind of levels of service it must achieve and so on before engaging into further analysis on functional and non-functional properties of the intended system.

These issues of early requirements are specifically tackled by the *strategy-service-support* (referred to as S^3) modelling approach (Loucopoulos, 2003). It is based on the premise that informal (c.f. (Galliers, 1993; Leymann et al., 1994), semi-formal (c.f. (Kavakli et al., 1999; Ould, 1995) or formal approaches (c.f. (Fuxman et al., 2003; Fuxman et al., 2001) to business process modelling do not fully address the issues relating to early requirements. The S^3 modelling approach advocates a process cycle of *hypothesis formulation, testing*, and *re-formulation* until stakeholders have enough confidence about the efficiency of the proposed design. Essentially, one is developing theories, externalised as conceptual models, about the Universe of Discourse and tests these theories for their validity. These models are subsequently subjected to scenario generation in consensus-building stakeholder workshops.

2 THE S^3 APPROACH

2.1 Overview

In terms of methodology the S^3 approach supports a reasoning cycle of *hypothesis formulation, testing,*

I. Seruca et al. (eds.), Enterprise Information Systems VI, 37–42.
© 2006 *Springer. Printed in the Netherlands.*

and *re-formulation*. Within this reasoning cycle, S^3 deals with strategic, service and support issues.

    a. Strategic issues are organisational and stakeholder goals for improving the organisation's performance.

    b. Service issues are the levels of improvement considered by the organisation.

    c. Support issues are the resources policies and actions required to reach the desired service levels.

The S^3 approach is a generic approach and has been applied to a variety of different domains and applications such as electricity deregulation (Kavakli et al., 1999), profiling of customers in the banking sector (Kardasis et al., 2000), electronic procurement projects (Kardasis et al., 2004) and co-ordination of systems in large-scale spectators' events (Loucopoulos, 2003).

The S^3 approach is motivated by four 'principles: (a) *Systems thinking* in considering all interrelations between different system components forming a whole (Chackland, 1999; Richmond, 1993); (b) *Abstract thinking* in moving away from the physical manifestation of processes (Walsham, 1994); (c) *Operational thinking* in considering the dynamics of a business process and in particular their behaviour over time (Sterman, 2000; Forrester, 1999); (d) *Solution-first thinking* in attempting to identify requirements by generating a provisional design whose purpose is to highlight potential functionality (Carroll, 2002).

In terms of method steps there are essentially two activities: (a) *model building and critiquing* (Andersen et al., 1997; Vennix, 1999) and (b) *simulation and group deliberation* (Fowler, 1996; Wolstenholme, 1995). Models are mainly built by analysts with input from domain experts but are critiqued and revised by stakeholders. Analysts also facilitate simulation sessions where model parameters are instantiated by stakeholders. Consensus building stakeholder workshops develop scenarios that facilitate deliberation of alternative future realizations.

To demonstrate the way the S^3 approach can be used to elicit and validate early requirements consider a number of examples will be given henceforth taken from a large application involving requirements for venue operations for the Athens 2004 Olympic Games (Loucopoulos et al., 2003). This problem domain is one of *process integration* that was phased by the Athens Organising Committee (ATHOC). There were many different *co-operating agents* (e.g. the distribution of results involves the co-ordination of systems concerned with timing, information structuring, information communication, reprographics, and physical distribution). Different stakeholders had *distinct goals* and expectations of systems (e.g. transportation is solely concerned with safe and timely arrival and departure of spectators whereas catering is concerned with meeting demand during the operation of a venue). Domain experts from 27 different functional areas had to arrive to a consensus of the functionality of an entire venue (e.g. transportation needs to be co-ordinated with crowd queuing control which in turn need to co-ordinate with security etc).

Co-development of business processes and support systems for this problem led to a number of complex decision making activities during early requirements. For example, addressing issues such as "what are the appropriate types and level of resources that will be needed by each functional area for each venue?", "what are the interrelationships and interdependencies of the various functional areas in providing the required services to the various customer groups?", "what is the trade-off between the desired service level and the resource allocation / requirements for each activity involved in a process?", "what is the optimal operational smoothing / resource levelling for the overall process pertaining to a given customer group?"

Ultimately, ATHOC had to specify the physical infrastructure (e.g. building works, public transportation etc), support systems (e.g. security systems, reporting systems, catering systems, ATMs etc) and procedures (e.g. protocols for dissemination of results, crowd control etc) in such a way so as to satisfy both the *individual* requirements of each functional area and the *systemic* requirements that arise from the process-oriented view of venue operations. It was therefore, profoundly important to reach agreement between stakeholders from all 27 functional areas on the way that their *interdependent requirements* were to be dealt in the most transparent, quantifiable and effective way possible.

2.1 Model Building

In eliciting the goals for the venue operations system, the aim was to understand what determined the successful operation of the system. This involved helping the various stakeholders externalise the (sometimes implicit) goals that they had, capturing these goals, and synthesising that knowledge with information from other sources, such as existing documentation, abstract descriptions of various systems and procedures, and so forth. Stakeholders' goals were thus an initial, high-level expression of system requirements viewed from the perspective of ATHOC, i.e. the *service provider* (as opposed to that of the *user*).

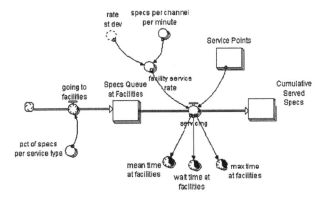

Figure 1: Model Fragment Regarding Venue Service Facilities

An example of high-level goal was expressed with respect to the overall presence of spectators in a venue. Given that a venue may hold more than one event during a day, at any time there may be spectators arriving at the venue area for one of the upcoming sessions, spectators leaving the venue from one of the past sessions, and spectators participating in a current session. The total number of spectators present has to be somehow controlled for practical reasons such as the availability of resources (e.g. space), but also due to safety concerns. This translates into the goal 'manage the total presence of spectators in the venue area'. This is an abstract goal that needs to be made more specific; to refine it, the stakeholders examined the factors influencing the presence of spectators in the venue and their distribution in the various areas of which it consists.

In order to understand the effects of choices that stakeholders made, it was essential to develop business process models that operationalised the stakeholders' goals. These models could be viewed at both a 'local' level and a 'global' level. Local level process view related to a single customer group, a small area of the venue, and a small part of venue resources and functions (workforce, machinery, consumables). Global level process view corresponded to the dynamic profiling of all venue components, over an extended time frame (e.g. an entire day of the Games), possibly with respect to the needs of more than one customer group.

A distinguishing feature of this type of situation is the large number of different service types that the model must represent, since the behaviour of the venue operations system is affected by each of these service sub-components. As a result, the degree of complexity in the resulting process model rises dramatically.

Process modelling in the S^3 approach is driven by the *strategy* as advocated in stakeholders' goals, by the *service* that one is attempting to offer in meeting this strategy and by the *support* that needs to be deployed in order for the specific level of service to be realised.

Consider the following strategic goal 'Minimise the time that a spectator has to wait in order to get serviced'. The service level will vary according to the spatial location of a particular catering outlet and the temporal demand according to games' schedule. Achieving a service level of less than 5 minutes response will depend in addition on the units and volume of support that is allocated to the particular catering outlet. There are two issues that make the definition of requirements for support systems less than straightforward. Firstly, there is dynamic demand and secondly, this particular service (i.e. catering) is itself dependent on other service units and in turn its behaviour influences other service units. At a basic, local level, the behaviour of each catering outlet is influenced by demand and supply as shown in the model fragment of Figure 1.

The demand is determined in part through the pct of specs per service type variable, which expresses the number of customers expected at each type of service facility per unit of time as a percentage of total spectator presence. Total spectator presence depends on overall spectators' behaviour in the venue area, which interacts with this model fragment through a number of feedback loops (not shown here due to the complexity of the complete model).

The supply is determined by two parameters: the number of Service Points available (e.g. 10 stands selling food), and the specs per channel per minute service rate (e.g. two spectators serviced per service point per minute). According to this

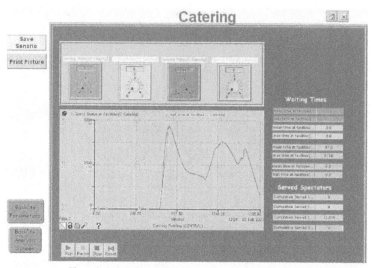

Figure 2: Stakeholder-Defined Parameters for Catering

representation, spectators arrive at the service facility (`going to facilities`), queue there for a while if no service point is available (`Specs Queue at Facilities`), and eventually get serviced (`servicing`).

Using this model fragment we can elaborate on the way that stakeholder goals were refined through the use of process modelling. We previously mentioned the high-level goal 'Minimise the time that a customer has to wait in order to get serviced'. The realisation of this goal for a given type of service facility, and for a given demand, depends on the availability of supply for that facility. Supply is composed of two independent factors, the number of service points and the service rate. Therefore, the initial goal was decomposed into two complementary (i.e. non-competing) goals: 'Maximise the number of service points' and 'maximise the service rate'. These goals are more accurate than the initial one, however they need to be analysed further in order to become quantifiable.

2.2   Scenarios

The generation of different scenarios concerning each problem studied, and the simulation of these scenarios with the help of the process models developed, is an essential part of requirements definition in the S³ approach. Evidence from the use of this approach on a number of industrial-strength applications indicate that scenarios are an indispensable tool for truly understanding the

implications of stakeholders in their deliberation of requirements. For example, in the components of the system model that deals with services (ATMs, merchandising, catering, etc), fragment of which is shown in Figure 1, there is a plethora of *stakeholder defined assumptions* regarding demand and supply for each service facility. Each set of parameter instantiation gives rise to a specific behaviour. For example, the example shown in Figure 2 is the result of the following choices: (a) all catering outlets are situated in a central area; (b) there are 44 catering outlets in this area.

These two sets of parameters define the way that support may be offered. In addition to these, stakeholders also defined the demand for service as shown in Figure 3. The choices available are: (a) the possible demand for catering set at 15 percent of all spectators and (b) the likely average response of each catering service which is set at 2 minutes per customer.

These 4 sets of parameters dictate the way that *strategy-service-support* interact to give rise to different system behaviours. Although in this example the focus of stakeholders was on catering, the interaction between requirements for catering and requirements for all other components of the system became highly visible. Catering for example, does not exist in isolation. It is influenced by other components and in turn it influences others. Other relevant factors, such as spectators' arrival and departure patterns, were taken into account. The stakeholders involved in scenario generation investigated the range of probable values for each of

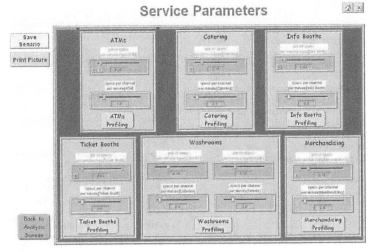

Figure 3: Simulation results for the 'Merchandising' service

these parameters, as well as some 'extreme' values that were less probable but worth investigating nonetheless. Each scenario was characterised by the values of *all* independent variables; the number of possible scenarios thus depended on the number of their feasible combinations.

The models were subjected to testing through simulation sessions, in workshops involving stakeholders in groups ranging from 5 to as many as 40. In all workshops the models were presented to project stakeholders together with the corresponding scenarios and simulated runs.

These features enabled stakeholders to reach a consensus about the underlying processes and the implications that each choice would have on overall system behaviour. The first type of result, i.e. results concerning specific components of the system, helped to answer operational questions concerning the rational allocation of resources and the resulting service provision capabilities of the system. The second type of result proved useful for understanding the overall behaviour of a venue, thus answering higher-level, management questions concerning customer presence and distribution, arrival and departure patterns etc.

3   CONCLUSIONS

In early requirements, when there is a great deal of vagueness and uncertainty about system goals that are often set against a background of social, organizational and political turbulence, the need for a systematic and systemic way of dealing with all co-development aspects seems to be of paramount importance.

The work presented in this paper is motivated by the premise that informal and textual descriptions need to give way to conceptual modelling languages with clear semantics and intuitive syntax so that an application can be defined at an appropriate level of abstraction. This greatly enhance visualisation of processes that in turn contribute to a more informed discussion and agreement between stakeholders.

Whilst qualitative-based conceptual modelling approaches seem to be an improvement on purely linguistic-based approaches, they fail to bridge the communication gap between client stakeholders and analysts. The issue of analyst-client relationship has been highlighted by many authors (Kennedy, 1994; Bashein et al., 1997). This type of modelling paradigm that has evolved from work on Databases, Software Engineering or Object-oriented Design, with its analyst orientation paradigms does little to enhance communication.

The S^3 approach argues that that qualitative models need to be enhanced with quantitative capabilities. These capabilities provide opportunities for the generation and evaluation of alternative scenarios with respect to stakeholder choices on their requirements. This way of working supports the way experts work on ill-structured problem settings such as planning and design (Carroll, 2002).

ACKNOWLEDGEMENTS

The author wishes to express his gratitude to his many colleagues, analysts and stakeholders, at the Athens 2004 Olympic Games Organising Committee. In particular to Nikos Prekas for managing the team of analysts and liaising with stakeholders in the most effective manner and to Dimitris Beis and Gregory Vgontzas for having the insight to adopt new innovative approaches towards the design of venue operations. The author would also like to acknowledge the contribution of Kostas Zografos of the Athens University of Economics and Business for the work on the design framework.

REFERENCES

D. F. Andersen, G. P. Richardson, and J. A. M. Vennix (1997) *Group Model Building: Adding More Science to the Craft*, System Dynamics Review, Vol. 13, No. 2, pp. 187-201.

B. Bashein and M. I. Markus (1997) *A Credibility Equation for IT Specialists*, Sloan Management Review, Vol. 38, No. 4, pp. 35-44.

J. M. Carroll (2002) *Scenarios and Design Cognition*, in proceedings of IEEE Joint International Conference on Requirements Engineering (RE'02), E. Dubois and K. Pohl (ed) Essen, Germany, pp. 3-5, 2002.

P. B. Checkland (1999) *Soft Systems Methodology : a 30-year Retrospective*, New ed. ed. Chichester: Wiley, 1999.

J. W. Forrester (1999) *Principles of Systems*. Waltham, MA: Pegasus Communications Inc., 1999.

A. Fowler (1996) *Simulations's Evolving Role In Management*, in proceedings of 1996 International System Dynamics Conference, G. P. Richardson and J. D. Sterman (ed) Cambridge, Massachusetts, pp. 162-165, 1996.

A. Fuxman, L. Liu, M. Pistore, M. Roveri, and J. Mylopoulos (2003) *Specifying and Analysing Early Requirements: Some Experimental Results*, in proceedings of 11th IEEE International Conference on Requirements Engineering, (ed) Monterey Bay, California, USA, pp. 105-116, 2003.

A. Fuxman, J. Mylopoulos, M. Pistore, and P. Traverso (2001) *Model Checking Early Requirements Specifications in Tropos*, in proceedings of 5th IEEE International Symposium on Requirements Engineering, (ed) Toronto, Canada, pp. 174-181, 2001.

R. D. Galliers (1993) *Towards a Flexible Information Architecture: Integrating Business Strategies, Information Systems Strategies and Business Process Redesign*, Journal of Information Systems, Vol. 3, No. 3, pp. 199-213.

P. Kardasis, N. Prekas, and P. Loucopoulos (2000) *A Framework of Patterns for the Banking Sector*, in proceedings of DEXA 2000 DomE - International Workshop on Enterprise and Domain Engineering, in conjunction with the DEXA 2000 Conference, (ed) Greenwich, UK, pp. 818-822, 2000.

P. Kardasis and P. Loucopoulos (2004) *Expressing and Organising Business Rules towards the Development of an Electronic Procurement System: An Empirical Study*, Information & Software Technology, Vol. 46, No. 11, pp. 701-718.

V. Kavakli and P. Loucopoulos (1999) *Goal-Driven Business Process Analysis - Application in Electricity Deregulation*, Information Systems, Vol. 24, No. 3, pp. 187-207.

S. Kennedy (1994) *Why Users Hate your Attitude*, Informatics, Vol. February, No. 1994, pp. 29-32.

F. Leymann and W. Altenhuber (1994) *Managing Business Processes as an Information Resource*, IBM Systems Journal, Vol. 33, No. 2, pp. 326-348.

P. Loucopoulos, K. Zografos, and N. Prekas (2003) *Requirements Elicitation for the Design of Venue Operations for the Athens2004 Olympic Games*, in proceedings of 11th IEEE International Requirements Engineering Conference, (ed) Monterey Bay, California, U.S.A., pp. 223-232, 2003.

P. Loucopoulos (2003) *The S3 (Strategy-Service-Support) Framework for Business Process Modelling*, in proceedings of Workshop on Requirements Engineering for Business Process Support (REBPS'03), J. Eder, R. Mittermeir, and B. Pernici (ed) Klagenfurt/Velden, Austria, pp. 378-382, 2003.

M. Ould (1995) *Business Processes: Modelling and Analysis for Re-engineering and Improvement*. Chichester: John Wiley & Sons, 1995.

B. M. Richmond (1993) *Systems Thinking: Critical Thinking Skills for the 1990s and beyond*, System Dynamics Review, Vol. 9, No. 2, pp. 113-133.

J. D. Sterman (2000) *Business Dynamics : Systems Thinking and Modeling for a Complex World*. Boston: Irwin/McGraw-Hill, 2000.

J. A. M. Vennix (1999) *Group Model-Building: Tackling Messy Problems*, System Dynamics Review, Vol. 15, No. 4, pp. 379-401.

G. Walsham (1994) *Virtual Organization: An Alternative View*, Information Society, Vol. 10, No. 4, pp. 289-292.

E. F. Wolstenholme (1995) *Decision Analysis Using Dynamic Simulation*, in proceedings of System Dynamics '95, T. Shimada and K. Saeed (ed) Tokyo, pp. 937-945, 1995.

ORGANIZATIONAL PATTERNS
Beyond Technology to People

James O. Coplien

PROG Group, Vrije Universiteit Brussel, PO Box 4557, Wheaton, IL 60540, USA
Email: JOCoplien@cs.com

Keywords: Pattern language, software development, architecture, anthropology, ethnography, Christopher Alexander.

Abstract: Most of the software discipline has come to honor the role of architecture to organize software development. The software pattern discipline has taken up the architectural metaphor quite literally, borrowing its key notions from Christopher Alexander, an innovative master builder of houses, neighborhoods, and towns. However, the software industry has missed the obvious: that architecture is a secondary concern that precipitates from the structure of the enterprise that builds it. Getting the architecture right means getting the enterprise structure right: it is certainly a necessary and potentially sufficient condition for achieving most of the goals that software engineering holds out for architectural activity.

Like most metaphors, the architectural metaphor breaks down somewhere. Unlike houses, whose structure tends to reflect the activities of the end users of the product, the structure of software exists more to serve those who build it than those who use it. This parallel has been shifting, but not on the software side: modern buildings, driven more by technology that make it possible to create 100-foot spans on the ground floor of a skyscraper, pay homage to the technology to be used in construction, and to the design techniques used to support that technology. Software, a largely technological field, has had this outlook almost from the beginning. As an industry focused on technology, it is no surprise that our software pattern discipline has taken up a largely technical agenda. Our current direction in patterns avoids the most central foundation of the pattern discipline: to build systems that are beautiful, morally profound, and "habitable" for the people they touch.

Yet there is hope: as a strong parallel to the structural concerns of software that are found in software architecture, *organizational patterns* give a voice to the crucial structural constructs of software development enterprises. It is these structures of human relationships, rather than the technological underpinnings, that drive architecture. That fact has long been known to the industry as Conway's Law, but most managers view Conway's Law more as a Dilbertesque joke than as a sober planning principle.

Organizational patterns are a major stride for creating the generative structure of the business—the structure of the enterprise itself—that gives rise to such other important structures as the system architecture and, by inference, the system's human interface. The first major pattern language of software organizational structure has been completed after a decade of research. There is much more that can be done—not just by organizational specialists, but also by "software people" of every job and description.

1   INTRODUCTION

Architecture is one of the longest-standing and widely known metaphors in computer science. Most software engineering communities—whether in software production, computer science education, or software management—harbour deeply held intuitions about its importance. Awe of architecture (and not, perhaps surprisingly, for either requirements or for coding) has propelled the popularity of notations such as UML, the methodologies that embed them, and the tools that express them.

Each software development organization has its own architectural principles. Such principles as coupling and cohesion and modularity are almost universal, and other principles such as the Laws of Demeter are peculiar to such design styles as object orientation.

Are these true principles, or just shadows of a deeper and more important principle that has come to be ignored?

I. Seruca et al. (eds.), Enterprise Information Systems VI, 43–52.
© 2006 *Springer. Printed in the Netherlands.*

2   THE ARCHITECTURAL METAPHOR

It all started at IBM in the early 1960s. Fred Brooks approached Jerry Weinberg with the idea that architecture might be a good metaphor for what we do in software development. Jerry encouraged him to pursue the metaphor, and the rest is history.

Of course, it didn't end there; many others would rediscover the metaphor from different perspectives over the years. One of them would be Peter Naur, who noted this in 1968:

> ...software designers are in a similar position to architects and civil engineers, particularly those concerned with the design of large heterogeneous constructions, such as towns and industrial plants. It therefore seems natural that we should turn to these subjects for ideas about how to attack the design problem. As one single example of such a source of ideas I would like to mention: Christopher Alexander: Notes on the Synthesis of Form. (Naur 1968)

As time progressed the metaphor took on a life of its own, and the word took on a meaning that might strike is originators as foreign or off-centre. This problem wasn't unique to software. The architect Christopher Alexander also maintained that architecture of the modern age had lost its roots. Alexander argued that in early human cultures and in contemporary rural cultures, people built their own houses from materials familiar to them from everyday life. They didn't hire architects and perhaps not even carpenters, but invested themselves in the building of their homes or businesses. Sometimes a community would come together for a barn raising, or neighbours would lend a hand if someone were re-building after a fire. However, the homeowner was in touch with the materials of the craft and with the details of the product itself.

Alexander faults technology with a decrease in the quality of construction and decay in beauty. That reinforced steel beams are available as construction materials makes it possible to create a 70-foot span in the lobby of a skyscraper hotel. That one can build such structures doesn't mean they are beautiful. Another key aspect of technology is its affinity for pre-manufactured and often mass-produced parts. Alexander noted that pre-manufactured parts have all their degrees of freedom fixed at the factory, and thus cannot be made to fit in the context where they belong.

But it is impossible to form anything which has the character of nature by adding preformed parts.

When parts are modular and made before the whole, by definition then, they are identical, and it is impossible for every part to be unique, according to its position in the whole. (Alexander, 1979: p. 368)

This key idea gained the attention of the object-oriented software community, a community that had developed a stake in pre-manufactured software parts called *objects*. The word of the day was reuse, and objects had offered hope that pre-manufactured objects could achieve this vision. The evidence suggested otherwise. Reuse wasn't working, certainly not in the object-oriented world.

The other aspect of Alexander's worldview that gained the attention of the object-oriented community was Alexander's attentiveness to the human side of design. Alexander's notion of design went far beyond utilitarianism to broader quality of human life and to the core itself of human existence. Patterns were ultimately about people.

At the time, the pattern community took this human element as a value and a watchword but failed to make it a central agenda. Having suffered lapses in architectural thinking over the years, the software community focused on the architectural aspect of patterns as its end. This led to a technological cornucopia of patterns, mostly lacking in the life that was central to Alexander's original work. Alexander initially offered this insight on software patterns ten years ago (and published the perspective in 1999), but not much has changed in the interim:

> Have you asked whether a particular system of patterns, taken as a system, will generate a coherent computer program? If so, I have not yet heard about that. But the point is, that is what we were looking for all the time. Again, I have no idea to what extent that is true for you and whether you are looking for the same thing when you work on software patterns.

> So far, as a lay person trying to read some of the works that have been published by you in this field, it looks to me more as though mainly the pattern concept, for you, is an inspiring format that is a good way of exchanging fragmentary, atomic ideas about programming. Indeed, as I understand it, that part is working very well. But these other two dimensions, (1) the moral capacity to produce a living structure and (2) the generativity of the thing, its capability of producing coherent wholes—I haven't seen very much evidence of those two things in software pattern theory. (Alexander 1999: p. 75)

In the world of buildings and towns, architecture is sometimes an end in itself: an artistic statement. Such is rarely the case in software. Good aesthetics compensate neither for lack of structural soundness nor for human inconvenience. The goal of architecture, and therefore of patterns, should be the morally profound, coherent wholes that generate human comfort.

2.1 Architecture and Process

Software developers sometimes use the term "architect" as a verb. Architecture is a *noun*; the verb is *design*. *Design* is the process we use to solve a problem. It starts with a vague understanding of the problem and gradually builds system structure. In doing so, it also builds an increased understanding of the problem.

The process is more than just mapping an understanding of the problem onto solution structures that can subsequently be built. Most of the work on a new system focuses on identifying what the system should do and then, to a lesser degree, on how the system should accomplish these ends. After the first release comes maintenance. The process of maintenance design focuses on recovering some understanding of what the system does and how it does it, understanding that has been lost over time. One does maintenance to fix problems in the software, problems that have arisen as the user community interfaces with the software architecture and its applications. It is perhaps only on the first round of maintenance that requirements become clear. Anything prior to that is either a hope or a guess.

The architecture of a system is therefore not a truth—or, if it is a truth, it is a truth at a given point of time that emerges from the process of development itself. Software design is dialectic between the development community and the architecture. The architecture "learns" from the processes of the organizations that build it, and serves the processes of the organizations that use it. In a healthy development, there is good feedback from the user process to the designer process. Architecture has meaning only in the context of these associated processes. These processes owe to the structure and values of the organizations in which they arise. Carried out well, these processes can improve quality of life for inhabitants of both the design and user communities.

3 THE HUMAN SIDE OF ARCHITECTURE

Alexander believed that the whole focus of architecture should be quality of life. He had no time for architecture as art for its own sake; the artistic quality of architecture should emanate from its human scale and its suitability to human needs. He went beyond the saw of "form follows function" to embrace form also as the source of beauty and as the foundation of harmony in a system. Architecture exists for the sake of those who inhabit it.

Software architecture in fact has, or should have, an analogous focus. The software itself doesn't care what its architecture is. In fact, many stock principles of architecture such as coupling and cohesion work against desiderata such as performance. Why, then, are we concerned about architecture?

In a 1968 *Datamation* article (Conway 1968), Conway proposed that the structure of any software architecture reflects the structure of the organization that builds it. Suppose you were going to form a company to write compilers. If the company were divided into three departments, it is almost certain that the company will produce a three-pass compiler. Software architecture must align with the structure of the organization that builds it. If the organization already exists, the architecture should reflect that existing structure.

We can think of software developers as "inhabiting" the code. We too often forget that the users of a program are also "inhabitants" of the code. That suggests that software architecture must align not only with the structure of the organization that builds it, but also with that of the organization that uses it. Consider a CAD system that will be used to build an airplane. The enterprise using the tool has a design group, a manufacturing group, and a maintenance group (and other groups as well, no doubt). Each group has its own culture and expertise. We will want to build the CAD system with one component optimized for the designers, another component optimized for manufacturing, and another for field maintenance. In short, the architecture of the CAD system should follow the structure of the *using* organization. One can elicit this structure using techniques such as domain analysis (Coplien 1998), which aligns the overall system architecture with the structure of the business. The final alignment to attend to is that between the software architecture and that of the development organization. Naïvely put, the business structure shapes the software architecture and the software architecture shapes the development teams. In reality, some development teams have historic structures that are difficult to change, so they may have more influence on both the architecture and on the business structure itself than in the ideal case. The fundamental principle is that the three structures align.

As an aside, it is instructive to consider one popular example of misalignment: that which results from geographically distributed development or outsourcing. Geographically distributed development comes about from internal business concerns, history, corporate acquisitions and partnerships, and sometimes from simple politics. It suggests a set of structures and patterns that can be arbitrarily different from the core structures of the business. Geographic boundaries are among the most difficult ones to change: distance is a compelling force in any joint endeavour. This is the great risk of geographic distribution and outsourcing. (Several of our organizational patterns address this problem by insisting that the geographic structure follow the business structure: e.g., ORGANIZATION FOLLOWS LOCATION and ORGANIZATION FOLLOWS MARKET are two such patterns.)

Software engineering—true to its name—usually views these as technological issues. It is true that technology opens new doors of opportunity in design. However, technology more often serves as a medium rather than as a form. While it extends the range of design into more useful and beautiful forms, it also extends the range of design in the other direction. Alexander notes that modern building technology has given us power to set our intuition aside and to build horrid structures. These structures lack the differentiation that owes to human design. Just as modern technology allows us to build buildings that appear to express art for its own sake, rather than for the sake of function, so modern software design technologies encourage us to use methodologies or design fads which rarely can be justified in terms of their contribution to quality of human life. Such benefits as are promised by these technologies are usually taken at face value. They usually relate more to near-term business considerations such as time to market and development cost, rather than to the amount of time it will take the user to learn to use the program, or the cost that the user will incur from the program's human/machine interface inefficiencies. Just as modern technology allows us to build ugly buildings, modern methods, languages, and GUI-builders allow us to build astonishingly ugly software.

4   ENTERPRISE-LEVEL HUMAN-CENTERED DESIGN

Software development culture is entering a phase where it is recognizing the importance of the human element. Much of the realization comes with widespread frustration with widely used software platforms. It was this notion of human-centred design that was at the heart of the Macintosh project at Apple, which in retrospect proved to be a leader in the way it gave stature to human concerns in the human interface.

This is not uniquely a human interface concern. Raskin (Raskin 2000) notes that computing is all about supporting the *users'* conceptual model of their workflows. Most of that relates to artefacts and information that travels between people; it is all about the structure of the *users'* organization. Beyer and Holtzblatt's great, common sense book (Beyer Holtzblatt 1999) on software design tells us how to build these conceptual models: Go and sit with your users and, as Yogi Berra would say, you can observe a lot just by watching.

The great folks of software have recognized for years that understanding the structure and behaviours of the organizations that use software and the people they comprise can lead to great design (e.g., Weinberg 1980). However, the human agenda never seemed to take root. Through the 1970s and 1980s, any human revolution in software seemed elusive.

This perspective took on new life in the early 1990s when eight leaders of the object-oriented programming community came together in a meeting in Colorado to ponder why object-oriented development hadn't delivered on its promises of reuse and productivity. Their conclusion was that object orientation had been ignoring the relationships between objects, and that programming had become a dehumanized industry. If you believe Conway's Law, and map the object-to-object relationships onto the groups of people that program those objects, the problem again reduces to organizational structure. That meeting crystallized the software pattern discipline.

Most early patterns from this discipline continued in the computer science tradition of software architecture: focusing on recurring structures within the software itself. But a small number of people took the next step to articulate patterns in the organizations that create or use this software, and suggested focusing on *that* structure to cure software ills. Those works included Norm Kerth's *Caterpillar's Fate* (Kerth 1995), Bruce Whitenack's RAPPeL (Whitenack 1995), and a collection of so-called *Development Process*

Generative Pattern Language patterns by this author (Coplien 1995).

Others would soon follow. In the following year, Alistair Cockburn published *Prioritizing Forces in Software Design* (Cockburn 1996) at the same time that Ward Cunningham's EPISODES pattern language appeared (Cunningham 1996). The former would become one of the foundations of the Agile Alliance, and the latter would become one of the foundations of Extreme Programming. Both of these foundations drew from similar principles that could be found in their counterparts of the previous year, and that would continue to be found in their successors. Unlike computer science design, which was master-planned according to some method, these techniques gave room to emergence: to design the same way that nature grows. Whereas computer science tried to employ formalism to omnisciently predict outcomes, these approaches embraced feedback. The dichotomy continues: controlling versus responsive, revenues versus costs, technology-centred versus people-centred.

Of course, both cost and revenues matter in real development; formalism has its place; truly mature processes may be repeatable and predictable. However, in the 1980s the pendulum had swung too far in the favour of the technological perspective. Patterns in general, and organizational patterns in particular, restored some balance to the object-oriented design community. While the architectural pattern folks wrote patterns of the structure of software, the organizational patterns folks wrote patterns of organizational structure. The human side of computing and technical side of computing had finally found a common language to express the common structure they each had been gazing at from their own perspective for decades.

The computer science path to design looks to mathematics, type theory, notations and methods to attain excellence. The human-cantered way looks to organizational structure and to the behaviours of people in those organizations. Great software design, if any different from organizational design, is too closely linked with it to be considered a separate discipline.

5 PATTERNS

If patterns had just been a notation or a language that allowed programmers and organizational people to communicate, that would have been one thing. But there is more to patterns than that, and what the deeper foundations portend for organizational structure and software development may be key to the human component of our discipline. It is important to explore these foundations.

5.1 Structure in Design

Design is all about solving problems by building something, and building has a lot to do with composition. In fact, most of our facilities for interacting with the world around us are based on structure and perception of structure. Human perception itself is based on structure, symmetry, and patterns (Alexander Huggings 1964). The core of what humans find beautiful isn't perfect symmetry: the fine structures of design are slightly asymmetric. This is no accident; there is no perfect symmetry in nature, and understanding the foundations of this nature of nature owes much to modern advances in physics (Close 2000). Physicists have a word they use to describe the configurations that result from these "broken symmetries:" *patterns*. Such deep stuff of the structure of the Universe underlies Alexander's design worldview:

> Nature, too, creates beautiful structures which are governed by repeated application of structure-preserving transformations. In this connection, I think it is useful to remark that what I call structure-preserving transformations are very closely related to what has become known as "symmetry · breaking" in physics. (Alexander 2002: p. 63)

5.2 Structure of Organizations

If these ideas underlie the structure of nature, they should underlie the structure software systems that interact with "nature" or the cultural structures that emerge from nature. You might object and say that culture is too far removed from nature for patterns to propagate to that level but, no: it's patterns all the way down. The classic texts on the structure of cultures use an almost perfectly analogous notion of pattern to describe even the architecture of human organizations:

> Patterns are those arrangements or systems of internal relationship which give to any culture its coherence or plan, and keep it from being a mere accumulation of random bits. They are therefore of primary importance. (Kroeber 1948: p. 119)

5.3 It's All About Change

Evolution has had a long time to produce a perfect human culture, but it doesn't seem to have fared well to that end. There are two reasons: differentiation of the contexts in which the cultures evolved (different climates, different geography), and the ongoing march of change. Human beings learn, and cultures and societies as a whole learn and change. Good software supports change. Good organizations support change.

Change is hard. Software change has little to do with softness; it is hard. Cultural change is even harder. One major goal of a culture is to maintain status quo: to keep familiar things familiar. Left to its own devices, a culture changes little or not at all. Given external stimuli that tend to undermine its rituals or assumptions, it changes slowly by default. A responsively changing organization requires active *learning* at the organizational level: the external stimulus must become an internal stimulus and focus. How does this learning take place?

Most modern software folks, and certainly those who have learned enough to know that organizations and people are important, will tell you that it is an issue of development process. If one can change the process, then one can accommodate most changes suffered by a culture such as a software development organization. This assessment is correct up to a point. The next and more interesting questions are: Where do processes come from, and how does process learning take place?

Swieringa and Wierdsma (1992) talk about three structures in an organization and about the different levels of learning that happen for these three structures. At the most surface level are organizational processes; they speak of *single-loop learning* that happens at this level, a learning of relationships between cause and effect. Beneath that level is the structure of the organization: the relationships, entities, and patterns that make the organization what it is. One might ask, for example, what caused the organization even to *want* to learn. The processes themselves don't beg for learning; there is something in the structure of the organization itself (or deeper) that encourages this learning. So, for example, learning how to learn might be an issue of organizational structure. That is a doubly recursive feedback loop with respect to the cause-and-effect model of the process level. Learning at this level is called *double-loop learning*. A third level of organizational learning answers the question of where structure comes from: it comes from principles and values. These properties go to the heart of the organization's identity. Learning at that level is *triple-loop learning*: re-inventing the organization.

For example, why do you have a code review process? We have code reviews because of functional differentiation within the organization.

Coders do code, but we need someone to review their code from the perspective of a different "place" in the organizational structure. This "place" may be the structure of another piece of code (code written by someone else), or the perspective of the tester, or the perspective of the people who understand the requirements and who want to know whether the code will do what it is supposed to do. This differentiation in structure is itself what gives rise to processes such as code reviews, integration builds, and test plans. Where does this structure come from? It comes from principles and values: principles such as divide and conquer (division of labour), and values such as quality (which creates those parts of structure that attend to testing and perhaps to process itself).

Re-inventing the business is hard, and some businesses haven't survived attempts to do themselves this favour. Yet single-loop learning can only be temporary because the deeper structural level will cause processes to revert to their former successions. Change must happen at the structural level. To make lasting changes to organizational processes means changing the organizational structure.

Changing the organizational structure means more than shuffling titles on an organizational chart. In the cultural sense, "organizational structure" means the patterns of relationships between roles, individuals, and groups within the enterprise. Having a piece of paper called an organizational chart that states what the organization is doesn't make it so; the structure of the real organization can be found around the water coolers, in Email exchanges, in the hallways where groups of people are collocated and, to some smaller degree, in the meetings that bring people together. There is a structure in these relationships. Swieringa and Wierdsma call this the *instrumental structure* of the organization.

Real change in an organization comes from evolution of the instrumental structure. Change is the only certainty in life. What are the units of change? Patterns fit the need very well for several reasons.

First, patterns are enduring. Because they work at the structural level, they aren't temporary in the sense that process changes are temporary.

Second, they are incremental. A good pattern is a structure-preserving transformation. It works locally, adding structure to some part of a system while sustaining the remaining overall structure. Big changes are hard; they best can be accomplished by series of small changes. Is this always possible? No. However, many organizational changes can and should be accomplished piecemeal while they are too often orchestrated through a Big Bang. Some organizations are never the same thereafter.

Third, this approach leads to a sound architecture. If the organizational structure grows according to a pattern language that draws on the key structures of the business domain, then the architecture will in turn reflect those key structures. That's what architecture is supposed to do—serve the business. We must continually remind ourselves that it should do so not for its own sake, but for the sake of the relationships between the people who inhabit it.

6 KEY PATTERNS OF SOFTWARE DEVELOPMENT

The key patterns of software development organizations have come together in several key collections, many of which were mentioned in Section 4 above. Many of those patterns have been woven together into a single pattern language of about 100 patterns for software development (Coplien Harrison 2004). Here are some of the key patterns from that pattern language.

6.1 Engage Customers

If you want to manage an incremental process that accommodates customer input, and if you want the customer to feel loved, *Then:* Engage customers after Quality Assurance and project management are prepared to serve them. Most of "engaging customers" means listening to them more than it means asking them questions or reviewing Use Cases or UML diagrams with them. Use Cases may have a place in dialogue with the customer but are secondary to the practice of listening. You can observe a lot, just by watching. And it should be a cold day in Hell before a customer sees a UML diagram. Customer engagement means making a customer feel cared for, and that as much means spending time with them as it does fixing their bugs and addressing their requirements.

6.2 Work Flows Inward

If you want information to flow to the producing roles in an organization, *Then:* put

the developer at the center and see that information flows *toward* the center, not *from* the center. If you always feed developers with the resources and information they need and if you allow them to control the process (DEVELOPER CONTROLS PROCESS is another one of our patterns) then the organization will be working its hardest to deliver the artifact that matters most: the software to be delivered to the customer. The alternative is to channel resources to management. But most managers do not directly produce anything delivered to the customer.

6.3 Architect Controls Product

If a project has a long life, *Then:* use the architect to carry the vision forward and serve as the long--term keeper of architectural style. The goal is to keep the conceptual integrity high for the project. The Architect doesn't dictate APIs or code but embodies the principles and styles that are key to success in this line of business.

6.4 Developer Controls Process

If you need to orchestrate the activities of a given location or feature, *Then:* put the Developer role in control of the succession of activities. The Developer role is the one who builds things that your customer pays for; other roles produce internal plans and artifacts that the customer never sees. If the schedule is planned around the Developer, then the Developer is never blocked and Developer productivity can be optimized.

6.5 Hallway Chatter

If developers tend to huddle around the organizational core or supporting roles are inadequately engaged with each other, *Then:* rearrange responsibilities in a way that encourages less isolation and

more interworking among roles and people. Do you think work gets done in meetings and through management channels? Guess again. Grinter and Herbsleb (Grinter Herbsleb 1999) argue that most of the useful communication in an organization takes place in the hallways. WATER COOLER is a closely related pattern.

6.6   Face to Face Before Working Remotely

If a project is divided geographically, *Then:* begin the project with a meeting of everyone in a single place. Of course, you want to avoid geographically distributed development when you can. If you must support remote development, invest in a travel budget so people can meet face to face. If you think it's too expensive, experience indicates that you pay now—or pay later. (The picture was taken at Camp Carson, Colorado, and shows Colonel Wilfrid M. Nlunt, the U.S. commanding officer shaking hands with Colonel Denetrius Xenos, military attaché of the Greek ambassador to the United States—a face-to-face meeting before working remotely.)

6.7 Apprenticeship

If you have difficulty retaining expertise, *Then:* grow expertise internally from existing employees or even new hires. Don't put everyone through one big training program. Nurture expertise (another one of our patterns is DOMAIN EXPERTISE IN ROLES).

7   TOWARDS A PATTERN LANGUAGE

Each one of these patterns incrementally adds structure to the organization: structure between the organization and the customer, structure between the organization and its developers, structure that cuts across formal structures, structure across geographic distance, and the establishment of a structural link to

a new hire. We can build these structures one at a time. These patterns, and dozens like them, combine and interact with each other in rich ways to yield an overall structure that is more powerful than the sum of its parts. We can put patterns together in many different ways to achieve many different organizational styles. Imagine patterns as being like words in a language, and imagine a grammar that defines legal combinations and sequences of these words. Such a collection of patterns, together with the rules for composing them, is called a *pattern language*.

Pattern languages rise to deal with system concerns. They can handle so called "wicked problems" where it's difficult to determine a proper solution given the observed symptoms. What most organizations do when faced with such symptoms is to just try anything—which, in fact, is better than doing nothing. Patterns are a more informed way of just trying anything. They build on years of experience, on the experience of hundreds of organizations that have faced analogous situations in the past.

Pattern languages build cultures. They bring development beyond something technological to create structures and processes at human scale. They help restore the human dimension to software development. We encourage organizations to use try these patterns, to write their own organizational patterns, and in general to use patterns to unleash their own instincts to do what is right, humane, and for the greater good. Many of these patterns are common sense. In a world full of methods, notations, and processes, common sense is so uncommon.

8   CONCLUSION

What is the bottom line? All of this talk about beauty and human value is fine, but it is profitability and market position that dominate software conferences and business plan. Any viable idea must ultimately stoop to that level of concern. So, then: Where does business success start?

Business success starts with business values: the principles and value systems that an enterprise uses to judge its success. Does success depend on usability of the software? Or does your company base success on sales? Can the latter be an accurate reflection of the former? Profitability owes to much more than to having a great product; it owes just as much to being first to market with a product, or to an effective sales campaign. Most markets focus on the so-called bottom line as the measure of success. Profit is an abstraction that has allowed businesses to distance themselves from the day-to-day business concerns of their customers. The modern corporate focus on stock value and quarterly earnings has repressed quality concerns to second-class standing. Requirements documents have become a way of insulating the corporation from engaging the customer in dialogue and in the ongoing process of feedback in development that can lead to true customer satisfaction. Business and technical perspectives have displaced the human perspective.

Involving customers as partners, as an organization that has every bit as much to do with the structure of your product as your own organization does, is a good first step in human-centred design. Such a bird's-eye view of your enterprise can offer rich insights into the architecture of your system, through techniques such as domain analysis. The architecture precipitates naturally from the human concerns. Organizational patterns are a guide to shaping the organizational structures that bode for success. The software architecture echoes that same structure by Conway's Law.

That structure in turn generates the processes that will guide your designers, systems engineers, architects, coders, testers, and marketing people in creating a product that will improve the quality of life for your customers. Good organizational patterns concern themselves with the quality of life of your own employees, too—a corporation should view them as stakeholders whose needs are as important as those of customers.

Patterns are small elements of organizational improvement that contribute to great systems. There probably is no single vision of what makes a great organization. Instead, great systems grow from small systems that work, and they grow through local adaptation and incremental improvement. Patterns capture those steps of improvement that we have found again and again contribute to the health of an enterprise.

Business success and quality of life both emanate from grounding in human concerns. There is no recipe for success, but principles of change based on human interaction and relationship have far-reaching benefits for the software development process and end users. Patterns explicitly embrace these human concerns and can serve as a foundation for so-called process improvement and process re-engineering. While patterns can guide an organization on the path to improvement, both the initiative to change and the pearls of insight must come from within the organization. Improvement proceeds one pattern at a time. In our changing world, the process never ends.

REFERENCES

Alexander, C., and A. W. F. Huggings. "On Changing the Way People See." *Perception and Motor Skills 19*, Southern University Press, 1964, pp. 235-253.

Alexander, Christopher. *The Timeless Way of Building.* New York: Oxford University Press, 1979.

Alexander, C. "The Origins of Pattern Theory, The Future of the Theory, and the Generation of a Living World." In *IEEE Software Special Issue on Architecture Design 16(5)*, September 1999.

Alexander, C. *The Nature of Order: Book One: The Process of Creating Life.* Berkeley, CA: The Center for Environment Structure, 2002.

Beyer, Hugh, and Karen Holtzblatt. *Contextual Design.* San Francisco: Morgan Kauffman, 1998.

Close, F. *Lucifer's Legacy: The Meaning of Asymmetry.* Oxford: Oxford University Press, 2000.

Cockburn, A. Prioritizing Forces in Software Design. In Vlissides, J., Jim Coplien and Norm Kerth, eds., *Pattern Languages of Program Design II.* Reading, MA: Addison-Wesley, 1996.

Conway, Melvin E. How do Committees Invent? *Datamation 14(4)*, April 1968.

Coplien, J. "A Development Process Generative Pattern Language." In Coplien, J., and D. Schmidt, eds., *Pattern Languages of Program Design.* Reading, MA: Addison-Wesley, 1995.

Coplien, J. *Multi-paradigm Design for C++.* Reading, MA: Addison, Wesley, 1998.

Coplien, J., and N. B. Harrison. Organizational Patterns of Agile Software Development. Upper Saddle River, NJ: Prentice-Hall, 2004.

Cunningham, W. "EPISODES: A Pattern Language of Competitive Development." In Vlissides, J., Jim Coplien and Norm Kerth, eds., *Pattern Languages of Program Design II.* Reading, MA: Addison-Wesley, 1996.

Grinter, R., and J. Herbsleb. "Architectures, Coordination, and Distance: Conway's Law and Beyond." *IEEE Software*, Sept/Oct 1999, pp. 63-70.

Kerth, N. "Caterpillars Fate: A Pattern Language for Transforming from Analysis to Design." In Coplien, J., and D. Schmidt, eds., *Pattern Languages of Program Design.* Reading, MA: Addison-Wesley, 1995.

Kroeber, A. Anthropology: *Culture, Patterns and Process.* New York: Harcourt, Brace and World, 1948.

Naur, P. and B. Randell, eds. *Proceedings of NATO Software Engineering Conference.* Garmisch, Germany, 1968.

Raskin, J. *The Humane Interface: New Directions for Designing Interactive Systems.* Reading, MA: Addison-Wesley, 2000.

Swieringa, J., and A. Wierdsma. *Becoming a Learning Organization: Beyond the Learning Curve.* Reading, MA: Addison-Wesley, 1992.

Weinberg, Gerald M. *Software Psychology.* Cambridge, MA: Winthrop Publishers, 1980.

Whitenack, B. "RAPPeL: A Requirements Analysis Pattern Language for Object-Oriented Development." In Coplien, J., and D. Schmidt, eds., *Pattern Languages of Program Design.* Reading, MA: Addison-Wesley, 1995.

PART 1

Databases and
Information Systems Integration

ASSESSING EFFORT PREDICTION MODELS FOR CORRECTIVE SOFTWARE MAINTENANCE
An empirical study

Andrea De Lucia
Dipartimento di Matematica e Informatica
University of Salerno
Via S. Allende, 84081 Baronissi (SA), Italy
Email: adelucia@unisa.it

Eugenio Pompella
EDS Italia Software S.p.A.
Viale Edison, Loc. Lo Uttaro
81100 Caserta, Italy
Email: eugenio.pompella@eds.com

Silvio Stefanucci
Department of Engineering
University of Sannio
Piazza Roma, 82100 Benevento, Italy
Email: stefanucci@unisannio.it

Keywords: Software Engineering, Corrective Software Maintenance, Management, Cost Estimation Models

Abstract: We present an assessment of an empirical study aiming at building effort estimation models for corrective maintenance projects. We show results from the application of the prediction models to a new corrective maintenance project within the same enterprise and the same type of software systems used in a previous study. The data available for the new project are finer grained according to the indications devised in the first study. This allowed to improve the confidence in our previous empirical analysis by confirming most of the hypotheses made and to provide other useful indications to better understand the maintenance process of the company in a quantitative way.

1 INTRODUCTION

Planning software maintenance work is a key factor for a successful maintenance project and for better project scheduling, monitoring, and control. To this aim, effort estimation is a valuable asset to maintenance managers in planning maintenance activities and performing cost/benefits analysis. In fact, it allows to:

- support software related decision making;
- reduce project risks;
- assess the efficiency and productivity of the maintenance process;
- manage resources and staff allocation, and so on.

Management can use cost estimates to approve or reject a project proposal or to manage the maintenance process more effectively. Furthermore, accurate cost estimates would allow organizations to make more realistic bids on external contracts.

Unfortunately, effort estimation is one of the most relevant problems of the software maintenance process (Banker et al., 1993; Kemerer & Slaughter, 1999; Jorgensen, 1995). Predicting software maintenance effort is complicated by the many typical aspects of software and software systems that affect maintenance activities. The maintenance process can be focused on several different types of interventions: correction, adaptation, perfection, etc.

(IEEE, 1998). Maintenance projects may range from ordinary projects requiring simple activities of understanding, impact analysis and modifications, to extraordinary projects requiring complex interventions such as encapsulation, reuse, reengineering, migration, and retirement (De Lucia et al., 2001). Moreover, software costs are the result of a large number of parameters (Boehm, 1981), so any estimation or control technique must reflect a large number of complex and dynamic factors. The predictor variables typically constitute a measure of size in terms of LOC or function points (Niessink & van Vliet, 1998) or complexity (Nesi, 1998) and a number of productivity factors that are collected through a questionnaire (Boehm, 1981). Quality factors that take into account the maintainability of the system are also considered to improve the prediction of the maintenance costs (Granja-Alvarez & Barranco-Garcia, 1997; Sneed, 2003).

The size of a maintenance task can also be used to estimate the effort required to implement the single change (Jorgensen, 1995; Sneed, 2003). However, while useful for larger adaptive or perfective maintenance tasks during software evolution (Fioravanti & Nesi, 2001), this approach is not very attractive for managers that have to estimate the effort required for a corrective maintenance project. Indeed, in this case the effort of a maintenance period greatly depends on the number of

55

I. Seruca et al. (eds.), Enterprise Information Systems VI, 55–62.

maintenance requests, whereas tasks of the same type typically require a similar effort (Basili *et al.*, 1996; Ramil, 2000).

In a recent work (De Lucia *et al.*, 2002), we presented an empirical study aiming at building corrective maintenance effort prediction models from the experience of the Solution Center setup in Italy (in the town of Caserta) by EDS Italia Software, a major international software company. This paper presents a replicated assessment of the effort prediction models described in (De Lucia *et al.*, 2002). We show results from the application of the prediction models to a new corrective maintenance project within the same enterprise and the same application domain as the projects used in the previous study. The data available for the new project were finer grained according to the indications devised in the first study. This allowed to improve the confidence in our previous empirical analysis by confirming most of the hypotheses made and to provide other useful indications to better understand the maintenance process of the company in a quantitative way.

The paper is organized as follows. Sections 2 and 3 report the experimental setting and the results of the previous experimental study, respectively. Section 4 describes the new project, while Sections 5-7 present and discuss the results achieved through the analysis of the finer grained data available for the new maintenance project. Concluding remarks are outlined in Section 8.

2 EXPERIMENTAL SETTING

Most of the business of the subject company concerns maintaining third party legacy systems. The subject company realizes outsourcing of system conduction and maintenance, including help desk services, for several large companies. Very often the customers ask for a very high service agreement level and this requires an accurate choice and allocation of very skilled maintainers, with adequate knowledge of the application domain and programming language of the maintenance project. This implies a careful definition of the maintenance process with well-defined activities, roles, and responsibilities to avoid inefficiencies (Aversano *et al.*, 2002). The phases of the life-cycle of the ordinary maintenance process are shown in Table 1. They closely follow the IEEE Standard for Software Maintenance (IEEE, 1998).

The data set available for our study is composed of a number of corrective software maintenance projects conducted on software systems of different customers. The subject systems are mainly business applications in banking, insurance, and public administration. These projects allow for general conclusions that can be applied to other corrective maintenance projects in the business application domains of the subject company.

Table 1: Phases of the corrective maintenance process

Phase	Short description
Define	Requirements identification and definition
Analyze	Requirements analysis
Design	Design of software modules and test cases
Produce	Implementation of software modules and execution of test cases
Implement	Delivery and introduction of the new modules in the software system

The main advantage of the data set is that it does not contain missing values. This is due to the careful manner in which the data was collected. In fact, the subject company is at CMM level 3 and is currently planning the assessment to achieve CMM level 4. At the CMM level 3, metrics are collected, analyzed, and used to control the process and to make corrections to the predicted costs and schedule, as necessary. Therefore, metric collection was crucial and supported by automatic tools, such as workflow management systems which are of aid to process automation and improvement (Aversano *et al.*, 2002). Technical metrics, such as software complexity metrics, were not available. In fact, for each new maintenance project, the subject company preliminarily collects a number of different technical metrics on a meaningful subset (about 20%) of the application portfolio to be maintained. The goal is to make an assessment of the software systems to make decisions about negotiations of the customer service levels, and to select the skills required by the maintenance team (De Lucia *et al.*, 2001).

3 PREVIOUS EMPIRICAL STUDY

In a previous work (De Lucia *et al.*, 2002), the data of five corrective maintenance projects was used in an empirical study aiming at constructing effort prediction models. We used multiple linear regression analysis to build prediction models and validated them on the project data using cross-validation techniques (Bradley & Gong, 1983).

The data set was composed of 144 monthly observations, collected from all the projects. For each observation, corresponding to monthly maintenance periods for each project, the following data was available and considered in our analysis (see Table 2):

- size of the system to be maintained;
- effort spent in the maintenance period;

- number of maintenance tasks, split in three categories:

  type A: the maintenance task requires software source code modification;

  type B: the maintenance task requires fixing of data misalignments through database queries;

  type C: the maintenance task requires interventions not included in the previous categories, such user disoperation, problems out of contract, and so on.

The cost estimation model previously used within the organization was based on the size of the system to be maintained and the total number of maintenance tasks. For this reason we decided to build a linear model taking into account these two variables (model A in Table 3). However, we observed that the effort required to perform a maintenance task of type A might be sensibly different than the effort required to perform a task of type B or C. Also the number of maintenance tasks of type A is sensibly lower than the number of maintenance tasks of the other two types. For this reason, we expected to achieve a sensible improvement by splitting the variable N into the two variables NA and NBC (see Table 2). The result of our regression analysis was model B in Table 3. Finally, we also built a model considering the effect of each different type of maintenance tasks (model C in Table 3), although this model is generally more difficult and risky to be used, because it requires more precise estimates of the number of tasks of type B and C. Indeed, the coefficients of this model seem to suggest that the effort required for these two types of maintenance tasks is different: in particular, tasks of type C seem to be more expensive than tasks of type B.

To evaluate the prediction performance, we performed cross-validation and computed MRE (Magnitude Relative Error) for each observation, MMRE (Mean Magnitude Relative Error) and MdMRE (Median Magnitude Relative Error). The MRE$_i$ on an observation i is defined as:

$$MRE_i = \frac{|\hat{y}_i - y_i|}{y_i}$$

where y_i is the value of the i-*th* value of the dependent variable as observed in the data set and $\hat{y}_i$ is the corresponding value predicted by the model. MMRE is the average of the MRE$_i$, while MdMRE is the median of the MRE$_i$.

Moreover, the following variants of the measure PRED (Conte *et al.*, 1986; Jorgensen, 1995) were computed:

- PRED$_{25}$ = % of cases with MRE <= 0.25.
- PRED$_{50}$ = % of cases with MRE <= 0.50.

The MMRE, MdMRE, and PRED measures resulting from the leave-one-out cross-validation are shown in Table 4.

The prediction performances of our models are nevertheless very interesting according to the findings of Vicinanza *et al.* (1991), in particular considering that what is really wanted by software management is not to predict accurately, but to control over the final results.

Table 2: Collected metrics

Metric	Description
NA	# of tasks requiring software modification
NB	# of tasks requiring fixing of data misalignment
NC	# of other tasks
NBC	NBC=NB+NC
N	N=NA+NB+NC
SIZE	Size of the system to be maintained [kLOC]
EFFORT	Actual Effort [man-hours]

Table 3: Effort prediction model parameters

Model	Var.	b$_i$ (Coeff.)	p-value	R^2	Adj R^2
A	N	1.342904	<10E-07	0.8257	0.8245
	SIZE	0.169086			
B	NA	9.053286	<10E-07	0.8891	0.8876
	NBC	0.138275	<10E-07		
	SIZE	1.164826	<10E-07		
C	NA	7.86988	<10E-07	0.8963	0.8941
	NB	0.514121	<10E-07		
	NC	2.81486	0.000001		
	SIZE	0.130507	<10E-07		

Table 4: Model predictive performances

	Model A	Model B	Model C
MMRE	42.53%	36.40%	32.25%
MdMRE	37.57%	29.16%	25.35%
PRED$_{25}$	31.25%	40.36%	49.31%
PRED$_{50}$	66.75%	74.56%	82.64%

4 NEW EMPIRICAL STUDY

The main limitation of the data set was the fact that only the total effort of each maintenance period was maintained, while data for the single maintenance tasks was not available.

Indeed, it would have been interesting to increase the granularity of the collected data, also considering the effort of all the tasks of the same type or, even better, the effort of the single maintenance task. The availability of this data would allow to:

- validate our hypothesis of considering different maintenance task types in the cost estimation models;

- assess the different task types in a quantitative way;
- discover outliers at different granularity levels, both for monthly observations, and for single maintenance requests;
- understand the process in a quantitative way.

To overcome the limitations of the first study concerning the granularity of the data, the subject company implemented a specific process management tool (PMT) and used it in a new maintenance project. The PMT is web-based and is used at three different geographical sites, corresponding to the different Solution Centers involved in this new project. Its main capabilities are recording time and effort needed to carry out each phase of the maintenance process, notifying events to the maintenance team members responsible to perform a task when this has to be started, interfacing existing tools for configuration management, tracking maintenance requests.

Each maintenance request coming from the customer is recorded by a fist level Help Desk using a tracking tool that is on-line consulted only on one site by the software analysts responsible for this maintenance project. The analysts have two options: accepting the request and routing it to other sites or discarding the request and providing the motivations directly to the Help Desk tracking tool. Each accepted request is assigned a typology, that can be Change (small evolution), Defect (trouble ticket), or Other. Moreover, if the request is classified as Defect, there are other attributes specifying the severity and the associated priority (High, Medium, Low). The maintenance process is composed of a set of phases (shown in Table 1), again decomposable in a set of elementary activities based on the typology of the maintenance request. Each phase can be assigned to different human resources allocated on the project.

The new project was still on when we started the empirical study, so the data concerning the first 6 months of the project were available. The PMT allowed to collect about 30,000 observations, concerning 7,310 maintenance requests received in these 6 months. In this case, each observation corresponds to one phase of the maintenance process applied to a maintenance request, while in the previous empirical study it corresponded to the aggregation of all the maintenance requests received in one month. For each maintenance request the following data was available:

- Effort spent on each phase of the maintenance process (measured in man-hours);
- Priority, split in three categories:

High: anomalies that entail the total unavailability of the system;
Medium: anomalies that entail the partial unavailability (one or more functions) of the system;
Low: anomalies that do not entail blocks of the system's functions, but degrade the performances of the system or cause incorrect operations or are limited to the user interface.

Table 5 shows the descriptive statistics for the monthly metrics of this maintenance project.

Table 5: Descriptive statistics of the new project

Metric	Min	Max	Mean	Median	Std.Dev.
NA	66	96	83.33	83.5	10.23
NB	276	472	353.83	348	69.39
NC	625	927	780.5	782	104.23
N	967	1423	1217.67	1223	164.51
EFFORT	3225	4857	3812.5	3768	539.58

5 ASSESSING PREDICTIVE PERFORMANCES ON THE NEW PROJECT

Our first analysis was evaluating the predictive performances of the models built in De Lucia *et al.* (2002) on the new maintenance project. We applied the models to the new data simulating their behavior as it was really applied for prediction purposes. In fact, for the first monthly observation we used directly the models and coefficients of Table 3; for the next observation, we added previous observations to the data learning set of the model and recalibrated the models calculating the coefficients again. Results are shown in Table 6.

Table 6: Assessed model predictive performances

	Model A	Model B	Model C
MMRE	36.91%	31.40%	16.60%
MdMRE	32.31%	27.29%	14.31%
PRED$_{25}$	0.00%	33.33%	83.33%
PRED$_{50}$	66.66%	66.66%	100.00%

For the best model (model C) only one prediction falls outside the 25% wall, producing a PRED$_{25}$ value of 83.33%. The MRE of each observation is reasonably low for all the predictions: if we discard the worst prediction (MRE = 35.56%), the MRE has a maximum value of 21.00%, that is surely an acceptable error value for the software maintenance effort prediction. The mean MRE is 16.60%, again an excellent value. It is worth noting that although the number of monthly periods is small, the performance parameters in Table 6 exhibit the same positive trends as in the previous study (see Table 4), in particular concerning MMRE e MdMRE. However, the small number of monthly periods seems to be the main reason for the greater variations of the PRED measures.

Our previous work was centered on the model construction and assessment of the prediction performance through cross-validation (Bradley & Gong, 1983). In this paper the granularity of the data collected for the last software project allows us to make further analyses: we have useful data to confirm (or to reject) the basic hypothesis of the effort prediction model, namely the assumption that the tasks of different type require different effort to be made and, in particular, tasks of type A generally require greater effort than the other two types. The box plot of Figure 1 and the data in Table 8 clearly confirm this hypothesis and provide us with a lot of other information about the maintenance process.

Each type of task has mean and median values sensibly different and presents a higher value for the coefficient of variation (it is the ratio of standard deviation by mean), thus indicating the presence of statistical outliers. However, rather than discarding all statistical outliers, we decided to analyze the data in a flexible way: we only discarded the maintenance requests with an effort that was clearly abnormal compared with all the other observations. These outliers represent isolated points with very high effort values almost of one magnitude order greater than the other observations (including other statistical outliers). On the other hand, besides abnormal outliers, it is common to have a relatively small number of maintenance requests requiring a great effort (compared to mean value); therefore, if we had discarded from our analysis also these observations that can be considered as outliers by a pure statistical point of view, we would have surely lost useful information about the software maintenance process.

It is worth noting that the effort required to accomplish the maintenance tasks corresponding to abnormal outliers is very large (almost two magnitude order greater than the mean). These maintenance requests can be easily identified as soon as they begin to be worked, as their resolution is usually non standard and requires more complex analysis and design. Sometimes, they are programmed maintenance requests, such as database restructuring operations. These can be viewed as the perfective interventions auspicated by Lehman's laws of software evolution to deal with the increasing complexity and declining quality of the software systems (Lehman & Belady, 1985). For this reason, the effort of these maintenance tasks should not be considered in the prediction model; rather, a project manager should account for a small number of such tasks when estimating the effort of the maintenance project.

According to this heuristic we identified five outliers, corresponding to five maintenance requests, one of type A, three of type C and one of type B. After this elimination we recalibrated the effort prediction models and obtained the new relative errors shown in Table 7: the performance values are improved in all the parameters, although slightly. Moreover, if we consider the model C, MRE sensibly decreases for all the months which have an outlier discarded; in particular, the maximum value of the monthly MRE shrinks from 35.56% to 26.48%.

Table 7: Assessed model predictive performances (without outliers)

	Model A	Model B	Model C
MMRE	37.72%	28.06%	15.69%
MdMRE	38.68%	30.40%	13.56%
PRED$_{25}$	16.66%	33.33%	83.33%
PRED$_{50}$	66.66%	83.33%	100.00%

6 ANALYSIS OF TASKS OF DIFFERENT TYPES AND PRIORITY

In this section we analyze the distribution of the effort among tasks of different type and priority. As shown in Figure 1, the height of the NA box indicates that tasks of type A have higher variability than the tasks of other types. Generally, this type of tasks:

- requires an effort great almost five or six times the effort required by the other two types, as it can be noted by comparing the values of the quartiles, of the medians, and of the box fences (adjacent values);
- has effort value ranges clearly higher than the other two types;
- has the main influence on the effort.

This confirms our hypothesis about the different influence on the effort determined by the type of tasks.

The other two types of tasks have similar boxes, indicating that the tasks of type B and C:

- generally require similar effort to be made, with a slight adjunctive effort for type B;
- have a small variability range, as the efforts of the maintenance tasks comprised between the 10th and 90th percentiles range between 0.4 and

4 hours for maintenance tasks of type B and between 0.4 and 3 hours for maintenance tasks of type C (see Table 8).

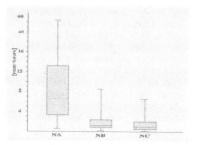

Figure 1: Effort distribution box plot with respect to maintenance request types

Table 8: Effort distribution among task types

	NA	NB	NC
Mean	12.78	2.43	1.94
StDev	20.30	6.86	7.25
10th Percentile	1.75	0.40	0.40
Median	6.75	1.20	1.00
90th Percentile	30.00	4.00	3.00

A consideration to make is the fact that while the coefficients of model C in Table 3 seems to suggest that in the previous projects the effort required for tasks of type C is greater than the effort required for tasks of type B, the detailed data of the new project seems to confute this hypothesis, as maintenance tasks of type B and C require a similar effort (slightly higher for tasks of type B). Therefore, the major improvement of model C with respect to model B (compare Tables 4 and Table 6) was unexpected, as the data of the new project seems to justify the aggregation of the tasks of type B and C and its use as a single variable in the prediction model B. The reason of the major improvement of the performances of model C can be justified by a compensation effect of the coefficients of the model. It is worth noting that due to the similarity of the efforts of maintenance tasks of type B and C and due to the fact that the number of maintenance tasks of type C is about twice the number of maintenance tasks of type B, applying model C is equivalent to apply model B with a lower coefficient for NA and a higher coefficient for NBC (see Table 3). Therefore, giving a greater weight to tasks of types B and C with respect to tasks of type A would result in better performances of model B in the new project.
The classification of each request by priority allows to make further considerations about the maintenance process execution. Almost all the outliers do not have high priority. From Table 9 and

Table 10 there is a low percentage of high priority tasks. The larger part of the effort is spent on the low priority tasks, which are resolved after an accurate scheduling of the activities. It is worth noting that, among the low priority tasks, the tasks of type A account only for 4.64% of the total number of maintenance requests, but consume 22.93% of the total effort. This suggests that a big part of maintenance requests that impacts on software code has low priority and a complexity level not trivial, as they need more effort to be made.

Table 9: Task type and priority distribution (%)

	Type A	Type B	Type C
High priority	0.60	2.18	2.08
Medium priority	1.59	3.97	15.35
Low priority	4.64	22.91	46.66

Table 10: Effort distrib. (%) among task type and priority

	Type A	Type B	Type C
High priority	2.23	4.12	1.96
Medium priority	5.80	4.03	12.40
Low priority	22.93	16.90	29.62

7 EFFORT DISTRIBUTION ANALYSIS

In this section we analyze the data about the distribution of the effort to the phases of the maintenance process. Figures 2 and 3 show the phase distribution distinguishing the tasks of type A from the tasks of type B and C. This distinction is needed because the maintenance process for a task of type A requires software code modifications: this operation and all the strictly correlated activities (such as document check-in/check-out, testing execution, etc.) are included in the phase called Produce, that is not present in the other task types.
There are not unexpected results: for type A the Produce phase is the most expensive, as it can be seen from the height of the box and of the upper fence. This is reasonable, as the effort needed for testing (that generally is an expensive operation), is accounted in this phase.
For type B and C the phase distribution is almost regular: all the boxes have similar height and have median value at 25%; there are no high values for the fences, and the phases require analogous time to be executed, with Analyze and Design generally more expensive than Define and Implement.
It is worth noting that the phases of the maintenance process for the tasks of type B and C have a very short time. In most cases, they are performed in less than one hour. In this case, the phase distribution

analysis clearly shows that there is no real utility to perform analyses aiming at reducing the time needed for the completion of a single phase. On the other hand, it is useful to analyze them to discover particular trends or phase distribution correlated to specific process characteristics. In our case, we have not discovered any of these properties, so we have limited our discussion to the simple description of the time distribution among the different phases.

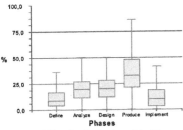

Figure 2: Effort distribution box plot with respect to phases (maintenance requests of type A)

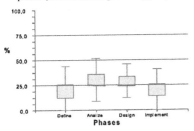

Figure 3: Effort distribution box plot with respect to phases (maintenance requests of type B and C)

8 CONCLUSION

In this paper we have presented an assessment of an empirical study aiming at building corrective maintenance effort estimation models. In a previous work (De Lucia et al., 2002) we used as a case study a data set obtained from five different corrective maintenance projects to experimentally construct, validate, and compare model performances through multivariate linear regression models. The main observation was to take into account the differences in the effort required to accomplish tasks of different types. Therefore, we built effort prediction models based on the distinction of the task types. The prediction performance of our models was very interesting according to the findings of Vicinanza et al. (1991).

A critique to the applicability of the cost estimation models might be the fact that they consider as independent variables the number of maintenance tasks that are not known at the beginning of a project and that should be in turn estimated. However, as far as our experience with these type of systems has demonstrated, the overall trend of the maintenance tasks of each type appears to follow the Lehman's laws of software evolution (Lehman & Belady, 1985), in particular the self regulation and the conservation of organizational stability laws: in general the number of maintenance tasks of each type oscillates around an average value across the maintenance periods. These average values can be calculated with a good approximation after a few maintenance periods and used to estimate the maintenance effort. Both the average values and the effort estimates can be improved as soon as new observations are available. A deeper discussion of this issue is out of the scope of this paper. More details and empirical data are available from the authors.

Although the results of the previous study were good, we identified some limitations concerning the granularity of the metrics used in the previous empirical study and auspicated the collection of further information useful to overcome them. The subject company is currently planning the assessment to move from CMM level 3 to CMM level 4. It is a requisite of the CMM level 3 that metrics are to be collected, analyzed, and used to control the process and to make corrections on the predicted costs and schedule, if necessary. Therefore, metric collection was crucial. The study presented in (De Lucia et al., 2002) suggested to record process metrics at a finer granularity level than a monthly maintenance period. The subject company applied these considerations in the definition of the metric plan of a new maintenance project, analyzed in this paper: productivity metrics have been collected and recorded for each maintenance request, allowing to obtain more accurate productivity data. Therefore, we performed a replicated assessment of the effort prediction models on a new corrective maintenance project. Thanks to the finer data, we have been able to:

- verify the prediction performances of the models on a new maintenance project, applying the effort prediction model to the new project data;
- verify the hypothesis of the different effort needed by the tasks of different types in a quantitative way, measuring the effort required by the different task types;
- identify outliers in the data at a finer granularity level, analyzing the single maintenance request instead of their aggregation;

- improve the understanding of the corrective maintenance process and its trends, by analyzing the distribution of the effort among the different process phases and different types and priorities of the maintenance tasks.

At the end of the assessment on the new project we had confirmation both of goodness of the prediction performances of the estimation models and of the validity of our hypotheses (different task types require different effort). From the distribution of the effort among the phases of the process, we also had evidence that the corrective maintenance process under study was quite stable. This is due to the long dated experience of the subject company and its maintenance teams in conducting corrective maintenance projects. Perhaps, this is one of the reasons why the company does not collect data for this type of projects concerning other factors, such as personnel skills that also generally influence maintenance projects (Jorgensen, 1995). This lack of available metric data is a limitation that should be considered before using the estimation models derived from our study outside the subject company and the analyzed domain and technological environment.

Future work will be devoted to introduce further metric plans in the maintenance projects of the subject organization. Besides statistical regression methods, we aim at investigating other techniques. For example, dynamic system theory can be used to model the relationship between maintenance effort and code defects (Calzolari *et al.*, 2001).

REFERENCES

Aversano, L., Canfora, G., De Lucia, A., & Stefanucci, S. (2002). Automating the Management of Software Maintenance Workflows in a Large Software Enterprise: a Case Study. *Journal of Software Maintenance and Evolution: Research and Practice*, 14(4), 229-255.

Basili, V., Briand, L., Condon, S., Kim, Y.M., Melo, W.L., & Valett, J.D. (1996). Understanding and Predicting the Process of Software Maintenance Releases. *Proc. of Int. Conf. on Software Engineering*, Berlin, Germany, pp. 464-474.

Banker, R.D., Datar, S.M., Kemerer, C.F., & Zweig, D. (1993). Software Complexity and Maintenance Costs. *Communications of ACM*, 36(11), 81-94.

Boehm, B.W. (1981). *Software Engineering Economics*. Prentice-Hall Inc., Englewood Cliffs, N.J., 1981.

Bradley E., & Gong, G. (1983). A Leisurely Look at the Bootstrap, the Jack-Knife and Cross-Validation. *Amer. Statistician*, 37(1), 836-848.

Calzolari, F., Tonella, P., & Antoniol, G. (2001). Maintenance and Testing Effort Modelled by Linear and Non Linear Dynamic Systems. *Information and Software Technology*, 43(8), 477-486

Conte, S., Dunsmore, H., & Shen, V. (1986). *Software Engineering Metrics and Models*. Benjamin-Cummings Publishing Company, 1986.

De Lucia, A., Fasolino, A., & Pompella, E. (2001). A Decisional Framework for Legacy System management. *Proceedings of IEEE Int. Conf. on Software Maintenance*, Florence, Italy, pp. 642-651.

De Lucia, A., Pompella, E., & Stefanucci, S. (2002). Effort Estimation for Corrective Software Maintenance. *Proc. of Int. Conf. on Software Engineering and Knowledge Engineering*, Ischia, Italy, pp. 409-416.

Fioravanti, F. & Nesi, P. (2001). Estimation and Prediction Metrics for Adaptive Maintenance Effort of Object-oriented Systems. *IEEE Trans. on Software Engineering*, 27(12), 1062-1084.

Granja-Alvarez, J.C. & Barranco-Garcia, M.J. (1997). A method for estimating maintenance cost in a software project: a case study. *Journal of Software Maintenance: Research and Practice*, 9(3), 161-175.

IEEE Std. 1219-1998 (1998). Standard for Software Maintenance, IEEE CS Press, Los Alamitos, CA.

Jorgensen, M. (1995). Experience With the Accuracy of Software Maintenance Task Effort Prediction Models. *IEEE Trans. on Software Engineering*, 21(8), 674-681.

Kemerer, C.F. & Slaughter, S. (1999). An Empirical Approach to Studying Software Evolution. *IEEE Trans. on Software Engineering*, 25(4), 493-509.

Lehman, M. & Belady, L. (1985). *Program Evolution: Processes of Software Change*. Academic Press, Austin, 1985.

Niessink, F. & van Vliet, H. (1998). Two Case Studies in Measuring Maintenance Effort. *Proc. of IEEE Int. Conf. on Software Maintenance*, Bethesda, Maryland, USA, pp. 76-85.

Nesi, P. (1998). Managing Object Oriented Projects Better, *IEEE Software*, 15(4), 50-60.

Ramil, J.F. (2000). Algorithmic Cost Estimation Software Evolution. *Proc. of Int. Conf. on Software Engineering*, Limerick, Ireland, pp. 701-703.

Sneed, H.M. (2003). Software Maintenance Cost Estimation. *Advances in Software Maintenance Management: Technologies and Solutions*. M. Polo editor, Idea Group Publishing, USA, pp. 201-227.

Vicinanza, S., Mukhopadhyay, T., & Prietula, M. (1991). Software Effort Estimation: an Exploration Study of Export Performance. *Information System Research*, 2(4), 243-262.

ORGANIZATIONAL AND TECHNOLOGICAL CRITICAL SUCCESS FACTORS BEHAVIOR ALONG THE ERP IMPLEMENTATION PHASES

José Esteves

Department of Lenguajes y Sistemas Informáticos , Universitat Politécnica de Catalunya, Jordi Girona Salgado 1-3 08034 Barcelona, Spain
Email: jesteves@lsi.upc.es

Joan A. Pastor

Universitat Internacional de Catalunya,Immaculada 22
08017 Barcelona, Spain
Email: jap@unica.edu

Keywords: Enterprise Resource Planning, critical success factors, implementation phases, ERP implementation project

Abstract: This paper analyzes the evolution of organizational and technological critical success factors along the ERP implementation phases. The identification of factors leading to success or failure of ERP systems is an issue of increasing importance, since the number of organizations choosing the ERP path keeps growing. Our findings suggest that while both good organizational and technological perspectives are essential for a successful ERP implementation project, their importance shifts as the project moves through its lifecycle.

1 INTRODUCTION

During the last years some studies have been published in relation to the Critical Success Factors (CSFs) topic in ERP implementations.. The identification of factors leading to success or failure of ERP implementations is an issue of increasing importance, since the number of organizations choosing the ERP path keeps growing.

In this paper we attempt to analyze how the organizational and technological perspectives are perceived along the ERP implementation phases. Specifically, we have analyzed how the unified model of CSFs for ERP implementation projects presented by Esteves and Pastor (2000) fits into a organizational-technological framework. In our study, to evaluate organizational and technological perspectives, we have used their CSFs unified model. Understanding the CSFs that help to lead to successful implementations of Information Systems (IS) has been a key interest for practitioners as well as many IS researchers (Haines and Goodhue 2000).

This paper is organized as follows. First, we present the unified model of CSFs and the SAP implementation methodology. Then we describe the research framework for evaluating CSFs relevance. Next, we discuss the relevance of each CSF taken into account organizational and technological perspectives. Finally we discuss the results and further work.

2 UNIFIED MODEL OF CSFS FOR ERP IMPLEMENTATIONS

The CSF approach has been applied to many aspects and tasks of information systems, and more recently to ERP systems implementations, (e.g. Dolmetsch et al. 1998, Holland et al. 1999, Parr et al. 1999, Nah et al. 2001). Based in a set of studies published by several authors, containing commented lists of CSFs in ERP implementations, Esteves and Pastor (2000) unified these lists and created a CSFs unified model

63

	Strategic	Tactical
Organizational	• Sustained management support • Effective organizational change management • Good project scope management • Adequate project team composition • Comprehensive business process reengineering • Adequate project champion role • User involvement and participation • Trust between partners	• Dedicated staff and consultants • Strong communication inwards and outwards • Formalized project plan/schedule • Adequate training program • Preventive trouble shooting • Appropriate usage of consultants • Empowered decision-makers
Technological	• Adequate ERP implementation strategy • Avoid customization • Adequate ERP version	• Adequate infrastructure and interfaces • Legacy systems knowledge • Formalized testing plan • Adequate data migration process

Figure 1: The critical success factors unified model for ERP implementations

for ERP implementation projects. The unified model is represented in figure 1. The advantage of this model is that it unifies a set of studies related with lists of CSFs identified by other authors; the CSFs are categorized in different perspectives and, each CSF is identified and defined.

In the authors' view, the nature of the ERP implementation issues includes strategic, tactical, organizational and technological perspectives. Therefore, we propose that the CSFs model should have these four perspectives. The organizational perspective is related with concerns like organizational structure and culture and, business processes. The technological perspective focuses on aspects related to the particular ERP product in consideration and on other related technical aspects, such as hardware and base software needs. The strategic perspective is related with core competencies accomplishing the organization's mission and long-term goals, while the tactical perspective affects the business activities with short-term objectives.

2.1 CSFs Relevance

In 1988, Pinto and Prescott (1988, p. 5), claimed that "the majority of the studies in the critical success factor research stream have been theoretical and have assumed a static view of the importance of various factors over the life of a project. In other words, a critical success factor was assumed to have the same degree of importance throughout the life of the project". Therefore, Pinto and Prescott (1988) examined changes in the criticality of project CSFs over the life cycle of a project. They concluded that the relevance of CSFs is subject to change at

different phases of the project life cycle. They stated that "this finding implies that future use of critical success factor analysis and implementation, regardless of the area to be examined, may be contingent on other organizational phenomena, such as project (or organizational) life cycle" (Pinto and Prescott, p. 17).

Subsequent studies on CSF approach have addressed not solely the identification of CSFs but also their relevance along the project life cycle. However, the number of these types of studies is still very limited with most studies only focusing on CSF identification. The assumption that CSFs relevance varying along the implementation phases is slightly different from some studies that try to define CSFs for each phase of the project life cycle. Pinto and Prescott (1988) use the same set of CSFs and examined their relevance along the project phases while some studies define different sets of CSFs for each project phase. These approaches are different although some researchers are empirically using the same assumption stated by Pinto and Prescott (1988) since they are providing what they call "the most critical" or "most relevant" or "the top" CSFs which means they are only defining the most relevant CSF but probably they are always using as a reference the same set of CSFs.

With regarding to the research approach, to study CSFs relevance researchers have used surveys and case studies using interviews. The typical procedure is to ask participants to rank the most relevant CSFs in each project phase and then create a list of the most relevant CSFs in each project phase or, they ask participants to evaluate CSFs relevance using a Likert scale. Some authors have studied CSFS along different IS project types: information centers (Magal et al. 1988), IS implementation projects (Pinto and Slevin 1988), Cooper and Zmud (1990), ERP lifecycle (Somers and Nelson 2001, Nah et al. 2001).

3 THE ASAP IMPLEMENTATION METHODOLOGY

In 1996, SAP introduced the Accelerated SAP (ASAP) implementation methodology with the goal of speeding up SAP implementation projects. ASAP was advocated to enable new customers to utilize the experience and expertise gleaned from thousands of implementations worldwide. This is specifically targeted for small and medium enterprises adopting SAP. The key phases of the ASAP methodology, also known as the ASAP roadmap, are:

- **Project preparation** – the purpose of this phase is to provide initial planning and preparation of SAP project. The steps of this phase help identify and plan the primary focus areas to be considered such as: objectives, scope, plan and definition of project team.
- **Business blueprint** - the purpose of this phase is to create the business blueprint, which is a detailed documentation of the results gathered during requirements workshops/meetings. It will allow the implementation project team to clearly define their scope, and only focus on the SAP processes needed to run the organization business.
- **Realization** - the purpose of this phase is to implement business and processes requirements on the business blueprint. The objectives are final implementation in the system, an overall test, and the release of the system for production (live) operation.
- **Final preparation** – the purpose of this phase is

to complete the final preparation, including testing, end user training, system management and cut over activities, to finalize the readiness to go live. The final preparation phase also serves to resolve all open issues.
- **Go live & support** - the purpose of this phase is to move from a pre-production environment to live production operation. A support organization must be set up for end users to provide long-term support. This phase is also used to monitor system transactions and to improve overall system performance. Finally the completed project is closed.

The structure of each phase is the following: each phase is composed of a group of work packages. These work packages are structured in activities, and each activity is composed of a group of tasks. An example of two work packages of ASAP, project kickoff and quality check, is described in table 1. For each task, a definition, a set of procedures, results and roles are provided in the ASAP roadmap documentation. According to a survey of Input company (Input 1999), organizations have been more satisfied with SAP tools and methodologies than with those of implementation partners. Implementations where ASAP or Powered by SAP methodologies were used averaged only 8 months, compared to 15 months for standard implementations.

4 OUR PROPOSED CSF RELEVANCE SCHEME

CSFs can either be ongoing, or they can be temporal (Khandewal and Ferguson 1999). Khandewal and Ferguson (1999) assert notwithstanding the earlier

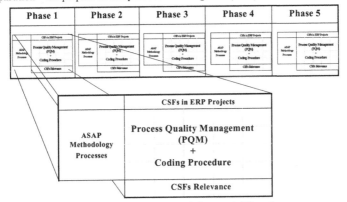

Figure 2: Research framework followed

statement that the CSFs can either be ongoing, or temporal that all CSFs can be defined in a way that they are temporal. For example, formal plan and schedule for the ERP implementation project can be defined as a temporal CSF. This CSF will then be considered having been achieved as soon as a project plan is developed. The assumption is that once the project plan is developed the ongoing updating of this plan would be an integral part of the project plan. All CSFs would thus belong to a point in time, although they may differ in their degree of temporality. Therefore, it is important to know these points in time were CSFs are more relevant. Next, we describe our research framework for evaluating CSFs relevance along SAP implementation phases and the relevance scheme obtained.

4.1 Research Framework for Evaluating CSFs Relevance

We have used the Process Quality Management (PQM) method (Ward 1990) to relate the CSFs with the ASAP processes. The PQM method developed by IBM is "designed to assist the management team reach consensus on the most critical business activities, i.e. those whose performance will have the biggest impact on the success or failure of the enterprise" (Ward 1990). PQM uses the concept of CSFs (Rockart 1979) to encourage management teams to focus their attention on the critical issues of the business, and then to base the IT strategy on these. Next, we describe the following steps of the PQM method, as we have applied them in our research case (see figure 2):

- **First step**: define the mission. We define the following mission: "To implement the ERP system, according to the organization's business and organizational needs" and then "to show that the ERP implementation will add value through the satisfaction of the organization requirements

previously defined". This mission reflects the intention of the whole group of people involved in an ERP implementation project;

- **Second step**: define CSFs. We will use the CSFs unified model proposed by Esteves and Pastor (2000);
- **Third step**: define the processes. In our case, the processes are those defined in the ASAP methodology;
- **Fourth step**: establish the relationship of CSFs versus ASAP processes. This is done through the creation of the matrix presented in figure 2 and table 1. For each one of the five SAP implementation phases a matrix was created.

Next, we describe how the matrix of CSFs versus ASAP processes was created.

According to Hardaker and Ward (1987), "the object is to single out the processes that have a primary impact on this particular CSF". What we are looking for are those essential activities and not all of them. The matrix in table 1 has been built in the following way. We focused on each CSF and asked this question: Which ASAP processes must be performed especially well for us to be confident of achieving this CSF? Then, we looked at all theprocesses and decided which ones were important for that CSF. Each time we established a relationship between a CSF and a process, we marked a '1' in the corresponding cell of the matrix (see table 1). A second process was used to validate and to get more reliability in the research. We used a coding procedure to analyze the ASAP documentation. The coding procedure consisted in coding line-by-line all the ASAP processes using a predefined list of codes, in this case the list of CSFs. Next, we present part of the full matrix of CSFs versus ASAP processes built for the first phase of ASAP, the project preparation phase.

Table 1: Example of the matrix CSFs versus ASAP processes for project preparation phase

	ASAP Processes \ CSFs in ERP implementations	Sustained management support	Effective organizational change management	Good project scope management	Adequate project team composition	Comprehensive business process redesign	User involvement and participation	Adequate project sponsor role	Adequate project manager role	Trust between partners	Dedicated staff and consultants	Strong communication	Formalize project plan/schedule	Adequate training program	Preventive trouble shooting	Usage of appropriate consultants	Empower decision makers	Adequate ERP implementation strategy	Avoid customization	Adequate ERP version	Adequate infrastructure and interfaces	Adequate legacy systems knowledge
W	Project Kickoff																					
A	Kickoff Meeting																					
T	Prepare for kickoff meeting						1					1										
T	Conduct kickoff meeting	1				1	1				1											
T	Company wide project introduction						1				1	1										
A	Project team standards meeting																					
T	Prepare for standard meeting						1					1										
T	Conduct standard meeting						1			1	1											
W	Quality Check																					
A	Perform quality check and approval																					
T	Conduct quality check						1															
T	Signoff project preparation phase	1					1															
	Number of CSFs occurrences	2				1	7			1	3	3										

4.2 CSFs Relevance

Table 2 represents the CSFs relevance for each CSF in each implementation phase. The values were calculated in the following way. We have built a matrix of CSFs versus ASAP processes such as the one in table 1 for each implementation phase, and for each CSF we sum the number of occurrences of that CSF. For instance, the sum of 2 in the CSF Sustained Management Support means that we defined 2 relationships between this CSF and 2 ASAP tasks. Then, we converted the number of occurrences (raw scores) into a normative scale of ten scores. In a scale of this kind, results from 1-3 are considered irrelevant, from 4-7 normal relevance, and 8-10 they are considered of high relevance. In our case, we see that almost all the factors are higher than 4. Thus, their relevance is normal or high in most cases. We do not pretend to say that a CSF with a low summation it is not important; what we say is that it is less relevant in that period of the project. CSFs have all the same importance. Therefore, all of them should be carefully respected and analyzed.

One of the main results from table 2 is that organizational CSFs have more relevance along the ERP implementation phases than technological ones. Once again, there is the need to focus more on people and process than on technology itself. This is not new, and other studies have proved the same aspect in other types of IS implementation projects. This aspect is very important since as Felix and Harrison (1984) quoted, "technical problems can usually be detected and repaired before the system is put in jeopardy. The cost may be high in terms of either budget or schedule, but the repair can be made. Organizational and personnel problems often cannot be redressed, and continue to jeopardize the success of the system itself".

Table 2: CSFs relevance along the SAP implementation phases

Perspectives		Critical Success Factors	SAP Implementation phases				
			1	2	3	4	5
Organizational Perspective	Strategic	Sustained management support	8	6	5	5	8
		Effective organizational change management	6	9	5	5	6
		Good project scope management	5	3	4	4	4
		Adequate project team composition	4	4	4	4	4
		Comprehensive business process redesign	4	7	4	3	4
		User involvement and participation	5	9	10	8	6
		Adequate project sponsor role	7	6	4	5	7
		Adequate project manager role	10	9	9	10	10
		Trust between partners	6	4	4	4	6
	Tactical	Dedicated staff and consultants	5	5	4	4	6
		Strong communication inwards and outwards	7	7	6	8	9
		Formalized project plan/schedule	8	7	7	7	7
		Adequate training program	5	5	5	7	4
		Preventive trouble shooting	4	4	8	8	7
		Usage of appropriate consultants	6	9	9	6	4
		Empowered decision makers	4	5	4	5	4
Technological Perspective	Strategic	Adequate ERP implementation strategy	5	4	4	4	6
		Avoid customization	4	4	5	3	4
		Adequate ERP version	4	3	3	3	4
	Tactical	Adequate infrastructure and interfaces	6	6	7	7	4
		Adequate legacy systems knowledge	4	4	4	4	4
		Formalized testing plan	4	4	8	6	4
		Adequate data migration process	4	4	5	6	4

Next, we describe each CSF relevance along the SAP phases, classified by organizational and technological perspectives.

4.2.1 Organizational Perspective

Sustained management support is more relevant at the beginning and at the end of the implementation. The reason is that at the beginning senior management should help in the rollout of the project, analyze the business benefits, define the mission and scope of the project and provide the resources needed for the project. At the end, there is the need to encourage the system usage and help in the commitment of user involvement.

Effective organizational change management and business process redesign are more relevant in the second phase. In this phase the business blueprint is defined, and the business processes are analyzed, redesigned (some) and documented. There is the need to understand how the organization intends to run its business within the SAP system and the changes in the organization.

Adequate project team composition has the same relevance along all the phases since they play an important part in the whole project. ASAP

methodology does not focus too much on this CSF since it assumes that the right people were chosen.

Good project scope management is relevant at the beginning when managers define the scope and in the last phase because the scope is usually revised and changed according to the results of the go live system tests.

Adequate project sponsor role is more relevant at the beginning when people need to be motivated to start the project and to obtain the necessary resources and in the last phase when project sponsor needs to encourage the use of the system.

Adequate project manager role is relevant in all phases. It is less relevant in the second and third phases than in with the others because these phases are dedicated to business modelling and configuration tasks and here the role of the project manager is to guarantee that everything goes according to the plan.

Trust between partners is relevant at the beginning when all the stakeholders involved in the project should share their goals and knowledge and at the end when they have to analyze and again share their knowledge to finish the project with success.

User involvement and participation is relevant in the phases where their know-how is important to achieve a good customization of the system to organizational needs. They participate in the definition of business requirements, help in the analysis of the ERP configuration and in conversion of data and the testing of the system.

Dedicated staff and consultants is more relevant in the last phase where there is the need to dedicated more effort in order to the system go live and also be available to help users answering their questions and reduce their doubts about the new system.

Appropriate usage of consultants is relevant especially in the second and third phases. On the second phase the knowledge of consultants is important to improve the business processes, and on the third phase consultants product knowledge on the ERP system parameterization.

Empowered decision makers is more relevant in the second and fourth phases because there is the need to take quickly decisions related with the business processes redesign (second phase) and the adequate customization of ERP system (fourth phase) in order to accomplish project plan/schedule on time.

Adequate training program is more relevant in phase 4 because it is when the training program of end users starts, but in the previous phases there are also training concerns related with project team training and to prepare end user training.

Strong communication inwards and outwards is more relevant at the first two phases where there is strong need of communication between senior management and the project team in the definition of project plan and scope, and in the last phase where there is the need of a strong communication with the whole organization to start the go & live of the SAP system.

Formalized plan and schedule relevance decreases during the implementation project. The reason is that at beginning it is important starting planning as early as possible. However, along the project, modifications to accomplish the results expected.

Preventive troubleshooting is more relevant in the last three phases, especially in the fourth phase during which issues arise when the production system is being tested and old data converted to the new system.

4.2.2 Technological Perspective

Avoid customization is more relevant in phase 3, when the SAP system is configured and more than 8.000 tables must be parameterized. The software configuration should follow the business requirements defined in the previous phase.

Adequate ERP implementation strategy is more relevant at the first phase because is in this phase that the SAP implementation strategy should be decided.

Adequate ERP version has the same relevance along all the phases. From the beginning until the end of the project implementation, SAP recommends that the project team follows the upgrade of SAP releases and should consider the adoption of new ones.

Adequate infrastructure and interfaces is more relevant in phases 3 and 4, when there is the need to configure the infrastructure for the production operation (go live). In these phases are also configured the interfaces with other systems, and the creation of reports and forms.

Adequate legacy systems knowledge is less relevant at the first phase because this phase is related with the preparation of project implementation. In phase 3 the need of knowledge of legacy systems is more relevant in order to minimize the effort of configuration, to help in conversion of data and the creation of interfaces.

Formalized testing plan is more relevant in phase 3 and 4 because in these phases the system needs to be tested after the parameterization process. The test should include not only functional testing but also the user's acceptance testing.

Adequate data migration process is more relevant in phase 4 because it is in this phase that data is migrated to the ERP system. The data migration process may be done using automatic procedures, or manually, or a mix of both. Finally, users must certify that they accept the data migration results.

5 DISCUSSION AND FURTHER RESEARCH

Based upon the schema presented in table 2, we analyzed the evolution of organizational and technological CSFs along the ERP implementation phases (see table 3). Our findings suggest that while both organizational and technological perspectives are essential for a successful ERP implementation project, their relevance shifts as the project moves through its lifecycle. Organizational issues are most important at the beginning, while technological issues gain in importance towards the middle as figure 3 shows. The organizational perspective has a high or normal relevance along the ERP implementation phases while the technological perspective starts by low and normal relevance and gradually increases to normal and high relevance.

Table 3: CSFs relevance along the SAP implementation phases

ERP implementation phase	Relevance Value	Perspective	
		Organizational	Technological
Project planning	Low	5	5
	Normal	7	2
	High	4	0
Business blueprint	Low	4	6
	Normal	8	1
	High	4	0
Realization	Low	7	3
	Normal	5	3
	High	4	1
Final preparation	Low	5	4
	Normal	7	3
	High	4	0
Go Live	Low	6	6
	Normal	7	1
	High	3	0

Next, we analyze our findings phase by phase:
- **Project preparation** – In this phase, organizational factors have more relevance than technological factors. Adequate project manager role, sustained management support and formalized plan/schedule are the most relevant strategic factors while adequate infrastructure and interfaces is the most relevant technological factor. The main reason for these CSFs relevance is due to the fact that this phase is dedicated mostly to define and organize the project.
- **Business blueprint** – Organizational factors are still the most relevant factors on this phase. However, organizational factor types change. Adequate project manager role is the most relevant in all phases, but sustained management support relevance decreases, organizational change, user involvement and participation, and usage of appropriate consultants arise as the most relevant organizational factors. Regarding technological factors, adequate infrastructure and interfaces is the most relevant one. This phase is mainly dedicated to the business analysis and modelling.
- **Realization** – In general we evidenced that organizational factors relevance decreases and technological factors gain relevance. Adequate project manager role, user involvement and participation, and usage of appropriate consultants are still the most relevant organizational factors, while formalized testing plan and adequate infrastructure and interfaces are the most relevant technological factors. This relevance is according to the fact that in this phase the ERP system is parameterized.

Therefore most of the technological tasks are done in this phase.
- **Final preparation** – Organizational factors increase a little their relevance while technological factors decrease their relevance. Adequate project manager and user involvement and participation remain the most relevant organizational factors. Strong communication inwards and outwards gains relevance in this phase. Adequate infrastructure and interfaces stills the highest relevant technological factor. This phase is dedicated to the system testing and users training. The final adjustments to the system are done in this phase.
- **Go live & support** – Again, organizational factors still have more relevance on this phase, while technological factors loose significantly their relevance. Adequate project manager role and strong communication inwards and outwards are the most relevant organizational factors. Regarding technological factors all have a normal relevance in this phase. This phase is dedicated to the system go live. Therefore is important to communicate and involve everyone in this process to achieve success.

These findings have implications in the way organizations should manage their ERP implementation projects. Some of these implications are:
- Organizations should consider organizational factors early in the project lifecycle, during project preparation and business blueprint and at the end.
- The transition from organizational to technological issues must be carefully managed

since it means changing the relevance of CSFs. Therefore, it should exist a careful monitoring of these new CSFs.

- ERP project monitoring and controlling involves a dynamic multi-success-factor management since the most relevant CSFs may change along the project.
- The adequate project manager role is the most relevant CSF along all the ERP implementation phases. Therefore, organizations must put special attention on the selection, motivation and retention of this person and try to select the most adequate person for this role.
- Project managers must have adequate skills for both dealing with organizational and technological issues, or at least he/she counts on other people that support he/she in this shift along the project.

In this study we used all the CSFs proposed in the CSFs unified model for ERP implementations and the ASAP methodology. However, we have developed a general criticality indicator that can be applied to any ERP implementation methodology (see Esteves and Pastor 2001). We are aware that CSFs vary from implementation to implementation. However, this does not mean that organizations should forget the less critical CSFs; Instead, organizations must still control and monitor them to minimize projects risks. In fact, the CSFs from the unified model should all be treated as perceived project risks. We are now trying to validate these preliminary findings using the case study method and interviews with people of various roles that have been involved in ERP implementation projects. We also want to analyze the implications of studying vertical implementation cases such as higher education ERP implementation projects. Finally, we also will compare our findings with other studies of ERP implementation projects in general in order to identify similarities and discrepancies that may help improve our work.

ACKNWOLEDGEMENTS

This work has been supported by Fundação para a Ciência e a Tecnologia (FCT), Portugal.

REFERENCES

Cooper, R., Zmud, R. 1990. Information Technology Implementation Research: A Technological Diffusion Approach. Management Science, 36(2), pp. 123-139.

Esteves, J., Pastor, J. 2000. Towards the Unification of Critical Success Factors for ERP Implementations. 10th Annual BIT Conference.

Felix, R., Harrison, W. 1984. Project Management Considerations for Distributed Processing Applications. MISQ Quarterly, Vol. 8, n. 3, pp. 161-170.

Haines, N., Goodhue, L. 2000. ERP Implementations: The Role of Implementation Partners and Knowledge Transfer. 11th International Conference of the Information Resource Management Association.

Holland, C., Light, B., Gibson, N. 1999. A Critical Success Factors Model for Enterprise Resource Planning Implementation", European Conference on Information Systems

Input 1999. Buyers's Guide to SAP Services Providers in the U.S", Input company.

Khandelwal, V., Ferguson, J. 1999. Critical Success Factors (CSFs) and the Growth of IT in Selected Geographic Regions. Hawaii International Conference on System Sciences

Kwon, T., Zmud, R. 1987. Unifying the fragmented models of information systems implementation. In: Boland, Hirschheim (Eds.), Critical Issues in Information Research, Wiley, New York, 1987.

Magal, S., Carr, H., Watson, H. 1988. Critical Success Factors for Information Centers. MIS Quarterly, 1988, 413-424.

Nah, F., Lau, J., Kuang, J. 2001. Critical Factors for Successful Implementation of Enterprise Systems", Business Process Management Journal, Vol. 7, n. 3, pp. 285-296.

Parr, A., Shanks, G., Darke, P. 1999. Identification of Necessary Factors for Successful Implementation of ERP Systems", in: New information technologies in organizational processes, field studies and theoretical reflections on the future work. Kluwer academic publishers, pp. 99-119.

Pinto J., Prescott J. 1988. Variations in Critical Success Factors over the Stages in the Project Life Cycle. Journal of Management, 14(1), pp. 5-18.

Rockart, J. 1979. Chief executives define their own information needs. Harvard Business Review, pp. 81-92.

Scott J., Vessey I. 2002. Managing Risks in Enterprise Systems Implementations", Communications of the ACM, 45(4), April 2002, pp. 74-81.

Somers T., Nelson, K. 2001. The Impact of Critical Success Factors across the Stages of Enterprise Resource Planning Implementations. Hawaii International Conference on System Sciences.

Ward, B. 1990. Planning for Profit. Chapter 5, in "Managing Information Systems for Profit. Edited by T. J. Lincoln, John Wiles & Sons Ltd., pp. 103-146.

ACME-DB: AN ADAPTIVE CACHING MECHANISM USING MULTIPLE EXPERTS FOR DATABASE BUFFERS

Faizal Riaz-ud-Din, Markus Kirchberg

Information Science Research Centre, Department of Information Systems,
Massey University, Private Bag 11-222, Palmerston North, New Zealand.
{F.Riaz-ud-din, M.Kirchberg}@massey.ac.nz

Keywords: Database caching, adaptive caching, buffer management

Abstract: An adaptive caching algorithm, known as Adaptive Caching with Multiple Experts (ACME), has recently been presented in the field of web-caching. We explore the migration of ACME to the database caching environment. By integrating recently proposed database replacement policies into ACME's existing policy pool, an attempt is made to gauge ACME's ability to utilise newer methods of database caching. The results suggest that ACME is indeed well-suited to the database environment and performs as well as the best currently caching policy within its policy pool at any particular moment in its request stream. Although execution time increases by integrating more policies into ACME, the overall processing time improves drastically with erratic patterns of access, when compared to static policies.

1 INTRODUCTION

One of the key factors affecting a database's performance is its ability to effectively and efficiently cache frequently requested data. Main memory access is approximately 170,000 times faster than disk accesses (Ramakrishnan and Gehrke, 2000). The challenge in main memory caching is to determine which page of data to replace (the 'victim') from the buffer pool once it is full, to make space for future data pages to be read in from secondary storage. The selection of victims is performed by a cache replacement algorithm, which chooses victims according to certain criteria based on past access patterns.

This paper attempts to trial and evaluate a recently presented adaptive cache replacement algorithm, known as ACME, or Adaptive Caching with Multiple Experts (Ari et al., 2002). ACME uses machine learning to dynamically select the cache victim from a number of policies, or experts, during the cache replacement process. Whilst ACME was originally presented for the web-caching environment, this paper describes the evaluation of the adaptation of ACME to the database environment. The rigidity and robustness of ACME is also tested by its ability to integrate more complex policies in its policy pool, including optimizations achieved in terms of overall processing time.

The remainder of this paper is presented as follows: Section 2 presents related work, including adaptive caching algorithms, with a focus on ACME. Sections 3 and 4 respectively, detail the way in which ACME has been adapted to the database environment and the issues concerned with implementation. Section 5 analyses the results obtained from driving the database-adapted ACME (referred to as ACME-DB in this paper) with live and synthetic traces. Finally, section 6 presents conclusions.

2 RELATED WORK

The main task of a buffer manager is to retrieve the data from secondary storage into main memory, thus allowing the data in the main memory to be accessed by the transactions that request information from the database. There are two purposes for accessing data in this manner: firstly it ensures that subsequent

72

I. Seruca et al. (eds.), Enterprise Information Systems VI, 72–81.

accesses to the same data are much faster in future references (since they are now in the main memory and do not need to be accessed from secondary storage again), and secondly, it ensures that the data is presented to the database in a synchronous manner, resulting in data consistency. Any data in the main memory that has been changed by a transaction is written back to where it was retrieved from on the secondary storage device.

This process of using the main memory area as an efficient data delivery mechanism is known as caching, whilst the main memory cache is also known as the buffer pool. A cache replacement algorithm is often referred to as a buffer replacement policy, and its function is to select a victim from the buffer pool.

Ideally, secondary storage devices would have I/O speeds at least as fast as main memory. However, because there is a latency issue involved with reading from secondary storage (Sacco and Schkolnick, 1986), and main memory is far more costly than secondary storage, the need to find an optimal practical buffer replacement policy still exists.

A number of buffer replacement policies have been presented in the literature in the quest for that optimal replacement policy. The more well-known amongst them have been FIFO (First-In-First-Out), LIFO (Last-In-First-Out), MRU (Most Recently Used), LRU (Least Recently Used), and LFU (Least Frequently Used), as well as others (Effelsberg and Haerder, 1984).

More recently, LRFU (Least Recently / Frequently Used), has been presented, which is a policy that attempts to combine the benefits of LRU and LFU (Lee et al., 1999). Whilst LRU-K (O'Neil et al., 1993) has succeeded in achieving a higher hit-rate than LRU, implementation is more difficult and execution time is higher. Even more recently, policies such as LIRS (Low Inter-reference Recency Set) (Jiang and Zhang, 2002), 2Q (Johnson and Shasha, 1994), and W^2R (Weighing Room / Waiting Room) (Jeon and Noh, 1998) have been presented. Whilst these recent policies suggest a marked improvement over their predecessors, implementation is not as simple as for LRU.

Adaptive caching algorithms go one step further by using two or more policies, in the attempt to reap their benefits, whilst avoiding their pitfalls (Castro et al., 1997).

Hybrid Adaptive Caching (HAC) is an adaptive caching algorithm presented by Castro et al. (Castro et al., 1997) within the environment of distributed objects. It combines the benefits of both page and object caching, whilst at the same avoiding their respective disadvantages. It behaves like a page caching system when spatial locality is good, and

when spatial locality degrades, it behaves like an object caching system, thereby adapting to the different access patterns in the request stream.

Adaptive Caching with Multiple Experts (ACME) is another adaptive caching algorithm presented recently by Ari et al. (Ari et al., 2002) within the context of the web-caching environment. ACME makes use of a policy pool that consists of a number of different static replacement policies ('experts'). Each of these experts has its own cache (known as a Virtual Cache). The request stream is processed by each of the experts and each performs its own caching independent of the others. When the actual cache that holds the data (the Real or Physical Cache) is full, and a page needs to be replaced, the experts are queried to see if they would have held the requested page in their virtual caches. If so, they are awarded a vote, otherwise they are penalised. The votes that each expert gains over time are used to determine its probability in choosing the next replacement victim.

ACME also possesses a machine-learning algorithm and it 'learns' to use the current best policy over time, based on the past successes and failures of the individual experts in the policy pool (Ari, 2002). The architecture of ACME is illustrated in Figure 1 below for clarity.

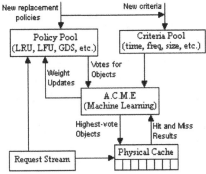

Figure 1: ACME architecture (Ari, 2002)

ACME is used as the basis of this research because it readily allows the incorporation of other policies within its architecture. Not only does this mean that ACME has the ability to use many different criteria when selecting a victim, but importantly, it provides the flexibility required to adapt it to the database environment (Ari et al., 2002). However, it should be noted that adding more policies increases the memory usage, and increases processing time. For detailed information on ACME, please refer to (Ari et al., 2002).

3 ADAPTING ACME FOR DATABASE CACHING

ACME was originally designed for use within a web-cache and as such, it includes certain features not necessarily required in a database-caching environment. With regard to the target database cache simulation in mind, ACME needed to be modified (Riaz-ud-Din, 2003).

3.1 Required Modifications

The original implementation of ACME allows for objects of different sizes to be cached. This ability is removed with the assumption that the pages that exist in memory are of the same size, thereby removing the need to correlate the sizes of the pages and freeing buffer space. This makes it easier to predict the number of I/O operations on the buffer pool.

The other modification required was to remove those policies from the ACME buffer pool that used the sizes of the objects to determine the object's priority in the cache. Since the size of all objects is the same in the database environment, these policies are redundant in that one of the criteria (the object size) used to determine the object's priority is no longer an issue. New policies have been added to the buffer pool, with an emphasis on using policies applicable to the implemented cache simulation.

3.2 Additional Demands

The additional demands of adapting ACME to the database environment include adding policies to the policy pool which are intrinsically dissimilar to the policies in the original ACME policy pool. The original ACME policies are based on single priority queues, and objects are assigned priorities based on pre-defined functions that use parameters such as time, size, and so on. However, the new policies that have been added to the policy pool for ACME-DB include policies that use more than one priority queue or divide the main buffer pool into a number of buffers. Using such policies requires more sophisticated buffering operations for caching and uncaching, and requires careful considerations to be made before integrating them into the ACME-DB buffer pool.

In addition, release mechanisms now need to be defined for each policy using more than a single queue or stack to manipulate the buffer pool. The literature that details the multi-buffer policies that have been added to the policy pool only describe the caching and uncaching operations of the respective policies. Consequently, the release mechanisms (described in Sub-Section 4.2) on arbitrary pages needed to be designed based on the heuristic analysis of the intrinsic behaviour of these policies.

4 IMPLEMENTATION

This section discusses issues related to implementing the additional database policies within the framework of the original ACME architecture, after applying the necessary adaptations as described in the previous section.

4.1 Release Mechanisms

In addition to being able to cache and uncache pages, each of the policies also needs to know how to release pages arbitrarily when required. The release functionality is invoked by each policy when one of the policies has selected a replacement victim to expel from the Real Cache. At this point the other policies would also need to expel the reference to the replacement victim from their physical caches as well. However, the replacement victim is not necessarily the same page that would be selected by each of the other policies' uncaching rules.

This process of releasing an arbitrary page from the physical cache of each policy requires a release mechanism that discards the selected page from cache. Discarding a page with the original ACME required removing a page from a priority queue. However, in the ACME-DB implementation, the release mechanisms are more complex since they affect more than one queue or stack for the new policies that have been added to the policy pool.

The release mechanisms have been determined based on the way in which the buffers are used by each of the policies concerned. In the same way that the caching and uncaching functionality needs to be separated from each other for the purposes of being able to integrate them into the overall ACME architecture, the release mechanism for each policy needs to be defined separately so that it can be invoked independent of caching and uncaching.

4.2 Choice of Policies

Random, FIFO, LIFO, LRU, LFU, LFUDA, MFU, and MRU were the only policies that were re-used from the original ACME implementation, and their release mechanisms simply evict victim pages from a priority queue. Six new policies were also added to the policy pool. These new policies are aimed more specifically to work in a database-specific environment, and have more complex behaviour that the other existing policies in the policy pool. The respective release mechanisms for each of the six policies that have been added as part of ACME-DB will now be described.

LIRS. This policy is described in (Jiang and Zhang, 2002). In the case of uncaching a page from the buffer, the page at the front of the List Q queue is ejected, creating space for a new page in the buffer pool. However, when releasing the page arbitrarily some other factors need to be taken into account.

(i) In the case that the page to be released exists in List Q, that is, the page is a resident HIR page, the page is released from List Q (wherever in the queue it may be). This case is identical to the case of uncaching, except that instead of replacing the page at the front of the queue, any page in the queue could be potentially replaced.

(ii) In the case that the page to be replaced exists in the LIR page set, that is, the page is an LIR page, the page is released from the LIR page set. This creates a space in the LIR page set, which needs to be filled in before normal caching / uncaching processes can proceed on the buffers. The space in the LIR page set is filled by ejecting the resident HIR page at the tail of List Q, and pushed onto the top of the LIR page set (the implementation employs a LIR page set to hold LIR pages). If this page was not in Stack S, it is pushed onto Stack S, and flagged as a resident LIR page.

The release mechanism is designed in this manner because it is presumed that the HIR page at the tail of List Q is the HIR page that had the least recency out of all the other resident HIR pages. In releasing one of the LIR pages from the LIR page set, it is considered that the HIR page in List Q with the least recency should be added to the LIR page set to fill the space left by the released page. Due to the fact that a resident HIR page is therefore turned into an LIR page, it needs to be added to Stack S, if it is not already there, and flagged as a resident LIR page. (Note: All pages are flagged as either resident or non-resident in the implementation).

LRFU. This policy is described in (Lee et al., 1999). The release mechanism in this case simply removes the page from the priority queue.

LRU-K. This policy is described in (O'Neil et al., 1993). The release mechanism in this case simply removes the page from the priority queue.

SFIFO. This policy is described in (Turner and Levy, 1981). The release mechanism in this policy checks the primary buffer for the page to be released, and releases it from there if found. If not, then the secondary buffer is checked for the page to be released, and is released from there. The release mechanism design in this policy reflects the fact that pages are not cached to the secondary buffer until the primary buffer is full, thereby enabling the arbitrary removal of pages from either buffer.

2Q. This policy is described in (Johnson and Shasha, 1994). The release mechanism in this policy checks to see whether the page to be released exists in the Am buffer, and releases it from there if found. If not, then the page to be released is searched for in the A1in buffer, and released from there if found. The release mechanism was designed in this manner so that the sizes of each of the A1in and A1out buffers are checked when uncaching occurs, thereby enabling the arbitrary release of a page from either the Am or A1in buffer.

W^2R. This policy is described in (Jeon and Noh, 1998). The release mechanism in this policy checks the Weighing Room buffer for the page to be released, and releases it from there if found. If not, the Waiting Room buffer is checked for the page to be released, and is released from there. The Weighing Room is implemented as a simple LRU queue, and the Waiting Room as a FIFO queue, enabling the simple arbitrary removal of a page from either queue, without needing any extra queue adjustments.

5 EVALUATION

This section describes the evaluation environment for which ACME-DB was implemented, the methodology used to design the experiments, the results of those experiments, and an analysis of the results.

5.1 Evaluation Environment and Traces

The ACME-DB simulation was implemented using C++, compiled and tested on Microsoft Windows XP, Linux RedHat 6.2 and Linux Debian. The execution time tests were performed on a Pentium IV 2GHz PC with 256 MB of RAM.

Two traces were used to simulate request streams. These traces are the DB2 and OLTP (On-Line Transaction Processing) traces used by Jeon and Noh (Jeon and Noh, 1998), Johnson and Sasha (Johnson and Shasha, 1994) and by O'Neil et al. (O'Neil et al., 1993). The DB2 trace was originally obtained by running a DB2 commercial application and contains 500,000 page requests to 75,514 distinct pages. The OLTP trace contains records of page requests to a CODASYL database for a window of one hour. It contains 914,145 requests to 186,880 distinct pages.

Further to these two live traces, five synthetic traces were also created to simulate well known susceptibilities in replacement policies, and to simulate request streams that would not favour any particular policy in the policy pool.

5.2 Experimental Methodology

This sub-section provides details on the experiments used to test and evaluate ACME-DB. Unless otherwise stated, all the experiments that tested hit rates in relation to the request stream were based on a cache size of 1000 pages. This cache size was chosen in an attempt to make comparisons with other experiments that used cache sizes of 1000 as well.

5.2.1 Combined Effect of all Policies

This experiment involved running ACME-DB across the two live traces with all fourteen policies enabled. This was to determine the combined effect of all the policies on the Real Cache hit rate, and to show the hit rates achieved by the virtual caches of the individual policies.

5.2.2 Real Cache Adaptation to the Current Best Policy

The second part of the experiment involved running ACME-DB with the best policy and an average-performing policy to determine the extent to which the Real Cache adapted to the best policy in terms of hit rate. The purpose of this test was to examine the switching of the current best policy and how this would affect the Real Cache in terms of hit rate.

5.2.3 The Adaptive Nature of ACME-DB

This experiment involved running ACME-DB with Synthetic Trace A to determine the behaviour of ACME when one of the policies switched from one performance extreme to the other and to illustrate how the presence of another policy in the policy pool has a stabilising effect during the performance degradation of the first policy.

5.2.4 Different Cache Sizes

ACME-DB was tested with all of its policies in the policy pool using cache sizes of between 100 and 10000 pages. The objective of this test was to determine the effect of the cache size on the cache hit rate.

5.2.5 Average Time Loss for Each Additional Policy

It is well known that the different replacement policies used in ACME-DB vary in performance with regard to time complexity. It is possible that the addition of certain policies to the policy pool could increase the overall time complexity of ACME-DB, and thus detract from the benefits of using policies that perform well in terms of hit rate.

5.2.6 Investigation of Susceptibilities to Well-known Weaknesses

Replacement policies were run using synthetic traces designed to expose the commonly known weaknesses of particular policies. This aimed to expose the susceptibility of other policies in the policy pool, and observe the effect on the Real Cache.

5.2.7 The Effect of Disk Reads on the Total Execution Time

This experiment gauged the effect of disk reads on total execution time, and whether the ability of the Real Cache to adapt to the current best policy would result in improved or poorer performance. The results of this test would provide the best value practically, since disk accesses are taken into account.

5.3 Simulation Results

This sub-section presents the main results and corresponding analyses. For the purposes of this paper, in most cases, only the results for the DB2 trace have been shown. For more details, please refer to (Riaz-ud-Din, 2003).

5.3.1 Relative Performance of Policies

Figure 2 below shows the hit rates with all policies in the policy pool using the methodology given in Sub-Section 5.2.1.

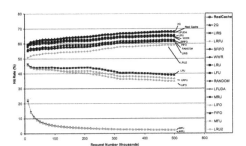

Figure 2: Requests vs. Hit rates

The graph above clearly defines three distinct groups of policies that are poor, average, and good in their relative performance. This reflects the relative strengths and weaknesses inherent in the heuristics that have been used to drive the victim selection processes of these policies. MRU and MFU performed poorly whilst 2Q and LFUDA performed particularly well.

5.3.2 The Performance of the Real Cache

In order to test the desired adaptive behaviour (that is, the Real Cache always stays closer to the best policy), only 2Q and FIFO were used in the policy pool (see Sub-Section 5.2.2 for methodology). Experiments in (Riaz-ud-Din, 2003) have shown that even when only two policies are in the policy pool, the Real Cache attempts to stay with the best performing (in terms of its cache hit rate) expert. Here the Real Cache is using the 2Q policy to do the majority of its caching, so its hit rates are similar to 2Q's hit rates. So if 2Q performs so well, is there any benefit in having other policies in the policy pool? Do the policies act synergistically to improve the Real Cache hit rate?

Results from tests performed in (Riaz-ud-Din, 2003) show no significant differences between the Real Cache hit rates where only 2Q and LFUDA are used, and where all the policies are used. Thus, having a large number of policies in the policy pool seems to neither help nor hinder the Real Cache hit rate. However, this would affect execution time and memory, which will be examined later in this paper.

Tests in (Riaz-ud-Din, 2003) also show that the Real Cache can only perform as well as the current best performing policy, which may not always have high hit rates. This shows the importance of finding the best mix of the minimum number of policies for inclusion in the policy pool.

5.3.3 The Adaptive Behaviour of ACME

Whilst 2Q has so far performed the best for the live requests, there may be other request patterns for which it may not do as well (refer figure 7). The methodology given in Sub-Section 5.2.3 is used to highlight this fact and Figure 3 below displays the results.

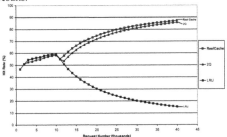

Figure 3: Request vs. Hit rate (2Q and LRU only)

It illustrates how LRU starts off with a higher hit rate than 2Q and at this point in time, the Real Cache adapts to LRU's caching behaviour. However, when the processing reaches the part of the trace that inhibits the performance of LRU, 2Q continues to climb the 'hit rate chart', while LRU's performance starts to degrade significantly. At this point, the Real Cache does not drop with LRU, but rather adapts to the new best policy (2Q) to clearly illustrate ACME's adaptive nature.

This is an important point because it indicates that having other policies should result in a 'safer' policy pool. Therefore, if at any particular moment, the performance of the current best policy degrades due to a known or un-known weakness, other policies in the policy pool would ensure that the Real Cache hit rate would not degrade as well, or at least not to the same extent.

In all of the relevant figures, it can be seen that the Real Cache hit rate starts with individual policy hit rates from one point and then starts to converge on the best policy as the number of requests increases. As more requests are made, the machine learning adjusts the weights until the best performing policies have a greater probability of being selected for performing caching and uncaching actions on the Real Cache, which then starts resembling the current best policy with respect to its hit rate.

5.3.4 The Effect of Having Different Cache Sizes

Live traces were driven using different cache sizes to show the effect of cache size on the Real Cache with Figure 4 below showing hit rate versus the cache size for the DB2 trace.

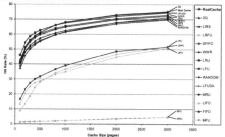

Figure 4: Cache Size vs. Hit rate, DB2 Trace

The effect of cache size on the Real Cache hit rate is summarised for each of the live traces in Table 1 below.

Table 1: Real Cache hit rates for different cache sizes

Cache Size	Real Cache Hit Rates (%)			
	DB2		OLTP	
	Value	% Increase	Value	% Increase
100	39.5	--	7.1	--
200	47.8	20.9	13.9	94.9
300	52.2	9.3	17.1	23.0
400	55.2	5.7	21.7	27.5
500	57.1	3.5	24.9	14.6
800	60.5	5.9	33.7	35.2
1,000	61.6	1.8	33.9	0.7
2,000	67.0	8.7	40.0	17.9
3,000	69.1	3.3	45.8	14.5
5,000	71.11	2.9	50.1	9.5
10,000	73.27	3.0	55.3	10.4

The choice of cache sizes shown above were determined by the cache sizes that have been used to test the new policies that have been added to the policy pool, in their respective papers. Doing so provides a basis for comparison with the other policies using similar cache sizes.

Figure 4 cumulatively shows that increasing the cache size also increases the individual policies' hit rates, and therefore the Real Cache hit rate (since the Real Cache follows the best policy at any time regardless of cache size). However, the major sacrifice for achieving better hit rates as a result of larger cache sizes is that the time required to process the requests also increases (since there are more pages to search through). This is largely due to the fact that processing time is positively correlated to the number of policies in the policy pool (as each of the virtual caches also perform their own caching).

5.3.5 Effect of Replacement Policies on Time Performance

Just as replacement policies vary in performance with regard to hit rates, so too do they vary with regard to their time complexities. Figure 5 below illustrates this point by showing the additional time each policy adds to the total time it takes for ACME-DB to process a request stream of 50,000 requests as described in the methodology outlined in Sub-Section 5.2.5.

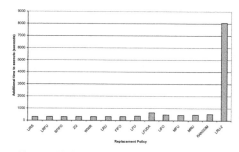

Figure 5: The increase in time by adding each policy

In the above figure, all policies (except LRU-2) increase the total time for ACME to process the request stream in similar magnitude (around 300 to 500 seconds) for 50,000 requests. Of this subset, LFUDA increased the time the most - by around 600 seconds (10 minutes). However, to put this in perspective, LRU-2 increased the total time by over 8000 seconds (more than 2 hours), which is 13 times slower than LFUDA. Thus, LRU-2's performance in this respect does not warrant its inclusion in the policy pool.

2Q, which has been shown to perform relatively on par with LFUDA using the live traces, only adds half as much time (around 300 seconds) as LFUDA does to the overall running time and therefore would arguably make it better for request streams similar to the DB2 or OLTP traces. Once again, this shows the importance of reducing the number of policies, and of finding a good mix of policies.

5.3.6 Effect on all Policies by Introducing Well-known Susceptibilities

Figure 6 below shows the effect of sequential flooding. Specifically, a synthetic trace was used to highlight the sequential flooding patterns to which LRU is susceptible.

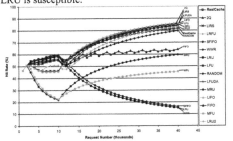

Figure 6: The effect of sequential flooding

As Figure 6 above shows, the hit rates for all of the policies dramatically change at 10,000 requests (this is where the sequential flooding patterns are introduced into the request stream). As expected, the hit rates for LRU, and W^2R (which is based on LRU in this implementation) significantly degrade. SFIFO also shows a similar weakness to this susceptibility, and this is because the primary and secondary buffers in SFIFO combine to act in a similar manner to LRU.

The remaining policies improve upon encountering the sequential flooding because most of them have been designed specifically to avoid this susceptibility. The erratic behaviour of the FIFO policy is due to the fact that the partial DB2 Trace that is included at the start of the synthetic trace used here has already referenced the same pages that are referenced in the sequential flooding part of the trace. Thus, the contents of the buffer pool upon encountering the sequential flooding includes some of those pages to be referenced, and when these pages are referenced during the sequential flooding part, the hit rates of the FIFO trace increases temporarily, and when other pages are not found the hit rates decrease again.

Introducing sequential scanning patterns in the request stream shows an immediate degradation of performance in terms of hits for all policies. Some policies recover, whilst others continue to degrade, but the Real Cache stays with the better policies. Please see (Riaz-ud-Din, 2003) for the details of this experiment.

Figure 7 below shows the effect of skewed high reference frequencies on the policies in the policy pool. A synthetic trace was designed to highlight the frequency patterns to which LFU is susceptible.

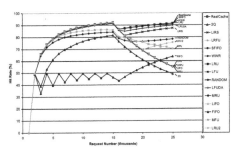

Figure 7: The effect of skewed high reference frequencies

The skewed high reference frequency patterns were introduced at 15,000 requests, as shown by the immediate degradation of hit rates for all policies. Interestingly, 2Q, which has performed the best with all of the tests so far, is the worst performing policy for this trace and along with other policies it continues to decline upon encountering the skewed high reference frequency patterns. This indicates that 2Q is susceptible to skewed high frequency patterns in request streams and once again confirms that having other policies results in a 'safer' policy pool than if just one policy, such as 2Q, was relied upon.

So far, it would seem that a good choice of policies for the policy pool would include 2Q and LRU in particular because 2Q performs very well with most of the request streams, and for those that it does not, LRU performs very well. Thus, they complement each other well and neither has a significant overhead in terms of execution time, in comparison to other policies such as LFUDA or LRU2.

The question of which policies and how many policies to use, is one that is well worth answering. However, this cannot be addressed by studying the effects of running through only two traces, but needs more in-depth examination across a wide range of live access patterns. It would depend highly on the databases expected access patterns.

5.3.7 The Effect of Misses on the Total Processing Time

Until now the discussion of processing time with regard to the time taken to find a victim and the additional time added per policy has only dealt with the time taken for ACME-DB to do the processing required to perform the caching, uncaching, release and other activities within the scope of the implementation. The time taken to read from disk, which occurs in the event of a miss, has until now been ignored. However, the time that is taken to read from disk is significant, and forms a major part of the latencies concerned with the overall database performance. As noted, the time needed to read from disk is some 170,000 times greater than reading from memory and each read from disk takes around 10 milliseconds.

To gauge the effect on the total time required for processing requests (including the time for disk reads), the methodology given in Sub-Section 5.2.7 was used. The trace used was intended to induce the best and worst behaviour of SFIFO and 2Q at opposite ends of the spectrum. The results are presented in Table 2 below.

Table 2: Execution times with and without disk reads

Policies in Policy Pool	Time to execute without disk reads (seconds)	Number of misses	Time to execute including disk reads (seconds)
2Q	12	28,197	**293.97**
SFIFO	8	58,196	**589.96**
2Q & SFIFO	18	4,852	**66.52**

The above table shows the time taken to execute the trace, the number of misses on the Real Cache, and the time to execute including disk reads, for the two policies. The column to note is right-most, which shows that the performance was significantly better by introducing two policies in the policy pool, each of which contributed to the hit rate when the other was susceptible to the pattern in the request stream. Overall a gain of 227.45 seconds (almost 4 minutes) over 96,000 requests is made.

The above experiment has shown that when ACME-DB encounters a request stream where the current best policy changes, the overall execution time (when accounting for the disk reads avoided by maintaining a higher hit rate) decreases substantially.

However, what if the current best policy is the same policy over a long period of time (or even the entire request stream), as with the live traces used here? In this case, what would the eventual loss in performance be by using ACME-DB, rather than the policy just by itself? In order to answer this all important question, the above experiment was run once again, but this time with the first 100,000 requests from the DB2 trace, which has shown to favour 2Q over all the other policies. The results are presented in Table 3 below.

Table 3: Execution times with and without disk reads

Policies in Policy Pool	Time to execute without disk reads (seconds)	Number of misses	Time to execute including disk reads (seconds)
2Q	15	367,020	**382.02**
SFIFO	4	392,900	**396.9**
2Q & SFIFO	34	371,170	**405.17**

Running 2Q by itself results in the fastest execution time overall, whilst the slowest is when running SFIFO and 2Q together. The loss in time by adding SFIFO is 23.15 seconds over 100,000 requests, compared to the 227.45 seconds gained in the previous experiment. This time loss is only a small fraction of the time that is potentially gained by using ACME-DB should a request pattern to which 2Q is susceptible be encountered. Furthermore, if 2Q continues to be the current best policy, the Real Cache's hit rate will continue to move closer to 2Q's hit rate. Consequently, the Real Cache's misses will be more or less the same as 2Q's misses, resulting in fewer disk reads, and ultimately faster execution times.

These experiments confirm that the net gain by introducing both policies would indeed result in better overall performance, especially where the request stream exhibits differing patterns of access with time.

6 CONCLUSIONS

The work described in this paper examines the implementation of a recently proposed adaptive algorithm, known as Adaptive Caching with Multiple Experts (ACME), within the database environment. The results indicate that ACME works well with single-sized page caches and with replacement policies that are readily applied to the database buffer pool. It has also been shown that ACME maintains its adaptive behaviour when caching database pages, and stays with the current best policy. Most significantly, it has also been shown that whilst adding more policies to the policy pool increases the execution time, the overall processing time is dramatically reduced due to a greater number of hits. The results are based on an implementation that is efficient, can be readily integrated into the real world environment, and should provide great incentive for further database research. The results of this work provide an excellent platform for further research in the field of database buffer replacement.

ACKNOWLEDGEMENTS

We would like to thank Ismail Ari for the original ACME source code and Xiaodong Zhang, Song Jiang, Sam H. Noh, and Heung Seok Jeon for the live traces.

REFERENCES

Ari, I. (2002). *Storage Embedded Networks (SEN) and Adaptive Caching using Multiple Experts (ACME)*, Ph.D. Proposal.

Ari, I., Amer, A., Miller, E., Brandt, S., and Long, D. (2002). Who is more adaptive? ACME: Adaptive Caching using Multiple Experts. *Workshop on Distributed Data and Structures (WDAS 2002)*.

Castro, M., Adya, A., Liskov, B., and Myers, A. C. (1997). HAC: Hybrid Adaptive Caching for Distributed Storage Systems. In *Proceedings of the 16th ACM Symposium on Operating Systems Principles (SOSP)*, 102–115.

Effelsberg, W. and Haerder, T. (1984). Principles of Database Buffer Management. In *ACM Transactions on Database Systems*, 9 (4), 560 – 595.

Jeon, H. S. and Noh, S. H. (1998). A Database Disk Buffer Management Algorithm Based on Prefetching. In *Proceedings of the ACM Conference on Information and Knowledge Management (CIKM '98)*, 167-174.

Jiang, S. and Zhang, X. (2002). LIRS: An Efficient Low Inter-Reference Recency Set Replacement Policy to Improve Buffer Cache Performance. In *Proceedings of the ACM SIGMETRICS Conference on Measurement and Modeling of Computer Systems*, 31-42.

Johnson, T. and Shasha, D. (1994). 2Q: A Low Overhead High Performance Buffer Management Replacement Algorithm. In *Proceedings of the 20th International Conference on Very Large Databases*, 439 - 450.

Lee, D., Choi, J., Kim, J. H., Noh, S. H., Min, S. L., Cho, Y. and Kim, C. S. (1999). On the Existence of a Spectrum of Policies that Subsumes the Least Recently Used (LRU) and Least Frequently Used (LFU) Policies. In *Proceedings of ACM SIGMETRICS'99 International Conference on Measurement and Modeling of Computer Systems*, 134 - 143.

O'Neil, E. J., O'Neil, P. E., and Weikum, G. (1993). The LRU-K Page Replacement Algorithm for Database Disk Buffering. In *Proceedings of ACM MOD International Conference on Management of Data*, 297 – 306.

Ramakrishnan, R. and Gehrke, J. (2000). *Database Management Systems*, McGraw Hill, USA.

Riaz-ud-din, F. (2003). *Adapting ACME to the Database Caching Environment*. Masters Thesis, Massey University.

Sacco, G. M. and Schkolnick, M. (1986). Buffer Management in Relational Database Systems. In *ACM Transactions on Database Systems*, 11, 473 – 498.

Turner, R. and Levy, H. (1981). Segmented FIFO Page Replacement. In *Proceedings of ACM SIGMETRICS*, 48 – 51.

RELATIONAL SAMPLING FOR DATA QUALITY AUDITING AND DECISION SUPPORT

Bruno Cortes

Instituto Politécnico do Cávado e Ave, Barcelos, Portugal
Email: bcortes@ipca.pt

José Nuno Oliveira

Departamento de Informática da Universidade do Minho, Braga, Portugal
Email: jno@di.uminho.pt

Keywords: Fuzzy logic, data sampling, estimation and data quality.

Abstract: This paper presents a strategy for applying sampling techniques to relational databases, in the context of data quality auditing or decision support processes. Fuzzy cluster sampling is used to survey sets of records for correctness of business rules. Relational algebra estimators are presented as a data quality-auditing tool.

1 INTRODUCTION

In the last few years, many companies around the world have spent large amounts of resources on process re-engineering encompassing both applications and data. Voluminous data sets, in particular those extracted from the Web, have become a serious problem to those companies whose intended information profit is eventually put at risk because of data management costs.

As a matter of fact, it is hard to support and maintain the quality of fast-growing data. These very rapidly become infected with so-called "dirty" data, a problem nowadays identified under the *data quality* heading. The risk of deterioration, which is a real menace, is worsened by the complexity of the information contained in many legacy systems (with many years of age) that are still in use today.

In this context, *data quality auditing* emerges as a relevant business area. Even the most advanced database management systems (DBMS) are still unable to cope with subtle semantic dependences that cannot be expressed in standard DBMS languages and systems. Popularly known as *business rules*, such dependencies can only be captured by mathematical formulae over the target data. Such (temporal) logic *predicates* are referred to as *datatype invariants* in the literature of formal methods for software design (Oliveira, 1997).

Data quality auditing of complex business rules requires resource-consuming batch processing, whose complexity is proportional to the volume of the data under test, mostly because of the CPU bandwidth needed to process the conjunction of logical predicates – some of them complementing themselves, others sharing the domain of analysis.

In the industrial world, *sampling* - a standard strategy for ensuring the quality of manufactured products - is easy to implement because the manufacturing process itself can be analysed independently of other processes in the organization. In the database domain, however, data is always inter-related and several processes can induce mutual dependencies that are not explicit in the database schema.

Until the last decade, there was a lack of knowledge about how to build good samples in databases (Olken, 1993). In creating samples, one has to deal with factors such as *existential* and *referential integrity*, data distribution and correlated variables, among other issues.

Some auditing processes often find it useful to consider closed and consistent samples (Bisbal and Grimson, 2000), because they can report the behaviour and performance of information systems and applications. In most cases, however, what auditors look for is the real state of data. Data samples must therefore reflect the same errors, the same behaviour and the same (lack of) quality as the original database.

I. Seruca et al. (eds.), Enterprise Information Systems VI, 82–88.

This paper describes the data sampling techniques developed as a basis for the data analysis component of a *data quality software system* based on formal methods (Ranito et al., 1998 and Neves, Oliveira et al. 1999).

2 FUZZY CLUSTERING FOR SAMPLING

Several methods can be used to approach sampling in databases (Olken, 1993) but, in particular, *weighted* and *stratified sampling* algorithms appear to produce best results on data quality auditing. Whenever processes are concerned with small amounts of data exhibiting similar behaviour, the exceptions and problems emerge in a faster way.

Fuzzy clustering is an interesting technique to produce weights and partitions for the sampling algorithms. The creation of partitions is not a static and disjoint process. Records have a chance to belong to more than one partition and this will reduce the sampling potential error, since it is possible to select a relevant record[1] during the sampling of subsequent partitions, even when it was not selected in the partition that shared more similar values with it. The same probabilities can also be used to produce universal weighted samples.

The *Partition Around Method* (Kaufman and Rousseeuw, 1990) is a popular partition algorithm where the *k-partitions* method is used to choose the centred (representative) element of each partition, whereupon the partitions' limits are established by neighbourhood affinity. The *fuzziness* introduced in the algorithm is related with the dependency between probability of inclusion in a partition and the *Euclidean* distance between elements, not only regarding the nearest neighbour but also other partitions' representatives.

2.1 K-partitions Method

For a given population, each record is fully characterized wherever it is possible to know every value in all **p** attributes. Let x_{it} represent the value of record **i** in attribute **t**, $1 \leq t \leq p$. The *Euclidean distance* $d(i,j)^2$ between two records, **i** and **j**, is given by:

$$d(i,j) = \sqrt{(x_{i1} - x_{j1})^2 + \dots + (x_{ip} - x_{jp})^2}$$

---

[1] Critical record in terms of data quality.
[2] $d(i,j) = d(j,i)$

If necessary, some (or all of the) attributes must be normalized to avoid that different domains affect with more preponderance the cluster definition. The common treatment is the calculation of the mean value of an attribute and its standard deviation (or mean absolute deviation as an alternative).

The *k-partitions* method defines as first partition's representative the element that minimizes the sum of all the Euclidean distances to all the elements in the population. The other representatives are selected according to the following steps:

1. Consider an element **i** not yet selected as a partition's representative.
2. Consider element **j** not yet selected and denote by D_j its distance to the nearest representative of a partition, already selected. As mentioned above, d(j,i) denotes its distance to element **i**.
3. If **i** is closer to **j** than its closest representative, then **j** will contribute for the possible selection **i** as a representative. The contribute of **j** for the selection of **i** is expressed by the following gain function:

$$C_{ji} = \max(D_j - d(j,i), 0)$$

4. The potential of selection of individual **i** as representative is then given by:

$$\sum_{j} C_{ji}$$

5. Element **i** will be selected as representative if it maximizes the potential of selection:

$$\max_i \sum_{j} C_{ji}$$

2.2 Fuzzy Clustering Probabilities

After defining the partitions' representatives, it is possible to set a probability of inclusion of each element in each one of the **k** partitions established, based on the Euclidean distance between elements.

A *representativeness factor* f_r is set according to the relevance of an element in the context of each cluster. Empirical tests indicate this factor to be 0.9 when dealing with a partition's representative and 0.7 for all the others (Cortes, 2002). The algorithm's definition is described below[3]:

---

[3] For a full description see (Cortes, 2002).

1. Let D_i be the sum of the Euclidean distances $d(i,m)$ of element i to all partition's representatives ($1 \leq m \leq k$) and j be its nearest partition's representative.
2. The probability of selection of i as an element of the partition represented by j is given by:

$$P_j = fr \times \left(1 - \frac{d(i,j)}{D_i}\right)$$

3. The probability of selection of i as an element of any other partition v, $v \neq j$, is given by:

$$P_v = 1 - \left(fr \times \left(1 - \frac{d(i,j)}{D_i}\right)\right),$$

when $k = 2$

$$P_v = \left(1 - \frac{d(i,v)}{D_i}\right) \times \left(\frac{1 - P_j}{k - 1 - \left(1 - \frac{d(i,j)}{D_i}\right)}\right)$$

when $k > 2$.

3   ESTIMATING ALGEBRA OPERATIONS

Data quality auditing processes, including business rules validation, can be implemented as a sequence of algebra operations over large sets of data.

As a rule, these operations are chained according to complex precedence graph. This is why auditing is a high resource consuming process. When the auditing reports are more concerned with relative errors than with their actual identification, sampling and estimation become less expensive alternatives to be taken into account.

3.1   Estimating Data Quality with Join Operations

Several studies have been made to try to determine the query size of a join operation between two tables (Lipton, Naughton et al., 1990), whether all the parameters are available for analysis or not (Sun, Ling et al., 1993), based on sampling analysis.

Join operation with key attributes

Starting with the work presented in (Lipton, Naughton et al., 1990), a query result can be analysed as a set of disjoint clusters, sharing the same values in the joining attributes. The query size equals the sum of the size of all clusters. If the join of two tables $R \bowtie S$ resorts to key attributes of R then the size of each cluster mentioned above depends on the number of records in S that share the same values in the joining attributes.

To estimate the query size α of such a join operation, we treat the result as a set of n clusters (there are n distinct values in the key attributes of relation R), and $\alpha = \Sigma_i\, a_i$, with $1 \leq i \leq n$, where a_i is the estimation of the number of records in S that share the same i key value of R.

Let b be a major limit of a_i and A the equivalent metric regarding α, the size of a cluster and the size of the join itself. Set a confidence level of p to the sampling process, with two limits, k_1 and k_2, determined by:

$$k_1 = \frac{1}{1 - \sqrt{p}}$$

$$k_2 \geq \frac{1}{1 - p}$$

Accuracy is established by two given parameters δ and ε, while the error in the estimator $\hat{A}$ will be limited by the maximum of A/δ and A/ε. The estimation process is described as follows:

```
let s ← 0
let m ← 0
while (s<k₁bδ(δ+1) ∧ m<k₂ε²) do
    s ← s + a_Sampling({1,...,n})
    m ← m + 1
wend
Â ← ns / m
```

The calculation of k_1 and k_2 and the proofs of the following theorems can be found in (Lipton, Naughton et al., 1990).

Theorem 3.1: If the estimation process ended because $s < k_1 b \delta(\delta+1)$ then the estimation error in $\hat{A}$ if less then A/δ with a confidence level of p.

Theorem 3.2: If the estimation process ended because $m < k_2 \varepsilon^2$, then the estimation error in $\hat{A}$ if less then A/ε, with a confidence level of p.

The major limit **A** of the operation is the actual size of the operation (and it is supposed to have existential and referential integrity problems, since we dealing with legacy, dirty data). Since estimator Â represents the estimated size of a supposed join operation with clean data, it is possible to assert, with confidence level **p**, that the number of records that must be ensured to guarantee the quality of a rule implemented using this join operation lay within the interval

$$[(A-(Â+err), A-(Â-err))]$$

when A-(Â+*err*)>0 and within the interval

$$[0, A-(Â-err))]$$

when A-(Â+*err*)<0, where **err** is **A/δ** or **A/ε**, depending on the stop condition of the process.

Join with non-key attributes

Should non-key attributes be used in a join operation R∞S then the query size will also depend on the number of records in **R** that share the same values in the join domain. In general terms, the major limit **A** is now depending on the average number of records in relation **R** that share the same values in join attributes; in other words, to produce a confident limit **A**, we must calculate the size of relation **S** times the size of relation **R** and divide the result by the number of distinct values in join attributes of relation **R**.

To estimate the number of distinct values of a population several estimators can be used, such as *Chao*, *Jackknife*, *Shlosser* or *Bootstrap*, among others (Hass, Naughton et al., 1995). From this set, *Jackknife* and *Shlosser* usually produce the best results[4].

The *Jackknife* estimator can be calculated from a sample of **n** records, with **d_n** distinct values in the sample, from an initial population with **N** records. For each **k** element in the sample, $1 \leq k \leq n$, let **d_{n-1}(k)** denote the number of distinct values in the sample after removing the **k** element (if **k** is unique **d_{n-1}(k)=d_n-1**, otherwise **d_{n-1}(k)=d_n**). Calculating **d_{n-1}(k)** for all the elements of the sample and dividing it by the sample size **n**, yields:

$$d_{(n-1)} = \frac{\sum_{k=1}^{n} d_{n-1}(k)}{n}$$

The first order of the *Jackknife* estimator is then:

$$\overline{D}_{jk} = d_n - (n-1)(d_{n-1} - d_n)$$

On the other hand, the *Shlosser* estimator is given by:

$$\overline{D}_{Shlosser} = d_n + \frac{f_1 \times \sum_{i=1}^{n} (1-q)^i \times f_i}{\sum_{i=1}^{n} iq \times (1-q)^{i-1} \times f_i}$$

where q represents the **n/N** sampling probability and **f_i** is the number of values in the sample that occur exactly **i** times.

To produce best results, the choice between the *Shlosser* and the *Jackknife* estimators is determined by a *uniformity* test χ^2 in the sampled population.

Considering a sample of size **n** with **d** distinct values, let **m = n/d** and

$$u = \sum_{j:n_j>0} \frac{(n_j - m)^2}{m}$$

For **n > 0** and **0 < φ < 1**, $x_{n-1,\varphi}$ is the real number that satisfies $P(\chi^2 < x_{n-1,\varphi}) = \varphi$, with **n-1** degrees of freedom.

According with the χ^2 test, if $u \leq x_{n-1,\varphi}$, then the sample is particularly uniform and the *Jackknife* estimator should be used. The *Shlosser* estimator should be used otherwise.

3.2 Estimating Data Quality with Selection Operations

The implementation of business rules over a sample of a selection operation σ_{pr} (which will select all records in the relation when **pr ≡ true**), is transparent to the validation process[5] because sampling and selection are commutative operations:

$$\psi(n,\sigma_{pr}(R)) \equiv \sigma_{pr}(\psi(n,R))$$

This holds because, in both situations, the sampling probability for those records that do not validate **pr** is null while the others share a probability of **p = n/Nσ_{pr}** when dealing with random sampling.

---

[4] Limitations of the mentioned estimators are out of the scope of this paper.

[5] When the selection is established for independent variables.

The same criteria can be used for dependent variables, namely those involved in a referential integrity dependencies. In these cases, it is necessary to look at the join operation as a unique independent set prior to dealing with the selection operation itself.

4 TESTS AND RESULTS

The theory presented in this paper has been implemented and tested in industrial environments, during the auditing and migration stages of decision support solutions, under the edge of national funded project *Karma* (*ADI P060-P31B-09/97*).

Table 1 refers to the auditing results in a Enterprise Resource Planning System of a small company, regarding its sales information.

In this database, although the relational model was hard-coded in the application, the engine didn't implement the concept of referential integrity.

The referential integrity between the *Orders* table and the *OrderDetails* table, as well as the referential integrity between *Orders* and *Customers* tables and between *OrderDetails* and *Products* tables, have been tested using sampling auditing and full auditing processes. To evaluate the samples' behaviour when dealing with independent variables, the mean value of a purchasing order as well as the number of items in regular order were calculated for the samples. These values were also compared with real observations in the entire tables. From the final results some conclusions were taken:

a) The validation of *referential integrity* over samples using a classification of the population presents poor results when dealing with small samples, with estimations above the real values.

b) The validation of *existential integrity* (for example the uniqueness), under the same circumstances, presents poor results when dealing with small samples, with estimations bellow the real values.

c) Mean values and distribution results are also influenced by the scope of the sample, and must be transformed by the sample size ratio.

For the referential integrity cases, this is an expected result since the set of records in the referring table (say T_1) is much larger than the strict domain of the referred table (say T_2). The error of the estimator must be affected by the percentage of records involved in the sample. Let:

- t_1 be the sample of the referring table T_1;
- t_2 be the sample of the referred table T_2;
- α_2 be the percentage of records of T_2 selected for the sample ($\#t_2/\#T_2$);
- $\beta(T_1,T_2)$ be the percentage of records in T_1 that validates the R.I. in T_2.

It would be expected that $E[\beta(t_1,t_2)] = \beta(T_1,T_2)$, but when dealing with samples in the referred table (T_2) the expected value will match $E[\beta(t_1,t_2)] = \beta(T_1,T_2) * \alpha_2$. The estimated error is given by $\varepsilon = 1-\beta$ and therefore $E[\varepsilon(t_1,t_2)] = 1-[1-\varepsilon(T_1,T_2)] * \alpha_2$. Table 1 and figures 1, 2 and 3 show the referential integrity problems detected $\varepsilon(T_1,T_2)$, the sampling error $\varepsilon(t_1,t_2)$ and the expected error value for each case $E[\varepsilon(t_1,t_2)]$.

It is possible to establish the same corrective parameter when dealing with existential integrity, frequencies or distributions.

Several other tests were made in medium size and large size databases, corroborating the results presented above (Cortes, 2002).

Table 1: Referential integrity tests on a ERP database (OD) OrderDetails, (O) Orders (P) Products and(C) Customers tables

R.I.	$\varepsilon(T_1,T_2)$	α_2	$\varepsilon(t_1,t_2)$	$E[\varepsilon(t_1,t_2)]$
Sample I	(90% confidence, 5% accuracy)			
OD→O	5.8%	25.3%	72.1%	76.1%
OD→P	12.9%	77.3%	30.4%	32.6%
O→C	4.7%	74.4%	27.2%	29.1%
Sample II	(95% confidence, 5% accuracy)			
OD→O	5.8%	32.5%	66.6%	69.3%
OD→P	12.9%	82.6%	23.0%	28.0%
O→C	4.7%	81.1%	22.0%	22.8%
Sample III	(98% confidence, 5% accuracy)			
OD→O	5.8%	40.4%	58.3%	61.9%
OD→P	12.9%	86.6%	22.0%	24.5%
O→C	4.7%	85.5%	19.0%	18.5%
Sample IV	(99% confidence, 2% accuracy)			
OD→O	5.8%	83.7%	19.5%	21.1%
OD→P	12.9%	97.3%	14.5%	15.2%
O→C	4.7%	97.7%	7.5%	6.9%
Sample V	(99.5% confidence, 1% accuracy)			
OD→O	5.8%	96.0%	9.4%	9.5%
OD→P	12.9%	98.8%	14.4%	14.1%
O→C	4.7%	98.8%	5.5%	5.8%

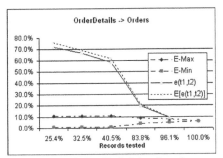

Figure 1: OrderDetails → Orders dependency

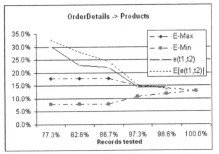

Figure 2: OrderDetails → Products dependency

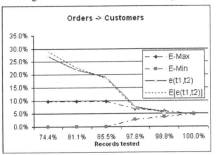

Figure 3: Orders → Customers dependency

The use of estimators to determine data quality based on join and selection operations produces good results, in particular when dealing with large volumes of data. Table 2 indicates the results of referential integrity estimations on an industrial environment. The testing environment was a major university database with data quality problems after a partial database migration.

Since several records of students, courses and grades were not completely migrated to the new database, the RDBMS presented a poor behaviour in terms of referential integrity, among other things.

To a more significant number of records (between 700.000 to 1.000.000 or more), estimation

must be taken into consideration as a preliminary auditing tool, saving time and resources. The equivalent tests in the entire database universe took several hours of CPU time in a parallel virtual machine with 8 nodes.

In this particular case, the choice of the best estimator was previously decided with an uniformity test as describe in the previous chapter. Comparing the number of students and courses in the university with the number of grades, we might say that data is contained within an almost uniform interval, which makes it appropriate for the use of *Jackknife* estimator. Several other tests were made and reported in (Cortes, 2002).

Table 2: Integrity estimation on university IS (G) Grades, (C) Courses and (S) Students tables

R.U.	#T1	$\epsilon(T_1,T_2)$	∞JK	$\epsilon(t_1,t_2)$
G→S	711043	12.4%	563019	20.5%
G→C	711043	59.4%	327185	55.0%

5 CONCLUSIONS AND FURTHER WORK

The research described in this paper presents a different strategy for data quality auditing processes based on data sampling. Our strategy is particularly useful if adopted at the earlier stages of an auditing project. It saves time and resources in the identification of critical inconsistencies and guides the detailed auditing process itself. The representative samples can further be used in determining association rules or evaluating times series, two areas more related with decision support itself.

But even though the results achieved are encouraging to proceed with this methodology, it is important to be aware that:

- There is no perfect recipe to produce an universal sample. Each case must be approached according to the data's profile – size, distribution, dependencies among other issues – and auditing purposes.

- Sampling will not produce accurate results, only good estimators. It will give us a general picture of the state of the art of a database, but more accurate processes – such as data cleansing – must involve an entire data set treatment.

The clustered analysis of data ("*divide and conquer*") maintaining data dependencies is an efficient and accurate method and can be optimised when implemented over parallel computing platforms (Cortes, 2002).

Further research is under way to determine the impact of incremental sampling of new data on the previous analysis results. This is relevant because information systems are living beings that evolve through time. Another approach regards the *fuzziness* of algebra operations (e.g. a selection is no longer a true or false result, but will produce a degree of selection (Andreasen, Christiansen et al., 1997) and its impact on the overall sampling analysis.

ACKNOWLEDGEMENTS

The work reported in this paper was funded by research contract *KARMA* (*ADI P060-P31B-09/97*) and Portuguese Governmental Institute (*FCT SFRH/BM/2358/2000*).

BIBLIOGRAPHY

T. Andreasen, H. Christiansen and H. Larsen, "Flexible Query Answering Systems", ISBN 0-7923-8001-0, Kluwer Academic Publishers, 1997

J. Bisbal and J. Grimson, "Generalising the Consistent Database Sampling Process". ISAS Conference, 2000

Bruno Cortes, "Amostragem Relacional", MsC. Thesis, University of Minho, 2002

P. Hass, J. Naughton et al., "Sampling-Based Estimation of the Number of Distinct Values of an Attribute", 21st VLDB Conference, 1995

Peter Haas and Arun Swami, "Sequential Sampling Procedures for Query Size Optimization", ACM SIGMOD Conference, 1992

L. Kaufman and P. Rousseeuw, "Finding Groups in Data – An Introduction to Cluster Analysis", Wiley & Sons, Inc, 1990

R. Lipton, J. Naughton et al., "Practical Selectivity Estimation through Adaptative Sampling", ACM SIGMOD Conference, 1990

F. Neves, J. Oliveira et al., "Converting Informal Meta-data to VDM-SL: A Reverse Calculation Approach", VDM workshop FM'99, France, 1999.

José N. Oliveira, "SETS – A Data Structuring Calculus and Its Application to Program Development", UNU/IIST, 1997

Frank Olken, "Random Sampling from Databases", PhD thesis, University of California, 1993

J. Ranito, L. Henriques, L. Ferreira, F. Neves, J. Oliveira. "Data Quality: Do It Formally?" Proceedings of IASTED-SE'98, Las Vegas, USA, 1998.

A. Shlosser, "On estimation of the size of the dictionary of a long text on the basis of sample", Engineering Cybernetics 19, pp. 97-102, 1981

Sun, Ling et at., "An Instant Accurate Size Estimation Method for Joins and Selection in a Retrieval-Intense Environment", ACM SIGMOD Conference, 1993

Hannu Toivonen, "Sampling Large Databases for Association Rules", 22nd VLDB Conference, 1996

TOWARDS DESIGN RATIONALES OF SOFTWARE CONFEDERATIONS

Jaroslav Král
Charles University
Malostranské nám. 25, 118 00 Praha 1, Czech Republic
jaroslav.kral@mff.cuni.cz

Michal Žemlička
Charles University
Malostranské nám. 25, 118 00 Praha 1, Czech Republic
michal.zemlicka@mff.cuni.cz

Keywords: Service orientation, software paradigm, user involvement, autonomous component, user-oriented component interface, software confederations.

Abstract: The paper discuss reasons why service-oriented architecture is a new software paradigm and the consequences of this fact for the design of enterprise information systems. It is shown that such systems called confederations need not use web services in the sense of W3C. It is, however, more or less a necessity in e-commerce. Confederations (service-oriented systems with known set of services) are typical for manufacturing systems. As business processes supported by enterprise systems must be supervised by businessmen, the same must hold for communication inside service-oriented systems. It implies that the interfaces of the services must be user-oriented (user-friendly). It can be easier achieved in confederations than in e-commerce systems. User oriented interface has positive consequences for the software engineering properties of the confederation. Confederations should sometimes include parts based on different implementation philosophies (e.g. data orientation). Pros and cons of it are discussed. Open issues of service orientation are presented.

1 INTRODUCTION

Enterprise information systems (EIS) tend to have the service-oriented architecture (SOA), i.e. a peer-to-peer (virtual) network of almost independent (autonomous) software units providing some services. EIS differ from the systems supporting e-commerce as EIS have

- known and almost fixed collection of services,

- user interface to whole system (often called portal), and

- known set of multistep business processes involving the services.

Information systems (and software systems in general) having such properties are called *(software) confederations* whereas the SOA systems supporting e-commerce are called *alliances* (see (Král and Žemlička, 2003a) for details). Note, that in e-commerce the set of business partners is not known and the partners must to be looked for. The emphasis of SOA on peer-to-peer principles is not commonly accepted (see e.g. (Tůma, 2003)). Peer-to-peer is a crucial property of SOA.

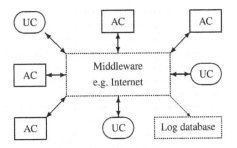

AC ... autonomous component

UC ... user interface component

(e.g. XSLT component or portal)

Figure 1: Software confederation

The structure of a confederation is given in Fig. 1. It can be meaningful not to limit middleware to be Internet-based. The middleware can even be based on a combination of different communication technologies and/or communication infrastructures. It follows that the services (peers) in confederations need not be web services in the sense of W3C (W3 Consortium,

I. Seruca et al. (eds.), Enterprise Information Systems VI, 89–96.
© 2006 *Springer. Printed in the Netherlands.*

2002; Jablonski and Petrov, 2003). We use SOA in this broader sense.

Software confederations appear quite often e.g. in e-government, health care systems, and public organizations. The user involvement in the activities of software confederation is deeper and wider than in classical logically monolithic software systems[1]. Confederations open new variants of user involvement into human interaction with the software systems.

A proper solution of human involvement in the development and the use of confederations usually results into better functions of the confederations and into enhancement of software engineering properties of the system (see section 3).

The application of service orientation is nowadays rather a paradigm than simply a new technique only. By a paradigm we understand according to the Webster Dictionary 'a generally accepted perspective of a particular discipline at a given time'. By a software paradigm we understand a consistent collection of methods, tools, examples of good practices, and development/activity patterns governed by a specific philosophy. New paradigms always require a new way of thinking and new methods and tools. Any new paradigm requires therefore a lot of effort and time to be governed and properly used. Old habits and intuitions must be changed or replaced by new ones. There should be changes in education and training of software experts (Král and Žemlička, 2004a; Král and Žemlička, 2004c).

One can object that service orientation is a quite old technique. It is true for e.g. soft real-time systems like flexible manufacturing systems (see e.g. (Král and Demner, 1979; Král et al., 1987)) but service orientation was not a paradigm in the above sense – it was no generally accepted philosophy at that time. Let us show that service orientation is becoming a leading software engineering paradigm now.

We exploit the experience with the development of the systems having some properties of SOA. The systems were several successful projects of Flexible Manufacturing System (later integrated into CIM systems), several automated warehouse projects (Kopeček, 2003; Skula, 2001) and analysis of the systems for municipal authorities. We often speak about services as about components to point out that a service is provided by a specific software component beeing often a complete application.

2   NEW PARADIGM

The concept of service-oriented architecture in the form of confederation is known for decades. The first

---

[1]Even if sometimes physically distributed.

application of SOA was in soft real-time system like the flexible manufacturing systems dated back in the seventies (compare e.g. (Král and Demner, 1979)). Some features of SOA were even present in COBOL systems. One can therefore argue that SOA is not a new paradigm. It is not so due to the following arguments:

1. SOA was not ten years ago in a leading edge of software development. The classical object-oriented paradigm was the main topic. Information systems typically had no service-oriented architecture.

2. The SOA-based philosophy differs from the object-oriented one like the data-oriented philosophy is different from the object-oriented one. First SOA systems used a very simple not too powerful middleware. SOA were therefore not able to be used in large distributed information systems. New middleware opens new ways for software systems how to be developed and/or used. These challenges are not investigated enough yet.

3. The conferences, publications and standards on SOA-related topics/problems has appeared recently only.

4. The concept of SOA was not generally accepted and strictly speaking there is now no complete consensus what is SOA about.

5. The practice indicates that it is not easy for the object-oriented people to accept and properly use the service-oriented philosophy.

Let us discuss the last point in more details as it also confirms the conjecture that the service-oriented paradigm is a new paradigm different e.g. from the object-oriented one. It is indicated e.g. by the following facts (compare (Brown et al., 1998)):

- The antipattern "Stovepipe Enterprise/Islands of Automation" ((Brown et al., 1998), pp. 147–157) is in service-orientation rather a pattern if a proper gate connecting the island to a middleware is available.

- The basic attitude in SOA is the decomposition of the system into large components providing complex functions. It is a turn near to the antipattern "Functional Decomposition". The modeling of such systems can use a modification of data flow diagrams, a tool that disappeared from object-oriented methodology during the last ten years (compare (Rumbaugh et al., 1991) and from the UML standard (Object Management Group, 2001)).

- Encapsulation and autonomous development of applications (e.g. legacy systems, third party products) is the main design pattern in SOA. It is, however, near to the stovepipe system antipattern

((Brown et al., 1998), pp. 159–190, although the recommendations from p. 162 can be applied).

Service-orientation simplifies refactoring of or even excludes the antipatterns: Lava Flow (the technology changes can be hidden inside the services behind their interfaces), Vendor Lock-In (possible but can be easily overcome), Reinvent the Wheel (legacy systems and third-party products can easily integrated), Corncob (unpleasant hacker can develop his own service), etc.

3   HUMAN INVOLVEMENT IN SERVICE-ORIENTED SYSTEMS

The lack of user involvement in requirements specifications is the main reason of software project failures. The novelty of service orientation is that the involvement of users in the system activities is deeper than in classical systems. The activities of human beings are not limited to UC from Fig. 1 only. The communication (dialog) in *e*-commerce is usually stateless. The dialog starts with looking for a service (autonomous component) that provides the contact and other information on potential business partners (e.g. supplier). This is often done using UDDI and WSDL. It implies that the communication between partners must be supported by a widely accepted middleware (Internet) and must use generally accepted message formats based on appropriate standards (XML).

The dialog is usually in a SOAP-based formats. The dialog is used to perform a business process (e.g. business agreement conclusion) under the (possible) personal supervision of businessmen of the partners. The business documents produced in this way are to be often formally confirmed by businessmen (signed traditionally or electronically).

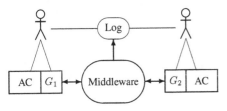

Figure 2: Semi-automated contract dialog scheme: Users should be able to supervise communication and to analyse Log datastore

Business processes are internal matters of the communicating parties. The coordination of the business processes of several partners can be therefore a quite

complicated task. Optimal requirements specification on the supervising activity of individual steps of business processes is a corner stone of requirement specification of the alliance as a whole.

As the businessmen must able to understand the communication between the autonomous components, they must be able to understand the formats of the messages produced and/or accepted by the gates G_1 and G_2 in Fig. 2. This is easy only if the message formats are based on the languages of the user knowledge domains. We say that the interfaces are user-oriented. It can be more easily achieved in confederations where the partners know each other and can agree message formats according their needs. As their knowledge domains are usually based on a long term activities and they are therefore in some sense "tuned", the user-oriented interfaces of G_1 and G_2 (i.e. the languages defined by message formats) tends to be stable (not so varying as IT technologies). It has important software engineering advantages described below.

In confederations users must be able to define and to supervise business process being networks of steps performable by particular services. The communication traffic in service-oriented systems can and should be logged. The confederations admit, however, a wider set of implementation principles than alliances.

The data defining business processes are best to store in user interface components (portals). The business steps are then supervised via the portal. An extreme solution is that there are no business processes (workflows) defining data and the business processes are completely controlled by users.

Business data analysis (via e.g. OLAP) must be based on data-oriented view. In this case the users (usually managers) must have a transparent access to data (tiers) of the components.

The notions and/or languages specifying the actions of components (e.g. bookkeeping) are often remarkably stable. The same can hold for the languages of the interfaces of corresponding services. It is quite possible that the interface of a component does not vary in spite of the fact that the component implementation varies. The stability of interfaces is important for the communication partners of the given component and for the stability of the whole confederations. It has further substantial software engineering advantages (modifiability, outsourcing opportunities, reduction of number of messages, integration of products of various vendors, openness, etc.).

It is not feasible to limit the philosophy and the software architecture to one choice. It is especially important for the confederations. So the crucial point of the requirements specification for confederations is what philosophy or combination of philosophies will be used. Examples of the philosophies are classical data flow batch systems (see (Yourdon, 1988)), data driven systems (see (Donnay Software Designs, 1999)), object-oriented systems (see (Rumbaugh et al., 1991; Jacobson and et all, 1995)). This issue is not addressed in existing CASE tools and only a little addressed by research.

4   DATA-FLOW BATCH SYSTEMS (DFBS)

DFBS were typical for the COBOL era more than thirty years ago when due to the limits of hardware (and to some degree to then state-of-art at that time) the possibilities of on-line (interactive) elaboration as well as of the use of modern database system were limited, if any. Such systems were usually written in COBOL. Note that COBOL compilers are still well supported.

DFBS has many important advantages. The case Y2K has shown that DFBS are extremely stable. In many enterprises they had been in use without almost any maintenance for years – sometimes even for decades. The enterprises had even no COBOL programmers about year 2000 although they had been using systems written in COBOL and DFBS's intensively.

DFBS is typically a collection of autonomous programs providing some services usually written in COBOL. The tasks of the programs were the transformation of massive data from several input files into (massive) data in several output files. The programs can be developed almost independently. The batch character of the systems simplifies the development and reduces maintenance effort. There are still many situations when DFBS can and should be used. Examples are massive data correctness control, data replication, off-line data filtering and transformations, and (statistic) data analysis. Note that the philosophy of DFBS can be easily adapted to the case when the data are in data stores (e.g. copies of databases), not necessarily in files. It is, however, assumed that the data elaboration can be off-line (i.e. performable in the batch mode). Batch systems can be necessary when data analysis is very time consuming.

The first DFBS's were based on the analysis of the data (originally paper documents) flows already existing in the organization. Such analysis is known as function decomposition. Function decomposition reflects the basic features of workflows in enterprises. It is an advantage that some other specification philosophies do not have. On the other hand the use of DFBS does not properly support the horizontal communication in organizations. It has further drawbacks especially in an object-oriented environment. It can make the business process (re)construction more difficult.

From technical point of view it can be difficult to synchronize DFBS with the every-day activities of on-line (interactive) systems. So DFBS are not often used but it does not mean that they are useless. If a DFBS can be used, we should specify the requirements as transformations of input data into output data. It is not equal to the way we specify the data and data operations in data-driven system and object-oriented system described below. DFBS use data-flow diagrams as a main system visualization tool and structured analysis and design as a system development tool (Yourdon, 1988). If a DFBS can be used, it can save a lot of effort and it can simplify the maintenance and increase the reusability of the system. DFBS has the architecture of a network of autonomous services – it is a property that has recently returned in a modified form in software confederations.

DFBS are still usually written in COBOL. The classical COBOL thinking is not obsolete here. The thinking oriented towards a network of autonomous services partly applicable during the implementation of DFBS substantially simplifies the task, provided that the network based architecture is possible. It is the case of DFBS being formed by a virtual network of autonomous programs (a predecessor of services). The autonomous programs can be autonomously developed using different methodologies and/or programming languages if necessary. The programs can be reused or they can be third party products. It is a great advantage having its counterpart in software confederations. It need not therefore be a good idea of some CIO's to avoid 'COBOL thinking' (compare (Sneed, 2002)) and to require every DFBS to be reengineered to be an object-oriented system.

Batch systems are usually very stable, well maintenable and have good software engineering properties. Such systems can be applied in confederations in the cases of massive data reconstructions, data replications and even in the time consuming cases of data analysis. In these cases the batch-oriented attitude is more or less a practical necessity. We know banks performing due to safety reasons financial transactions in two steps. In on-line mode the transaction data are stored in a temporal database. The transactions are completed in batch mode by DFBS.

The use of batch system can impose some limitations on the system performance as some operations cannot be done on-line. The importance of such limitations is often overestimated and advantages of the application of batch system underestimated. The consequence is that the batch philosophy is wrongly considered to be obsolete and useless. Due to this prejudice some opportunities are missed as the analysis does not include the question whether some applications should not be implemented via a batch subsystem.

DFBS attitude can be an optimal solution in massive data filtering, presentation (report generation) and other task performable in batch mode.

The modeling of batch systems is possible via data-flow diagrams known from structured analysis and design (Yourdan, 1988) or by the tools of functional design.

5   DATA DRIVEN SYSTEM (DDS)

Data driven systems appeared after the success of modern database systems. The aim at that time was usually to computerize operative level of an enterprise (warehouses, bookkeeping, business data). Data types were known and various operations could be defined over the same data. Moreover properly designed data structures can be used for many other potential operations – i.e. the data enable many further operations not specified yet. It was and still is supported by the power of the SQL language.

The substantial properties of the architecture of the developed system was the data model expressed by ER-diagrams often accompanied by data-flow model (Donnay Software Designs, 1999). The condition for the application of such a strategy was a proper quality of hardware (servers, client workplaces, data networks).

Data driven systems are still a good solution in the situations when the kernel of the problem is in the data area, i.e.:

• The main problem is to define data and data structures and to collect data in an electronic form.

• The operations can be easily derived from data and data concepts, there are many possible operations over the same data (i.e. a value can be used by many different operations in different ways).

• The properties of the system depend heavily on the optimality of the operations on data.

• There is a need to work with and analyze massive data (statistics, OLAP, etc.).

The requirements specification starts from the data specifications and/or data model and from basic operations. As data enables a broad set of operations the system is open in this sense.

Data oriented philosophy is appropriate in the case when a system is built from scratch starting from data tier.

The existence of data orientation in modern systems is confirmed by the existence of resource definition framework (RDF (W3 Consortium, 1999)) and (meta)data oriented research. Data orientation is typical for management information systems. Such systems assume a flexible open system of operations over massive data.

The fact that the collection of operations is open can be felt sometimes disadvantageous (optimality issues, some important operations need not be detected). The practice indicates that DDS are usually not felt as a system of collaborating autonomous services. Note, however, that common database with triggers can be quite easily adapted to serve as middleware. The message transfer can be implemented as a storing some data including an activation of a trigger causing proper activation of the addressee of the message. The integration of software pieces is in this case via a common data tier. The used tools are SQL, ER-diagrams, RDF, data-flow-diagrams. A strong point of DDS is their openness and support for data analysis. Weak points are:

• the problems with definition of common data structure/database,

• issues connected with data replication and unification (common format/structure),

• large systems are difficult to reconstruct,

• inflexibility of "middleware" services (data routing) compared with the middleware implementation and message passing via e.g. Internet.

Elements of DDS must be often applied in the parts performing on-line (interactive) data analysis (e.g. OLAP/ROLAP[2]) and generally the management tier of information systems. Elements of data orientation can appear on quite low level. In (Král and Žemlička, 2003b; Král and Žemlička, 2004b) a practical implementation of the interface between Scheduler and an automated machine tool workshop is described. The interface was based on a common database and its presentation tool having features of data analysis. The implementation facilitated the success of several projects of several flexible manufacturing systems.

6   IMPLEMENTATION OF SOFTWARE CONFEDERATIONS

Technically a legacy system AC is integrated into a confederation via adding a gate G to AC (Fig. 3). G connects AC to a middleware. AC is also redesigned to be a permanent process (if not already one). The software confederation has then the structure from Fig. 3.

AC can be implemented using object-oriented philosophy. Sometimes it can happen that a system can (seemingly) be designed as a confederation or as a

---

[2]OLAP = on-line analytical processing, ROLAP = relational OLAP.

monolithic system in which all autonomous components should be completely rewritten and "dissolved" in the system.

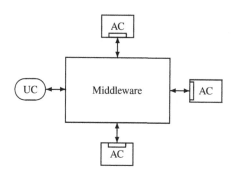

Figure 3: Software confederation with gates

Although the choice between the two alternatives seems to be a quite technical one, it should be included into requirements specification. The requirements specification should be adapted to the fact whether the monolithic or confederated philosophy is to be used as it influences substantially user properties of the system and the set of feasible solutions. If a particular autonomous component AC "belongs" to some department/division (being e.g. its local information system), the department is satisfied with AC, and AC can provide all required information/services to other collaborating autonomous components, then AC can and often should be integrated. Note that it reduces development effort as substantial parts of code are reused. The department people feel that they still (mentally) 'own' AC. It is well known that of such ownership feeling is advantageous and often necessary.

Confederative architecture can make feasible requirement types raised by CEO like the transformation of the enterprise organization structure into a decentralized form, selective outsourcing of some parts of the information system, selling out some divisions/departments, integration of newly purchased firms/divisions, support for supply chain management, and forming various business coordination groups (Král and Žemlička, 2002). Autonomous components can be developed as a "black boxes" using any of the developing strategies mentioned above.

7   BUSINESS PROCESSES IN CONFEDERATIONS; USERS AS SERVICES

The business processes in confederations can be quite complex, they can be a complex networks of activities (variants of workflow). There can be various levels of automation of business processes and their particular steps. It is highly desirable that the processes can be (in principle) supervised by users. Users can:

- define or modify the definition of processes,
- can start processes, supervise/influence/perform their steps, on-line redefine and reschedule process steps,
- change the run of the running (active) processes (change the sequence of the steps, etc.),
- replace some services intended to be provided by software by 'manual activities'.

The last requirement is especially important during the system development as it can serve as the prototyping tool and even substitution of not yet developed (implemented) services. It is a very useful tool for run-time of the system as it can happen that some services will be always provided by human beings or that users will have to simulate or provide services not available due a failure at the given moment. The condition is that user interface components (UC, portals) are able to accept the messages for the missing services, present it to the users and to produce answers defined by users. It is often a quite simple task to implement it (Král et al., 1987) – provided that the interfaces of gates are user-oriented in the above sense.

More complicated business processes should use (should be controlled) by some process defining data. There is a problem where to store business process' states and data. The most promising seems the strategy to include the data into the data of the associated user 'owning' (responsible for) the process. It is also possible to generate a new service S associated with UC. The purpose of S is then to serve as an agent controlling business processes owned by some user.

8   SOFTWARE ENGINEERING ISSUES

The user-oriented interfaces of components enhance the following software engineering properties of the service-oriented systems:

1. User involvement. The governance of business processes by users is easier than in classical systems.

2. Modifiability

- implementation changes in services can be hidden, it simplifies maintainability as well;
- some autonomous components can be purchased, insourced or outsourced.

3. Incremental development as well as iterative development.

4. Prototyping and temporal replacement of the services that are currently not available.

5. Short milestones (autonomous services can be not too large software units).

6. Solution/refactoring of many antipatterns (Brown et al., 1998), see above.

7. New turns, e.g. testing the response time of real-time control systems (Král, 1998).

8. Reduction of development effort due:

   - integration of legacy systems,
   - purchasing autonomous component from vendors,
   - decomposition the system into small units that due to dependency between the system size and the development effort reduces the effort (Effort $\doteq c \cdot \text{Size}^{1+a}$, $a > 0$), see COCOMO II,
   - shorter feedback between developers and users.

The are open issues:

1. It is not clear what services should be good to be provided as a central (infrastructure) ones. Central services can be a bottleneck (access traffic, too strong influence of big vendors, data correctness checking, service modification, etc.).

2. Confederative architecture can make customers less dependent on large vendors. The vendors are not happy with it and try to resist it.

3. As a new paradigm the confederations need the developers to precisely understand the user knowledge and needs. This opposes the strong computer-oriented feeling and interests of software experts. To avoid it they should understand and accept the thinking and philosophy of experimental sciences (e.g. physics, to some degree economy) and mathematical statistics. It is quite difficult to achieve it.

4. Data intensive functions (for management and DDS in general) can benefit from service orientation but there is no good methodology available for it now.

5. In some parts of confederations some seemingly obsolete techniques (COBOL) can be used. The traditional integration (into object-oriented or database applications/systems) of such services need not be a simple matter.

6. There are problems with security and effectiveness. Note, however, that the user-oriented interfaces imply reduction of the number of messages and therefore can enhance system performance and can limit threats due to misuse of RPC.

9   MAIN POINTS OF DESIGN OF SERVICE-ORIENTED SYSTEMS

As there is no common agreement what service orientation and service-oriented architecture are about (Barry and Associates, 2003), it is necessary to decide first whether the architecture of the system will be a virtual peer-to-peer network. We believe that the choice of peer-to-peer is the best one and we shall discuss this case. The components (peers of the network) should be quite large applications behaving like services in human society. The services should be specified via their interfaces and integrated therefore as black boxes.

The services (their interfaces) should mirror the real-world services provided by the organizational units of enterprises or by people. Their interfaces should be (and due to the above conditions can be) user-oriented, i.e. understandable to system users. The system then behaves like the human society being also a network of autonomous services.

Users should be deeply involved in the specification and design of the interfaces.

The development process of SOA system depends on the variants of decomposition and integration. The implementation of interfaces can be different in confederations (known collection of services) and alliances (e-commerce).

There can be problems with the acceptance of the philosophy in the above sense, as service orientation is a new paradigm for many people especially for the strongly object-oriented beings. The acceptance and governing of a new paradigm need many years.

It is preferable for the development, debugging and use of service-oriented system to design services/programs so that they can be substituted by discussion with human bodies via user interface. It is good to support the human involvement as much possible (i.e. automate as little as possible). The development process should be incremental using Pareto 80-20 law as much as possible. It is against the strategy computerize as much as possible promoted by software vendors and accepted by some users.

10 CONCLUSIONS

The service-oriented architecture is a very powerful and in many areas a quite new paradigm. There are, however, several issues to be solved yet:

1. Education of people to be able to use service orientation properly. Service orientation is not any simple and straightforward modification of the object-oriented techniques and object-oriented philosophy.

2. Design patterns as well as new tools of modeling are not available yet.

3. The SOA influences the specification of requirements more substantially than other architectures do.

4. The collaboration of users (*including their top management*) with developers as well as users involvement should be tighter than before.

5. The developers should have a deeper knowledge of the user problem and knowledge domain.

Important issues are the prejudices of software developers like insisting on full computerization, belief that users are too stupid to take part in requirements specifications, etc.

Service orientation is, however, today already an attitude promising to develop software of the quality known from the other branches of industry.

Supported by the Czech Science Foundation, grant No. 201/02/1456.

REFERENCES

Barry and Associates (2003). http://www.service-architecture.com.

Brown, W. J., Malveau, R. C., Hays W. "Skip" McCormick, I., and Mowbray, T. J. (1998). *AntiPatterns: Refactoring Software, Architectures, and Projects in Crisis.* John Wiley & Sons, New York.

Donnay Software Designs (1999). Mature, portable, data-driven systems. http://www.dclip.com/datadr.htm.

Jablonski, S. and Petrov, I. (2003). Web services, workflow and metadata management as the integration means in the electronic collaboration era. Tutorial at the ICEIS'03 conference.

Jacobson, I. and et all (1995). *Object Oriented Software Engineering: A Use Case Driven Approach.* Addison Wesley.

Kopeček, P. (2003). Private communication.

Král, J. (1998). *Informační Systémy, (Information Systems, in Czech).* Science, Veletiny, Czech Republic.

Král, J. and Demner, J. (1979). Towards reliable real time software. In *Proceedings of IFIP Conference Construction of Quality Software*, pages 1–12, North Holland.

Král, J., Černý, J., and Dvořák, P. (1987). Technology of FMS control software development. In Menga, G. and Kempe, V., editors, *Proceedings of the Workshop on Information in Manufacturing Automation*, Dresden.

Král, J. and Žemlička, M. (2002). Autonomous components. In Hamza, M. H., editor, *Applied Informatics*, pages 125–130, Anaheim. ACTA Press.

Král, J. and Žemlička, M. (2003a). Software confederations and alliances. In *CAiSE'03 Forum: Information Systems for a Connected Society*, Maribor, Slovenia. University of Maribor Press.

Král, J. and Žemlička, M. (2003b). Software confederations and manufacturing. In Camp, O., Filipe, J., Hammoudi, S., and Piattini, M., editors, *ICEIS 2003: Proceedings of the Fifth International Conference on Enterprise Information Systems*, volume 3, pages 650–653, Setúbal. EST Setúbal.

Král, J. and Žemlička, M. (2004a). Architecture, specification, and design of service-oriented systems. In reviewing process.

Král, J. and Žemlička, M. (2004b). Service orientation and the quality indicators for software services. Accepted for EMCSR'04 in Vienna.

Král, J. and Žemlička, M. (2004c). Systemic of human involvement in information systems. Technical Report 2, Charles Univerity, Faculty of Mathematics and Physics, Department of Software Engineering, Prague, Czech Republic.

Object Management Group (2001). Unified modeling language. http://www.omg.org/technology/documents/formal/uml.htm.

Rumbaugh, J., Blaha, M., Premerlani, W., Eddy, F., and Lorensen, W. (1991). *Object-Oriented Modeling and Design.* Prentice-Hall, Englewood Cliffs, New Jersey 07632.

Skula, J. (2001). Private communication.

Sneed, H. (2002). Position statement at panel discussion at CSMR 2002, Budapest, Hungary.

Tůma, P. (2003). Modern software architectures: Novel solutions or old hats? In Popelínský, L., editor, *DATAKON 2003*, pages 151–162, Brno, Czech Republic. Masaryk University.

W3 Consortium (1999). Resource description framework. A proposal of W3C Consortium. http://www.w3.org/RDF/.

W3 Consortium (2002). Web services activity. http://www.w3.org/2002/ws/ – as visited on 31st October 2003.

Yourdon, E. (1988). *Modern Structured Analysis.* Prentice-Hall, 2nd edition.

MEMORY MANAGEMENT FOR LARGE SCALE DATA STREAM RECORDERS *

Kun Fu and Roger Zimmermann
Integrated Media System Center
University of Southern California
Los Angeles, California 90089
Email: [kunfu,rzimmerm]@usc.edu

Keywords: Memory management, real time, large-scale, continuous media, data streams, recording.

Abstract: Presently, digital continuous media (CM) are well established as an integral part of many applications. In recent years, a considerable amount of research has focused on the efficient retrieval of such media. Scant attention has been paid to servers that can record such streams in real time. However, more and more devices produce direct digital output streams. Hence, the need arises to capture and store these streams with an efficient data stream recorder that can handle both recording and playback of many streams simultaneously and provide a central repository for all data.
In this report we investigate memory management in the context of large scale data stream recorders. We are especially interested in finding the minimal buffer space needed that still provides adequate resources with varying workloads. We show that computing the minimal memory is an $\mathcal{NP}$-complete problem and will require further study to discover efficient heuristics.

1 INTRODUCTION

Digital continuous media (CM) are an integral part of many new applications. Two of the main characteristics of such media are that (1) they require real time storage and retrieval, and (2) they require high bandwidths and space. Over the last decade, a considerable amount of research has focused on the efficient retrieval of such media for many concurrent users (Shahabi et al., 2002). Algorithms to optimize such fundamental issues as data placement, disk scheduling, admission control, transmission smoothing, etc., have been reported in the literature.

Almost without exception these prior research efforts assumed that the CM streams were readily available as files and could be loaded onto the servers offline without the real time constraints that the complementary stream retrieval required. This is certainly a reasonable assumption for many applications where the multimedia streams are produced offline (e.g., movies, commercials, educational lectures, etc.). However, the current technological trends are such that more and more sensor devices (e.g., cam-

eras) can directly produce digital data streams. Furthermore, many of these new devices are network-capable either via wired (SDI, Firewire) or wireless (Bluetooth, IEEE 802.11x) connections. Hence, the need arises to capture and store these streams with an efficient data stream recorder that can handle both recording and playback of many streams simultaneously and provide a central data repository.

The applications for such a recorder start at the low end with small, personal systems. For example, the "digital hub" in the living room envisioned by several companies will in the future go beyond recording and playing back a single stream as is currently done by TiVo and ReplayTV units (Wallich, 2002). Multiple camcorders, receivers, televisions, and audio amplifiers will all connect to the digital hub to either store or retrieve data streams. An example for this convergence is the next generation of the DVD specification that also calls for network access of DVD players (Smith, 2003). At the higher end, movie production will move to digital cameras and storage devices. For example, George Lucas' "Star Wars: Episode II Attack of the Clones" was shot entirely with high-definition digital cameras (Huffstutter and Healey, 2002). Additionally, there are many sensor networks that produce continuous streams of

*This research has been funded in part by NSF grants EEC-9529152 (IMSC ERC) and IIS-0082826, and an unrestricted cash gift from the Lord Foundation.

I. Seruca et al. (eds.), Enterprise Information Systems VI, 97–106.
© *2006 Springer. Printed in the Netherlands.*

data. For example, NASA continuously receives data from space probes. Earthquake and weather sensors produce data streams as do web sites and telephone systems.

In this paper we investigate issues related to memory management that need to be addressed for large scale data stream recorders (Zimmermann et al., 2003). After introducing some of the related work in Section 2 we present a memory management model in Section 3. We formalize the model and compute its complexity in Section 4. We prove that because of a combination of a large number of system parameters and user service requirements the problem is exponentially hard. Conclusions and future work are contained in Section 5.

2 RELATED WORK

Managing the available main memory efficiently is a crucial aspect of any multimedia streaming system. A number of studies have investigated buffer and cache management. These techniques can be classified into three groups: (1) *server buffer management* (Makaroff and Ng, 1995; Shi and Ghandeharizadeh, 1997; Tsai and Lee, 1998; Tsai and Lee, 1999; Lee et al., 2001), (2) *network/proxy cache management* (Sen et al., 1999; Ramesh et al., 2001; Chae et al., 2002; Cui and Nahrstedt, 2003) and (3) *client buffer management* (Shahabi and Alshayeji, 2000; Waldvogel et al., 2003). Figure 1 illustrates where memory resources are located in a distributed environment.

In this report we aim to optimize the usage of server buffers in a large scale data stream recording system. This focus falls naturally into the first category classified above. To the best of our knowledge, no prior work has investigated this issue in the context of the design of a large scale, unified architecture, which considers both retrieving and recording streams simultaneously.

3 MEMORY MANAGEMENT OVERVIEW

A streaming media system requires main memory to temporarily hold data items while they are transferred between the network and the permanent disk storage. For efficiency reasons, network *packets* are generally much smaller than disk *blocks*. The assembly of incoming packets into data blocks and conversely the partitioning of blocks into outgoing packets requires main memory buffers. A widely used solution in servers is double buffering. For example, one buffer

Table 1: Parameters for a current high performance commercial disk drive.

Model	ST336752LC
Series	Cheetah X15
Manufacturer	Seagate Technology, LLC
Capacity C	37 GB
Transfer rate R_D	See Figure 2
Spindle speed	15,000 rpm
Avg. rotational latency	2 msec
Worst case seek time	$\approx$ 7 msec
Number of Zones Z	9

is filled with a data block that is coming from a disk drive while the content of the second buffer is emptied (i.e., streamed out) over the network. Once the buffers are full/empty, their roles are reversed.

With a stream recorder, double buffering is still the minimum that is required. With additional buffers available, incoming data can be held in memory longer and the deadline by which a data block must be written to disk can be extended. This can reduce disk contention and hence the probability of missed deadlines (Aref et al., 1997). However, in our investigation we are foremost interested in the minimal amount of memory that is necessary for a given workload and service level. Hence, we assume a double buffering scheme as the basis for our analysis. In a large scale stream recorder the number of streams to be retrieved versus the number to be recorded may vary significantly over time. Furthermore, the write performance of a disk is usually significantly less than its read bandwidth (see Figure 2b). Hence, these factors need to be considered and incorporated into the memory model.

When designing an efficient memory buffer management module for a data stream recorder, one can classify the interesting problems into two categories: (1) *resource configuration* and (2) *performance optimization*.

In the resource configuration category, a representative class of problems are: *What is the minimum memory or buffer size that is needed to satisfy certain playback and recording service requirements?* These requirements depend on the higher level QoS requirements imposed by the end user or application environment.

In the performance optimization category, a representative class of problems are: *Given certain amount of memory or buffer, how to maximize our system performance in terms of certain performance metrics?* Two typical performance metrics are as follows:

i Maximize the total number of supportable streams.

ii Maximize the disk I/O parallelism, i.e., minimize the total number of parallel disk I/Os.

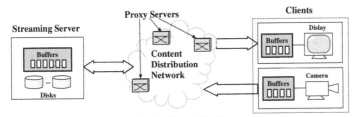

Figure 1: Buffer distribution in a traditional streaming system

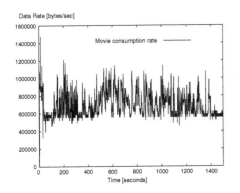

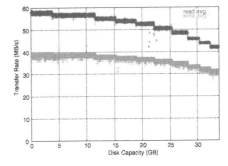

Figure 2a: The consumption rate of a movie encoded with a VBR MPEG-2 algorithm ("Twister")

Figure 2b: Maximum read and write rate in different areas (also called *zones*) of the disk. The transfer rate varies in different zones.i The write bandwidth is up to 30% less than the read bandwidth.

Figure 2: Variable bit rate (VBR) movie characteristics and Disk characteristics of a high performance disk drive (Seagate Cheetah X15, see Table 1)

We focus on the resource configuration problem in this report, since it is a prerequisite to optimizing performance.

4   MINIMIZING THE SERVER BUFFER SIZE

Informally, we are investigating the following question: *What is the minimum memory buffer size S_{min}^{buf} that is needed to satisfy a set of given streaming and recording service requirements?*

In other words, the minimum buffer size must satisfy the *maximum* buffer resource requirement under the given service requirements. We term this problem the *Minimum Server Buffer* or MSB. We illustrate our discussion with the example design of a large scale recording system called HYDRA, a High-

performance Data Recording Architecture (Zimmermann et al., 2003). Figure 3 shows the overall architecture of HYDRA. The design is based on random data placement and deadline driven disk scheduling techniques to provide high performance. As a result, statistical rather than deterministic service guarantees are provided.

The MSB problem is challenging because the media server design is expected to:

i support multiple simultaneous streams with different bandwidths and variable bit rates (VBR) (Figure 2a illustrates the variability of a sample MPEG-2 movie). Note that different recording devices might also generate streams with variable bandwidth requirements.

ii support concurrent reading and writing of streams. The issue that poses a serious challenge is that disk drives generally provide considerably less write than read bandwidth (see Figure 2b).

iii support multi-zoned disks. Figure 2b illustrates how the disk transfer rates of current generation

Table 2: List of terms used repeatedly in this study and their respective definitions

Term	Definition	Units
B_{disk}	Block size on disk	MB
T_{svr}	Server observation time interval	second
ξ	The number of disks in the system	
n	The number of concurrent streams	
p_{iodisk}	Probability of missed deadline by reading or writing	
$\overline{R_{Dr}}$	Average disk read bandwidth during T_{svr} (no bandwidth allocation for writing)	MB/s
p_{req}	The threshold of probability of missed deadline, it is the worse situation that client can endure.	
$\overline{R_{Dw}}$	Average disk write bandwidth during T_{svr} (no bandwidth allocation for reading)	MB/s
$t_{seek}(j)$	Seek time for disk access j, where j is an index for each disk access during a T_{svr}	ms
$R_{Dr}(j)$	Disk read bandwidth for disk access j (no bandwidth allocation for writing)	MB/s
$\mu_{t_{seek}}(j)$	Mean value of random variable $t_{seek}(j)$, where j is an index for each disk access during a T_{svr}	ms
$\sigma_{t_{seek}}(j)$	Standard deviation of random variable $t_{seek}(j)$	ms
β	Relationship factor between R_{Dr} and R_{Dw}	
$\overline{t_{seek}}$	The average disk seek time during T_{svr}	ms
$\mu_{t_{seek}}$	Mean value of random variable $\overline{t_{seek}}$	ms
$\sigma_{t_{seek}}$	Standard deviation of random variable $\overline{t_{seek}}$	ms
α	Mixed-load factor, the percentage of reading load in the system	
m_1	The number of movies existed in HYDRA	
D_i^{rs}	The amount of data that movie i is consumed during T_{svr}	MB
μ_i^{rs}	Mean value of random variable D_i^{rs}	MB
σ_i^{rs}	Standard deviation of random D_i^{rs}	MB
n_i^{rs}	The number of retrieving streams for movie i	
m_2	The number of different recording devices	
D_i^{ws}	The amount of data that is generated by recording device i during T_{svr}	
μ_i^{ws}	Mean value of random variable D_i^{ws}	MB
σ_i^{ws}	Standard deviation of random D_i^{ws}	MB
n_i^{ws}	The number of recording streams by recording device i	
N_{max}	The maximum number of streams supported in the system	
S_{min}^{buf}	The minimum buffer size needed in the system	MB

drives is platter location dependent. The outermost zone provides up to 30% more bandwidth than the innermost one.

iv support flexible *service requirements* (see Section 4.1 for details), which should be configurable by Video-on-Demand (VOD) service providers based on their application and customer requirements.

As discussed in Section 3, a double buffering scheme is employed in HYDRA. Therefore, two buffers are necessary for each stream serviced by the system. Before formally defining the MSB problem, we outline our framework for service requirements in the next section. Table 4 lists all the parameters and their definitions used in this paper.

4.1 Service Requirements

Why do we need to consider *service requirements* in our system? We illustrate and answer this question with an example.

Assume that a VOD system is deployed in a five-star hotel, which has 10 superior deluxe rooms, 20 deluxe rooms and 50 regular rooms. There are 30 movies stored in the system, among which five are new releases that started to be shown in theaters during the last week. Now consider the following scenario. The VOD system operator wants to configure the system so that (1) the customers who stay in superior deluxe rooms should be able to view any one of the 30 movies whenever they want, (2) those customers that stay in deluxe rooms should be able to watch any of the five new movies released recently at anytime, and finally (3) the customers in the regular rooms can watch movies whenever system resources permit.

The rules and requirements described above are formally a set of service constraints that the VOD operator would like to enforce in the system. We term these type of service constraints *service requirements*. Such service requirements can be enforced in the VOD system via an admission control mechanism. Most importantly, these service requirements will affect the server buffer requirement. Next, we will describe how to formalize the memory configuration problem and find the minimal buffer size in a streaming media system.

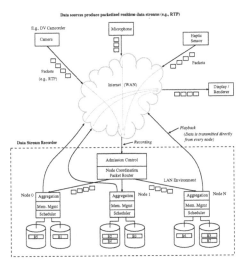

Figure 3: HYDRA: Data Stream Recorder Architecture. Multiple source and rendering devices are interconnected via an IP infrastructure. The recorder functions as a data repository that receives and plays back many streams concurrently

4.2 MSB Problem Formulation

4.2.1 Stream Characteristics and Load Modeling

Given a specific time instant, there are m_1 movies loaded in the HYDRA system. Thus, these m_1 movies are available for playback services. The HYDRA system activity is observed periodically, during a time interval T_{svr}. Each movie follows an inherent bandwidth consumption schedule due to its compression and encoding format, as well as its specific content characteristics. Let D_i^{rs} denote the amount of data that is consuming during T_{svr}. Furthermore, let μ_i^{rs} and σ_i^{rs} denote the mean and standard deviation of D_i^{rs}, and let n_i^{rs} represent the number of retrieval streams for movie i.

We assume that there exist m_2 different recording devices which are connected to the HYDRA system. These recording devices could be DV camcorders, microphones or haptic sensors as shown in Figure 3. Therefore, in terms of bandwidth characteristics, m_2 types of recording streams must be supported by the recording services in the HYDRA system. Analogous with the retrieval services, D_i^{ws} denotes the amount of data that is generated by recording device i during time interval T_{svr}. Let μ_i^{ws} and σ_i^{ws} denote the mean

and standard deviation of D_i^{ws} and let n_i^{ws} represent the number of recording streams generated by recording device i. Consequently, we can compute the total number of concurrent streams n as

$$n = \sum_{i=1}^{m_1} n_i^{rs} + \sum_{i=1}^{m_2} n_i^{ws} \qquad (1)$$

Thus, the problem that needs to be solved translates to finding the combination of $< n_1^{rs}...n_{m_1}^{rs}, n_1^{ws}...n_{m_2}^{ws} >$, which maximizes n. Hence, N_{max} can be computed as

$$N_{max} = max(n) = max(\sum_{i=1}^{m_1} n_i^{rs} + \sum_{i=1}^{m_2} n_i^{ws}) \quad (2)$$

under some *service requirements* described below. Note that if the double buffering technique is employed, and after computing N_{max}, we can easily obtain the minimum buffer size S_{min}^{buf} as

$$S_{min}^{buf} = 2B_{disk}N_{max} \qquad (3)$$

where B_{disk} is the data block size on the disks. Note that in the above computation we are considering the worst case scenario where no two data streams are sharing any buffers in memory.

4.2.2 Service Requirements Modeling

We start by assuming the example described in Section 4.1 and following the notation in the previous section. Thus, let $n_1^{rs}, ..., n_{30}^{rs}$ denote the number of retrieval streams corresponding to the 30 movies in the system. Furthermore, without loss of generality, we can choose $n_1^{rs}, ..., n_5^{rs}$ as the five newly released movies.

To enforce the *service requirements*, the operator must define the following constraints for each of the corresponding service requirements:

C1: $n_1^{rs}, ..., n_{30}^{rs} \geq 10$.
C2: $n_1^{rs}, ..., n_{30}^{rs} \geq 20$.

Note that we do not define the constraint for the third service requirement because it can be automatically supported by the statistical admission model defined in the next section.

The above constraints are equivalent to the following linear constraints:

C1: $n_1^{rs}, ..., n_5^{rs} \geq 30$.
C2: $n_6^{rs}, ..., n_{30}^{rs} \geq 10$.

These linear constraints can be generalized into the following linear equations:

$$\begin{array}{l} \sum_{j=1}^{m_1} a_{ij}^{rs} n_j^{rs} + \sum_{k=1}^{m_2} a_{ik}^{ws} n_k^{ws} \leq b_i \\ n_j^{rs} \geq 0 \\ n_k^{ws} \geq 0 \\ n_j^{rs} \text{ and } n_k^{ws} \text{ are integers} \end{array} \qquad (4)$$

where $i \in [0, w]$, w is the total number of linear constraints, $j \in [1, m_1]$, $k \in [1, m_2]$, and a_{ij}^{rs}, a_{ik}^{ws}, b_i are linear constraint parameters.

4.2.3 Statistical Service Guarantee

To ensure high resource utilization in HYDRA, we provide statistical service guarantees to end users through a comprehensive three random variable (3RV) admission control model. The parameters incorporated into the random variables are the variable bit rate characteristic of different retrieval and recording streams, a realistic disk model that considers the variable transfer rates of multi-zoned disks, variable seek and rotational latencies, and unequal reading and recording data rate limits.

Recall that system activity is observed periodically with a time interval T_{svr}. Formally, our 3RV model is characterized by the following three random variables: (1) $\sum_{i=1}^{m_1} n_i^{rs} D_i^{rs} + \sum_{i=1}^{m_2} n_i^{ws} D_i^{ws}$, denoting the amount of data to be retrieved or recorded during T_{svr} in the system, (2) $\overline{t_{seek}}$, denoting the average disk seek time during each observation time interval T_{svr}, and (3) $\overline{R_{Dr}}$ denoting the average disk read bandwidth during T_{svr}.

We assume that there are ξ disks present in the system and that p_{iodisk} denotes the probability of a missed deadline when reading or writing, computed with our 3RV model. Furthermore, the statistical service requirements are characterized by p_{req}: the threshold of the highest probability of a missed deadline that a client is willing to accept (for details see (Zimmermann and Fu, 2003)).

Given the above introduced three random variables — abbreviated as X, Y and Z — the probability of missed deadlines p_{iodisk} can then be evaluated as follows

$$
\begin{aligned}
p_{iodisk} &= P\left[(X, Y, Z) \in \Re\right] \\
&= \iiint_{\Re} f_X(x) f_Y(y) f_Z(z) dx dy dz \\
&\leq p_{req}
\end{aligned}
\tag{5}
$$

where $\Re$ is computed as

$$
\begin{aligned}
&\Re \\
&= \left\{ (X, Y, Z) \mid \frac{X}{\xi} > \left(\frac{(\alpha Z + (1-\alpha)\beta Z) \times T_{svr}}{1 + \frac{Y \times (\alpha Z + (1-\alpha)\beta Z)}{B_{disk}}} \right) \right\}
\end{aligned}
\tag{6}
$$

In Equation 6, B_{disk} denotes the data block size on disk, α is the mixload factor, which is the percentage of reading load in the system and is computed by Equation 10, and β is the relationship factor between the read and write data bandwidth. The necessary probability density functions $f_X(x)$, $f_Y(y)$, and

$f_Z(z)$ can be computed as

$$
\begin{aligned}
&f_X(x) \\
&= \frac{e^{-\frac{\left[x - (\sum_{i=1}^{m_1} n_i^{rs}\mu_i^{rs} + \sum_{i=1}^{m_2} n_i^{ws}\mu_i^{ws})\right]^2}{2 \times (\sum_{i=1}^{m_1} n_i^{rs}(\sigma_i^{rs})^2 + \sum_{i=1}^{m_2} n_i^{ws}(\sigma_i^{ws})^2)}}}{\sqrt{2\pi(\sum_{i=1}^{m_1} n_i^{rs}(\sigma_i^{rs})^2 + \sum_{i=1}^{m_2} n_i^{ws}(\sigma_i^{ws})^2)}}
\end{aligned}
\tag{7}
$$

while $f_Y(y)$ similarly evaluates to

$$
\begin{aligned}
&f_Y(y) \\
&\approx \frac{e^{-\frac{(\sum_{i=1}^{m_1} n_i^{rs}\mu_i^{rs} + \sum_{i=1}^{m_2} n_i^{ws}\mu_i^{ws})}{2B_{disk}}\left[\frac{y - \mu_{t_{seek}}(j)}{\sigma_{t_{seek}}(j)}\right]^2}}{\sqrt{2\pi\sigma_{t_{seek}}^2(j)}}
\end{aligned}
\tag{8}
$$

with $\mu_{t_{seek}}(j)$ and $\sigma_{t_{seek}}$ being the mean value and the standard deviation of the random variable $t_{seek}(j)$, which is the seek time[2] for disk access j, where j is an index for each disk access during T_{svr}. Finally, $f_Z(z)$ can be computed as

$$
\begin{aligned}
&f_Z(z) \\
&\approx \frac{e^{-\frac{(\sum_{i=1}^{m_1} n_i^{rs}\mu_i^{rs} + \sum_{i=1}^{m_2} n_i^{ws}\mu_i^{ws})}{2B_{disk}}\left[\frac{z - \mu_{R_{Dr}}(j)}{\sigma_{R_{Dr}}(j)}\right]^2}}{\sqrt{2\pi\sigma_{R_{Dr}}^2(j)}}
\end{aligned}
\tag{9}
$$

where $\mu_{R_{Dr}}(j)$ and $\sigma_{R_{Dr}}(j)$ denote the mean value and standard deviation for random variable $R_{Dr}(j)$. This parameter represents the disk read bandwidth limit for disk access j, where j is an index for each disk access during a T_{svr}, and α can be computed as

$$
\alpha \approx \frac{\sum_{i=1}^{m_1} n_i^{rs}\mu_i^{rs}}{\sum_{i=1}^{m_1} n_i^{rs}\mu_i^{rs} + \frac{\sum_{i=1}^{m_2} n_i^{ws}\mu_i^{ws}}{\beta}}
\tag{10}
$$

We have now formalized the MSB problem. Our next challenge is to find an efficient solution. However, after some careful study we found that there are two properties — integer constraints and linear equation constraints — that make it hard to solve. In fact, MSB is a $\mathcal{NP}$-complete problem. We will prove it formally in the next section.

4.3 NP-Completeness

To show that MSB is $\mathcal{NP}$-complete, we first need to prove that $MSB \in \mathcal{NP}$.

Lemma 4.1: $MSB \in \mathcal{NP}$

Proof: We prove this lemma by providing a polynomial-time algorithm, which can verify MSB with a given solution $\{n_1^{rs} \ldots n_{m_1}^{rs}, n_1^{ws} \ldots n_{m_2}^{ws}\}$.

We have constructed an algorithm called *Check-Optimal*, shown in Figure 4. Given a set $\{n_1^{rs} \ldots n_{m_1}^{rs}, n_1^{ws} \ldots n_{m_2}^{ws}\}$, the algorithm *CheckOptimal* can verify the MSB in polynomial-time for the following reasons:

---

[2] $t_{seek}(j)$ includes rotational latency as well.

Procedure CheckOptimal $(n_1^{rs} \ldots n_{m_1}^{rs}, n_1^{ws} \ldots n_{m_2}^{ws})$
/* Return TRUE if the given solution satisfies */
/* all the constraints and maximize n, */
/* otherwise, return FALSE. */
(i) $S=\{n_1^{rs} \ldots n_{m_1}^{rs}, n_1^{ws} \ldots n_{m_2}^{ws}\}$,
    If CheckConstraint(S) == TRUE
    Then continue;
    Else return FALSE;
(ii) For $(i = 1; i \leq m_1; i++)$
    {
        $S' = S; S'.n_i^{rs} = S'.n_i^{rs} + 1;$
        If CheckConstraint(S') == TRUE
        Then return FALSE;
        Else continue;
    }
(iii) For $(i = 1; i \leq m_2; i++)$
    {
        $S' = S; S'.n_i^{ws} = S'.n_i^{ws} + 1;$
        If CheckConstraint(S') == TRUE
        Then return FALSE;
        Else continue;
    }
(iv).return TRUE;
end CheckOptimal;

Procedure CheckConstraint $(n_1^{rs} \ldots n_{m_1}^{rs}, n_1^{ws} \ldots n_{m_2}^{ws})$
/* Return TRUE if the given solution satisfies */
/* all the constraints, otherwise return FALSE. */
(i) $S=\{n_1^{rs} \ldots n_{m_1}^{rs}, n_1^{ws} \ldots n_{m_2}^{ws}\}$,
    If S satisfies all the linear constraints defined
    in Equation 4.
    Then continue;
    Else return FALSE;
(ii) If S satisfies the statistical service guarantee
    defined in Equation 5.
    Then return TRUE;
    Else return FALSE;
end CheckConstraint;

Figure 4: An algorithm to check if a given solution $\{n_1^{rs} \ldots n_{m_1}^{rs}, n_1^{ws} \ldots n_{m_2}^{ws}\}$ satisfies all the constraints specified in Equation 4 and 5 and maximizes n as well

1 Procedure *CheckConstraint* runs in polynomial time because both step (i) and step (ii) run in polynomial time. Note that the complexity analysis of step (ii) is described in details elsewhere (Zimmermann and Fu, 2003).

2 Based on the above reasoning, we conclude that procedure *CheckOptimal* runs in polynomial time because each of its four component steps runs in polynomial time.

Therefore, $MSB \in \mathcal{NP}$. ∎

Next, we show that MSB is $\mathcal{NP}$-hard. To accomplish this we first define a restricted version of MSB, termed RMSB.

Definition 4.2 : The *Restricted Minimum Server Buffer Problem* (RMSB) is identical to MSB except

that $p_{req} = 1$. ∎

Subsequently, RMSB can be shown to be $\mathcal{NP}$-hard by reduction from *Integer Linear Programming* (ILP) (Papadimitriou and Steiglitz, 1982).

Definition 4.3 : The *Integer Linear Programming* (**ILP**) problem:
    Maximize $\sum_{j=1}^{n} C_j X_j$
    subject to
        $\sum_{i=1}^{n} a_{ij} X_j \leq b_i$ for $i = 1, 2, \ldots, m$, and
        $X_j \geq 0$ and X_j is integer for $j = 1, 2, \ldots, n$.
∎

Theorem 4.4: *RMSB is $\mathcal{NP}$-hard.*

Proof: We use a reduction from ILP. Recall that in MSB, Equation 5 computes the probability of a missed deadline during disk reading or writing p_{iodisk}, and p_{iodisk} is required to be less than or equal to p_{req}. Recall that in RMSB, $p_{req} = 1$. Therefore, it is obvious that $p_{iodisk} \leq (p_{req} = 1)$ is always true no matter how the combination of $\{n_1^{rs} \ldots n_{m_1}^{rs}, n_1^{ws} \ldots n_{m_2}^{ws}\}$ is selected. Therefore, in RMSB, the constraint of statistical service guarantee could be removed, which then transforms RMSB into an ILP problem. ∎

Theorem 4.5: *MSB is $\mathcal{NP}$-hard.*

Proof: By *restriction* (Garey and Johnson, 1979), we limit MSB to RMSB by assuming $p_{req} = 1$. As a result – based on Theorem 4.4 – MSB is $\mathcal{NP}$-hard. ∎

Theorem 4.6: *MSB is $\mathcal{NP}$-complete.*

Proof: It follows from Lemma 4.1 and Theorem 4.5 that MSB is $\mathcal{NP}$-complete. ∎

4.4   Algorithm to Solve MSB

Figure 5 illustrates the process of solving the MSB problem. Four major parameter components are utilized in the process: (1) *Movie Parameters* (see Section 4.2.1), (2) *Recording Devices* (see Section 4.2.1), (3) *Service Requirements* (see Section 4.2.2), and (4) *Disk Parameters* (for details see (Zimmermann and Fu, 2003)). Additionally, there are four major computation components involved in the process: (1) *Load Space Navigation*, (2) *Linear Constraints Checking*, (3) *Statistical Admission Control*, and (4) *Minimum Buffer Size Computation*.

The *Load Space Navigator* checks through each of the possible combinations $\{n_1^{rs} \ldots n_{m_1}^{rs}, n_1^{ws} \ldots n_{m_2}^{ws}\}$ in the search space. It also computes the temporary maximum stream number N_{max} when it receives the results from the admission control module. Each of the possible solutions $\{n_1^{rs} \ldots n_{m_1}^{rs}, n_1^{ws} \ldots n_{m_2}^{ws}\}$ is first checked

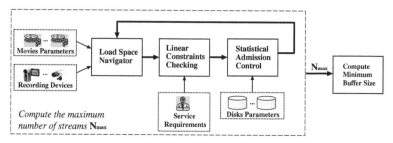

Figure 5: Process to solve the MSB problem

by the *Linear Constraints Checking* module, which enforces the service requirements formulated in Section 4.2.2. The solutions that satisfy the service requirements will be further verified by the *Statistical Admission Control* module described in Section 4.2.3, which provides the statistical service guarantees for the recording system. After exhausting the search space, the load space navigator forwards the highest N_{max} to the *Minimum Buffer Size Computation* module, which computes the minimal buffer size S_{min}^{buf}.

We conclude by providing an algorithm that solves the MSB problem in exponential time shown in Figure 6, based on the process illustrated in Figure 5.

5   CONCLUSIONS AND FUTURE RESEARCH DIRECTIONS

We have presented a novel buffer minimization problem (*MSB*) motivated by the design of our large scale data stream recording system HYDRA. We formally proved that MSB is $\mathcal{NP}$-complete, and we also provided an initial exponential-time algorithm to solve the problem. As part of our future work, we will focus on finding an approximation algorithm which solves the MSB problem in polynomial-time. Furthermore, we plan to evaluate the memory management module in the context of the other system components that manage data placement, disk scheduling, block prefetching and replacement policy, and QoS requirements. Finally, we plan to implement and evaluate the memory management module in our HYDRA prototype system.

REFERENCES

Aref, W., Kamel, I., Niranjan, T. N., and Ghandeharizadeh, S. (1997).   Disk Scheduling for Displaying and Recording Video in Non-Linear News Editing Systems.   In *Proceedings of the Multimedia Computing and Networking Conference*, pages 228–239, San Jose, California.   SPIE Proceedings Series, Volume 3020.

Chae, Y., Guo, K., Buddhikot, M. M., Suri, S., and Zegura, E. W. (2002). Silo, rainbow, and caching token: Schemes for scalable, fault tolerant stream caching. *Special Issue of IEEE Journal of Selected Area in Communications on Internet Proxy Services*.

Cui, Y. and Nahrstedt, K. (2003).   Proxy-based asynchronous multicast for efficient on-demand media distribution.   In *The SPIE Conference on Multimedia Computing and Networking 2003 (MMCN 2003), Santa Clara, California*, pages 162–176.

Garey, M. R. and Johnson, D. S. (1979). *Computers and Intractability: A Guide to Theory of NP-Completeness*. W.H.Freeman and Company, New York.

Huffstutter, P. J. and Healey, J. (2002). Filming Without the Film. *Los Angeles Times*, page A.1.

Lee, S.-H., Whang, K.-Y., Moon, Y.-S., and Song, I.-Y. (2001).   Dynamic Buffer Allocation in Video-On-Demand Systems. In *Proceedings of the international conference on Management of data (ACM SIGMOD'2001), Santa Barbara, California, United States*, pages 343–354.

Makaroff, D. J. and Ng, R. T. (1995).   Schemes for Implementing Buffer Sharing in Continuous-Media Systems. *Information Systems, Vol. 20, No. 6.*, pages 445–464.

Papadimitriou, C. H. and Steiglitz, K. (1982). *Combinatorial Optimization: Algorithms and Complexity*. Prentice Hall, Inc., Englewood Cliffs, New Jersey 07632.

Ramesh, S., Rhee, I., and Guo, K. (2001). Multicast with cache (mcache): An adaptive zero delay video-on-demand service. In *IEEE INFOCOM '01*, pages 85–94.

Sen, S., Rexford, J., and Towsley, D. F. (1999). Proxy prefix caching for multimedia streams. In *IEEE INFOCOM '99*, pages 1310–1319.

Shahabi, C. and Alshayeji, M. (2000). Super-streaming: A new object delivery paradigm for continuous media servers. *Journal of Multimedia Tools and Applications*, 11(1).

Shahabi, C., Zimmermann, R., Fu, K., and Yao, S.-Y. D. (2002). Yima: A Second Generation Continuous Media Server. *IEEE Computer*, 35(6):56–64.

Shi, W. and Ghandeharizadeh, S. (1997). Buffer Sharing in Video-On-Demand Servers. *SIGMETRICS Performance Evaluation Review*, 25(2):13–20.

Smith, T. (2003). Next DVD spec. to offer Net access not more capacity. *The Register*.

Tsai, W.-J. and Lee, S.-Y. (1998). Dynamic Buffer Management for Near Video-On-Demand Systems. *Multimedia Tools and Applications, Volume 6, Issue 1*, pages 61–83.

Tsai, W.-J. and Lee, S.-Y. (1999). Buffer-Sharing Techniques in Service-Guaranteed Video Servers. *Multimedia Tools and Applications, Volume 9, Issue 2*, pages 121–145.

Waldvogel, M., Deng, W., and Janakiraman, R. (2003). Efficient buffer management for scalable media-on-demand. In *The SPIE Conference on Multimedia Computing and Networking 2003 (MMCN 2003), Santa Clara, California*.

Wallich, P. (2002). Digital Hubbub. *IEEE Spectrum*, 39(7):26–29.

Zimmermann, R. and Fu, K. (2003). Comprehensive Statistical Admission Control for Streaming Media Servers. In *Proceedings of the 11th ACM International Multimedia Conference (ACM Multimedia 2003)*, Berkeley, California.

Zimmermann, R., Fu, K., and Ku, W.-S. (2003). Design of a large scale data stream recorder. In *The 5th International Conference on Enterprise Information Systems (ICEIS 2003)*, Angers - France.

Procedure FindMSB

/* Return the minimum buffer size */

(i) N_{max} = FindNmax; /* Find the maximum number of supportable streams */

(ii) Compute S_{min}^{buf} using Equation 3.

(iii) return S_{min}^{buf};

end FindMSB;

Procedure FindNmax

/* Return the maximum number of supportable streams */

(i) Considering only statistical service guarantee p_{req}, let N_i^{rs} denote the maximum of supportable retrieving streams of movie i without any other system load. Find the N_i^{rs}, where $i \in [1, m_1]$.

(ii) Considering only statistical service guarantee p_{req}, let N_i^{ws} denote the maximum of supportable recording streams of generated by recording device i without any other system load. Find the N_i^{ws}, where $i \in [1, m_2]$.

(iii) $N_{curmax} = 0$; $S_{curmax} = \{0 \ldots 0, 0 \ldots 0\}$

(iv) For $(X_1^{rs} = 1; X_1^{rs} \le N_1^{rs}; X_1^{rs} + +)$

$\ldots\ldots$

    For $(X_{m_1}^{rs} = 1; X_{m_1}^{rs} \le N_{m_1}^{rs}; X_{m_1}^{rs} + +)$

    For $(X_1^{ws} = 1; X_1^{ws} \le N_1^{ws}; X_1^{ws} + +)$

    $\ldots\ldots$

    For $(X_{m_2}^{ws} = 1; X_{m_2}^{ws} \le N_{m_2}^{ws}; X_{m_2}^{ws} + +)$

    {

        $S' = \{X_1^{rs} \ldots X_{m_1}^{rs}, X_1^{ws} \ldots X_{m_2}^{ws}\}$;

        If CheckConstraint(S') == TRUE /* CheckConstraint is defined in Figure 4 */

        Then

        {

           If $\sum_{i=1}^{m_1} X_i^{rs} + \sum_{i=1}^{m_2} X_i^{ws} > N_{curmax}$

           Then

               $N_{curmax} = \sum_{i=1}^{m_1} X_i^{rs} + \sum_{i=1}^{m_2} X_i^{ws}$; $S_{curmax} = \{X_1^{rs} \ldots X_{m_1}^{rs}, X_1^{ws} \ldots X_{m_2}^{ws}\}$

        }

    }

(v) return N_{curmax};

end FindNmax;

Figure 6: Algorithm to solve MSB problem

PART 2

Artificial Intelligence and Decision Support Systems

COMPREHENSIBLE CREDIT-SCORING KNOWLEDGE VISUALIZATION USING DECISION TABLES AND DIAGRAMS

Christophe Mues, Johan Huysmans, Jan Vanthienen
K.U.Leuven
Naamsestraat 69, B-3000 Leuven, Belgium
Email: {Christophe.Mues; Johan.Huysmans; Jan.Vanthienen}@econ.kuleuven.ac.be

Bart Baesens
University of Southampton
School of Management, SO17 1BJ Southampton, UK
Email: B.M.M.Baesens@soton.ac.uk

Keywords: Credit scoring, neural network rule extraction, decision tables, decision diagrams.

Abstract: One of the key decision activities in financial institutions is to assess the credit-worthiness of an applicant for a loan, and thereupon decide whether or not to grant the loan. Many classification methods have been suggested in the credit-scoring literature to distinguish good payers from bad payers. Especially neural networks have received a lot of attention. However, a major drawback is their lack of transparency. While they can achieve a high predictive accuracy rate, the reasoning behind how they reach their decisions is not readily available, which hinders their acceptance by practitioners. Therefore, we have, in earlier work, proposed a two-step process to open the neural network black box which involves: (1) extracting rules from the network; (2) visualizing this rule set using an intuitive graphical representation. In this paper, we will focus on the second step and further investigate the use of two types of representations: decision tables and diagrams. The former are a well-known representation originally used as a programming technique. The latter are a generalization of decision trees taking on the form of a rooted, acyclic digraph instead of a tree, and have mainly been studied and applied by the hardware design community. We will compare both representations in terms of their ability to compactly represent the decision knowledge extracted from two real-life credit-scoring data sets.

1 INTRODUCTION

One of the key decisions financial institutions have to make as part of their daily operations is to decide whether or not to grant a loan to an applicant. With the emergence of large-scale data-storing facilities, huge amounts of data have been stored regarding the repayment behavior of past applicants. It is the aim of credit scoring to analyze this data and build data-mining models that distinguish good applicants from bad applicants using characteristics such as amount on savings account, marital status, purpose of loan, etc. Many machine-learning and statistical techniques have been suggested in the literature to build credit-scoring models (Baesens et al., 2003c; Thomas, 2000). Amongst the most popular are traditional statistical methods (e.g. logistic regression (Steenackers and Goovaerts, 1989)), nonparametric statistical models (e.g. k-nearest neighbor (Henley and Hand, 1997) and classification trees (David et al., 1992)) and neural networks (Baesens et al., 2003b).

However, when looking at today's credit-scoring practice, one typically sees that the estimated classification models, although often based on advanced and powerful algorithms, fail to be successfully integrated into the credit decision environment. One of the key underlying reasons for this problem, is that the extracted knowledge and patterns can not easily be represented in a way that facilitates human interpretation and validation. Hence, properly visualizing the knowledge and patterns extracted by a data-mining algorithm is becoming more and more a critical success factor for the development of decision-support systems for credit scoring.

Therefore, in this paper, we report on the use of different knowledge visualization formalisms for credit scoring. Starting from a set of propositional if-then rules previously extracted by a powerful neural network rule extraction algorithm, we will investigate both decision tables and decision diagrams as alternative knowledge visualization schemes. The latter are a generalization of decision trees taking on the form of a rooted, acyclic digraph instead of a tree, and have mainly been studied and applied by the hardware design community. We will compare both representations in terms of their ability to compactly represent the decision knowledge extracted from two real-life credit-scoring data sets.

I. Seruca et al. (eds.), Enterprise Information Systems VI, 109–115.
© 2006 *Springer. Printed in the Netherlands.*

This paper is organized as follows. Section 2 discusses the basic concepts of decision tables. Section 3 then elaborates on how decision diagrams may provide an alternative, more concise view of the extracted patterns. Empirical results are presented in section 4. Section 5 concludes the paper.

2   DECISION TABLES

Decision tables (DTs) are a tabular representation used to describe and analyze decision situations (e.g. credit-risk evaluation), where the state of a number of conditions jointly determines the execution of a set of actions. A DT consists of four quadrants, separated by double-lines, both horizontally and vertically. The horizontal line divides the table into a condition part (above) and an action part (below). The vertical line separates subjects (left) from entries (right). The condition subjects are the criteria that are relevant to the decision-making process. They represent the attributes of the rule antecedents about which information is needed to classify a given applicant as good or bad. The action subjects describe the possible outcomes of the decision-making process (i.e., the classes of the classification problem: applicant = good or bad). Each condition entry describes a relevant subset of values (called a state) for a given condition subject (attribute), or contains a dash symbol ('-') if its value is irrelevant within the context of that column ('don't care' entry). Subsequently, every action entry holds a value assigned to the corresponding action subject (class). True, false and unknown action values are typically abbreviated by '×', '-', and '.', respectively. Every column in the entry part of the DT thus comprises a classification rule, indicating what action(s) apply to a certain combination of condition states. E.g., in Figure 1 (b), the final column tells us to classify the applicant as good if owns property = no, and savings amount = high.

If each column only contains simple states (no contracted or don't care entries), the table is called an expanded DT, whereas otherwise the table is called a contracted DT. Table contraction can be achieved by combining logically adjacent (groups of) columns that lead to the same action configuration. For ease of legibility, we will allow only contractions that maintain a lexicographical column ordering, i.e., in which the entries at lower rows alternate before the entries above them; see Figure 1 (Figure 2) for an example of an (un)ordered DT, respectively. As a result of this ordering restriction, a decision tree structure emerges in the condition entry part of the DT, which lends itself very well to a top-down evaluation procedure: starting at the first row, and then working one's way down the table by choosing from the relevant condition states,

one safely arrives at the prescribed action (class) for a given case. The number of columns in the contracted table can be further minimized by changing the order of the condition rows. It is obvious that a DT with a minimal number of columns is to be preferred since it provides a more parsimonious and comprehensible representation of the extracted knowledge than an expanded DT (see Figure 1).

1. Owns property?	yes				no			
2. Years client	≤ 3		>3		≤ 3		>3	
3. Savings amount	low	high	low	high	low	high	low	high
1. Applicant=good	-	×	×	×	-	×	-	×
2. Applicant=bad	×	-	-	-	×	-	×	-

(a) Expanded DT

1. Owns property?	yes			no	
2. Years client	≤ 3		>3		
3. Savings amount	low	high		low	high
1. Applicant=good	-	×	×		×
2. Applicant=bad	×	-	-	×	-

(b) Contracted DT

1. Savings amount	low			high
2. Owns property?	yes		no	-
3. Years client	≤ 3	>3	-	-
1. Applicant=good	-	×		×
2. Applicant=bad	×	-	×	-

(c) Minimum-size contracted DT

Figure 1: Minimizing the number of columns of a lexicographically ordered DT

1. Savings amount	high	-	low	low
2. Owns property?	-	yes	no	-
3. Years client	-	>3	-	≤ 3
1. Applicant=good	×	×	-	-
2. Applicant=bad	-	-	×	×

Figure 2: Example of an unordered DT

Note that we deliberately restrict ourselves to single-hit tables, wherein columns have to be mutually exclusive, because of their advantages with respect to verification and validation (Vanthienen et al., 1998). It is this type of DT that can be easily checked for potential anomalies, such as inconsistencies (a particular case being assigned to more than one class) or incompleteness (no class assigned). The decision table formalism thus facilitates the expert's assessment of the knowledge extracted by e.g. a neural network rule extraction algorithm. What's more, consulting a DT in a top-down manner, as suggested above, should prove more intuitive, faster, and less prone to human error, than evaluating a set of rules one by one.

3   DECISION DIAGRAMS

Decision diagrams are a graph-based representation of discrete functions, accompanied by a set of graph algorithms that implement operations on these functions. Given the proper restrictions (cf. infra), decision diagrams have a number of valuable properties:

- they provide a canonical function representation;
- they can be manipulated efficiently;
- for many practically important functions, the corresponding descriptions turn out to be quite compact.

Precisely these properties explain why various types of diagrams have been used successfully in efficiently solving many logic synthesis and verification problems in the hardware design domain. Especially binary decision diagrams (BDDs) have, since the work of Bryant (Bryant, 1986), who defined the canonical subclass of reduced ordered binary decision diagrams, pervaded virtually every subfield in the former areas. There are on the other hand relatively few reported applications so far in the domain of artificial intelligence (Horiyama and Ibaraki, 2002) and machine learning (Kohavi, 1996), while their use for the visual representation of rules extracted from neural networks, or in the application domain of credit scoring, has to our knowledge not been proposed before (note that our approach differs from that presented in (Kohavi, 1996) in that we apply MDDs in a separate visualization step instead of during the learning itself).

Since we are dealing with general discrete (as opposed to binary) attributes, we will apply *multi-valued decision diagrams* (MDDs), a representation similar to BDDs but which does not restrict the outdegree of internal nodes or the number of sink nodes (Kam et al., 1998). An MDD is a rooted, directed acyclic graph, with m sink nodes for every possible output value (class). Each internal node v is labelled by a test variable $var(v) = x_i$ $(i = 1, ..., n)$, which can take values from a finite set $range(x_i)$. Each such node v has $| range(x_i) |$ outgoing edges, and its successor nodes are denoted by $child_k(v)$, for each $k \in range(x_i)$, respectively. An MDD is ordered (OMDD), iff, on all paths through the graph, the test variables respect a given linear order $x_1 < x_2 < ... < x_n$; i.e., for each edge leading from a node labelled by x_i to a node labelled by x_j, it holds that $x_i < x_j$.

An OMDD is meant to represent an n-variable discrete function. For a given assignment to the variables, the function value is determined by tracing a path from the root to a sink, following the edges indicated by the values assigned to the variables. The label of the sink node specifies the function value (class) assigned for that input. Figure 3 displays an example of an OMDD representation for a two-variable function, $\{0, 1, 2, 3\} \times \{0, 1, 2\} \rightarrow \{0, 1\}$, with respect to the variable order $x_1 < x_2$.

Up to here, OMDDs are not yet uniquely determined for each function. However, by further restricting the representation, a canonical form of MDDs is obtained, namely reduced OMDDs (ROMDD). An OMDD is said to be reduced, iff it does not contain a

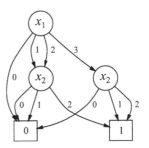

Figure 3: MDD example

node v whose successor nodes are all identical, and no two distinct nodes u, v exist such that the subgraphs rooted in u and v are isomorphic, i.e., for which: $var(u) = var(v)$, and $child_k(u) = child_k(v)$ for all $k \in range(var(u))$. For a given variable ordering, the ROMDD representation of any function is uniquely determined (up to isomorphism), as a result of which several properties (e.g., functional equivalence, constant functions, etc.) become easily testable. Conceptually, a reduced decision diagram can be interpreted as the result of the repeated application of two types of transformations on a decision tree or graph: one reduction rule is to bypass and delete redundant nodes (*elimination rule*), the other is to share isomorphic subgraphs (*merging rule*). In Figure 4, both rules are illustrated for a simple binary example. Note that, in practice, efficient implementations of diagram operations are used that directly produce a reduced form as the diagrams are being built. From here on, we will use the term 'MDD' to denote ROMDDs in particular.

Over the years, several BDD packages have been developed, which implement and provide interfaces for the manipulation of BDDs (in our experiments, we have applied David Long's package (Long, 2003), developed at Carnegie Mellon University. Most often, MDDs are implemented indirectly using these same packages, by binary encoding multi-valued variables (as explained in (Kam et al., 1998)). Direct MDD implementations have also been proposed, e.g. in (Miller and Drechsler, 1998).

4   EMPIRICAL EVALUATION

In previous research, we applied neural network rule extraction methods to extract a set of propositional if-then rules from a trained neural network (Baesens et al., 2003a; Baesens et al., 2003b). The experiments were conducted on two real-life credit-scoring data sets and the publicly available German credit data set.

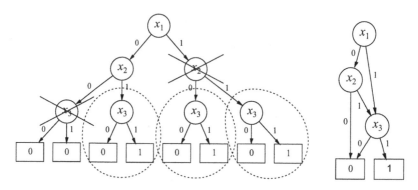

Figure 4: Decision trees (left) versus diagrams (right)

Figure 5 depicts the rule set that was extracted on the Bene1 data set obtained from a major Benelux financial institution (3123 Obs., 33 inputs).

If Term >12 months **and** Purpose = cash provisioning **and** Savings Account ≤ 12.40 € **and** Years Client ≤ 3 **then** Applicant = bad

If Term >12 months **and** Purpose = cash provisioning **and** Owns Property = no **and** Savings Account ≤ 12.40 € **then** Applicant = bad

If Purpose = cash provisioning **and** Income > 719 € **and** Owns Property = no **and** Savings Account ≤ 12.40 € **and** Years Client ≤ 3 **then** Applicant = bad

If Purpose = second-hand car **and** Income > 719 € **and** Owns Property = no **and** Savings Account ≤ 12.40 € **and** Years Client ≤ 3 **then** Applicant = bad

If Savings Account ≤ 12.40 € **and** Economical sector = Sector C **then** Applicant = bad

Default class: Applicant = good

Figure 5: Rules extracted for Bene1

It was shown that the extracted rule sets achieve a very high classification accuracy on independent test set data. The rule sets are both concise and easy to interpret and thus provide the credit-scoring expert with an insightful explanation. However, while propositional rules are an intuitive and well-known formalism to represent knowledge, they are not necessarily the most suitable representation in terms of structure and efficiency of use in case-by-case decision making. Research in knowledge representation suggests that graphical representation formalisms can be more readily interpreted and consulted by humans than a set of symbolic propositional if-then rules (see e.g.

(Santos-Gomez and Darnel, 1992)).

Decision tables provide an alternative way of representing the extracted knowledge (Wets, 1998). We have used the PROLOGA (Prologa, 2003) software to construct the decision tables for the extracted rule sets. PROLOGA is an interactive modelling tool for computer-supported construction and manipulation of DTs (Vanthienen and Dries, 1994). A powerful rule language is available to help specify the DTs, and automated support is provided for several restructuring and optimization tasks.

Table 1 summarizes the properties of the DTs built from the extracted rule sets for the Bene1 and German credit data sets. For German credit (Bene1), the fully expanded decision table contained 6600 (192) columns, respectively. Subsequently, we converted each of these expanded DTs into a more compact DT, by joining nominal attribute values that do not appear in any rule antecedent into a common 'other' state, and then performing optimal table contraction (using a simple exhaustive search method). As a result of this reduction process, we ended up with two minimum-size contracted DTs, consisting of 11 and 14 columns for the German credit and Bene1 data sets, respectively (cf. right column of Table 1). Figure 6 depicts the resulting decision table for the Bene1 data set. While retaining the predictive accuracy of the original rule set, the top-down readability of such a DT, combined with its conciseness, makes the latter a very attractive visual representation of the extracted knowledge. Furthermore, the DT can be easily verified: clearly, there are no missing rules or inconsistencies in Figure 6.

However, a well-known property that can undermine the visual interpretability of decision trees, and hence also of lexicographically ordered DTs, is the inherent replication of subtrees or -tables implementing terms in disjunctive concepts (e.g. (Kohavi, 1996)).

Table 1: The number of columns in the expanded and minimized DTs

Data set	Columns in expanded DT	Columns in minimized DT
German	6600	11
Bene1	192	14

Table 2: MDD size results

Data set	Intern. nodes in MDD (1)	Intern. nodes in dec. tree (2)	Size saving
German	8	8	0%
Bene1	9	12	25%

For example, in the DT for Bene1 (cf. Figure 6), column blocks $\{2, 3, 4, 5\}$ and $\{9, 10, 11, 12\}$, though having the same respective action values, are not eligible for contraction, because they differ in more than one condition entry (viz., with respect to the attributes 'purpose' and 'term'). On the other hand, a decision diagram, which allows the sharing of one such instance through multiple incoming edges, might be smaller than the corresponding tree or table. Therefore, in addition to the DT, we have built an equivalent MDD representation based on the extracted rule set, thereby adhering to the same ordering of attributes as in the minimum-size DT. Figure 7 presents the resulting diagram for Bene1. It was produced using the Graphviz graph-drawing software (Gansner et al., 1993; AT&T, 2003).

Unlike in Figure 6, the part of the MDD representation that matches the replicated table segment is included only once: the subgraph rooted at the rightmost of the two 'years client'-nodes is effectively shared through its two incoming edges. Hence, describing the function in MDD format results in a more compact representation, because the merging rule, unlike the DT contraction rule, does apply here. This empirically confirms why we consider a decision diagram to be a valuable alternative knowledge visualization aid. Nevertheless, decision diagrams are so far seldom considered in this context, despite their being a graph-based generalization of the far more frequently applied decision tree representation.

We have repeated the same exercise for the German credit data set, but in the latter case, no further size savings could be obtained vis-à-vis the DT representation. In Table 2, we have summarized the results of the MDD construction process for both data sets. Note that, because of the aforementioned relation between a decision tree and a lexicographically ordered DT, the figures in column (2) also match the number of splits appearing in the condition entry part of the corresponding DT. Consequently, the final column provides a measure of the additional size gains of MDD reduction over DT contraction (i.e., the added effect of graph sharing).

Both decision tables and diagrams facilitate the development of powerful decision-support systems that can be integrated in the credit-scoring process. A DT consultation engine typically traverses the table in a top-down manner, inquiring the user about the condition states of every relevant condition encountered along the way. A similar decision procedure is induced when consulting the decision diagram representation, and following the proper path through the graph. Hence, both types of representations provide efficient decision schemes that allow a system implementation to ask targeted questions and neglect irrelevant inputs during the question/answer-dialog. Furthermore, given the availability of efficient condition reordering operations for both types of representations, questions can be easily postponed during this process. For example, in PROLOGA, the available answer options always include an additional 'unknown' option, which allows the user to (temporarily) skip the question. When that happens, the DT's conditions are first reordered internally: moving the corresponding condition to the bottom of the order and then recontracting the DT may result in new don't care entries being formed for it. After that, the session continues with the next question. If, at some point, a conclusion is reached regarding the DT's actions, the former question could effectively be avoided; else, it eventually pops up again.

In the Bene1 example, suppose that we are deciding on a particular applicant whose properties will eventually be found to match against the condition entries of column 12, which tells us to accept the loan. Before arriving at that conclusion, we are required to provide only 4 of the 7 inputs to make a classification decision: 'term', 'owns property' and 'income' successively turn out to be irrelevant for this case. If, on the other hand, we would consult the rule description shown in Figure 5, we would need to evaluate every single rule, thereby testing its antecedent until a condition is found that fails, before we may conclude that none of the rules applies and that the default class (applicant = good) must be chosen.

5 CONCLUSIONS

In this paper, we have shown how credit-scoring knowledge can be compactly visualized either in the form of decision tables or diagrams. For two real-life cases, it was first of all shown how a set of propositional if-then rules, extracted by a neural network rule extraction algorithm, can be represented as a decision table. The constructed decision tables

1. Savings Account				≤12.40 €									> 12.40 €
2. Economical sector	Sector C	other											-
3. Purpose	-	cash provisioning							second-hand car		other		-
4. Term	-	≤ 12 months			> 12 months		-						
5. Years Client	-	≤ 3		>3	≤ 3	>3		≤ 3			> 3		
6. Owns Property	-	Yes	No		-	-	Yes	No	Yes	No		-	-	-
7. Income	-	-	≤ 719 €	> 719 €	-	-	-	-	-	≤ 719 €	> 719 €	-	-	-
1. Applicant=good	-	×	×	-	×	-	×	-	×	×	-	×	×	×
2. Applicant=bad	×	-	-	×	-	×	-	×	-	-	×	-	-	-
	1	2	3	4	5	6	7	8	9	10	11	12	13	14

Figure 6: Decision table for the rules extracted for Bene1

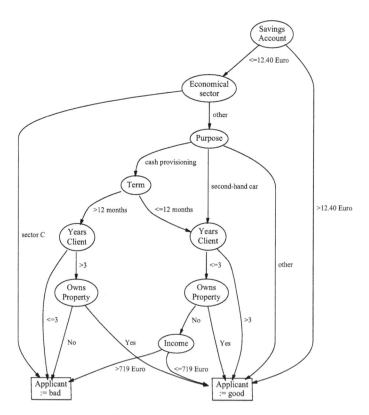

Figure 7: MDD for the Bene1 data set

were then reduced in size using lexicographical order-preserving contraction and condition row order minimization routines which in both cases yielded a parsimonious representation of the extracted rules, while preserving their predictive power. Secondly, we have advocated the use of multi-valued decision diagrams as an alternative visualization that can provide additional size savings compared to the former DT representation. What's more, we have seen empirical confirmation of this property on one of the two data sets. Subsequently, we have demonstrated that the use of either decision tables or diagrams facilitates an efficient case-by-case consultation of the knowledge (e.g., by limiting the number of questions that the user must answer in order to reach a conclusion). Hence, using decision tables and/or diagrams in combination with a rule extraction algorithm provides an interesting approach for developing powerful yet transparent credit-scoring models.

REFERENCES

AT&T Laboratories (2003). Graphviz, graph-drawing tool. http://www.research.att.com/sw/tools/graphviz/.

Baesens, B., Mues, C., Setiono, R., De Backer, M., and Vanthienen, J. (2003a). Building intelligent credit scoring systems using decision tables. In *Proceedings of the Fifth International Conference on Enterprise Information Systems (ICEIS'2003)*, pages 19–25, Angers, France.

Baesens, B., Setiono, R., Mues, C., and Vanthienen, J. (2003b). Using neural network rule extraction and decision tables for credit-risk evaluation. *Management Science*, 49(3):312–329.

Baesens, B., Van Gestel, T., Viaene, S., Stepanova, M., Suykens, J., and Vanthienen, J. (2003c). Benchmarking state of the art classification algorithms for credit scoring. *Journal of the Operational Research Society*, 54(6):627–635.

Bryant, R. (1986). Graph-based algorithms for boolean function manipulation. *IEEE Transactions on Computers*, C-35(8):677–691.

David, R., Edelman, D., and Gammerman, A. (1992). Machine learning algorithms for credit-card applications. *IMA Journal of Mathematics Applied In Business and Industry*, 4:43–51.

Gansner, E. R., Koutsofios, E., North, S. C., and Vo, K. P. (1993). A technique for drawing directed graphs. *IEEE Transactions on Software Engineering*, 19(3):214–230.

Henley, W. and Hand, D. (1997). Construction of a k-nearest neighbour credit-scoring system. *IMA Journal of Mathematics Applied In Business and Industry*, 8:305–321.

Horiyama, T. and Ibaraki, T. (2002). Ordered binary decision diagrams as knowledge-bases. *Artificial Intelligence*, 136(2):189–213.

Kam, T., Villa, T., Brayton, R. K., and Sangiovanni-Vincentelli, A. L. (1998). Multi-valued decision diagrams: Theory and applications. *International Journal on Multiple-Valued Logic*, 4(1-2):9–62.

Kohavi, R. (1996). *Wrappers for Performance Enhancement and Oblivious Decision Graphs*. PhD thesis, Department of Computer Science, Stanford University.

Long, D. (2003). OBDD package. http://www-2.cs.cmu.edu/~modelcheck/bdd.html.

Miller, D. and Drechsler, R. (1998). Implementing a multi-valued decision diagram package. In *Proceedings of the International Symposium on Multiple-Valued Logic*, pages 52–57, Fukuoka, Japan.

Prologa (2003). Decision table modelling tool. http://www.econ.kuleuven.ac.be/prologa/.

Santos-Gomez, L. and Darnel, M. (1992). Empirical evaluation of decision tables for constructing and comprehending expert system rules. *Knowledge Acquisition*, 4:427–444.

Steenackers, A. and Goovaerts, M. (1989). A credit scoring model for personal loans. *Insurance: Mathematics and Economics*, 8:31–34.

Thomas, L. (2000). A survey of credit and behavioural scoring: forecasting financial risk of lending to customers. *International Journal of Forecasting*, 16:149–172.

Vanthienen, J. and Dries, E. (1994). Illustration of a decision table tool for specifying and implementing knowledge based systems. *International Journal on Artificial Intelligence Tools*, 3(2):267–288.

Vanthienen, J., Mues, C., and Aerts, A. (1998). An illustration of verification and validation in the modelling phase of kbs development. *Data and Knowledge Engineering*, 27:337–352.

Wets, G. (1998). *Decision Tables in Knowledge-Based Systems: Adding Knowledge Discovery and Fuzzy Concepts to the Decision Table Formalism*. PhD thesis, Department of Applied Economic Sciences, Catholic University of Leuven, Belgium.

DYNAMIC MULTI-AGENT BASED VARIETY FORMATION AND STEERING IN MASS CUSTOMIZATION

Thorsten Blecker, Nizar Abdelkafi

Departement of Production/Operations Management, University of Klagenfurt, Austria
Email: blecker@ieee.org, nizar.abdelkafi@uni-klu.ac.at

Gerold Kreutler, Gerhard Friedrich

Computer Science and Manufacturing, University of Klagenfurt, Austria
Email: gerold.kreutler@uni-klu.ac.at, gerhard.friedrich@uni-klu.ac.at

Keywords: Product Configuration, Mass Customization, Variety Formation and Steering, Multi Agent System

Abstract: Large product variety in mass customization involves a high internal complexity level inside a company's operations, as well as a high external complexity level from a customer's perspective. To cope with both complexity problems, an information system based on agent technology is able to be identified as a suitable solution approach. The mass customized products are assumed to be based on a modular architecture and each module variant is associated with an autonomous rational agent. Agents have to compete with each other in order to join coalitions representing salable product variants which suit real customers' requirements. The negotiation process is based on a market mechanism supported by the target costing concept and a Dutch auction. Furthermore, in order to integrate the multi-agent system in the existing information system landscape of the mass customizer, a technical architecture is proposed and a scenario depicting the main communication steps is specified.

1 INTRODUCTION

Mass customization is a business strategy that aims at satisfying individual customers' needs nearly with mass production efficiency (Pine, 1993). The development of mass customization is essentially due to the advances realized in modular product architectures and flexible manufacturing systems. However, the progress in the fields of information technologies and artificial intelligence for the support of Internet based customer-supplier interactions can be considered as the most relevant enablers for a successful implementation of the strategy. Rautenstrauch et al. (2002) pointed out that information systems provide the necessary support for enterprises pursuing mass customization.

The information which arises during the interaction process between the customer and supplier serves to build up a long-lasting individual customer relationship (Piller, 2001). Due to high customer orientation, mass customization induces a variety-rich environment. However, customers generally do not seek out variety per se. They do only want the choice that fits to their needs.

The resulting variety in mass customization triggers a high complexity level that leads to additional costs. Moreover, because of the limited human information processing capacity and lack of technical product knowledge, excessive variety confuses customers who are overwhelmed by the complexity of the decision making process. Therefore, the main goal should be to find an optimal product variety which leads to the optimal cost-benefit-relation. For example, Blecker et al. (2003) propose a key metrics system to cope with the internal variety-induced complexity and emphasize the importance of the interaction systems to reduce the external complexity experienced by customers during the buying process.

From this point of view, we can identify two challenges. Firstly, the mass customizer must be supported by an information system to efficiently cope with variety. Secondly, it is relevant to assist customers with adequate information tools during the individualization process in order to lead them in a fast paced manner and with a low amount of effort to their optimal choice. In this paper, after a short description of the main variety problems in mass customization, we formally define a multi-agent based approach supporting dynamic variety-forma-

I. Seruca et al. (eds.), Enterprise Information Systems VI, 116–126.

tion and steering enabling mass customizers to face both depicted challenges. Then, we suggest a technical infrastructure for the implementation of the multi-agent system.

2 VARIETY PROBLEMS IN MASS CUSTOMIZATION

Due to the high individualization level in mass customization, final products are not manufactured until a customer order arrives. This customer-pull system improves the planning situation in dynamic markets and avoids costs such as those due to final products' inventory and special offers to incur. However, the huge variety induced in mass customization is associated with a high complexity and involves costs which arise in the form of overheads. Rosenberg (1997) mentions that product complexity is essentially due to two main reasons which are (a) the variety of product types and groups and (b) the number of components being built in the products, as well as their connections with each other.

An empirical study of Wildemann (2001) has shown that with the doubling of the number of product variants, the unit costs would increase about 20-35% for firms with traditional manufacturing systems. For segmented and flexible automated plants the unit costs would increase about 10-15%. Wildemann concluded that an increase of product variety is associated with an inverted learning curve. Furthermore, Rathnow (1993) depicts a huge product variety is not usually profitable and points out that there is a point $V_{opt.}$ (optimal variety) from which the cost effects of product variety overcompensate its beneficial effects. Lingnau (1994) qualitatively examines cost effects which are involved when increasing variety. He considers a functional organization structure and scrutinizes the effects of variety on sales, production, purchasing and research and development. Lingnau points out that variety generates additional costs in each function. For example, when introducing new variants, new distribution channels could be necessary. Increased variety also complicates the production planning and control and more setups leading to longer idle times in which are required. With higher variety the work-in-process inventory also increases and quality assurance measures should be intensified.

The introduction or elimination of product variants are decisions which are made within the scope of variety steering. Blecker et al. (2003) make the distinction between variety management and variety steering. Variety management embraces the concepts that can be applied in order to increase compo-

nent and process commonality levels during a company's operations such as part families, building blocks, modular product architectures, etc. Unlike variety management concepts, variety steering concepts essentially deal with external variety, which can be perceived by customers. In this paper, we assume that the mass customizer has already implemented a variety management concept and that the main decisions concern variety steering.

The excess of variety and the resulting complexity can endanger the success of mass customized products whose prices should not dramatically differ from the corresponding ones manufactured with a mass production system. That is why, it is relevant to efficiently cope with the internal effects of variety in mass customization. In addition to high internal complexity level during a company's operations, variety induces external complexity that has bad effects from a customer's perspective.

Due to the limited human information processing capacity, excessive variety could confuse customers. Furthermore, customers are not aware of their needs until they see them violated. By looking for suitable products in huge assortments, customers can experience stress, frustration or regret. Iyengar/Lepper (2000) also claim that in limited-choice contexts people are engaged in rational optimization, whereas in extensive-choice contexts people simply end their choice-making when they find a choice that is merely satisfactory, rather than optimal. Furthermore, Schwartz (2000) indicates that by adding new options, the choice situation would be less rather than more attractive and that some people would look for the help of e.g. experts, who make the decision for them.

On the one hand, in order to avoid customers getting lost in huge product assortments, the mass customizer should support them during the interaction process to help them find the product variants corresponding to their optimal choice. On the other hand, the mass customizer has to strongly consider the internal complexity by efficiently steering variety. Therefore, a comprehensive solution approach must integrate both customer's and supplier's perspectives in one information system.

3 A MULTI-AGENT APPROACH FOR VARIETY FORMATION AND STEERING

Common configuration systems for mass customization necessitate specific product knowledge and often overstrain customers. Therefore, we are convinced that these systems should be improved to better support customers during the elicitation process. Blecker et al. (2004) opt for interaction systems which are capable of assisting customers through advisory. Thus, the interaction system should be able to capture a customers' preferences and profile in order to display only the subset of relevant product variants which would better fulfil customers' requirements. From the huge product assortment, only the best variants succeed to be short-listed and displayed to customers. Consequently, in the long run these will better contribute to a supplier's success. Those which are not short-listed will only trigger high complexity and are not relevant for customers. This would suggest that the product variants would compete with each other. That is why it is necessary to define a mechanism setting the rules which organize the competition between variants. This leads one to consider a market mechanism supported by multi-agent technology. The complexity and fuzziness of the problem are further reasons for the use of a multi-agent approach.

The multi-agent based system should dynamically support each user during the interaction process. This means that the system should iteratively generate and refine product variants according to specific customers' needs. Concurrently, it supports the long term supplier's variety steering. This is realized by the decentralization of variety decisions which are supported by autonomous agents.

At first, we present the assumption and definitions required to build up the multi-agent system. Then, we conceptually describe how agents can reach agreements in order to form product variants.

3.1 Assumption and Definitions

Pine (1993) pointed out that the best method to achieve mass customization is to develop products around modular architectures. Ericsson and Erixon (1999) defined modules as building blocks with defined interfaces. By combining only a few modules, it is possible to construct a huge number of product variants. The economies of scale are reached through modules instead of products and economies of scope are attained when modules are built in different products. That is why the assumption of this paper is as follows:

Assumption: Modular product architecture
We assume that the complete set of product variants can be manufactured on the basis of modules.

The main idea is to consider the module variants to be built in the different product variants as autonomous rational agents. It is more reasonable to

consider the module variants as agents than the product variants because with a few modules, one can build up a very large number of product variants which can go up to billions. Thus, by considering modules as agents the problem remains manageable and the computational resources are not overstrained. Therefore, we provide the following definition:

Definition 1: Module agent
Let M be the set of all modules, $M = \{M_1, M_2, \ldots, M_m\}$. We call M_i a module class. A module class M_i contains a set of module variants $MV_{i1}, MV_{i2}, \ldots, MV_{ip(i)}$. p is a function associating an index i of a module class with the index $p(i)$ referring to the number of module variants in a module class. With each module variant $MV_{ij}, j = 1, \ldots, p(i)$ we associate an autonomous rational agent, called a module agent $MA_{ij}, j = 1, \ldots, p(i)$ which disposes of resources and is able to perform tasks.

Modules can be classified in must- and can-modules. Must-modules are indispensable for ensuring the basic product functionalities, whereas can- modules are optional. For example, an engine is a must-module for a car. Without an engine a car cannot ensure its basic functionality consisting of mobility. In contrast to the engine, an air-conditioner is a can-module because it does not disturb the main functionalities a car must perform. In this context the term platform is defined in the technical literature in two distinctive views:

- A product platform is the set of all modules required for the manufacturing of all possible product variants (e.g. Ericsson/Erixon, 1999).
- A product platform can also be the appellation of a specific *common module* which is used in a great range of product variants (e.g. Piller/Waringer, 1999; Wildemann, 2003). This definition is commonly used in the automobile industry.

The second definition of platforms will be adopted in this paper because it considers the platform as a module having an additional relevance in comparison to other modules, which is mainly due to its implementation frequency in product variants. The corresponding agents are called platform agents to make the distinction vis-à-vis other module agents. Furthermore, the set of all platform and module agents are grouped in an agent pool. All different agents are members of a multi-agent system whose main goal is to present only a *subset* of product variants, which would best fit customers' needs.

Because only a subset is allowed to be displayed to customers, the product variants have to compete with each other. Due to the modular architecture of products, we can argue that the module variants also compete to be existent in the set of the presented product configurations. Being driven by a further motivation of this work to support variety steering decisions in mass customization, the module variants which do not resist competition should be eliminated. Therefore, it is legitimate to provide the second definition:

Definition 2: Self-preservation
Each module agent MA_{ij} strives for ensuring its existence by having enough resources to survive.

Definition 2 leads us to consider evolutionary theory which sees evolution as the result of selection by the environment acting on a population of organisms competing for resources. The winners of the competition, those who are most fit to gain the resources necessary for survival, will be selected, the others are eliminated (Kauffman, 1993). The resources of an agent are stored in an account which is defined as follows:

Definition 3: Module agent's account
Each module agent MA_{ij} has revenues and expenses that are summed up in an account Acc_{ij} of monetary units. Acc_{ij} constantly diminishes in the course of time.

It is relevant to mention that the monetary units that a module agent has on its account do not relate to the prices customers pay. The account only serves as an internal steering mechanism for a multi-agent system. The account surplus rather refers to the actual resources of an agent MA_{ij}. From definitions 2 and 3, we can conclude that each agent endeavors to maximize its account surplus. A surplus of zero will mean that the module agent risks death leading to the elimination of the module variant. Furthermore, the second part of definition 3 means that the agent's resources diminish in the course of time even if the agent does not carry out any task. To explain what a task is, we provide the following definition:

Definition 4: Module agent's task
The task T_{ij} of module agent is to form product variants by joining coalitions $C_k, k = 1, ..., n$.

The allocation of tasks to groups of agents is necessary when tasks cannot be performed by a single agent. The module agents on their own are not able to provide a solution. They need to cooperate in order to fulfill tasks. However, the autonomy principle of agents is preserved because each agent can decide whether to take part or not in a product variant. By forming coalitions each agent strives for its personal utility/account via cooperation. Module agents follow the economic principle of rationality

and attempt to form a coalition which will maximize their own utilities. Furthermore, because of the heterogeneity of customer requirements, module agents may have different efficiencies in task performance due to their different capabilities.

In order to participate in a coalition, the module agent has to pay a certain fee. It is noteworthy that as opposed to other work in multi-agent systems (e.g. Shehory and Kraus, 1995), one agent may participate in more than one coalition. Moreover, these coalitions are dynamic and take place in real-time, after capturing customers' preferences. However, a coalition may succeed or fail. This primarily depends on the coalition's result, which can be complete or incomplete:

Definition 5: Complete vs. incomplete coalitions
We say that a coalition is complete if the coalition formed by the module agents builds up a salable product variant. A coalition is incomplete if the coalition formed by the module agents does not build up a salable product variant.

Note that an agent will join a coalition only if the payoff it will receive in the coalition is greater than, or at least equal to, what it can obtain by staying outside the coalition (Shehory and Kraus, 1995). In our case a module agent that does not participate in any coalition has a payoff of zero. Because the account surplus of an agent diminishes in the course of time, each agent should be interested in participating in beneficial coalitions to be able to reconstruct its resources and thus better ensuring its existence. However, there is no certainty about the success of coalition results. As aforementioned, each agent has to pay a certain fee in order to be allowed to participate in a coalition. But if the coalition that subsequently forms is incomplete or fails because it is not powerful enough to be displayed to customers, then the participation of an agent in a coalition is a waste of resources. Therefore, each agent has to be capable of estimating in advance the likelihood of the success of the coalitions it joins. However, the module agents should remain as simple as possible and should not become very complex. The whole multi-agent system has to contribute to problem solving and one agent should only dispose of the intelligence it requires in order to not waste computational resources.

3.2 The Negotiation Process

Firstly, it is relevant to determine the mechanism initiating a coalition. This being in reference to decisions about (a) which module agents are able to begin the formation of coalitions and (b) which reaching agreement process should be implemented to coordinate the module agents. We agree that platform agents are most suitable for initiating coalitions. We also assume that these agents dispose of an infinite account surplus. Therefore, they do not have to care about their existence. This is a legitimate assumption because the development of product platforms is generally cost-intensive. The development process itself may last for a duration of many years. Platforms are also created to be the basic module of a wide range of product variants for a long period of time. For example, by canceling a platform in the automobile industry, this would mean to cancel all models and the corresponding variants which are supported by this platform. Thus, such a decision is strategic and should not be allocated to automated software agents. As in each decision in variety steering it should be supported by human agents who have the required competencies and information. However, it is conceivable that each platform agent strives for being successful as much as possible, e.g. by contributing to the most sales' volumes.

On the basis of customers' preferences, the type and the number of product platforms to form coalitions are determined. Note that:

- a platform agent can be selected more than once,
- each product variant is based on one platform,
- each platform can be found in several product variants and,
- the total number of the selected platform agents is also the utmost limit of the product variants which can be formed by coalitions.

The coalitions take place at a certain point in time and form in order to fulfill the needs of one customer. When all resulting coalitions are complete, then the number of product variants will be exactly equal to the number of selected platform agents provided that no identical coalitions form. The platform agents have the ability to steer the formation of coalitions by (a) fixing the set of module agents which could contribute to the fulfillment of customers' requirements and by (b) determining the mechanism according to which module agents can join coalitions.

We propose to base the coalition formation mechanism on the target costing concept and a Dutch auction. Target costing is based on the price the customer is willing to pay. Starting from this price, it is possible to determine the utmost limit of the costs of each product function that is allowed to incur by taking into account the contribution of each function to the fulfillment of customer requirements. Further on, because each product component or module makes a certain contribution to the realization of a product function it is possible to distribute the function costs on the modules respectively components (Seidenschwarz, 2001). Thus, the result of target costing is an utmost limit for modules' or components' costs. The platform agents which are the auctioneers use these costs to initiate a Dutch auction. The module agents which compete to join the coalitions are the bidders. A Dutch auction is legitimate in this case because each agent tends to delay as much as possible in joining a sub-coalition in order to (a) better evaluate whether to participate or not in a hitherto sub-coalition and (b) minimize as much as possible the fees to pay. But due to the product configuration constraints, when a module agent wins the bid, it may impose constraints on the other bidding agents which intend to take part of the sub-coalition. Thus, the intelligence of the module agent should enable it to proficiently estimate when and for which coalition it bids. These auctions will continue until all coalitions are formed.

Although platform agents have an infinite account, we assume that they will also try to maximize the revenues they receive from module agents. We will describe in the next section how the product variants resulting from the coalitions are filtered after their formation. Only the set of product variants that are displayed to customers will receive revenues which are distributed on modules. The total collected monetary units from all module agents are collected in an account and then distributed on the module agents participating in the few successful product variants by considering their contribution in the fulfillment of the product functions and their participation level.

Up to now, we have only described what module and platform agents should perform and how the whole multi-agent system can reach agreements in order to form coalitions. But we have not mentioned what are the abilities an agent should have, to effectively carry out its tasks. Module and platform agents have different tasks. Therefore, they have different abilities. Module agents strive for maximizing their utilities (accounts). That is why, they have to develop strategies in order to survive. Subsequently, they should be able to evaluate in advance the success of the coalitions by estimating the probability that the formed product variants can be displayed to customers. Furthermore, they have to know when to bid and which coalition would be beneficial to join. Generally, as intelligent agents module agents have to update their knowledge from their own experience and the behavior of the other module agents pertaining to the multi-agent environment, which means that they have to learn.

In opposition to module agents, platform agents do not care about their existence due to their infinite account surplus. Furthermore, they decide which module agents are allowed to participate in the coalitions. Therefore, they are more powerful than module agents. Platform agents initiate and coordinate the formation of coalitions. They are also capable of communicating with each other to avoid the formation of identical coalitions. Platform agents have the overview of the coalition while forming and can forbid the further bidding of module agents by considering the constraints imposed by module agents which have already joined the coalition.

In the following we concentrate on module agents. We assume that the product platforms are capable of initiating the Dutch auction and that only product constraints may restrain the participation of module agents in coalitions. In order to represent the module agents, we use a mathematical tool from decision theory. Decision theory defines a rational agent as one that maximizes the expected utility. The expected utility EU of an action is defined as (Russel/Norvig, 1995):

$$EU(\alpha) = \square_{\omega \in \Omega} U(\omega) P(\omega \mid \alpha)$$

where

$\alpha \in Ac$; Ac: the set of all possible actions available to an agent,

$\Omega = \{\omega, \omega', ...\}$: the set of all possible outcomes

$U: \Omega \to IR$ a utility function associating an outcome with a real

P: a probability distribution over possible outcomes given the performance of actions

Let the function f_{opt} take as input a set of possible actions, a set of outcomes, a probability distribution and a utility function and let this function return an action. The defined behavior of f_{opt} is defined as follows (Russel/Norvig, 1995):

$$f_{opt}(Ac, \Omega, P, U) = \arg\max_{\alpha \in Ac} \square_{\omega \in \Omega} U(\omega) P(\omega \mid \alpha)$$

Wooldridge (2000) criticizes f_{opt} for building rational agents because f_{opt} requires an unconstrained search which can be very expensive when the space of all actions and their outcomes is very wide. But, in our case this critic does not seem to be strong enough because the action types that a module agent can perform are (a) to participate in a coalition (Participating is the action $\alpha = 1$) or (b) not to participate (Not participating is the action $\alpha = 0$). Thus, the number of action types a module agent disposes of are only two. Furthermore, the outcome of actions may be that either (a) the module agent is a member of a product variant which is selected in

the final subset (Success of a coalition is the outcome $\omega = 1$) or (b) the module agent is a member of a product variant which is not selected in the subset to be presented to customers (Failure of a coalition is the outcome $\omega = 0$). That is why, we argue that it is legitimate to consider f_{opt} to build module agents. However, f_{opt} should be adapted to the requirements of the multi-agent system problem that was presented above.

Suppose at a point in time t=0 the platform agents initiate coalitions. Each platform agent chooses which module agents are allowed to bid. For each module agent, the platform agent communicates a function to a module class i having the following form:

$$K_i(t) = K_i g_i(t)$$

where

$K_i(t)$: the Dutch auction function decreasing in the course of time,

K_i: a constant representing the first price of the Dutch auction,

$g_i: [0,T] \to]0,1] / g_i(0) = 1$;

g_i: a steadily decreasing function and,

T: the maximal bidding time

As aforementioned, when a module agent joins a coalition, it may restrain the participation of other module agents also intending to join the coalition. Therefore, each module agent must be capable of evaluating the behavior of the other agents that could prohibit its participation. This behavior should be captured by the function $Risk$ which is a risk function of a module agent MA_{ij}:

$$Risk: [0,T] \to [0,1] / Risk(0) = 0 \text{ and } Risk(T) = R$$

where

$Risk$ is a steadily increaing function

$R \in [0,1]$ is a constant reflecting the risk willingness of the module agent

Note that the function $Risk$ is a function that leads the module agent to bid as early as possible in order to increase its chances in being a participant of a coalition. Let Re $venue$ be the function which takes the value 0 when the agent is not a member of the coalitions representing the product variants displayed to customers and the value Re v when the product variants are displayed to customers. The utility function U of a module agent depends on the risk function which is supposed to decrease revenue during the auction process, the revenue function and the Dutch auction function. The adapted f_{opt} for our case is:

$$f_{opt}(Ac, \Omega, Risk, \mathrm{Re}\, venue, g_i, P, U) =$$
$$\arg \max_{t \in [0,T]} \Box \{[1 - Risk(t)] \mathrm{Re}\, v - K_i g_i(t)\} P(\omega \mid \alpha)$$

The adapted f_{opt} returns the point in time t at which the module agent has to bid for the Dutch auction to maximize its utility. But note that if $t \in [0,T]$ then $\alpha = 1$ and if there is no $t \in [0,T]$ maximizing the utility ($t > T$) then $\alpha = 0$ and the module agent intends on not participating in the coalition.

Furthermore, suppose that a module agent MA_{ij} is allowed to participate in p coalitions: $C_k, k \in \{1, ..., p\}$. For each coalition the module agent estimates f_{opt} and at the point in time t=0 where an auction begins, the module agent has to develop a plan

$$(Plan_{t=0})_{ij} = \left(\left(\alpha_1^0, t_1^0\right)..., \left(\alpha_k^0, t_k^0\right)... \left(\alpha_p^0, t_p^0\right)\right)_{ij}$$

which indicates whether or not and when to bid for each coalition. For notation purposes, when $\alpha_k = 0$, the module agent allocates to t_k^0 an infinite value ($t_k^0 = \infty$), which is in accordance with the fact that an agent will never bid and then not to participate. Moreover, by developing a plan the module agent has to consider its account constraint. It is not allowed to pay for coalitions more than the account surplus. This means that $\Box$ $fees \leq Account\ surplus$. It is also conceivable that the module agent wants to allocate only a certain sum of monetary units for the coalitions which should be formed to be presented to one customer. This depends on the self-preservation strategy the module wants to pursue.

However, the agent plan determined at $t = 0$ is not fixed for the whole auction process. The module agent has to adapt this plan according to the changes which could occur in its environment. Suppose that the tuples of $(Plan_{t=0})_{ij}$ are arranged so that $t_1^0 \leq ... \leq t_k^0 \leq ... \leq t_p^0$. Suppose that $t_1^0 \neq \infty$ and $t_2^0 \neq \infty$ and that at a point in time $t < t_1^0$ an agent from the same class wins the bid or an agent from another class imposes participation constraints. At this point in time, the module agent has to estimate once again f_{opt} for the remaining coalitions to determine whether and when to bid. This is legitimate because when the participation in one coalition fails the module agent can allocate the resources he has planed to expend differently. The resulting plan at a point in time $t = 1$ is:

$$(Plan_{t=1})_{ij} = \left(\left(\alpha_2^1, t_2^1\right)..., \left(\alpha_k^1, t_k^1\right)... \left(\alpha_p^1, t_p^1\right)\right)_{ij}.$$

The application of the described process will continue until different coalitions are formed.

Recapitulating, we can say that the main advantages of the developed multi-agent approach are:

- the easy maintenance of the system: when introducing new module variants or eliminating old ones, it is sufficient to introduce or eliminate module agents,
- the dynamic variety generation during the interaction process and variety steering as well as,
- the application of a market mechanism concept which lets the intelligent agents themselves decide according to the current situation about their suitability to fulfill real customers' requirements. Such a market mechanism based approach enables us to efficiently carry out the coordination mechanism, even for a high number of involved agents (Shehory et al., 1998).

4 TECHNICAL ARCHITECTURE

In this section we present a complete model for variety formation and steering based on the multi-agent system approach developed in the previous section. We propose to interface the module agents' pool to a customer advisory system to support dynamic variety formation during the real time customer advisory process.

Advisory systems are software systems that guide customers according to their profile and requirements through a „personal", customer oriented advisory process to elicit their real needs from an objective point of view (Blecker et al., 2004). During the advisory process, the system suggests the customer product variants according to his profile and refines them through the dialog. At the end of the advisory process, the customer is supported with product variants which fulfill his real needs.

At each advisory session the multi-agent system dynamically creates coalitions of product variants that can be recommended to the user. Therefore, we aim at integrating the system into the existing information system landscape. Figure 1 depicts the architecture of such a system.

Beside the agents' pool the architecture consists of the following main elements:

- an online interface to the data of the advisory system that provides a customer's preferences,
- an interface to the supplier's back office which for instance comprises a CRM or OLAP system,
- additional filtering and target costing data sources,

- librarian agents that have access to all back office systems and make proper data available for the other components,
- coordination agents that coordinate the variety formation in the agents' pool and,
- a blackboard that supports communication between the module agents' pool and its environment.

The system also supports variety steering. As was mentioned in the previous section, the account balance of the agents provides a measurement of the

decision on the product level; otherwise the system gathers his needs, which can be captured in e.g. a language different form product specification. For instance, data can contain personal data such as the customer's age or marital status, his personal preferences or desired product attributes. In the automotive domain it could be about a male customer with two children who is sporty, but prefers an economical car.

(2) The information about the customer is supplemented by the librarian agent: Depending on

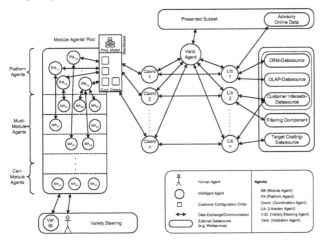

Figure 1: Technical architecture for an agent based variety formation and steering

success of a module variant which constantly can be analyzed by a variety steering agent or humans.

Before we technically describe the system, we will describe the main idea on the basis of a scenario: During the advisory process the system captures the customer's requirements according to his knowledge level. During the advisory dialog the system presents the user a proposal of several product variants according to his profile and preferences. These are refined through the advisory dialog which leads to dynamically refined suggestions for product variants. Finally, the system generates suggestions of product variants that meet real customer needs.

The creation of a valid subset of product variant coalitions is dynamically carried out by following steps:

(1) A so-called librarian agent obtains data from the online advisory data source. These data can contain both user data and product preferences – depending on the knowledge level of the user. If the user is familiar to the domain, he can make a

whether the customer is recognized (e.g. by a login process) this data can be obtained from the CRM data source where both the customer's interests and his past buying behavior are stored. Otherwise the information can be provided from the OLAP data source where traditional web mining techniques such as clustering are used to extend the customer's profile. The result of this process is an improved profile of the customer's needs.

(3) In order to support the negotiation process in the module agents' pool, the librarian agent calls for service from the filtering component in order to convert the customer attributes to product attributes. For instance, this can be based on expert rules or statistical methods. As an example the attributes of (1) could be inferred that the car should be a sedan with no automatic transmission that runs on diesel.

(4) The target costing component is used to estimate the costs of the product's functions that the cus-

tomer probably will have to pay for. For instance, this could be based on past sales of a clustered customer group.

(5) The data is passed on to the coordination agent who monitors the load of the module agents' pool. If the number of customer configuration orders is below a certain limit, the coordination agent sets forth a request for new product variants with the desired product properties onto the blackboard. Note that these product properties derived from the customer attributes only support the negotiation process, they are not constraints. Besides for that, the coordination agent selects both appropriate platform agents who should carry out the auction, and the number of coalitions of product variants they should form. This decision is based on the customer's profile and the product model.

(6) Now the negotiation process is carried out as described in the previous chapter, until all coalitions are formed. The resulting coalitions are put back onto the blackboard where they are removed from the coordination agents and passed to the validation agent.

(7) The validation agent requests data from information agents in order choose a subset of the available coalitions of variants to present them to the customer. This task is performed on the basis of validation which is a kind of „reverse mapping". That means that the properties of the selected coalitions are mapped to customer attributes as a kind of verification. The best coalitions are presented and rewarded with monetary revenue for the accounts.

(8) If the customer makes the decision to buy a certain product variant of the presented subset, it is conceivable that an additional reward would be sent back to the accounts of the corresponding module agents.

(9) Additionally, we propose the use of the account level of each module agent as an indicator to support variety steering decisions. In an independent process the system makes suggestions to eliminate module variants. If the account level is negative or low in comparison with competing module variants, this is an indicator to remove the module variant. Furthermore, the introduction of new module variants can affect the internal and external complexities which can be estimated by computing suitable key metrics (Blecker et al., 2003).

In conclusion we can see that the complexity is spread throughout all system components in the multi agent system:

- The module agents' pool is responsible for carrying out a negotiation for forming product variant coalitions,

- coordination agents manage the blackboard and the general interface between the agents' pool and its environment,
- librarian agents not only interface the back office systems, they independently obtain data and process them in an intelligent way to support the other agents optimally,
- a validation agent carries out the validation of the module variants coalition independently of the decisions of the other system components.

For the implementation of such, we propose to base the system on Java technology. This not only ensures platform independence, it also provides a uniform framework for the implementation of all components.

All back office systems such as CRM, OLAP or other data sources must be connected via custom interfaces, for example by XML. On the variety formation system, data can be provided by web services so that the agents can access the services. The agents' pool can be realized in one virtual machine. Due to the decision to represent module variants instead of product variants as agents, this assumption is admissible. This way we can lower the communication costs because this enables a direct interaction between the agent instances. The coordination between the agents' pool and the external agents is carried out via a blackboard where all agents are registered. Coordination agents, validation agents and librarian agents can be distributed for reasons of load balancing. Communication between these agents can be performed via Java's RMI (Remote Method Invocation) or CORBA to support other systems.

5 CONCLUSIONS

In this paper, we have depicted the main problems which are triggered by increasing variety in mass customization. Variety involves an internal complexity inside a company's operations, as well as an external complexity from a customer's perspective. To mitigate both complexities' problems, the main idea is to provide an information system solution which is capable of both supporting customers during the interaction process by proposing and refining product variants and simultaneously supporting variety steering decisions. The agent technology is able to be identified as a suitable approach to cope with this problem in a decentralized, self-coordinating way.

The developed system integrates both customer's and supplier's perspectives in one information system. We outlined how module variants can be represented as intelligent agents that negotiate with each other to ensure their survival within the scope of variety steering. Based on the decision theory's model for rational agents, we formally define the function that an agent strives to optimize. The negotiation process between the intelligent agents is based on the target costing concept and a Dutch auction. This is also described in a formal way defining the possible functions which have to be determined. Because we intend to carry out simulations of the entire system, several functions which determine the intelligence of the defined agents should be tested. Based on these simulations we will decide which implementation will lead to a working prototype. Furthermore, a technical architecture for the agent-based variety formation and steering in mass customization is proposed.

The main advantages of the developed approach are the easy maintenance of the system, the dynamic variety generation and variety steering, as well as the application of a market mechanism concept supported by agent technology. The adopted market mechanism presents a relevant approach enabling one to overcome the shortcomings of existing interaction systems and variety steering methods. Thus, instead of building rigid rules in the interaction system that map customer requirements into product attributes, the proposed market mechanism approach lets the intelligent agents themselves decide according to the current situation about their suitability to fulfill real customers' requirements. Furthermore, the market mechanism enables us to connect two relevant concepts in mass customization, namely which product variants should be retained in the product assortment and which specific ones from this assortment should be selected and offered to a particular customer.

REFERENCES

Blecker, T., Abdelkafi, N., Kaluza, B., and Friedrich, G., 2003. Key Metrics System for Variety Steering in Mass Customization. In *MCPC'03, 2nd Interdisciplinary World Congress on Mass Customization and Personalization, Munich*, October 6-8, 2003.

Blecker, T., Abdelkafi, N., Kreutler, G., and Friedrich, G., 2004. An Advisory System for Customers' Objective Needs Elicitation in Mass Customization. In *4th Workshop on Information Systems for Mass Customization, Madeira Island*, February 29-March 3, 2004.

Ericsson, A., and Erixon, G., 1999. *Controlling Design Variants: Modular Product Platforms*, Society of Manufacturing Engineers. Dearborn, Michigan.

Iyenger, S. S., and Lepper, M. R., 2000. When Choice is Demotivating: Can One Desire Too Much of a Good Thing?, URL: http://www.columbia.edu/~ss957/publications.html (Retrieval 10. Oct. 2003).

Kauffman, S. A., 1993. *The Origins of Order: Self-Organization and Selection in Evolution*, Oxford University Press, New York.

Lingnau, V., 1994. *Variantenmanagement: Produktionsplanung im Rahmen einer Produktdifferenzierungsstrategie*, Erich Schmidt Verlag GmbH & Co. Berlin.

Piller, F. T., 2001. *Mass Customization: Ein wettbewerbsstrategisches Konzept im Informationszeitalter, Gabler Verlag*. Wiesbaden, 2nd edition.

Piller, F. T., and Waringer, D., 1999. *Modularisierung in der Automobilindustrie – neue Formen und Prinzipien*, Shaker Verlag. Aachen.

Pine II, J., 1993. *Mass Customization: The New Frontier in Business Competition*, Harvard Business School Press. Boston.

Rathnow, P. J., 1993. *Integriertes Variantenmanagement: Bestimmung, Realisierung und Sicherung der optimalen Produktvielfalt*, Vandenhoeck und Ruprecht. Goettingen.

Rautenstrauch, C., Taggermann, H., and Turowski, K., 2002. Manufacturing Planning and Control Content Management in Virtual Enterprises Pursuing Mass Customization. In Rautenstrauch, C., Seelmann-Eggebert, R., and Turowski, K. (Eds.). *Moving into Mass Customization: Information Systems and Management Principles*, Springer-Verlag. Berlin Heidelberg, pp. 103-118.

Rosenberg, O., 1997. Kostensenkung durch Komplexitaetsmanagement. In Franz, K.-P., and Kajueter, P. (Eds.). *Kostenmanagement: Wertsteigerung durch systematische Kostensenkung*, Schaeffer Poeschel Verlag. Stuttgart, pp. 225-245.

Russel, S., and Norvig, P., 1995. *Artificial Intelligence: A Modern Approach*, Prentice-Hall, Inc. New Jersey.

Schwartz, B., 2000. Self-Determination: The Tyranny of Freedom, URL: http://www.swarthmore.edu/SocSci/bschwar1/self-determination.pdf

Seidenschwarz, W., 2001. *Target Costing. Marktorientiertes Zielkostenmanagement*, Vahlen. Muenchen, 2nd edition.

Shehory, O., and Kraus, S., 1995. Coalition formation among autonomous agents: Strategies and complexity. In Castelfranchi, C., and Muller, J. P., (Eds.). *From Reaction to Cognition*, Springer Verlag. pp. 57-72.

Shehory, O., Sycara, K.P., and Jha, S., 1998. Multi-agent coordination through coalition formation. In Singh, M.P., Rao, A.S., and Wooldridge, M.J., (Eds.). *Proceedings of ATAL '97*, Springer Verlag. pp 143-154.

Wildemann, H., 2001. *Das Just-In-Time Konzept – Produktion und Zulieferung auf Abruf*, TCW Transfer-Centrum GmbH. Muenchen, 5th edition.

Wildemann, H., 2003. *Produktordnungssysteme: Leitfaden zur Standardisierung und Individualisierung des Produktprogramms durch intelligente Plattformstrategien*, TCW Transfer-Centrum GmbH. Muenchen, 2nd edition.

Wooldrige, M., 2000. *Reasoning about rational agents*, The MIT Press. Cambridge et al.

MULTIPLE ORGAN FAILURE DIAGNOSIS USING ADVERSE EVENTS AND NEURAL NETWORKS

Álvaro Silva
Hospital Geral de Santo António
Porto, Portugal
a.moreirasilva@mail.telepac.pt

Paulo Cortez
DSI, Universidade do Minho
Guimarães, Portugal
pcortez@dsi.uminho.pt

Manuel Santos
DSI, Universidade do Minho
Guimarães, Portugal
mfs@dsi.uminho.pt

Lopes Gomes
Inst. de Ciências Biomédicas Abel Salazar
Porto, Portugal
cardiologia.hgsa@mail.telepac.pt

José Neves
DI, Universidade do Minho
Braga, Portugal
jneves@di.uminho.pt

Keywords: Intensive Care Medicine, Classification, Clinical Data Mining, Multilayer Perceptrons.

Abstract: In the past years, the *Clinical Data Mining* arena has suffered a remarkable development, where *intelligent data analysis* tools, such as *Neural Networks*, have been successfully applied in the design of medical systems. In this work, *Neural Networks* are applied to the prediction of organ dysfunction in *Intensive Care Units*. The novelty of this approach comes from the use of *adverse events*, which are triggered from four bedside alarms, being achieved an overall predictive accuracy of 70%.

1   INTRODUCTION

Scoring the severity of illness has become a daily routine practice in *Intensive Care Units (ICUs)*, with several metrics available, such as the *Acute Physiology and Chronic Health Evaluation System (APACHE II)* or the *Acute Physiology Score (SAPS II)*, just to name a few (Teres and Pekow, 2000). Yet, most of these prognostic models (given by *Logistic Regression*) are static, being computed with data collected within the first 24 hours of a patient's admission. This will produce a limited impact in clinical decision making, since there is a lack of accuracy of the patient's condition, with no intermediate information being used.

On the other hand, the *Clinical Data Mining* is a rapidly growing field, which aims at discovering patterns in large clinical heterogeneous data (Cios and Moore, 2002). In particular, an increasing attention has been set of the use of *Neural Networks* (connectionist models that mimic the human central nervous system) in *Medicine*, with the number of publications growing from two in 1990 to five hundred in 1998 (Dybowski, 2000).

The interest in *Data Mining* arose due to the rapid emergence of electronic data management methods, holding valuable and complex information (Hand et al., 2001). However, human experts are limited and may overlook important details, while tecniques such as *Neural networks* have the potential to solve some of these hurdles, due to capabilities such as nonlinear learning, multi-dimensional mapping and noise toler-

ance (Bishop, 1995).

In *ICUs, organ failure diagnosis* in real time is a critical task. Its rapid detection (or even prediction) may allow physicians to respond quickly with therapy (or act in a proactive way). Moreover, multiple organ dysfunction will highly increase the probability of the patient's death.

The usual approach to detect organ failure is based in the *Sequential Organ Failure Assessment (SOFA)*, a diary index, ranging from 0 to 4, where an organ is considered to fail when its *SOFA* score is equal or higher than 3 (Vincent et al., 1996). However, this index takes some effort to be obtained (in terms of time and costs).

This work is motivated by the success of previous applications of *Data Mining* techniques in *ICUs*, such as *predicting hospital mortality* (Santos et al., 2002). The aim is to study the application of *Neural Networks* for organ failure prediction (identified by high *SOFA* values) of six systems: *respiratory, coagulation, liver, cardiovascular, central nervous* and *renal*. Several approaches will be tested, using different *feature selection, training* and *modeling* configurations. A particular focus will be given to the use of daily intermediate adverse events, which can be automatically obtained from four hourly bedside measurements, with fewer costs when compared to the *SOFA* score.

The paper is organized as follows: first, the *ICU* clinical data is presented, being preprocessed and transformed into a format that enables the classifica-

I. Seruca et al. (eds.), Enterprise Information Systems VI, 127–134.
© 2006 *Springer. Printed in the Netherlands.*

tion task; then, the neural models for organ failure diagnosis are introduced; next, a description of the different experiments performed is given, being the results analyzed and discussed; finally, closing conclusions are drawn.

2   MATERIALS AND METHODS

2.1   Clinical Data

In this work, a part of the *EURICUS II* database (www.frice.nl) was adopted which contains data related to 5355 patients from 42 *ICUs* and 9 European Union countries, collected during a period of 10 months, from 1998 to 1999. The database has one *entry* (or *example*) per each day (with a total of 30570), being its main features described in Table 1:

- The first six rows denote the *SOFA* values (one for each organ) of the patient's condition in the previous day. In terms of notation, these will be denoted by $SOFA_{d-1}$, where d represents the current day.

- The *case mix* appears in the next four rows, an information that remains unchanged during the patient's internment, containing: the *admission type* (1 - Non scheduled surgery, 2 - Scheduled surgery, 3 - Physician); the *admission origin* (1 - Surgery block, 2 - Recovery room, 3 - Emergency room, 4 - Nursing room, 5 - Other *ICU*, 6 - Other hospital, 7 - Other sources); the *SAPSII* score (a mortality prediction index, where higher values suggest a high death probability) and the patient's age. Figure 1 shows the frequency distributions of these attributes.

- Finally, the last four rows denote the intermediate outcomes, which are triggered from four monitored biometrics: the *systolic Blood Pressure (BP)*; the *Heart Rate (HR)*; the *Oxygen saturation (O2)*; and the *URine Output (UR)*. A panel of *EURICUS II* experts defined the normal ranges for these four variables (Tables 2 and 3). Each *event* (or *critical event*) is defined as a binary variable, which will be set to 0 (false), if the physiologic value lies within the advised range; or 1 (true) else, according to the time criterion.

Before attempting modeling, the data was preprocessed, in order to set the desired classification outputs. First, six new attributes were created, by sliding the $SOFA_{d-1}$ values into each previous example, since the intention is to predict the patient's condition ($SOFA_d$) with the available data at day d ($SOFA_{d-1}$, *case mix* and adverse events). Then, the last day of the patient's admission entries were discarded (remaining a total of 25309), since in this cases, no $SOFA_d$ information is available. Finally,

the new attributes were transformed into binary variables, according to the expression:

$$0 \ , \ if \ SOFA_d < 3 \quad (false, \text{ no organ failure})$$
$$1 \ , \ else \quad\quad\quad\quad\ (true, \text{ organ dysfunction})$$
$$(1)$$

2.2   Neural Networks

In *MultiLayer Perceptrons*, one of the most popular *Neural Network* architectures, *neurons* are grouped into *layers* and only *forward connections* exist (Bishop, 1995). Supervised learning is achieved by an iterative adjustment of the network *connection weights* (the *training* procedure), in order to minimize an error function, computed over the training examples (*cases*).

The state of a neuron (s_i) is given by (Haykin, 1999):

$$s_i = f(w_{i,0} + \sum_{j \in I} w_{i,j} \times s_j) \quad (2)$$

where I represents the set of nodes reaching node i, f the activation function (possibly of nonlinear nature), $w_{i,j}$ the weight of the connection between nodes j and i (when $j = 0$, it is called *bias*); and $s_1 = x_1, \ldots, s_n = x_n$, being $x_1, \ldots, x_n$ the input vector values for a network with n inputs.

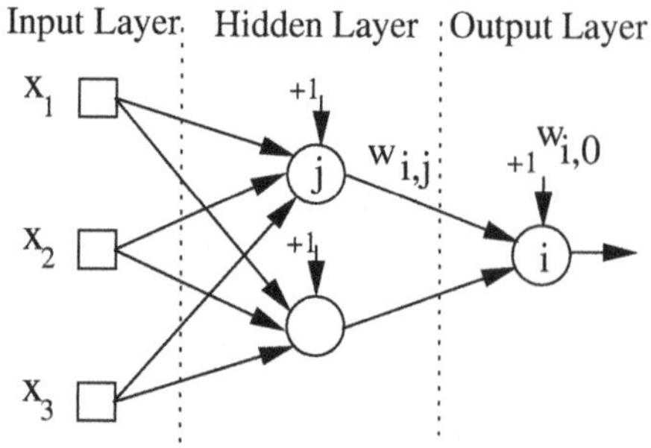

Figure 2: A fully connected network with 3 inputs, 2 hidden nodes, 1 output and *bias* connections

All experiments reported in this work will be conducted using a neural network object oriented programming environment, developed in *JAVA*.

Fully connected *Multilayer Perceptrons* with *bias* connections, one hidden layer (with a fixed number of hidden nodes) and logistic activation functions ($f(x) = \frac{1}{1+e^{-x}}$) were adopted for the organ failure classification (Figure 2). Only one output node is used, since each organ system will be modeled by a different network. This splitting is expected to facilitate the *Neural Network* learning process. Therefore,

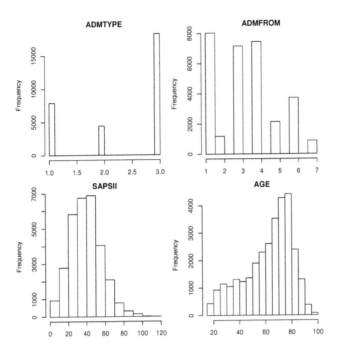

Figure 1: The *case mix* histograms.

Table 1: The clinical data attributes.

Attribute	Description	Domain Values
respirat	Respiratory	$\{0, 1, 2, 3, 4\}$
coagulat	Coagulation	$\{0, 1, 2, 3, 4\}$
liver	Liver	$\{0, 1, 2, 3, 4\}$
cardiova	Cardiovascular	$\{0, 1, 2, 3, 4\}$
cns	Central nervous system	$\{0, 1, 2, 3, 4\}$
renal	Renal	$\{0, 1, 2, 3, 4\}$
admtype	Admission type	$\{1, 2, 3\}$
admfrom	Admission origin	$\{1, 2, \ldots, 7\}$
sapsII	SAPSII score	$\{0, 1, \ldots, 160\}$
age	Patients' age	$\{18, 19, \ldots, 100\}$
NBP	Number of daily *BP* events and critical events	$\{0, 1, \ldots, 28\}$
NHR	Number of daily *HR* events and critical events	$\{0, 1, \ldots, 26\}$
NO2	Number of daily *O2* events and critical events	$\{0, 1, \ldots, 30\}$
NUR	Number of daily *UR* events and critical events	$\{0, 1, \ldots, 29\}$

the predicted class (P_k) for the k example is given the nearest class value:

$$P_k = \begin{cases} 0 \text{ , } if \text{ } s_{k,o} < 0.50 \\ 1 \text{ , } else \end{cases} \quad (3)$$

where $s_{k,o}$ denotes the output value for the o output

node and the k input example.

Before feeding the *Neural Networks*, the data was preprocessed: the input values were standardized into the range $[-1, 1]$ and a *1-of-C* encoding (one binary variable per class) was applied to the nominal attributes (non ordered) with few categories

Table 2: The *event* time ranges

Event	Suggested Range	Continuously Out of Range	Intermittently Out of Range
BP (mmHg)	90 – 180	≥ 10′	≥ 10′ in 30′
O2 (%)	≥ 90	≥ 10′	≥ 10′ in 30′
HR (bpm)	60 – 120	≥ 10′	≥ 10′ in 30′
UR (ml/hour)	≥ 30	≥ 1 hour	

Table 3: The *critical event* time ranges

Critical Event	Suggested Range	Continuously Out of Range	Intermittently Out of Range	Event Anytime
BP (mmHg)	90 – 180	≥ 60′	≥ 60′ in 120′	BP < 60
O2 (%)	≥ 90	≥ 60′	≥ 60′ in 120′	O2 < 80
HR (bpm)	60 – 120	≥ 60′	≥ 60′ in 120′	HR < 30 ∨ HR > 180
UR (ml/hour)	≥ 30	≥ 2 hours		≤ 10

($SOFA_{d-1}$, *admtype* and *admfrom*). For example, the *admtype* variable is fed into 3 input nodes, according to the scheme:

$$1 \rightarrow \quad -1 \quad -1 \quad 1$$
$$2 \rightarrow \quad -1 \quad 1 \quad -1$$
$$3 \rightarrow \quad -1 \quad -1 \quad 1$$

At the beginning of the training process, the network weights are randomly set within the range [-1,1]. Then, the *RPROP* algorithm (Riedmiller, 1994) is applied, due to its faster convergence and stability, being stopped when the training error slope is approaching zero or after a maximum of E epochs (Prechelt, 1998).

2.2.1 Statistics

To insure statistical significance, 30 runs were applied in all tests, being the accuracy estimates achieved using the *Holdout* method (Flexer, 1996). In each simulation, the available data is divided into two mutually exclusive partitions, using stratified sampling: the *training set*, used during the modeling phase; and the *test set*, being used after training, in order to compute the accuracy estimates.

A common tool for classification analysis is the *confusion matrix* (Kohavi and Provost, 1998), a matrix of size $L \times L$, where L denotes the number of possible classes (*domain*). This matrix is created by matching the *predicted* (*test result*) and *actual* (*patients real condition*) values. When $L = 2$ and there are four possibilities (Table 4): the number of *True Negative (TN)*, *False Positive (FP)*, *False Negative (FN)* and *True Positive (TP)* classifications.

From the matrix, three accuracy measures can be defined (Essex-Sorlie, 1995): the *Sensitivity* (also

Table 4: The 2 × 2 *confusion matrix*

↓ actual \ predicted →	negative	positive
negative	TN	FP
positive	FN	TP

known as *recall* and *Type II Error*); the *Specificity* (also known as *precision* and *Type I Error*); and the *Accuracy*, which gives an overall evaluation. These metrics can be computed using the following equations:

$$\begin{aligned} Sensitivity &= \tfrac{TP}{FN+TP} \times 100 \ (\%) \\ Specificity &= \tfrac{TN}{TN+FP} \times 100 \ (\%) \\ Accuracy &= \tfrac{TN+TP}{TN+FP+FN+TP} \times 100 \ (\%) \end{aligned} \quad (4)$$

3   RESULTS

3.1   Feature Selection

Four different feature selection configurations will be tested, in order to evaluate the input attribute importance:

A - which uses only the $SOFA_{d-1}$ values (1 variable).

B - where all available input information is used ($SOFA_{d-1}$ of the corresponding organ system, the *case mix* and the *adverse events*, in a total of 9 attributes);

C - in this case, the $SOFA_{d-1}$ is omitted (8 variables); and

D - which uses only the four *adverse outcomes*.

Since the *SOFA* score takes costs and time to obtain, in this study, a special attention will be given to the last two settings.

In the initial experiments, it was considered more important to approach feature selection than model selection. Due to time constrains, the number of hidden nodes was set to $round(N/2)$, where N denotes the number of input nodes ($N = 5$, $N = 21$, $N = 16$ and $N = 4$, for the **A**, **B**, **C** and **D** setups, respectively); and $round(x)$ gives nearest integer to the x value.

The commonly used $2/3$ and $1/3$ partitions were adopted for the *training* and *test* sets (Flexer, 1996), while the maximum number of training epochs was set to $E = 100$. Each input configuration was tested for all organ systems, being the accuracy measures given in terms of the mean of thirty runs (Table 5).

The **A** selection manages to achieve a high performance, with an *Accuracy* ranging from 86% to 97%, even surpassing the **B** configuration. This is not surprising, since it is a well established fact that the *SOFA* is a adequate score for organ dysfunction. Therefore, the results suggest that there is a high correlation between $SOFA_{d-1}$ and $SOFA_d$.

When the *SOFA* index is omitted (**C** and **D**), the *Accuracy* values only decay slightly. However, this measure (which is popular within *Data Mining* community) is not sufficient in *Medicine*. Ideally, a test should report both high *Sensitivity* and *Specificity* values, which suggest a high level of confidence (Essex-Sorlie, 1995). In fact, there seems to be a trade-off between these two characteristics, since when the *SOFA* values are not present (Table 5), the *Sensitivity* values suffer a huge loss, while the *Specificity* values increase.

3.2 Balanced Training

Why do the **A/B** selections lead to high *Accuracy* /*Specificity* values and low *Sensitivity* ones? The answer may be due to the biased nature of the organ dysfunction distributions; i.e., there is a much higher number of *false* (0) than *true* (1) conditions (Figure 3).

One solution to solve this handicap, is to *balance* the training data; i.e., to use an equal number of true and false learning examples. Therefore, another set of experiments was devised (Table 6), using random sampling training sets, which contained $2/3$ of the true examples, plus an equal number of false examples. The test set was composed of the other $1/3$ positive entries. In order to achieve a fair comparison with the previous results, the negative test examples were randomly selected from the remaining ones, with a distribution identical to the one found in the original dataset (as given by Figure 3).

The obtained results show a clear improvement in the *Sensitivity* values, specially for the **C** configuration, stressing the importance of the *case mix* attributes. Yet, the overall results are still far from the ones given by the **A** selection.

3.3 Improving Learning

Until now, the main focus was over selecting the correct training data. Since the obtained results are still not satisfactory, the attention will move towards better *Neural Network* modeling. This will be achieved by changing two parameters: the *number of hidden nodes* and the *maximum number of training epochs*. Due to computational power restrictions, these factors were kept fixed in the previous experiments. However, the adoption of *balanced training* leads to a considerable reduction of the number of training cases, thus reducing the required training time.

Several experimental trials were conducted, using different combinations of hidden nodes ($H = 4$, 8, 16 and 32) and maximum number of epochs ($E = 100$, 500 and 1000), being selected the configuration which gave the lowest training errors ($H = 16$ and $E = 1000$). These setup lead to better results, for all organ systems and accuracy measures (Table 6).

To evaluate the obtained results, a comparison with other *Machine Learning* classifiers was performed (Table 7), using two classical methods from the *WEKA Machine Learning* software (Witten and Frank, 2000): *Naive Bayes* - a statistical algorithm based on probability estimation; and *JRIP* - a learner based on "IF-THEN" rules.

Although presenting a better *Accuracy*, the *Naive Bayes* tends to emphasize the *Specificity* values, giving poor *Sensitivity* results. A better behavior is given by the *JRIP* method, with similar *Sensitivity* and *Specificity* values. Nevertheless, the *Neural Networks* still exhibit the best overall performances.

4 CONCLUSIONS

The surge of novel bio-inspired tools, such as *Neural Networks*, has created new exciting possibilities for the field of *Clinical Data Mining*. In this work, these techniques were applied for *organ failure diagnosis* of *ICU* patients.

Preliminary experiments were drawn to test several feature selection configurations, being the best results obtained by the solely use of the *SOFA* value, measured in the previous day. However, this score takes much more time and costs to be obtained, when compared with the physiologic adverse events. Therefore, another set of experiments were conducted, in order

Table 5: The *feature selection* performances (in percentage)

Organ	A			B			C			D		
	Acc.	Sen.	Spe.	Acc.	Sen.	Spe.	Acc.	Sen.	Spe.	Acc.	Sen.	Spe.
respirat	86.3	72.4	90.2	86.2	70.0	90.8	77.9	4.4	98.8	77.6	1.8	99.4
coagulat	97.4	68.8	98.7	97.3	59.6	99.0	95.8	4.6	99.9	95.7	0.0	100
liver	98.3	68.6	99.1	98.3	60.2	99.4	97.3	7.6	99.9	97.3	0.0	100
cardiova	94.2	84.1	96.3	94.2	84.0	96.3	82.8	7.5	99.0	82.2	0.5	99.8
cns	95.7	92.7	96.4	95.7	92.3	96.4	83.5	23.4	97.1	81.6	0.4	99.9
renal	95.5	71.3	97.8	95.3	66.6	98.1	91.4	5.7	99.7	91.1	0.3	100
Mean	94.6	76.3	96.4	94.5	72.1	96.7	88.1	8.9	99.1	87.6	0.5	99.96

Acc. - Accuracy, Sen. - Sensitivity, Spe - Specificity.

Table 6: The balanced **C**, **D** and **C** improved performances (in percentage)

Organ	C			D			C (improved)		
	Acc.	Sen.	Spe.	Acc.	Sen.	Spe.	Acc.	Sen.	Spe.
respirat	61.3	66.4	59.8	67.1	41.1	74.5	63.3	70.4	61.3
coagulat	67.6	66.8	67.7	73.7	41.5	75.1	70.0	72.0	69.9
liver	70.0	71.6	70.0	66.9	36.5	67.8	72.5	77.3	72.4
cardiova	65.9	62.5	66.7	68.2	37.9	74.8	69.1	66.3	69.8
cns	73.6	63.9	75.7	66.8	36.3	73.7	75.2	72.2	75.8
renal	67.8	65.6	68.0	73.2	37.6	76.6	71.9	70.5	72.0
Mean	67.7	66.2	68.0	69.3	38.5	73.8	70.3	71.5	70.2

Acc. - Accuracy, Sen. - Sensitivity, Spe - Specificity.

Table 7: The classifiers performances for the **C** selection balanced data (in percentage)

Organ	Naive Bayes			JRIP			Neural Networks		
	Acc.	Sen.	Spe.	Acc.	Sen.	Spe.	Acc.	Sen.	Spe.
respirat	73.5	25.2	87.3	62.8	61.9	63.0	63.3	70.4	61.3
coagulat	83.3	24.8	85.8	67.8	62.4	68.0	70.0	72.0	69.9
liver	70.8	54.3	71.2	75.7	73.7	75.7	72.5	77.3	72.4
cardiova	73.4	33.4	82.0	66.6	70.3	65.8	69.1	66.3	69.8
cns	76.3	41.3	84.2	77.6	74.4	78.3	75.2	72.2	75.8
renal	76.8	45.6	79.9	69.1	68.5	69.2	71.9	70.5	72.0
Mean	75.7	37.4	81.7	69.9	68.5	70.15	70.3	71.5	70.2

Acc. - Accuracy, Sen. - Sensitivity, Spe - Specificity.

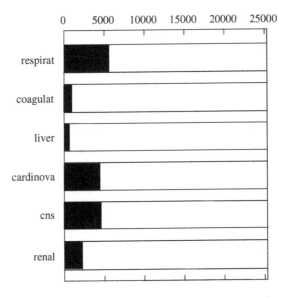

Figure 3: The organ failure *true* (in black) and *false* (in white) proportions

to improve the use of the latter outcomes. First, the training sets were balanced to contain similar proportions of positive and negative examples. Then, the number of hidden nodes and training epochs was increased. As the result of these changes, an improved performance was gained, specially in terms of *sensitivity*.

A final comparison between the SOFA score and the proposed solution (the **C** improved setup), still favors the former, although the *Sensitivity* values are close (being even higher for the **C** configuration in the *coagulation* and *liver systems*). Nevertheless, it is important to stress the main goal of this work: to show that is it possible to diagnose organ failure by using cheap and fast intermediate outcomes (within our knowledge this is done for the first time). The results so far obtained give an overall accuracy of 70%, which although not authoritative, still back this claim. In addiction, the proposed approach opens room for the development of automatic tools for clinical decision support, which are expected to enhance the physician response.

In future research it is intend to improve the performances, by exploring different *Neural Network* types, such as *Radial Basis Functions* (Bishop, 1995). Another interesting direction is based in the use of alternative *Neural Network* training algorithms, which can optimize other learning functions (e.g., *Evolutionary Algorithms* (Rocha et al., 2003)), since the gradient-based methods (e.g., the *RPROP* (Riedmiller, 1994)) work by minimizing the *Sum Squared Error*, a target which does not necessarily correspond to maximizing the *Sensitivity* and *Specificity* rates. Finally, it is intended to enlarge the experiments to other *ICU* applications (e.g., predicting *life expectancy*).

REFERENCES

Bishop, C. (1995). *Neural Networks for Pattern Recognition*. Oxford University Press.

Cios, K. and Moore, G. (2002). Uniqueness of Medical Data Mining. *Artificial Intelligence in Medicine*, 26(1-2):1–24.

Dybowski, R. (2000). Neural Computation in Medicine: Perspectives and Prospects. In et al., H. M., editor, *Proceedings of the ANNIMAB-1 Conference (Artificial Neural Networks in Medicine and Biology)*, pages 26–36. Springer.

Essex-Sorlie, D. (1995). *Medical Biostatistics & Epidemiology: Examination & Board Review*. McGraw-Hill/Appleton & Lange, International edition.

Flexer, A. (1996). Statistical evaluation of neural networks experiments: Minimum requirements and current practice. In *Proceedings of the 13th European Meeting on Cybernetics and Systems Research*, volume 2, pages 1005–1008, Vienna, Austria.

Hand, D., Mannila, H., and Smyth, P. (2001). *Principles of Data Mining*. MIT Press, Cambridge, MA.

Haykin, S. (1999). *Neural Networks - A Compreensive Foundation*. Prentice-Hall, New Jersey, 2nd edition.

Kohavi, R. and Provost, F. (1998). Glossary of Terms. *Machine Learning*, 30(2/3):271–274.

Prechelt, L. (1998). *Early Stopping – but when?* In: *Neural Networks: Tricks of the trade*, Springer Verlag, Heidelberg.

Riedmiller, M. (1994). Supervised Learning in Multilayer Perceptrons - from Backpropagation to Adaptive Learning Techniques. *Computer Standards and Interfaces*, 16.

Rocha, M., Cortez, P., and Neves, J. (2003). Evolutionary Neural Network Learning. In Pires, F. and Abreu, S., editors, *Progress in Artificial Intelligence, EPIA 2003 Proceedings, LNAI 2902*, pages 24–28, Beja, Portugal. Springer.

Santos, M., Neves, J., Abelha, A., Silva, A., and Rua, F. (2002). Augmented Data Mining Over Clinical Databases Using Learning Classifier System. In *Proceedings of the 4th Int. Conf. on Enterprise Information Systems - ICEIS 2002*, pages 512–516, Ciudad Real, Spain.

Teres, D. and Pekow, P. (2000). Assessment data elements in a severity scoring system (Editorial). *Intensive Care Med*, 26:263–264.

Vincent, J., Moreno, R., Takala, J., Willatss, S., Mendonca, A. D., Bruining, H., Reinhart, C., Suter, P., and Thijs, L. (1996). The SOFA (Sepsis-related Organ Failure Assessment) score to describe organ dysfunction / failure. *Intensive Care Med*, 22:707–710.

Witten, I. and Frank, E. (2000). *Data Mining: Practical Machine Learning Tools and Techniques with Java Implementations*. Morgan Kaufmann, San Francisco, CA.

MINING THE RELATIONSHIPS IN THE FORM OF THE PREDISPOSING FACTORS AND CO-INCIDENT FACTORS AMONG NUMERICAL DYNAMIC ATTRIBUTES IN TIME SERIES DATA SET BY USING THE COMBINATION OF SOME EXISTING TECHNIQUES

Suwimon Kooptiwoot, M. Abdus Salam

School of Information Technologies, The University of Sydney, Sydney, Australia
Email:{ suwimon, msalam }@it.usyd.edu.au

Keywords: Temporal Mining, Time series data set, numerical data, predisposing factor, co-incident factor

Abstract: Temporal mining is a natural extension of data mining with added capabilities of discovering interesting patterns, inferring relationships of contextual and temporal proximity and may also lead to possible cause-effect associations. Temporal mining covers a wide range of paradigms for knowledge modeling and discovery. A common practice is to discover frequent sequences and patterns of a single variable. In this paper we present a new algorithm which is the combination of many existing ideas consists of the reference event as proposed in (Bettini, Wang et al. 1998), the event detection technique proposed in (Guralnik and Srivastava 1999), the large fraction proposed in (Mannila, Toivonen et al. 1997), the causal inference proposed in (Blum 1982) We use all of these ideas to build up our new algorithm for the discovery of multi-variable sequences in the form of the predisposing factor and co-incident factor of the reference event of interest. We define the event as positive direction of data change or negative direction of data change above a threshold value. From these patterns we infer predisposing and co-incident factors with respect to a reference variable. For this purpose we study the Open Source Software data collected from SourceForge website. Out of 240+ attributes we only consider thirteen time dependent attributes such as Page-views, Download, Bugs0, Bugs1, Support0, Support1, Patches0, Patches1, Tracker0, Tracker1, Tasks0, Tasks1 and CVS. These attributes indicate the degree and patterns of activities of projects through the course of their progress. The number of the Download is a good indication of the progress of the projects. So we use the Download as the reference attribute. We also test our algorithm with four synthetic data sets including noise up to 50 %. The results show that our algorithm can work well and tolerate the noise data.

1 INTRODUCTION

Time series mining has wide range of applications and mainly discovers movement pattern of the data, for example stock market, ECG(Electro-cardiograms) weather patterns, etc. There are four main types of movement of data: 1. Long-term or trend pattern 2. Cyclic movement or cyclic variation 3. Seasonal movement or seasonal variation 4. Irregular or random movements.

Full sequential pattern is kind of long term or trend movement, which can be cyclic pattern like machine working pattern. The idea is to catch the error pattern which is different from the normal pattern in the process of that machine. For trend movement, we try to find the pattern of change that can be used to estimate the next unknown value at the next time point or in any specific time point in the future.

A periodic pattern repeats itself throughout the time series and this part of data is called a segment. The main idea is to separate the data into piecewise periodic segments.

There can be a problem with periodic behavior within only one segment of time series data or seasonal pattern. There are several algorithms to separate segment to find change point, or event.

There are some works (Agrawal and Srikant 1995; Lu, Han et al. 1998) that applied the Apriori-like algorithm to find the relationship among attributes, but these work still point to only one dynamic attribute. Then we find the association

135

I. Seruca et al. (eds.), Enterprise Information Systems VI, 135–142.

among static attributes by using the dynamic attribute of interest. The work in (Tung, Lu et al. 1999) proposed the idea of finding inter-transaction association rules such as

RULE1: If the prices of IBM and SUN go up, Microsoft's will most likely (80 % of time) go up the next day.

Event detection from time series data (Guralnik and Srivastava 1999) utilises the interesting event detection idea, that is, a dynamic phenomenon is considered whose behaviour changes over time to be considered as a qualitatively significant change.

It is interesting if we can find the relationship among dynamic attributes in time series data which consist of many dynamic attributes in numerical form. We attempt to find the relationship that gives the factors that can be regarded as the cause and effect of the event of interest. We call these factors as the predisposing and co-incident factors with respect to a reference variable. The predisposing factor can tell us the event of other dynamic attributes which mostly happen before the reference event happens. And the co-incident factor can tell us the event of other dynamic attributes which mostly happens at the same time or a little bit after the reference event happens.

2 TEMPORAL MINING

An interesting work in (Roddick and Spiliopoulou 2002), they review research related to the temporal mining and their contributions related to various aspects of the temporal data mining and knowledge discovery and also briefly discuss the relevant previous work .

In majority of time series analysis, we either focus on prediction of the curve of a single time series or the discovery of similarities among multiple time series. We call time dependent variable as dynamic variable and call time independent variable as static variable.

Trend analysis focuses on how to estimate the value of dynamic attribute of interest at the next time point or at a specific time point in the future.

There are many kinds of patterns depending on application data. We can separate pattern types into four groups.

1. Cyclic pattern is the pattern which has the exact format and repeat the same format to be cyclic form, for example, ECG, tidal cycle, sunrise-sunset

2. Periodic pattern is the pattern which has the exact format in only part of cycle and repeat this exact format at the same part of cycle, for example, "Everyday morning at 7:30-8:00 am., Sandy has breakfast", the rest of the day Sandy has many

activities which no exact pattern. The cycle of the day, every day the exact format happen only in the morning at 7:30-8:00 am.

3. Seasonal pattern is the pattern which is a sub type of cyclic pattern and periodic pattern. There is a pattern at a specific range of time during the year's cycle, for example, half year sales, fruit season, etc.

4. Irregular pattern is the pattern which doesn't have the exact pattern in cycle, for example, network alarm, computer crash.

2.1 Trend Analysis Problem

Trend analysis works are normally done by finding the cyclic patterns of one numerical dynamic attribute of interest. Once we know the exact pattern of this attribute, we can forecast the value of this attribute in the future. If we cannot find the cycle pattern of this attribute, we can use moving average window or exponential moving average window (Weiss and Indurkhya 1998; Kantardzic 2003) to estimate the value of this dynamic attribute at the next time point or at the specific time point in the future.

2.2 Pattern Finding Problem

In pattern finding problem, we have to find the change point to be the starting point and the end point of cycle or segment. Then we try to look for the segment or cycle pattern that is repeated in the whole data set. To see which type of pattern it is, that is, the cyclic pattern of periodic pattern, seasonal pattern or irregular pattern and observe the pattern.

The pattern matching problem is to find the way of matching the segment patterns. Pattern matching, can be exact pattern (Dasgupta and Forrest 1995) or rough pattern matching (Hirano, Sun et al. 2001; Keogh, Chu et al. 2001; Hirano and Tsumoto 2002), depending on the data application. The exact pattern is, for example, the cycle of machine working. The rough pattern is, for example, the hormone level in human body.

Another problem is the multi-scale pattern matching problem as seen in (Ueda and S.Suzuki 1990; Hirano, Sun et al. 2001; Hirano and Tsumoto 2001) to match patterns in different time scales.

One interesting work is Knowledge discovery in Time Series Databases (Last, Klein et al. 2001) . Last et al. proposed the whole process of knowledge discovery in time series data bases. They used signal processing techniques and the information-theoretic fuzzy approach. The computational theory of perception (CTP) is used to reduce the set of extracted rules by fuzzification and aggregation.

Another interesting work done in time series (Keogh, Lonardi et al. 2002) proposed an algorithm that detects surprising patterns in a time series database in linear space and time. This algorithm is named TARZAN. The definition of surprising in this algorithm is general and domain independent, describing a pattern as surprising if the frequency with which we encounter it differs greatly from that expected given previous experience.

3   PROBLEM

We get an OSS data set from http://sourceforge.net which is the world's largest Open Source software development website. There are 1,097,341 records, 41,540 projects in this data set. This data set consists of seventeen attributes include time attribute. The time attribute of each record in this data set is monthly. Each project in this data set is a software. There are many attributes that show various activities. We are interested in thirteen attributes which indicate the number of activities in this data set. The data of these thirteen attributes are all numeric. The value of the Download attribute is the number of the downloads. So the Download attribute is the indicator showing how popular the software is and show how successful the development of the software is. We are interested in the significant change of the number of the Download attribute. Then we employ the idea of the event detection technique proposed by (Guralnik and Srivastava 1999) to detect the event of the Download attribute. The event of our interest is the direction of the significant change of the data which can be up or down.

We want to find the predisposing factor and the co-incident factor of the Download event. We employ the same idea about the reference event as proposed in (Bettini, Wang et al. 1998) which is the fixed event of interest and we want to find the other events related to the reference event. So we call the Download attribute as the reference attribute and call the event of the Download attribute as the reference event.

The predisposing factor of the reference event can possibly be the cause of the reference event or the cause of the other event which is the cause of the reference event. And the co-incident factor of the reference event can possibly be the effect of the reference event or the effect of the other event which is the effect of the reference event somehow or be the event happening at the same time as the reference event happens or can be the result from the same cause of the reference event or just be the result from the other event which happens at the same time of the

reference event happens. To make this concept clear, see the example as follow

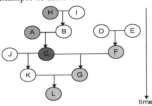

Figure1: The relationships among the events over time

If we have the event A, B, C, D, E, F, G, H, I, J, K, L and the relationships among them as shown in Figure 1. That is H and I give B; A and B give C; D and E give F; C and F give G; J and C give K; K and G give L. But in our data set consists of only A, C, F, G, H, L. And the reference event is C. We can see that H and A happen before C, we may say that A is the cause of C and/or H is the cause of C. But in the real relationship as shown above, we know that H is not the cause of C directly or it is not because A and H give C. So we call A and H are the predisposing factors of C. And we find that F happens at the same time as C happens. And G and L happen after C. We call F as the co-incident factor of C. We can see from the relationship that G is the result from C and F. L is the result from G which is the result from C. And F is the co-factor of C that gives G. Only G is the result from C directly. L is the result from G which is the result from C.

We want to find the exact relationships among these events. Unfortunately, no one can guarantee that our data set of consideration consists of all of the related factors or events. We can see from the diagram or the relationship shown in the example that the relationship among the events can be complex. And if we don't have all of the related events, we cannot find all of the real relationships. So what we can do with the possible incomplete data set is mining the predisposing factor and co-incident factor of the reference event. Then the users can further consider these factors and collect more data which related to the reference event and explore more in depth by themselves on the expert ways in their specific fields.

The main idea in this part is the predisposing factor can possibly be the cause of the reference event and the co-incident factor can possible be the effect of the reference event. So we employ the same idea as proposed in (Blum 1982; Blum 1982) that cause happens before the effect. The effect happens after the cause. We call the time point when the reference event happens as the current time point. We call the time point before the current time point as the previous time point. And we call the time point after the current time point as the post time point. Then we define the predisposing factor of the reference event as the event which happens at the previous time point. And we define the co-incident factor of the reference event as the event happens at the current time point and/or the post time point.

4 BASIC DEFINITIONS AND FRAMEWORK

The method to interpret the result is selecting the large fraction of the positive slope and the negative slope at each time point. If it is at the previous time point that means it is the predisposing factor. If it is at the current time point and/or the post time point that means it is the co-incident factor.

Definition 1: A time series data set is a set of records r such that each record contains a set of attributes and a time attribute. The value of time attribute is the point of time on time scale such as month, year.

$$r_j = \{ a_1, a_2, a_3, \ldots, a_m, t_j \}$$

where

r_j is the jth record in data set

Definition 2: There are two types of the attribute in time series data set. Attribute that depends on time is dynamic attribute ($\square$), other wise, it is static attribute (S).

Definition 3: Time point (t_i) is the time point on time scale.

Definition 4: Time interval is the range of time between two time points $[t_1, t_2]$. We may refer to the end time point of interval (t_2).

Definition 5: An attribute function is a function of time whose elements are extracted from the value of attribute i in the records, and is denoted as a function in time, $a_i(t_x)$

$$a_i(t_x) = a_i \in r_j$$

where

a_i attribute i;

t_x time stamp associated with this record

Definition 6: A feature is defined on a time interval $[t_1, t_2]$, if some attribute function $a_i(t)$ can be approximated to another function $\Phi(t)$ in time, for example,

$$a_i(t) \approx \Phi(t), \ \forall t \in [t_1, t_2]$$

We say that Φ and its parameters are features of $a_i(t)$ in that interval $[t_1, t_2]$.

If $\Phi(t) = \alpha_i t + \beta_i$ in some intervals, we can say that in the interval, the function $a_i(t)$ has a slope of α_i where slope is a feature extracted from $a_i(t)$ in that interval

Definition 7: Slope (α_i) is the change of value of a dynamic attribute (a_i) between two adjacent time points.

$$\alpha_i = (a_{i(t_x)} - a_{i(t_{x-1})}) / t_x - t_{x-1}$$

where

$a_{i(t_x)}$ is the value of a_i at the time point t_x

$a_i(t_{x-1})$ is the value of a_i at the time point t_{x-1}

Definition 8: Slope direction $d(\alpha_i)$ is the direction of slope.

If $\alpha_i > 0$, we say $d_\alpha = 1$

If $\alpha_i < 0$, we say $d_\alpha = -1$

If $\alpha_i \cong 0$, we say $d_\alpha = 0$

Definition 9: A significant slope threshold (δI) is the significant slope level specified by user.

Definition 10: Reference attribute (a_t) is the attribute of interest. We want to find the relationship between the reference attribute and the other dynamic attributes in the data set.

Definition 11: An event ($E1$) is detected if $\alpha_i \geq \delta I$

Definition 12: Current time point (t_c) is the time point at which reference variable's event is detected.

Definition 13: Previous time point (t_{c-1}) is the previous adjacent time point of t_c

Definition 14: Post time point (t_{c+1}) is the post adjacent time point of t_c

Proposition 1: Predisposing factor of a_t denoted as $PE1a_t$ is an ordered pair (a_i, d_α) when $a_i \in \square$

If $^{np}a_i\, t_{c-1} > \,^{nn}a_i\, t_{c-1}$, then $PE1a_t \approx (a_i, 1)$

If $^{np}a_i\, t_{c-1} < \,^{nn}a_i\, t_{c-1}$, then $PE1a_t \approx (a_i, -1)$

where

$^{np}a_i\, t_{c-1}$ is the number of positive slope of $E1$ of a_i at t_{c-1}

$^{nn}a_i\, t_{c-1}$ is the number of negative slope of $E1$ of a_i at t_{c-1}

Proposition 2: Co-incident factor of a_t denoted as $CE1a_t$ is an ordered pair (a_i, d_α) when $a_i \in \square$

If $((^{np}a_i\, t_c > \,^{nn}a_i\, t_c) \vee (^{np}a_i\, t_{c+1} > \,^{nn}a_i\, t_{c+1}))$, then $CE1a_t \approx (a_i, 1)$

If $((^{np}a_i\, t_c < \,^{nn}a_i\, t_c) \vee (^{np}a_i\, t_{c+1} < \,^{nn}a_i\, t_{c+1}))$, then $CE1a_t \approx (a_i, -1)$

where

$^{np}a_i\, t_c$ is the number of positive slope of $E1$ of a_i at t_c

$^{nn}a_i\, t_c$ is the number of negative slope of $E1$ of a_i at t_c

$^{np}a_i\, t_{c+1}$ is the number of positive slope of $E1$ of a_i at t_{c+1}

$^{nn}a_i\, t_{c+1}$ is the number of negative slope of $E1$ of a_i at t_{c+1}

5 ALGORITHM

Now we present a new algorithm.

Input: The data set which consists of numerical dynamic attributes. Sort this data set in ascending order by time, a_t, δI

Output: $^{np}a_i\, t_{c-1}$, $^{nn}a_i\, t_{c-1}$, $^{np}a_i\, t_c$, $^{nn}a_i\, t_c$, $^{np}a_i\, t_{c+1}$, $^{nn}a_i\, t_{c+1}$, $PE1a_t$, $CE1a_t$

Method:

For all a_i

    For all time interval $[t_x , t_{x+1}]$

        Calculate α_i

           For a_t

               If $\alpha_i \geq \delta I$

                    Set that time point as t_c

                    Group record of 3 time points t_{c-1} t_c t_{c+1}

Count $^{np}a_i$ t_{c-1} , $^{nn}a_i$ t_{c-1} , $^{np}a_i$ t_c , $^{nn}a_i$ t_c , $^{np}a_i$ t_{c+1} , $^{nn}a_i$ t_{c+1}

// interpret the result

If $^{np}a_i$ t_{c-1} > $^{nn}a_i$ t_{c-1} , then $PE1a_t \approx (a_i , 1)$

If $^{np}a_i$ t_{c-1} < $^{nn}a_i$ t_{c-1} , then $PE1a_t \approx (a_i , -1)$

If $^{np}a_i$ t_c > $^{nn}a_i$ t_c , then $CE1a_t \approx (a_i , 1)$

If $^{np}a_i$ t_c < $^{nn}a_i$ t_c , then $CE1a_t \approx (a_i , -1)$

If $^{np}a_i$ t_{c+1} > $^{nn}a_i$ t_{c+1} , then $CE1a_t \approx (a_i , 1)$

If $^{np}a_i$ t_{c+1} < $^{nn}a_i$ t_{c+1} , then $CE1a_t \approx (a_i , -1)$

For the event, the data change direction, we employ the method proposed by (Mannila, Toivonen et al. 1997) that is using the large fraction to judge the data change direction of the attribute of consideration.

Using the combination of the ideas mentioned above, we can find the predisposing factor and the co-incident factor of the reference event of interest. The steps to do this task are

1. Set the threshold of the data change of the reference attribute.

2. Use this data change threshold to find the event which is the change of the data of the reference attribute between two adjacent time point is equal to or higher than the threshold, and mark that time point as the current time point

3. Look at the previous adjacent time point to find the predisposing factor and the post adjacent time point of the current time point to find the co-incident factor

4. Separate the case of the reference event to be the positive direction and the negative direction

4.1 For each case, count the number of the positive change direction and the number of the negative change direction of the other attributes in consideration.

4.2 Select the large fraction between the number of the positive change direction and the number of the negative change direction. If the number of the positive direction is larger than the number of the negative direction, we say that the positive change direction of the considered attribute is the factor. Otherwise, we say that the negative change direction of the considered attribute is the factor. If the factor is found at the previous time point, we say that the factor is the predisposing factor. If the factor is found at the current time

point or the post time point, we say that the factor is the co-incident factor.

We don't use the threshold to find the event of the other attributes because of the idea of the degree of importance (Salam 2001). For example, the effects of the different kind of chilly on our food are different. Only small amount of the very hot chilly make our food very hot. Very much of sweet chilly make our food not so spicy. We see that the same amount of the different kind of chilly creates the different level of the hotness in our food. The very hot chilly has the degree of importance in our food higher than the sweet chilly. Another example, about the number of Download of the software A, we can see that normal factors effect on the number of Download are still there. But in case there is a lecturer or a teacher assign his/her 300 students in his/her class to test the software A and report the result to him/her within 2 weeks. This assignment makes the number of Download of the software A increase significantly in very short time. For the other software, software B, is in the same situation or the same quality or the same other factors as the software A which should get the same number of Download as the software A, but there is no lecturer or teacher assigning his/her 300 students to test it. The number of Download of the software B is lower than the software A. Or in case there is a teacher or lecturer assign his/her 500 students to test 2 or 3 softwares and report the results to him/her within one month. This event makes the number of Download of many softwares increase in very short time. Such incidental factors have the potential to skew the results. Such factors may have high degree of importance that effect on the number of Download of the software. It is the same as the only small amount of the data change of some attributes can make the data of the reference attribute change very much. So we do not specify the threshold of the event of the other attributes to be considered as the predisposing factor or the co-incident factor. For example, the graph of the data is shown in Graph 1

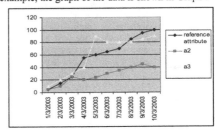

Graph 1: the data in the graph

We calculate the slope value showing how much the data change and the direction of the data change per time unit.

Then we set the data change threshold as 15. We use this threshold to find the reference event. We find the reference event at the time 4/03. Then we mark this time point as the current time point. Next we look at the previous time point, 3/03, for the predisposing factor, we find that a2 with the positive direction and a3 with positive direction are the predisposing factor of the reference event. Then we look at the current time point and the post time point, 4/03 and 5/03, for the co-incident factor, we find that at the current time point, a2 with the negative direction and a3 with the positive direction are the co-incident factor. And at the post time point, a2 with the positive direction and a3 with the positive direction are the co-incident factor. We can summarize the result in the pattern table as shown in Table 1.

Table 1: the direction of each attribute at each time point

	Previous time point	Current time point	Post time point
a2	Up	down	up
a3	Up	up	up

6 OSS DATA

The OSS data on SourceForge website has been collected over the last few years. Initially some projects were listed with the SourceForge at various developmental stages. Since then a large number of new projects have been added at different time points and are progressing at different pace. Though they are at different developmental stages, there data is still collected at regular intervals of one month. Due to this a global comparison of all of the projects poses many problems. Here we wish to explore local trends at each event.

The main idea is to choose an event in the reference variable as a reference time point and mine the relationship with other numerical dynamic attributes. By using this method, we wish to explore the predisposing and co-incident factors of the reference event of interest in time series data set. The predisposing factor is the factor which can be the cause of the reference event or the factor that has effect on the reference event somehow. The co-incident factor is the factor that can be the effect of the reference attribute or the factor that is also the result of the predisposing factor of the reference event or the reference event effect on it somehow.

7 EXPERIMENTS

We apply our method with one OSS data set which consists of 17 attributes (Project name, Month-Year, Rank0, Rank1, Page-views, Download, Bugs0, Bugs1, Support0, Support1, Patches0, Patches1, Tracker0, Tracker1, Tasks0, Tasks1, CVS. This data set consists of 41,540 projects, 1,097,341 records

7.1 Results

We select the Download attribute to be the reference attribute. And we set the significant data change threshold as 50. The results are separated into two cases. The first case is the data change direction of the Download is positive. The second is the data change direction of the Download is negative. The results are shown in Table 2 and Table 3 accordingly.

7.1.1 Slope Direction of the Download is Positive

Table 2: Summary of the results in case the slope direction of the Download is positive

	previous	current	post
P/V	Up	up	down
Bugs0	Up	up	down
Bugs1	Up	up	down
Support0	up	up	down
Support1	up	up	down
Patches0	up	up	down
Patches1	up	up	down
Tracker0	up	up	down
Tracker1	up	up	down
Tasks0	down	down	down
Tasks1	up	up	down
CVS	up	up	down

From this finding we can see that the predisposing factors of the number of the Download significantly increases are the number of Tasks0 decreases and the rest of other attributes which consists of Page views, Bugs0, Bugs1, Support0, Support1, Patches0, Patches1, Tracker0, Tracker1, Tasks1, CVS increase. At the same time interval, the co-incident factors of the number of Download significantly increases are the same as its predisposing factors but after that the number of all of the other attributes decreases.

7.1.2 Slope Direction of the Download is Negative

Table 3: Summary of the result in case the slope direction of the Download is negative

	previous	current	post
P/V	up	down	down
Bugs0	up	down	down
Bugs1	up	down	up
Support0	up	down	down
Support1	up	down	up
Patches0	up	down	up
Patches1	up	down	up
Tracker0	up	down	down
Tracker1	up	down	up
Tasks0	down	down	down
Tasks1	down	down	down
CVS	down	down	down

From these results, we find that the predisposing factors of the number of the Download significantly decreases are the number of almost all of the other attributes increases, except only the number of Tasks0, Tasks1 and CVS decrease. And the co-incident factors of the number of Download significantly decrease are the number of all of the other attributes decrease at the same time interval. After that the number P/V, Bugs0, Support0, Tracker0, Tasks0, Tasks1, CVS decrease and the number of Bugs1, Support1, Patches0, Patches1, Tracker1 increase .

8 PERFORMANCE

Our methods consume time to find the predisposing factor and the co-incident factor of the reference event just in $O(n)$ where n is the number of the total records. The most time consuming is the time for calculating the slope (the data change) of every two adjacent time points of the same project which take

time $O(n)$. And we have to spend time to select the reference event by using the threshold which takes time $O(n)$. We have to spend time to group records around the reference event (at the previous time point, the current time point and the post time point) which is $O(n)$. And the time for counting the number of events of the other attributes at each time point around the current time point is $O(n)$. The time in overall process can be approximate to $O(n)$, which is not exponential. So our methods are good enough to apply in the big real life data set.

In our experiments we use PC PentiumIV 1.6 GHz, RAM 1 GB. The operating system is MS WindowsXP Professional. We implement these algorithms in Perl 5.8 on command line. The data set test has 1,097,341 records, 41, 540 projects with total 17 attributes. The number of attributes of consideration is 13 attributes. The size of this data set is about 48 MB.

We want to see if our program consume running time in linear scale with the size of the data or not. Then we test with the different number of records in each file and run each file at a time. The result is shown in Graph 2.

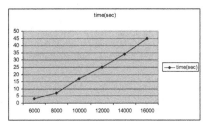

Graph 2: Running time (in seconds) and the number of records to be run at a time

From this result confirm us that our algorithm consumes execution time in linear scale with the number of records.

8.1 Accuracy Test with Synthetic Data Sets

We synthesize 4 data sets as follow
1. Correct complete data set
2. Put 5 % of noise in the first data set
3. Put 20 % of noise in the first data set
4. Put 50 % of noise in the first data set

We set the data change threshold as 10. The result is almost all of four data sets correct, except only at the third data set with 20 % of noise, there is only one point in the result different from the others, that is, the catalyst at the current point changes to be positive slope instead of steady.

9 CONCLUSION

The combination of the existing methods to be our new algorithm can be used to mine the predisposing factor and co-incident factor of the reference event very well. As seen in our experiments, our proposed algorithm can be applied to both the synthetic and the real life data set. The performance of our algorithm is also good. They consume execution time just in linear time scale and also tolerate to the noise data.

10 DISCUSSION

The threshold is the indicator to select the event which is the significant change of the data of the attribute of consideration. When we use the different thresholds in detecting the events, the results can be different. So setting the threshold of the data change have to be well justified. It can be justified by looking at the data and observing the characteristic of the attributes of interest. The users have to realize that the results they get can be different depending on their threshold setting. The threshold reflects the degree of importance of the predisposing factor and the co-incident factor to the reference event. If the degree of importance of an attribute is very high, just little change of the data of that attribute can make the data of the reference attribute change very much. So for this reason setting the threshold value is of utmost importance for the accuracy and reliability of the results.

REFERENCES

Agrawal, R. and Srikant R., 1995. *Mining Sequential Patterns*. In Proceedings of the IEEE International Conference on Data Engineering, Taipei, Taiwan.

Bettini, C., Wang S., et al. 1998. *Discovering Frequent Event Patterns with Multiple Granularities in Time Sequences*. In IEEE Transactions on Knowledge and Data Engineering 10(2).

Blum, R. L., 1982. *Discovery, Confirmation and Interpretation of Causal Relationships from a Large Time-Oriented Clinical Databases: The Rx Project*. Computers and Biomedical Research 15(2): 164-187.

Dasgupta, D. and Forrest S., 1995. *Novelty Detection in Time Series Data using Ideas from Immunology*. In Proceedings of the 5th International Conference on Intelligent Systems, Reno, Nevada.

Guralnik, V. and Srivastava J., 1999. *Event Detection from Time Series Data*. In KDD-99, San Diego, CA USA.

Hirano, S., Sun X., et al., 2001. *Analysis of Time-series Medical Databases Using Multiscale Structure Matching and Rough Sets-Based Clustering Technique*. In IEEE International Fuzzy Systems Conference.

Hirano, S. and Tsumoto S., 2001. *A Knowledge-Oriented Clustering Technique Based on Rough Sets*. In 25th Annual International Computer Software and Applications Conference (COMPSAC'01), Chicago, Illinois.

Hirano, S. and Tsumoto S., 2002. *Mining Similar Temporal Patterns in Long Time-Series Data and Its Application to Medicine*. In IEEE: 219-226.

Kantardzic, M., 2003. *Data Mining Concepts, Models, Methods, and Algorithms*. USA, IEEE Press.

Keogh, E., Chu S., et al., 2001. *An Online Algorithm for Segmenting Time Series*. In Proceedings of IEEE International Conference on Data Mining, 2001.

Keogh, E., Lonardi S., et al., 2002. *Finding Surprising Patterns in a Time Series Database in Linear Time and Space*. In Proceedings of The Eighth ACM SIGKDD International Conference on Knowledge Discovery and Data Mining (KDD '02), Edmonton, Alberta, Canada.

Last, M., Klein Y., et al., 2001. *Knowledge Discovery in Time Series Databases*. In IEEE Transactions on Systems, Man, and Cybernetics 31(1): 160-169.

Lu, H., Han J., et al., 1998. *Stock Movement Prediction and N-Dimensional Inter-Transaction Association Rules*. In Proc. of 1998 SIGMOD'98 Workshop on Research Issues on Data Mining and Knowledge Discovery (DMKD'98) ,, Seattle, Washington.

Mannila, H., Toivonen H., et al., 1997. *Discovery of frequent episodes in event sequences*. In Data Mining and Knowledge Discovery 1(3): 258-289.

Roddick, J. F. and Spiliopoulou M., 2002. *A Survey of Temporal Knowledge Discovery Paradigms and Methods*. In IEEE Transactions on Knowledge and Data Mining 14(4): 750-767.

Salam, M. A., 2001. *Quasi Fuzzy Paths in Semantic Networks*. In Proceedings 10th IEEE International Conference on Fuzzy Systems, Melbourne, Australia.

Tung, A., Lu H., et al., 1999. *Breaking the Barrier of Transactions: Mining Inter-Transaction Association Rules*. In Proceedings of the Fifth International on Knowledge Discovery and Data Mining [KDD 99], San Diego, CA.

Ueda, N. and Suzuki S., 1990. *A Matching Algorithm of Deformed Planar Curves Using Multiscale Convex/Concave Structures*. In JEICE Transactions on Information and Systems J73-D-II(7): 992-1000.

Weiss, S. M. and Indurkhya N., 1998. *Predictive Data Mining*. San Francisco, California, Morgn Kaufmann Publsihers, Inc.

INFORMATION ACCESS VIA TOPIC HIERARCHIES AND THEMATIC ANNOTATIONS FROM DOCUMENT COLLECTIONS

Hermine Njike Fotzo, Patrick Gallinari

Université de Paris6 – LIP6, 8 rue du Capitaine Scott, 75015 Paris, France
Email : Hermine.Njike-Fotzo@lip6.fr, Patrick.Gallinari@lip6.fr

Keywords: Concept hierarchies, typed hyperlinks generation, thematic annotations, text segmentation.

Abstract: With the development and the availability of large textual corpora, there is a need for enriching and organizing these corpora so as to make easier the research and navigation among the documents. The Semantic Web research focuses on augmenting ordinary Web pages with semantics. Indeed, wealth of information exists today in electronic form, they cannot be easily processed by computers due to lack of external semantics. Furthermore, the semantic addition is an help for user to locate, process information and compare documents contents. For now, Semantic Web research has been focused on the standardization, internal structuring of pages, and sharing of ontologies in a variety of domains. Concerning external structuring, hypertext and information retrieval communities propose to indicate relations between documents via hyperlinks or by organizing documents into concepts hierarchies, both being manually developed. We consider here the problem of automatically structuring and organizing corpora in a way that reflects semantic relations between documents. We propose an algorithm for automatically inferring concepts hierarchies from a corpus. We then show how this method may be used to create specialization/generalization links between documents leading to document hierarchies. As a byproduct, documents are annotated with keywords giving the main concepts present in the documents. We also introduce numerical criteria for measuring the relevance of the automatically generated hierarchies and describe some experiments performed on data from the LookSmart and New Scientist web sites.

1 INTRODUCTION

Large textual and multimedia databases are nowadays widely available but their exploitation is restricted by the lack of meta-information about their structure and semantics. Many such collections like those gathered by most search engines are loosely structured. Some have been manually structured, at the expense of an important effort. This is the case of hierarchies like those of internet portals (Yahoo, LookSmart, Infoseek, etc) or of large collections like MEDLINE: documents are gathered into topics, which are themselves organized into a hierarchy going from the most general to the most specific [G. Källgren, 1988]. Hypertext multimedia products are another example of structured collections: documents are usually grouped into different topics and subtopics with links between the different entities. Generally speaking, structuring collections makes easier navigating the collection, accessing information parts, maintaining and enriching the collection. Manual structuring relies on a large amount of qualified human

resources and can be performed only in the context of large collaborative projects like e.g. in medical classification systems or for specific commercial products. In order to help this process it would be most needful to rely on automatic or semi-automatic tools for structuring document collections.

The Semantic Web whose goal is to help users to locate, organize, process information and compare documents contents, has for now focalised on the standardization, internal structuring of documents and sharing of ontologies in a variety of domains. The short-term goal is to transform existing sources (stored as HTML pages, in databases...) into a machine-understandable form. RDF (resources description form) has been created for computers but Semantic Web should be equally accessible by computers using specialized languages and interchange formats, and humans using natural language. Although the general framework of Semantic Web includes provisions for natural language technology, such techniques have largely been ignored. Nevertheless we can quote [B. Katz, J. Lin, 2002] who propose a method to augment

I. Seruca et al. (eds.), Enterprise Information Systems VI, 143–150.

RDF with natural language to be more familiar for users.

In this context, we study here how to automatically structure collections by deriving concept hierarchies from a document collection and how to automatically generate from that a document hierarchy. The concept hierarchy relies on the discovering of "specialization/generalization" relations between the concepts which appear in the documents of a corpus. Concepts are themselves automatically identified from the set of documents.

This method creates "specialization / generalization" links between documents and document parts. It can be considered as a technique for the automatic creation of specific typed links between information parts. Such typed links have been advocated by different authors as a mean for structuring and navigating collections. It also associates to each document a set of keyword representative of the main concepts in the document.

The proposed method is fully automatic and the hierarchies are directly extracted from the corpus, and could be used for any document collection. It could also serve as a basis for a manual organization.

The paper is organized as follows. In section 2 we introduce previous related work. In section 3, we describe our algorithm for the automatic generation of typed relations "specialization/generalization" between concepts and documents and the corresponding hierarchies. In section 4 we discuss how our algorithm answers some questions of the Web Semantic research. In section 5 we propose numerical criteria for measuring the relevance of our method. Section 6, describes experiments performed on small corpus extracted from Looksmart and New Scientists hierarchies.

2 PREVIOUS WORK

In this section we present related work on automatically structuring document collection. We discuss work on the generation of concept hierarchies and on the discovering of typed links between document parts. Since for identifying concepts, we perform document segmentation into homogeneous themes, we also briefly present this problematic and describe the segmentation method we use. We also give some pointers on work on natural language annotations for the Semantic Web.

Many authors agree about the importance of typed links in hypertext systems. Such links might prove useful for providing a navigation context or for improving research engines performances.

Some authors have developed links typologies. [Randall Trigg, 1983] proposes a set of useful types for

scientific corpora, but many of the types can be adapted to other corpora. [C. Cleary, R. Bareiss, 1996] propose a set of types inspired by the conversational theory. These links are usually manually created.

[J. Allan, 1996] proposes an automatic method for inferring a few typed links (revision, abstract/expansion links). His philosophy is close to the one used in this paper, in that he chose to avoid complex text analysis techniques. He deduces the type of a link between two documents by analysing the similarity graph of their subparts (paragraphs). We too use similarity graphs (although of different nature) and corpus statistics to infer a relation between concepts and documents.

The generation of hierarchies is a classical problem in information retrieval. In most cases the hierarchies are manually built and only the classification of documents into the hierarchy is automatic. Clustering techniques have been used to create hierarchies automatically like in the Scatter/Gather algorithm [D. R. Cutting et al. 1992]. Using related ideas but by using a probabilistic formalism, [A. Vinokourov, M. Girolami, 2000], propose a model which allows to infer a hierarchical structure for unsupervised organization of documents collection. The techniques of hierarchical clustering were largely used to organize corpora and to help information retrieval. All these methods cluster documents according to their similarity. They cannot be used to produce topic hierarchies or to infer generalization/specialization relations.

Recently, it has been proposed to develop topic hierarchies similar to those found in e.g. Yahoo. As in Yahoo, each topic is identified by a single term. These term hierarchies are built from "specialization/generalization" relations between the terms, automatically discovered from the corpus. [Lawrie and Croft 2000, Sanderson and Croft 1999] propose to build term hierarchies based on the notion of subsumption between terms. Given a set of documents, some terms will frequently occur among the documents, while others will only occur in a few documents. Some of the frequently occurring terms provide a lot of information about topics within the documents. There are some terms that broadly define the topics, while others which co-occur with such a general term explain aspects of a topic. Subsumption attempts to harness the power of these words. A subsumption hierarchy reflects the topics covered within the documents, a parent term is more general than its child. The key idea of Croft and co-workers has been to use a very simple but efficient subsumption measure. Term x subsumes term y if the following relation holds :

$P(x|y) > t$ and $P(y|x)<P(x|y)$, where t is a preset threshold. Using related ideas, [K. Krishna, R.

Krishnapuram 2001] propose a framework for modelling asymmetric relations between data.

All these recent works associate the notion of concept to a term and rely on the construction of term hierarchies and the classification of documents within these hierarchies. Compared to that, we propose two original contributions. The first is the extension of these approaches to the construction of real concept hierarchy where concepts are identified by set of keywords and not only by a single term, all concepts being discovered from the corpus. These concepts better reflect the different themes and ideas which appear in documents, they allow for a richer description than single terms. The second contribution is the automatic construction of a hierarchical organization of documents also based on the "specialization/generalization" relation. This is described in section 3.

For identifying concepts, we perform document segmentation into homogeneous themes. We used the segmentation technique of [G. Salton et al. 1996] which relies on a similarity measure between successive passages in order to identify coherent segments. In [G. Salton et al. 1996], the segmentation method proceeds by decomposing texts into segments and themes. A segment is a bloc of text about one subject and a theme is a set of such segments. In this approach, the segmentation begins at the paragraph level. Then paragraphs are compared each other via a similarity measure.

For Now, Semantic Web Research focalises on the standardization, internal structuring of documents and sharing of ontologies in a variety of domains with the short-term to transform existing sources into a machine-understandable form (i.e. RDF). The researchers of the field realise that this language is not intuitive for common user and that it is difficult for them to understand formal ontologies and defined vocabularies. Therefore they preach as another mean of semantics augmentation, the annotation in natural language which is more intuitive for humans.

[B. Katz, J. Lin, 2002] propose a method to augment RDF with natural language to make RDF friendlier to humans and to facilitate the Web Semantic adoption by many users. Our approach is complementary to their work. Indeed, at the end of our structuring algorithm we have derived all the concepts present in the collection and for each document the set of concepts it is about. Then we are able to annotate documents with the set of its concepts. Each concept is represented by a set of keywords in the corpus language.

3 AUTOMATIC CONSTRUCTION OF TOPICS AND DOCUMENTS HIERARCHIES

3.1 Basic Ideas

This work started while studying the automatic derivation of typed links "specialization / generalization" between the documents of a corpus. A link from document $D1$ to document $D2$ is of the type specialization (generalization from $D2$ to $D1$), if $D2$ is about specifics themes of $D1$. For example, $D1$ is about war in general and $D2$ is about the First World War in particular. This type of relation allows to build hierarchical organizations of the concepts present in the corpus which in turn allows for the construction of a hierarchical corpus organization.

In hierarchies like Yahoo!, the concepts used to organize documents are reduced to words. This gives only basic indications on the content of a document and the corresponding hierarchies are relatively poor. For this reason, we have tried to automatically construct hierarchies where each concept will be identified by a set of words. In order to do this, we need the knowledge of all themes present in the collection and of the specialization/generalization relations that do exist among them. From now on, we will identify a concept to a set of keywords.

For identifying the concepts present in a document, we use Salton segmentation method [G. Salton et al. 1996] which outputs a set of themes extracted from the corpus. Each theme is identified by a set of representative keywords.

For the detection of specialization/generalization relations between detected concepts, we will first build a term hierarchy like [Mark Sanderson, Bruce Croft, 1999], we then construct from that a concept hierarchy. After that, documents may be associated to relevant concepts in this hierarchy thus producing a document hierarchy based on the "specialization/generalization" relation between documents.

To summarize, the method is built around three main steps:

- Find the set of concepts of a given corpus
- Build a hierarchy (of type specialization /generalization) of these concepts
- Project the documents in the concepts hierarchy and infer typed links "specialization/generalization" between documents.

3.2 Algorithm

3.2.1 Concept Extraction from a Corpus

The goal here is to detect the set of concepts within the corpus and the words that represent them. For that, we extend Salton work on text segmentation:

We decompose a document into semantic themes using Salton's method [G. Salton et al. 1996], which can be viewed as a clustering on document paragraph.

Each document being decomposed in set of semantic themes, we then cluster all the themes in all documents to retain the minimal set of themes that ensure a correct coverage of the corpus.

We find for each concept the set of words that represent the concept. A concept is be represented here by its most frequent words.

3.2.2 Building the Concepts Hierarchy

The next step is to detect the "specialization/generalization" relations between extracted concepts so as to infer the concept hierarchy.

First, we build the hierarchy of terms within the corpus using Croft and Sanderson subsumption method [Mark Sanderson, Bruce Croft, 1999].

Then we create a concept hierarchy as follows. For each couple of concepts, we compute from the terms hierarchy the percentage x of words of concept $C2$ generalized by words of concept $C1$ and y the percentage of words of $C1$ generalized by words of $C2$. If $x > S1 > S2 > y$ ($S1$ and $S2$ are thresholds) then we deduce a relation of specialization/generalization between these concepts ($C1$ generalizes $C2$).[1]

After that, we have a hierarchical organization of concepts. It is therefore possible to attach indexed documents to the nodes in the hierarchy. One document may belong to different nodes if it is concerned with different concepts. Note that all concepts are not comparable by this "specialization / generalization" relation.

At this stage we already have an interesting organization of the corpus which rely on a richer semantic than those offered on classical portals or by term hierarchies [Lawrie and Croft 2000, Sanderson and Croft 1999]. However we can go further and establish "specialization/generalisation" links between corpus documents as explained below.

---

[1] Note that we briefly describe in section 6 an alternative method for directly building concept hierarchies without the need to first build the term hierarchy.

3.2.3 "Specialisation/Generalization" Relation Between Documents

Each document may be indexed by the set of corpus concepts and annotated by the set of keywords of the relevant concepts of its content. We then proceed in a similar way as for building concepts hierarchies from terms hierarchies:

For each couple of documents $D1$, $D2$, we compute from the concepts hierarchy the percentage of the concepts of D2 generalized by the concepts of $D1$ and vice versa. This allows to infer a "specialization/generalization" relation between the two documents.

Note that it is a global relation between two documents, but we could also envisage relations between parts of documents. In particular, our "specialization/generalization" relation excludes the fact that two documents generalize one another which could happen when they deal with different concepts. $D1$ could be a specialization of $D2$ for concept $C1$ and a generalization for concepts $C2$. However, we made this hypothesis for simplification.

Instead of building a hierarchy of documents, we could use the "specialization/generalization" relation to indicate links between documents. Such links could also be built between the document segments identified during the first step of the algorithm. This would result into an alternative representation of the document collection.

4 OUR ALGORITHM AND SEMANTIC WEB

This section will discuss how our algorithm answers some questions of Semantic Web research. The Semantic Web research can be view as an attempt to address the problem of information access by building programs that help users to locate, collect, and compare documents contents. In this point of view our structuring algorithm addresses some of these problems:

- The set of themes extracted from the collection, where each theme has a label in natural language, is a good synthesis of the collection for the user

- If one of the themes interests the user, he has all the documents treating the theme in the hierarchy node and each document has an annotation which reflects all the themes in it. This allows the user to target the subset of document likely to interest him.

- All documents are annotated by the themes they are about. The annotations are in natural language and give a summary of the document.

Two others motivations are in the scope of Semantic Web research:

- Generate new knowledge from existing documents. Now this is not possible because computers cannot understand the contents of documents

- Synthesize and compile knowledge from multiples sources. To do this computers should be able to relate the contents of multiple documents, this is not the case.

For the second point typed links could be a part of the response. Indeed, typed links show a relation between documents contents and defined the relation. They are useful for users because they give them a navigation context when retrieving a corpus. We can also imagine that a search engine knowing the existing typed links could use them to improve the information retrieval.

In our algorithm we only derived the specialization/generalization link between documents contents. We are developing automatic method for other Trigg typology link typed.

5 EVALUATION MEASURES

Evaluating the relevance of a concept or document hierarchy is a challenging and open problem. Evaluations on user groups generally give ambiguous and partial results while automatic measures only provide some hints on the intrinsic value of the hierarchies. However, for avoiding at this stage the heavy process of human evaluation, we resort to automatic criteria to judge the quality of learned hierarchies. We therefore propose two measures of similarity between hierarchies. This will allow to compare the coherence of our automatic hierarchies to reference manual hierarchies (here a part of LookSmart hierarchy), but will not provide an indication of its absolute quality, neither will it tell us which hierarchy is the best.

5.1 A Measure Based on the Inclusion

Documents in the hierarchy are said to share a relation of :

- "Brotherhood" if they belong to the same node
- "Parents-child" if they belong to nodes of the same branch

The first measure of similarity we propose is based on the mutual inclusion degree of hierarchies. The

inclusion degree of hierarchy A with respect to hierarchy B is:

Inclusion(A,B) = $(N_f + Np)/(|F_A|+|P_A|)$

Where N_f is the number of couples of "brothers" in A which belong to B.

N_p is the number of couples "parents-child" in A which belong to B.

$|F_A|$ is the number of couples of "brothers" documents in A.

$|P_A|$ is the number of couples of "parents-child" in A

Finally, the similarity between A and B is the average of their mutual inclusion:

Similarity(A, B) = (inclusion(A, B) + inclusion(B,A)) / 2

5.2 A Measure Based on Mutual Information

This similarity measure is inspired by the similarity measure between two clustering algorithms proposed in [T. Draier, P. Gallinari, 2001]. Let X and Y be the labels (classes) of all elements from a dataset according to the two different clustering algorithms and X_i be the label for the ith cluster in X, $P_X(C = K)$ the probability that an object belongs to the cluster K in X, and $P_{XY}(C_X=k_x, C_Y=k_y)$ the joint probability that an object belongs to the cluster k_x in X and to the cluster k_y in Y. To measure the similarity of the two clustering methods, the authors propose to use the mutual information between the two probability distributions:

$MI(X,Y) = \Sigma_{i \in CX} \Sigma_{j \in CY} P_{XY}(C_X = i, C_Y = j)* \log [(P_{XY}(C_X = i, C_Y = j)) / (P_X(C_X = i) * P_Y(C_Y = j))]$. If MI is normalized between 0 and 1 the more $MI(X, Y)$ is close to 1 the more similar are the two set of clusters and therefore the methods.

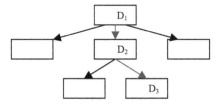

Figure 1 : An example of documents hierarchy. We showed three nodes with only one document D_i. if we considered the node labelled D_3 it contains one document $\{D_3\}$, and for relation «parent-child »it contains the couples $\{(D_1, D_3), (D_2, D_3)\}$

In the case of hierarchical organization of documents, for measuring the similarity between two hierarchies, we need to measure how objects are grouped together (inside the hierarchy nodes) and to measure the similarity of the relations "parent-child" between objects in the two hierarchies. For simplifying the description, we will first consider that in each hierarchy one object may belong only to one node. The extension to the case where one object may appear in different nodes is easy but it is not exposed here.

For a hierarchy X let us note X_i a node of the hierarchy. A hierarchy of documents is described by two relations which are the relations "brotherhood" shared by the documents within a node and the relation of generalization between couples of documents sharing a relation of "parent-child". A hierarchy can thus be seen like two simultaneous regroupings relating respectively on the documents and on the couples "parent-child". The hierarchy is defined by the groups of documents which are linked by these two types of relation.

The mutual information $MI(X, Y)$ between two hierarchies will be the combination of two components: $MI_D(X_D, Y_D)$ the mutual information between the groups of documents, corresponding to the nodes of the two hierarchies (it is the same measure as for a traditional clustering) and $MI_{P-C}(X_{P-C}, Y_{P-C})$ the mutual information measured on the groups of couples "parent-child" of the hierarchies. The mutual information between hierarchies X and Y will then be calculated by:

$$MI(X,Y) = \alpha * MI_D(X_D, Y_D) + (1 - \alpha) * MI_{P-C}(X_{P-C}, Y_{P-C}),$$

where α is a parameter which allow to give more or less importance to the regrouping of documents in same the node or to the hierarchical relations "parent-child" documents. With this measure we can compare hierarchies of different structures.

6 EXPERIMENTS AND DATA

6.1 LookSmart and New-Scientist Data

The data we used for our experiments are a part of the www.looksmart.com and www.newscientist.com sites hierarchies. First, we extracted a sub-hierarchy of LookSmart consisting of about 100 documents and 7000 terms about artificial intelligence. In a second experiment, we extract a sub-hierarchy of New-Scientist site consisting of about 700 documents. New-Scientist Web site is a weekly science and technology news magazine which contains all the latest science and technology news. Here the sub-hierarchy is heterogeneous sub-hierarchy whereas LookSmart data concern only AI. Documents are about AI, Bioterrorism, cloning, Dinosaurs, and Iraq. For each

theme there are sub-categories concerning specifics aspects of the theme. In both cases, we compare the document hierarchies induced by our method and the term hierarchies to the original hierarchies, using the methods described in section 3.

6.2 Experiments and Results

6.2.1 Segmentation, Annotations

In this section due to the place limitations we will give few examples of themes extract from the corpus, links between themes.

Comparing to the initial hierarchy of Looksmart with five categories, the hierarchy derived by our algorithm on the same corpus is more larger and deeper. Indeed, more of the original categories are specialized by our algorithm and it discovers new themes across the original ones. For example, many sub-categories emerge from "Knowledge Representation": ontologies, building ontologies, KDD (where paper are about the data representation for KDD)... and most of the emerging categories are themselves specialized. In the same way, "Philosophy-Morality" is subdivided in many categories like AI definition, Method and stakes, risks and so on... Table 1 shows some examples of extracted themes on LookSmart data.

Table 1: examples of five concepts extracted from looksmart corpus, with a relation of generalization/ specialization between (2, 3), (2, 4), (2, 5)

1	Definition AI intelligence learn knowledge solve build models brain Turing test thinking machine
2	Informal formal ontology catalog types statement natural language name axiom definition logic
3	FCA technique pattern relational database data mining ontology lattice category
4	ontology Knowledge Representation John Sowa category artificial intelligence philosopher Charles Sanders Peirce Alfred North Whitehead pioneer symbolic logic
5	system KR ontology hierarchy category framework distinction lattice chart

Each document can then be annotated with the set of keywords of its index concepts (remember that after the step of concepts extraction all documents are indexed with their concepts).

6.2.2 Hierarchies Similarities

In this section we compare the hierarchies induced by our method and term hierarchies to the original hierarchy using the measures of section 5.

Table 2: similarities between Looksmart and NewScientist data and others hierarchies (term, concept, concept_version2)

LookSmart			
	Terms.	Concepts1.	Concept2.
Inclusion	0.4	0.46	0.65
Mutual Information	0.3	0.6	0.7
NewScientist			
	Terms.	Concepts1.	Concept2.
Inclusion	0.3	0.2	0.6
Mutual Information	0.2	0.2	0.65

The concept hierarchy is large compared to the originals ones, and only a few documents are assigned to each concept. The greater width of the concepts hierarchy is due to the fact that some themes detected through corpus segmentation are not present in originals hierarchies which exploit poorer conceptual representations.

Nevertheless, the similarity between our hierarchy and LookSmart's is quite high. The inclusion similarity is about **0.5**, and the similarity based on the mutual information is around **0.6** (table 3). But the similarity between our hierarchy and New-Scientist one is low. This result point out the weakness of subsumption method our algorithm is based on, when the data are heterogeneous. We decide to modify our algorithm to be free from terms hierarchy induction for computing the subsumption relation between concepts. Remember that in our definition, concept $C1$ subsumes concept $C2$ if most terms of $C2$ are subsumed by terms from $C1$. This relation was inferred from the term hierarchy (section 3.2.2). However it is also possible to directly derive the concept hierarchy without relying on the term hierarchy. For that we directly estimate P(concept C_i | concept C_j) by the number of documents containing both concepts divided by the number of documents containing concept C_j.

This hierarchy (denoted Concepts2. in table 2) seems closer to the manual hierarchy. It detects less

subsumption relations between concepts on looksmart data; therefore it is less wide than the first concept hierarchy. Why does the number of subsumption between concepts fall down in the second method? A reason might be that in the construction of the first concept hierarchy, concept C2 is generalized by concept C1 if most of the terms of C2 are generalized by C1 terms. Let us take the extreme case where only one word $w1$ of $C1$ generalizes the $C2$ terms. In this case, we will say that $C1$ generalizes $C2$. Actually, we can say that the presence of $C2$ in a document implies the presence of $w1$, but it is not sure that it implies the presence of $C1$. For the second concept hierarchy the subsumption of $C2$ by $C1$ ensures that $C2$ implies $C1$.

For the newscientist data, due to the heterogeneity of the vocabulary, subsumption test fail for many pairs of word and this effect is more drastic when projecting theme on term hierarchy. The consequence is that many theme nodes is compose by one document. Therefore the hierarchy is far from the original one. Modifying the definition of subsumption concept gives a hierarchy more similar than the original one. One way to reduce the influence of vocabulary heterogeneity is to consider synonyms in the computation of P(term1|term2).

These experiments shed some light on the algorithm behaviour. The hierarchies we obtain are coherent (particularly the second those obtain with the second method) compared to LookSmart and New-Scientists hierarchies, particularly on the groups of documents detected, but some of the documents pairs sharing the relation "Parent-Child" in the concept hierarchy do not appear in Looksmart hierarchy. This is inherent to the difference of nature between the two hierarchies.

If we compare the automatically built term hierarchy with that of LookSmart, we see that inclusion similarity is **0.4** and the mutual information is **0.3**. Both hierarchies use terms to index and organize documents. However, the term hierarchy uses all terms in the collection, whereas LookSmart uses a much smaller vocabulary. Therefore the hierarchy term is very large compared to LookSmart. Nevertheless some groups of documents are still common to the two hierarchies.

The similarity of the concept hierarchy with Looksmart seems higher than that of the term hierarchy.

7 CONCLUSIONS AND PERSPECTIVES

We have described a method to automatically generate a hierarchical structure from a documents collection. The same method can be used to build specialization/generalization links between documents or document parts and augmented documents with metadata in natural language. We have also introduced two new numerical measures for the open problem of the comparison and evaluation of such hierarchies. These measures give an indication on the proximity of two hierarchies; this allows measuring the coherence of two different hierarchies. On the other hand, they do not say anything on the intrinsic quality of the hierarchies. We are currently working on the development of measures for quantifying how much a hierarchy respects the "specialization/generalization" property.

Our method applied to LookSmart and New-Scientists data gives interesting first results although there is still place for improvements. The experiments also show that our concepts hierarchies are nearer to original hierarchies than a reference method which automatically builds terms hierarchies. Further experiments on different collections and on a larger scale are of course needed to confirm this fact.

We also show that our algorithm could give some answers to Semantic Web research concerns:

- Thematic hierarchies make easier information access and navigation, they are also a mean to synthesize a collection
- The algorithm allow to automatically related document sharing a specialization/generalization relation.
- At the end of the method each document is augmented with a set of keywords which reflects the concepts it is about

A perspective could be the use of automatically extracted concepts to build or enrich ontologies in a specific domain.

REFERENCES

J. Allan, 1996. Automatic hypertext link typing. Proceeding of the ACM Hypertext Conference, Washington, DC pp.42-52.

C. Cleary, R. Bareiss, 1996. Practical methods for automatically generating typed links. Hypertext '96, Washington DC USA

D. R. Cutting, D. R. Karger, J. O. Pedersen, J. W. Tukey, 1992. Scatter/gather: A cluster-based approach to browsing large document collections. In ACM SIGIR.

T. Draier, P. Gallinari, 2001. Characterizing Sequences of User Actions for Access Logs Analysis, User Modelling, LNAI 2109.

G. Källgren, 1988. Automatic Abstracting on Content in text. Nordic Journal of Linguistics. pp. 89-110, vol. 11.

B. Katz, J. Lin, 2002. Annotating the Semantic Web Using Natural Language. In Proceedings of the 2nd Workshop on NLP and XML (NLPXML-2002) at COLING 2002.

B. Katz, J. Lin, D. Quan, 2002. Natural Language Annotations for the Semantic Web. In Proceedings of the International Conference on Ontologies, Databases and Applications of Semantics (ODBASE2002).

K. Krishna, R. Krishnapuram, 2001. A Clustering Algorithm for Asymmetrically Related Data with Applications to Text Mining. Proceedings of the 2001 ACM CIKM International Conference on Information and Knowledge Management. Atlanta, Georgia, USA. Pp.571-573

Dawn Lawrie and W. Bruce Croft, 2000. Discovering and Comparing Topic Hierarchies. In proceedings of RIAO 2000.

G. Salton, A. Singhal, C. Buckley, M. Mitra, 1996. Automatic Text Decomposition Using Text Segments and Text Themes. Hypertext 1996: 53-65

Mark Sanderson, Bruce Croft, 1999. Deriving concept hierarchies from text. In Proceedings ACM SIGIR Conference '99, 206-213.

Randall Trigg, 1983. A network-based approach to text handling for the online scientific community. University of Maryland, Department of Computer Science, Ph.D dissertation, November 1983.

A. Vinokourov, M. Girolami, 2000. A Probabilistic Hierarchical Clustering Method for Organizing Collections of Text Documents. Proceedings of the 15th International Conference on Pattern Recognition (ICPR'2000), Barcelona, Spain. IEEE computer press, vol.2 pp.182-185.

NEW ENERGETIC SELECTION PRINCIPLE IN DIFFERENTIAL EVOLUTION

Vitaliy Feoktistov

Centre de Recherche LGI2P, Site EERIE, EMA
Parc Scientifique Georges Besse, 30035 Nimes, France
Vitaliy.Feoktistov@ema.fr

Stefan Janaqi

Centre de Recherche LGI2P, Site EERIE, EMA
Parc Scientifique Georges Besse, 30035 Nimes, France
Stefan.Janaqi@ema.fr

Keywords: differential evolution, evolutionary algorithms, heuristics, optimization, selection.

Abstract: The Differential Evolution algorithm goes back to the class of Evolutionary Algorithms and inherits its philosophy and concept. Possessing only three control parameters (size of population, differentiation and recombination constants) Differential Evolution has promising characteristics of robustness and convergence. In this paper we introduce a new principle of Energetic Selection. It consists in both decreasing the population size and the computation efforts according to an energetic barrier function which depends on the number of generation. The value of this function acts as an energetic filter, through which can pass only individuals with lower fitness. Furthermore, this approach allows us to initialize the population of a sufficient (large) size. This method leads us to an improvement of algorithm convergence.

1 INTRODUCTION

Evolutionary Algorithms increasingly become the primary method of choice for optimization problems that are too complex to be solved by deterministic techniques. They are universal, robust, easy to use and inherently parallel. The huge number of applications and continuous interest prove it during several decades (Heitkötter and Beasley, 2000; Beasley, 1997). In comparison with the deterministic methods Evolutionary Algorithm require superficial knowledge about the problem being solved. Generally, the algorithm only needs to evaluate the cost function for a given set of input parameters. Nevertheless, in most cases such heuristics take less time to find the optimum than, for example, gradient methods. One of the latest breakthroughs in the evolutionary computation is the *Differential Evolution* algorithm.

2 DIFFERENTIAL EVOLUTION

Differential Evolution (DE) is a recently invented global optimization technique (Storn and Price, 1995). It can be classified as an *iterative stochastic method*. Enlarging the Evolutionary Algorithms' group, DE turns out to be one of the best *population-based* optimizers (Storn and Price, 1996; Feoktis-tov and Janaqi, 2004c; Feoktistov and Janaqi, 2004a; Feoktistov and Janaqi, 2004b). In the following lines we give a brief description of DE algorithm.

An optimization problem is represented by a set of variables. Let these variables form a D-dimensional vector in continuous space $X = (x_1, \ldots, x_D) \in \mathbb{R}^D$. Let there be some criterion of optimization $f : \mathbb{R}^D \to \mathbb{R}$, usually named *fitness* or *cost* function. Then the goal of optimization is to find the values of the variables that minimize the criterion, i.e. to find

$$X^* : f(X^*) = \min_X f(X) \qquad (1)$$

Often, the variables satisfy boundary constraints

$$L \leq X \leq H : \quad L, H \in \mathbb{R}^D \qquad (2)$$

As all Evolutionary Algorithms, DE deals with a *population* of solutions. The population $\mathbb{P}$ of a generation g has NP vectors, so-called *individuals* of population. Each such individual represents a potential optimal solution.

$$\mathbb{P}^g = X_i^g, \quad i = 1, \ldots, NP \qquad (3)$$

In turn, the individual contains D variables, so called *genes*.

$$X_i^g = x_{i,j}^g, \quad j = 1, \ldots, D \qquad (4)$$

The population is *initialized* by randomly generating individuals within the boundary constraints,

$$\mathbb{P}^0 = x_{i,j}^0 = rand_{i,j} \cdot (h_j - l_j) + l_j \qquad (5)$$

151

I. Seruca et al. (eds.), Enterprise Information Systems VI, 151–157.

where $rand$ function generates values uniformly in the interval $[0, 1]$.

Then, for each *generation* the individuals of the population are updated by means of a *reproduction* scheme. Thereto for each individual ind a set of other individuals π is randomly extracted from the population. To produce a new one the operations of *Differentiation* and *Recombination* are applied one after another. Next, the *Selection* is used to choose the best. Now briefly consider these operations.

Here, we show the typical model of the *Differentiation*, others can be found in (Feoktistov and Janaqi, 2004a; Feoktistov and Janaqi, 2004c). For that, three different individuals $\pi = \{\xi_1, \xi_2, \xi_3\}$ are randomly extracted from a population. So, the result, a *trial* individual, is

$$\tau = \xi_3 + F \cdot (\xi_2 - \xi_1), \quad (6)$$

where $F > 0$ is the *constant of differentiation*.

After, the trial individual τ is recombined with updated one ind. The *Recombination* represents a typical case of a genes' exchange. The trial one inherits genes with some probability. Thus,

$$\omega_j = \begin{cases} \tau_j & \text{if } rand_j < Cr \\ ind_j & \text{otherwise} \end{cases} \quad (7)$$

where $j = 1, \dots, D$ and $Cr \in [0, 1)$ is the *constant of recombination*.

The *Selection* is realized by comparing the cost function values of updated and trial individuals. If the trial individual better minimizes the cost function, then it replaces the updated one.

$$ind = \begin{cases} \omega & \text{if } f(\omega) \le f(ind) \\ ind & \text{otherwise} \end{cases} \quad (8)$$

Notice that there are only three control parameters in this algorithm. These are NP – population size, F and Cr – constants of differentiation and recombination accordingly. As for the terminal conditions, one can either fix the number of generations g_{max} or a desirable precision of a solution VTR (*value to reach*).

The pattern of DE algorithm is presented in Algorithm 1.

3 DIFFERENTIATION

Differentiation occupies a quite important position in the reproduction cycle. So, we try to analyze it in detail.

Geometrically, Differentiation consists in *two* simultaneous operations: the first one is the choice of a Differentiation's direction and the second one is the calculation of a step length in which this Differentiation performs. From the optimization point of view we have to answer the next two questions:

Algorithm 1 Differential Evolution

Require: F, Cr, NP – control parameters
   initialize $\mathbb{P}^0 \leftarrow \{ind_1, \dots, ind_{NP}\}$
   evaluate $f(\mathbb{P}^0)$
   while (terminal condition) **do**
     for all $ind \in \mathbb{P}^g$ **do**
       $\mathbb{P}^g \rightarrow \pi = \{\xi_1, \xi_2, \dots, \xi_n\}$
       $\tau \leftarrow Differentiate(\pi, F)$
       $\omega \leftarrow Recombine(\tau, Cr)$
       $ind \leftarrow Select(\omega, ind)$
     end for
     $g \leftarrow g + 1$
   end while

---

1. How to choose the optimal direction from all available ones?

2. What step length is necessary in order to better minimize the cost function along the chosen direction?

Let us remind that the principle of Differentiation is based on a random extraction of several individuals from the population and the geometrical manipulation of them.

Possible directions of Differentiation entirely depend on the disposition of extracted individuals. Also, their disposition influences the step length. Furthermore by increasing either the size of population or the number of extracted individuals we augment the diversity of possible directions and the variety of step lengths. Thereby we intensify the exploration of the search space. But on the other hand, the probability to find the best combination of extracted individuals goes considerably down.

Example. We take the typical differentiation strategy $u = x_1 + F \cdot (x_2 - x_3)$, where for each current individual three other individuals are randomly extracted from the population.

- In the first case we suppose that the population consists only of *four* individuals. So there are $(4-1)(4-2)(4-3) = 3 \cdot 2 \cdot 1 = 6$ possible directions and 6 possible step lengths. Imagine then that only one combination gives the best value of the cost function. Therefore the probability to find it, is $1/6$.

- In the second case the population size is equal to *five* individuals. It gives $(5-1)(5-2)(5-3) = 4 \cdot 3 \cdot 2 = 24$ directions and as many step lengths. But, in this case, the probability to find the best combination is much less – $1/24$.

If we choose another strategy consisting of two randomly extracted individuals, $u = x_1 + F \cdot (x_2 - x_1)$ for example, then for the population size of five individuals the diversity of possible directions and step lengths is equal now to $(5-1)(5-2) = 12$ (two times less then in the previous case).

As we can see only two factors control the capability of the search space exploration. These are the population size NP and the number of randomly extracted individuals k in the strategy. In the case of the consecutive extraction of individuals the dependence of the potential individuals diversity from both the population size and the number of extracted individuals is shown in the Formula 9.

$$f(NP, k) = \prod_{i=1}^{k}(NP - i) \qquad (9)$$

But, where is the compromise between the covering of the search space (*i.e.* the diversity of directions and step lengths) and the probability of the best choice? This question makes us face with a dilemma that was named *"The Dilemma of the search space exploration and the probability of the optimal choice"*.

During the evolutionary process the individuals learn the cost function surface (Price, 2003). The step length and the difference direction adapt themselves accordingly. In practice, the more complex the cost function is, the more exploration is needed. The balanced choice of NP and k defines the efficiency of the algorithm.

4 ENERGETIC APPROACH

We introduce a new energetic approach which can be applied to population-based optimization algorithms including DE. This approach may be associated with the processes taking place in physics.

Let there be a population $\mathbb{P}$ consisting of NP individuals. Let us define the *potential* of individual as its cost function value $\varphi = f(ind)$. Such potential shows the remoteness from the optimal solution $\varphi^* = f(ind^*)$, *i.e.* some energetic distance (potential) that should be overcome to reach the optimum. Then, the population can be characterized by superior and inferior potentials $\varphi_{max} = \max f(ind_i)$ and $\varphi_{min} = \min f(ind_i)$. As the population evolves the individuals take more optimal energetic positions, closest possible to the optimum level. So if $t \to \infty$ then $\varphi_{max}(t) \to \varphi_{min}(t) \to \varphi^*$, where t is an elementary step of evolution. Approaching the optimum, apart from stagnation cases, can be as well expressed by $\varphi_{max} \to \varphi_{min}$ or $(\varphi_{max} - \varphi_{min}) \to 0$. By introducing the *potential difference* of population $\Delta\varphi(t) = \varphi_{max}(t) - \varphi_{min}(t)$ the theoretical condition of optimality is represented as

$$\Delta\varphi(t) \to 0 \qquad (10)$$

In other words, the optimum is achieved when the potential difference is closed to 0 or to some desired precision ε. The value $\Delta\varphi(t)$ is proportional to the algorithmic efforts, which are necessary to find the optimal solution.

Thus, the *action A* done by the algorithm in order to pass from one state t_1 to another t_2 is

$$A(t_1, t_2) = \int_{t_1}^{t_2} \Delta\varphi(t)dt \qquad (11)$$

We introduce then the *potential energy* of population E_p that describes total computational expenses.

$$E_p = \int_{0}^{\infty} \Delta\varphi(t)dt \qquad (12)$$

Notice that the equation (12) graphically represents the area S_p between two functions $\varphi_{max}(t)$ and $\varphi_{min}(t)$.

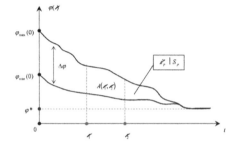

Figure 1: Energetic approach

Let us remind that our purpose is to increase the speed of algorithm convergence. Logically, the convergence is proportional to computational efforts. It is obvious the less is potential energy E_p the less computational efforts are needed. Thus, by decreasing the potential energy $E_p \equiv S_p$ we augment the convergence rate of the algorithm. Hence, the convergence increasing is transformed into a problem of potential energy minimization (or S_p minimization).

$$E_p^* = \min_{\Delta\varphi(t)} E_p(\Delta\varphi(t)) \qquad (13)$$

5 NEW ENERGETIC SELECTION PRINCIPLE

5.1 The Idea

We apply the above introduced *Energetic Approach* to the DE algorithm. As an elementary evolution step t we choose a *generation g*.

In order to increase the convergence rate we minimize the potential energy of population E_p (Fig.1). For that a supplementary procedure is introduced at the end of each generation g. The main idea is to replace the superior potential $\varphi_{max}(g)$ by so called *energetic barrier* function $\beta(g)$. Such function artificially underestimates the potential difference of generation $\triangle \varphi(g)$.

$$\beta(g) - \varphi_{min}(g) \le \varphi_{max}(g) - \varphi_{min}(g)$$
$$\Leftrightarrow \quad \beta(g) \le \varphi_{max}(g), \quad \forall g \in [1, g_{max}] \quad (14)$$

From an algorithmic point of view this function $\beta(g)$ serves as an *energetic filter* for the individuals passing into the next generation. Thus, only the individuals with potentials less than the current energetic barrier value can participate in the next evolutionary cycle (Fig.2).

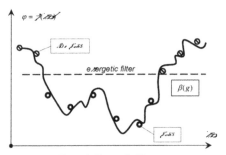

Figure 2: Energetic filter

Practically, it leads to the decrease of the population size NP by rejecting individuals such that:

$$f(ind) > \beta(g) \quad (15)$$

5.2 Energetic Barriers

Here, we show some examples of the energetic barrier function. At the beginning we outline the variables which this function should depend on. Firstly, this is the generation variable g, which provides a passage from one evolutionary cycle to the next. Secondly, it should be the superior potential $\varphi_{max}(g)$ that presents the upper bound of the barrier function. And thirdly, it should be the inferior potential $\varphi_{min}(g)$ giving the lower bound of the barrier function (Fig.3).

Linear energetic barriers. The simplest example is the use of a proportional function. It is easy to obtain by multiplying either $\varphi_{min}(g)$ or $\varphi_{max}(g)$ with a constant K.

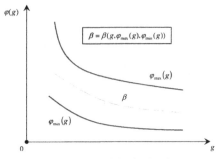

Figure 3: Energetic barrier function

In the first case, the value $\varphi_{min}(g)$ is always stored in the program as the current best value of the cost function. So, the energetic barrier looks like

$$\beta_1(g) = K \cdot \varphi_{min}(g), \quad K > 1 \quad (16)$$

The constant K is selected to satisfy the energetic barrier condition (14).

In the second case, a little procedure is necessary to find superior potential (maximal cost function value of the population) $\varphi_{max}(g)$. Here, the energetic barrier is

$$\beta_2(g) = K \cdot \varphi_{max}(g), \quad K < 1 \quad (17)$$

K should not be too small in order to provide a smooth decrease of the population size NP.

An advanced example would be a superposition of the potentials.

$$\beta_3(g) = K \cdot \varphi_{min}(g) + (1 - K) \cdot \varphi_{max}(g) \quad (18)$$

So, with $0 < K < 1$ the energetic barrier function is always found between the potential functions. Now, by adjusting K it is easier to get the smoothed reduction of the population without condition violation (14). Examples of the energetic barrier functions are shown on the figure (Fig.4).

Nonlinear energetic barriers. As we can see the main difficulty of using the linear barriers appears when we try to define correctly the barrier function in order to provide a desired dynamics of the population reduction. Taking into consideration that $\varphi_{max} \to \varphi_{min}$ when the algorithm converges locally, the ideal choice for the barrier function is a function which begins at a certain value between $\varphi_{min}(0)$ and $\varphi_{max}(0)$ and converges to $\varphi_{max}(g_{max})$.

Thereto, we propose an exponential function $K(g)$

$$K(g) = K_l + (K_h - K_l) \cdot e^{\left(-\frac{T}{g_{max}} \cdot g\right)} \quad (19)$$

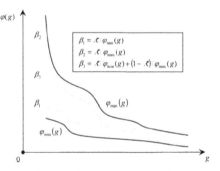

Figure 4: Linear energetic barriers

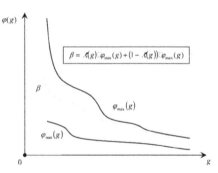

Figure 6: Nonlinear energetic barriers

This function, inspired by the color-temperature dependence from Bernoulli's low, smoothly converges from K_h to K_l. The constant T, so called *temperature*, controls the convergence rate. The functional dependence on the temperature constant $K(T)$ is represented on the figure (Fig.5).

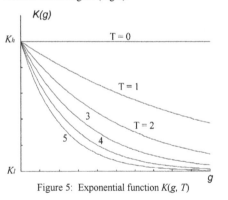

Figure 5: Exponential function $K(g, T)$

By substituting the constant K in the equations (16-18) for the exponential function (19) we can supply the energetic barrier function with improved tuning (Fig.6).

5.3   Advantages

Firstly, such principle of energetic selection permits to initialize the population of a sufficiently large size. This fact leads to better (careful) exploration of a search space during the initial generations as well as it increases the probability of finding the global optimum.

Secondly, the introduction of the energetic barrier function decreases the potential energy of the population and thereby increases the algorithm rate.

Thirdly, a double selection principle is applied. The first one is a usual DE selection for each individual of a population. Here, there is no reduction of the population size. And the second one is a selection of the best individuals which pass in the next generation, according to the energetic barrier function. It leads to the reduction of the population size.

Remark. Notice that a considerable reduction of the population size occurs at the beginning of the evolutionary process. For more efficient exploitation of this fact a population should be initialized with greatly larger size NP_0 than usually. Then, when the population shrinks to a certain size NP_f, it is necessary to stop the energetic selection procedure. This forced stopping is explained by possible stagnation and not enough efficient search in a small size population. In fact, the first group of generations locates a set of promising zones. The selected individuals are conserved in order to make a thorough local search in these zones.

6   COMPARISON OF RESULTS

In order to test our approach we chose three test functions (20) from a standard test suite for Evolutionary Algorithms (Whitley et al., 1996). The first two functions, Sphere f_1 and Rosenbrock's function f_2, are classical De Jong testbads (Jong, 1975). Sphere is a "dream" of every optimization algorithm. It is smooth, unimodal and symmetric function. The performance on the Sphere function is a measure of the general efficiency of the algorithm. Whereas the Rosenbrock's function is a nightmare. It has a very narrow ridge. The tip of the ridge is very sharp and it runs around a parabola. The third function, Rotated Ellipsoid f_3, is a true quadratic non separable optimization problem.

$$f_1(X) = \sum_{i=1}^{3} x_i^2$$

$$f_2(X) = 100(x_1^2 - x_2)^2 + (1 - x_1)^2 \qquad (20)$$

$$f_3(X) = \sum_{i=1}^{20} \left(\sum_{j=1}^{i} x_j \right)^2$$

We fixed the differentiation F and recombination Cr constants to be the same for all functions. $F = 0.5$. Recombination $Cr = 0$ (there is no recombination) in order to make the DE algorithm rotationally invariant (Salomon, 1996; Price, 2003). The terminal condition of algorithm is a desirable precision of optimal solution VTR (*value to reach*). It is fixed for all tests as $VTR = 10^{-6}$. We count the *number of function evaluations* NFE needed to reach the VTR. The initial data are shown in the Table 6.

Table 1: Initial test data

f_i	D	NP	NP_0	NP_f	K
1	3	30	90	25	0.50
2	2	40	120	28	0.75
3	20	200	600	176	0.15

For DE with energetic selection principle the initial population size was chosen three times larger than in the classical DE scheme: $NP_0 = 3 \cdot NP$. The forced stopping was applied if the current population became smaller than NP. Hence $NP_f \leq NP$. As an energetic barrier function the linear barrier $\beta_3(g)$ was selected (18). So, K is an adjusting parameter for barrier tuning, which was found empirically. D is the dimension of the test functions.

The average results of 10 runs for both the classical DE scheme and DE with energetic selection principle are summarized in the Table 2.

Table 2: Comparison the classical DE scheme (cl) and DE with energetic selection principle (es)

f_i	NFE_{cl}	NFE_{es}	$\delta, \%$
1	1088.7	912.4	16,19
2	1072.9	915.3	14,69
3	106459.8	94955.6	10,81

The numbers of function evaluations (NFE's) were compared. It is considered that NFE_{cl} value is equal to 100% therefore the relative convergence

amelioration in percentage wise can be defined as

$$\delta = 1 - \frac{NFE_{es}}{NFE_{cl}} \qquad (21)$$

Thus, δ may be interpreted as the algorithm improvement.

Remark. We tested DE with a great range of other functions. The stability of results was observed. So, in order to demonstrate our contribution we have generated only 10 populations for each test function relying on the statistical correctness. Nevertheless farther theoretical work and tests are necessary.

7 CONCLUSION

The variation of the population size of population-based search procedures presents a rather promising trend. In this article we have examined its decrease. The proposed energetic approach explains a theoretical aspect of such population reduction. The efficiency of the new energetic selection principle based on this energetic approach is illustrated by the example of the DE algorithm. The given innovation provides more careful exploration of a search space and leads to the convergence rate improvement. Thus, the probability of the global optimum finding is increased. Further works are carried on the methods of increasing the population size.

REFERENCES

Beasley, D. (1997). Possible applications of evolutionary computation. In Bäck, T., Fogel, D. B., and Michalewicz, Z., editors, *Handbook of Evolutionary Computation*, pages A1.2:1–10. IOP Publishing Ltd. and Oxford University Press, Bristol, New York.

Feoktistov, V. and Janaqi, S. (2004a). Generalization of the strategies in differential evolutions. In *18th Annual IEEE International Parallel and Distributed Processing Symposium. IPDPS – NIDISC 2004 workshop*, page (accepted), Santa Fe, New Mexico – USA. IEEE Computer Society.

Feoktistov, V. and Janaqi, S. (2004b). Hybridization of differential evolution with least-square support vector machines. In *Proceedings of the Annual Machine Learning Conference of Belgium and The Netherlands. BENELEARN 2004.*, pages 53–57, Vrije Universiteit Brussels, Belgium.

Feoktistov, V. and Janaqi, S. (2004c). New strategies in differential evolution. In Parmee, I., editor, *6-th International Conference on Adaptive Computing in Design and Manufacture, ACDM 2004*, page (accepted), Bristol, UK. Engineers House, Clifton, Springer-Verlag Ltd.(London).

Heitkötter, J. and Beasley, D. (2000). *Hitch Hiker's Guide to Evolutionary Computation: A List of Frequently Asked Questions (FAQ)*.

Jong, K. A. D. (1975). *An analysis of the behavior of a class of genetic adaptive systems*. PhD thesis, University of Michigan.

Price, K. (2003). *New Ideas in Optimization, Part 2: Differential Evolution*. McGraw-Hill, London, UK.

Salomon, R. (1996). Re-evaluating genetic algorithm performance under coordinate rotation of benchmark functions: A survey of some theoretical and practical aspects of genetic algorithms. *BioSystems*, 39:263–278.

Storn, R. and Price, K. (1995). Differential evolution - a simple and efficient adaptive scheme for global optimization over continuous spaces. Technical Report TR-95-012, International Computer Science Institute, Berkeley, CA.

Storn, R. and Price, K. (1996). Minimizing the real functions of the ICEC'96 contest by differential evolution. In *IEEE International Conference on Evolutionary Computation*, pages 842–844, Nagoya. IEEE, New York, NY, USA.

Whitley, D., Rana, S. B., Dzubera, J., and Mathias, K. E. (1996). Evaluating evolutionary algorithms. *Artificial Intelligence*, 85(1-2):245–276.

AN EXPERIENCE IN MANAGEMENT OF IMPRECISE SOIL DATABASES BY MEANS OF FUZZY ASSOCIATION RULES AND FUZZY APPROXIMATE DEPENDENCIES [1]

J. Calero, G. Delgado, M. Sánchez-Marañón
Department of Pedology and Agricultural Chemistry. University of Granada
{varanda,gdelgado,masanche}@ugr.es

D. Sánchez, M.A.Vila
Department of Computer Science and A.I. University of Granada
{daniel,vila}@decsai.ugr.es

J.M. Serrano
Department of Computer Science. University of Jaen
jschica@ujaen.es

Keywords: Expert soil knowledge, aggregated soil databases, imprecision factors in soil knowledge, fuzzy data mining.

Abstract: In this work, we start from a database built with soil information from heterogeneous scientific sources (Local Soil Databases, LSDB). We call this an Aggregated Soil Database (ASDB). We are interested in determining if knowledge obtained by means of fuzzy association rules or fuzzy approximate dependencies can represent adequately expert knowledge for a soil scientific, familiarized with the study zone. A master relation between two soil attributes was selected and studied by the expert, in both ASDB and LSDB. Obtained results reveal that knowledge extracted by means of fuzzy data mining tools is significatively better than crisp one. Moreover, it is highly satisfactory from the soil scientific expert's point of view, since it manages with more flexibility imprecision factors (IFASDB) commonly related to this type of information.

1   INTRODUCTION

Soil survey data is required for different kinds of environmental and agronomic studies, specially for estimation of soil quality indicators and other very important soil characteristics over large areas (Cazemier et al., 2001). Many of these parameters present a high degree of spatial variability, and they obstruct knowledge extraction when soil survey scale is small or very small (1:200000 or lower). In other order of things, obtaining a high precision map can be very expensive in time and resources, as a minimum number of measures would be desirable for resource optimization. Due to costs related to the schedule of a cartography or soil survey at a high scale in large geographic areas, researchers must recur in many occasions to knowledge fusion from different local soil databases for regional or national level studies (Bui and Moran, 2003).

Information sources in local soil databases present a very heterogeneous nature, combining not only soil cartographies but also Ph.D. thesis, monographes and other diverse works. This fact implies that resulting databases from local soil databases fusion (Ag-

gregated soil databases, ASDB) present an additional imprecision or uncertainty degree related to local information aggregation processes.

Statistical analysis techniques are frequently applied in soil study: analysis of variance (Ulery and Graham, 1993), regression analysis (Qian et al., 1993), main components analysis (Sánchez-Marañón et al., 1996) and discriminant analysis (Scheinost and Schwertmann, 1999). These techniques, based on statistical probability theory, are adequate for dealing with uncertainty derived from randomness. Nevertheless, they are not suitable when managing imprecision or uncertainty related to qualitative character in many attributes (soil structure, consistency), of subjective nature and hard for mathematical treatment (Webster, 1977), as the ones in the ASDB.

Data mining techniques (such as association rules or approximate dependencies) have been proven as effective tools when looking for hidden or implicit relations between attributes in a large database (ASDB) and they do not have the limitations of statistical procedures commented above. In particular, fuzzy data mining tools can be specially suitable when we consider intrinsically fuzzy information, as soil data.

In this work, our objective is to extract knowledge from an ASDB obtained from local heterogeneous information sources. We want to test that fuzzy data

[1]This work is supported by the research project Fuzzy-KIM, CICYT TIC2002-04021-C02-02.

I. Seruca et al. (eds.), Enterprise Information Systems VI, 158–166.

mining tools can manage the increment in imprecision or uncertainty degree related to an aggregation process, better than crisp tools. In order to accomplish this, we introduce a methodology of knowledge extraction and interpretation on an ASDB real case, in a large area in Iberian Peninsula Southeast. From this, the domain expert will estimate the suitability of the proposed tools for this particularly difficult case of databases.

2   PROBLEM STATEMENT

We consider several soil databases with an analogous structure, but obtained from different sources, by means of different criteria. Modelling these sources and criteria as discriminant attributes, we can fuse all these databases into an ASDB. Also, in order to model soil data more accurately, we consider fuzzy similarity relations and sets of linguistic labels over some soil attributes.

Formally, let $RE = \{A_1, \ldots, A_m, B\}$ be a relational scheme, and r an instance of RE. Let $S_{RE} = \{S_{A_k}\}$ be a set of fuzzy similarity relations over attributes in RE. Also, given $t \in r$ a tuple, let $t[A_k]$ be the intersection of t and A_k, and $\mu_{t[A_k]}$ the membership degree of the value.

Finally, let B be a discriminant attribute, and $dom(B) = \{b_1, \ldots, b_l\}$ the set of possible values of B. Our idea when using discriminant attributes is to generate more homogenous sets of objects from a database, according to the attribute values. That is, we can perform a query as the following,

`select` $A_1, \ldots, A_m$ `from` r `where` $B = b_j$;

obtaining r_j, a subset of r. Each subrelation r_j can be viewed as a LSDB, obtained according to a given criterium.

Moreover, if we apply some data mining techniques (i.e., association rules or approximate dependencies, see below), we can obtain the following,

- R_G, the set of all rules from r.
- R_j, the set of all rules from r_j.

We are interested in the study of possible existing correspondences between these sets of rules:

- Can we find rules in R_j that do not hold in R_G, and viceversa?
- Can imprecision or uncertainty management in data generate more accurate rules from domain experts' point of view, at both levels R_G and R_j?

Our proposed methodology is the following:

1. To define a set of criteria for decomposition of a given ASDB (r) into several LSDB (r_j), according to B, discriminant attribute, values.

2. To extract (fuzzy) approximate dependencies between attributes in r and in every subset of r.

3. To describe the obtained dependencies at a local level, by means of (fuzzy) association rules.

4. To compare the resulting sets of rules and dependencies in order to discover possible couplings at different levels.

5. To study in which real world problems imprecision and uncertainty management in data can generate better rules or dependencies, that is, when domain experts find more interesting and reasonable the obtained results.

3   DATA MINING TOOLS

In this section we summarize the techniques we have employed to analyze data corresponding to soil color and properties.

3.1   Association Rules

Given a set I ("set of items") and a set of transactions T (also called T-set), each transaction being a subset of I, association rules are "implications" of the form $A \Rightarrow C$ that relate the presence of itemsets (sets of items) A and C in transactions of T, assuming $A, C \subseteq I$, $A \cap C = \emptyset$ and $A, C \neq \emptyset$.

In the case of relational databases, it is usual to consider that items are pairs $\langle attribute, value \rangle$, and transactions are tuples in a table. For example, the item $\langle X, x_0 \rangle$ is in the transaction associated to a tuple t iff $t[X] = x_0$.

The ordinary measures proposed in (Agrawal et al., 1993) to assess association rules are *confidence* (the conditional probability $p(C|A)$) and *support* (the joint probability $p(A \cup C)$).

An alternative framework was proposed in (Berzal et al., 2001; Berzal et al., 2002). In this framework, accuracy is measured by means of Shortliffe and Buchanan's certainty factors (Shortliffe and Buchanan, 1975), in the following way: the certainty factor of the rule $A \Rightarrow C$ is

$$CF(A \Rightarrow C) = \frac{(Conf(A \Rightarrow C)) - S(C)}{1 - S(C)} \quad (1)$$

if $Conf(A \Rightarrow C) > S(C)$, and

$$CF(A \Rightarrow C) = \frac{(Conf(A \Rightarrow C)) - S(C)}{S(C)} \quad (2)$$

if $Conf(A \Rightarrow C) < S(C)$, and 0 otherwise.

Certainty factors take values in $[-1, 1]$, indicating the extent to which our belief that the consequent is true varies when the antecedent is also true. It ranges from 1, meaning maximum increment (i.e., when A is true then C is true) to -1, meaning maximum decrement.

3.2   Approximate Dependencies

A functional dependence $V \rightarrow W$ holds in a relational scheme RE if and only if $V, W \subseteq RE$ and for every instance r of RE

$$\forall t, s \in r \; if \; t[V] = s[V] \; then \; t[W] = s[W] \quad (3)$$

Approximate dependencies can be roughly defined as functional dependencies with exceptions. The definition of approximate dependence is then a matter of how to define exceptions, and how to measure the accuracy of the dependence (Bosc and Lietard, 1997). We shall follow the approach introduced in (Delgado et al., 2000; Blanco et al., 2000), where the same methodology employed in mining for AR's is applied to the discovery of AD's.

The idea is that, since a functional dependency "$V \rightarrow W$" can be seen as a rule that relates the equality of attribute values in pairs of tuples (see equation (3)), and association rules relate the presence of items in transactions, we can represent approximate dependencies as association rules by using the following interpretations of the concepts of item and transaction:

- An item is an object associated to an attribute of RE. For every attribute $At_k \in RE$ we note it_{At_k} the associated item.

- We introduce the itemset I_V to be

$$I_V = \{it_{At_k} \mid At_k \in V\}$$

- T_r is a T-set that, for each pair of tuples $< t, s > \in r \times r$ contains a transaction $ts \in T_r$ verifying

$$it_{At_k} \in ts \; \Leftrightarrow \; t[At_k] = s[At_k]$$

It is obvious that $|T_r| = |r \times r| = n^2$.

Then, an approximate dependence $V \rightarrow W$ in the relation r is an association rule $I_V \Rightarrow I_W$ in T_r (Delgado et al., 2000; Blanco et al., 2000). The support and certainty factor of $I_V \Rightarrow I_W$ measure the interest and accuracy of the dependence $V \rightarrow W$.

3.3   Fuzzy Association Rules

In (Delgado et al., 2003), the model for association rules is extended in order to manage fuzzy values in databases. The approach is based on the definition of fuzzy transactions as fuzzy subsets of items. Let $I = \{i_1, \ldots, i_m\}$ be a set of items and T' be a set of fuzzy transactions, where each fuzzy transaction is a fuzzy subset of I. Let $\tilde{\tau} \in T'$ be a fuzzy transaction,

we note $\tilde{\tau}(i_k)$ the membership degree of i_k in $\tilde{\tau}$. A fuzzy association rule is an implication of the form $A \Rightarrow C$ such that $A, C \subset RE$ and $A \cap C = \emptyset$.

It is immediate that the set of transactions where a given item appears is a fuzzy set. We call it *representation* of the item. For item i_k in T' we have the following fuzzy subset of T':

$$\tilde{\Gamma}_{i_k} = \sum_{\tilde{\tau} \in T'} \tilde{\tau}(i_k)/\tilde{\tau} \quad (4)$$

This representation can be extended to itemsets as follows: let $I_0 \subset I$ be an itemset, its representation is the following subset of T':

$$\tilde{\Gamma}_{I_0} = \bigcap_{i \in I_0} \tilde{\Gamma}_i = min_{i \in I_0} \tilde{\Gamma}_i \quad (5)$$

In order to measure the interest and accuracy of a fuzzy association rule, we must use approximate reasoning tools, because of the imprecision that affects fuzzy transactions and, consequently, the representation of itemsets. In (Delgado et al., 2003), a semantic approach is proposed based on the evaluation of quantified sentences (see (Zadeh, 1983)). Let Q be a fuzzy coherent quantifier:

- The support of an itemset $\tilde{\Gamma}_{I_0}$ is equal to the result of evaluating the quantified sentence Q of T' are $\tilde{\Gamma}_{I_0}$.

- The support of the fuzzy association rule $A \Rightarrow C$ in the FT-set T', $Supp(A \Rightarrow C)$, is the evaluation of the quantified sentence Q of T are $\tilde{\Gamma}_{A \cup C} = Q$ of T are $(\tilde{\Gamma}_A \cap \tilde{\Gamma}_C)$.

- The confidence of the fuzzy association rule $A \Rightarrow C$ in the FT-set T', $Conf(A \Rightarrow C)$, is the evaluation of the quantified sentence Q of $\tilde{\Gamma}_A$ are $\tilde{\Gamma}_C$.

As seen in (Delgado et al., 2003), the proposed method is a generalization of the ordinary association rule assessment framework in the crisp case.

3.4   Fuzzy Approximate Dependencies

As seen in (Bosc and Lietard, 1997), it is possible to extend the concept of functional dependence in several ways by smoothing some of the elements of the rule in equation 3. We want to consider as much cases as we can, integrating both approximate dependencies (exceptions) and fuzzy dependencies. For that purpose, in addition to allowing exceptions, we have considered the relaxation of several elements of the definition of functional dependencies. In particular we consider membership degrees associated to pairs (attribute, value) as in the case of fuzzy association rules, and also fuzzy similarity relations to smooth the equality of the rule in equation 3.

We shall define fuzzy approximate dependencies in a relation as fuzzy association rules on a special FT-set obtained from that relation, in the same way that approximate dependencies are defined as association rules on a special T-set.

Let $I_{RE} = \{it_{At_k} | At_k \in RE\}$ be the set of items associated to the set of attributes RE. We define a FT-set T'_r associated to table r with attributes in RE as follows: for each pair of rows $< t, s >$ in $r \times r$ we have a fuzzy transaction ts in T'_r defined as

$$\forall it_{At_k} \in T'_r, ts(it_{At_k}) =$$

$$min(\mu_t(At_k), \mu_s(At_k), S_{At_k}(t(At_k), s(At_k))) \quad (6)$$

This way, the membership degree of a certain item it_{At_k} in the transaction associated to tuples t and s takes into account the membership degree of the value of At_k in each tuple and the similarity between them. This value represents the degree to which tuples t and s agree in At_k, i.e., the kind of items that are related by the rule in equation 3. On this basis, we define fuzzy approximate dependencies as follows (Berzal et al., 2003; Serrano, 2003):

Let $X, Y \subseteq RE$ with $X \cap Y = \emptyset$ and $X, Y \neq \emptyset$. The fuzzy approximate dependence $X \to Y$ in r is defined as the fuzzy association rule $I_X \Rightarrow I_Y$ in T'_r.

The support and certainty factor of $I_X \Rightarrow I_Y$ are calculated from T'_r as explained in sections 3.3 and 3.1, and they are employed to measure the importance and accuracy of $X \to Y$.

A FAD $X \to Y$ holds with total accuracy (certainty factor $CF(X \to Y) = 1$) in a relation r iff $ts(I_X) \leq ts(I_Y)\ \forall ts \in T'_r$ (let us remember that $ts(I_X) = \min_{At_k \in X} ts(it_{At_k})\ \forall X \subseteq RE$). Moreover, since fuzzy association rules generalize crisp association rules, FAD's generalize AD's.

Additional properties and an efficient algorithm for computing FAD's can be found in (Berzal et al., 2003; Serrano, 2003).

3.5   Fuzzy Association Rules with Fuzzy Similarity Relations

Fuzzy logic can be an effective tool for representation of heterogeneous data. In fact, fuzzy similarity relations allow us to establish semantic links between values.

Several fuzzy association rules definitions can be found in the literature but, to our knowledge, none of them contemplates fuzzy similarity relations between values. Given two items $i_0 = < A, a_0 >$ and $i_1 = < A, a_1 >$, and a similarity degree $S_A(a_0, a_1) = \alpha$, it would be desirable to have into account how the support of an item is affected by appearances of similar items.

In (Sánchez et al., 2004), we extend the definition of fuzzy association rule (section 3.3)in the following

way. Let $A \in RE$ be an attribute, and $dom(A) = \{a_1, \ldots, a_p\}$ the set of possible values of A. For each $a_i \in A$, we define a linguistic label E_{a_i} as the function

$$E_{a_i} : A \to [0, 1]; E_{a_i}(a) = S_A(a_i, a) \quad (7)$$

where $S_A(a_i, a)$ is the similarity degree between a_i and a. Let I_A be the set of items where each item is associated to a pair $< A, E_{a_i} >$, $|I_A| = |dom(A)|$. This way, each time an item appears, we reflect its similarity with other items as the compatibility degree returned by its linguistic label. Moreover, according to this representation, we can apply the same methodology proposed in (Delgado et al., 2003) in order to obtain fuzzy association rules.

4   EXPERIMENTS

To carry out the aggregation process, we started from 14 databases, created from local information sources, that constitute the so called Local Soil Databases (LSDB). In this context, we denominated *"local"* information source each one of the categories for Discriminant Attributes in Table 1. Likewise, the Aggregated Soil Database (ASDB) results from the *"aggregation"* or inclusion in one large database of every local information source. During this process, a number of factors, that we called imprecision factors in Aggregated Soil Databases (IFASDB), appeared, causing a loss of accuracy and effectiveness in representation, extraction and management of knowledge allusive to the problem in the real world at ASDB level. We could describe several IFASDB, but in this work we considered only three that resume, in great part, all the others. This factors are: the ecogeographical variability, the bibliography from we extracted data and the set of protocols and standard techniques used by authors to describe and analyze soils (discriminant attributes *Mesoenvironment, Bibliographic Source* and *Protocol*, respectively, in Table 1). At this point, we must also describe the mesoenvironments (Sierra Nevada, Sierra of Gádor and Southeast). Relations between soil attributes and values that can be studied by means of our data mining techniques are numerous. The expert can enumerate a huge amount of basic well-known relations in Soil Science, i.e: mean annual rainfall and altitude, % of slope and % of clay, % of $CaCO_2$ and pH, original material and effective soil thickness, structure type and Horizon type, etc. We called all this rules *A Priori Expert Rules* (PER). From the set of PERs, we selected the rules derived from the dependence

$$HorizonType \to \%OrganicCarbon$$

This relates two very meaningful attributes in Soil Science:

- The horizon type definition and classification are conditioned for OC (Organic Carbon) content, a diagnostic feature in most employed systems of soil classification (Soil-Survey-Staff, 1975; FAO, 1998).

- OC content is highly sensitive to ecological and geographical variability in Mediterranean climate type.

- Both attributes are good indicators for several soil forming processes as melanization, accumulation, vertisolation, isohumification, horizonation, mineralization. . .

- OC content is an useful index for physical and biochemical degradation of soils, and it is in strict dependence with management.

- Analytical methods for OC content determination are not very sensitive to uncertainty, as opposed to the type of horizon. The latter is highly imprecise and is closely related with the analyst's competence and finality.

Once PERs are selected, we study the obtained ARs, ADs, FARs and FADs at both local and aggregated levels (LSDB and ASDB, respectively). By means of CF, we assess the extracted knowledge and suggest appropriate considerations for use of this data mining techniques, from an expert's point of view.

4.1   Knowledge Sources. Pretreatment of Soil Information

The ASDB included soil information about three mesoenvironments from the South and Southeast of the Iberian Peninsula under Mediterranean climate: Sierra Nevada, Sierra of Gádor and Southeast (involving part of the provinces of Murcia and Almería). Table 1 shows the main characteristics of local information sources. We used two Ph.D. Thesis and five cartographic sheets from LUCDEME, scale 1:100000.

Data from Sierra of Gádor was extracted from (Oyonarte, 1990) and consists of 70 soil profiles and 176 horizons. Altitude fluctuates from 100 to 2200 m, and rainfall from 213 mm/year (semiarid climate) to 813 mm/year (wet climate), with a mean annual rainfall of 562 mm/year. Lowest annual mean temperature is 6.4 C and the highest is 21.0 C, with a mean of 12.7 C. Original soil materials are of carbonated type, mainly limestones and dolomites.

Data from Southeast was extracted from LUCDEME soil maps, specifically from sheets 1041 from Vera, Almería (Delgado et al., 1991), 911 from Cehegin, Murcia (Alias, 1987), 1030 from Tabernas, Almería (Pérez Pujalte, 1987), 912 from Mula, Murcia (Alias, 1986) and 1031 from Sorbas, Almería (Pérez Pujalte, 1989). There is a total of 89 soil profiles and 262 horizons. Altitude fluctuates from 65 to 1120 m, and rainfall from 183 mm/year (arid climate) to 359 mm/year (semiarid climate), with a mean annual rainfall of 300 mm/year. Lowest annual mean temperature is 13.2 C and the highest is 19.0 C, with a mean of 17.0 C. Geological environment and Original soil materials are extremely different, we can find carbonated, acids and volcanic rocks.

Data from Sierra Nevada was extracted from (Sánchez-Marañón, 1992). There is a total of 35 soil profiles and 103 horizons. Altitude fluctuates from 1320 to 3020 m, and rainfall from 748 mm/year (semihumid climate) to 1287 mm/year (hiperhumid climate), with a mean annual rainfall of 953 mm/year. Lowest annual mean temperature is 0.0 C and the highest is 12.1 C. Geological environment and Original soil materials are mainly acids, but it is not strange to find basic rocks.

Attributes with numeric domains were discretized, following some of the methodologies discussed in (Hussain et al., 1999), under supervision of domain experts. A set of linguistic labels $\{Low, Medium, High\}$ was defined for every numeric attribute. Attributes with categorical domains were fuzzified considering fuzzy similarity relations.

4.2   Analyzing Discovered Knowledge

4.2.1   Crisp Case

When we considered crisp relations from ASDB (Table 2), we found only one AD, $HorizonType \rightarrow \%OrganicCarbon$ with CF 0.089, that reveal a strong grade of independence between these attributes. Provisionally, this conclusion contradicts the expert experience, confirmed in the bibliography. As we could expect, we obtained only four ARs, mainly with consequent $[\%OrganicCarbon = Low]$. This fact was not surprising to us, because the "Low" category had a high support (70%) ASDB. As the support threshold for rules was 10%, rules having "Medium" and "High" categories, were not found. In both cases, crisp data mining was not satisfactory enough for Soil Scientists, and we could not "fuse" ASDB and expert knowledge. Otherwise, when we considered separately the information stored in LSDBs (Table 3), we obtained approximate dependencies with higher CF than in ASDB. This phenomenon could reflect the action of IFASDB. Despite of this, some local dependencies showed smaller CF values than in the aggregated case, and express a total independence.

4.2.2 Fuzzy Case

Observing FADs from ASDB, a CF of 0.31 is found (Table 2). Despite of this low CF, the dependence degree shown between $HorizonType$ and OC content was more informative than in the crisp case. It reflected better the expert knowledge. Even though, initially, the soil scientist expected a higher degree, it can be explained due to the influence of soils placed at Southeast Mesoenvironment in ASDB. Indeed, due to the arid nature of this climate, it could be expected that one of the main soil forming factors, OC content incorporated to soil from vegetation, were low and homogenous. The latter conclusion can be checked regarding Table 4. Moreover, fuzzy data mining let us obtain a higher number of rules than in crisp case. This supposes, quantitatively, a higher volume of discovered knowledge.

A good example of correspondence or *"fusion"* between databases and expert knowledge could be obtained comparing ARs from Sierra de Gádor with Southeast ones. The former had rules with *"moderate"* and *"high"* OC content in consequent, whereas the latter had a *"low"* value in consequent. Sierra of Gádor has a higher mean altitude and mean annual rainfall, and, consequently, more vegetation in soil and horizons (especially in Ah type). Looking at this, the fuzzy model reflects more accurately soil forming processes as melanization and accumulation. We can also examine others IFSDB in addition to *Mesoenvironment*. I.e., *Protocol* constitute an important source of variability in ASDB. Comparing *"Perez"* and *"Alias"* categories, the former has more ARs (Table 6) and relates more categories, reflecting a more detailed and precise knowledge than *"Alias"*. *"Perez"* protocols (including field description, analysis and other techniques) seem to be more reliable than *"Alias"* ones.

5 CONCLUSIONS

We have seen how large databases can be divided into homogeneous subsets defining one or more discriminant attributes. This division, followed by a knowledge discovery process, can allow us to discover previously unnoticed relations in data.

We conclude that, for this particular case, knowledge extracted by means of fuzzy data mining was more suitable to *"fusion"* or comparison with expert knowledge that crisp. Moreover, fuzzy data mining was sensitive to low support categories as $[\%OrganicCarbon = Low]$ or $[HorizonType = Bk\ or\ Btk]$, discarded in crisp data mining.

We could confirm that fuzzy data mining is highly sensitive to latent knowledge in ASDBs. That fact is very important for a soil scientist, since lets us apply it with the assurance that imprecision and uncertainty factors (IFASDB) will not distort or alter the knowledge discovery process.

As a future task, we propose to solve this same problem in a general case. With a domain expert aid, we must define the set of criteria for database decomposition but also discern when fuzzy techniques get better results than crisp ones.

REFERENCES

Agrawal, R., Imielinski, T., and Swami, A. (1993). Mining association rules between sets of items in large databases. In *Proc. Of the 1993 ACM SIGMOD Conference*, pages 207–216.

Alias, J. (1986). *Mapa de suelos de Mula. Mapa 1:100000 y memoria*. LUCDEME; MAPA-ICONA-University of Murcia.

Alias, J. (1987). *Mapa de suelos de Cehegin. Mapa 1:100000 y memoria*. LUCDEME; MAPA-ICONA-University of Murcia.

Berzal, F., Blanco, I., Sánchez, D., Serrano, J., , and Vila, M. (2003). A definition for fuzzy approximate dependencies. *Fuzzy Sets and Systems*. Submitted.

Berzal, F., Blanco, I., Sánchez, D., and Vila, M. (2001). A new framework to assess association rules. In Hoffmann, F., editor, Advances in Intelligent Data Analysis. Fourth International Symposium, IDA'01. Lecture Notes in Computer Science 2189, pages 95–104. Springer-Verlag.

Berzal, F., Blanco, I., Sánchez, D., and Vila, M. (2002). Measuring the accuracy and interest of association rules: A new framework. *Intelligent Data Analysis*. An extension of (Berzal et al., 2001), submitted.

Blanco, I., Martín-Bautista, M., Sánchez, D., and Vila, M. (2000). On the support of dependencies in relational databases: strong approximate dependencies. *Data Mining and Knowledge Discovery*. Submitted.

Bosc, P. and Lietard, L. (1997). Functional dependencies revisited under graduality and imprecision. In Annual Meeting of NAFIPS, pages 57–62.

Bui, E. and Moran, C. (2003). A strategy to fill gaps in soil over large spatial extents: An example from the murray-darlin basin of australia. *Geoderma, 111*, pages 21–44.

Cazemier, D., Lagacherie, P., and R., M.-C. (2001). A possibility theory approach from estimating available water capacity from imprecise information contained in soil databases. *Geoderma, 103*, pages 113–132.

Delgado, G., Delgado, R., Gamiz, E., Párraga, J., Sánchez Marañon, M., Medina, J., and Martín-García, J. (1991). *Mapa de Suelos de Vera*. LUCDEME, ICONA-Universidad de Granada.

Delgado, M., Marín, N., Sánchez, D., and Vila, M. (2003). Fuzzy association rules: General model and applications. *IEEE Transactions on Fuzzy Systems 11(2)*, pages 214–225.

Delgado, M., Martín-Bautista, M., Sánchez, D., and Vila, M. (2000). Mining strong approximate dependencies from relational databases. In Proceedings of IPMU'2000.

FAO (1998). The world reference base for soil resources. world soil resources. Technical Report 84, ISSS/AISS/IBG/ISRIC/FAO, Rome.

Hussain, F., Liu, H., Tan, C., and Dash, M. (1999). Discretization: An enabling technique. Technical report, The National University of Singapore.

Oyonarte, C. (1990). *Estudio Edáfico de la Sierra de Gádor (Almera). Evaluación para usos forestales*. PhD thesis, University of Granada.

Pérez Pujalte, A. (1987). *Mapa de suelos de Tabernas. Mapa 1:100000 y memoria*. LUCDEME; MAPA-ICONA-CSIC.

Pérez Pujalte, A. (1989). *Mapa de suelos de Sorbas. Mapa 1:100000 y memoria*. LUCDEME; MAPA-ICONA-CSIC.

Qian, H., Klinka, K., and Lavkulich, L. (1993). Relationships between color value and nitrogen in forest mineral soils. *Can. J. Soil Sci., 73*, pages 61–72.

Sánchez, D., Sánchez, J. R., Serrano, J. M., and Vila, M. A. (2004). Association rules over imprecise domains involving fuzzy similarity relations. To be submitted to Estylf 2004.

Sánchez-Marañón, M. (1992). *Los suelos del Macizo de Sierra Nevada. Evaluación y capacidad de uso (in Spanish)*. PhD thesis, University of Granada.

Sánchez-Marañón, M., Delgado, R., Párraga, J., and Delgado, G. (1996). Multivariate analysis in the quantitative evaluation of soils for reforestation in the sierra nevada (southern spain). *Geoderma, 69*, pages 233–248.

Scheinost, A. and Schwertmann, U. (1999). Color identification of iron oxides and hydroxisulfates: Uses and limitations. *Soil Sci. Soc. Am. J., 65*, pages 1463–1461.

Serrano, J. (2003). *Fusin de Conocimiento en Bases de Datos Relacionales: Medidas de Agregacin y Resumen (in Spanish)*. PhD thesis, University of Granada.

Shortliffe, E. and Buchanan, B. (1975). A model of inexact reasoning in medicine. Mathematical Biosciences, *23*, pages 351–379.

Soil-Survey-Staff (1975). *Soil Taxonomy*. U.S. Dept. Agri. Handbook No. 436.

Ulery, A. and Graham, R. (1993). Forest-fire effects on soil color and texture. *Soil Sci. Soc. Am. J., 57*, pages 135–140.

Webster, R. (1977). *Quantitative and Numerical Methods in Soil Classification and Survey*. Claredon Press, Oxford.

Zadeh, L. (1983). A computational approach to fuzzy quantifiers in natural languages. *Computing and Mathematics with Applications*, 9(1):149–184.

Table 1: Discriminant attributes for the soil database

Mesoenvironment	Soil profile	Horizon
Sierra Nevada [SN]	35	103
Sierra Gádor[SB]	70	176
Southeast [SE]	89	262
Bibliographic source	**Soil profile**	**Horizon**
Ph.D. Thesis [MARAÑON]	35	103
Ph.D. Thesis [OYONARTE]	70	176
LUCDEME sheet 1014, Vera.[VERA]	29	76
LUCDEME sheet 1030, Tabernas. [TABERNA]	14	37
LUCDEME sheet 1031, Sorbas. [SORBAS]	24	72
LUCDEME sheet 912, Cehegn. [CEHEGIN]	10	32
LUCDEME sheet 911, Mula. [MULA]	12	45
Acting protocol	**Soil profile**	**Horizon**
Sánchez-Marañon, M. [SANCHEZ]	35	103
Oyonarte, C. [CECILIO]	70	176
Pérez-Pujalte, A. [PEREZ]	67	185
Alías, L. [ALIAS]	22	77

Table 2: Obtained CF in ASDB ($HorizonType \rightarrow \%OrganicCarbon$)

Approx. Dep.	CF 0.09
Assoc. Rules	$[C] \Rightarrow [L]$, CF 0.8
	$[Bw] \Rightarrow [L]$, CF 0.7
	$[Ah] \Rightarrow [L]$, CF -0.39
	$[Ah] \Rightarrow [M]$, CF 0.41
F. Approx. Dep.	CF 0.31
F. Assoc. Rules	$[Ck] \Rightarrow [L]$, CF 0.53
	$[C] \Rightarrow [L]$, CF 0.69
	$[Bwk] \Rightarrow [L]$, CF 0.23
	$[Bw] \Rightarrow [L]$, CF 0.41
	$[Bw] \Rightarrow [M]$, CF 0.25
	$[Btk] \Rightarrow [L]$, CF 0.81
	$[Bt] \Rightarrow [L]$, CF 1
	$[Bk] \Rightarrow [L]$, CF 0.49
	$[Ap] \Rightarrow [L]$, CF 0.50
	$[Ah] \Rightarrow [L]$, CF -0.01
	$[Ah] \Rightarrow [M]$, CF 0.13
	$[Ah] \Rightarrow [H]$, CF 0.28

Table 3: Obtained CF in crisp LSDB ($HorizonType \rightarrow$ %$OrganicCarbon$)

Mesoenv.	AD	AR
SE	CF 0.01	$[Ap] \Rightarrow [L]$, CF 0.56 $[Bw] \Rightarrow [L]$, CF 0.81 $[Ah] \Rightarrow [L]$, CF -0.19 $[Ah] \Rightarrow [M]$, CF 0.23
SB	CF 0.37	$[Bw] \Rightarrow [L]$, CF 0.65 $[Ah] \Rightarrow [L]$, CF -0.58 $[Ah] \Rightarrow [M]$, CF 0.57
SN	CF 0.11	$[C] \Rightarrow [L]$, CF 1 $[Bw] \Rightarrow [L]$, CF 1 $[Ah] \Rightarrow [L]$, CF -0.35 $[Ah] \Rightarrow [M]$, CF 0.35
Bib. source	**AD**	**AR**
CEHEGIN	CF 0.12	$[Ck] \Rightarrow [L]$, CF -0.15 $[Ap] \Rightarrow [L]$, CF 1 $[Ah] \Rightarrow [L]$, CF -0.32
MARAÑON	CF 0.11	$[C] \Rightarrow [L]$, CF 1 $[Bw] \Rightarrow [L]$, CF 1 $[Ah] \Rightarrow [L]$, CF -0.35 $[Ah] \Rightarrow [M]$, CF 0.35
MULA	CF 0.73	$[C] \Rightarrow [L]$, CF 1 $[Ap] \Rightarrow [L]$, CF 1
OYONARTE	CF 0.37	$[Bw] \Rightarrow [L]$, CF 0.65 $[Ah] \Rightarrow [L]$, CF -0.58 $[Ah] \Rightarrow [M]$, CF 0.57
SORBAS	CF -0.01	$[C] \Rightarrow [L]$, CF 1 $[Bw] \Rightarrow [L]$, CF 1 $[Ap] \Rightarrow [L]$, CF -0.07 $[Ah] \Rightarrow [M]$, CF -0.02
TABERNAS	CF -0.02	$[C] \Rightarrow [L]$, CF -0.03 $[Bw] \Rightarrow [L]$, CF 1 $[Ap] \Rightarrow [L]$, CF -0.13 $[Ah] \Rightarrow [L]$, CF -0.01
VERA	CF 0.07	$[C] \Rightarrow [L]$, CF 0.5 $[Ap] \Rightarrow [L]$, CF -0.23
Acting prot.	**AD**	**AR**
ALIAS	CF 0.53	$[Ck] \Rightarrow [L]$, CF -0,23 $[Ck] \Rightarrow [L]$, CF 1 $[Ck] \Rightarrow [L]$, CF 1
CECILIO	CF 0.37	$[Bw] \Rightarrow [L]$, CF 0.65 $[Ah] \Rightarrow [L]$, CF -0.58 $[Ah] \Rightarrow [M]$, CF 0.57
SANCHEZ	CF 0.11	$[C] \Rightarrow [L]$, CF 1 $[Bw] \Rightarrow [L]$, CF 1 $[Ah] \Rightarrow [L]$, CF -0.35 $[Ah] \Rightarrow [M]$, CF 0.35
PEREZ	CF -0.04	$[C] \Rightarrow [L]$, CF 0.41 $[Bw] \Rightarrow [L]$, CF 0.81 $[Ah] \Rightarrow [L]$, CF -0.16 $[Ah] \Rightarrow [M]$, CF 0.19

Table 4: Obtained CF in fuzzy LSDB ($HorizonType \rightarrow$ %$OrganicCarbon$) (i)

Mesoenv.	FAD	FAR
SE	CF 0.38	$[Ck] \Rightarrow [L]$, CF 0.54 $[C] \Rightarrow [L]$, CF 0.73 $[Bwk] \Rightarrow [L]$, CF 0.43 $[Bw] \Rightarrow [L]$, CF 0.80 $[Btk] \Rightarrow [L]$, CF 0.88 $[Bt] \Rightarrow [L]$, CF 0.61 $[Bk] \Rightarrow [L]$, CF -0.03 $[Ap] \Rightarrow [L]$, CF 0.66 $[Ah] \Rightarrow [L]$, CF 0.23 $[Ah] \Rightarrow [M]$, CF 0.18
SB	CF 0.35	$[C] \Rightarrow [M]$, CF -0.05 $[C] \Rightarrow [H]$, CF -0.05 $[Bwk] \Rightarrow [M]$, CF 0.57 $[Bwk] \Rightarrow [H]$, CF 0.06 $[Btk] \Rightarrow [M]$, CF -0.05 $[Btk] \Rightarrow [H]$, CF -0.05 $[Bw] \Rightarrow [M]$, CF 0.48 $[Bw] \Rightarrow [H]$, CF 0.11 $[Bt] \Rightarrow [M]$, CF 0.31 $[Bt] \Rightarrow [H]$, CF -0.05 $[Ap] \Rightarrow [M]$, CF 0.30 $[Ap] \Rightarrow [H]$, CF -0.05 $[Ah] \Rightarrow [M]$, CF 0.07 $[Ah] \Rightarrow [H]$, CF 0.37
SN	CF 0.34	$[Ck] \Rightarrow [L]$, CF 0.80 $[C] \Rightarrow [L]$, CF 0.72 $[Bwk] \Rightarrow [L]$, CF 0.81 $[Bw] \Rightarrow [L]$, CF 0.41 $[Bw] \Rightarrow [M]$, CF 0.30 $[Bt] \Rightarrow [L]$, CF -0.01 $[Ap] \Rightarrow [L]$, CF -0.01 $[Ah] \Rightarrow [L]$, CF 0.26 $[Ah] \Rightarrow [M]$, CF 0.15 $[Ah] \Rightarrow [H]$, CF 0.05

Table 5: Obtained CF in fuzzy LSDB ($HorizonType \rightarrow$ $\%OrganicCarbon$) (ii)

Bib. source	FAD	FAR
CEHEGIN	CF 0.52	$[Ck] \Rightarrow [L]$, CF 0.55 $[C] \Rightarrow [L]$, CF 0.80 $[Bwk] \Rightarrow [L]$, CF 0.85 $[Bw] \Rightarrow [L]$, CF 0.85 $[Ap] \Rightarrow [L]$, CF 0.34 $[Ap] \Rightarrow [M]$, CF 0.26 $[Ah] \Rightarrow [L]$, CF 0.09 $[Ah] \Rightarrow [M]$, CF 0.48
MULA	CF 0.72	$[Ck] \Rightarrow [L]$, CF 0.77 $[C] \Rightarrow [L]$, CF 0.81 $[Bwk] \Rightarrow [L]$, CF -0.03 $[Bw] \Rightarrow [L]$, CF -0.03 $[Ap] \Rightarrow [L]$, CF 0.80 $[Ah] \Rightarrow [L]$, CF 0.33
SORBAS	CF 0.65	$[Ck] \Rightarrow [L]$, CF 0.96 $[C] \Rightarrow [L]$, CF 0.96 $[Bw] \Rightarrow [L]$, CF 0.95 $[Bt] \Rightarrow [L]$, CF 0.96 $[Ap] \Rightarrow [L]$, CF 0.85 $[Ah] \Rightarrow [L]$, CF 0.66
TABERNAS	CF 0.52	$[Ck] \Rightarrow [L]$, CF 0.93 $[C] \Rightarrow [L]$, CF 0.78 $[Bwk] \Rightarrow [L]$, CF 0.93 $[Bw] \Rightarrow [L]$, CF 0.91 $[Bt] \Rightarrow [L]$, CF 0.93 $[Ap] \Rightarrow [L]$, CF 0.72 $[Ah] \Rightarrow [M]$, CF 0.52
VERA	CF 0.25	$[Ck] \Rightarrow [M]$, **CF 0.79** $[C] \Rightarrow [L]$, CF 0.44 $[Bwk] \Rightarrow [L]$, **CF 0.77** $[Bw] \Rightarrow [L]$, CF 0.60 $[Btk] \Rightarrow [L]$, CF 0.78 $[Bt] \Rightarrow [L]$, CF 0.24 $[Bt] \Rightarrow [M]$, CF 0.37 $[Ap] \Rightarrow [L]$, CF 0.45 $[Ap] \Rightarrow [M]$, CF 0.14 $[Ah] \Rightarrow [L]$, CF 0.05 $[Ah] \Rightarrow [M]$, CF 0.16 $[Ah] \Rightarrow [H]$, CF 0.23

Table 6: Obtained CF in fuzzy LSDB ($HorizonType \rightarrow$ $\%OrganicCarbon$) (iii)

Acting prot.	FAD	FAR
ALIAS	CF 0.61	$[Ck] \Rightarrow [L]$, CF 0.50 $[C] \Rightarrow [L]$, CF 0.85 $[Bwk] \Rightarrow [L]$, CF 0.44 $[Bw] \Rightarrow [L]$, CF 0.44 $[Ap] \Rightarrow [L]$, CF 0.62 $[Ah] \Rightarrow [L]$, CF 0.19 $[Ah] \Rightarrow [M]$, CF 0.33
PEREZ	CF 0.33	$[Ck] \Rightarrow [L]$, CF 0.57 $[C] \Rightarrow [L]$, CF 0.66 $[Bwk] \Rightarrow [L]$, CF 0.43 $[Bw] \Rightarrow [L]$, CF 0.82 $[Btk] \Rightarrow [L]$, CF 0.87 $[Bt] \Rightarrow [L]$, CF 0.60 $[Bk] \Rightarrow [L]$, CF -0.01 $[Ap] \Rightarrow [L]$, CF 0.67 $[Ah] \Rightarrow [L]$, CF 0.25 $[Ah] \Rightarrow [M]$, CF 0.15 $[Ah] \Rightarrow [H]$, CF 0.24

PART 3

Information Systems Analysis and Specification

ANALYSIS AND RE-ENGINEERING OF WEB SERVICES

Axel Martens

Humboldt-Universität zu Berlin,
Department of Computer Science
E-mail: martens@informatik.hu-berlin.de

Keywords: Web services, Business Processes, Analysis, Usability, Petri nets

Abstract: To an increasing extend software systems are integrated across the borders of individual enterprises. The Web
              service approach provides group of technologies to describe components and their composition, based on well
              established protocols. Focused on business processes, one Web service implements a local subprocess. A
              distributed business processes is implemented by the composition a set of communicating Web services.
              At the moment, there are various modeling languages under development to describe the internal structure of
              one Web service and the choreography of a set of Web services. Nevertheless, there is a need for methods for
              stepwise construction and verification of such components.
              This paper abstracts from concrete syntax of any proposed language definition. Instead, we apply Petri nets to
              model Web services. Thus, we are able to reason about essential properties, e. g. *usability* of a Web service –
              our notion of a quality criterion. Based on this framework, we present an algorithm to analyze a given Web
              service and to transfer a complex process model into a appropriate model of a Web service.

1 INTRODUCTION

In this paper, we focus on the application of Web service technology to distributed business processes: One Web service implements a local subprocess. Thus, we regard a Web services as a stateful system. From composition of a set of Web services there arises a system that implements the distributed business processes.

Within this setting, the quality of each single Web service and the compatibility of a set of Web services are questions of major interest. In this paper, we define the notion of *usability* – our quality criterion of a Web service and present an algorithm to verify this property. Based on this analysis, we present an approach to restructure and simplify a given Web service model.

1.1 Web Services

A *Web service* is a self-describing, self-contained modular application that can be described, published, located, and invoked over a network, e. g. the World Wide Web. A Web service performs an encapsulated function ranging from a simple request-reply to a full business process.

A Web service has a standardized interface and can be accessed via well established protocols. Thus, the Web service approach provides a homogenous layer to address components upon a heterogenous infrastructure.

Instead of one new specific technology, the Web service approach provides group of closely related, established and emerging technologies to model, publish, find and bind Web services – called the *Web service technology stack* (Gottschalk, 2000). This paper is concerned with the application of Web service approach towards the area of business processes. Thus, we focus on the behavior of a Web service, defined by its internal structure.

1.2 Business Processes

A business process consists of a self-contained set of causally ordered activities. Each activity performs a certain functionality, produces and consumes data, requires or provides resources and is executed manually or automatically. A distributed business process consists of local subprocesses that are geographically distributed and/or organizationally independent.

I. Seruca et al. (eds.), Enterprise Information Systems VI, 169–176.
© 2006 *Springer. Printed in the Netherlands.*

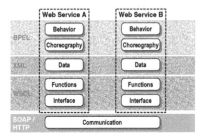

Figure 1: Business processes and Web services

The communication between these subprocesses (via a standardized interface) realizes the coordination of the distributed process. Figure 1 sketches the mapping between the business terms and the Web service technologies.

For each aspect of a distributed business process the Web service technology stack provides an adequate technology, as shown in Figure 1. The *core layers* cover the technical aspects: data are represented by *XML documents*, the functionality and the interface are defined by help of the *Web service Description Language WSDL* and the communication uses standardized protocols, e. g. the *Simple Object Access Protocol SOAP* .

The internal structure of a process and the organizational aspects are covered by the *emerging layers*. There are different proposals towards a specification language. We focus on the *Business Process Execution Language for Web services BPEL4WS* (BEA et al., 2002). In combination with the core layers, BPEL4WS allows to model a business process precisely, such that the model can be directly executed by the middleware. Moreover, an abstract model of the process can be expressed by help of BPEL4WS, too. Such an abstract model is published to the repository such that a potential service requestor can decide, whether or not that service is compatible to his own component.

Although the technological basement is given, there is a lot of open questions: Do two Web services fit together in a way, that the composition yields a deadlock-free system? – the question of *compatibility*. Can one Web service be exchanged by another within a composed system without running into problems? – the question of *equivalence*. Can we reason about the quality of one given Web service without considering the environment it will by used in? In this paper we present the notion of *usability* – our quality criterion of a Web service. This criterion is intuitive and can be easily proven locally. Moreover, this notion allows to answer the other questions mentioned above.

1.3 Solution

The current paper is part of larger framework for modeling and analyzing distributed business processes by help of Web services (Martens, 2004). This framework is based on Petri nets. Petri nets are a well established method for distributed business processes (van der Aalst, 1998b; van der Aalst, 1998a). As we will show, Petri nets are also an adequate modeling language for Web services.

Based on this formalism, we are able to discuss and define *usability* of a Web service – our notion of a quality criterion, and further properties. Due to our abstract view on behavior and structure of Web services, the results presented here can be adopted easily to every concrete modeling language, e. g. BPEL4WS (Martens et al., 2004).

The remaining paper is structured as follows: Section 2 presents very succinctly our modeling approach. Section 3 establishes the core section of this paper: Applied to an example, we present the algorithm to verify usability. Besides the verification of usability, the algorithm generates useful information for re-engineering. Section 4 presents our approach. Finally, Section 5 gives an overview of the methods that belong to our framework.

2 MODELING

The following section presents our modeling approach. To deal with the problems of distributed business processes in a generic manner, we use Petri nets. Thus, we give a short introduction to Petri nets and show how to model a Web service. Afterwards we deal with the composition of those models and discuss their essential properties.

2.1 Modeling Web Services

A distributed business process comes into existence because of composition of Web services. Each of these Web services represents a local subprocess. Figure 2 shows the model of such two subprocess – the Web service of a travel agency and the Web service of a customer.

A business process consists of a self-contained set of activities which are causally ordered. A Petri net $N = (P, T, F)$ consists of a set of *transitions* T (boxes), a set of *places* P (ellipses) and a *flow relation* F (arcs) (Reisig, 1985). A transition represents an active element, i. e. an activity (e. g. Get Itinerary). A place represents a passive element, i. e. a state between activities, a resource or a message channel (e. g. Itinerary).

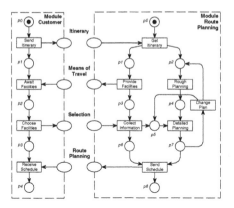

Figure 2: A workflow module and its environment

A Web service consists of internal structures that realize a local subprocess and an interface to communicate with its environment, i. e. other Web services. Thus, we model a Web service by help of a workflow net – a special Petri net, that has two distinguished places $\alpha, \omega \in P$ to denote the begin (α) and the end (ω) of a process (van der Aalst, 1998a) – supplemented by an interface, i. e. a set of places representing directed message channels. Such a model we call *workflow module*.

Definition 2.1 (Module).
A finite Petri net $M = (P, T, F)$ is called *workflow module* (*module* for short), iff:

(i) The set of places is divided into three disjoint sets: *internal places* P^N, *input places* P^I and *output places* P^O.

(ii) The flow relation is divided into *internal flow* $F^N \subseteq (P^N \times T) \cup (T \times P^N)$ and *communication flow* $F^C \subseteq (P^I \times T) \cup (T \times P^O)$.

(iii) The net $\mathcal{N}(M) = (P^N, T, F^N)$ is a workflow net.

(iv) Non of the transitions is connected both to an input place and an output place.   *

Figure 2 shows on the right side the workflow module of a travel agency. The module is triggered by an incoming Itinerary. Then the control flow splits into two concurrent threads. On the left side, an available Means of travel are offered to the customer and the service awaits his Selection. Meanwhile, on the right side, a Rough Planning may happen . The Detailed Planning requires information from the customer. Finally, the service sends a Route Planning to the customer.

2.2   Composing Web Services

A distributed business process is realized by the composition of a set of Web services. We will now define the pairwise composition of workflow modules. Because this yields another workflow module, recurrent application of pairwise composition allows us to compose of more than two modules.

Figure 2 shows the module of a travel agency and the module of a customer. Obviously, both modules can be composed. As a precondition for composition, we will define the property of *syntactical compatibility* of two modules.

Definition 2.2 (Syntactical compatibility).
Two workflow modules A and B are called *syntactically compatible*, iff the internal processes of both modules are disjoint, and each common place is an output place of one module and an input place of the other.   *

Two syntactically compatible modules do not need to have a completely matching interface. They might even have a completely disjoint interface. In that case, the reason of composition is at least dubious. When two modules are composed, the common places are merged and the dangling input and output places become the new interface. To achieve a correct module as the result of the composition, we need to add new components for initialization and termination. For more illustrating examples see (Martens, 2004).

Definition 2.3 (Composed system).
Let $A = (P_a, T_a, F_a)$ and $B = (P_b, T_b, F_b)$ be two syntactically compatible modules. Let $\alpha_s, \omega_s \notin (P_a \cup P_b)$ two *new* places and $t_\alpha, t_\omega \notin (T_a \cup T_b)$ two *new* transitions. The *composed system* $\Pi = A \oplus B$ is given by (P_s, T_s, F_s), such that:

• $P_s = P_a \cup P_b \cup \{\alpha_s, \omega_s\}$
• $T_s = T_a \cup T_b \cup \{t_\alpha, t_\omega\}$
• $F_s = F_a \cup F_b \cup \{(\alpha_s, t_\alpha), (t_\alpha, \alpha_a), (t_\alpha, \alpha_b),$
  $(\omega_a, t_\omega), (\omega_b, t_\omega), (t_\omega, \omega_s)\}$

If the composed system contains more than one components for initialization and termination, the corresponding elements are merged.   *

Syntactically, the result of the composition is again a workflow module. Hence, recurrent application of pairwise composition allows us to compose of more than two modules.

Corollary 2.1 (Composing modules): Whenever A and B are two syntactically compatible workflow modules, the composed system $\Pi = A \oplus B$ is a workflow module too.   *

This corollary can be easily proven. We therefore omit the proof here, it can be found in (Martens, 2004).

2.2.1 Usability

This paper focusses on distributed business processes. The composition of two workflow modules A and B represents a business process, if the composed system $\Pi = A \oplus B$ has an empty interface, i.e. Π is a workflow net. In that case, we call A an *environment* of B.

If a module U is an environment of M, obviously M is an environment of U too. Thus, the module Customer shown in Figure 2 is an environment of the module Route Planning.

In the real world, the environment of a Web service may consist of several other Web services. If we want to reason about that specific Web service, we don't have any assumption on its potential environment. Thus, without loss of generality, we may consider its environment as one, arbitrary structured Web service.

Given a workflow module and one environment, it is possible to reason about the quality of the composed system. The notion of *soundness* (van der Aalst, 1998a) is an established quality criterion for workflow nets. Basically, soundness requires each initiated process to come to a proper final state. Because a business process arises from composition of existing components, we use the slightly different notion of *weak soundness*. See (Martens, 2004) for a precise definition.

Obviously, the purpose of a workflow module is to be composed with an environment such that the resulting system is a proper workflow net, i.e. we require the resulting workflow net to be weak sound. Thus, we define *usability* based on weak soundness.

Definition 2.4 (Usability).
Let M be a workflow module.

(i) An environment U *utilizes* the module M, iff the composed system $\Pi = M \oplus U$ is weak sound.

(ii) The module M is called *usable*, iff there exists at least one environment U, such that U utilizes M. ∗

Concerning this definition, the module Customer utilizes the module Route Planning and vice versa. Thus, both modules are called usable. The notion of usability forms the base to derive further properties, e.g. a detailed discussion on compatibility can be found in (Martens, 2003a).

3 ANALYSIS

In the previous section we have introduced the notion of usability. Further essential properties of Web services (e.g. compatibility) can be derived from this notion. The definition of usability itself is based on the existence of an environment. Thus, we cannot disprove the usability of a given Web service, because we have to consider all its possible (infinitely many) environments.

Hence, this section provides a different approach: We derive an adequate representation of the behavior of a given Web service – the *communication graph*. Illustrated by help of an example, we present the algorithm to *decide* usability. Besides the verification of usability, we use the communication graph of a Web service for re-engineering in Section 4.

3.1 Example

To reason about usability, we first take a look on an example that is complex enough to reflect some interesting phenomenons, but small enough to be easily understood. Figure 3 shows this example.

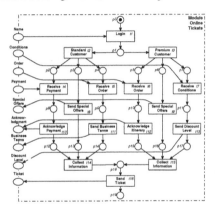

Figure 3: Module online tickets

In this paper, a Web service implements a local business process. Thus, the model of a Web service often is derived from an existing business process model and the structure of the model therefore reflects the organization structure within the process. As we will see later, such a Web service model should be restructured before publishing.

Figure 3 shows a model of a Web service selling online tickets. Basically, the workflow module consists of two separated parts. After the module receives the Name of the customer, an internal decision is made: either the customer is classified as Standard Customer or as Premium Customer. In the first case, only the left part of the module is used, and the right part otherwise. At the end, both cases are join by sending the ordered Ticket.

Within each case, there are three independent threads of control – representing three independent departments: the *marketing dept.* sends Special Offers, the *canvassing dept.* receives the Order and answers by sending the Business Terms or an Acknowledgment, and the *accounts dept.* manages the financial part.

To prove the usability of the workflow module Online Tickets, we try to derive an environment that utilizes this module. Consider a customer who claims to be a Premium Customer. He might send his Name and waits for the Special Offers. Afterwards he sends his Conditions and expects the information on his current Discount Level.

Unfortunately, by some reasons he has lost his status and he is classified as a Standard Customer. In that case, the module ignores the Conditions and waits for the Order and for Payment. The composed system of such a customer and the module Online Tickets has reached a deadlock.

Our first approach to find an utilizing environment was based on the *structure* of a given module. Although the module Online Tickets is usable – as we will see later – this approach went wrong. Hence, our algorithm to decide the usability is based on the behavior of a workflow module.

3.2 The Communication graph

A workflow module is a reactive system, it consumes messages from the environment and produces answers depending on its internal state. The problem is, an environment has no explicit information on the internal state of the module. But each environment does know the structure of the module and can derive some information by considering the communication towards the module. Thus, an environment has implicit information. We reflect exactly that kind of information within a data structure – called the *communication graph*.

Definition 3.1 (communication graph).
A communication graph (V, H, E) is a directed, strongly connected, bipartite graph with some requirements:

- There are two kinds of nodes: *visible* nodes V and *hidden* nodes H. Each edge $e \in E$ connects two nodes of different kinds.

- The graph has a definite root node $v_0 \in V$, each leaf is a visible node, too.

- There exists a labeling $m = (m_v, m_e)$, such that m_v yield an definite set of states for each visible node and m_e yields a bag of messages to each edge.

*

For the precise, mathematical definition see (Martens, 2004). Figure 4 shows the communication graph of module Online Tickets. Some parts of the graph a drawn with dashed lines – we will com to this later.

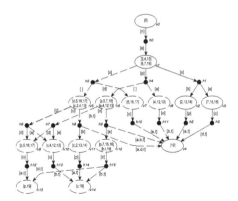

Figure 4: Communication graph

The root node v0 is labeled with the initial state of the module ([0] stands for one token on place p0). An edge starting at a visible node is labeled with a bag of messages send by the environment – called *input*, an edge starting at a hidden node is labeled with a bag of messages send by the module – called *output*. Thus, a path within this graph represents a communication sequence between the module an an environment.

Some visible nodes are labeled with more than one state (e. g. v1). In that case, after the communication along the path towards this node, the module has reached or will reach one of these states.

The communication graph of a given module is well defined and we present an algorithm for its calculation. But before we can do so, we have to introduce some functions on workflow modules:

Activated input Concerning a given state of a module, an activated input is a minimal bag of messages the module requires from an environment either to produce an output or to reach the final state. The function INP yields the set of activated inputs.

Successor state Concerning a given state of a module, a successor state is a reachable state that is maximal concerning one run of the module. The function NXT yields the set of successor states.

Possible output Concerning a given state of a module, a possible output is a maximal bag of messages the is send by the module while reaching a successor state. The function OUT yields the set of possible outputs.

Communication step The tuple (z, i, o, z') is called communication step, if z, z' are states of a module, i is an input and o is an output and $(z' + o)$ is a successor state of $(z + i)$. $\mathcal{S}(M)$ denotes the set of all communication steps for a given module M.

All notions mentioned above are well defined based on partial ordered run of the workflow module (see (Martens, 2004)). Because of the limited space, we do not go into further details. Applying these notions, we are now able to present the construction of the communication graph. The algorithm starts with the root node v_0 labeled with the initial state:

1. For each state within the label of v_i calculate the set of activated inputs: $\bigcup_{z \in m(v_i)} \text{INP}(z)$.

2. For each activated input i within this set:

   (a) Add a new hidden node h, add a new edge (v_i, h) with the label i.

   (b) For each state within the label of v_i calculate the set of possible outputs: $\bigcup_{z \in m(v_i)} \text{OUT}(z + i)$.

   (c) For each possible output o within this set:

      i. Add a new visible node v_{i+1}, add a new edge (h, v_{i+1}) with the label o.

      ii. For each state $z \in m(v_i)$ and for each communication step $(z, i, o, z') \in \mathcal{S}(M)$ add z' to the label of v_{i+1}.

      iii. If there exists a visible node v_j such that $m(v_{i+1}) = m(v_j)$ then merge v_j and v_{i+1}. Otherwise, goto step 1 with node v_{i+1}.

The communication graph of a module contains that information, a "good natured" environment can derive. That means, the environment always sends as little messages as possible, but as much as necessary to achieve an answer resp. to terminate the process in a proper state. By considering all reachable successor states together with all possible outputs, the choices within the module are not restricted.

3.3 The Usability Graph

By help of the communication graph we can decide the usability of a module. A communication graph may have several leaf nodes: none, finitely or infinitely many. Figure 4 shows a graph with three leaf nodes: v4, v13 and v14. In each communication graph there is at most one leaf node labeled with the defined final state of the workflow module (v4). All other leaf nodes contain at least one state, where there are messages left or which marks a deadlock within the module (v13 and v14).

That means: If we build an environment that communicates with the module according to the labels along the path to such a leaf node, this environment does not utilize the module. Therefore, we call the communication sequence defined by such a path an erroneous sequence. Now we can try to eliminate all erroneous sequences. We call a subgraph of the communication graph that does not contain any erroneous sequences an *usability graph* of that module.

Definition 3.2 (Usability graph).

A subgraph U of the communication graph C is called *usability graph*, iff

• U contains the root node and the defined leaf node (labeled with the defined final state of the workflow module) of C.

• For each hidden node within U all outgoing edges are within U, too.

• Each node within U lies on a path between the root node and the defined leaf node.   ∗

A usability graph of a module describes, how to use that module. For the precise, mathematical definition see (Martens, 2004). A communication graph may contain several usability graphs.

Figure 4 shows the only usability graph of module Online Tickets drawn by solid lines. Now we can construct a more clever customer than we did at the beginning of this section: A customer send its name [n] and awaits the special offers [s]. Afterwards, he sends the order [o].

If he receives the business terms [b], he was classified as standard customer. Thus, he pays [p] and gets an acknowledgement and the ticket [a, t]. Otherwise, he is a premium customer and receives an acknowledgement [a]. In that case, he transmits his conditions [c] and receives finally the current discount level and the ticket [d, t].

If we look at Figure 4, there is a path from the node v1 to the defined leaf node v4 via h5, i.e. the module might serve properly the customer from beginning of this section. But, the decision wether or not the path to h5 is continued towards the node v4 is up to the module. An environment has no further influence. Hence, a utilizing environment must prevent to reach this node.

3.4 Theorem of Usability

An usability graph U can easily be transformed into an environment of the workflow module – we call it the *constructed environment*, denoted by $\Gamma(U)$. The next section presents the generation of an abstract representation for a given workflow module (Figure 5). The construction of the environment takes place analogically, just by switching the directions of communication. We need the constructed environment to decide the usability of some cyclic workflow modules.

Now we can formulate the correlation between the usability of a workflow module and the existence of a usability graph:

Theorem 3.1 (Usability).
Let M be a workflow module and let C be the communication graph of M.

• The module M is *not* usable, if C contains no finite usability graph.

- An acyclic module M is usable, if and only if C contains at least one finite usability graph.
- An cyclic module M is usable, if C contains at least one finite usability graph U and the composed system $M \oplus \Gamma(U)$ is weak sound.   ⋆

The proof applies the precise definition and underlying structures of Petri net theory. Hence, we omit the proof here. All proofs together with information about the complexity of our algorithms can be found in (Martens, 2004). The algorithms are also implemented within an available prototype (Martens, 2003b).

4   RE-ENGINEERING

As we have shown, the workflow module of the online ticket service is usable. Nevertheless, the representation is not adequate for publishing the service within a public repository. We already have address the problems of a customer who wants to use this service.

4.1   Views on Web Services

Anyhow, it is not correct to call the module shown in Figure 3 a "bad" model in general. The quality of a model always depends on its purpose. Concerning Web services we can distinguish two purposes, that come along with totally different requirements.

On the one hand, a Web service is modeled to describe the way it is executed. Such a model is useful for the provider of the service. Hence, it is called the *private view model* and needs to contain a lot of details on the internal structure. The module shown in Figure 3 is a good candidate for a *private view model*, because it reflects the organization structure (three independent departments).

On the other hand, a Web service is modeled to describe how to use it. Such a model has to be easily understandable, because a potential requestor of the service wants to decide, whether or not that service is compatible to his own component. Hence, such a model is called the *public view model*. For that purpose the module Online Tickets is no adequate model of the services.

As a consequence thereof, we need another model of this services. Because of many reasons, it is not efficient to build a new public view model from scratch. Instead the public view model should be automatically derived from the private view model.

4.2   Transformation

Basically, the transformation of private view model into a public view model is an abstraction from de-

tails. Hence, a common approach focusses on elimination and fusion of elements within a given model. In this paper, we present a different approach. A potential requestor of a Web service ist not urgently interested in the (possibly simplified) structure of a process. For him, the behavior is of vital importance. As we have discussed, the usability graph is an adequate representation of the usable behavior for a given Web service. Thus, the public view model should be derived from the usability graph of the private view model.

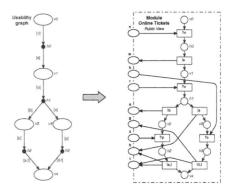

Figure 5: A module and its environment

Figure 5 shows on the left side the usability graph of the module Online Tickets. We have omit the labeling of the visible states, because this is of no interest for the transformation. On the right side, Figure 5 shows public view model of the online ticket service. The transformation is very simple: Each node of the usability graph is mapped to a place within the module and each edge of the graph is mapped to a transition that is put in between the two places representing the source and target nod of the edge. Finally, the interface places are added and each transition is connected to these places according to the label of the edge.

As the result, a customer can easily understand, how to use the service. The independency between the canvassing department and the accounts department was replaced be a causal order, because now utilizing environment of this module could communicate with both departments concurrently.

A public view model of a Web service, that is generated by our algorithm contains only the usable behavior of the original model. Thus, the both views on the process are not equivalent. We require just a simulation relation: Each utilizing environment of the public view model has to be a utilizing environment of the private view model. In the very most cases this property holds per construction. There are a few abnormal cases, where we have to prove the simulation relation and to adjust the result in case. More details can be found in (Martens, 2004).

5 SUMMARY

In this paper, we have sketched a framework for modeling business processes and Web services by help of Petri nets. This framework has enabled us to specify a fundamental property of such components – *usability*. We have also presented algorithms to verify this property locally. Moreover, the our approach yields a concrete example how to use a given Web services.

Beside the results presented here, the notion of usability and the formalism of communication graphs are the basis for further investigations on Web services. On the one hand, the analysis of usability offers a starting point for the simplification of Web service models and for re-engineering of such components. On the other hand, the equivalence of two Web services can be decided. This is exceedingly important for a dynamic exchange of components within a running system: Does the new component behave exactly the way the replaced component did?

All presented algorithms are implemented within a prototype. Currently, we try to improve the efficiency of the algorithms by the application of partial order reduction techniques. Due to this approach we will be able to handle much larger workflow modules which emerge by transformation of a real world modeling language into our framework, i. e. BPEL4WS (BEA et al., 2002).

REFERENCES

BEA, IBM, Microsoft, and SAP (2002). *BPEL4WS– Business Process Execution Language for Web Service* Version 1.1.

Gottschalk, K. (2000). *Web Services architecture overvie* IBM developerWorks, Whitepaper. http://ibm com/developerWorks.

Martens, A. (2003a). On compatibility of web service *Petri Net Newsletter*, (65):12–20.

Martens, A. (2003b). WOMBAT4WS– *Workflow Mo eling and Business Analysis Toolkit for Web Se vices*. Humboldt-Universität zu Berlin, Mai ual. http://www.informatik.hu-berlin de/top/wombat.

Martens, A. (to appear 2004). *Verteilte Geschäftsprozesse Modellierung und Verifikation mit Hilfe von Web Se vices*. PhD thesis, Humboldt-Universität zu Berlin.

Martens, A., Stahl, C., Weinberg, D., Fahland, D., and He dinger, T. (2004). BPEL4WS– Semantik, Analy und to workflow management. *Journal of Circui* Universität zu Berlin.

Reisig, W. (1985). *Petri Nets*. Springer-Verlag, Berlin, He delberg, New York, Tokyo, eatcs monographs on the oretical computer science edition.

van der Aalst, W. M. P. (1998a). The application of pe netsVisualisierung. Informatik-Bericht, Humboldt- *Systems and Computers*, 8(1):21–66.

van der Aalst, W. M. P. (1998b). Modeling and analy ing interorganizational workflows. In Lavagno, and Reisig, W., editors, *Proceedings of CSD'98*, page 262–272. IEEE Computer Society Press, Fukushim Japan.

BALANCING STAKEHOLDER'S PREFERENCES ON MEASURING COTS COMPONENT FUNCTIONAL SUITABILITY

Alejandra Cechich

Departamento de Ciencias de la Computación, Universidad del Comahue, Neuquén, Argentina
Email: acechich@uncoma.edu.ar

Mario Piattini

Escuela Superior de Informática, Universidad de Castilla-La Mancha, Ciudad Real, España
Email: Mario.Piattini@uclm.es

Keywords: Component-Based System Assessment, COTS components, Software Quality.

Abstract: COTS (Commercial Off-The-Shelf) components can be incorporated into other systems to help software developers to produce a new system, so that both artefacts – components and the system – form a single functional entity. In that way, developing software becomes a matter of balancing required and offered functionality between the parties. But required functionality is highly dependent on component's users, i.e. stakeholders of a COTS component selection process. Inputs to this process include discussions with composers, reuse architects, business process coordinators, and so forth. In this paper, we present an approach for balancing stakeholder's preferences, which can be used in the process of measuring functional suitability of COTS candidates. We describe and illustrate the use of our proposal to weight requirements of components and determine suitable COTS candidates for given software.

1 INTRODUCTION

The last decade marked the first real attempt to turn software development into engineering through the concepts of component-based software engineering (CBSE) and commercial Off-The-Shelf (COTS) components. It is clear that CBSE affects software quality in several ways, ranging from introducing new methods for selecting COTS components to defining a wide scope of testing principles and measurements (Cechich et al., 2003).

The idea is to create high-quality parts and put them together. However, joining high quality parts not necessarily produces a high-quality system.

At the same time, defining quality features able to be measured might mitigate the impact of selecting and integrating COTS components. Although measures are not straightforward to take, it might be possible to focus on different aspects of a component, which directly – or perhaps indirectly – in some cases – provide metrics on the resulting composition. In that way, metrics might be used to improve the process of selecting and integrating

components by reducing risks on decision-making tasks (Sedigh-Ali et al., 2001).

Components are plugged into a software architecture that connects participating components and enforces interaction rules. The architectural options are high-level descriptions of components and their expected interactions. For instance, the model in Alexander and Blackburn (1999), supposes that there is an architectural definition of a system, whose behaviour has been depicted by scenarios or using an architecture description language (ADL). The model explores the evaluation of components using a specification-based testing strategy, and proposes a semantics distance measure that might be used as the basis for selecting a component from a set of candidates.

Our proposal (Cechich and Piattini, 2004), has adapted this model as a basement for quality measurement. We express the semantics distance in terms of functional suitability measures, which provide a better identification of the different COTS functionalities. To do so, a system can be extended or instantiated through the use of some component type. Due several instantiations might occur, an

I. Seruca et al. (eds.), Enterprise Information Systems VI, 177–184.
© 2006 *Springer. Printed in the Netherlands.*

assumption is made about what characteristics the actual components must possess from the architecture's perspective. Thus, the specification of the architecture A (SA) defines a specification S_C for the abstract component type C (i.e. $SA \Rightarrow S_C$). Any component K_i, that is a concrete instance of C, must conform to the interface and behaviour specified by S_C.

We should remark the importance of determining behavioural incompatibilities through the use of scenario specifications, even thought the scenario S is not explicitly included into our measure definitions. This is due to the fact that we consider the definition of metrics as a process included into a broader measurement process, which defines some activities for setting the measurement context – such as defining scenario specifications or identifying stakeholders (Cechich and Piattini, 2003).

Determining the needed quality is difficult when different stakeholders have different needs. One might be tempted to state that the stakeholder requiring the highest component quality should determine the overall level of quality to the CBS. But what if that component use is rather minor and unimportant to the CBS, whereas the major component use does not require anywhere near such a level of quality? Thus it is necessary to balance conflicting requirements for CBS quality.

Weighting requirements for COTS component selection can be problematic. Sometimes these weights are inconsistent and lead to confusion about which are the most essential customer requirements (Maiden and Ncube, 1998). Using more sophisticated methods, such as the AHP method (Saaty, 1990), has received some interest in the application of well-known COTS component selection procedures. However, simpler decision-making techniques can also be appropriate to resolve disagreements promoting a cost-effective use. In any case, clearly defining a way of balancing preferences on requirements is essential to the selection process.

On the other hand, the requirements elicitation techniques have widely used a family of goal-oriented requirements analysis (GORA) methods – I* (I* homepage; Mylopoulos et al., 1999), KAOS (KAOS homepage; Dardenne et al., 1993), and GRL (GRL homepage) – as an approach to refine and decomposing the needs of customers into more concrete goals that should be achieved.

In this paper, we describe a proposal to balance stakeholder's preferences during a COTS component selection process. Our proposal extends a version of a Goal-Oriented Requirements Analysis Method called AGORA (Kaiya et al., 2002) by considering additional features of COTS components. The proposal might be combined with other techniques for weighting preferences such as the Goals-Skills-Preferences Framework (Hui et al., 2003) and the AHP method. Then, the balanced requirements are included into the computation of a compact suite of measures on functional suitability of the COTS component candidates.

In Section 2 of the paper we briefly introduce our measurement approach for COTS component's functional suitability. Section 3 then presents the notion of AGORA graphs as it might be used in COTS component selection to balance stakeholder's preferences. Finally, section 4 introduces our weighting procedure to functional suitability based on measures derived from the graph. We conclude with an overview of research directions and future extensions.

2 MEASUREMENT OF COTS FUNCTIONAL SUITABILITY

In the previous section, we have emphasized the fact that the output from the system should satisfy the user's requirements by using the functionality supplied by at least one COTS component. They are plugged into a software architecture that connects participating components and enforces interaction rules.

Given a specification S_C for an abstract component type C, a candidate component K to be a concrete instance of C must conform to the interface and behaviour specified by S_C.

Although the process of selecting a component K consists of evaluating interface and semantic mappings, in our work only semantic mappings are addressed. Mappings in S_C, which represent the different required functionalities, are established between input and output domains. We focus on incompatibilities derived from functional differences between the specification in terms of mappings of a component K_i (S_{Ki}) and the specification in terms of mappings of S_C.

Let's illustrate the measurement procedure by using an E-payment system as an example. We suppose the existence of some scenarios describing the two main stages of the system – *authorisation* and *capture*. Authorisation is the process of checking the customer's credit card. If the request is accepted, the customer's card limit is reduced temporarily by the amount of the transaction. Capture is when the card is actually debited.

The scenarios will provide an abstract specification of the mappings of S_C that might be composed of:

-   Input domain: (AID) Auth_IData{#Card, Cardholder_Name, Exp-Date}; (CID) Capture_Idata{Bank_Acc, Amount}.
-   Output domain: (AOD) Auth_Odata{ok-Auth}; (COD) Capture_Odata{ok_capture, DB_update}.
-   Mapping: {AID → AOD};{CID → COD}

Suppose we pre-select two components to be evaluated, namely K_1 and K_2 respectively. A typical situation for inconsistency in the functional mappings between S_{K1}, S_{K2} and S_C is illustrated in Figure 1, where dashed lines indicate (required) mappings with respect to S_C, and the solid lines are (offered) mappings with respect to S_{K1} (grey) and S_{K2} (black). Note that the input domain of the component K_1 does not include all the values that the specification S_C requires, i.e. the capture functionality is not provided. Besides, the input domain of the component K_2 includes more values than the required by S_C, although the mapping satisfies the required functionality. We should also note that there is another functionality provided by K_2, i.e. {Taxes → Statistics}, which might inject harmful effects to the final composition.

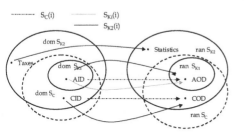

Figure 1: Functional mappings of S_C and S_{K1}/S_{K2}

Our measures of functional suitability have been classified into two different groups: component-level measures and solution-level measures. The first group of measures aims at detecting incompatibilities on a particular component K, which is a candidate to be analysed. However, it could be the case that we need to incorporate more than one component to satisfy the functionality required by the abstract specification S_C. In this case, the second group of measures evaluates the functional suitability of all components that constitute the candidate solution.

To clarify the use of the specification S_C during the measurement procedure, we briefly introduce some metrics. At the component-level, we have defined the following measures (Cechich and Piattini, 2004):

- "Compatible Functionality" (CF_C) as the amount of functional mappings provided by S_K and required by S_C in the scenario S.
- "Missed Functionality" (MF_C) as the amount of functional mappings required by S_C in the scenario S and not provided by S_K.
- "Added Functionality" (AF_C) as the amount of functional mappings not required by S_C in the scenario S and provided by S_K.
- "Component Contribution"(CC_F) as the percentage in which a component contributes to get the functionality required by S_C in the scenario S.

Now, let's calculate the functional suitability measures on K_2 for the E-payment example. Considering the functional mappings provided by K_2 ({AID → AOD; CID → COD; Taxes → Statistics}), the component-level measure results are as follows:

$$CF_C(K_2) = 2; \ MF_C(K_2) = 0, \ AF_C(K_2) = 1;$$
$$CC_F(K_2) = 1.$$

These values indicate that the component K_2 is a candidate to be accepted for more evaluation; i.e. the component is completely functionally suitable. But there is one added function that could inject harmful side effects into the final composition. Besides, there are another types of analysis the component should be exposed before being eligible as a solution – such as analysis of non-functional properties (Chung et al., 2000), analysis of vendor viability (Ballurio et al., 2002), and so forth.

Adaptation required by the components should also be quantified. For example, measurement might be defined at three levels: (1) size measures will be basically in terms of the amount of adaptability needed by a component-based solution; (2) complexity of adaptation will be measured in terms of interactions with target components that are identified to determine all potential mismatches; and finally, (3) architectural adaptability might define calculations for measures of changes that affect system's stability (Cechich and Piattini, 2003) in terms of architectural adaptability.

3 STAKEHOLDER'S PREFERENCES ON COTS FUNCTIONALITY

Stakeholders might try to find the best component (or set of components) decomposing and weighting the goals of the abstract specification S_C, as it was presented in the previous section. For example, a *reuse architect* may be interested in identifying and acquiring components promoting the value of reuse and ensuring consistency of design across projects; a *certifier* may be interested in setting component specification standards and ensuring compliance and consistency of components across different teams; or a *business process coordinator* may be interested in demonstrating the value of components with respect to business processes (Allen and Frost, 2001). Hence, functional requirements are affected by different views that should be conciliated.

Generally speaking, goals can be decomposed to calculate a preference value for each stakeholder. The extended version of a Goal-Oriented Requirements Analysis Method called AGORA, (Kaiya et al., 2002), is a top-down approach for refining and decomposing the needs of customers into more concrete goals that should be achieved for satisfying the customer's needs.

An AGORA goal graph, is an attributed version of AND-OR goal graphs, whose parts can be described as follows:

- Attribute values are attached to nodes and edges, in addition to structural characteristics of the graph. There are two types of attributes:
  - A preference matrix is attached to a node, i.e. a goal, and stands for the degree of preference or satisfiability of the goal for each stakeholder; and
  - A contribution value is attached to an edge to express the degree of the contribution of the goal to the achievement of its connected parent goal.
- Rationale can be attached to an attribute as well as a node and an edge. It represents decomposition decisions associated to goal refinement and attribute value definition.

The procedure to construct an AGORA goal graph involves:

- Establishing initial goals as customers' needs.
- Decomposing and refining goals into sub-goals.
- Choosing and adopting the goals from the alternatives of decomposed goals.
- Detecting and resolving conflicts on goals.

The stakeholders attach the value subjectively. However, they can use some systematic techniques, such as the AHP method (Saaty, 1990), to assign more objective values.

The contribution values and preference matrices help to choose suitable sub-goals. Basically, when a sub-goal is connected to an edge having a high contribution, it can be a candidate to be chosen as a successor of his parent goal

Since a preference matrix includes the preference degree for each stakeholder, we can identify the conflicts among them by analysing the variance on the diagonal elements of the matrix.

In the following subsection, we introduce an extension of the AGORA graph to include some necessary elements when evaluating COTS components. Our approach explicitly considers some characteristics of COTS components to balance stakeholder's preferences on functional goals.

3.1 AGORA Graphs in COTS Selection

Initial goals are typically considered as the customer needs and assigned to nodes of the graph. But when incorporating COTS components, goals should be balanced against COTS services. For example, using the main concepts of goal-oriented requirements engineering, the goal acquisition and specification process (Alves, 2003; Alves and Finkelnstein, 2002) includes the necessity of identify goals that help to distinguish between products (called core goals) from those that are provided by most available products (called peripheral goals). Then, our proposal extends the AGORA graph to include a first categorisation of goals into *core* and *peripheral*.

A second categorisation is due to the traditional separation of requirements into functional and non-functional properties. This classification remains relevant due to the different treatments given to the properties when defining quality attributes and measurements. In this work, only functional suitability is considered. Then, we limit the scope of this paper to analysing functional properties.

Initial goals, as considered in AGORA graphs, are the needs of the customers that will be refined and decomposed into sub-goals one after another. It is possible to have more than one sub-goal of a parent goal, and it is also possible to use two types of decomposition corresponding to the logical combination of the sub-goals – one is AND-decomposition and the other is OR-decomposition.

Therefore, with the functional goals of the component specified by mappings in S_C, the next step is to refine the goals considering the perspectives of different stakeholders – reuse architect, certifier, business process coordinator, etc. Then, the computation of stakeholder's preference values for the refined goals will allow us to add preferences to mappings of S_C, distinguishing between core and peripheral functional goals.

In our context of component-based systems, an AGORA graph describes the abstract specification of a required component (S_C) according to the scenario S. Figure 2 shows a snapshot of a possible AGORA graph for our E-payment case.

There are two types of conflicts on goals; one is the conflict between goals and the other one is the conflict on a goal between stakeholders. The first type of conflicts appears in Figure 2 between the goals "Prevent unauthorised debits" and "No authorisation", whose edge has a negative contribution value. The second type appears in the figure on the goal "Input AID data". The diagonal elements of the preference matrix show that the reuse architect gave the preference value 8 by himself, while the business process coordinator's preference is –5 given by himself (Figure 3 shows the preference matrix where the stakeholders are identified).

When we find a large variance on the diagonal elements of the preference matrix, there is a possibility of conflict among the stakeholders for the goal. In this case, the relevant stakeholders would be forced to negotiate for the conflict resolution of the goal. Negotiation can be supported by methods such as the WinWin (Boehm et al., 1995).

In Figure 2, final goals are identified to achieve the initial goals, i.e. the sub-goals "Input AID data", "Issue AOD data", "Register formally with the bank", and "Input the user identification by Web page by user".

It seems that information to apply a traditional negotiation process is enough. But, we have already remarked the importance of distinguishing between core and peripheral goals when selecting COTS components. This characterisation would lead to dealing with a third type of conflicts on goals: conflicts between the abstract specification of a component and its possible instantiations. These conflicts should be resolved when the COTS component selection actually take place. Then, it is important to add some extra information on the graph, so the negotiation will be possible.

Then, the AGORA graph in Figure 2 has been extended adding the labels <core>/<peripheral> to facilitate the future negotiation. For example, suppose that we evaluate the components K_1 and K_2 introduced in section 2. We easily note that component K_1 should be withdrawn from analysis

because it does not offer one core functionality. We should search for other components or combination of components, such as K_2, to instantiate the three core goals of the graph. On the other hand, there is a peripheral goal ("Input the user identification by Web page by user") on the graph, which would be desirable to have. However, its categorisation as peripheral makes this functionality a candidate to be discharged (or to be added by an adapter), when there are no COTS candidates offering it.

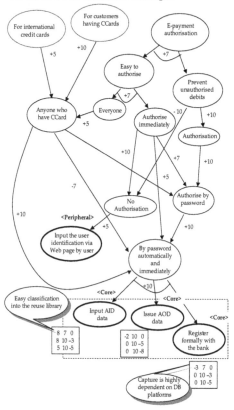

Figure 2: A snapshot of the AGORA graph for the E-payment case

RA CE BC

	RA CE BC	
RA	8 7 0	RA: Reuse Architect
CE	8 10 –3	CE: Certifier
BC	5 10 -5	BC: Business Process Coordinator

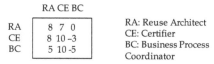

Figure 3: An example of a preference matrix

4 MEASURING DESIRABILITY AND MODIFIABILITY OF GOALS

Besides the classification of goals as core and peripheral, the attributes desirability (level of importance for a goal to be met), and modifiability (level in which a goal can be modified) are proposed as attributes for goal description when selecting COTS components (Alves and Filkenstein, 2002).

By using an AGORA graph, we can estimate the quality of several properties of the adopted goals. Particularly, correctness is assumed as a quality factor that represents how many goals in a specification meet stakeholder's needs. Correctness in AGORA is strongly related to contribution values on the path of the adopted goal as well as on its stakeholder's preference value. Particularly, the average stakeholder's preference value of the adopted final goals (Cup) is defined by Kaiya et al. (2002) as:

$$Cup = \text{AVE} \ (\cup_{f \ \in FinalGoal, \ s \ \in \ Stakeholder, \ m \ \in \ Preference} \ \{m_{s,customer} \mid has(f,m)\})$$

where $m_{s,customer}$ means a stakeholder's preference value evaluated by the stakeholder s in the preference matrix m. The results of the calculation for all the core goals of Figure 2 are as follows:

$Cup(RA) = ((8 + 8 + 5) + (-2 + 0 + 0) + (-3 + 0 + 0)) / (3 + 3 + 3) / 10 = 0.18$
$Cup(CE) = ((7 + 10 + 10) + (10 + 10 + 10) + (7 + 10 + 10)) / (3 + 3 + 3) / 10 = 0.93$
$Cup(BC) = ((0 - 3 - 5) + (0 - 5 - 8) + (0 - 3 - 5)) / (3 + 3 + 3) / 10 = -0.32$

$Cup = (0.18 + 0.93 - 0.32) / 3 = 0.26$

In COTS component selection, this measure might indicate the degree of agreement on stakeholder's preferences, i.e. on the *desirability* of the core goals of the abstract specification S_C. Lower results of Cup, such as 26% in our case, show a need of further discussion on the required functionality of the component C; i.e. causes of disagreement should be detected. For example, stakeholders have different goals, even their perceptions of reality vary significantly. Then, scenarios may drive the agreement process and establish partial consistency among existing systems – all systems involved in using the COTS component.

On the other hand, *modifiability* is about the degree in which committed goals can be changed when selecting COTS components. Let's briefly clarify the point: suppose there is a strong agreement on a set of goals (Cup = 80%), however the search of COTS candidates offering the functionalities shows that there are no candidates available. In this case, evaluators should have agreed on the degree in which the goals (even categorised as core) can be modified. Then, the modifiability of the goals will help to decide on acquiring COTS components with less functionality than required, adding the functionality by means of an adapter (such as a wrapper), or building the missed functionality from scratch.

In (Kaiya et al., 2002), the quality metrics for modifiability include how an AND-OR graph is closed to a tree structure. When there are many incoming edges to a goal, the goal contributes to an achievement of many goals. In consequence, these many goals should be under consideration in case of changing the goal. The quality metric is defined as follows:

$$Tre = \frac{\#\{g \in RefinedGoals \mid \#\{e \mid incoming(g,e)=1\}\}}{\#RefinedGoals}$$

$$RefinedGoals = Goals - Initial \ Goals$$

Calculations for Figure 2 show that there are 3 initial goals and 13 refined goals, from which only 9 have one incoming edge. Then, the result of calculation of *Tre (modifiability)* for Figure 2 is 9 / 13 = 0.69. In other words, the figure shows four goals whose incoming edges are more than one (13 – 4 = 9), out of 13 refined goals.

We should note that other quality metrics such as unambiguity, completeness, and consistency might be calculated on AGORA graphs. However, desirability and modifiability are the main properties when we apply the analysis on abstract specifications of COTS components aiming at being included into a selection procedure.

4.1 Weighting the Functional Requirements of *Sc*

Functional mappings of S_C, as introduced in section 2, are associated to one or more refined goals of the graph. By doing so, an agreement among stakeholders might be achieved by calculating the desirability of each group of refined goals representing a particular mapping. For the example in Figure 2, calculations should be split into three groups: one containing the core goals referring to the authorisation functionality (two core refined goals), another containing the capture functionality (one core refined goal), and another containing the peripheral goal. Then, desirability of the three groups should be calculated and decisions should be made based on the following cases, where "agreement-threshold" is a suggested value between 0.6 and 0.7 and "core/peripheral" is the type of refined goal:

- Case 1: desirability(refined goal/s) < agreement-threshold ∧ core ⇒ Try other scenarios to get agreement
- Case 2: desirability(refined goal/s) < agreement-threshold ∧ peripheral ⇒ decision to discharge
- Case 3: desirability(refined goal/s) ≥ agreement-threshold ∧ peripheral ⇒ decision to retain
- Case 4: desirability(refined goal/s) ≥ agreement-threshold ∧ core ⇒ keep for the selection process

Modifiability is calculated to be used during the selection procedure, whether decisions on buying or developing should be made.

Let's consider again the E-payment example. The functional suitability measures introduced in section 2 were calculated for two COTS candidates – K_1 and K_2. Before starting the selection procedure, an abstract specification of the component (S_C) was defined as a reference to be used when comparing candidates, and the component K_2 was indicated as the most functionality suitable. However, the agreement on the functionality required by the abstract specification S_C is not enough (*Cup* indicator is around 26%). It would indicate that we should have tried other scenarios to get agreement (case 1). Hence, the desirability measure might have been used to avoid further investment in searching candidates while required functionality is still not clear, i.e. we should not proceed comparing the functionality offered by candidates until desirability of all core requirements has reached the agreement-threshold.

Of course, actually classifying the requirements as "core" or "peripheral" is another different concern. We assume that the classification is valid and it remains stable during the selection process. However, 69% of modifiability would indicate that there is a good chance of negotiating (and changing) the requirements when balancing between offered services of candidates. But it also could indicate that the classification as "core" should be reviewed. Having higher values on modifiability (around 90%) on a core requirement would indicate that we could potentially resign most of our expectations on this requirement letting offered services prevail. For example, we could keep some of the alternative goals resigning others whether COTS candidates are hard to find or adapt.

Summing up, desirability might reduce search and selection efforts by detecting functionality on which there is no enough agreement; and modifiability might help to predict a space of negotiation and change when constraints from actual candidates are applied.

5 CONCLUSIONS

Assessing component-based systems, especially systems with COTS components, differs in several ways from the usual situation. Now, stakeholders must be willing to resign some of their requirements trying to adjust their expectations to what actual candidates offer in a marketplace. In this context, balancing requirements among offerings is an outstanding concern when selecting COTS components. In this paper, we have introduced a proposal for calculating a preference value for each functional requirement, and we have weighted the desirability and modifiability of core and peripheral goals. These calculations are some of the inputs required by a broader measurement procedure, which would lead to a more objective evaluation of COTS candidates.

However, an aspect that needs further discussion is the possibility of establishing a set of main stakeholders or roles on a selection process. Furthermore, when an organisation implements the approach, it needs to identify which specific roles and priorities it should address and what does or does not work for that organisation. Preference matrices should be limited to these specific roles, so calculations are kept between practical and meaningful boundaries.

Another aspect that needs more attention is the diverse possibilities of documenting the specification S_C. We have chosen scenarios because of their wide use on evaluating architectures, however other representations might be more suitable depending on specific constraints of the system.

Finally, the classification of requirements as core or peripheral needs to be derived from a previous analysis on factors that traditionally influence software requirements elicitation processes.

ACKNOWLEDGMENTS

This work was partially supported by the CyTED (Ciencia y Tecnología para el Desarrollo) project VII-J-RITOS2, by the UNComa project 04/E048, and by the MAS project supported by the Dirección General de Investigación of the Ministerio de Ciencia y Tecnología (TIC 2003-02737-C02-02).

REFERENCES

Alexander R. and Blackburn M., 1999. Component Assessment Using Specification-Based Analysis and Testing. *Technical Report SPC-98095-CMC, Software Productivity Consortium.*

Allen P. and Frost S., 2001. Planning Team Roles for CBD. In *Component-Based Software Engineering - Putting the Pieces Together*, Addison-Wesley. Edited by G. Heineman and W. Council.

Alves C., 2003. COTS-Based Requirements Engineering. In *Component-Based Software Quality: Methods and Techniques*, Springer-Verlag LNCS 2693.

Alves C. and Filkenstein A., 2002. Challenges in COTS-Decision Making: A Goal-Driven Requirements Engineering Perspective. In *Proceedings of the Fourteenth International Conference on Software Engineering and Knowledge Engineering*, SEKE'02.

Ballurio K., Scalzo B., and Rose L, 2002. Risk Reduction in COTS Software Selection with BASIS. In *Proceedings of the First International Conference on COTS-Based Software Systems*, ICCBSS 2002, Springer-Verlag LNCS 2255 , pp. 31-43.

Boehm B., Bose P., Horowitz E., and Lee M., 1995. Software Requirements Negotiation Aids: A Theory-W Based Spiral Approach. In *Proceedings of the 17th International Conference on Software Engineering*, pp. 243-253.

Cechich A., Piattini M., and Vallecillo A., (eds.) 2003. *Component-Based Software Quality: Methods and Techniques*, Springer-Verlag LNCS 2693.

Cechich A. and Piattini M., 2003. Defining Stability for Component Integration Assessment. In *Proceedings of the 5th International Conference on Enterprise Information Systems*, ICEIS 2003, pp. 251-256.

Cechich A. and Piattini M., 2004. On the Measurement of COTS Functional Suitability. In *Proceedings of the 3rd International Conference on COTS-based Software Systems*, ICCBSS 2004, Springer-Verlag LNCS.

Chung L., Nixon B., Yu E., and Mylopoulos J., 2000. *Non-Functional Requirements in Software Engineering*. Kluwer Academic Publisher.

Dardenne A., van Lamsweerde A., and Fickas S, 1993. Goal-directed Requirements Acquisition. *Science of Computer Programming*, Vol. 20, pp. 3-50.

GRL homepage, http://www.cs.toronto.edu/k-m/GRL/

Hui B., Lisakos S., and Mylopoulos J., 2003. Requirements Analysis for Customizable Software: A Goals-Skills-Preferences Framework, In *Proceedings of the 11th IEEE International Requirements Engineering Conference*, pp. 117-126.

I* homepage, http://www.cs.toronto.edu/km/istar

Kaiya H., Horai H., and Saeki M., 2002. AGORA: Attributed Goal-Oriented Requirements Analysis Method. In *Proceedings of the IEEE International Conference on Requirements Engineering*, pp. 13-22.

KAOS homepage, http://www.info.ucl.ac.be/research/projects/AVL/ReqEng.html

Maiden N. and Ncube C., 1998. Acquiring COTS Software Selection Requirements. In *IEEE Software*, Vol. 15(2), pp. 46-56.

Mylopoulos J., Chung L., and Yu E., 1999. From Object-Oriented to Goal-Requirements Analysis, *Communications of the ACM, 42*(1), pp. 31-37.

Saaty T.L., 1990. *The Analytic Hierarchy Process.* McGraw-Hill.

Sedigh-Ali S., Ghafoor A., and Paul R., 2001. Software Engineering Metrics for COTS-Based Systems. *IEEE Computer Magazine*, pp. 44–50.

A POLYMORPHIC CONTEXT FRAME
TO SUPPORT SCALABILITY AND EVOLVABILITY
OF INFORMATION SYSTEM DEVELOPMENT PROCESSES

Isabelle Mirbel

I3S Laboratory
Les Algorithmes
Route des Lucioles
BP 121
06903 Sophia Antipolis Cedex
FRANCE
isabelle.mirbel@unice.fr

Keywords: Information System, Method Engineering, Fragment, Reuse, Evolution

Abstract: Nowadays, there is an increasing need for flexible approaches, adaptable to different kinds of Information System Development (ISD). But customization of ISD processes have mainly be thought of for the person in charge of building processes, i.e. the methodologists, in order to allow him/her to adapt the process to the need of its company or projects. But there is also a need for customizations dedicated to project team members (application engineers), to provide them with customized guidelines (or heuristics) which are to be followed while performing their daily task. The knowledge capitalization framework we propose supports evolvability and customization of ISD processes. Reuse and customization are handled through *process fragments* stored in a dedicated *repository*. Our purpose is not to propose a new way to built processes, as several approaches already exist on this topic, but to ease the use of existing ones by making them less rigid and allowing their adaptation to the need of the company, the project and most of all, the project team member. Therefore, in addition to a *repository* of *process fragments*, we propose a scalable and polymorphic structure allowing methodologists to define a working space through a *context* made of *criterias*. Thanks to this *context* the project team members better qualify their ISD problem in order to find a suitable solution. A solution is made of *process fragments* organized into a *route-map* specially built to answer the project team member need and directly usable by him/her.
The *context-frame* we focus on in this paper is a scalable structure which supports evolution and tailoring by the methodologists for the project team member's need with regards to project and process features.

1 INTRODUCTION

Information System Development (ISD) is different each time, depending on the situation and context. A given technique, notation or mechanism may be used in a different way depending on the development under consideration. A process (or method) that has proved its power for certain kinds of development may be quite unsuitable for others. There is no universal applicability of processes (Ralyte, 2001). Therefore, there is a need for flexible approaches, adaptable to different kinds of development. The need for situation-specific processes, to better satisfy particular situation requirements, has already been emphasized (van Slooten and Hodes, 1996; Brinkkemper et al., 1998).

Moreover, there is an increasing need for lightweight processes by opposition to heavyweight ones. Lightweight processes increase project team members (or application engineers) involvement on the contrary of heavyweight processes where the only significant choice is made by methodologists who chose the development process. Lightweight processes focus on finding the best way for the current situation. Project team members choose from as many alternative paths as possible.

Indeed customization of ISD processes (Ralyte, 2001; Brinkkemper et al., 1998) have mainly be thought of for the person in charge of building a new process, i.e. the methodologists, in order to allow him/her to adapt the process to the need of its company or projects. But there is also a need for customizations dedicated to project team members, to provide them with guidelines (or heuristics) which are to be followed while performing their daily task (Gnatz et al., 2001; Mirbel and de Rivieres, 2002b). The adaptation is handled through the breaking down of guidelines (heuristics) into fragments, which may then be selected if they answer to the project team member need.

I. Seruca et al. (eds.), Enterprise Information Systems VI, 185–192.
© 2006 *Springer. Printed in the Netherlands.*

It is recognized as important to benefit from the experiences acquired during the resolution of previous problems through reuse and adaptation mechanisms (Cauvet et al., 2001). With regards to software development, reuse has been widely studied from the product point of view (Gamma et al., 1995; Fowler, 1997), but it is now also a challenging issue to handle it from the process point of view.

Moreover, the constant evolution of techniques, mechanisms and technologies provided to support ISD requires evolution-oriented development processes. Adapted processes have to be developed to take advantage of new technologies. Real world evolves and implies changes of the supporting information system. Handling correctly information system evolution also means to use appropriate ISD processes.

We propose a knowledge capitalization framework to support evolvability of ISD processes. Reuse and customization are handled through *process fragments* stored in a dedicated *repository*. This framework is mainly dedicated to project team members and allow them to let others benefit from their experience in solving ISD problem by storing their solution in terms of fragments inside the repository. Our framework also allows them to retrieve fragments corresponding to their ISD problem by using the *process fragment repository*. The key element of such a repository is the means proposed to store and retrieve fragments.

From the methodologist point of view, we believe capitalization could be much more useful if driven to focus on critical aspects of development process ; and customization much more efficient if kept inside the boundaries of the company development process.

To answer this twofold need (fragment manipulation means for project team members and process control for methodologists), we propose a scalable and polymorphic structure, the *context frame*. It helps project team members to specify fragments in a way anticipating their reuse, and to well express their ISD problem to find a suitable solution. The *context frame* can be seen as an ontology dedicated to ISD processes. Ontology for development processes is a current high topic of work in the field of method engineering (Saeki, 2003). Our *context frame* is managed by methodologists allowing them both to drive the project team members on critical aspects when creating and retrieving fragments and to keep customization (supported by fragment selection) inside the boundaries of the company development process. The *context frame* is not a fixed structure and evolves through the time. Its content is controlled by the methodologists, giving them a way to support the evolvability of development processes and project needs. It is the purpose of this paper to present this *context frame*.

We start first by presenting the whole framework

in section 2. Then, the *context frame* is described in section 3. The different kinds of context required to support scalability in ISD processes are first presented in section 4. Then, in section 5, their usefulness for ISD *by* reuse, as well as for ISD *for* reuse is discussed. Finally, we conclude in section 6.

2 A FRAMEWORK TO CAPITALIZE KNOWLEDGE ABOUT ISD PROBLEM SOLVING

During ISD, heuristics are elaborated and may be useful to other teams facing close situations in different projects independently of the functional domain as well as the technical domain. Our approach allows to reassemble heuristics accumulated by project team members to help focusing on critical aspects of development and to take advantage of the way to solve problems. We focus on the re-use of the way of working, on the way to apprehend ISD tasks.

Our approach aims at guiding project team members to most appropriately apply a set of techniques and methods so as to focus on critical aspects of ISD in order to better handle its complexity. Therefore, we propose a *context frame* which allow methodologists to define the working context and project team members to situate their work with regards to this context. The *context frame* is managed by the methodologists and allows them to set the boundaries inside which customization will be possible with regards to the project team members needs. It allows methodologists to provide customized processes and to keep project team members inside the framework of the process used by the company. Project team members use the *context frame* defined by methodologists to characterize the new *fragments* they introduce in the repository. By situating their fragment with regards to the criterias of the context frame, they anticipate their reuse in the framework of the company development process. Project team members also express their ISD *problem* with the help of the *context frame* to select and reuse fragments from the repository through ISD *by* reuse.

The main goal of the *process fragment repository* is to help project team members through their daily tasks. Most of the time, ISD processes are defined with regards to the phase they are involved in (Henderson-Sellers and Edwards, 1990; Boehm, 1988; Royce, 1970), with regards to the results to be obtained (Finkelstein et al., 1990; Franckson and Peugeot, 1991). But to get a valuable result, it is not enough to use the dedicated diagram(s) and concept(s) at the right moment. It is also necessary for the project team members to understand what he/she is working on and why he/she is using such a diagram or concept has to be taken into account (Potts, 1989; Rolland and Souyeyet, 1995; si Said and Rolland, 1998). In our approach, ISD tasks are driven by the problem one may face through his/her daily work, instead of the result he/she wants to get.

Notations provided to support ISD tasks are more and more richer (Object Management Group, 2001). They also become more and more complex and therefore seems to be the heart of ISD: project team members focus on the use of the different diagrams or concepts provided by the notation much more than on the tasks to be performed. Our approach helps in re-centering the work on tasks instead of notation.

With regards to ISD *for* reuse, *fragments* are defined through an *intention* inciting them to carefully specify the aim of the fragment. A *fragment context* is associated to each new-built fragment to enforce its definition with regards to the working framework.

With regards to ISD *by* reuse, requests are expressed in terms of *problem* and *problem context*. *Solutions* are given in terms of *route-map* made of *fragments* including guidelines and heuristics to help in ISD tasks.

An example of fragment is given in figure 1. In this figure, a fragment named `Requirement-out-of-scope` is presented. Its *fragment context* indicates it presents guidelines for when dealing with a running software. There is an associate fragment `DB-out-of-scope`, which is complementary. There is no incompatible fragments. The intention explain the purpose of the fragment which is to help in documenting the running part of the application under which the development will take place. Associated guidelines in UML are then given.

Name	Requirement–Out–of–Scope
Fragment Context	({base – software – running software})
Related Fragments	BusinessDomain–Out–of–Scope – complementarity – 0.75
Non–compatible Fragments	–
Intention To document existing parts of the running software useful to understand the purpose of the new software but not directly related to the new development.	
Guidelines	**Notation** UML use–case diagrams
	Description Add use–cases dedicated to running functionalities increasing the understanding of the software. Stereotype them with <<out–of–scope>>.
	Group all the use–cases stereotyped <<out–of–scope>> in a package (or set of packages) also stereotyped <<out–of–scope>>

Figure 1: An example of fragment

Figure 2 summarizes the structure of our framework with the two main sources of information: the *context frame* and the *process fragment repository*, on top of which mechanisms for ISD *by* re-use and *for* re-use are provided to the project team members, while means of context management are provided to methodologists.

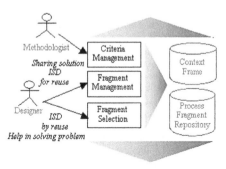

Figure 2: Framework overview

In this paper, we focus on the *context frame*. And we show how useful it is for ISD *by* reuse and *for* reuse.

3 A SCALABLE AND POLYMORPHIC CONTEXT FRAME

The *context frame* allows methodologists to define a common working frame for all the project team members and all the projects in the company. The working frame is defined through a *context* made of *criterias* and allowing then project team members to better qualify their ISD problem in order to get a customized solution.

A criteria represents a point of view or an aspect on the development process that methodologists want to highlight in order to help project team members to apply techniques and methods to focus on critical aspects of the development process. Through ISD *for* reuse, criterias help in qualifying fragments to anticipate and ease their reuse. Through ISD *by* reuse, criterias help in specifying the problem to solve in order to get adapted fragments. Information characterizing the software to develop (*Software to develop includes a* `User Interface`, *Software to develop includes a* `database`, *Software to develop is* `distributed`, *Software to develop is build on a* `running` *application*), the competence of the project team members in charge of the development (*expert, medium, beginner*), and the project management features (*Delivery strategy, Realization strategy, Time pressure*) are example of useful criterias to customize the process.

In the following, we discuss first the structure of the *context frame*. Then, we show how to use it.

4   CONTEXT FRAME DEFINITIONS

A *context frame* is a tree which root-node is the most generic criteria called *Base*. Leaf-nodes correspond to *criterias* or *families* of criteria.

- A *criteria* is a leaf node in the tree. It is described by its *name*. Examples of criterias are *software to develop includes a* database, or *guidelines dedicated to* expert *designers*.

- A *family* of criteria is a non-leaf node with at least two sub-nodes (which could be *criteria* or *family* nodes). A *family* is described by a *name* and information about relationships among the different criterias or sub-families constituting the current family. Families are interesting to allow a better understanding of criterias entered in the framework, from the project team member point of view as well as from the methodologist point of view. For instance, as we deal with different criterias characterizing the software to be developed: *Software to develop includes a* User Interface, *Software to develop includes a* database, *Software to develop is* distributed, *Software to develop is build on a* running *application*, we can group all these criterias into a family called Software *to develop*. This non-leaf node helps methodologists to maintain the context frame and project team members to understand and use the grouped criterias.

The objective of the context frame is to help:

- through ISD *for* reuse by providing a means to organize fragments and
- through ISD *by* reuse by providing a means to select the right fragments to build a *solution* corresponding to a *problem*.

Therefore, additional information aiming at better specifying the way criterias belong to a family helps in using them to constitute a coherent context. Two kinds of information are provided:

- The *order* field indicates if direct criterias or sub-families are ordered (*o d* = *o*) or not (*o d* = *no*). For instance, if development process phase is a *family*, analysis, design, implementation and test are criterias which are ordered (analysis is processed before design, which is processed before implementation, which is processed before test). It is interesting to indicate it because when retrieving fragments associated with the design criteria for instance, it may also be interesting to look at fragments associated with the analysis and implementation criterias, especially if one is interested in the beginning and ending steps of the design phase.

- The *exclusion* field indicates if direct criterias or sub-families are exclusive (*ex* = *e*) or not (*ex* = *ne*). For instance, there is in the repository a criteria related to project time pressure. Guidelines may be given for project under high time pressure as well as project under low time pressure. Therefore time pressure is a *family* and low time pressure and high time pressure are criterias. We specify them as exclusive criterias because guidelines associated to high time pressure project are not compatible with guidelines associated with low time pressure project and could not be provided in the same *solution* to a ISD *problem*.

The *exclusion* field is associated to the family because if only some of the sub-nodes are exclusive among them, it means that a sub-family has to be isolated for these specific sub-nodes.

Definition 1 (Context frame). A context frame, CF, is a tree where:

- the root node is defined as <name=*base*, exc=*ne*, ord=*no*, type=*root*>,

- non-leaf nodes are *family* defined as <name, exc, ord, type=*family*>,

- leaf nodes are *criterias* defined as <name, exc, ord, type=*criteria*>

Figure 3 shows the structure of the *context frame*.

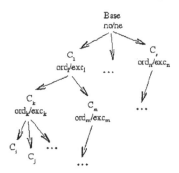

Figure 3: Context frame

Definition 2 (Criteria). A criteria is fully defined as a path from the root node base to a node n_n of the context frame.

$$C = [ba\ e, n_1, ..., n_n]\ with\ ba\ e, n_1, ..., n_n \in CF$$

If n_n is a *family* node, then the *exclusion* field must be different from *e* because one of its *criterias* has to be chosen inside the *family*.

$$if\ type_{n_n} = fami\ y,\ ex\ _{n_j} = e$$

Definition 3 (Compatibility). Two criterias are compatible if they do not share in their definition a common *family* node n_i with an *exclusion* field equal to e.

$$C\ _1\ omp\ C\ _2$$
$$n_i \in C\ _1\ and\ n_j \in C\ _2$$
$$if\ n_i = n_j\ then\ ex\ _{n_i} = e$$

Definition 4 (Context). A context is defined as a set of *compatible* criterias.

$$Co = \{C\ _1, ..., C\ _n\},$$
$$C\ _i, C\ _j \in Co, C\ _i\ omp\ C\ _j$$

An example of *context frame* is given in figure 4. Three families of criterias are presented in this figure: Designer expertise, Software to develop and Project. The Designer expertise family helps in specifying for whom the guidelines are dedicated to: Experts are distinguished from Medium and Beginners. This family is specified as *ordered* because guidelines associated with the Beginner criteria may for instance complete guidelines associated with the Medium criteria when someone doesn't know exactly how to consider the expertise of the designers under consideration. And they are specified as *non-exclusive* because it could be meaningful to extract for instance fragment dedicated to Medium and Beginner designers in a same solution.

The Software to develop family groups criterias related to the qualification of the software to be developed (Mirbel and de Rivieres, 2002a). We distinguish the fact that the application to be developed includes a user-interface (UI), a database (BD), is distributed (Distributed) or is built on top of a running application (Running software). This last criteria is presented as a *family* because different aspects of a running software may be considered : Functional domain, Interface and Code (Mirbel and de Rivieres, 2003). Again a distinction is done among weak, medium and strong reuse of existing code, functional domain and interface. The Software to develop criteria is described as *non-ordered* because the different sub-families are non-related criterias. And they are described as *non-exclusive* because they may be associated with a same problem, solution or fragment. Weak, Medium and Strong criterias are considered as *non-ordered* because a fragment dedicated to guidelines to weakly keep the code for instance may not necessary be complementary to the one dedicated to keep the code in a medium way. And on the contrary, it is not forbidden also to search for a solution including for instance Medium and Strong criterias. Therefore, they are specified as *non-exclusive*.

The last family, project, groups criterias characterizing the project. It has been shown that it is important to take into account project features when working on methodological aspects of ISD (van Slooten and Hodes, 1996). In this example, Delivery strategy, Realization strategy and Time pressure aspects are taken into consideration. The three *families* are examples of *exclusive* criterias: there is only one Delivery strategy chosen for a project and the different kinds of strategies (At once, incremental and evolutionary) can't be mixed. The remark is the same for the Realization strategy. With regards to Time pressure, the associated criterias are also *exclusive*, because guidelines for project under a high time pressure are not compatible with guidelines dedicated to project under a low time pressure.

An example of *criteria* taken from figure 4 is: [base - software to develop - running software - code - weak]. An example of *context* is { [base - software to develop - running software - code - weak], [base - software to develop - DB], [base - Designer expertise - Medium] }

5   CONTEXT FRAME IN USE

The *context frame* is a key element of our framework. In the following, we show how it is useful for the methodologists and for the project team members to support ISD *for* reuse and ISD *by* reuse.

Indeed, one unique context, called the *global context*, is created and maintained by the methodologists in the company. They are the only one allowed to build the *global context* customized for the company development process. It represents the ontology shared by all the projects and project team members with regards to ISD. The *global context* is used by the project team members when they build new fragments and when they search the repository for fragments organized in route-map dedicated to their problem. Contexts associated to fragments and problems, as it will be explained in the following, are subsets of the *global context*.

5.1   Context and Criteria Management

A *global context* is defined and managed by the methodologists. It allows them to define a single working space shared by all the projects and project team members in the company.

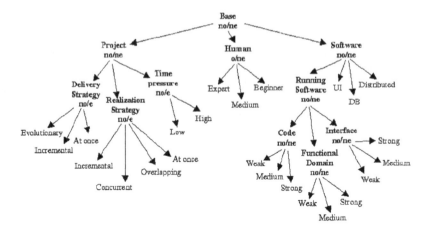

Figure 4: Example of context frame

Definition 5 (Global context). The *global context* is defined as a set of (at least one) compatible criterias.

$$C = [ba e, C_1, ..., C_n]$$

The *global context* is shared by all the project team members who select in it the criterias they are interested in when building a new fragment or when searching for fragments in the repository. Project team members can not add new criterias. They have to use the ones defined by the methodologists. Methodologists make the *global context* evolve by refining existing criterias or adding new nodes under the *base* node.

Evolution is a key issue of the structure because it allows to always drive the project team members to focus on critical aspect(s) of the development whatever the process evolution is.

When they refine existing criterias, methodologists have to take care about the associated fragments. Indeed, fragments are always associated to *criteria* node of the global context. If a *criteria* node n (leaf node) is refined into a *family* node (non-leaf node) with *criteria* sub-nodes $n_1, .., n_n$ (leaf nodes), then methodologists have to modify each fragment associated to n in order to associate it to at least one of the sub-nodes n_n ($n_n \in n_1, .., n_n$).

5.2 Context and ISD for Reuse

A *fragment context* is associated with each fragment. It helps in situating the fragment in the repository with regards to the aspects of the development process which have been emphasized by methodologists; it anticipates fragment reuse and allows to provide a suitable solution to a given ISD problem when searching the repository.

Definition 6 (Fragment context). The *fragment context* is defined as a set of at least one compatible criteria taken from the *global context*.

$$FC = \{C_1, ..., C_n\}$$
$$C_i \in FC, C_i \in C$$
$$C_i, C_j \in FC, C_i \ comp \ C_j$$

Each criteria constituting the *fragment context* has to end with a *criteria* node (leaf node):

- by definition it is not allowed to end a criteria with a *family* node (non-leaf node) which *exclusion* field is equal to e (cf section 4).

- An *exclusion* field equals to ne would be equivalent to a *fragment context* including all the sub-nodes of the *family* node (non-leaf node) under consideration, which means that the criteria would not be discriminant.

Therefore, only *criteria* nodes (leaf node) are allowed as terminal nodes in the *criteria* definition of the *fragment context*.

$$C_i \in FC, C_i = [ba e, ..., n_j], type_{n_j} = fami y$$

5.3 Context and ISD by Reuse

A *problem context* is associated to each problem (and its solution expressed in terms of fragment route-maps) to help in focusing on solutions dedicated to the problem. By comparing the *fragment contexts* and the *problem context*, fragments are selected and adapted solutions are elaborated. The *problem context* is given within the problem definition to search the repository. *Necessary* criterias indicate aspects the project team member is interested in. *Forbidden* criterias indicate aspects the project team member is not interested in. It could be useful to specify it sometimes to be sure the fragments including these (forbidden) aspects will be removed from the solution before it is presented.

Definition 7 (Problem context). A *problem context* is defined as a set of at least one compatible *necessary criterias* and a set of compatible *forbidden criterias*. All criterias are taken from the *global context*.

$$PC = <CN, CF> \text{ where}$$
$$CN = \{C_1, .., C_n\}, CF = \{C_1, .., C_m\}$$
$$C_i \in CN, \nexists C_i \in CF$$
$$C_i \in CN, C_i \in \quad C$$
$$C_i \in CF, C_i \in \quad C$$
$$C_i, C_j \in CN, C_i \quad omp \ C_j$$
$$C_i, C_j \in CF, C_i \quad omp \ C_j$$

By definition, it is not allowed to end a criteria with a *family* node (non-leaf node) which *exclusion* field is equal to *e* (cf section 4). And an *exclusion* field of the terminal node describing the criteria equals to *ne* is equivalent to a *problem context* including all the sub-nodes.

6 CONCLUSION

In this paper we presented the *context frame*, a polymorphic structure to help supporting evolvability and scalability of ISD processes through knowledge capitalization and sharing. The framework we propose is mainly based on a *process fragment repository* and a *global context frame*. The *process fragment repository* is dedicated to the storing of process fragments which may be reused through ISD *by* reuse. The *global context frame* supports evolvability of ISD processes through the use of criterias to better specify *fragments*, *problems* and *solutions*.

From the methodologists point of view, there is a need for a common framework for all the project team members working in the company and for means to keep project team members in the boundaries of the company development process. The *context frame* encourages project team members to focus on specific/critical aspects of the project they are involved in and the development process they use. It should help project team members to always take as much advantage as possible from the last version of the development process chosen, adapted and used in the company. It is a scalable structure which supports evolution and tailoring by the methodologists for the project team member's need with regards to project and process features.

From the project team member point of view, means are provided:

- to help to select the right fragments to solve his/her problems and
- to allow him/her to qualify its reusable element of solution when he/she add it as a new fragment in the repository.

The *context frame* we propose answers these needs. Criterias are a means to closely match project team member's need and to take into account their evolution.

A case tool is under development to validate the approach on a real case in companies where attempts have already been made to customize the development processes and to provide dedicated solutions through process fragments (Mirbel and de Rivieres, 2002a).

In the future, we would like to weight fragments with regards to the expertise level of the project team members introducing the fragments into the repository. We will also introduce support to fragment comparison needed when entering a new fragment in the repository.

As the main goal of this approach is still to benefit from the experiences acquired during the resolution of previous problems, it is also crucial for us to provide means to capitalize information about the way fragments and route-maps are reused through the proposed framework. Therefore, our future works include the integration of *tracking information* to capitalize about the way ISD *by* reuse is handled.

REFERENCES

Boehm, B. (1988). A spiral model of software development and enhancement. *Computer*, 21:61–72.

Brinkkemper, S., Saeki, M., and Harmsen, F. (1998). Assembly techniques for method engineering. In *10th International Conference on Advanced Information Systems Engineering*, Pisa, Italy.

Cauvet, C., Rieu, D., Fron-Conte, A., and Ramadour, P. (2001). *Ingienie des systmes d'information*, chapter Rutilisation dans l'ingienie des systmes d'information, pages 115–147. Hermes.

Finkelstein, A., Kramer, J., and Goedicke, M. (1990). Viewpoint oriented software developement. In *Le gnie logiciel et ses applications*, Toulouse, France.

Fowler, M. (1997). *Analysis Patterns: Reusable Object Models*. Object Technology Series. Addison-Wesley, Reading, Massachusetts.

Franckson, M. and Peugeot, C. (1991). Spcification of the object and process modeling language ESF. Technical Report D122-OPML-1.0.

Gamma, E., Helm, R., Johnson, R., and Vlissides, J. (1995). *Design Patterns: Elements of Reusable Object-Oriented Software*. Addison-Wesley Professional Computing Series. Addison-Wesley Publishing Company, New York, NY.

Gnatz, M., Marschall, F., Popp, G., Rausch, A., and Schwerin, W. (2001). Modular process patterns supporting an evolutionary software development process. *Lecture Notes in Computer Science*, 2188.

Henderson-Sellers, B. and Edwards, J. (1990). The object-oriented systems life cycle. *Communications of the ACM*, 33(9):142–159.

Mirbel, I. and de Rivieres, V. (2002a). Adapting Analysis and Design to Software Context: the JECKO Approach. In *8th International Conference on Object-Oriented Information S ystems*.

Mirbel, I. and de Rivieres, V. (2002b). Introducing Flexibility in the Heart of Analysis and Design. In *6th world multiconference on systemics, cybernetics and informatics (SCI)*.

Mirbel, I. and de Rivieres, V. (2003). *UML and the Unified Process*, chapter Towards a UML profile for building on top of running software. IRM Press.

Object Management Group (2001). Uml specification.

Potts, C. (1989). A generic model for representing design methods. In *11th International Conference on Software Engineering*.

Ralyte, J. (2001). *Ingenierie des methodes a base de composants*. PhD thesis, Universite Paris I - Sorbonne.

Rolland, C. and Souveyet, C. (1995). An approach for defining ways-of-working. *Information Systems Journal*.

Royce, W. (1970). Managing the development of large software systems: Concepts and techniques. In *WESCON*.

Saeki, M. (2003). Toward automated method engineering: Supporting method assembly in came. In *First International Workshop on Engineering methods to support information systems evolution*, Geneva, Switzerland.

si Said, S. and Rolland, C. (1998). Formalising guidance for the CREWS goal-scenario approach to requirements engineering. In *Eight European-Japanese Conference on Information Modelling and Knowledge Bases*.

van Slooten, K. and Hodes, B. (1996). Characterizing IS development projects. In S. Brinkkemper, K. Lyytinen, R. W., editor, *IFIP TC8, WG 8.1/8.2*, pages 29–44.

FEATURE MATCHING IN MODEL-BASED SOFTWARE ENGINEERING

Alar Raabe

Department of Computer Engineering, Tallinn Technical University, Ehitajate tee 5, 19086 Tallinn, Estonia
Email: alar.raabe@profitsoftware.ee

Keywords: Model-based development, model-driven architecture (MDA), domain modeling, feature models, software engineering

Abstract: There is a growing need to reduce the cycle of business information systems development and make it independent of underlying technologies. Model-driven synthesis of software offers solutions to these problems. This article describes a method for synthesizing business software implementations from technology independent business models. The synthesis of business software implementation performed in two steps, is based on establishing a common feature space for problem and solution domains. In the first step, a solution domain and a software architecture style are selected by matching the explicitly required features of a given software system, and implicitly required features of a given problem domain to the features provided by the solution domain and the architectural style. In the second step, all the elements of a given business analysis model are transformed into elements or configurations in the selected solution domain according to the selected architectural style, by matching their required features to the features provided by the elements and configurations of the selected solution domain. In both steps it is possible to define cost functions for selecting between different alternatives which provide the same features. The differences of our method are the separate step of solution domain analysis during the software process, which produces the feature model of the solution domain, and usage of common feature space to select the solution domain, the architectural style and specific implementations.

1 INTRODUCTION

Today business processes become increasingly dependent on the software, and must change rapidly in response to market changes. Initial results from software development should be delivered with a very short delay and have to be deployable with minimal costs. When the business volume grows, or the business processes change, supporting software systems must be able to grow and change along, without impeding the business process and without a major reimplementation effort. To achieve different non-functional requirements (e.g. quality of service) needed for business information systems, different implementation technologies, which themselves are rapidly evolving, are to be used and combined.

As a result, there is a growing need to shorten the development cycle of business information systems, and to achieve its independence of underlying technologies, which often evolve without offering backward compatibility. Therefore the main body of reusable software assets of an enterprise should be independent of implementation technologies.

These problems are addressed by model-based approaches to software development, e.g. model-based software synthesis (Abbott et al., 1993), model-based development (Mellor, 1995), and model driven architecture (MDA) (OMG, 2001a). In the model-based software development, the primary artifact is a model of the required software system, which becomes the source of the specific implementation of a given software system created through synthesis or generation.

We treat the development of business information systems as similar to domain-oriented application development technologies (SEI, 2002 and Honeywell, 1996), where business, in general, is treated as a large general domain containing several more specific domains (business areas), which refer to common elements from the general business domain.

In this article we describe a method that is applicable to synthesizing business software implementations from technology independent business models.

Our method is based on establishing a common

I. Seruca et al. (eds.), Enterprise Information Systems VI, 193–202.
© 2006 *Springer. Printed in the Netherlands.*

feature space for problem and solution domains for the business information systems and using the features of problem domain elements for synthesizing the implementation from the solution domain elements.

The problems analyzed in this article are:

- existence and contents of a common feature space for problem and solution domains,
- a method for the synthesis of implementation from analysis models based on the common features of problem and solution domain elements.

Presented method requires a separate step of solution domain analysis during the software engineering process described in (Raabe, 2003). During both the problem domain and solution domain analysis, the previously described techniques of using the extended meta-models (Raabe, 2002) are used to incorporate feature models.

The rest of this paper is organized as follows. Section 2 analyzes briefly the usage of models in software engineering, section 3 describes the feature -based methods suitable for solution domain analysis, and section 4 proposes a feature matching technique for implementation synthesis from analysis models.

2 USAGE OF MODELS IN SOFTWARE ENGINEERING

In the software engineering process, models are traditionally used for documentation purposes and in certain cases as source artifacts for automatic derivation (e.g. generation) of other artifacts.

Models as documentation could be used to document results of analysis, design, or implementation phases of software projects.

Models as source artifacts could be used to represent results of analysis (e.g. description of a problem statement), or to represent results of design (e.g. high level description of a solution). In both cases, models are a source for either a compilation or generation process where new dependent artifacts are created or for the interpretation or execution process, where the models directly drive the implementation.

2.1 Definitions

We will use the following definitions from UML:

- a *domain* is an area of knowledge or activity characterized by a set of concepts and terminology understood by practitioners in that area (OMG, 2001b);
- a *model* is a more or less complete abstraction of a system from a particular viewpoint (Rumbaugh, Jacobson & Booch, 1999).

We assume that domains may themselves contain more specific sub-domains, i.e. there can exist a generalization relationship between domains (Simos et al., 1996). Based on this generalization relationship, domains form a taxonomic hierarchy.

We extend the meaning of the model to represent not only abstractions of physical systems (OMG, 2001b) but also abstractions of logical systems.

We will use the following definition from Organization Domain Modeling (ODM) (Simos et al., 1996):

- a *feature* is a distinguishable characteristic of a concept (e.g. system, component) that is relevant to some stakeholder of this concept.

Features of a given software system are organized into feature model(s).

Additionally, we introduce the following definitions:

- a *domain model* is a body of knowledge in a given domain represented in a given modeling language (e.g. UML);
- a *problem domain* of a software system is a domain which is the context for requirements of that software system;
- a *solution domain* of a software system is a domain which describes the implementation technology of that software system;
- an *analysis model* is a model of a software system which contains elements from the relevant problem domain models and is a combination and specialization of relevant problem domain models specified by the set of functional requirements for a given software;
- an *implementation model* is a model of specific implementation of some software system which contains elements from the relevant solution domain models and a combination and specialization of relevant solution domain models specified by the set of non-functional requirements for a given software system;
- a *feature space* is a set of features, which are used in a given set of feature models;
- a *configuration* (or topology) is a set of interconnected domain elements or concepts, which collectively provide a certain set of features.

We use the term *implementation model* instead of the design model to stress that this model represents not only the logical level of design, but the design of the software system for the specific combination of solution domains – a specific implementation.

2.2 Model-based Software Engineering Methods

Model-based software engineering covers software development methods, where models are the main artifacts and some or all other artifacts are derived from the models.

Model-based software engineering was first taken into use in application domains where the correctness and reliability of software were very important (i.e. in real-time and embedded systems). In these cases, extensive usage of models during analysis and design was inevitable due to the complexity of the domain and high-level quality requirements for resulting systems. Existence of up-to-date models and the need to retain properties of models in the implementation facilitated their use as a source for other artifacts during the software engineering process.

Examples of this approach to the engineering of embedded and real-time software are Model-Integrated Computing (MIC) developed in Vanderbilt University ISIS (Abbott et al., 1993) and Model-Based Development (MBD) developed by Shlaer and Mellor (Mellor, 1995).

Later, model-based software engineering was also taken into use in other application domains like:
- for generative programming with reusable components – GenVoca developed in Texas University (Batory and O'Malley, 1992),
- for the development and configuration of members of software system families (i.e. product line architectures) – Family-Oriented Abstraction, Specification, and Translation (FAST) developed in AT&T (Weiss, 1996),

and
- for the integration and interoperability of distributed systems – Model-Driven Architecture (MDA) proposed by OMG (OMG, 2001a).

In the traditional approach to model-based software engineering, implementation can be derived either from the description of very high-level solution to the problem or from the problem description itself.

In the first case, an analyst creates an analysis model which describes the problem, based on the problem domain knowledge. Next a designer, based on the solution domain knowledge, creates a design model that will be automatically transformed to the actual implementation of the system.

In the second case, the analysis model itself is directly transformed into an implementation.

These cases both need previously prepared description of transformation, which incorporates the knowledge of problem and solution domains. This description of transformation will then be reusable for several problem descriptions which all belong to the same problem domain.

In the present approaches to model-based software engineering, the knowledge about the problem and solution domains is implicit (i.e. embedded into the transformation description) and the transformation from the problem domain into the solution domain often depends on the chosen transformation technology.

While model-based approaches apply the model-based software engineering paradigm to the development of actual software, the development of transformations is usually following the old software engineering paradigms.

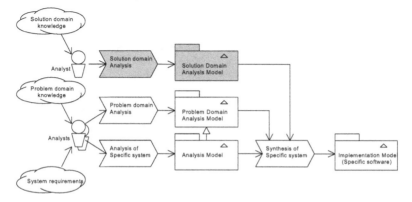

Figure 1: Model-based software engineering process with a separate solution domain analysis step

2.3 Proposed Model-based Software Engineering Method

In (Raabe, 2003), we proposed solution domain analysis as an additional step during the software process (as shown in Fig. 1). Introducing this additional step will produce a solution domain model and will allow us to use formalized results of problem domain analysis and solution domain analysis as a basis for deriving the description of transformation from the analysis model to the implementation model.

3   DOMAIN ANALYSIS

Domain engineering (SEI, 2002) encompasses domain analysis, domain design, and domain implementation. Domain analysis contains the following activities:

- *domain scoping*, where relevant domain with its sub-domains will be selected and the main area of focus will be defined, and
- *domain modeling*, where relevant domain information is collected and integrated into a coherent domain model.

Domain model defines the scope (i.e. boundary conditions) of the domain, elements or concepts that constitute the domain (i.e. domain knowledge), generic and specific features of elements and configurations, functionality and behavior.

According to the different domain engineering approaches, there are several different domain analysis methods (Czarnecki and Eisenecker, 2000).

3.1   Feature-Oriented DomaiAnalysis

Feature modeling, also known as feature analysis, is the activity of modeling the common and the variable properties of concepts and their interdependencies.

Feature-oriented domain analysis methods describe the characteristics of a problem and the required characteristics of a solution independently of their structure.

Examples of feature-oriented domain analysis methods are:

- Feature-Oriented Domain Analysis (FODA) from SEI (Kang et al., 1990), which became a part of their MBSE framework (SEI);
- Feature-Oriented Reuse Method (FORM) developed by K. Kang (Kang, 1998);
- Domain Engineering Method for Reusable Algorithmic Libraries (DEMRAL) by Czarnecki and Eisenecker (Czarnecki and

Eisenecker, 2000).

Feature model consists of the following elements:

- *concepts* – any elements and structures of the domain of interest and
- *features* – qualitative properties of the concepts.

A feature model represents feature types and definitions, hierarchical decomposition of features, composition rules (i.e. dependencies between concepts) and rationale for features. It consists of a feature diagram and additional information.

Feature diagram is a tree-like diagram, where the root node represents a concept and other nodes represent features of this concept and sub-features of features. An example of a feature diagram is shown in Fig. 2.

From the composition point of view, the following feature types are most commonly used in feature models:

- mandatory features (e.g. $f_1, f_2, f_5, f_6, f_7, f_8, f_9$),
- optional features (e.g. f_3, f_4),
- alternative features (e.g. f_5, f_6), and
- or-features (e.g. f_7, f_8, f_9).

Composition rules between features are constraints for composing features for instances of concepts (e.g. "requires", "excludes").

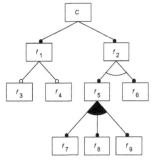

Figure 2: Example of a feature diagram

From the domain point of view, it is possible to describe different feature classes.

FODA (Kang et al., 1990) distinguishes between context features (non-functional characteristics of application), operational features (application functions), and representation features (interface functions).

FORM (Kang, 1998) distinguishes between capability features (further divided into functional and non-functional features), operating environment features, domain technology features, and implementation technique features.

DEMRAL (Czarnecki and Eisenecker, 2000) distinguishes between the following feature classes:

- features for all the concepts: attributes, data structures, operations, error handling, memory management, synchronization, persistence, perspectives, and subjectivity, and
- features for container-like concepts: element type, indexing, and structure.

Additionally, domain features in DEMRAL are annotated with the priorities representing the typicality and importance of a given feature.

During the domain analysis, the following models are created:

- traditional models for
  - static structures (e.g. class models, object models),
  - functionality (e.g. use-case models, scenario models), and
  - interactions or behavior (e.g. sequence models, collaboration models);
- feature models for functional and non-functional features.

Characteristic configurations of a given domain are identified during the domain analysis before the feature modeling and are represented as models of the static structures.

A feature set of a configuration might be larger than the sum of feature sets of all the concepts in the configuration.

Similarly to configurations, it is also possible to attach a set of non-functional features to the entire domain.

3.2 Problem Domain Analysis

Taking the insurance domain as an example of a problem domain, we will study the feature model of some concepts from this domain. Let us take as an example a concept *Policy* which represents an insurance agreement between an insurer and a policy holder. In the insurance domain model, this concept represents an independent business entity. As such, it has the following features:

- characteristic to the problem domain (insurance):
  - attributes (e.g. policy number, policy holder);
  - processing states (e.g. quote, offer);
  - attached business rules (e.g. validity and consistency conditions);
  - business processes attached (e.g. offering, renewal);

- services (e.g. computing the price, change of state);
- generic – independent of the problem domain:
  - it has identity;
  - it exists independently of other concepts in a given problem domain;
  - it has a state represented by the attributes;
  - it is transactional;
  - it is persistent and searchable;
  - it is viewable and modifiable.

Another example is a concept *Renewal*, which represents a process of renewing some of the characteristics of an insurance agreement. In the insurance domain model, this concept represents a business process. As such it has the following features:

- characteristic to the problem domain (insurance):
  - parameters (e.g. target date);
  - attached business rules (e.g. precondition and post condition);
  - it operates on other specific elements of a problem domain (e.g. policy);
- generic – independent of the problem domain:
  - it has no identity;
  - it has no state represented by the attributes;
  - it is transient.

These examples show that apart from features which are domain dependent, elements of a problem domain have certain generic features.

3.3 Solution Domain Analysis

Taking J2EE (Singh et al., 2002) as an example of a solution domain, we will study the feature model of some concepts from J2EE. Let us take as an example a concept *EntityBean*, which represents persistent data. As such, it has the following features:

- characteristic to the solution domain (J2EE):
  - attributes (e.g. context, primary key, handle);
  - processing states (e.g. active, passive);
  - attached rules (e.g. constraints on the state);
  - attached processes (e.g. passivation, activation, etc.);
  - services (e.g. create, find);
- generic –independent of the solution domain:

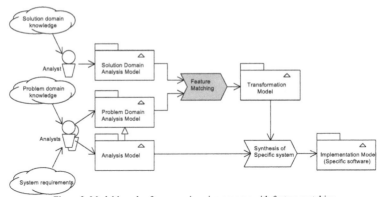

Figure 3: Model-based software engineering process with feature matching

- ° it has identity;
- ° it exists independently of other concepts;
- ° it has a state represented by the attributes;
- ° it is transactional;
- ° it is persistent and searchable.

Another example is a concept *Stateless SessionBean*, which represents a functional service. As such, it has the following features:

- • characteristic to the solution domain (J2EE):
  - ° parameters (e.g. context, handle);
  - ° processing states (e.g. active, passive);
  - ° attached rules (e.g. constraints on the state);
  - ° attached processes (e.g. passivation, activation);
- • generic – independent of the solution domain:
  - ° it has no identity;
  - ° it has no state represented by attributes;
  - ° it is transient;
  - ° it is scalable.

These examples show that apart from the features, which are domain dependent, elements of a solution domain and elements of problem domain have similar generic features.

These generic features, which are common for the problem and solution domain elements, stem from the generic requirements toward the software systems and describe various domain independent qualities of these elements. In nature, these generic features may be either functional or non-functional.

Analyzing J2EE as a solution domain, we see that certain generic features, which we identified in the problem domain example, require a configuration of concepts which will collectively provide them.

For example, to achieve the generic features of persistence, searchability, viewability, and modifiability in J2EE, we would have to construct a configuration consisting of *EntityBean*, some database domain concepts (e.g. table), and some user interface concepts (e.g. JSP).

4   FEATURE MATCHING

If the results of solution domain analysis are formalized into the models following the same analysis paradigm as the problem domain analysis, it will be possible to develop automatic synthesis of transformation rules. These rules will be transforming the analysis model of a system in the problem domain into an implementation model of the same system in the solution domain, producing the implementation of the specified system.

If this automatic synthesis of transformation rules is based on the features of the solution domain and problem domain elements, we call it *feature matching* (shown in Fig. 3.).

In the proposed method, synthesis of business software implementation from the technology independent business analysis model is performed in two steps.

First, a solution domain and software architecture style are selected by matching the explicitly required features of a given software system and implicitly required features of a given problem domain to the features provided by the software architecture style.

Next, all elements of a given business analysis model are transformed into elements or sets of interconnected elements of the selected architecture style, by matching their required features to the features provided by the elements of the selected architecture style. During this step, the common feature model drives the design of software implementation.

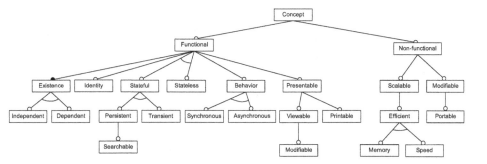

Figure 4: Common feature space

In both steps it is possible to define the cost functions for selecting between different alternatives that provide the same features.

4.1 Common Feature Space

In the previous study of applying feature modeling to problem domain analysis and solution domain analysis, we discovered that there exists a set of features which is common to both domains.

Elements of both domains:
- have the following functional features:
  - may have or may not have identity,
  - can be independent in their existence or dependent on other elements,
  - may have or may not have a state represented by the attributes (be stateful or stateless),
  - can be transient or persistent,
  - in case they are persistent, can be searchable,
  - can be viewable,
  - in case they are viewable, can be modifiable,
  - have asynchronous or synchronous behavior,
- have the following non-functional features:
  - efficiency (in terms of speed or space),
  - scalability,
  - modifiability,
  - portability.

These common features form a common feature space (Fig. 4), which is a basis to the synthesis of the implementation of an actual system from a problem description. This synthesis is a process of finding mapping between the model in the problem domain and the model in the solution domain, guided by the common features of model elements.

4.2 Solution Domain Selection

Usually, in the software engineering process, there are several different implementation technologies and architectural styles (Shaw and Garlan, 1996) available to choose from. In principle, it should be possible to make a decision on the architectural style and implementation technology independently, but often the implementation technology prescribes certain architectural styles, which are better supported than others.

In the process of synthesizing implementation from the model in the problem domain, the first task is to select the suitable solution domain. This will be based mainly on non-functional features of solution domains (e.g. scalability, modifiability). At that stage, it might happen that one solution domain does not provide all the required features. In this case, it would be necessary to combine several solution domains. This combination of solution domains (e.g. Java language combined with certain RDBMS to provide persistence) forms a new solution domain that is applicable to a given problem.

Examples of selecting architectural style:
- a suitable architectural style for data-entry application is "central repository", a front-end application with the back-end data storage (e.g. RDBMS);
- a suitable architectural style for signal processing application is "pipes and filters", where "filters" implement transformations on signals and are connected with "pipes";
- a suitable architectural style for decision support system is "blackboard", where relatively autonomous agents are cooperating via common model of situation.

4.3 Implementation Synthesis

The next step in the feature matching, when the solution domain is selected, is actual implementation synthesis. During this process, for every element of the problem domain model, a suitable element or a suitable configuration of elements of the solution domain model is selected. The result is a mapping from the problem domain model to the solution domain model (i.e. implementation). Suitability of the solution domain element(s) for a given problem domain model element is decided by their corresponding features.

Descriptions of concepts (or domain elements) are given by the sets of their features:

$$C = F = \{f_i\}$$

and sets of features of configurations of concepts are the unions of all the feature sets of elements in the configuration:

$$\{C_1, ..., C_n\} = F_1 \cup ... \cup F_n$$

We represent the mapping between the concepts of the problem domain and those of the solution domain:

or simply:
$$f : \{C^P\} \to \{C^S\}$$
$$\{C^P\} \to \{C^S\}$$

We reduce finding a suitable configuration in the solution domain for the generic case to different specific cases, which cover all situations.

The first case is trivial – when the feature set of a problem domain element is a subset of the feature set of a certain solution domain element, then the problem domain element is mapped directly to this solution domain element:

$$F^P \subseteq F^S \Rightarrow \{C^P\} \to \{C^S\}$$

The second case – when the feature set of a problem domain element is a subset of the union of feature sets of a configuration of solution domain elements, then the problem domain element is mapped directly to this configuration of the solution domain elements:

$$F^P \subseteq F^S_1 \cup ... \cup F^S_m \Rightarrow \{C^P\} \to \{C^S_1, ... , C^S_m\}$$

The third case – when there exists a configuration of problem space elements consisting of n elements, then if the union of feature sets of these elements is a subset of the feature set of a

certain solution domain element, the given configuration of problem domain elements is mapped to this solution domain element:

$$F^P_1 \cup ... \cup F^P_n \subseteq F^S \Rightarrow \{C^P_1, ... , C^P_n\} \to \{C^S\}$$

The last case is the most complex and describes also the generic case – when there exists a configuration of problem space elements consisting of n elements, then if the union of feature sets of these elements is a subset of union of feature sets of a certain configuration of solution domain elements, the given configuration of the problem domain elements is mapped to this configuration of solution domain elements:

$$F^P_1 \cup ... \cup F^P_n \subseteq F^S_1 \cup ... \cup F^S_m \Rightarrow \{C^P_1, ..., C^P_n\} \to \{C^S_1, ..., C^S_m\}$$

This step is driven by the structure of the problem domain model and the analysis model.

4.4 Selecting Between Alternatives

Different solution domains usually have different non-functional features or quality attributes (Bass, Clements & Kazman, 1998). These non-functional features could be divided to run-time features (e.g. performance, security, availability, usability) and maintenance features (e.g. modifiability, portability, reusability, integrability, testability). The combination of non-functional features corresponds to a certain set of business goals (e.g. time to market, cost, projected lifetime, market share, rollout schedule).

The non-functional requirements connected to the problem specification can be used to choose between possible solution domains and usage styles of the given solution domain elements (e.g. software architecture style).

Inside a solution domain there may exist many configurations of solution domain elements, which can be used to implement the same functional or non-functional requirements. There feature matching algorithm can use different strategies of choosing between elements and configurations of the solution domain.

There can be alternatives between the elements or configurations of the solution space, which offer similar feature sets:

$$F^P \subseteq F^S_1 \text{ \& } F^P \subseteq F^S_2$$

In this case, during the feature matching, it is possible to use different strategies to make the decision between alternatives. Possible feature matching strategies are maximal, minimal, or optimal.

The maximal strategy, where the solution domain element or configuration is selected, if it provides most additional features for implementing a given problem domain element:

$$|F^S_1 \setminus F^P| < |F^S_2 \setminus F^P| \Rightarrow \{C^P\} \rightarrow \{C^S_2\}$$

The minimal strategy, where the solution domain element or configuration is selected, if it provides least additional features for implementing a given problem domain element:

$$|F^S_1 \setminus F^P| < |F^S_2 \setminus F^P| \Rightarrow \{C^P\} \rightarrow \{C^S_1\}$$

The optimal strategy, where a solution domain element or a configuration is selected, based on the cost function:

$$\mathrm{cost}(F^S_1) < \mathrm{cost}(F^S_2) \Rightarrow \{C^P\} \rightarrow \{C^S_1\}$$

where the cost function $\mathrm{cost}(F)$ is based on non-functional features of C^S_i.

For example, if we take into account the scalability requirements in the case described above, we would select the configuration built around the *SessionBean* instead of *EntityBean* for the concept *policy*.

When selecting a suitable solution, the domain can be viewed as global optimization, selecting suitable configurations in the selected solution domain can be viewed as local optimization.

5 RELATED WORK

A similar problem has been analyzed in the context of domain engineering approach in SEI (Peterson and Stanley, 1994). Peterson and Stanley have studied mapping of the domain model to a generic design. In their work, they presented mapping from the domain analysis results presented in FODA into the predefined architecture (OCA – Object Connection Architecture) by architecture elements.

Another similar technique is presented in the Feature-Oriented Reuse Method (FORM) developed by K. C. Kang (Kang, 1998). In this method, also a feature space (result form FODA) is mapped into a predefined artifact space (an architecture) by using kinds of features identified in the feature modeling.

Both of these methods allow mapping of the problem domain results only into predefined architecture.

The difference of our approach from these two approaches is that we allow synthesis of implementations in different, not predefined solution domains.

Selection of the architectural style, based on reasoning about the quality attributes of architectural styles is dealt with in the Attribute-Based Architecture Styles (ABAS) method (Bass, Clements & Kazman, 1998).

Lately the MDA initiative from OMG (OMG, 2001a) has been establishing modeling standards needed to develop supporting tools for mapping platform independent models (PIMs) into platform specific models (PSMs). Techniques and tools presented in the article are in line with MDA and useful when the MDA approach is applied to the development of large-scale business systems.

6 CONCLUSIONS

The difference of our method from other domain specific and model-based methods is the separate step of solution domain analysis, which results in a reusable solution domain model, and using a feature space that is common to the problem and solution domains, for selecting the solution domain, the architecture style, and specific implementations.

We have shown that there exists a common feature space for both the problem domain and solution domain elements.

We have presented an algorithm based on this common feature space for selecting the solution domain, architectural style, and for synthesizing an implementation.

We have also shown that it is possible to drive the solution domain selection and implementation synthesis algorithm with a suitable cost function.

The presented method allows shorter software development cycles due to the automation of the implementation phase, reusability of the problem domain knowledge (i.e. business analysis models) with different solution domains (i.e. implementation technologies), and better usability of solution domain knowledge. It is applicable to OMG MDA for transformation or mapping of the platform independent model (PIM) to platform specific models (PSMs).

In the future, providers of implementation technologies (e.g. J2EE) may supply also the models of their solution domains (incl. feature models), together with other artifacts of a given implementation technology. Together with the development of tools that could synthesize implementations based on the problem domain models by using feature matching, this would dramatically reduce the threshold of using new implementation technologies for software engineering. This would require establishment of a standard for common feature space, and a standard for representing feature models.

In our next research steps we will study the common feature space for consistency and completeness and solution domain configurations (e.g. emerging new feature sets during synthesis and the relationship of solution domain configurations to design patterns).

ACKNOWLEDGEMENTS

Author wishes to gratefully acknowledge Profit Software Ltd. (Finland) and the Estonian Science Foundation for their support (Grant 4721).

Author wishes to thank Riina Putting and Kert Uutsalu for discussions on the subject and many useful suggestions for improving this paper.

REFERENCES

Abbott, B., Bapty, T., Biegl, C., Karsai, G., Sztipanovits, J., 1993, Model-Based Software Synthesis, *IEEE Software*, May, 10 (3), 1993, pp.42-52.

Bass, L., Clements, P. and Kazman, R., 1998, *Software Architecture in Practice*, Addison-Wesley.

Batory, D. and O'Malley, S., 1992, The design and implementation of hierarchical software systems with reusable components, *ACM Transactions on Software Engineering and Methodology*, Vol. 1, No. 4, pp. 355-398.

Czarnecki, K., Eisenecker, U., W., 2000, *Generative Programming, Methods, Tools, and Applications*, Addison-Wesley.

Honeywell, 1996, Domain-Specific Software Architectures, www.htc.Honeywell.com/projects/dssa

Kang, K. C., Cohen, S. G., Hess, J. A., Novak, W. E., Peterson, A. S., 1990, Feature-Oriented Domain Analysis (FODA) Feasibility Study, SEI CMU, CMU/SEI-90-TR-021

Kang, K. C., Kim, S., Lee, J., Kim, K., Shin, E., and Huh., M., 1998, FORM: A feature-oriented reuse method with domain-specific reference architectures. *Annals of Software Engineering*, Vol. 5, pp. 143-168.

Medvidovic, N., Taylor, R. N., 1997, A Framework for Classifying and Comparing Architecture Description Languages, *Proceedings of the Sixth European Software Engineering Conference (ESEC/FSE 97)*, Ed. by M. Jazayeri and H. Schauer, Springer Verlag, pp. 60-76.

Mellor, S. J., 1995, Reuse through automation: Model-Based Development, *Object Magazine*, September 1995.

OMG, 2001a, *Model Driven Architecture*, OMG 01-07-01, ftp.omg.org/pub/docs/ormsc

OMG, 2001b, *OMG Unified Modeling Language Specification Version 1.4*, OMG 01-09-67, ftp.omg.org/pub/docs/formal

Peterson, A. S., Stanley, J. L., 1994, Mapping a Domain Model and Architecture to a Generic Design, SEI CMU, CMU/SEI-94-TR-008

Raabe, A., 2002, Techniques of combination of metamodel extensions, *Proceedings of the Estonian Academy of Sciences, Engineering*, 8 (1), 2002, pp. 3-17.

Raabe, A., 2003, Software Engineering Environment for Business Information Systems, In *Proceedings of ICEIS 2003, 5th International Conference on Enterprise Information Systems, Angers, France, 23-26 April, 2003*, Volume 3, pp. 129-137.

Rumbaugh, J., Jacobson, I., and Booch, G., 1999, *The Unified Modeling Language Reference Manual*, Addison-Wesley, Reading, Massachusetts.

SEI, 2002, Domain Engineering: A Model-Based Approach, www.sei.cmu.edu/domain-engineering

Simos, M., Creps, D., Klinger, C., Levine, L., and Allemang, D., 1996, *Organization Domain Modeling (ODM) Guidebook, Version 2.0*, Technical Report for STARS, STARS-VC-A025/001/00, June 14, 1996.

Singh, I., Stearns, B., Johnson, M. and the Enterprise Team, 2002, Designing Enterprise Applications with the J2EE Platform, Second Edition, Addison-Wesley.

Shaw, M., Garlan, D., 1996, *Software Architecture: Perspectives on an Emerging Discipline*, Prentice-Hall.

Weiss, D., 1996, Family-Oriented Abstraction, Specification, and Translation The FAST Process, Keynote talk at *Computer Assurance Conference (COMPASS), 19 June 1996*, www.research.avayalabs.com/user/weiss/pubs/compass96.ps

TOWARDS A META MODEL FOR DESCRIBING COMMUNICATION
How to address interoperability on a pragmatic level

Boriana Rukanova, Kees van Slooten, Robert A. Stegwee

School of Business, Public Administration and Technology, University of Twente, P.O.Box 217, 7500 AE Enschede, The Netherlands
Email: {b.d.rukanova, c.vanslooten, r.a.stegwee}@utwente.nl

Keywords: business information systems, interoperability, pragmatics, standard

Abstract: The developments in the ICT led companies to strive to make parts of the business transaction electronic and raised again the issue of interoperability. Although interoperability between computer systems has been widely addressed in literature, the concept of interoperability between organizations is still to a large extent unexplored. Standards are claimed to help achieving interoperability. However, experience with the implementation of EDI standards shows that many EDI implementation projects led to technical solutions with unclear business benefits. New standards are currently being developed, however their implementation can also lead again to purely technical solution, if the social context is not taken sufficiently into account. In this paper we address the problem on how to identify interoperability problems on a pragmatic level that can occur between organizations that want to carry out business transactions electronically. We also point out that, in order to identify interoperability problems on a pragmatic level, it is necessary to capture the communication requirements of the business parties and to evaluate to what extent a standard is capable to meet these requirements. To perform that evaluation we develop a meta model for describing communication. The meta model is based on theory of speech-act and communicative actions. The use of the meta model to identify interoperability problems on a pragmatic level is illustrated with an example.

1 INTRODUCTION

The developments in the area of ICT made possible disparate information systems to exchange data electronically. This raised the question of how to achieve interoperability. The issue of interoperability between software systems has already been widely addressed (Goh et al., 1999; Heiler, 1995; Wegner, 1996). Further, it is expected that the use of standards can help in resolving the interoperability problems. However, experience with the implementation of EDI standards shows that often the result is a technical interoperability between software systems with unclear business benefit (Covington, 1997; Huang, 1998). Other standards are currently being developed. Examples are RosettaNet, and HL7. However, there is a danger that an implementation of such a standard could lead again only to a technical solution, rather than improving the way of doing business. This means that more than technical interoperability between computer systems is needed, but rather interoperability between organizations (business

information systems) is to be achieved (Stegwee & Rukanova, 2004).

To achieve interoperability between organizations, it is important to realize first, that an organization is a combination of people and technology. Second, each organization operates in its own context. Thus, the organizations need to define a shared communication context in order to enter into business transactions together (Stamper, 1996; Vermeer, 2000).

If the business parties decide to use computers to perform parts of the business transaction electronically, then the relevant shared context needs to be made explicit, formalized and embedded in the computer systems. In case where standards are used to formalize the relevant shared context, a standard needs to be evaluated to what extent it is capable to cover the relevant shared context (Rukanova et al., 2003a). This check is important to indicate where interoperability problems might arise. One possibility to make the comparison between the requirements of the communication context and the

I. Seruca et al. (eds.), Enterprise Information Systems VI, 203–210.
© 2006 *Springer. Printed in the Netherlands.*

capabilities of a standard is by using a meta model, which captures elements of a business transaction (Rukanova et al., 2003b).

To capture the context of a business transaction, a number of views can be defined (Rukanova et al., 2003c). These views can help to look at the business transaction from different perspectives and provide a holistic understanding of the context of a business transaction. The analysis of the different views can contribute to the identification of interoperability problems that can occur, when different organizations decide to do business transactions electronically.

In this paper we will investigate only one of the views: "the communicative acts view", which is concerned with how to describe the conversations and the intentions in a business transaction. This view is concerned with the pragmatics aspect in a business transaction. The pragmatics underlines the importance that it is not sufficient to understand what is communicated, but also what is the intention behind it, how you interpret the communicated information and how you act upon it. This paper is concerned with *how to identify interoperability problems on a pragmatic level.*

To achieve interoperability on a pragmatic level, it is necessary to be able to express and compare the requirements of the business transaction (on a pragmatic level) and the capability of the standard to cover these requirements. In this paper we create a meta model for describing conversations to help make that comparison.

The remaining part of the paper is structured as follows. In part two, a number of theoretical constructs to describe communication are identified. In part three these constructs are used as a basis for defining a meta model for describing communication. In part four we use the meta model to evaluate the capabilities of a standard to cover the business requirements (on a pragmatic level).

2   ELEMENTARY UNITS TO DESCRIBE COMMUNICATION

As it was mentioned in the introduction, the main concern in this paper is how to achieve interoperability on pragmatic level, if organizations want to use standards in order to carry out their business transactions electronically. Thus, it is necessary to identify key elements that can capture communication requirements of a business transaction and further to use these elements to evaluate the extent to which a standard is capable of capturing the communication requirements. As we are currently interested in the pragmatic aspect of

communication, it means that the elements that we need to identify have to address the problem of what is communicated, and how is it interpreted. Further, as we are interested in the whole business transaction, we need to identify what communication takes place during the entire transaction lifecycle.

2.1   E-message and Ae-message

The research done in the area of information systems and language-action perspective can provide us with substantial input to be able to identify key elements, which describe communication. As this research addresses communication in general, we can apply some of the findings to describe communication specific for business transactions. To define what is communicated and what is the intention behind the communicated information, we will make use of the notions of elementary message (e-message) and action elementary message (ae-message).

The notion of e-message is defined by Langefors (Langefors, 1973). According to Langefors, an e-message consists of four basic terms to give information about the property of an object: the identity of an object, the kind of property, the specification of that property for that object, the point in time at which the information is valid. Further we add that an object can have multiple properties. Thus each combination of object (id), property, property value and time can result in an e-message. If we want to describe the different properties of an object at a given time, a number of e-messages can be defined. This can be schematically presented as illustrated in figure 1. The ORM notation (Halpin, 1996) is used as a means for representation of the models in this paper.

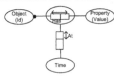

Figure 1: An object defined in terms of elements of e-messages

Although using the elements of e-message is a good starting point for describing communication, it provides a limited view, as it implies a purely descriptive approach toward information. (Goldkuhl & Lyytinen, 1982; Winograd & Flores, 1986). However, language can be used not only to describe things, but also to perform actions (Austin, 1962; Goldkuhl, 1995; Habermas, 1984; Searle, 1969). In order to capture the intention behind the communicated information, the notion of action elementary message (ae-message) can be used (Agerfalk, 1999, 2002; Goldkuhl & Agerfalk, 2002). The notion of the ae-message is built upon the notion of e-message, and extended to capture the intention. An ae-message is composed of four elements: the communicator, the interpreter, propositional content (the content that is communicated), and the communicative function (the intention behind the communicated information) (see Figure 2).

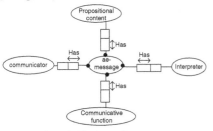

Figure 2: Elements of an ae-message

We will elaborate further on the concepts of communicative function and the propositional content. The propositional content consists of a number of e-messages. The propositional content is the content, which is communicated, that is information about objects and their properties at a certain time. (See Figure 3)

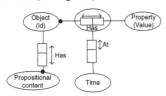

Figure 3: Elements of a propositional content

There are relationships between the objects, which are part of the prepositional content, however, for simplicity reasons this relationship is not explicitly represented in the model

The other concept included in the ae-message, which deserves attention, is the communicative function (synonyms are illocutionary acts and action mode). The communicative function contains the intention of the speech act. Different types of communicative functions (illocutionary acts) can be identified (see (Habermas, 1984; Searle, 1969)). Examples of communicative functions are order and promise. The main point that we want to make here is to stress the importance of the communicative function in capturing intentions behind the communicated information. We will not go further into describing the different types of communicative functions. However, in part 2.2 of this paper, we will

come back to the concept of communicative functions to explore their role in forming patterns of conversations.

So far we have identified some elementary constructs for describing communication. However, although describing ae-messages is a big step in describing communication, the speech acts theories are criticized in two directions. The first one is that they do not pay much attention to the content of what is communicated (the propositional content) (Schoop, 2003). The second one is that they focus mainly on the individual speech acts, and not on the whole conversation. This issue will be further addressed in the next section.

2.2 Sequence of Utterances

The Speech-act approaches focus mainly on the individual speech-acts rather than the whole conversation, thus the speech-act theory cannot be used to explain the organization of communication (Goldkuhl, 2003). The research done by Winograd and Flores (Winograd & Flores, 1986) can help in addressing this problem, as the authors argue that the main focus should not be on the individual speech-acts, but the conversation, in which individual speech acts are related to one another. Their key contribution is in the identification of basic patterns for describing conversations- the "conversation for action" scheme (see figure 4).

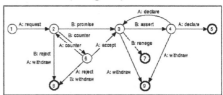

Figure 4: The basic "Conversation for Action" Adopted form Winograd and Flores, 1986, p. 65

The schema describes different states that a conversation can take and how the states are altered through the performance of speech acts. For example, actor A can make a request to another actor B. B can either promise to fulfil the request, counter the request or reject it. Here we can see how different communicative functions (e.g. request, promise) can interplay to form a conversation. Flores and Winograd have influenced a number of researchers in the field of Language action perspective. Based on the conversation for action scheme, a number of communication patterns have been derived. However, the derived patterns seem to be rather prescriptive. The result of this is that, when describing a real life situation, one might end up with actually changing the requirements of the real-life situation so that they can fit into the pre-defined pattern. This however is undesirable. Thus, although interaction patterns can be helpful in eliciting the conversation requirements, their use should be done with caution (Goldkuhl, 2003).

In the introduction we started with the problem of how to identify interoperability problems (on a pragmatic level) that can occur if companies decide to do business transactions electronically by using standards. So far, we have identified a number of elements, which can help us to describe conversations. This enables us to move to the next step for addressing the interoperability on pragmatic level: linking these elements in a meta model for describing conversations.

3 A META MODEL FOR DESCRIBING CONVERSATIONS

In the previous section we have identified a number of concepts to describe a conversation. However, these concepts alone provide a fragmented view of elements of conversation. In this section, we link these concepts into a meta model.

The meta model is presented in Figure 5 below.

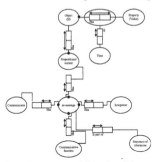

Figure 5: A meta model for describing conversations

Although most of the concepts were already introduced earlier, a brief description and explanation of the meta model is provided below. A key concept around which the meta model is built is the ae-message. An action elementary message has a communicator, an interpreter, a propositional content, and a communication function. Further, an ae-message is part of a conversation, and the conversation can be described with sequence of utterances. We consider the real life situation as a starting point for identifying sequence of utterances. Communication patterns (such as the "conversation for action" scheme of Winograd and Flores) can be

used as a support tool to describe the sequence of utterances, once they have been identified based on the real-life situation. Although the scheme of Winograd and Flores is very powerful in expressing different possibilities that a conversation can follow, there could be real-life situations, where this scheme can turn to be limited. Thus, the Winograd and Flores scheme, as well as any other patterns of conversations (whenever available) should be used with caution.

To overcome the critique that speech acts do not focus on the content of what is communicated (see 2.1), the notion of propositional content is explicitly includes in the model. The propositional content contains information about objects, the properties of objects, the values of the properties and the time the value is valid.

In that way, the meta model captures information about the content of the message that is communicated, who is the communicator and the interpreter of that message, what is the intention of that message and how it forms part of a conversation.

The main benefit from the meta model is that it can be used to describe both the communication requirements of a business transaction and the capabilities of the standard in the same terms. When both, the requirements of the business transaction and the capabilities of the standard are expressed in terms of the meta model, they can be easily compared (see also (Rukanova et al., 2003a, b). A mismatch between the two will mean that some of the requirements of the business transaction cannot be covered by the standard, which would signal interoperability problems (on a pragmatic level). In the section below we will illustrate the use of the meta model.

4 THE META MODEL IN USE

In this section we will illustrate the use of the meta model to identify whether interoperability on a pragmatic level can be achieved. We will first introduce a standard (the (HL7) standard will be used for our example). Further we will describe a simple business transaction, which needs to be automated using the HL7 standard. We will translate the requirements of the business transaction in terms of the meta model. We will also translate the capabilities of the standard in terms of the meta model. Once expressed in the same terms, we will be able compare the requirements of the business transaction and the capability of the standard to meet these requirements. A mismatch between the two will mean that there could be interoperability problems on a pragmatic level, which can hinder the way of doing business. Due to space limits, in this example we will not elaborate in full detail the elements describing the propositional content. However, such a description can be done and is important part of the analysis.

4.1 The HL7 Standard

For this example we will look at the HL7 v.3 standard. HL7 is one of the leading Healthcare standards for clinical data interchange. The standard covers transactions in several areas, some of which are accounting and billing, claims and reimbursement, and diagnostic orders and observations. For the purpose of this example we will look at how the interactions are defined in the HL7 standard and we will limit our analysis to the interactions related to Laboratory observations. Before going further we will provide some background information about the HL7 v.3 standard.

In the basis of the HL7 v.3 is the HL7 Reference Information Model (RIM). The RIM models, on a very high abstract level, the major things of interest in the healthcare domain. It consists of six major classes, defines the attributes of these classes and the relationships between them. The messages that are exchanged in the clinical communication are derived from the RIM. However, the link between the RIM and the message that is actually exchanged is not straightforward, but it requires intermediary steps. As the concepts in the RIM are very general, a procedure called cloning is defined. After this procedure, a domain message information model is defined (DMIM). This model is derived from the RIM, and provides further restrictions on the defined information (by for example restricting the attributes of the classes). This domain message information model is then used to create the Hierarchical message description, which defines in full detail the messages that are later exchanged in the interactions. A central class in the RIM is the "Act". The act represents actions that are executed and must be represented as the healthcare processes take place. An example of Act is (Lab) Order. The information provided above is important in order to understand how interactions are defined in the HL7 standard.

In the HL7 v.3 Guide, an interaction is defined as " a unique association between a specific message type (information), a particular trigger event, and the application roles that send and receive a message type. It is a unique, one-way transfer of information." From this definition we can derive, that an interaction is uniquely defined using four components: the sending application role (a system component which sends a message), the receiving

application role (a system component, which receives the message), the trigger event (the reason to send a message), and the message type (what message to send) (see Figure 6).

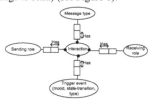

Figure 6: Description of the HL7 interactions

To better understand the interactions, as defined in the HL7 standard, some further elaboration is needed on the notion of a trigger event. According to the HL7 v.3 Guide, "a trigger event is an explicit set of conditions that initiate the transfer of information between system components (application roles). It is a real-world event such as the placing of a laboratory order or drug order." The trigger event is expressed as a combination of mood, state-transition, and type. The "mood" is a very important concept in the HL7 v.3 standard. It distinguishes between statements of facts that the ordered service (act) has been completed, or it specifies the intent to perform such a service. Examples of moods as defined in the HL7 are "order" (an order of a service), "promise" (a promise that the service will be performed), and "event" (a statement that the service has been performed). Another important attribute of act is act status. The act status captures the defined state of an act. Examples of act status are "active" (the act can be performed or is performed), and "completed" (an act that has terminated normally after all of its constituents have been performed). A change in the act status can lead to a state-transition (for example an act status can become from "active" to "completed". The third element defining the event is type. There are three types of events defined in the HL7 standard: user request based, interaction based and state-transition based trigger events. Within this paper we will not go into describing these concepts into full detail. However, it is important to say that the combination of mood, state-transition, and type can capture the intent behind the message.

Based on the analysis of the HL7 concerning lab order, we found out that the HL7 trigger events supports the following intentions: request to fulfil an order, promise to fulfil the order, rejection to fulfil the order, statement that the order has been fulfilled. We will come back to these elements in the next section.

4.2 Evaluation of the HL7 Standard

In section three of this paper we have presented a meta model for describing conversations. In section 4.1. we have introduced a brief description of how interactions are described in the HL7 standard. The aim of this section is to express the capabilities of the HL7 standard concerning Lab order in terms of the meta model.

From the meta model for describing conversations it can be said that an ae-message has propositional content, communicator, interpreter, and communicative function. The interactions defined in the HL7 standard correspond to the ae-messages defined in the meta model. The sending role and the receiving role (as defined in HL7) can be translated as communicator and interpreter in terms of the meta model. The trigger event can be translated as communicative function in terms of the meta model and the hierarchical message description can be seen as propositional content. Further, the trigger events defined for Lab order in the HL7 standard support the following communicative functions: request to fulfil an order, promise to fulfil the order, rejection to fulfil the order, statement that the order has been fulfilled. For illustrative purposes, we can map these communicative functions to the scheme of Winograd and Flores (see figure 4). Note, we have first identified the interactions supported by the standard and after that we check whether the interactions can be mapped to the scheme of Winograd and Flores. Further, for this example the scheme provides a good visualization of the different interactions. From the mapping we can see that the HL7v.3 standard supports the individual interactions *request (1,2)*, *promise (2,3)*, *reject (2,8)* and *declare (3,4)* (see Figure 4).

Different elements of the propositional content are covered in an HL7 message. In the HL7 message, information about objects of interest for the transactions is captured. Examples of such information is information about the patient (and how one can identify a patient), or the about the properties of a patient, such as name and the sex. Further, the HL7 standard defines the reference values for such properties. Although we will not be able to further elaborate on the propositional content due to limitations of space that we have for this paper, such an analysis is important and can be done in practice.

In the next section we describe a business transaction, parts of which would need to be automated using the HL7 standard.

4.3 Description of the Business Transaction

For the purpose of this example, we use an imaginary business transaction, which we describe below. Let us imagine that a doctor sees a patient and decides to order a lab tests for him. Thus, the doctor has to enter into a business transaction with the Lab. For the communication between the doctor and the Lab there is an agreement to communicate in the following way. The doctor orders a lab test. The Lab either accepts to perform the lab test and confirms the order, or rejects the order. Once the lab test is performed, the Lab sends the Observation result to the doctor and the doctor either does not communicate back (in case that he does not have objections to the test result), or asks for correction, if he thinks that there is a mistake. Currently this communication is paper-based. However, this way of communication is time consuming and time is critical in the Healthcare domain. Also, a double entry of data is required.

To reduce the time for carrying out a transaction and to avoid double entry of information, a decision is made to automate the communication between the doctor and the Lab. Further, the HL7 standard is chosen to support the electronic communication.

4.4 Describing the Business Transaction in Terms of the Meta Model

In this section we will translate the requirements of the business transaction described in 4.3. in terms of the meta model. We start with analysing the elements of an ae-message again. If a message is send from the doctor to the Lab, then the doctor can be translated as a communicator in the ae-message and the Lab as the interpreter of the ae-message. If the Lab sends a message to the doctor, then the Lab is the communicator of the ae-message and the doctor is the interpreter. In case the transaction is electronic, these roles can be played by the applications used by the doctor and the interpreter.

The propositional content corresponds to the content of the paper documents exchanged between the Doctor and the Lab. The communicative functions that are used in the communication between the doctor and the Lab are: Ordering of a lab test, acceptance to perform the lab test, rejection to perform the test, statement that the test is completed, questioning of the result of the test. To visualize the communicative functions, we can again map them to the scheme of Winograd and Flores. This would result in the following interactions:

request (1,2), promise (2,3), reject (2,8), assert (3,4), declare (4,3).

So far, we have expressed the requirements of the business transaction and the characteristics of the standard, both in terms of the meta model. This enables us to compare the two, which will be done in the next section.

4.5 Comparing the Standard and the Requirements

Table 1 below provides a comparison of the requirements of the business transaction and the characteristics of the HL7 standard.

Table 1: Comparing the requirements of the business transaction and the capabilities of the HL7 standard.

Meta model element	Requirement of the Business Transaction	HL7 Standard Lab Orde
Specification of the propositional content	Required	Capable to cover (only for the communicative functions supported by HL7)
Identification of the communicator	Required	Capable to cover (identification of the sending application role)
Identification of the Interpreter	Required	Capable to cover (identification of the receiving application role)
Communication functions	Required: *Request (1,2)*, *promise (2,3)*, *reject (2,8)*, *assert (3,4)*, *declare (4,3)*.	Capable to cover: *Request (1-2)*, *promise (2,3)*, *reject (2,8)*, *assert (3,4)*,
Sequence of utterances	Successful completion *(1,2), (2,3), (3,4)* Failure *(1,2), (2,8)* Questioning the outcome *(1,2), (2,3), (3,4), (4,3)*	Successful completion *(1,2), (2,3), (3,4)* Failure *(1,2), (2,8)*

From the analysis it is clear that the HL7 standard (concerning Lab orders) is a good standard to cover the communication requirements between the doctor and the Lab. It has the capability to identify the communicator and the interpreter of a message, as well as the content of the message and the intention behind it. It can support both the conversation that can lead to successful completion of the business transaction as well as to failure. For the interactions that are supported by the HL7 standard, the HL7 standard specifies in detail the propositional content in terms of objects, properties, and it defines the reference values that these properties can have. Thus, we consider that the propositional content defined in the HL7 standard can cover the requirements of the business transaction. However, as we mentioned earlier, we will not go further in detail in elaborating the propositional content.

However, the HL7 does not support situations where the doctor can question the results of a lab test, thus a conversation that can lead to questioning of the outcome is not supported. Neither is the propositional content for this type of interaction. This can be a problem for achieving full interoperability between the Doctor and the Lab, unless additional measures to compensate for that are undertaken.

The aim of this example was mainly to illustrate how the meta model can be used. Although we looked at a simple transaction, the principles of the analysis can be applied to analyse very complex situations. This can be done by first, identifying the different parties that take part in a business transaction. And second, by applying a separate analysis of the conversations between each two parties separately, as illustrated in the example.

5 CONCLUSIONS AND FURTHER RESEARCH

In the introduction we stated that it is important to explore the concept of interoperability, going beyond interoperability between software systems. We further addressed the issue of interoperability on a pragmatic level between organizations, which would like to do business transactions electronically by using standards. We also pointed out that in order to identify interoperability problems on a pragmatic level, it is necessary to capture the communication requirements of the business parties and to evaluate to what extent a standard is capable to meet these requirements. The contribution of this paper can be seen in two main directions. It stresses the importance to look beyond the interoperability between software systems. Second, it addresses the issue of identifying interoperability problems on a pragmatic level and provides a meta model to help in that problem identification. We also provided an example on how the meta model can be used in practice.

The example used in this paper describes a rather simple transaction. The purpose of the example was to illustrate how the meta model can be used. However, the steps illustrated in this example can be used to analyse very complex transactions.

The future research on this topic can continue in two main directions. The first one is to empirically test the usefulness of the meta model in real life situations. The second one is to explore the concept of interoperability between organizations, capturing other aspects, apart form pragmatics.

REFERENCES

Agerfalk, P. J. (1999). *Pragmatization of Information Systems: A Theoretical and Methodological Outline*, Licentiate Thesis. Linkoping University.

Agerfalk, P. J. (2002). Messages are Signs of Action-From Langefors to Speech Acts and Beyond. *In Proceedings of LAP'02*, 80-100

Austin, J. L. (1962). How to do Things with Words, Oxford University Press.

Covington, M. A. (1997). On Designing a Language for Electronic Commerce. *International Journal of Electronic Commerce* 1(4): pp. 31-48.

Goh, C. H., S. Bressan, et al. (1999). Contex Interchange: New Features and Formalisms for the Intelligent Integration of Information. *ACM Transactions on Information Systems* 17(3): pp.270-292.

Goldkuhl, G. (1995). Information as Action and Communication. *The Infological Equation: Essay in the Honour of B. Langefors*: 63-79.

Goldkuhl, G. (2003). Conversational Analysis as a Theoretical Foundation for Language Action Perspective.*In proceedings of LAP 2003*, 51-69

Goldkuhl, G. and P. J. Agerfalk (2002). Actability: A Way to Understand Information Systems Pragmatics. In Liu K. Clarke, R., Andersen, P., Stamper, R. (eds.) *Coordination and Communication Using Signes*. Boston, Kluwer Academic Publishers.85-115

Goldkuhl, G. and K. Lyytinen (1982). A Language Action View on Information Systems. In proceedings of the *Third International Conference on Information Systems*, Ann Arbor, MI.

Habermas, J. (1984). *The Theory of Communicative Action 1. Reason and the Rationalization of Society*. Cambridge, Polity Press.

Halpin, T. (1996). Business Rules and Object Role Modeling. Database Programming and Design (October 1996).

Heiler, S. (1995). Semantic interoperability. *ACM Computing Servey* 27(2).271-273

HL7 "http://www.hl7.org/."

Huang, K. (1998). *Organizational Aspects of EDI: a Norm-oriented Approach* (PhD thesis).

Langefors, B. (1973). *Theoretical analysis of Information Systems*, Studentlitteratur.

Rukanova, B. D., Slooten, C. v, Stegwee, R.A. (2003)a. Beyond the Standard Development and the Standard Adoption. In proceedings of *8th EURAS Workshop on Standardization, Germany*., Mainz Publishers. 120-138

Rukanova, B. D., Slooten, C. v, Stegwee, R.A. (2003)b. Towards a Meta Model for Distributed Business Transactions. In proceedings of *CAiSE '03 Forum Information Systems for a Connected Society*.141-144

Rukanova, B. D., Slooten, C. v, Stegwee, R.A. (2003)c. Capturing the Context of a Business Transaction. In proceedings of *3rd International Interdisciplinary Conference on Electronic Commerce"ECOM-03"*, Gdansk, Poland. 135-141

Schoop, M. (2003). A Language-Action Approach to Electronic Negotiations. *In proceedings of LAP 2003*, 143-160

Searle, J. R. (1969). *Speech Acts. An Essay in the Philosophy of Language*. London, Cambridge University Press.

Stamper, R. (1996). Organisational Semiotics. F. S. J. M. (eds.). *Information Systems: An Emerging Discipline*. London and New York, McGraw-Hill.

Stegwee, R.A., Rukanova, B.D. (2003). Identification of Different Types of Standards for Domain-Specific Interoperability. In: *Proceedings of MIS Quarterly Pre-Conference Workshop* ICIS 2003. pp. 161- 170, Retrieved January, 2004 from http://www.si.umich.edu/misq-stds/proceedings/

Vermeer, B. (2000). How Important is Data Quality for Evaluating the Impact of EDI on Global Supply Chain. *Proceedings of the 33 Hawaii International Conference on System Science*.

Wegner, P. (1996). "Interoperability." *ACM Computing Servey* 28(1): 285-287.

Winograd, T. and F. Flores (1986). *Understanding Computers and Cognition: A New Foundation for Design*. Norwood, Ablex.

INTRUSION DETECTION SYSTEMS USING ADAPTIVE REGRESSION SPLINES

Srinivas Mukkamala, Andrew H. Sung
Department of Computer Science, New Mexico Tech, Socorro, U.S.A.
srinivas@cs.nmt.edu, sung@cs.nmt.edu

Ajith Abraham
Bio Inspired Grid (BIG) Lab, Department of Computer Science, Oklahoma State University, Tulsa, U.S.A.
ajith.abraham@ieee.org

Vitorino Ramos
CVRM-IST, Instituto Superior Técnico,Technical University of Lisbon, Lisbon, Portugal
vitorino.ramos@alfa.ist.utl.pt

Keywords: Network security, intrusion detection, adaptive regression splines, neural networks, support vector machines

Abstract: Past few years have witnessed a growing recognition of intelligent techniques for the construction of efficient and reliable intrusion detection systems. Due to increasing incidents of cyber attacks, building effective intrusion detection systems (IDS) are essential for protecting information systems security, and yet it remains an elusive goal and a great challenge. In this paper, we report a performance analysis between Multivariate Adaptive Regression Splines (MARS), neural networks and support vector machines. The MARS procedure builds flexible regression models by fitting separate splines to distinct intervals of the predictor variables. A brief comparison of different neural network learning algorithms is also given.

1 INTRODUCTION

Intrusion detection is a problem of great significance to protecting information systems security, especially in view of the worldwide increasing incidents of cyber attacks. Since the ability of an IDS to classify a large variety of intrusions in real time with accurate results is important, we will consider performance measures in three critical aspects: training and testing times; scalability; and classification accuracy.

Since most of the intrusions can be located by examining patterns of user activities and audit records (Denning, 1987), many IDSs have been built by utilizing the recognized attack and misuse patterns. IDSs are classified, based on their functionality, as misuse detectors and anomaly detectors. Misuse detection systems use well-known attack patterns as the basis for detection (Denning, 1987; Kumar, 1994). Anomaly detection systems use user profiles as the basis for detection; any deviation from the normal user behaviour is considered an intrusion (Denning, 1987; Kumar, 1994; Ghosh, 1999; Cannady, 1998).

One of the main problems with IDSs is the overhead, which can become unacceptably high. To analyse system logs, the operating system must keep information regarding all the actions performed, which invariably results in huge amounts of data, requiring disk space and CPU resource.

Next, the logs must be processed to convert into a manageable format and then compared with the set of recognized misuse and attack patterns to identify possible security violations. Further, the stored patterns need be continually updated, which would normally involve human expertise. An intelligent, adaptable and cost-effective tool that is capable of (mostly) real-time intrusion detection is the goal of the researchers in IDSs. Various artificial intelligence techniques have been utilized to

211

I. Seruca et al. (eds.), Enterprise Information Systems VI, 211–218.

automate the intrusion detection process to reduce human intervention; several such techniques include neural networks (Ghosh, 1999; Cannady, 1998; Ryan 1998; Debar, 1992a-b), and machine learning (Mukkamala, 2002a). Several data mining techniques have been introduced to identify key features or parameters that define intrusions (Luo, 2000; Cramer, 1995; Stolfo, 2000; Mukkamala, 2002b).

In this paper, we explore Multivariate Adaptive Regression Splines (MARS) (Steinberg, 1999), Support Vector Machines (SVM) and Artificial Neural Networks (ANN), to perform intrusion detection based on recognized attack patterns. The data we used in our experiments originated from MIT's Lincoln Lab. It was developed for intrusion detection system evaluations by DARPA and is considered a benchmark for IDS evaluations (Lincoln Laboratory, 1998-2000).

We perform experiments to classify the network traffic patterns according to a 5-class taxonomy. The five classes of patterns in the DARPA data are (normal, probe, denial of service, user to super-user, and remote to local).

In the rest of the paper, a brief introduction to the data we use is given in section 2. Section 3 briefly introduces to MARS. In section 4 a brief introduction to the connectionist paradigms (ANNs and SVMs) is given. In section 5 the experimental results of using MARS, ANNs and SVMs are given. The summary and conclusions of our work are given in section 6.

2 INTRUSION DETECTION DATA

In the 1998 DARPA intrusion detection evaluation program, an environment was set up to acquire raw TCP/IP dump data for a network by simulating a typical U.S. Air Force LAN. The LAN was operated like a real environment, but being blasted with multiple attacks (Kris, 1998; Seth, 1998). For each TCP/IP connection, 41 various quantitative and qualitative features were extracted (Stolfo, 2000; University of California at Irvine, 1999). Of this database a subset of 494021 data were used, of which 20% represent normal patterns. Attack types fall into four main categories:

- Probing: surveillance and other probing
- DoS: denial of service
- U2Su: unauthorized access to local super user (root) privileges
- R2L:unauthorizedaccess from a remote machine.

2.1 Probing

Probing is a class of attacks where an attacker scans a network to gather information or find known vulnerabilities. An attacker with a map of machines and services that are available on a network can use the information to look for exploits. There are different types of probes: some of them abuse the computer's legitimate features; some of them use social engineering techniques. This class of attacks is the most commonly heard and requires very little technical expertise.

2.2 Denial of Service Attacks

Denial of Service (DoS) is a class of attacks where an attacker makes some computing or memory resource too busy or too full to handle legitimate requests, thus denying legitimate users access to a machine. There are different ways to launch DoS attacks: by abusing the computers legitimate features; by targeting the implementations bugs; or by exploiting the system's misconfigurations. DoS attacks are classified based on the services that an attacker renders unavailable to legitimate users.

2.3 User to Root Attacks

User to root exploits are a class of attacks where an attacker starts out with access to a normal user account on the system and is able to exploit vulnerability to gain root access to the system. Most common exploits in this class of attacks are regular buffer overflows, which are caused by regular programming mistakes and environment assumptions.

2.4 Remote to User Attacks

A remote to user (R2L) attack is a class of attacks where an attacker sends packets to a machine over a network, then exploits machine's vulnerability to illegally gain local access as a user. There are different types of R2U attacks; the most common attack in this class is done using social engineering.

3 MULTIVARIATE ADAPTIVE REGRESSION SPLINES (MARS)

Splines can be considered as an innovative mathematical process for complicated curve drawings and function approximation. To develop a spline the X-axis is broken into a convenient number of regions. The boundary between regions is also known as a knot. With a sufficiently large number of knots virtually any shape can be well approximated. While it is easy to draw a spline in 2-dimensions by keying on knot locations (approximating using linear, quadratic or cubic polynomial etc.), manipulating the mathematics in higher dimensions is best accomplished using basis functions. The MARS model is a regression model using basis functions as predictors in place of the original data. The basis function transform makes it possible to selectively blank out certain regions of a variable by making them zero, and allows MARS to focus on specific sub-regions of the data. It excels at finding optimal variable transformations and interactions, and the complex data structure that often hides in high-dimensional data (Friedman, 1991).

Given the number of records in most data sets, it is infeasible to approximate the function $y=f(x)$ by summarizing y in each distinct region of x. For some variables, two regions may not be enough to track the specifics of the function. If the relationship of y to some $x's$ is different in 3 or 4 regions, for example, the number of regions requiring examination is even larger than 34 billion with only 35 variables (Steinberg, 1999). Given that the number of regions cannot be specified a priori, specifying too few regions in advance can have serious implications for the final model. A solution is needed that accomplishes the following two criteria:

- judicious selection of which regions to look at and their boundaries
- judicious determination of how many intervals are needed for each variable.

Given these two criteria, a successful method will essentially need to be adaptive to the characteristics of the data. Such a solution will probably ignore quite a few variables (affecting variable selection) and will take into account only a few variables at a time (also reducing the number of regions). Even if the method selects 30 variables for the model, it will not look at all 30 simultaneously. Such simplification is accomplished by a decision tree at a single-node, only ancestor splits are being considered; thus, at a depth of six levels in the tree, only six variables are being used to define the node.

3.1 MARS Smoothing, Splines, Knots Selection and Basis Functions

To estimate the most common form, the cubic spline, a uniform grid is placed on the predictors and a reasonable number of knots are selected. A cubic regression is then fit within each region. This approach, popular with physicists and engineers who want continuous second derivatives, requires many coefficients (four per region), in order to be estimated. Normally, two constraints, which dramatically reduce the number of free parameters, can be placed on cubic splines: curve segments must join, and continuous first and second derivatives at knots (higher degree of smoothness).

Figure 1 shows typical attacks and their distribution while Figure 2 (section 5) depicts a MARS spline with three knots (actual data on the right). A key concept underlying the spline is the knot. A knot marks the end of one region of data and the beginning of another. Thus, the knot is where the behavior of the function changes. Between knots, the model could be global (e.g., linear regression). In a classical spline, the knots are predetermined and evenly spaced, whereas in MARS, the knots are determined by a search procedure. Only as many knots as needed are included in a MARS model. If a straight line is a good fit, there will be no interior knots. In MARS, however, there is always at least one "pseudo" knot that corresponds to the smallest observed value of the predictor (Steinberg, 1999). Finding the one best knot in a simple regression is a straightforward search problem: simply examine a large number of potential knots and choose the one with the best R^2. However, finding the best pair of knots requires far more computation, and finding the best set of knots when the actual number needed is unknown is an even more challenging task. MARS finds the location and number of needed knots in a forward/backward stepwise fashion. A model that is clearly over fit with too many knots is generated first; then, those knots that contribute least to the overall fit are removed. Thus, the forward knot selection will include many incorrect knot locations, but these erroneous knots will eventually (although this is not guaranteed), be deleted from the model in the backwards pruning step (Abraham, 2001; Steinberg, 1999).

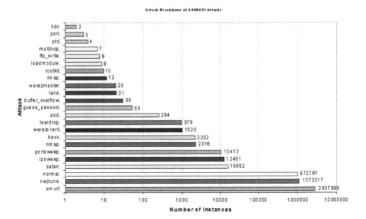

Figure1: Intrusion Detection Data Distribution

4 CONNECTIONIST PARADIGMS

The artificial neural network (ANN) methodology enables us to design useful nonlinear systems accepting large numbers of inputs, with the design based solely on instances of input-output relationships.

4.1 Resilient Back Propagation (RP)

The purpose of the resilient backpropagation training algorithm is to eliminate the harmful effects of the magnitudes of the partial derivatives. Only the sign of the derivative is used to determine the direction of the weight update; the magnitude of the derivative has no effect on the weight update. The size of the weight change is determined by a separate update value. The update value for each weight and bias is increased by a factor whenever the derivative of the performance function with respect to that weight has the same sign for two successive iterations. The update value is decreased by a factor whenever the derivative with respect to that weight changes sign from the previous iteration. If the derivative is zero, then the update value remains the same. Whenever the weights are oscillating the weight change will be reduced. If the weight continues to change in the same direction for several iterations, then the magnitude of the weight change will be increased (Riedmiller, 1993).

4.2 Scaled Conjugate Gradient Algorithm (SCG)

The scaled conjugate gradient algorithm is an implementation of avoiding the complicated line search procedure of conventional conjugate gradient algorithm (CGA). According to the SCGA, the Hessian matrix is approximated by

$$E^{"}(w_k)p_k = \frac{E^{'}(w_k + \sigma_k p_k) - E^{'}(w_k)}{\sigma_k} + \lambda_k p_k$$

where E' and E'' are the first and second derivative information of global error function $E\ (w_k)$. The other terms p_k, σ_k and λ_k represent the weights, search direction, parameter controlling the change in weight for second derivative approximation and parameter for regulating the indefiniteness of the Hessian. In order to get a good quadratic approximation of E, a mechanism to raise and lower λ_k is needed when the Hessian is positive definite (Moller, 1993).

4.3 One-Step-Secant Algorithm (OSS)

Quasi-Newton method involves generating a sequence of matrices $G^{(k)}$ that represents increasingly accurate approximations to the inverse Hessian (H^{-1}). Using only the first derivative information of E the updated expression is as follows:

$$G^{(k+1)} = G^{(k)} + \frac{pp^T}{p^T v} - \frac{(G^{(k)}v)v^T G^{(k)}}{v^T G^{(k)}v} + (v^T G^{(k)}v)uu^T$$

where

$$p = w^{(k+1)} - w^{(k)}, \quad v = g^{(k+1)} - g^{(k)},$$

$$u = \frac{p}{p^T v} - \frac{G^{(k)} v}{v^T G^{(k)} v}$$

and T represents transpose of a matrix. The problem with this approach is the requirement of computation and storage of the approximate Hessian matrix for every iteration. The One-Step-Secant (OSS) is an approach to bridge the gap between the conjugate gradient algorithm and the quasi-Newton (secant) approach. The OSS approach doesn't store the complete Hessian matrix; it assumes that at each iteration the previous Hessian was the identity matrix. This also has the advantage that the new search direction can be calculated without computing a matrix inverse (Bishop, 1995).

4.4 Support Vector Machines (SVM)

The SVM approach transforms data into a feature space F that usually has a huge dimension. It is interesting to note that SVM generalization depends on the geometrical characteristics of the training data, not on the dimensions of the input space (Bishop, 1995; Joachims, 1998). Training a support vector machine (SVM) leads to a quadratic optimization problem with bound constraints and one linear equality constraint. Vapnik (Vladimir, 1995) shows how training a SVM for the pattern recognition problem leads to the following quadratic optimization problem (Joachims, 2000):

Minimize:

$$W(\alpha) = -\sum_{i=1}^{l} \alpha_i + \frac{1}{2} \sum_{i=1}^{l} \sum_{j=1}^{l} y_i y_j \alpha_i \alpha_j k(x_i, x_j) \quad (1)$$

Subject to $\sum_{i=1}^{l} y_i \alpha_i$ (2)

$$\forall i : 0 \le \alpha_i \le C$$

where l is the number of training examples α is a vector of l variables and each component α_i corresponds to a training example (x_i, y_i). The solution of (1) is the vector α^* for which (1) is minimized and (2) is fulfilled.

5 EXPERIMENT SETUP

In our experiments, we perform 5-class classification. The (training and testing) data set contains 11982 randomly generated points from the data set representing the five classes, with the number of data from each class proportional to its size, except that the smallest classes are completely

included. The normal data belongs to class1, probe belongs to class 2, denial of service belongs to class 3, user to super user belongs to class 4, remote to local belongs to class 5. A different randomly selected set of 6890 points of the total data set (11982) is used for testing MARS, SVMs and ANNs. Overall accuracy of the classifiers is given in Tables 1-4. Class specific classification of the classifiers is given in Table 5.

5.1 MARS

We used 5 basis functions and selected a setting of minimum observation between knots as 10. The MARS training mode is being set to the lowest level to gain higher accuracy rates. Five MARS models are employed to perform five class classifications (normal, probe, denial of service, user to root and remote to local). We partition the data into the two classes of "Normal" and "Rest" (Probe, DoS, U2Su, R2L) patterns, where the Rest is the collection of four classes of attack instances in the data set. The objective is to separate normal and attack patterns. We repeat this process for all classes. Table 1 summarizes the test results of the experiments.

5.2 Neural Network

The same data set described in section 2 is being used for training and testing different neural network algorithms. The set of 5092 training data is divided in to five classes: normal, probe, denial of service attacks, user to super user and remote to local attacks. Where the attack is a collection of 22 different types of instances that belong to the four classes described in section 2, and the other is the normal data. In our study we used two hidden layers with 20 and 30 neurons each and the networks were trained using training functions described in Table 2. The network was set to train until the desired mean square error of 0.001 was met. As multi-layer feed forward networks are capable of multi-class classifications, we partition the data into 5 classes (Normal, Probe, Denial of Service, and User to Root and Remote to Local).

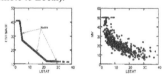

Figure 2: MARS data estimation using splines and knots

Table 1: MARS Test
Performance

Class	Accuracy
Normal	96.08 %
Probe	92.32 %
DOS	94.73 %
U2Su	99.71 %
R2L	99.48 %

Table 2: Test Performance of Different Neural Network Training Functions

Training Algorithm	No of Epochs	Accuracy (%)
Gradient descent	3500	61.70
Gradient descent with momentum	3500	51.60
Adaptive learning rate	3500	95.38
Resilient back propagation	67	97.04
Fletcher-Reeves conjugate gradient	891	82.18
Polak-Ribiere conjugate gradient	313	80.54
Powell-Beale conjugate gradient	298	91.57
Scaled conjugate gradient	351	80.87
BFGS quasi-Newton method	359	75.67
One step secant method	638	93.60
Levenberg-Marquardt	17	76.23
Bayesian regularization	533	64.15

Table 3: Performance of the Best Neural Network Training Function (Resilient Back Propagation)

Class of Attack	Normal	Probe	DoS	U2Su	R2L	%
Normal	1394	5	1	0	0	99.6
Probe	49	649	2	0	0	92.7
DoS	3	101	4096	2	0	97.5
U2Su	0	1	8	12	4	48.0
R2L	0	1	6	21	535	95.0
%	96.4	85.7	99.6	34.3	99.3	

Table 4: Detection Accuracy of SVMs

Class of Attack	Training Time (sec)	Testing Time (sec)	Accuracy (%)
Normal	7.66	1.26	99.55
Probe	49.13	2.10	99.70
DoS	22.87	1.92	99.25
U2Su	3.38	1.05	99.87
R2L	11.54	1.02	99.78

Table 5: Performance Comparison of Testing for 5 Class Classifications

Class of Attack	Accuracy (%)				
	SVM	RP	SCG	OSS	MARS
Normal	98.42	99.57	99.57	99.64	96.08
Probe	98.57	92.71	85.57	92.71	92.32
DoS	99.11	97.47	72.01	91.76	94.73
U2Su	64.00	48.00	0.00	16.00	99.71
R2L	97.33	95.02	98.22	96.80	99.48

We used the same testing data (6890), same network architecture and same activations functions to identify the best training function that plays a vital role for in classifying intrusions. Table 2 summarizes the performance of the different learning algorithms. The top-left entry of Table 3 shows that 1394 of the actual "normal" test set were detected to be normal; the last column indicates that 99.6 % of the actual "normal" data points were detected correctly. In the same way, for "Probe" 649 of the actual "attack" test set were correctly detected; the last column indicates that 92.7% of the actual "Probe" data points were detected correctly. The bottom row shows that 96.4% of the test set said to be "normal" indeed were "normal" and 85.7% of the test set classified, as "probe" indeed belongs to Probe. The overall accuracy of the classification is 97.04 with a false positive rate of 2.76% and false negative rate of 0.20.

5.3 SVM

Since SVMs are only capable of binary classifications, we will need to employ five SVMs, for the 5-class classification problem in intrusion detection, respectively. We partition the data into the two classes of "Normal" and "Rest" (Probe, DoS, U2Su, R2L) patterns, where the Rest is the collection of four classes of attack instances in the data set. The objective is to separate normal and attack patterns. We repeat this process for all classes. Training is done using the radial bias kernel option; an important point of the kernel function is that it defines the feature space in which the training set examples will be classified. Table 4 summarizes the overall results of the experiments using the test dataset. The empirical values presented depict the accuracy to detect the various attacks (reduction in false alarm rate) and helps to estimate the volume of false alarms if SVMs were deployed.

6 CONCLUSIONS

A number of observations and conclusions are drawn from the results reported: MARS is superior to SVMs in respect to classifying the most important classes (U2Su and R2L) in terms of the attack severity. SVMs outperform ANNs in the important respects of scalability (the former can train with a larger number of patterns, while would ANNs take a long time to train or fail to converge at all when the number of patterns gets large); training time and running time (SVMs run an order of magnitude faster); and prediction accuracy. Resilient back propagation achieved the best performance among the neural network learning algorithms in terms of accuracy (97.04 %) and faster convergence (67 epochs). We note, however, that the difference in accuracy figures tend to be very small and may not be statistically significant, especially in view of the fact that the 5 classes of patterns differ in their sizes tremendously. More definitive conclusions can only be made after analysing more comprehensive sets of network traffic data.

Finally, another gifted research line includes the potential use of MARS hybridized with self-organized ant-like evolutionary models as proposed in past works (Ramos, 2003; Abraham, 2003). The implementation of this swarm intelligence along with *Stigmergy* (Ramos, 2002) and the study of ant colonies behaviour and their self-organizing capabilities are decisively of direct interest to knowledge retrieval/management and decision support systems sciences. In fact they can provide new models of distributed, adaptive and collective organization, enhancing MARS data estimation on ever changing environments (e.g. dynamic data on real-time), as those we now increasingly tend to face over new disseminated information systems paradigms and challenges.

ACKNOWLEDGEMENTS

Support for this research received from *ICASA* (Institute for Complex Additive Systems Analysis, a division of *New Mexico Tech*), *U.S. Department of Defense IASP* and *NSF* capacity building grant is gratefully acknowledged, as well as for *FCT PRAXIS XXI* research fellowship, *Science & Technology Foundation* - Portugal. Finally, we would also like to acknowledge many insightful conversations with Dr. *Jean-Louis Lassez* and *David Duggan* that helped clarify some of our ideas.

REFERENCES

Abraham A., Ramos V., 2003. Web Usage Mining Using Artificial Ant Colony and Genetic Programming, *Congress on Evolutionary Computation* (CEC'03), IEEE Press, pp. 1384-1391.

Abraham A., Steinberg D., 2001. MARS: Still an Alien Planet in Soft Computing? *International Conference on Computational Science*, Springer-Verlag Germany, Lecture Notes in Computer Science 2074, pp. 235-244.

Bishop C. M., *Neural Networks for Pattern Recognition*, Oxford Press, 1995.

Cannady J., 1998. Artificial Neural Networks for Misuse Detection. *National Information Systems Security Conference*.

Cramer M., et. al. 1995. New Methods of Intrusion Detection using Control-Loop Measurement. *Proceedings of the Technology in Information Security Conference* (TISC), pp. 1-10.

Debar H., Becke M., Siboni D., 1992a. A Neural Network Component for an Intrusion Detection System. *Proceedings of the IEEE Computer Society Symposium on Research in Security and Privacy.*

Debar H., Dorizzi. B., 1992b. An Application of a Recurrent Network to an Intrusion Detection System. *Proceedings of the International Joint Conference on Neural Networks,* pp.78-83.

Denning D., 1987. An Intrusion-Detection Model. *IEEE Trans. on Software Engineering*, Vol.SE-13, N° 2.

Friedman, J. H, 1991. Multivariate Adaptive Regression Splines, *Annals of Statistics*, Vol 19, pp. 1-141.

Ghosh A. K., 1999. Learning Program Behavior Profiles for Intrusion Detection. *USENIX.*

Joachims T., 1998. Making Large-Scale SVM Learning Practical. University of Dortmund, LS8-Report, LS VIII-Report.

Joachims T., 2000. SVMlight is an Implementation of Support Vector Machines (SVMs) in C. *University of Dortmund. Collaborative Research Center on Complexity Reduction in Multivariate Data (SFB475)*: <http://ais.gmd.de/~thorsten/svm_light>.

Kendall K., 1998. A Database of Computer Attacks for the Evaluation of Intrusion Detection Systems. *Master's Thesis, Massachusetts Institute of Technology.*

Kumar S., Spafford E. H., 1994. An Application of Pattern Matching in Intrusion Detection. *Technical Report CSD-TR-94-013*, Purdue University.

Lincoln Laboratory, Massachusetts Institute of Technology (MIT), 1998-2000. *DARPA Intrusion Detection Evaluation*: <www.ll.mit.edu/IST/ideval/data/data_index.html>.

Luo J., Bridges S. M., 2000. Mining Fuzzy Association Rules and Fuzzy Frequency Episodes for Intrusion Detection. *International Journal of Intelligent Systems*, John Wiley & Sons, pp. 687-703.

Moller A.F., 1993. A Scaled Conjugate Gradient Algorithm for Fast Supervised Learning. *Neural Networks*. Vol. (6), pp. 525-533.

Mukkamala S., Janoski G., Sung A. H., 2002a. Intrusion Detection Using Neural Networks and Support Vector Machines. *Proceedings of IEEE International Joint Conference on Neural Networks*, pp. 1702-1707.

Mukkamala S., Sung A. H., 2002b. Identifying Key Features for Intrusion Detection Using Neural Networks. *Proceedings of ICCC International Conference on Computer Communications 2002.*

Ramos V., Abraham A., 2003. Swarms on Continuous Data. *Congress on Evolutionary Computation* (CEC), IEEE Press, pp. 1370-1375.

Ramos V., Muge F., Pina P., 2002. Self-Organized Data and Image Retrieval as a Consequence of Inter-Dynamic Synergistic Relationships in Artificial Ant Colonies. *Soft-Computing Systems – Design, Management and Applications*, IOS Press, Frontiers in Artificial Intelligence and Applications, pp. 500-509.

Riedmiller M., Braun H., 1993. A direct adaptive method for faster back propagation learning: The RPROP algorithm. *Proceedings of the IEEE International Conference on Neural Networks.*

Ryan J., Lin M-J., Miikkulainen R., 1998. Intrusion Detection with Neural Networks. *Advances in Neural Information Processing Systems* 10, Cambridge, MA: MIT Press.

Steinberg, D, Colla P. L., Martin K., 1999. MARS User Guide. *Salford Systems*, San Diego, CA.

Stolfo J., Fan W., Lee W., Prodromidis A., Chan P.K., 2000. Cost-based Modeling and Evaluation for Data Mining with Application to Fraud and Intrusion Detection. *DARPA Information Survivability Conference.*

University of California at Irvine, 1999. *KDD Cup*: <http://kdd.ics.uci.edu/databases/kddcup99/task.htm>.

Vladimir V. N., *The Nature of Statistical Learning Theory*, Springer-Verlag, Germany, 1995.

Webster S.E., 1998, The Development and Analysis of Intrusion Detection Algorithms. *S.M. Thesis, Massachusetts Institute of Technology*, June 1998.

A USER-CENTERED METHODOLOGY TO GENERATE VISUAL MODELING ENVIRONMENTS

Gennaro Costagliola, Vincenzo Deufemia, Filomena Ferrucci and Carmine Gravino

Dipartimento Matematica e Informatica, Università di Salerno
84081 Baronissi (SA), Italy
{gcostagliola, deufemia, fferrucci, gravino}@unisa.it

Keywords: Meta-modeling techniques, Grammar formalisms, CASE tools, Visual modeling languages

Abstract: CASE tools supporting many activities of the software development process embed visual modeling environments. Indeed, visual languages are practical means to allow engineers to define models and different views of software systems. However the effectiveness of visual modeling environments strongly depends from the process and tools used for their development. In this paper we present a user-centered methodology for the development of customized visual environments, and a tool to support it. The use of UML meta-modeling techniques and formal methods characterizes the proposed approach. Moreover, incremental development and rapid prototyping are ensured by the use of an automatic generation tool that allows designers to focus on structural features of the target language disregarding the visual environment creation.

1 INTRODUCTION

The observation that the human visual system is more inclined toward processing visual information rather than textual one, and the decreasing cost of hardware technologies and graphics software have caused the development of a large number of visual languages in many different application fields. Their use in the problem solving process allows for the construction of a problem representation, which gives insight into the structure of the problem, and helps to find a possible solution. For that reason, CASE tools embedding visual modeling environments are widely employed to support many activities of the software development process, such as specification, analysis and design. Indeed, they allow engineers to devise solutions and design systems by enabling to construct abstract models and different views of software systems.

However, the development of visual modeling environments is a cumbersome and time-consuming activity, which requires the adoption of suitable methodologies and powerful tools. It is worth noting that one of the major risks concerned with the development of visual environments is the lack of an effective look and feel due to the unsuitability of the designed icons to resemble their meaning, and/or the missing correspondence between user's intention and visual models interpretation. Such a risk is espe-

cially high for domain specific languages which are adopted in domain specific software methods (Nokia Mobile Phones, 1999)(Schmidt et al., 2002). Indeed, in such a case visual models are constructed by suitably arranging icons representing objects that should be part of the domain problem space, and be easily understood by end user by resembling their meaning through their physical representation.

In this paper we describe a user-centered methodology specifically conceived for the development of customized visual modeling environments and we propose a tool designed to support this methodology. The use of UML meta-modeling techniques and formal methods characterizes the proposed approach, which is based on an incremental development and rapid prototyping. The prototyping is essential because it is impossible to pre-specify the look and feel of a visual modeling language in an effective way, and its use can reduce requirement risks by revealing errors and omissions. Indeed, since requirements are usually expressed in the language of the application domain, they are often not understood by the designer developing the visual modeling environment. Thus, in order to enhance the communication between designer and user, the methodology proposes to define language requirements using UML class diagrams making them more understandable by users who do not have detailed technical knowledge.

I. Seruca et al. (eds.), Enterprise Information Systems VI, 219–226.

The rapid development of the language environment is essential for adopting a prototyping approach. To this aim, we propose the use of a grammar-based tool, named GENIE, that starting from the formal specification of the language is able to generate the corresponding visual modeling environment. The tool extends the 'compiler-compiler' approach widely adopted for the generation of programming environments to visual oriented environments. Moreover, the choice of a context-free style grammar formalism underlying GENIE allows for an incremental approach which notably simplifies the definition of visual environments. Another distinguishing characteristic of the proposed approach is the adoption of the GXL format as data representation for visual sentences (Holt et al., 2000). This choice allows for a more easy integration of the generated visual environments with other tools.

The paper is organized as follows. Section 2 illustrates the GENIE system and the design process supported by it. Section 3 is devoted to present the development of a visual environment for Data Flow Diagrams. Related work and final remarks conclude the paper.

2   THE GENIE SYSTEM

In this section we describe the GENIE (GENerator of Interoperable visual Environments) system for the automatic generation of visual modeling environments. In the following, first we present the methodology underlying the system, and then its architecture.

2.1   The Methodology Underlying GENIE

It is worth noting that one of the major risks concerned with the development of visual modeling environments is the lack of an effective look and feel due to the unsuitability of the designed icons to resemble their meaning, and/or the missing correspondence between user's intention and visual models interpretation. Such a situation can be related to the lack of a clear and unambiguous comprehension of the user's domain and needs, and the inadequacy of the communication between designer and end user.

In order to reduce such risk and obtain effective modeling languages a user centered approach is usually recommended. Such an approach should be based on rapid prototyping which requires the adoption of effective tools and formalisms. As we show in Figure 1, GENIE can be profitably exploited to carry out such a task since it supports a design process where the user plays a crucial rule. In particular, such design process is characterized by incremental and rapid prototyping aspects, and it is based on the use of UML meta-modeling techniques and formal methods.

Step 1. UML meta-modeling techniques are exploited during the requirements analysis. In particular, the designer starts by addressing the tasks concerned with domain understanding and requirements collection. After analyzing the risks and evaluating the alternatives (also due to the possible presence of conflicting end users) the designer provides a high-level specification of domain requirements in terms of annotated UML class diagrams. This notation represents a natural way of reflecting the real world entities that should be captured by the language, and allows the designer to describe the aggregation between domain objects and to organize them into a hierarchy that highlights specialization/generalization relationships. Moreover, the meta-model produced in this phase is enriched with layout information, which is associated to the classes representing visual symbols of the modeled language. The specified meta-model is input to GENIE that generates a first release of the visual editor by exploiting the visual environments generator module. Such a facility of GENIE allows the designer to focus on structural features of the target language disregarding the visual environment creation, which is automatically performed by the system.

This facilitates the combination of development and validation, and promotes the iterative design and interactive prototyping, by providing the capability of simulating the language in early stages of development. This editor is exposed to the user's judgement, who can experiment with the environment to verify the look of the language by editing visual sentences. Based on the user's feedback, the designer can refine the layout of the visual symbols, and resubmit the new version of the editor to the user's evaluation giving rise to an iteration cycle.

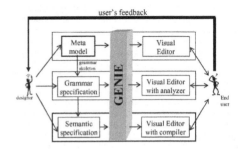

Figure 1: The design process supported by GENIE

Step 2. Once the visual editor satisfies the user needs, the UML specification is validated, and the designer carries out the second phase of the proposed methodology that is focused on the development of a syntax analyzer for the target language. To this aim, he/she again benefits from the availability of GENIE that allows him/her to provide a grammar specification by refining a previously generated draft, and to obtain the corresponding parser. The produced visual environment is exposed to the user's judgement, who can experiment with the environment by editing visual sentences and verifying if they are embedded in such an environment (i.e., they belong to the language specified by the grammar). Thus, he/she determines the aspects with which he/she is satisfied and the ones which need further enhancement or modification. The use of the prototype may also allow the user to better understand and express his/her requirements. Based on the user's feedback, the designer can refine the syntax specification of the language. The refined version is submitted again to the user's evaluation giving rise to an iteration cycle which is only stopped when the prototype fully satisfies the user.

Step 3. The third phase concern with the specification of the machine interpretation of visual sentences. In particular, the grammar specification is enriched with semantic rules in order to map visual sentences of the language into host-language programs or reports. Furthermore, semantic rules can be specified to statically analyze semantic properties of the sentences. Again the designer exploits the generator to obtain the visual modeling environment that besides the visual editor encompasses a compiler for the language. Such an environment can be exploited to verify the look and feel of the generated visual language, by editing visual sentences and requiring their interpretation. So, the user can test the system to validate the visual modeling environment or suggest further modifications.

Step 4. The final task of the designer is to provide means for visual language interchanging. Indeed, this is crucial to ensure a more easy integration of the generated visual environments with other tools, and this is an issue especially felt in the context of modeling languages. In the proposed approach, the issue is addressed by enriching the grammar specification with suitable semantic rules able to associate a XML-based representation to any sentence of the target language.

In the next subsection we will show the GENIE architecture and how the proposed system supports designer in carrying out such a task exploiting a versatile XML approach.

2.2   The GENIE Architecture

GENIE consists of two modules, namely the *UML Class Diagram Environment* (CDE), and the *Visual Language Compiler-Compiler* (VLCC) system (see Figure 2). The first environment allows designers to

draw and modify class diagrams, while the second module assists him/her in the syntactic and semantic specification of the visual modeling language and automatically generates the corresponding visual environment.

In the following, first we will describe in more detail the architecture of VLCC, and then we will illustrate the main features of the CDE module.

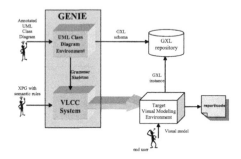

Figure 2: The architecture of GENIE

VLCC is a grammar-based visual environment generation system based on the *eXtended Positional Grammar* (XPG) model. The characteristics of such a grammar model allow VLCC to inherit and extend to the visual field, concepts and techniques of compiler generation tools like YACC (Johnson, 1978). In particular, the XPG model allows for an extension of LR parsing (Aho et al., 1985), named *XpLR methodology*, which is able to analyze very complex visual languages. The architecture of VLCC is shown in Figure 3.

It consists of three modules, namely the *Symbol Editor*, the *Production Editor*, and the *Visual Modeling Environment Generator*.

The designer creates the terminal and the nonterminal symbols of the grammar by using the Symbol Editor. This editor works in two modes, the drawing mode and the symbol mode allowing the designer to easily define and customize the icons that will form the sentence of the target visual modeling environment. Indeed, in drawing mode the designer can create or modify images using the usual graphical editor facilities. In symbol mode the designer can transform an image into a grammar symbol (terminal or non-terminal) by adding the syntactic and the semantic attributes, or can modify the syntactic or semantic attributes of a symbol. The set of terminal and nonterminal symbols are used by the designer to create the productions using the Production Editor (see Figure 3) that allows us to define the grammar in an assistant way.

A distinguishing characteristic of the environments

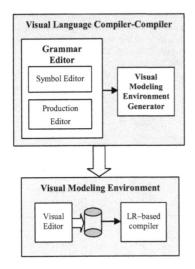

Figure 3: The VLCC architecture

generated by GENIE is the adoption of GXL (*Graph eXchange Language*) format as data representation for visual sentences. This allows for a more easy integration of the generated visual environments with other tools. The choice of GXL has been motivated by its characteristics of versatility, scalability and extensibility (Holt et al., 2000)(Winter, 2002). Indeed, although GXL was designed to be a standard data exchange format for graph-based tools it can be used in the context of visual languages because a graph structure can be identified in any diagrammatic visual sentence. Exchanging graphs with GXL deals with both *instance graphs* and their corresponding *graph schemas* in terms of XML documents (Extended Markup Language) (Winter, 2002). The graph schema provides the graph structure, i.e. the definition of nodes and edges, their attribute schemas and their incidence structure, and the instance graph represents a visual sentence.

Thus, GXL allows us to improve interoperability between visual modeling environments. As a matter of fact, some groups from industry and research committed to provide facilities to import and export GXL documents to their tools (Winter et al., 2002).

It is worth noting that the CDE module forming the front-end of GENIE has been obtained by exploiting VLCC. In particular, an XPG specifying the UML class diagrams language was input to the system together with suitable semantic rules able to create an environment which could provide further support to the designer during the language development

process. As a matter of fact, the front-end of GENIE not only assists him/her in the construction of a UML class diagram representing a high-level specification of a visual modeling language, but it is also able to translate such a diagram into a corresponding GXL schema and a context-free grammar skeleton. Due to the limit space, the set of rules to accomplish this translation are not reported here. The GXL schema produced from the meta-models are stored in the GXL repository, and will be exchanged together with their GXL instances, whenever the visual sentence are imported by other GXL-based tools.

3   AN EXAMPLE: GENERATING AN ENVIRONMENT FOR DFD

In this section we show how to generate a visual modeling environment for Data Flow Diagrams (DFDs) by using GENIE. DFDs are a graphical notation which is extensively employed in the software engineering field and provides one of the most successfully paradigms underlying several visual programming languages, such as, Show and Tell (Kimura et al., 1990), LabVIEW (Vose and Williams, 1986), Vampire (McIntyre, 1995). Languages based on this model exploit dataflow diagrams to visually depict dependencies between data and processes. Indeed, in these diagrams boxes represent processing steps and data flow along the connecting edges.

Figure 4 shows the meta-model for DFD specified by using the CDE module of GENIE.

It is worth noting that the UML class diagrams specified in this phase are by no means concerned with technical details of language implementation, but only describe the entities of the problem domain, and the annotation provides the concrete syntax of the language, i.e. physic, syntactic and semantic features of the symbols (see Figure 5). As an example the class STORE of the diagram in Figure 4 is annotated with information specifying that the symbol will be visualized as two parallel lines and will have a label describing data. Moreover, note that symbols PROCESS, STORE, ENTITY have one *attaching region* as syntactic attribute, and symbol EDGE has two attaching points as syntactic attributes corresponding to the start and end points of the edge. Observe that each attaching region is represented by a bold line and is identified by the number 1, whereas the two attaching points of EDGE are represented by bullets and are identified each by a number.

Thus, such UML class diagrams allow for a more effective communication between designer and end user, which can benefit from the comprehension of the specification and make suggestions and modifications in early phases of visual language development.

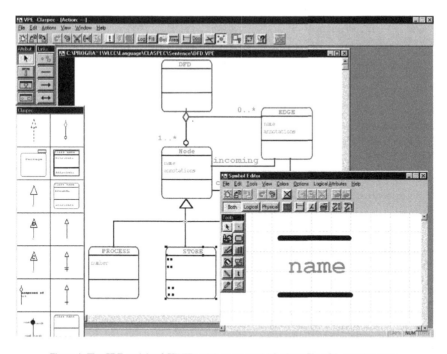

Figure 4: The CDE module of GENIE and the meta-model for Data Flow Diagram language

PROCESS   STORE   ENTITY   EDGE

Figure 5: The visual representation of symbols of DFD language

GENIE generates a visual editor and translates the meta-model into a corresponding GXL schema, and a context-free grammar skeleton that is shown in Figure 6.

In order to construct the XPG productions, the designer identifies the relations used to relate the symbols in the visual sentences by analyzing the annotations on the syntax and the associations of the grammar skeleton. As an example, the associations *incoming* and *outcoming* of the skeleton will be specified by using a relation **LINK** $_k$ which is a connection relation defined as: a graphical symbol A is in relation **LINK** $_k$ with a graphical symbol B iff attaching region h of A is connected to attaching region k of B, and will be denoted as h_k to simplify the notation. Moreover, we use the notation $\overline{h\_k}$ when describing the absence of a connection between two attaching areas h and kK.

Terminals = {PROCESS, ENTITY, STORE, EDGE}
Non Terminals = {DFD, Node}
Productions = {
  (1) DFD   □   Node
  (2) DFD   □   DFD EDGE *incoming* Node
  (3) DFD   □   DFD EDGE *outcoming* Node
  (4) Node   □   PROCESS
  (5) Node   □   STORE
  (6) Node   □   ENTITY
}

Figure 6: The grammar skeleton obtained from the UML class diagram of Figure 4

Thus, the following XPG productions can be obtained from the grammar skeleton. Notice that the superscripts are used to distinguish different occurrences of the same symbol.

(1) DFD   Node
    : $(DFD_1 = Node_1)$

(2) DFD   DFD′ **1.1** , $\overline{\mathbf{1.2}}$ EDGE **2.1** Node
    : $(DFD_1 = DFD'_1 - EDGE_1)$
    : $(PLACEHOLD; Node_1 \; 1; PLACEHOLD_1 = Node_1 - EDGE_2)$

(3) DFD   DFD′ **1.2**   **1̄.1̄**   EDGE **1.1** Node
    : $(DFD_1 = DFD_1' - EDGE_2)$
    : $(PLACEHOLD; \ Node_1 \quad 1; PLACEHOLD_1 = Node_1 - EDGE_1)$

(4) DFD   DFD′ *any* PLACEHOLD
    : $(DFD_1 = DFD_1' + PLACEHOLD_1)$

(5) Node   STORE
    : $(Node_1 = STORE_1)$

(6) Node   PROCESS
    : $(Node_1 = PROCESS_1)$

(7) Node   ENTITY
    : $(Node_1 = ENTITY_1)$

(8) Node   PLACEHOLD
    : $(Node_1 = PLACEHOLD_1)$

According to these rules, a data flow diagram is defined as

- a *Node* (production 1) or, recursively, as
- a *DFD* connected to a node through an outgoing (production 2) or incoming (production 3) edge.

A Node can be either a data store node (production 5), or a processing step node (production 6), an entity (production 7).

Let us observe that the relation identifier *any* denotes a relation that is always satisfied between any pair of symbols. PLACEHOLD is a fictitious terminal symbol to be dynamically inserted in the input sentence during the parsing process. It has one attaching region as syntactic attribute. Moreover, notice that $DFD_1 = DFD_1' \quad EDGE_1$ indicates set difference and has to be interpreted as follows: "the attaching area 1 of DFD has to be connected to whatever is attached to the attaching area 1 of DFD′ except for the attaching point 1 of EDGE". Moreover the notation $|Node_1|$ indicates the number of connections to the attaching area 1 of Node.

Now, by adding semantic rules to the XPG productions it is possible to translate any DFD sentence into the corresponding GXL instance in agreement with the data flow diagram GXL schema.

It is worth noting that the verification of properties of visual languages can be carried out during a static semantic analysis by exploiting the syntax structure given in output by the syntactic analysis. To this aim, semantic attributes and semantic rules can be added to the symbols and to the productions of the XPG specification in order to obtain a syntax structure summarizing the information of the input visual sentence.

As an example, let us consider the data flow diagram depicted in Figure 7 which violates the property that Data Stores can only be read or written by Processes. Such constraint can be checked by visiting the syntax graph of Figure 8 constructed from the DFD.

From the XPG specification the VLCC automatically generates a visual environment for data flow diagrams.

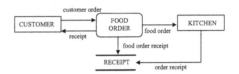

Figure 7: A data flow diagram with a data flow from an entity to a data store

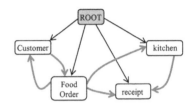

Figure 8: The syntax graph corresponding to the DFD in Figure 7

4 RELATED WORK

The development of effective modeling environments is a costly and time-consuming activity. Thus, it is widely recognized the need for the adoption of suitable and powerful tools supporting their implementation. In the last decades, several tools have been proposed, which differ in several aspects. We can classify such tools into two broad classes, named "meta-modeling tools" and "formal-based tools".

Systems falling in the first class are characterized by the use of a specification model, named *meta-model*, to define the visual language. In this category can be count systems such as MetaEdit+ (Kelly et al., 1996), Kogge (Ebert et al., 1997), ATOM[3] (de Lara and Vangheluwe, 2002). The most used meta-modeling techniques are usually classified into the following three main categories: ER-based, OO-based or graph based. The choice of the meta-model language is critic, since if it is too simple then it can be not sufficient to specify sophisticated languages; on the other hand, if it is too complicated then it can be very difficult to model a new visual language. However, meta-modeling languages do not possess precisely defined syntax and semantic, and cannot be used for verifying certain properties of the language under construction. For that reason, the meta-modeling techniques are usually supplemented with more formal languages, such as OCL, Z notation, etc. MetaEdit+ uses as meta-model GOPRR (Graph, Objects, Properties, Relationships, Roles) that adds the concept of graph to OPRR model. It allows the integration of concepts and rules for checking model integrity, consistency, and completeness by defining constraints rules. KOGGE (Ebert et al., 1997) supports the generation of visual languages such as Bon. The meta-model used to describe the abstract syntax is EER/GRAL. GRAL is used to provide integrity conditions, which cannot be expressed by EER descriptions.

Such tools do not provide adequate support for code generation. In particular, they have ad-hoc languages able to generate simple documentation but are not suitable to describe complicated dependencies. On the contrary GENIE allows us to easily perform translation by adding suitable semantic rules in order to realize appropriate code and report generation.

An approach similar to ours has been proposed in ATOM^3 (de Lara and Vangheluwe, 2002). It generates modeling tools by combining the use of a meta-modeling technique and graph grammars. In particular, the ER formalism extended with constraints is available at the meta-meta-level, where constraints can be specified as OCL, or Python expressions. Models are internally represented using *Abstract Syntax Graphs* and model manipulations such as simulation, optimization, transformation and code generation are expressed by means of graph grammars by advantages of graph transformation technique.

The "formal-based tools" are characterized by the use of a formal method for the specification of the modeling languages. In this context, special attention deserves systems that employ grammar formalisms for specifying the syntax and the semantics of a visual language (Bardohl, 2002)(Chok and Marriott, 1998)(Minas, 2002)(Rubin et al., 1990)(Zhang et al., 2001)(Uskudarli and Dinesh, 1995). This approach allows us to exploit the well-established theoretical background and techniques developed for string languages in the setting of visual languages. The main differences between the existing grammar-based systems lie in the characteristics of the underlying grammar formalism, its expressive power and the parsing efficiency.

5   FINAL REMARKS

In this paper we presented a user-centered methodology for the development of customized visual modeling environments, and a tool to support it. The use of UML meta-modeling techniques and formal methods characterizes the proposed approach. This allows us to inherit the appealing features of both the approaches. As a matter of fact, an UML class diagram is used during the requirements analysis in order to provide a high-level specification of the modeling language, which allows us to describe the entities of the problem domain, so that they are more understandable by language users. Moreover, a visual editor

is automatically generated from the specified meta-model. Note that the use of UML meta-model for the specification of visual languages is gaining interest in recent years. As a matter of fact, a meta-model approach is underlying most generators of diagrammatic editors. As an example, Metabuilder (Ferguson et al., 2000) automatically generates an editor for a new visual language starting from the class diagram modeling the language. UML meta-modeling has also been exploited to characterize families of diagrammatic languages through an abstract syntax given as a class diagram and a set of constraints in a logical language.

The specified UML meta-models are translated into formal specifications (in XPG format) that also include constraints on the modeling languages. Thus, due to the use of this grammar formalism the system exhibits several advantages. In particular, it allows us to extend the 'compiler-compiler' approach widely adopted for the generation of programming workbenches to visual oriented workbenches. Moreover, it allows us to easily perform several tasks on the defined language such as customization and modifications as well as the maintenance and the debug. Suitable semantic rules can be defined to realize appropriate code and report generation, as well as to realize static verification of the languages. The language specification can be notably simplified by the adoption of an incremental approach supported by context-free style grammars. Furthermore, the approach supports the software reuse through a central repository.

Another interesting characteristic of the visual environments generated by GENIE is the use of GXL format as data representation of the sentences. This feature makes easier the interoperability of the environments with other tools. As a matter of fact, some groups from industry and research committed to provide facilities to import and export GXL documents to their tools (Winter et al., 2002). However, the choice of GXL does not prevent from the use of other XML-based languages for import/export facilities. For example, for UML visual environments, we may need to represent the sentence also with the XMI format (XMI, 2003).

Now, several remarkable future researches can be foreseen. The proposed meta-model/grammar approach is based on a semi-automatic transformation of a meta-model into the corresponding XPG specification. As a consequence, it could be interesting to further investigate such an aspect in order to obtain a more automatic transformation mechanism. Finally, we intend to carry out usability studies of the proposed meta-model/grammar approach for generating visual modeling environments.

REFERENCES

Aho, A., Sethi, R., and Ullman, J. (1985). *Compilers, principles, techniques and tools*. Addison-Wesley.

Bardohl, R. (2002). A visual environment for visual languages. *Science of Computer Programming*, 44(2):181–203.

Chok, S. and Marriott, K. (1998). Automatic Construction of Intelligent Diagram Editors. In *Proceedings of the ACM Symposium on User Interface Software and Technology UIST98*, pages 185–194, San Francisco, California.

de Lara, J. and Vangheluwe, H. (2002). AToM^3: A tool for multi-formalism and meta-modelling. In *5th International Conference FASE 2002*, pages 174–188, Grenoble, France.

Ebert, J., Suttenbach, R., and Uhe, I. (1997). Meta-CASE in practice: A case for KOGGE. In *Proceedings of 9th International Conference CaiSE'97*, LNCS 1250, pages 203–216, Barcelona, Spain. Springer-Verlag.

Ferguson, R., Hunter, A., and Hardy, C. (2000). Metabuilder: The diagrammer's diagrammer. In *Proceedings Diagrams 2000*, LNCS 1889, pages 407–421, Edinburgh, Scotland, UK. Springer-Verlag.

Holt, R. C., Winter, A., and Schürr, A. (2000). GXL: Toward a standard exchange format. In *Proceedings of the 7th Working Conference on Reverse Engineering (WCRE 2000)*, pages 162–171, Los Alamitos. IEEE Computer Society.

Johnson, S. (1978). *YACC: Yet Another Compiler Compiler*. Bell Laboratories, Murray Hills, NJ.

Kelly, S., Lyytinen, K., and Rossi, M. (1996). MetaEdit+: A fully configurable multi-user and multi-tool CASE and CAME environment. In Constantopoulos, P., Mylopoulos, J., and Vassiliou, Y., editors, *Proceedings 8th International Conference CAiSE'96*, LNCS 1080, pages 1–21, Crete, Greece. Springer.

Kimura, T., Choi, J., and Mack, J. (1990). Show and Tell: A visual programming language. In Glinert, E. P., editor, *Visual Programming Environments: Paradigms and Systems*, pages 397–404. IEEE Computer Society Press, Los Alamitos.

McIntyre, D. (1995). *Design and implementation with Vampire*, pages 129–159. Manning Publications Co.

Minas, M. (2002). Concepts and realization of a diagram editor generator based on hypergraph transformation. *Science of Computer Programming*, 44(2):157–180.

Nokia Mobile Phones (1999). *Press Release: Nokia expects increased mobile growth and raises subscriber estimates*.

Rubin, R., Walker II, J., and Golin, E. (1990). Early experience with the visual programmer's workbench. *IEEE Transactions on Software Engineering*, 16(10):1107–1121.

Schmidt, C., Pfahler, P., and Fischer, U. K. C. (2002). SIMtelligence Designer/J: A Visual Language to Specify SIM Toolkit Applications. In *Procs of (OOPSLA'02), Second Workshop on Domain Specific Visual Languages*, pages 32–39.

Uskudarli, S. and Dinesh, T. (1995). Towards a Visual Programming Environment Generator for Algebraic Specifications. In *Procs. 11th IEEE International Symposium on Visual Languages*, pages 234–241, Darmstadt, Germany.

Vose, G. M. and Williams, G. (1986). LabVIEW: Laboratory virtual instrument engineering workbench. *Byte*, pages 84–92.

Winter, A. (2002). Exchanging graphs with GXL. In Mutzel, P., Jnger, M., and Leipert, S., editors, *Graph Drawing*, LNCS 2265, pages 485–500. Springer-Verlag.

Winter, A., Kullbach, B., and Riediger, V. (2002). An overview of the GXL graph exchange language. In S.Diehl, editor, *Software Visualization*, LNCS 2269, pages 324–336. Springer-Verlag.

XMI (2003). OMG document formal/03-05-02.

Zhang, K., Zhang, D., and Cao, J. (2001). Design, construction, and application of a generic visual language generation environment. *IEEE Transactions on Software Engineering*, 27(4):289–307.

PART 4

Software Agents and
Internet Computing

TEAMBROKER: CONSTRAINT BASED BROKERAGE OF VIRTUAL TEAMS

Achim P. Karduck

Department of Computer Science in Media, Furtwangen university of applied sciences
Robert-Gerwig-Platz 1, 78120 Furtwangen, Germany
karduck@fh-furtwangen.de

Amadou Sienou

Department of Computer Science in Media, Furtwangen university of applied sciences
Robert-Gerwig-Platz 1, 78120 Furtwangen, Germany
amadou@sienou.net

Keywords: Computer supported team formation, resource allocation, constraints satisfaction optimization

Abstract: Some consulting projects are carried out in virtual teams, which are networks of people sharing a common purpose and working across organizational and temporal boundaries by using information technologies. Multiple investigations covering these teams focus on coordination, group communication and computer supported collaborative work. However, additional perspectives like the formation of teams are also important. Here one should deal with the question: how to form the best team?

To approach this question, we have defined team formation as the process of finding the right expert for a given task and allocating the set of experts that best fulfills team requirements. This has been further transformed into a problem of constraint based optimal resource allocation.

Our environment for computer supported team formation has been developed by having adopted the brokerage view that consists of mediating experts between peers requesting a team and the ones willing to participate in a team. Computer supported brokerage of experts has been realized as a distributed problem solving that involves entities representing experts, brokers and team initiators.

1 INTRODUCTION

Let us suppose, *SAM & associates systems, Inc.* is an organization of experts, member of a worldwide heterogeneous network of consultants. This company intends to develop a knowledge management system. For this purpose, it decides to form a virtual team of experts.

Because of the "virtualness" of the team, members may not know each other. Therefore, the decision to engage a candidate will be based on few factors like expertise, knowledge and cost. After the identification of the factors, the problem of forming the team can be solved by evaluating first the outcome of each candidate related to these factors, then selecting the candidates with the highest score. However, the same procedure is launched whenever an expert revokes his application. In this case a new team should be formed. What about a computational support to the formation of the team?

Basically, virtual teams are networks of people bound by a common purpose, who work across organizational and temporal boundaries in a collaborative environment supported by information technologies (Lipnack and Stamps, 1997) like Computer Supported Collaborative Work (CSCW) systems. Some CSCW systems are optimized in order to support multiple facets of virtual teaming with features like communication and document management, timetabling a.s.o. Teaming virtually seems to be interpreted as the operation in CSCW whereby the process anterior to team working is neglected. We exactly aim to support this process.

2 FORMING VIRTUAL TEAMS

2.1 What is Team Formation

A virtual team, like any team, goes through the phases forming, storming, norming, performing and adjourning (Lipnack and Stamps, 2000; Tuckman, 1965; Tuckman and Jensen, 1977) to get performed while producing results. During the first step, "forming", members are brought together for the first time. Focusing on this, the question "how does the team emerge to enter the forming stage" is justified. The step anterior to the "forming" stage is what we call team formation. It consists in the identification and

I. Seruca et al. (eds.), Enterprise Information Systems VI, 229–236.
© 2006 *Springer. Printed in the Netherlands.*

the selection of candidates for each activity of the project in question. The process of team formation is subdivided into the steps (Deborah and Nancy, 1999) summarized as follows:

1. **Requirements definition.** Identification of potentials and definition of requirements for experts' profiles.

2. **Candidate identification.** Exploration of the search space to identify experts who seem to meet the requirements.

3. **Candidate analysis.** Multidimensional Analysis of experts's profiles, the generation of alternative teams and the evaluation of their performance values. Here, the question that really matter is to find out who the best candidates for a team are.

4. **Contact establishment.** Subsequent to the evaluation of alternative teams, one will select the best team and contact members.

The dimensions of candidate analysis are measurable criteria that affect the team work. Since the focus is on the formation phase, factors essential to start the "forming" stage of team development are those that really matter. In the literature, some factors have been empirically evaluated or applied to other teams (Anderson, 1996; Deborah and Nancy, 1999; Lipnack and Stamps, 2000; Tuckman and Jensen, 1977; Schutz, 1955). In previous investigations we have considered the following factors necessary in order to start a team.

Table 1: Factors affecting team formation

Factors	Description
Interest	What the members desire
Competencies	Skills and experiences of members
Risk	The risk of having a member
Availability	When are members available
Commitment	Deliberate attachment to the team
Budget	Amount available for the project
Project constraints	Cost constraints

Certainly these factors are interdependent. However competency is the most complex one, which affects the rest. It is therefore an object of a deeper analysis.

2.2 Conceptualizing Competency

Competency or *"a specific, identifiable, definable, and measurable knowledge, skill, ability and/or other deployment-related characteristic (e.g. attitude, behavior, physical ability) which a human resource may possess and which is necessary for, or material to, the performance of an activity within a specific business context"* (Chuck Allen (ed.), 2001) has following basic properties:

- **Measurability and scales.** Although competencies are generally measurable, some are difficult to quantify because of their nature or the complexity of the metrics.

- **Context/Taxonomy.** Taxonomies are semantical descriptions of competencies, recursions, implications and equivalence relations between classes. In the scope of our investigation the concept of taxonomy is a model describing skills, levels, positions, equivalence and implication.

- **Recursion (inclusion).** Competencies are not always expressed as single values; they may include or extend other measurable competencies.

- **Equivalence and implication.** In a given context, there are equivalence and implication relations between competencies. Equivalent competencies are those that give evidence of semantically identic competencies without using lexically identic expressions. Implication is a relation between two competencies expressing that the semantic meaning of the first competency implies the one of the seconde.

- **Attributes.** Competencies are described with multiple attributes like "evidence" and "weights" which express its existence or sufficiency and its relative importance respectively.

In order to compute competency, it has been necessary to conceptualize the even described model. Following (Deborah and Nancy, 1999) we have organized a competency in a three layered structure consisting of *area of competence, knowledge* and *knowledge item*. Here the area of competence is a wide context of knowledge. Knowledge items are single attributes specifying a given knowledge in a real-life domain.

A skill is a tuple (A, B, C) where A is the area of competence, B the knowledge, C the knowledge item.

A competency owned by an expert is the tuple (A, B, C, ℓ, e) where ℓ is the level of skill and e the experience expressed in number of months.

A competency required for a task is a tuple $(A, B, C, \ell^{min}, e_{min}, \omega_\ell, \omega_e)$ where ℓ^{min}, e_{min}, ω_ℓ, ω_e are the minimum level of skill, the minimum experience required, the weight of the level of skill and the weight of the experience respectively.

The competency (A, B, C, ℓ, e) of an expert is valid regarding to a given requirement $(A', B', C', \ell^{min}, e_{min}, \omega_\ell, \omega_e)$ if the skills (A, B, C) and (A', B', C') match and the constraints $\ell \geq \ell^{min}$ and $e \geq e_{min}$ hold.

Since interests are also competencies, we have adopted similar representations for them, i.e an interest is a tuple (A, B, C, ℓ) where ℓ is the level of interest.

Based on these concepts of team formation and the conceptualization of factors affecting the formation process, we have developed the TeamBroker system to support the formation of virtual project teams. In the literature, investigations cover just the pre-configuration of teams and workflow systems. In our research project, we have adopted a brokerage approach which consists in the brokerage of optimal solutions (set of experts) to a constraint based specification of a project.

3   TEAMBROKER

3.1   A Model for Team Formation

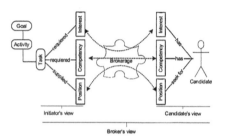

Figure 1: A model for team formation

According to (Pynadath et al., 1999; Lipnack and Stamps, 2000; Petersen and Gruninger, 2000), a team is defined in order to execute activities which are grouped around a goal. In figure 1 we have refined the model from (Petersen and Gruninger, 2000) by subdividing activities into single tasks able to be carried out by single experts. The problem of assigning tasks is therefore simplified to single resource allocation which is more tractable than the allocation of multiple resources (Bar-Noy et al., 2001).

A task, in order to be performed, requires a position, a set of competencies and interests. Candidates are entities with interests and competencies who are looking for positions. Team brokerage consists of finding candidates for a task so that the positions, the competencies and the interests match (doted arrows). In this model, the team initiator defines tasks and requirements while experts provide information concerning their interests, their competencies and the positions in which they are interested.

Here, allocating a set of resources (experts) to the set of tasks defined in the context of a project is

viewed as a Resource Allocation Problem (RAP). There are different approaches to solve RAP. Constraint programming, a framework used to solve combinatorial problems, is one of the successful approaches to these problems (Tsang, 1993). Key concepts of constraint programming are variables, their domains and constraints. Here, constraints are restrictions on the values to which a variable may be instantiated. The goal is to find an instantiation of all variables that satisfy all constraints.

Team formation is the Constraint Satisfaction Problem (CSP) (Z, D, C) specified as follows:

1. $\mathbf{Z} = \{\mathbf{z_1}, .., \mathbf{z_n}\}$ is the set of variables, each standing for the task to which experts should be allocated.

2. $\mathbf{D} = \{\mathbf{d_1}, .., \mathbf{d_n}\}$ is the set of domains of values to which variables z_i can be instantiated. Let us call elements of d_i instances indexed I which are conceptualized as follows:

   - **Budget.** Amount of money planned for the task to be assigned; indexed $B(I)$.
   - **Cost.** A value representing the cost of assigning a task to an expert; indexed $C(I)$. We define the cost as follows:

     $$C(I) = h_w(I) \times d(I) \times h_d(I) \qquad (1)$$

     Where $h_w(I)$ is the hourly wage, $d(I)$ the duration in days and $h_d(I)$ the number of work hours per day.

   - **Level of Commitment.** We refer to the aspect of commitment from (Petersen and Divitini, 2002) as the *level of commitment* expressed in the term of *commitment breaking cost*, which is the amount that a partner will have to pay if he leaves the organization before the achievement of goals. The level of commitment is indexed $L(I) \in [0, 1]$.
   - **Performance.** A value, indexed $P_{instance}$ that expresses the performance value of the instance.

3. C is a set of constraints in Z and D. We have categorized them into availability constraint, position constraint, instance constraints and team constraints.

   - **Availability constraint.** An expert is eligible for a team if he/she is available during the executing time of the tasks for which he/she is applying.
   - **Position constraint.** An expert applying for a task will be considered only if the position posted in the context of this task is the one that he/she is looking for.
   - **Instance constraints.** These constraints are restrictions to the level of interest, level of skill and experience. An expert is considered having an interest, skill or experience only if his/her levels

of skills or experience are at least equal to the level defined in the constraints.

- **Team constraints.** In contrast to instance constraints where only single experts are taken into consideration, team constraints affect the whole team.

Let us introduce a binary variable $x_I \in \{0, 1\}$ expressing whether an instance is activated; i.e. if the task z_i is assigned to a given expert and the resulting assignment is indexed I, the value $x_I = 1$; otherwise $x_I = 0$. A team is a n-dimensional vector the components of which are the indexes of activated instances.

Based on the properties of single resource allocation we have defined the following constraints:

C_1. The total budget planned for a project should not be exceeded:

$$\sum_i^n \sum_{I \in z_i} C(I) \times x_I \leq \sum_i^n \sum_{I \in z_i} B(I) \times x_I \quad (2)$$

For convenience, let us define the quotient

$$\Delta_{budget} = \frac{\sum_i^n \sum_{I \in z_i} C(I) \times x_I}{\sum_i^n \sum_{I \in z_i} B(I) \times x_I} \quad (3)$$

and specify this constraint as follows:

$$\Delta_{budget} \leq 1 \quad (4)$$

C_2. All tasks must be assigned and each only once:

$$\forall z_i \in Z, \quad \sum_{I \in z_i} x_I = 1 \quad (5)$$

Like any constraint satisfaction problems, this one will also have one, none or multiple solutions $X = \langle I_1, ..., I_n \rangle$. A solution is valid if both constraints C_1 and C_2 hold. The solution space has a size of $\prod_{i=1}^n |d_i|$. Therefore, we need to support the selection of a team by introducing the concept of team performance value P, which maps each solution X to a value $P(X)$. The value $P(X)$ depends on single performance values of the experts involved in the team X.

3.2   Evaluating Performance Values

Selecting an expert for a given task is a decision problem depending on multiple criteria. The decision is based on the performance of an instance which is an aggregate value of the factors cost, synergy, skills, experiences, commitment and risk. By using the technique of objectives hierarchies (Keeney, 1992) in order to transform these factors, we have eliminated interdependencies and have obtained the following criteria:

- Δ_{cost}. There are many candidates for a given task. The cost of assigning this task to an expert indexed i is $C(i)$. Let $C(max)$ be the cost of assigning the task to the most expensive expert. Δ_{cost} is the standardized value of the deviation of $C(i)$ from $C(max)$; i.e. how expensive is an expert compared to the worst case.

$$\Delta_{cost} = 1 - \frac{C(I)}{C(max)} \quad (6)$$

- **Level of commitment.** Value defined in the previous section as $L(I)$.

- **Synergy.** We have defined the *value of synergy* as the similarity V_s of candidate interests to the interests required for the task in question.

Let $S^{task} = \{(A_i, B_i, C_i, \ell_i^{min}), i = 1...n\}$ be the set of interests required for a given task;
$\Omega = \{\omega_i, \ \omega_i \in [0, 1], \ \sum_{i=1}^n \omega_i = 1, \ i = 1...n\}$ be a set of weighting factors representing the relative importance of interests;
ℓ_i^{min} be the minimum level required for each interest ;
$S = \{(A_i, B_i, C_i, \ell_i), i = 1...n\}$ be the set of experts' interests.

The vector X^{expert} representing the computed values of an expert's interest is defined as follows:

$$X^{expert} = \langle ..., \ell_i \times \omega_i \times \tau_i, ... \rangle, \quad (7)$$

$$\tau_i = \begin{cases} 1 & \ell_i \geq \ell_i^{min} \\ 0 & \ell_i < \ell_i^{min} \end{cases}, \quad i = 1...n \quad (8)$$

Here, ℓ_i is the expert's level of the ith interest. The value of synergy is finally defined as follows:

$$V_s = 1 - \frac{\sqrt{\sum_{i=1}^n \left(X_i^{ideal} - X_i^{expert} \right)^2}}{\sqrt{\sum_{i=1}^n \left(X_i^{ideal} \right)^2}} \quad (9)$$

Here X^{ideal} represents the virtual ideal expert according to this factor:

$$X^{ideal} = \langle ..., \ell^{max} \times \omega_i, ... \rangle, \quad i = 1...n \quad (10)$$

- **Competency (skills and experience).** The execution of a task requires a set of skills and experiences. Since experience depends on skills, we have introduced the concept of Competency to explain the aggregate value of both.

Let $S^{task} = \{(A_i, B_i, C_i, \ell_i^{min}, expe_i^{min}), i = 1...n\}$ be the set of skills and experiences required for a task.
$\Omega^s = \{\omega_i^s, \ \omega_i \in [0, 1], \ i = 1...n\}$ be a set of weights representing the relative importance of skills.
$\Omega^e = \{\omega_i^e, \ \omega_i \in [0, 1], \ i = 1...n\}$ be a set of weights representing the relative importance of experiences.

The vector X^{expert} represents the computed values

of the skills of an expert:

$$X^{expert} = \langle ..., \ell_i \times \omega_i^s \times \tau_i, ...\rangle, \qquad (11)$$

$$\tau_i = \begin{cases} 1 & \ell_i \geq \ell_i^{min} \\ 0 & \ell_i < \ell_i^{min} \end{cases}, \quad i = 1...n \qquad (12)$$

The vector Y^{expert} represents the computed values of the corresponding experiences.

$$Y^{expert} = \langle ..., expe_i \times \omega_i^e \times \tau_i, ...\rangle, \qquad (13)$$

$$\tau_i = \begin{cases} 1 & expe_i \geq expe_i^{min} \\ 0 & expe_i < expe_i^{min} \end{cases}, \quad i = 1...n \qquad (14)$$

The fused view of skills and experience is the matrix $C = \langle X_i, Y_i \rangle$. The aggregate value of expert's competencies is processed with the vector $Z^{expert} = \langle \|C_1\|, ..., \|C_i\|, ..., \|C_n\| \rangle$. Let Z^{ideal} be the virtual expert with the highest possible values of competencies. The aggregate value of an expert's competencies is the similarity of his/her competencies to the ones of the ideal virtual expert:

$$V_c = 1 - \frac{\sqrt{\sum_{i=1}^n \left(Z_i^{ideal} - Z_i^{expert} \right)^2}}{\sqrt{\sum_{i=1}^n \left(Z_i^{ideal} \right)^2}} \qquad (15)$$

Let us consider the following table illustrating the levels of skills and experiences of 3 experts candidates for a task requiring 2 skills. Since $V_{c2} = 0.996 > V_{c1} = 0.819 > V_{c3} = 0.667$, we conclude that considering this factor, $expert_2$ is the best one for this task.

Table 2: Sample competencies.

Requirement	skilled experts					
	$expert_1$		$expert_2$		$expert_3$	
	ℓ	expe	ℓ	expe	ℓ	expe
$competency_1$	3	30	3	36	4	36
$competency_2$	4	20	3	25	3	12
$competency_1$ =programming,java,2,24,60,45						
$competency_2$ = programming,ejb,2,6,40,55						
level: none=0, 1=low, 2=medium, 3=high, 4=expert						

Let $\omega_i, i = 1...4$ be weighting factors representing the initiator's relative preferences for the criteria Δ_{cost}, V_s, V_c and $L(I)$ respectively. Since the factors are preferential independents and the values are standardized, the weighted sum aggregation procedure is applicable to evaluate the performance $P_{instance}$ of an instance I as follows:

$$P_{instance}(I) = \sum_{i=1}^4 \omega_i \times I_i^{value} \qquad (16)$$

where

$$I_{i=1..4}^{value} = \langle \Delta_{cost}, V_s, V_c, L(I) \rangle$$

This value expresses "how well" the profile of an expert fulfills the requirement specification of a given task. For each task, the expert having the highest score is the best one.

Given that it was possible to order experts interested to tasks, it is now necessary to find the best constellation of experts. For this purpose, one will refer to the team performance value $P(X)$ which is the weighted sum of the utility of assigning single tasks to experts:

$$P(X) = \sum_{i=1}^n \omega_i \times \sum_{I \in z_i} P_{instance}(I) \times x_I \qquad (17)$$

Here $\omega_i \in [0, 1]$ is a weight representing the relative importance of the instance I and $\sum_{i=1}^n \omega_i = 1$.

3.3   Searching the Best Team

At this stage of the formation process, the main problem to deal with is to find the team with the highest utility so that all tasks are assigned to exactly one expert and the total cost does not exceed the total budget. This is a single resource allocation and Constraint Satisfaction Optimization Problem (CSOP) defined as follows (see eq. 17 for $P(X)$):

$$\begin{aligned} &find && X = \langle I_1, ..., I_n \rangle \\ &s.t. && maximize \; P(X) \\ &subject \; to && \\ & && \Delta_{budget}(X) \leq 1 \\ & && \forall z_i \in Z, \; \sum_{I \in z_i} x_I = 1 \\ & && \forall I \in z_i, \; x_I \in \{0, 1\} \end{aligned} \qquad (18)$$

Since it is algorithmically possible to satisfy the last constraint ($\forall z_i \in Z$, $\sum_{I \in z_i} x_I = 1$) by instantiating each variable exactly once, this one is no longer relevant to the solution if the control of the algorithm forces single allocations. The objective consists henceforth in maximizing the team utility without exceeding the total budget.

Note that $\forall I \in z_i, i = 1...n, \omega_i \geq 0$ and ω_i is constant; i.e. the weighting factor of each task is positive and constant during the formation process. Since $\sum_{I \in z_i} P_{instance}(I) \times x_I \geq 0$, $\forall I \in z_i$, the value $P(X)$ is maximal if the values $P_{instance}(I)$ are maximal; i.e. the team performance is maximal if tasks are assigned always to experts having the highest performance value. The set of the best experts is however not necessarily a valid solution because the constraints must be satisfied.

Let us suppose that the experts are ranked according to decreasing order of the values of $P_{instance}$. In case that the best team is not a valid solution, one will examine the next best team. This one is formed by replacing exactly one candidate for a task by the seconde best one for the same task. This process is a 1-flip operation used to expand the search space. In order to find the best team without executing an exhaustive search of the space, we have developed a search strategy extending the iterated hill-climbing search. The hill-climbing search is a local search strategy simulating a hill climber, who aims to reach the peak of a landscape by iteratively jumping from an initial peak to the peak of the neighborhood until he reaches the maximum (Michalewicz and Fogel, 1999). Hill-climbing strategies are confronted with the problem of local maxima. To deal with this problem, we have adopted the tabu approach that consists of recording all visited non-solution nodes in order to avoid them in the future. In order to select always the best team, we have adopted an approach similar to the best search strategy by defining an open-list to store the non-visited neighborhood of a node. The algorithm always selects the best state of the open-list and expands the space by executing the 1-flip operator until a solution is found or the whole space has been processed. The flip-process guarantees to select the next best expert applying for the task in question.

After the definition of the model, the metrics and the search strategy, it has been necessary to develop a technical environment that supports the concept.

3.4 Technical Realization

Figure 2 is the architecture of a technical environment supporting our model of team formation. TeamBroker, TeamCandidate, TeamInitiator are Java RMI (Remote Method Invocation) (Sun Microsystems, 2002) servers.

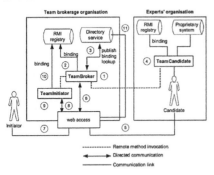

Figure 2: Architecture of the team brokerage system

The business of the team brokerage organization consists in forming teams of experts that fulfills requirements defined by initiators. It runs TeamBroker (1) RMI servers. Services provided by TeamBroker are published in a directory server (3). Using this information, experts identify and select (5) the suit-

able TeamBroker to which they send requests for registration. Upon reception of these requests, TeamBroker stores the reference of the server into its directory (3) by using the RMI registry service provider for JNDI (Java Naming and Directory Interface) (Sun Microsystems, 1999). When needed the suitable candidate is searched in the directory. Team initiators and experts use a web interface (7) to search, select and interact with a TeamBroker.

Experts' organizations are networks of experts looking for positions in virtual teams. Each of them runs a TeamCandidate (4) server, which is extensible to wrappers able to convert profiles described in proprietary formats into the one used in TeamBroker.

The initiator is an organization asking for virtual teams. It is responsible for the specification of requirements that the team should fulfill. Initiators access the brokerage system by using a web-interface (7,8,9). TeamInitiator is a RMI server that represents a human initiator. For each initiator requesting a registration, the system starts a TeamInitiator (9), which is bound (10) to the naming service of the broker.

At this level, team formation is an interaction of TeamBroker, TeamCandidate and TeamInitiator as shown in the sequence diagram of figure 3.

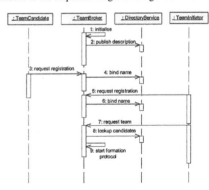

Figure 3: Sequences of team brokerage

1. A TeamBroker starts running

2. Publication of services into a directory server

3. A TeamCandidate requests registration and supplies its JNDI name.

4. TeamBroker binds the JNDI name of the TeamCandidate to its own directory service.

5. Initiators use the web-interface to request for registration. An instance of TeamInitator is started to forward the request to TeamBroker.

6. TeamBroker binds the TeamInitiator to its directory service.

7. TeamInitiator requests a team by sending a message to TeamBroker.

3. TeamBroker queries the directory for RMI names of TeamCandidate servers which are bound in the naming context of the position defined in initiator's request for the team.

9. TeamBroker connects finally to the RMI servers listed in the result of the previous query and starts the team formation protocol of figure 4.

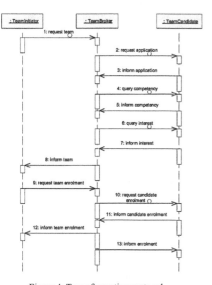

Figure 4: Team formation protocol

The team formation protocol is a set of communication messages shared by TeamBroker, TeamInitiator and TeamCandidate. As outlined in figure 4, it consists of the following six steps:

- **Request team (1).** The TeamInitiator requests the TeamBroker to form teams which fulfills requirements defined in the content of the message. The message contains the list of required positions, schedule, constraints, skills, experiences, interests and budgets.

- **Request application (2)/Inform application (3).** The TeamBroker identifies all potentially interested experts by searching in the directory. In a next step, it requests TeamCandidate to explicitly apply to the position within a deadline. The message addressed to the experts contains information concerning the position and the schedule. Instances of TeamCandidate answer by sending an application message. This message contains the state of the

application, the hourly wage and the level of commitment of the expert. The state of the application is either "accepted" or "rejected". If the state is "accepted" TeamBroker continues the formation process with the TeamCandidate. Otherwise this one is no longer considered as a candidate.

- **Query competency (4)/Query interest (6).** During this process, TeamBroker communicates with instances of TeamCandidate having accepted the application by sending an "inform application" message qualified "accepted". TeamBroker queries instances of interested TeamCandidate for level of competencies and experiences. The responses are "inform competency (5)" and "inform interest (7)" respectively.

- **Inform team (8).** At this stage of the formation protocol, TeamBroker has collected all information necessary to form teams. The result (teams and performances) is sent to the TeamInitiator.

- **Request team enrollment (9)/Inform team enrollment (12).** TeamInitiator selects the best team and requests TeamBroker to enroll it.

- **Request candidate enrollment (10)/inform candidate enrollment(11).** TeamBroker requests single experts to confirm the enrollment. When an instance of TeamCandidate receives this message, the expert represented by this instance should decide whether to join the team or not. If all members agree in the enrollment, the team is definitively formed and all entities (initiator and candidates) are informed about the success. Otherwise, a fail message is broadcasted (13).

4   RELATED WORK

Works related to our project are the ones from (Rub and Vierke, 1998) and (Petersen and Divitini, 2002; Petersen and Gruninger, 2000). In contrast to the first concept which supports the configuration of virtual enterprizes, we have emphasized the formation of virtual teams of humans. Both concepts share the aspects of optimal resource allocation.

Unlike the second approach, where the virtual team initiator is the entity processing partners' outcome and evaluating their utilities, we have adopted a brokerage approach. In our project, the formation process is a behavior of a configurable mediator called broker, which is able to use multiple taxonomies of knowledge description and different metrics to appraise candidates and form teams for the initiators. Furthermore, we suppose that there is no negotiation between the peers. In contrast to (Petersen and Divitini, 2002; Petersen and Gruninger, 2000), our performance metrics are based on the definition of non-interdependent criteria.

5   CONCLUSION

In our research projet, we have conceptualized factors affecting the formation of teams by defining models and metrics able to evaluate experts and teams. Based on this conceptualization of performance values and the formalization of constraints imposed by the project that a team has to carry out, we have transformed the problem of forming teams into a resource allocation problem. We have solved the resulting RAP by extending the iterated hill-climbing search strategy.

The TeamBroker system has been realized as a distributed system consisting of Java RMI servers. The successful application to our scenario has led to the conclusion that it supports the formation of virtual teams. However, the specification of a concrete project has to suit basic assumptions concerning (1) the structure of the criteria and competencies, (2) performance metrics, (3) aggregation procedures and (4) constraints.

As stated in (Deborah and Nancy, 1999) there are different types of virtual teams. Since for project or product development teams activities are clearly defined in form of technical requirements with fixed duration and measurable results, the TeamBroker system aims to support the formation of this kinds of teams. It is necessary to note that the system can also support the formation or pre-formation of non-virtual product development teams when rational measurable competencies of members are more important than emotional aspects.

In the future we intend to use advanced techniques of knowledge representation and processing in order to handle high inter-related skills.

In contrast to the current system, where the type of constraints are static, in our future work, we intend to assist team initiators by enabling them to add interactively new constraints to the system and to parameterize the resolution strategy by supporting for example partial constraints satisfaction.

We plan to integrate the TeamBroker system into a CSCW environment by adopting a service oriented architecture. This integration should support an automatic tracking of skills used by members while working in the CSCW environment.

REFERENCES

Anderson, W. (1996). Human resource development challenges in a virtual organization. In *IEMC Proceedings: Managing the Virtural Enterprise*, Vancouver, B.C.: IEMC.

Bar-Noy, A., Bar-Yehuda, R., Freund, A., Naor, J., and Schieber, B. (2001). A unified approach to approximating resource allocation and scheduling. *Journal of the ACM (JACM)*, 48(5):1069–1090.

Chuck Allen (ed.), H.-X. C. (2001). Competencies 1.0 (measurable characteristics). http://www.hr-xml.org [15.10.2002 20:00].

Deborah, L. D. and Nancy, T. S. (1999). *Mastering virtual teams : strategies, tools, and techniques that succeed.* Jossey-Bass Pub, San Francisco.

Keeney, L. R. (1992). *Value-focused thinking: a path to creative decision making.* Harvard University Press.

Lipnack, J. and Stamps, J. (1997). *Virtual Teams - Reaching across space, time and organizations with technology.* John Wiley & Sons.

Lipnack, J. and Stamps, J. (2000). *Virtual Teams.* John Wiley & Sons, 2 edition.

Michalewicz, Z. and Fogel, D. B. (1999). *How to solve it: modern heuristics.* Springer Verlag.

Petersen, S. A. and Divitini, M. (2002). Using agents to support the selection of virtual enterprise teams. In *Proceedings of Fourth International Bi-Conference Workshop on Agent-Oriented Information Systems (AOIS-2002)*, Bologne, Italy. AAMAS 2002.

Petersen, S. A. and Gruninger, M. (2000). An agent-based model to support the formation of virtual enterprises. In *International ICSC Symposium on Mobile Agents and Multi-agents in Virtual Organisations and E-Commerce (MAMA'2000)*, Woolongong, Australia.

Pynadath, D. V., Tambe, M., Chauvat, N., and Cavedon, L. (1999). Toward team-oriented programming. In *Agent Theories, Architectures, and Languages*, pages 233–247.

Rub, C. and Vierke, G. (1998). Agent-based configuration of virtual enterprises. In Holsten, A. e. a., editor, *Proc. of the Workshop on Intelligent Agents in Information and Process Management KI'98*, volume 9.

Schutz, W. (1955). What makes groups productive? *Human Relations*, 8:429–465.

Sun Microsystems, I. (1999). Java naming and directory interface, application programming interface (jndi). http://www.java.sun.com/jndi [10.10.2002 09:00].

Sun Microsystems, I. (2002). Java remote method invocation specification. http://www.java.sun.com/rmi [05.08.2002 18:00].

Tsang, R. (1993). *Foundations of constraint satisfaction.* Academic Press.

Tuckman, B. and Jensen, N. (1977). Stages of small-group development revised. *Group and Organizational Studies*, 2(4):419–427.

Tuckman, B. W. (1965). Developmental sequence in small groups. *Psychological Bulletin*, 63:384–389.

SEMANTIC E-LEARNING AGENTS
Supporting E-learning by semantic web and agents technologies

Jürgen Dunkel, Ralf Bruns

Department of Computer Science, University of Applied Sciences and Arts Hannover,
Ricklinger Stadtweg 120, D-30459 Hannover, Germany
Email: [juergen.dunkel, ralf.bruns]@inform.fh-hannover.de

Sascha Ossowski

AI Group, E.S.C.E.T.,Universidad Rey Juan Carlos Madrid,
Campus de Mostoles, Calle Tulipan s/n, E-28933 Madrid, Spain
Email: sossowski@escet.urjc.es

Keywords: Semantic Web, Ontology, Software Agents, E-learning

Abstract: E-learning is starting to play a major role in the learning and teaching activities at institutions of higher education worldwide. The students perform significant parts of their study activities decentralized and access the necessary information sources via the Internet. Several tools have been developed providing basic infrastructures that enable individual and collaborative work in a location-independent and time-independent fashion. Still, systems that adequately provide personalized and permanent support for using these tools are still to come.
              This paper reports on the advances of the Semantic E-learning Agent (SEA) project, whose objective is to develop virtual student advisors, that render support to university students in order to successfully organize und perform their studies. The E-learning agents are developed with novel concepts of the Semantic Web and agents technology. The key concept is the semantic modeling of the E-learning domain by means of XML-based applied ontology languages such as DAML+OIL and OWL. Software agents apply ontological and domain knowledge in order to assist human users in their decision making processes. For this task, the inference engine JESS is applied in conjunction with the agent framework JADE.

1 INTRODUCTION

E-learning has established itself as a significant part of learning and teaching at institutions of higher education worldwide. The students perform significant parts of their study activities decentralized and access the necessary information sources via the Internet. The emerged individual means of work are location-independent and time-independent, consequently requiring a permanent available and direct support that can only be provided by a software system.
The main focus of current E-learning systems is to provide an appropriate technical infrastructure for the information exchange between all user groups involved in the E-learning process. A recent comparison of modern E-learning environments (CCTT, 2002) revealed, that intelligent advisory agents are not applied so far in E-learning systems. However, the necessity of an intelligent support is unquestioned due to the individual and decentralized means of study (Cuena et al., 1999, Ossowski et al. 2002).

The objective of the semantic E-learning agent project is to develop virtual student advisors, that render support to university students, assisting them to successfully organize und perform their studies. These advisors are to behave both reactive and proactive: setting out from a knowledge base consisting of E-learning and user ontologies, their recommendations must be tailored to the personal needs of a particular student. For example, they should be able to answer questions regarding the regulations of study (e.g.: does a student possess all requirements to participate in an examination or a course?, is a student allowed to register for his/her

I. Seruca et al. (eds.), Enterprise Information Systems VI, 237–244.
© 2006 Springer. Printed in the Netherlands.

thesis?, etc). In addition, advisors should be capable of announcing new opportunities for students that are looking for suitable practical training jobs or thesis subjects.

To achieve these goals, we propose a software architecture (Dunkel et al., 2003) where virtual student advisors are developed with novel concepts from Semantic Web (Berners-Lee et al., 2001) and Intelligent Agent (Wooldbridge et al. 1995) technology. The basic idea is to model the structure of our E-learning domain by means of ontologies, and to represent it by means of XML-based applied ontology languages such as DAML+OIL and OWL. Due to the standardization of these technologies, knowledge models can easily be shared und reused via the Internet. Software agents apply the knowledge represented in the ontologies during their intelligent decision making process. Again, the use of widespread inference engines, such as JESS (Friedman-Hill, 2000a), and of agent frameworks that comply with the FIPA standard (FIPA, 2003) as JADE (Bellifemine et al., 2002), which facilitates maintenance and fosters interoperability with our system. We claim that this is quite a promising approach because – although first concrete practical application scenarios with Semantic Web technologies have been published, e.g. (Horrocks et al. 2002) – E-learning systems that successfully combine these techniques in order to render support to users are still to come.

This paper reports on the lessons learnt from the construction of a real-world application in the E-learning domain that draws upon an effective integration of both, Semantic Web and Intelligent Agent technology. It is organized as follows: In the next section the employed knowledge representation techniques and the developed knowledge models are presented in detail. The third section shows how automated inference can be carried out on base of the knowledge models, and how agents can provide reasoning capabilities using this ontology. In the following section the software architecture of the agent system is outlined. Finally, the last section summarizes the most significant features of the project and provides a brief outlook to the direction of future research.

2 ONTOLOGIES

The key concept of a semantic advisory system for university students is the semantic modeling of the E-learning domain knowledge (e.g. university regulations, course descriptions, admission regulations) as well as an individual user model, which reflects the current situation of study (e.g.

passed exams, current courses). In these models the fundamental structures of the available domain knowledge as well as the basic facts (e.g. offered courses) are defined.

In our system, the structural part of this E-learning knowledge is modeled by means of ontologies which formally define domain entities and the relations among them. For this purpose, we use Semantic Web technology based on XML and RDF/ RDF Schema (WWW-RDF, 2003), respectively. Software agents use this information as the basis for their reasoning and, due to the standardization of these technologies, they are able to access distributed information sources from different universities. Thus the developed ontologies can serve as standardized and open interfaces for the interoperability of E-learning systems.

The ontology language DAML+OIL is an attempt to address the shortcomings of the RDF/ RDF Schema specification by incorporating additional features (DAML, 2003). DAML+OIL includes support for classification, property restriction and facilities for type definitions. In the last years, ontology languages have converged to the new W3C standard OWL (Web Ontology Language) (WWW-OWL, 2003), which is currently under development. In a first step, we have chosen the DAML+OIL language to model the E-learning knowledge. The main reason was the availability of different tools for the development of the knowledge base. As soon as possible, the knowledge base will be migrated to the new W3C standard language OWL.

Two different ontologies have been developed for our E-learning agents: on the one hand, an ontology describing the organization structure of a university department, on the other hand, an ontology holding the knowledge about a specific user of the system.

2.1 Department Ontology

The department ontology models the essential parts of the organizational structure of a university. The emphasis lies on the individual departments, the different roles of persons in a department and the courses.

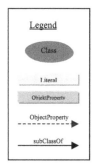
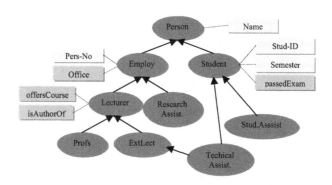

Figure 1: Department Ontology – person branch

It is modeled as follows. Every organizational unit is defined as a subclass of organization. For this super class a transitive property is defined, thus a hierarchy of instances can easily be modeled. In DAML this transitivity is modeled as follows:

```
<daml:TransitiveProperty
                  rdf:ID="subOrg">
   <rdfs:label>subOrg of</rdfs:label>
   <rdfs:domain
       rdf:resource="#Organization"/>
   <rdfs:range
       rdf:resource="#Organization"/>
</daml:TransitiveProperty>
```

The transitivity is used in the instance files to model a concrete hierarchy. For example, a student project is a sub-organization of a department and the computer science department is a sub-organization of the university FH Hannover.

```
<fbi:department rdf:ID="CS">
   <fbi:subOrg>
      <fbi:FH rdf:about="#FHHannover"/>
   </fbi:subOrg>
</fbi:department>
<fbi:project rdf:ID="Project1">
   <fbi:subOrg>
      <fbi:department
              rdf:about="#CS"/>
   </fbi:subOrg>
</fbi:project>
```

All further parts of the ontology belong to an organization. This is modeled by the property `<daml:ObjectProperty rdf:ID="isPartOf"/>`, which is restricted to a concrete subclass of organization.

The part of the ontology that models a person is shown in figure 1. The semantic of inheritance in this taxonomy is slightly different compared to object-oriented programming. In object-oriented programming it expresses a specialization of an "is-a"-relation, while in the context of ontologies, it serves mainly as a categorization of knowledge.

For the sake of clarity, the graphical representation does not show all information of the relations. In particular, is not shown which class or property of another branch of the ontology is referred to. One example is the property `offersCourse` of the class `Lecturer`. In the XML notation it is defined as follows:

```
<daml:ObjectProperty
                 rdf:ID="offersCourse">
   <rdfs:label> offers course
   </rdfs:label>
   <rdfs:domain
           rdf:resource="#Lecturer"/>
   <rdfs:range
     rdf:resource="#Course"/>
   <daml:minCardinality>1
   </daml:minCardinality>
</daml:ObjectProperty>
```

A lecturer teaches one or more courses and it is possible to navigate from a lecturer to a specific

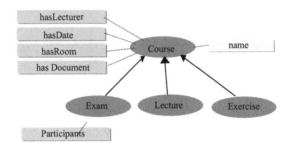

Figure 2: Department Ontology – course branch

course. In the course branch of the ontology one can find a property hasLecturer with a similar semantics with inverse direction of navigation. This can be defined as an inverse property in DAML.

```
<daml:ObjectProperty
              rdf:ID="hasLecturer">
  <daml:label>is offered by
  </daml:label>
  <daml:inverseOf
rdf:resource="#offersCourse"/>
</daml:ObjectProperty>
```

Figure 2 displays the course branch of the E-learning ontology. Not visualized by the graphical notation are further characteristics of subclasses. For example a course is a disjunctive union of its subclasses. In DAML this is modeled as follows.

```
<daml:Class
      rdf:about="#Course">
  <daml:disjointUnionOf rdf:parseType=
   "http://www.daml.org/2001/
            03/daml+oil#collection">
    <daml:Class rdf:about="#Lecture"/>
    <daml:Class rdf:about="#Exercise"/>
    <daml:Class rdf:about="#Exam"/>
  </daml:disjointUnionOf>
</daml:Class>
```

This construct ensures that a course is either a lecture, an exercise or an examination.

2.2 User Ontology

The user ontology serves as the knowledge model of a specific user, e.g. a student or a faculty member. The core class of the ontology is User. A user is a

person with respect to the department ontology. This is modeled by the object property sameClassAs, which is the DAML element to model inter-ontological equivalence.

```
<daml:Class rdf:about="#User">
  <daml:sameClassAs rdf:resource=
    "http://localhost:8080/Agents/
               FB_Onto.daml#Person"/>
</daml:Class>
```

The additional properties model all relevant data of a person, e.g. login name, student ID, current semester, passed/failed courses, last login date, skills etc.

3 AGENTS AND INFERENCE

The semantic E-learning agents should act like a human advisor according to the knowledge modeled in the ontology. This is achieved by using a rule-based inference engine to carry out the automated inferences entailed by the semantics of DAML.

3.1 Inference

To provide the semantic E-learning agents with reasoning capabilities, the rule-based Expert System Shell JESS (Java Expert System Shell) (Friedmann-Hill, 2000] is employed. JESS was initially developed as a Java version of CLIPS (C Language Integrated Productions System) and provides a convenient way to integrate reasoning capabilities into Java programs. With the JESS language complex rules, facts and queries can be specified.

3.2 Ontology Reasoning

To make use of the knowledge modeled in the ontology, the DAML semantics must be mapped into facts and rules of a production system, like JESS.

Because JESS does not provide any interface to import a DAML ontology in its knowledge base, we choose DAMLJessKB (Kopena et al., 2003), a reasoning tool for DAML that uses JESS as inference engine. In some more detail DAMLJessKB processes the following steps.

First DAMLJessKB loads and parses RDF documents using the RDF-Parser ARP of the Jena toolkit (Hewlett Packard Labs, 2003). ARP generates RDF triples. DAMLJessKB reorders the triples from subject-predicate-object form into predicate-subject-object form. Each RDF triple represents an unordered fact in JESS.

To assert triples in JESS minor transformations are necessary. DAMLJessKB translates URIs (Uniform Resource Identifiers) into JESS symbols by removing invalid characters (e.g. ~), and inserts the dummy predicate `PropertyValue` in front of each triple. The following example shows a generated fact for JESS, which means, that `Professor` is a subclass of `Lecturer`.

```
(PropertyValue
    http://www.w3.org/2000/01/rdf-
                schema#subClassOf
        file:///C:/FB_Onto.daml#Professor
        file:///C:/FB_Onto.daml#Lecturer )
```

Because in our DAML ontology `Lecturer` is defined as a subclass of `Person`, it follows that `Professor` is also a subclass of `Person`.

To support reasoning, DAMLJessKB includes some built-in rules of the DAML semantics, which are asserted into JESS, e.g. that an instance of a subclass is also an instance of the super class:

```
(defrule subclassInstances
    (PropertyValue daml:subClassOf
                    ?child ?parent)
    (PropertyValue rdf:type
                    ?instance ?child)
    =>
    (assert
    (PropertyValue rdf:type
                ?instance ?parent)
    )
)
```

The semantics of a JESS rule is similar to an if-then-statement in a programming language. Whenever the `if` part (the left-hand-side) which consists of several patterns is satisfied, the rule is executed, i.e. in our example a new fact is asserted into JESS. Details about the JESS language can be found in (Friedman-Hill, 2000).

Beside the DAML rules, which are directly supplied by DAMLJessKB, it is necessary to develop own domain-specific rules to model the complete expert knowledge. These rules make it possible to cope with complex queries related to a domain.

First, all facts are produced; then, the DAML rules are added; and finally the domain-specific rules are asserted into JESS. The reasoning process is performed by JESS applying all rules to deduce new facts which are successively added to the knowledge base.

DAMLJessKB can be considered as an interface to JESS, which is capable of translating DAML documents in accordance with their formal semantics. We are aware of several other tools with similar functionality, for example DAML API (DAML API, 2003), or the SWI Prolog distribution (SWI-Prolog 2003), which includes a package to parse RDF and assert as Prolog facts, but none of them fully meet the integration requirements of our E-learning system

3.3 Agent Access to the Knowledge Base

In order to cope with their specific tasks, semantic E-learning agents can pose queries to access the JESS knowledge base. These queries are special rules with no right-hand sides. The results of a query are those facts, which satisfy all patterns. For example, if a personal agent for a lecturer `tom` is interested in all courses he has to give, it can use the query:

```
(defquery getCourses
    "find IDs of all my courses"
    (declare (variables ?lecturerID)
        (PropertyValue lecture:givesCourse
            ?lectureID ?course)
    )
```

where `lecturerID` is the identifier of the lecturer, which serves as parameter of the query, and `?course` is an internal variable. All elements in a query must be fully qualified with their namespace, as they are used in the knowledge base. Executing the query yields all facts that satisfy all patterns specified in the query. E.g. a fact that fits the query could be:

```
(PropertyValue
    file://C:/FB_User.daml#givesCourse
    file://C:/FB_User.daml#tom
    file://C:/FB_Onto.daml#Math1)
```

In this case the lecturer `tom` gives the `Math1` course. The following example shows a more complex query that yields all documents of a course that are more recent than a certain time. It has two parameters: the time `mydate` and the identifier of a course, e.g. `file://C:/FB_Onto.daml#Math1`.

```
(defquery getNewerDocs
    (declare (variables ?mydate ?course))
        (PropertyValue rdf:type
                    ?course fb:course)
        (PropertyValue fb:hasDocument
                    ?course ?doc)
        (PropertyValue fb:changeDate
                    ?doc ?doc_modified)
        (PropertyValue date:longDate
                    ?doc_modified? long_date)
        (PropertyValue rdf:value
                    ?long_date
        ?doc_date&:(>= ?doc_date ?mydate))
)
```

The last pattern contains the condition that the last time the document was modified is greater than mydate.

4 JADE-AGENTS

In the previous sections we have modeled the knowledge of the E-learning system in two different ontologies: the department and the user ontology. The two knowledge bases are related to different domain concepts: to a department advisor and to a specific user. A human advisor and a human user communicate and exchange information to find a solution for an individual problem.

To implement a software system reflecting this situation we chose agent technology. Software agents provide a direct way to implement conversations or negotiations. The FIPA (Foundation of Intelligent Physical Agents)

organization (FIPA, 2003) has defined several standards for agent communication, e.g. ACL (Agent Communication Language). Agent technology provides natural means of communication and information exchange, which is on a high abstraction level and independent of certain technologies, e.g. protocols or inter-process communication mechanisms.

The semantic E-learning agents are developed with JADE (Java Agent Development Framework) (Bellifemine et al., 2002), which complies with the FIPA standards. JADE is completely written in Java and includes two main components: a FIPA-compliant agent platform and a framework to develop Java agents.

4.1 Agent Structure

Figure 3 outlines the structure of the E-Learning system with two different types of agents: a user and a department agent.

User Agent
The user agent is implemented in a class `UserAgent` and contains the user ontology with all relevant information about personal data, courses, skills, etc. When the user agent is started, it reads in the user ontology with its personal data using DAMLJessKB. Then the user agent-specific rules and queries are loaded and asserted in JESS.

```
void setUP(){
    damljesskb = new DAMLJessKB();
    damljesskb.loadDAMLResource(
                    userOntology);
    ...
    loadRules(userRules);
    ...
```

Corresponding to each JESS query the agent includes a dedicated method like `getCourses()`, which execute the query via DAMLJessKB, and receives an iterator object containing the query result.

```
String[] getCourses(){
    ...
    Iterator e = damljesskb.query (
        "getCourses", new String[] {""});
```

Department Agent
The department agent has all knowledge about the department, e.g. the curriculum and the examination regulations, which are modeled in its own DAML

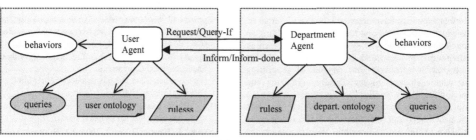

Figure 3: Agent structure

ontology. The corresponding class `Department-Agent` has a similar structure as `UserAgent`: In its `setup()`-Method DAMLJessKB is used to load the department ontology, specific rules and the necessary Jess queries. Each query can be executed in a corresponding agent method. One example is `getNewerDocs()`, which yields all documents related to a course which are newer than a specified date.

4.2 Agent Behavior and Communication

An agent must be able to execute several parallel tasks in response to different external events. In JADE all agent tasks are modeled as objects of the `Behavior` subclass, which determine the reactions of an agent: e.g. when it receives a message, and how it reacts on requests from another agent.

The JADE-method `addBehavior()` adds a behavior to the task queue of a specific agent. Behaviors a registered in an agent's `setup()`-method or on response to an user event.

In a round-robin policy a scheduler executes the `action()`-method of each behavior in the task queue. If the `action()`-method is finished, the `done()`-method is invoked. If it returns `true`, the task is removed from the event queue. To model cyclic tasks `done()` returns always `false`. Details about behaviors can be found in (Bellifemine et al., 2002).

For example, the following behaviors are defined in the E-learning system.

The user and the department agent use the `RegisterAtDF` behavior, which registers an agent with its name and type at the agent platform.

The user agent uses the `UA_SearchDepartment-Agent`-behavior to ask the name service of the platform, the Directory Facilitator (DF) for all department agents, and to establish a connection to them.

The `UA_SendRequest`-behavior requests information from the department agent. This behavior object is created by an event on the agent GUI. According to a parameter `content` (e.g. `SEND_DOCUMENTS`) the user agent collects the necessary request parameters, e.g. the courses of a user, and sends them via an ACL message to the department agent. Furthermore a command string (here: DOCUMENTS) is set to specify the request.

```
void action() {
    ...
    if(content== SEND_DOCUMENTS){
        ...
        parameters.setCourses(
            this.getCourses());
        ...
        msg.setContentObject(parameters);
        msg.setLanguage(DOCUMENTS);
        ...
    }
    msg.addReceiver(agent);
    myAgent.send(msg);
```

The `UA_ReceiveRequests`-behavior waits in an infinite loop for messages from a department agent. If a message arrives it is analyzed and the results are sent to the agent's GUI.

The department agent uses the `DA_SearchUser-Agent`-behavior to get all user agents, and to establish a connection to them.

The `DA_ReceiveRequest`-behavior analyzes arriving messages from user agents. It extracts the command string and the parameters of the message, to execute the specified query. Then the query results are packed into a message and returned to the corresponding user agent.

5 CONCLUSION

In this paper, we have described the use of Semantic Web languages and agent technology for building an intelligent advisory system for E-learning environments. Our goal is to create and deploy semantic E-learning agents capable of supporting university students in successfully organizing and performing their studies. In the project we have developed a software architecture, which integrates Semantic Web and Intelligent Agent technologies.

Due to the use of Semantic Web languages the developed knowledge models can easily be used in distributed systems and shared among software agents via the Internet.

The major difficulty encountered was the integration of the different concepts – on the one hand the knowledge base written in RDF and DAML+OIL, on the other hand the inference engine JESS and the agent environment JADE. Further problems emerged from the unsatisfactory tool support for developing the ontology and the concrete instances of the ontology. However, after the mentioned problems were solved we could implement a prototype system, where the agents were able to reason upon the knowledge base in the desired manner. Actually the migration of our system to the upcoming W3C standard language OWL is under work.

REFERENCES

Berners-Lee, T., Hendler, J., Lassila, O., 2001. The Semantic Web. Scientific American.

Bellifemine, F, Giovanni, C., Trucco, T., Rimassa, G., 2002, JADE Programmers's Guide, http://sharon.cs-elt.it/projects/jade/, retrieved October, 2003.

Dunkel, J. Holitschke, A., Software Architecture (In German), 2003. Springer Verlag.

Bruns, R., Dunkel, J., von Helden, J., 2003. Secure Smart Card-Based Access To An eLearning Portal. In ICEIS'03, 5th International Conference on Enterprise Information Systems. ICEIS Press.

CCTT - Center for Curriculum, Transfer and Technology, 2002.http://www.edutools.info/course/compare/all.jsp, retrieved October, 2003.

Cuena J., Ossowski S., 1999. Distributed Models for Decision Support. In: Weiß (ed.): Multi-Agent Systems — A Modern Approach to DAI. MIT Press, 459–504.

DAML-The DARPA Agent Markup Language Homepage: http://www.daml.org, retrieved October 10, 2003.

DAML API, 2003. http://codip.grci.com/Tools/Components.html, retrieved October, 2003.

Friedman-Hill, E., 2000a. JESS, The rule engine for the Java platform,. http://herzberg.ca.sandia.gov/jess/ retrieved October, 2003.

Friedman-Hill, E., 2000b, Jess. The Rete Algorithm, Sandia National Laboratories, http://herzberg.ca.sandia.gov/jess/docs/52/rete.html, retrieved October, 2003.

FIPA - Foundation of Intelligent Physical Agents, 2003. www.fipa.org, retrieved October, 2003.

Horrocks, I., Hendler, J. (eds.), 2002. The Semantic Web, First International Semantic Web Conference, Sardinia, Italy, Springer LNCS 2342.

Hewlett Packard Labs: Jena Semantic Web Toolkit, 2003. http://www.hpl.hp.vom/semweb, retrieved October, 2003.

Kopena, J. Regli, W., 2003, DAMLJessKB: A Tool for reasoning with the Semantic Web. IEEE Intelligent Systems, 18(3).

Ossowski, S., Hernández, J., Iglesias, C.A.; Fernández, A., 2002. Engineering Agent Systems for Decision Support. In: Engineering Societies in an Agent World III (Petta, Tolksdorf & Zambonelli, eds.), Springer-Verlag.

Ossowski, S., Omicini, A., 2002. Coordination Knowledge Engineering. Knowledge Engineering Review 17(4), Cambridge University Press.

SWI-Prolog, 2003. http://www.swi-prolog.org, retrieved October, 2003.

WWW – The World Wide Web Consortium, 2003a. RDF Primer – W3C Working Draft 05 September 2003: http://www.w3.org/TR/2002/WD-rdf-primer-20020319/, retrieved October 10, 2003.

WWW – The World Wide Web Consortium, 2003b. OWL (Web Ontology Language): http://www.w3.org/TR/-owl-ref/ , retrieved October 10, 2003.

Wooldridge, M.; Jennings, N., 1995. Intelligent Agents - Theory and Practice. Knowledge Engineering Review 10 (2), pp. 115–152.

SEAMLESS COMMUNICATION AND ACCESS TO INFORMATION FOR MOBILE USERS IN A WIRELESS ENVIRONMENT

Golha Sharifi, Julita Vassileva and Ralph Deters

University of Saskatchewan, Computer Science Department,
57 Campus Drive, Saskatoon, Saskatchewan S7N 5A9, Canada Phone:+1 306 966-4886,Fax:+1 306 966-4884
Email: {gos787, jiv, ralph}@cs.usask.ca

Keywords: Mobile Devices, Agents

Abstract: Providing mobile workers with mobile devices such as a Compaq iPaq with a CDPD card can support them in retrieving information from centralized information systems. More specifically, mobile devices can enable mobile users to make notifications for schedule changes and add new data into the information system. In addition these devices can facilitate group communication anytime and anywhere. This paper presents different ways of providing non-critical information in a timely fashion for nomadic users of mobile devices using a wireless network. A distributed application prototype to support nomadic users is proposed, and a simulated environment is used to evaluate the prototype. Since solutions for seamless access are highly domain specific, the study involves homecare workers at Saskatoon District Health (SDH). By keeping track of the users' current context (time, location etc.) and a user task model, it is possible to predict the information needs of mobile users and to provide context dependent adaptation of both the content and the functionality. Moreover, to avoid interrupts in the user's interaction with the main information sources, methods for mobile transactions management using agent-based smart proxies that buffer, delay or pre-fetch information/data are introduced.

1 INTRODUCTION

The development of wireless technology and the commercial success of small screen appliances, especially cellular phones and Personal Digital Assistants (PDAs) have advanced the development of mobile and ubiquitous computing (Weiser, 1991). Mobile and ubiquitous computing allows nomadic users to remain "connected" without depending on a wired infrastructure.

Nomadic workers who use mobile and small screen devices often need access to existing information services to enable them to browse multimedia information anytime and anywhere with ease. Nomadic workers in specific domains who might require these services include healthcare, emergency services, sales, and education. However, a major problem for the nomadic user using a thin client is the varying quality of the connection. Though connections remain fairly stable and good in areas close to network stations, for instance, Cellular Digital Packet Data (CDPD) towers, it is not uncommon to have zones of low connectivity or even no connection due to physical structures, for example, high concrete buildings blocking the signals.

We have investigated different ways of enabling seamless access of non-critical information for nomadic users. In this paper we focus on the needs of homecare workers of the Saskatoon District Health (SDH). The rest of the paper is organized as follows: in the next section the domain for this study and the current problems faced by mobile users are introduced; next, the general approach to solving these problems is described, which is explained in more detail in the third, fourth and fifth sections; the sixth section outlines an evaluation procedure; a comparison with other work is presented in the seventh section; the final section concludes the paper.

2 RESEARCH DOMAIN

The SDH was chosen as a result of an ongoing collaboration between Sasktel, TR-Labs and the University of Saskatchewan. Currently, the focus of this research is on the use of resource rich devices,

245

I. Seruca et al. (eds.), Enterprise Information Systems VI, 245–252.

like the Compaq iPaq and the CDPD network to support homecare workers in SDH.

Our research focuses on the problems of nomadic homecare workers in SDH. In SDH each patient has a team of homecare workers assigned to him or her, which consists of nurses, physiotherapists, home health aides, social workers, and dieticians responsible for looking after the patient. Each team meets on a periodic basis to discuss and coordinate necessary treatment for an individual patient. Tasks and duties are divided among the homecare workers based on skills and available time slots. The relation between patients and homecare workers can be described as M:N.

Though each of the homecare team members has different tasks and responsibilities, they all have one task in common: treatment of a patient. Homecare workers visit their patients in their homes. The offices of the homecare workers are usually scattered throughout different buildings and maintain separate scheduling and information systems. To date there has been no centralized information system for their use, which limits their ability to share and exchange information regarding schedules and patients' medical records.

Homecare workers provide health care services in different district areas in SDH. The wireless network's bandwidth they use is low (< 1 megabits per second (Mbps)) and varies significantly from one area to another. Currently, Saskatoon mobile homecare workers do not have access to patients' information outside the office, i.e. there is no available remote access to data files, such as health records and daily schedules.

A preliminary study was conducted on the usability of the electronic health records system for homecare at the SDH (Pinelle and Gutwin, 2001). The study describes the way that groups of homecare workers care for a patient and identifies the existing problems. Results from this study suggest that there are several obstacles for communication between the members of a group, which have led to difficulties in making changes in the treatment of patients, coordination among homecare workers, and the scheduling of patient visits. These difficulties are also observed in accessing information while the groups of homecare workers are mobile. In order to address these problems two approaches are proposed: increasing awareness and supporting communication.

Following the recommendations given (Pinelle and Gutwin, 2001), we would like to create a system that supports the access to information and the communication between homecare workers. Because of data-security and safety reasons, we decided not to focus on core health care data but on ways to improve the availability of non-critical information,

such as scheduling information and personal patient data, e.g., address and phone number. Access to the patient medical record data requires, according to the general regulation, permission from the patients, which is hard to obtain.

In SDH, homecare workers work in a variety of contexts, such as in the office, on the road, and at the patient's home. When an office scheduler or a homecare worker makes a schedule, she must have knowledge of the other team members' schedules in order to avoid conflicts in visiting the same patient. However, since there is no access to a centralized scheduling system, it is difficult to coordinate schedule changes and take into account new data regarding the patient. For instance, if a homecare worker visits a patient and notices that the patient's condition has worsened, ideally, s/he would immediately enter this information into the patient's record so that the other team members of the group can access the information and perhaps revise their schedules. However, this is not possible due to absence of centralized data storage. We classify the problems encountered by the homecare workers in two categories. The first category has to do with lack of efficient communication between homecare workers, and the second is related to the inefficient system of accessing and updating information.

Providing homecare personnel with mobile devices e.g. iPaq and access to the wireless network based on CDPD will allow them to retrieve information, receive and send notification of schedule changes, update the data/information system and communicate with other workers. Mobile devices come in varieties of types and capabilities. For instance, small screen computing devices differ in their features and abilities compared to desktop computers. Their most notable limitations are their smaller screen size, less powerful processors, less main memory and limited bandwidth because of the wireless network. To ensure scalability, performance, and speed, it is necessary to develop tools and techniques to compensate for these limitations.

In this paper we introduce tools and techniques that enable content and presentation adaptation to improve the access of workers to information/data. In particular, we have introduced the use of proxies that create the illusion of a seamless connection. Moreover, the adaptation is based on user, task, and context models. Further, to ensure that the users have the illusion of seamless access, intelligent agent-based (Jennings et al., 1998) proxies are used, which can delay write operations, pre-fetch data and cache data, as well as use the task, context, and user models to decide when and how to cache, pre-fetch or delay.

3 GENERAL APPROACH

In order to address these problems, we propose combining techniques from agent technologies, distributed database transaction management, and user and task modeling. One of the goals is to ensure seamless access to the information despite the frequent interruptions in the connection caused by the mobility of the homecare workers and the unequal coverage of the area. The interface has to be designed for small wireless devices allowing homecare workers to conveniently perform typical operations, including the following:
- Retrieving information from the system (downloading files)
- Entering new data into the health records (uploading/updating files)
- Accessing the schedule (reading schedules and making appointments)
- Communicating with other members of the home care division (sending/receiving messages)
It has been noted (Vassileva, 1996) that healthcare and homecare workers have typical tasks, which have standard information needs, e.g., the task of visiting a patient requires information regarding the patient's address. Therefore, it is possible to (1) predict what kind of information will be needed by the homecare worker using her schedule and (2) prefetch and/or adapt information appropriate for the task and (3) present it according to the user's preferences and the limitations of the device on which the information is going to be viewed. More specifically, the techniques proposed to achieve the goals stated in the previous section are listed below:
The use of agents: we use agents to give the users the impression of seamless connection. Agents hide the changes in the network bandwidth from the user by providing the needed information for the users before their information needs arise by the means of task, user, and context modeling and adaptation techniques.
The identification of read/write operations: To ensure data consistency, we identified two different kinds of read and write operations in the SDH domain. The first kind is reading or writing to data types needing a lock which prevents users from accessing and/or modifying the data simultaneously (e.g. a schedule); the second kind is information that will not be updated simultaneously and therefore does not require a lock (e.g. a patient's record).
Providing only necessary functionalities: When the context (time, location) and the current task of the user is known, the interface can provide only the functionalities needed by the user to perform the task in the specific context. In this way, the interface can be adapted to the constraint of the small device.

4 USER AND TASK MODELING

The combination of techniques described in the previous section is integrated in an application architecture called "Mobi-Timar" (Farsi for "mobile caregiver"), which has an interface for homecare workers, an agent middleware and a server side. The following assumptions are made to help us undertake the design:
- There is a centralized schedule for all homecare workers.
- The mobile devices are resource-rich, e.g., have at least 64 megabytes (MB) RAM, a wireless connection with a bandwidth of at least 19.2 kilobits per second (kbps), and the ability to run third party applications.
- Patient and schedule-related data is stored in a centralized repository.
- The wireless network coverage in the area has varying but known bandwidth and latency.
The next sections describe the main components of the Mobi-Timar architecture.

4.1 User Model

In the SDH, the homecare workers can be classified based on their profession as nurses, physiotherapists, social workers, home aide workers and dieticians. Therefore, the user models are based on the stereotype approach, as there are stereotypes corresponding to the professions of the homecare workers. There is a general stereotype for "homecare workers" which has subclass stereotypes corresponding to the professions. The stereotype user model is retrieved and initialized when the user logs in for the first time (she has to enter her profession). The stereotype user model does not change over time i.e., it is a long-term model, since the profession of a homecare worker remains the same. The individual user models are instances of the stereotype user classes containing specific individual preferences that may change over time, for example, "personal info", "Chief" or "expert" in Figure 2.
Figure 1 shows an example of the stereotype hierarchy. There are two different relations in this hierarchy. One relation is the inheritance between a subclass stereotype and the general stereotype, e.g., all nurses are homecare workers (see Figure 1). The other relationship that is shown in the stereotype hierarchy is the relation between a type of profession referred to as "user class" and its task hierarchies, e.g. the user class "Nurse" has a nurse task hierarchy.

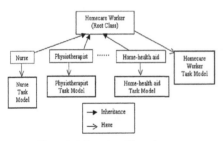

Figure 1: A Stereotype Hierarchy

The individual user model extends the stereotype of the particular user class with the personal information, preferences, rank and the experience of the user. Figure 2 shows an example of an individual user model and illustrates the relationship between this model and the stereotype user model.

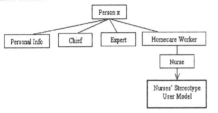

Figure 2: An Example of Individual User Model

4.2 Task Model

In SDH each class of users has to perform standardized tasks. Each task in this domain needs specific types of information to be successfully performed, and the information needs of tasks typically do not vary over time. The task hierarchies for each profession contain all the tasks that can be performed by that class of users. Figure 3 shows the task hierarchy for the user class "Nurse."

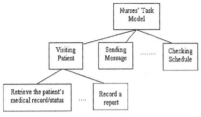

Figure 3: The Task Hierarchy of Nurses Stereotype Class

A detailed view of one task from this task model is shown in Figure 4. The task model is designed hierarchically, and each task is decomposed to subtasks (see Figures 3 and 4). Some of the subtasks are restricted to certain user classes. For the task "Visiting patient" in Figure 4, if the user is a nurse, he needs to perform the following three tasks sequentially:
- Retrieve the patient's medical record
- Retrieve the patient's personal information
- Record the report.

However, if the user is a home-health aide, she will perform only the latter two subtasks. The reason for having task hierarchies defined separately from user task hierarchies is that there can be more than one class of users performing this task. Depending on the user class, different subtasks and different information may be relevant. For example, when a nurse and physiotherapist perform the same task, i.e. retrieving a patient's record, the information that is provided to them is different. Again, depending on the users' profession, access rights to different information are given in each task. For example, in Figure 4, if the user is in the nurse class, he has the right to access the patient's medical record while other classes of users (e.g. social aide workers) do not have access to that information. The lower levels of the task model contain the detailed decompositions for each task and the information needed to perform each subtask. The description of each subtask includes information, such as the users' class and context in which the task can be performed.

As can be seen from Figure 4, each successive level in the task model differentiates subtasks based on either user type or context parameters. At the second level in Figure 4, the task hierarchy is user profession-specific because each task can be carried out differently and can provide different information based on the user's class. In the second level task decomposition takes place. At the third level in Figure 4, the subtasks are organized based on network bandwidth because different available bandwidth allows the task to be carried out differently. Depending on the current bandwidth

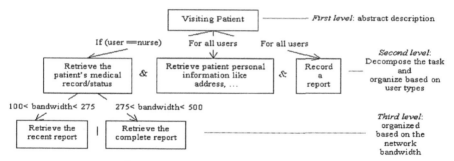

Figure 4: Task Hierarchy for Task "Visiting Patient"

availability, only one of the subtasks will be performed. The changes of task structures and the required information for tasks are regulated and can be changed only by the system administrator.

4.3 Schedule

The schedule is used to predict the task that a user will perform and the context (time, location), so the needed information can be pre-fetched according to the task model. Therefore, based on the schedule, which gives the time and location in which a task will be performed, the system uses the context model to predict the network bandwidth at a specific location.

4.4 Connectivity Model

The system's connectivity model contains a map of the network connectivity in the various known locations shown as an interval of available bandwidth for each location.

4.5 Library of Cases

Case-based reasoning (CBR) binds user model, task model and connectivity model together. It is possible to create a library of cases based on the task and the type of location of homecare workers. Figure 5 shows the way a case is constructed. In Figure 5, the *User description* represents the stereotype user model, *Task* represents the task model and *Connection interval* represents the connection model. The cases are indexed by task-ID (t4 in Figure 5) and the bandwidth necessary to achieve the task.

Case1: *User description:* nurse, physiotherapist
 Task: (t4) retrieve the patient's personal information
 Connection interval: [100,375]
 Result: load the address and the name of the patient

Figure 5: An Example of Case

The process of pre-fetching consists of predicting network connectivity using the connectivity model and the user's schedule (time, location and task) and pre-fetching/hoarding the needed information using the user's task model. Figure 6 shows this process of pre-fetching information. The current location of the user and the current time is used to find the next appointment from the user's schedule (step 1). Knowing the current location and the next location, the bandwidth is retrieved from the connectivity model (step2). When the task is known from the schedule, the necessary information for the completion of the task is retrieved from the task model (step 3). Having knowledge of the bandwidth and the task, the user model is checked for any specific preferences (step 4). These four steps represent the process of retrieving an appropriate case from the case library. The fifth step is to pre-fetch/hoard the necessary information. In Mobi-Timar if a user performs different tasks which are not included in her/his schedule, the system will not guarantee the availability of information in disconnected condition.

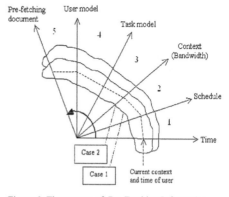

Figure 6: The process of Pre-Fetching Information

5 ADAPTATION

The proposed Mobi-Timar is based on client-server architecture in which the agents are the middleware. The client is a Mobile Device (MD) and the server runs on a desktop computer. The server side contains the adaptation mechanism, the library of cases, the schedule, the user model, the task model, the context model, the user agents and proxy agents. The server side is encoded in Java and uses the JADE [4] platform. A proxy agent and a user agent on the server side represent each client. The client side contains a proxy agent, user agent, an application agent and an individual user model. The client side is encoded in C#. The agents in C# and Java communicate through ACL messages. Figure 7 illustrates the communication architecture.

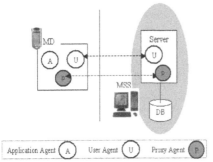

Figure 7: The Mobi-Timar Architecture

5.1 The Use of Agents

To give the users the impression of a seamless connection, agents are used. Agents hide changes in the network bandwidth from the user by automatically pre-fetching/hoarding the needed information from/to the server ahead of time (as shown in Figure 6).

5.2 The Identification of Read/Write Operations

To ensure that the read and write operations are transparent, we use two sets of agents (user agent and proxy agent) and two copies of data, one on the MD and the other on the server (data on the MD is a copy of the data on server). The user agent on the server side looks at any changes and updates on the server side. In the case of disconnection the user agent on the client and the server side will priorize the queue of tasks and messages that are waiting to be executed based on the user's preferences from the

user model. The proxy agent of a client on the server side plays the client role during disconnection mode, while the proxy agent on the MD plays the server role during disconnection mode. The proxy agent receives the messages from server/client, waits for the connection, and then forwards the messages to the client/server. The user agent performs automatic hoarding, and the proxy agent performs automatic reintegration. The needed data for the user is cached on the MD, and the primary copy of the data is stored on the server. If the client side is disconnected and the client is executing a write operation, client will continue with the task on MD. When the client is finished with the task on MD, the agents will wait for the connection and then execute the task on the server side and let the user know the result of the task. The status of the network bandwidth is also available for the user, so the user knows the accuracy of the data that she is using.

There are two different kinds of read and write operations, one that needs a lock and one that does not need a lock. When a user reads/writes to the schedule or the agent is pre-fetching/updating the schedule, the server side will lock the schedule to avoid any inconsistencies, such as the loss of information updates. If the client gets disconnected while reading the schedule, the schedule lock will be broken after a certain amount of time. If the client stays connected or only has a brief disconnection, the schedule stays locked until the client finishes the transaction. For agents/clients that are writing to the schedule, the schedule is locked and will not be updated until the transaction is committed. In case of an abort, the client on the MD will be notified.

Access to patient records does not require locking since information cannot be deleted or modified by homecare workers, who can only add more data. But adding the new information to the existing information cannot change the old content due to SDH policy, which states that all transactions related to homecare workers and patients should be recorded and archived. This is illustrated in Figure 8. After visiting a Patient at time *t1*, the Physiotherapist adds information to the Patient's record using her mobile device in an area of poor connection. Some time later at time *t2* in an area of good connection, a Nurse adds information to the Patient's record. Her transaction is committed on the server side fairly quickly at time *t3*. Therefore, at a later time, *t4*, when the Physiotherapist's transaction is finally committed on the server side, the additions to the Patient's record will be ordered based on the time when each transaction was originally performed on the client's mobile device. For this reason the clocks of all mobile devices are synchronized with server's clock.

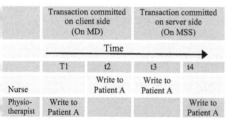

	Transaction committed on client side (On MD)		Transaction committed on server side (On MSS)	
	Time ⟶			
	T1	t2	t3	t4
Nurse		Write to Patient A	Write to Patient A	
Physio-therapist	Write to Patient A			Write to Patient A

Figure 8: An Example for Second Type of Read/Write

5.3 Providing Only Necessary Functionalities

The user agent can predict the next type of information access to be performed by the homecare worker using the task model (known from the user class), the connection model, the schedule and a library of cases. Based on the screen size limitation of mobile devices, the user agent provides only the suitable functionalities for the homecare worker's current access to information and not the full functionality of Mobi-Timar since it knows which operations are going to be performed. This allows a consistent way to design the user interface around specific user tasks.

6 EVALUATION

The evaluation of the Mobi-Timar architecture is done using a simulation environment for the location and available bandwidth. This simulation depicts a virtual world that provides the location and the network bandwidth. The movement of each user with her MD is represented with a moving avatar in the virtual world. Each user has a pre-assigned schedule, which instructs her to move to certain locations (visit patients) and perform certain tasks. The user moves her avatar in the simulated location and performs the tasks requiring access to the patient data and schedule on her MD.

Figure 9 illustrates one of the network coverage models for this simulation. Since it is important to test the ability of Mobi-Timar to adapt quickly to drastic changes in network coverage, different models are considered, which allows for a more realistic discontinuous pattern of coverage.

The simulation shows the movement of the user through different network areas, which allows testing the transparent read and write operations and the availability of data access regardless of the location and the network bandwidth. By testing these two aspects, we will be able to evaluate the functionality of Mobi-Timar.

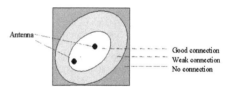

Figure 9: Different Network Coverage in the Simulation GUI

The evaluation of Mobi-Timar will be conducted by running experiments involving a centralized database containing information for four patients. Two graduate students will take the roles of a nurse and a physiotherapist. Each homecare worker will perform either a full-day or a half-day schedule, which includes all six types of operations: downloading files, updating and uploading files, sending messages, receiving messages, reading schedules, making or changing appointments. All these operations will be performed in two different conditions: connected and disconnected mode. This will allow us to evaluate the process of pre-fetching information based on the available bandwidth, accessing information during disconnection, reintegrating information and maintaining the consistency of data and user preferences on both client and server side.

The evaluation procedure involves the following two steps:

- Analyzing log data drawn from running the Mobi-Timar in several different bandwidth simulation models. The log file contains the homecare workers and agents transactions plus all the information transferred between the clients' devices and the server with time stamp allowing the computation of the speed of task execution.
- Using interviews to perform a usability study based on the following criteria:
  - Ease of use
  - User satisfaction
  - Interface design and the availability of information and tasks

The evaluation process will enable us to determine the number of failures and successful read/write operations. It will also be possible to deduce how well the system performs when the design assumptions made earlier are valid. We will also be able to ascertain how transparent the read/write operations were by looking at the consistency of data on both client and server side and the numbers of failed and successful operations.

7 RELATED WORK

There is a great deal of research on adaptation of the application and web infrastructure for mobile devices. Most of this research, for example CRUMPET (Poslad et al., 2001a; Poslad et al., 2001b), MyCampus (Sadeh et al., 2002) and Hippie (Oppermann et al., 1999; Specht and Oppermann, 1999), focuses on content adaptation, information retrieval, interface adaptation and representation adaptation. Furthermore, the focus of most of this research is on adaptation based on the user type and the level of experience of the user. In contrast, Mobi-Timar adapts also based on context (e.g. current time, user task, and connection availability). Projects, such as Broad-Car (Console et al., 2002), propose adaptation based on the context of the user and use multimedia output, e.g. voice, video or text, for presenting the data to the user. In these studies, parameters used for adaptation are bandwidth, user type, task, screen size, output channels of the device, and the location. However, there are no write transactions performed in any of these systems, and synchronization and transaction management are not needed. Unlike previous approaches, as in CRUMPET, Hippie and MyCampus, our Mobi-Timar addresses the problem of disconnection. Agents are used to pre-fetch information relevant to the user task and context. This research doesn't focus on just-in-time retrieval; instead, it aims to support seamless access to information and modification in a timely fashion.

8 CONCLUSIONS

In this paper we described Mobi-Timar, an architecture for a mobile communication and information system for homecare workers, which uses a variety of techniques including user modeling, task modeling, case-based adaptation, multi-agent systems and mobile transaction management.

The result of this research is an application and a middleware for a mobile environment that can be used in other domains with similar characteristics, for example, supporting mobile technicians, salespeople, real estate agents, etc. The application ensures seamless access to data by using mobile transaction management performed by the user agent and the proxy agent. The user model, task model and context model allow the agents to select and pre-fetch relevant information needed for the user's next task and to create the illusion of seamless connection for the users even when the bandwidth is low or the user is disconnected.

ACKNOWLEDGEMENT

This research has been supported by TR-Labs.

REFERENCES

CDPD (Cellular Digital Packet Data), http://www2.picante.com:81/~gtaylor/cdpd.html
Compaq iPaq, http://athome.compaq.com/showroom/static/ipaq/handheld_jumppage.asp
Console, L., Gioria, S., Lombardi, I., Surano, V., Torre, I., 2002. Adaptation and Personalization on Board Cars: A Framework and Its Application to Tourist Services. In *2nd International Conference on Adaptive Hypermedia and Adaptive Web Based Systems, AH 2002*, 112-121.
JADE: http://sharon.cselt.it/projects/jade/
Jennings, N., Sycara, K. and Wooldridge, M., 1998. A RoadMap of Agent Research and Development. *Journal on Autonomous Agents and Multi-Agent Systems*, 1, 275-306.
Oppermann, R., Specht, M., Jaceniak, I., 1999. Hippie: A Nomadic Information System. *Gellersen. W. (Ed.): Proceedings of the First International Symposium Handheld and Ubiquitous Computing (HUC'99)*, Karlsruhe, September 27 - 29, 330 - 333.
Pinelle, D. and Gutwin, C., 2001. Collaboration Requirements for Home Care. *Research Report, University of Saskatchewan*, http://hci.usask.ca/publications/index.xml
Poslad S., Laamanen H., Malaka R., Nick A., Buckle P. and Zipf, A., 2001a. CRUMPET: Creation of User-friendly Mobile Services Personalised for Tourism. *Proceedings of: 3G 2001 - Second International Conference on 3G Mobile Communication Technologies*. London, UK, 26-29.
Poslad S., Charlton P. In Marik V., Stepankova O., 2001b. Standardizing agent interoperability: the FIPA approach. *Proceedings of the Multi-Agent Systems & Applications Conference, ACAI-01 (invited paper)*.
Sadeh, N., Chan, E., Shimazaki, Y., Van, 2002. MyCampus: An Agent-Based Environment for Context-Aware Mobile Services. *In AAMAS02 Workshop on Ubiquitous Agents on Embedded, Wearable, and Mobile Devices*, Bologna, Italy.
Specht, M., and Oppermann, R., 1999. User Modeling and Adaptivity in Nomadic Information Systems. *Proceedings of the 7. GI-Workshop Adaptivität und Benutzermodellierung in Interaktiven Softwaresystemen (ABIS99)*, Universität Magdeburg, September 27 - October 1, 325 -328.
Vassileva, J., 1996. A Task-Centered Approach for User Modeling in a Hypermedia Office Documentation System. *User Modeling and User Adapted Interaction*, 6, 2-3, 185-223.
Weiser, M., 1991. The computer for the twenty-first century. *Scientific American*, September, 94-100.

AGENT PROGRAMMING LANGUAGE WITH INCOMPLETE KNOWLEDGE - AGENTSPEAK(I)

Duc Vo and Aditya Ghose
Decision Systems Laboratory
School of Information Technology and Computer Science
University of Wollongong
NSW 2522, Australia
Email: {vdv01,aditya}@uow.edu.au

Keywords: Agent programming language, AgentSpeak, BDI agent, default theory, incomplete knowledge, replanning

Abstract: This paper proposes an agent programming language called AgentSpeak(I). This new language allows agent programs (1) to effectively perform while having incomplete knowledge of the environment, (2) to detect no-longer possible goals and re-plan these goals correspondingly, and (3) to behave reactively to changes of environment. Specifically, AgentSpeak(I) uses default theory as agent belief theory, agent always act with preferred default extension at current time point (i.e. preference may changes over time). A belief change operator for default theory is also provided to assist agent program to update its belief theory. Like other BDI agent programming languages, AgentSpeak(I) uses semantics of transitional system. It appears that the language is well suited for intelligent applications and high level control robots, which are required to perform in highly dynamic environment.

1 INTRODUCTION

In modelling rational agents, modelling agent's attitudes as *Belief, Desire, Intention* (BDI agent) has been the best known approach. This model was first introduced by a philosopher Michael Bratman (Bratman, 1987) in 1987 and 1988. There has been number of formalizations and implementations of BDI Agents such as (Rao, 1996; Rao and Georgeff, 1995; Rao and Georgeff, 1991; Hindriks et al., 1999; Riemsdijk et al., 2003; Dastani et al., 2003; Wooldridge, 2000). Belief, desire, intention attitudes of a rational agent represents the information that the agent has about the environment, the motivation of what it wants to do, and finally the plans that the agent intends to execute to achieve its desired goals. These mental attitudes are critical for achieving optimal performance when deliberation is subject to resource bounds (Bratman, 1987).

Although, researchers have tackled most issues of BDI agents from logical systems (Rao and Georgeff, 1991; Wobcke, 2002; Wooldridge, 2000) to logic programming (D'Inverno and Luck, 1998; Rao, 1996), the issue of acting with incomplete knowledge about the environment has not been addressed in BDI agent programming languages. Rational agent is desired to work in a highly dynamic environment, while having incomplete knowledge about the environment.

In literature, there has been much work to address the problem of incompleteness of belief theory such as (Reiter, 1980; Delgrande et al., 1994; Brewka and Eiter, 2000; Alferes et al., 1996; Meyer et al., 2001; Ghose and Goebel, 1998; MaynardReidII and Shoham, 1998; Alchourrón et al., 1985). Another problem normally faced in open-dynamic environment is to adapt with changes of environment both to react to changes and to adjust strategies to achieve previously adopted goals. Again, this problem has not been focused by available BDI agent programming languages.

In this paper, we propose a new agent programming language called AgentSpeak(I) which allows agent programs to effectively perform with incomplete knowledge about the environment, and to dynamicly adapt with changes of the environment but persistently commit to its goals.

This paper includes six sections. The next section describes an scenario of rescue robot where agent (RBot) needs to reason, act, and react with incomplete knowledge about its highly dynamic environment. This example will be use throughout the paper in the subsequent sections to demonstrate presented theory. Section three discusses definition, syntax, and properties of agent programs in AgentSpeak(I): agent belief theory; goals and triggers; plans; intention; and events. Section four defines operational semantics for

I. Seruca et al. (eds.), Enterprise Information Systems VI, 253–260.
© 2006 Springer. Printed in the Netherlands.

AgentSpeak(I). Section five compares AgentSpeak(I) with existing agent programming languages: AgentSpeak(L), 3APL, and ConGolog. Finally, conclusion and future research section will remark what has been done in the paper and proposes research directions from this work.

2 EXAMPLE

Let us consider a scenario of rescue robot (named RBot). RBot works in disaster site. RBot's duty is to rescue trapped person from a node to the safe node A. The condition of the site is dynamic and unsure. The only definite knowledge that RBot has about the area is the map. RBot can only travel from one node to another if the path between two nodes is clear. Because of the limitation of its sensor, RBot can only sense the conditions between its node and adjacent nodes.

RBot has knowledge of where its locate at, where there is a $trapped$ human, $path$ between nodes, if a node is on_fire, if it is $carry$ing a person, and finally its goal to $rescue$ trapped human. Basic actions of RBot are $move$ between node, $pick$ a person up, and $release$ a person. RBot can only move from one node to another node if there is a direct path between two nodes and this path is clear. RBot can only pick a person up if it is located at the node where the person is trapped. RBot can only release a carried person at node A. Table below defines predicate symbols for RBot.

$at(x)$: The robot is at node x
$clear(x, y)$: Path between nodes x and y is clear
$path(x, y)$: There is a path between nodes x and y
$trapped(p, x)$: There is a person p trapped at node x
$carry(p)$: The robot is carrying person p
$on\_fire(x)$: node x is on fire (i.e. danger for RBot)
$rescue(p, x)$: Goal to rescue person p at node x
$move(x, y)$: Move from node x to an adjacent node y on an available $path(x, y)$
$pick(p)$: Pick person p up
$release(p)$: Release carried person p

In such high-dynamic environment, to accomplish the rescuing task, RBot should be able to make default assumptions when reasoning during its execution, and RBot should also be able to adapt with changes of the environment by modifying its plans, intentions.

3 AGENT PROGRAMS

Agent belief theory

In this section, we introduce the agent belief theory. Agents usually have incomplete knowledge about the

world requiring a suitably expressive belief representation language. We take the usual non-monotonic reasoning stance insisting on the ability to represent *defaults* on a means for dealing with this incompleteness. In the rest of this paper we explore the consequences of using default logic (Reiter, 1980) as the belief representative language. However, most of our results would hold had some other non-monotonic reasoning formalism had been used instead.

We augment the belief representation language in AgentSpeak (L) with default rules. If p is a predicate symbol, $t_1, ..., t_n$ are terms, then an atom is of the form $p(t_1, ..., t_n)$ denoted $p(\vec{t})$ (e.g. $at(x)$, $rescue(p, x)$, $clear(A, B)$). If $b_1(\vec{t_1})$ and $b_2(\vec{t_2})$ are belief atoms, then $b_1(\vec{t_1}) \wedge b_2(\vec{t_2})$ and $\neg b_1(\vec{t_1})$ are beliefs. A set S of beliefs is said to be consistent iff S does not have both a belief b and its negation $\neg b$. A belief is called ground iff all terms in the belief are ground terms (e.g. $at(A)$, $trapped(P, F)$, $path(C, F) \wedge clear(C, F)$).

Let $\alpha(\vec{x})$, $\beta(\vec{x})$, and $\omega(\vec{x})$ be beliefs. A default is of the form $\frac{\alpha(\vec{x}):\beta(\vec{x})}{\omega(\vec{x})}$ where $\alpha(\vec{x})$ is called the *prerequisite*; $\beta(\vec{x})$ is called the *justification*; and $\omega(\vec{x})$ is called the *consequent* of the default (Reiter, 1980). Interpretation of a default depends on variants of default logics being used (note that several exist (Reiter, 1980; Delgrande et al., 1994; Brewka and Eiter, 2000; Giordano and Martelli, 1994) exploring different intuitions). Informally, a default is interpreted as follows: "If for some set of ground terms $\vec{c}$, $\alpha(\vec{c})$ is provable from what is known and $\beta(\vec{c})$ is consistent, then conclude by default that $\omega(\vec{c})$".

A *default theory* is a pair (W, D), where W is a consistent set of beliefs and D is a set of default rules. Initial default theory of RBot is presented in table 1.

Example 1 *Initial default theory* $\Delta_{RBot} = (W_{RBot}, D_{RBot})$ *of RBot*

$$W_{RBot} = \left\{ \begin{array}{ll} path(A, B), & path(B, C), \\ path(C, D), & path(C, E), \\ path(C, F) & path(D, F), \\ path(E, F), & at(x) \wedge at(y) \rightarrow \\ x = y \end{array} \right\}$$

$$D_{RBot} = \left\{ \begin{array}{ll} \frac{:at(A}{at(A)}, & \frac{:clear(A,B}{clear(A,B)}, \\ \frac{:\neg carry(p)}{\neg carry(p)}, & \frac{:trapped(P,F)}{trapped(P,F)}, \\ \frac{path(x,y):clear(x,y)}{clear(x,y)}, \\ \frac{:\neg trapped(p,y)}{\neg trapped(p,y)}, & \frac{:\neg path(x,y)}{\neg path(x,y)}, \\ \frac{:\neg clear(x,y)}{\neg clear(x,y)}, \end{array} \right\}$$

Much of out discussion is independent of the specific variant being used. We only require that at least an extension must exist. This is not generally true for Reiter's default logic (Reiter, 1980). However, if one restricts attention to semi- normal default theories, there is a guarantee that an extension will always

exist. We make this assumption here. i.e belief theories must necessarily only be semi-normal default theories.

Example 2 *With Reiter semantics, default extensions
of* Δ_{RBot} *would be*

$$E_{RBot1} \quad = \quad Cn(\{ \quad at(A), \quad path(A,B),$$
$$clear(A,B), \quad path(B,C), \quad path(C,F), \quad \neg carry(p),$$
$$trapped(P,F), \quad clear(B,C), \quad \neg clear(B,D),$$
$$\neg clear(D,F), clear(C,F),...\})'$$
$$E_{RBot2} \quad = \quad Cn(\{ \quad at(A), \quad path(A,B),$$
$$clear(A,B), \quad path(B,C), \quad path(C,F), \quad \neg carry(p),$$
$$trapped(P,F), \quad clear(B,D), \quad clear(D,F),$$
$$\neg clear(C,F),...\})$$
etc.

To operate, an agent program needs to commit with
one extension of its default theory. There is an extension selection function for agent to select most preferred extension from set of extensions of its default
theory for further execution. Let $S_{\mathcal{E}}$ be a extension
selection function, if $B = S_{\mathcal{E}}(\Delta)$, then (1) B is a default extension of Δ and (2) B is the most preferred
extension by the agent at the time where $S_{\mathcal{E}}$ is applied. In the rest of this paper, the *current agent belief
set* will be denoted by $B = S_{\mathcal{E}}(\Delta)$ given an agent
belief theory $\mathcal{B} = \langle \Delta, S_{\mathcal{E}} \rangle$.

Belief Change Operators
Belief change is a complicated issue. There have
been several well known work on belief change such
as (Alchourrón et al., 1985; Ghose et al., 1998; Meyer
et al., 2001; Darwiche and Pearl, 1997; Ghose and
Goebel, 1998). In this paper, we do not discuss this
issue in detail. However for the completeness of out
system, we adopt belief change framework of (Ghose
et al., 1998). We denote $\circ_g$ (respectively $-_g$) as
Ghose's revision (respectively contraction) operator.
When updating agent belief theory, we assumes
that (1) the belief to be revised must be a consistent
belief, (2) the belief to be revised must be consistent
with the set of the base facts of belief theory, (3) the
belief to be contracted must not be a tautology and (4)
the belief to be contracted must not be entailed by the
base facts.

Goals, Triggers, Plans and Intentions
We follow the original definitions in (Rao, 1996) to
define goals and triggering events. Two types of goals
are of interest: *achievement goals* and *test goals*. An
achievement goal, denoted $!g(\vec{t})$, indicates an agent's
desire to achieve a state of affairs in which $g(\vec{t})$ is true.
A test goal, denoted $?g(\vec{t})$, indicates an agent's desire
to determine if $g(\vec{t})$ is true relative to its current beliefs. Test goals are typically used to identify unifiers
that make the test goal true, which are then used to
instantiate the rest of the plan. If $b(\vec{t})$ is a belief and
$!g(\vec{t})$ is an achievement goal, then $+b(\vec{t})$ (add a belief $b(\vec{t})$), $-b(\vec{t})$ (remove a belief $b(\vec{t})$), $+!g(\vec{t})$ (add

an achievement goal $!g(\vec{t})$), and $-!g(\vec{t})$ (remove the
achievement goal $g(\vec{t})$) are *triggering events*.

An agent program includes a *plan library*. The
original AgentSpeak (Rao, 1996) definition views a
plan as a triple consisting of a *trigger*, a *context* (a
set of pre-conditions that must be entailed by the current set of beliefs) and a *body* (consisting of a sequence of atomic actions and sub-goals). We extend
this notion to distinguish between an *invocation context* (the pre-conditions that must hold at the time that
the plan in invoked) and an *invariant context* (conditions that must hold both at the time of plan invocation
and at the invocation of every plan to achieve sub-
goals in the body of the plan and their sub-goals). We
view both kinds of contexts to involve both *hard pre-
conditions* (sentences that must be true relative to the
current set of beliefs) and *soft pre- conditions* (sentences which must be consistent with the current set
of beliefs). Soft pre-conditions are akin to *assumptions, justifications* in default rules (Reiter, 1980) or
constraints in hypothetical reasoning systems (Poole,
1988).

Definition 1 *A plan is a 4-tuple* $\langle \tau, \chi, \chi^*, \pi \rangle$ *where*
τ *is a trigger,* χ *is the invocation context,* χ^* *is
the invariant context and* π *is the body of the plan.
Both* χ *and* χ^* *are pairs of the form* (β, α) *where*
β *denotes the set of hard pre-conditions while* α *denotes the set of soft pre-conditions. A plan* p *is
written as* $\langle \tau, \chi, \chi^*, \pi \rangle$ *where* $\chi = (\beta, \alpha)$ *(also referred to as* $InvocationContext(p)$*),* $\chi^* = (\beta^*, \alpha^*)$
(also referred to as $InvariantContext(p)$*),* $\pi =<
h_1, \ldots, h_n >$ *(also referred to as* $Body(p)$*) and each
h_i is either an atomic action or a goal. We will also
use* $Trigger(p)$ *to refer to the trigger* τ *of plan* p.

Example 3 *RBot's plan library:*
$$p_1 = \quad \langle +!at(y),(\{at(x)\},\{\emptyset\}),$$
$$(\{\emptyset\},\{clear(x,y)\}), \langle move(x,y)\rangle\rangle$$
$$p_2 = \quad \langle +!at(y),(\{\neg at(x),path(x,y)\},\{\emptyset\}),$$
$$(\{\emptyset\},\{clear(x,y)\}),$$
$$\langle !at(x),?clear(x,y),move(x,y)\rangle\rangle$$
$$p_3 = \quad \langle +!rescue(p,x),(\{\emptyset\},\{\emptyset\}),$$
$$(\{\emptyset\},\{trapped(p,x) \quad \lor \quad carry(p)\}),$$
$$\langle !at(x),pick(p),!at(A),release(p)\rangle\rangle$$
$$p_4 = \quad \langle +on\_fire(x),(\{at(x),\neg on\_fire(y),$$
$$path(x,y)\},\{clear(x,y)\}),$$
$$(\{\emptyset\},\{\emptyset\}), \langle move(x,y)\rangle\rangle$$
$$p_5 = \quad \langle +trapped(p,x),(\{\emptyset\},\{\emptyset\}),$$
$$(\{\emptyset\},\{\emptyset\}), \langle !rescue(p,x)\rangle\rangle$$
$$P_{RBot} = \{p_1,p_2,p_3,p_4,p_5\}$$

In example 3, plan p_1 and p_2 are RBot strategies to
get to a specific node on the map. Plan p_3 is the strategy assisting RBot to decide how to rescue a person
trapped in a node. Plan p_4 is a reactive-plan for RBot
to get out of on-fire node. Plan p_5 is another reactive-
plan for RBot to try rescue a person, when RBot adds
a new belief that person is trapped at some node.

As with (Rao, 1996), a plan p is deemed to be a relevant plan relative to a triggering event τ if and only if there exists a most general unifier σ such that $d\sigma = \tau\sigma$, where $Trigger(p) = \tau$. σ if referred to as the *relevant unifier* for p given τ.

Definition 2 *A plan* p *of the form* $\langle \tau, \chi, \chi^*, \pi \rangle$ *is deemed to be an* applicable plan *relative to a triggering event* τ' *and a current belief set* B *iff:*

(1) There exists a relevant unifier σ *for* p *given* τ'.
(2) There exists a substitution θ *such that* $\beta\sigma\theta \cup \beta^*\sigma\theta \subseteq Th(B)$
(3) $\alpha\sigma\theta \cup \alpha^*\sigma\theta \cup B$ *is satisfiable.*

$\sigma\theta$ *is referred to as the* applicable unifier *for* τ' *and* θ *is called its* correct answer substitution.

Thus, a relevant plan is applicable if the hard pre- conditions (both in the invocation and invariant contexts) are entailed by its current set of beliefs and the soft pre- conditions (both in the invocation and invariant contexts) are consistent with its current set of beliefs.

Example 4 *Plan* p_3 *is intended by trigger* $+!rescue(P, F)$ *and agent belief set* E_1 *with correct answer substitution* $\{p/P, x/F\}$
$(p_3)\sigma\{p/P, x/F\} =$
$\langle +!rescue(P, F), (\{\emptyset\}, \{\emptyset\}), (\{\emptyset\}, \{trapped(P, F)$
$\lor carry(p)\}), \langle !at(F), pick(P), !at(A), release(P)$
$\rangle\rangle$

Definition 3 *An intended (partially instantiated) plan* $\langle \tau, \chi, \chi^*, \pi \rangle$ $\sigma\theta$ *is deemed to be executable with respect to belief set* B *iff*

(1) $\beta^*\sigma\theta \subseteq Th(B)$
(2) $\alpha^*\sigma\theta \cup B$ *is satisfiable*

Example 5 *Plan* $(p_3)\sigma\{p/P, x/F\}$ *is executable with respect to belief set* E_2.

Syntactically, our plan is not much different to the one in (Rao, 1996), however, the partition of context to four parts will give the agent more flexible when applying and executing a plan. This way of presenting a plan also provides agent's ability to discover when thing goes wrong or turns out not as expected (i.e. when invariant context is violated).

An intention is a state of intending to act that a rational agent is going to do to achieve its goal (Bratman, 1987).

Formally, an intention is defined as

Definition 4 *Let* $p_1, ..., p_n$ *be partially instantiated plans (i.e. instantiate by some applicable substitution), an intention* ι *is a pre- ,ordered tuple* $\langle p_1, ..., p_n \rangle$. *Where*

(1) $Trg_P(p_1)$ *is called original trigger of* ι,
    denote $Trg_I(\iota) = Trg_P(p_1)$
(2) An intention $\iota = \langle p_1, ..., p_n \rangle$ *is said to be valid with respect to current belief set* B *iff* $\forall i\ p_i$ *is executable with respect to* B *(definition 3).*

(3) An intention is said to be true intention if it is of the form $\langle \rangle$ *(empty). A true intention is always valid.*
(4) An intention $\iota = \langle p_1, ..., p_n \rangle$ *is said to be in-valid with respect to current belief set* B *if it is not valid.*
(5) Another way of writing an intention ι *is* $\langle \iota', p_n \rangle$ *with* $\iota' = \langle p_1, ..., p_{n-1} \rangle$ *is also an intention.*

Example 6 *At node* A, *RBot may have an intention to rescue a trapped person at node* F *as*

$$\iota_1 = \langle p_3\sigma\{p/P, x/F\}\rangle$$

Events

We adopt notion of agent events in AgentSpeak(L) (Rao, 1996). An events is a special attribute of agent internal state, an event can be either external (i.e. events are originated by environment e.g. users or other agents) or internal (i.e. evens are originated by internal processes of agent).

Definition 5 *Let* τ *be a ground trigger, let* ι *be an intention, an event is a pair* $\langle \tau, \iota \rangle$.

(1) An event is call external event if its intention is a true intention, otherwise it is called internal event.
(2) An event is valid with respect to agent current belief set B *if its intention is valid with respect to* B, *otherwise it is invalid event.*
(3) Let $e = \langle \tau, \iota \rangle$ *be an event, denote*
$$Trg_E(e) = \left\{ \begin{array}{ll} \tau & \text{if } e \text{ is external} \\ Trg_I(\iota) & \text{if } e \text{ is internal} \end{array} \right\}$$

Example 7 *External Event:*
$e_1 = \langle +!rescue(P, F), \langle\rangle\rangle$
Internal Event:
$e_2 = \langle +!at(F), \langle p'_3 \rangle\rangle$
where
$p'_3 = \langle +!rescue(P, F), \quad (\{\emptyset\}, \quad \{\emptyset\}), \quad (\{\emptyset\}, \{trapped(P, F) \lor carry(p)\}), \langle pick(P), !at(A), release(P) \rangle\rangle$

Corollary 1 *All external events of an agent are valid in respects of its current belief set.*

4 OPERATIONAL SEMANTICS

Like other BDI agent programming languages (Rao, 1996; Hindriks et al., 1999; Levesque et al., 1997), we use transitional semantics for our system.

Informally, an agent program in AgentSpeak(I) consists of a belief theory $\mathcal{B}$, a set of events E, a set of intention I, a plan library P, and three selection functions $\mathcal{S}_E$, $\mathcal{S}_P$, $\mathcal{S}_I$ to select an event, a plan, an intention (respectively) to process.

Definition 6 *An agent program is a tuple*

$$\langle \mathcal{B}, P, E, I, \mathcal{S}_P, \mathcal{S}_E, \mathcal{S}_I \rangle$$

where

(1) $\mathcal{B} = \langle \Delta, \mathcal{S}_\mathcal{E} \rangle$ *is agent belief theory of the agent.*

(2) *At any time denote* $B = \mathcal{S}_\mathcal{E}(\Delta)$ *is current belief set of the agent.*

(3) E *is set of events (including external events and internal events).*

(4) P *is agent plan repository, a library of agent plans.*

(5) I *is a set of intentions.*

(6) $\mathcal{S}_E$ *is a selection function which selects an event to process from set* E *of events.*

(7) $\mathcal{S}_P$ *is a selection function which selects an applicable plan to a trigger* τ *from set* P *of plans.*

(8) $\mathcal{S}_I$ *is a selection function which selects an intention to execute from set* I *of intentions.*

(9) $\mathcal{S}_E/\mathcal{S}_P/\mathcal{S}_I$ *returns null value if it fails to select an extension/intention/plan*

Example 8 *The initial agent program of RBot at node a would be like*

$\langle \mathcal{B}_{RBot}, P_{RBot}, \{\langle +!rescue(person, f), \langle\rangle\rangle\}, \langle\rangle,$
$\mathcal{S}_E, \mathcal{S}_P, \mathcal{S}_I \rangle$
Where $\mathcal{S}_E$, $\mathcal{S}_P$, $\mathcal{S}_I$ *are some valid selection functions (e.g. select the first valid option).*

There are two types of transits in AgentSpeak(I): *Transit to process events* and *Transit to execute intention*. These transitions may run in sequent or in parallel. The choice of using which method depends on specific domain.

As shown in definitions 4 and 5, an agent intention or an event can be sometime invalid. A good agent program should appropriately response to such cases. We propose two functions $Repair_I$ and Val_E for the purposes repairing invalid intentions and validate events when executing AgentSpeak(I) agent programs. The $Repair_I$ function takes an invalid intention as its input and outputs an event which is then valid with respect to agent current belief set. The Val_E function is slightly different. It takes an event as its input and outputs an valid event.

Definition 7 *Let* $\mathbb{I}$ *be set of all intentions,* $\mathbb{E}$ *be set of all events,* $\mathbb{B}$ *be set of all belief sets. Let* $Repair_I$: $\mathbb{I}, \mathbb{B} \rightarrow \mathbb{E}$ *be a repairing function which modify an invalid intention* ι *with respect to belief set* B *to return an valid event* ϵ *with respect to belief set* B.

The function Rep_i must satisfy following conditions

RI-1. if $\langle \tau, \iota' \rangle = Rep_i(\iota, B)$, then (1) ι' and ι are in the forms of $\langle p_1, ..., p_k \rangle$ and $\langle p_1, ..., p_k, p_{k+1}, ...p_n \rangle$ respectively where $(k < n)$, and (2) ι' is valid with respect to belief set B.

RI-2. if if $\langle \tau, \iota' \rangle = Rep_i(\iota, B)$, where $\iota' = \langle p_1, ..., p_k \rangle$ and $\iota = \langle p_1, ..., p_k, p_{k+1}...p_n \rangle$, then $\tau = Trg_P(p_{k+1})$.

Definition 8 *Let* $\mathbb{E}$ *be set of all events,* $\mathbb{B}$ *be set of all belief sets. If* B *is current agent belief set,* $e = \langle \tau, \iota \rangle$ *is an event, then function* Val_E :: $\mathbb{E}, \mathbb{B} \rightarrow \mathbb{E}$ *is defined as*

$$Val_E(e, B) = \left\{ \begin{array}{ll} e & \text{if } e \text{ is valid wrt } B \\ Rep_i(\iota, B) & \text{if } e \text{ is invalid wrt } B \end{array} \right\}$$

When an event $e = \langle \tau, \iota \rangle$ is selected by event selection function $\mathcal{S}_E$. Val_E function helps to make sure that e valid with respect to agent current belief set B, and ready to be processed.

Event Processing

Transition of agent program to process events depends on the event triggers. An event trigger can be

1. Add an achievement goal $+!g(\vec{t})$

2. Remove an achievement goal $-!g(\vec{t})$

3. Add a belief $+b$

4. Remove a belief $-b$

In case of adding an achievement goal $+!g(\vec{t})$, our agent (1) selects an applicable plan p from the plan library, (2) partially instantiate p with applicable substitution θ by unifier σ, (3) appends $p\sigma\theta$ to intention part of the event, and (4) adds that intention into the agent's intention set.

Definition 9 *Let* $Val_E(\mathcal{S}_E(E)) = \langle +!g(\vec{t}), \iota \rangle$, *let* $\mathcal{S}_P(P) = p$, *and where partially instantiated plan* p *is an applicable plan relative to triggering event* $+!g(\vec{t})$ *and current belief set* B. *e is said to be processed iff* $\langle \iota, p \rangle \in I$

In case of removing an achievement goal $-!g(\vec{t})$ (remind that $-g(\vec{t})$ is grounded), our agent (1) removes any plans which are triggered by ground trigger $+!g(\vec{t})$ from agent sets of intentions and events, (2) removes any sub-plans of those plans (i.e. plans which have higher priorities in the same intention).

Definition 10 *Let* $Val_E(\mathcal{S}_E(E)) = e$ *where* $e = \langle -!g(\vec{t}), \iota \rangle$. *e is said to be processed iff for any intention*

$$\iota \in I \cup \{\iota' | \langle \tau, \iota' \rangle \in E\}$$

if (1) ι *is in the form of* $\langle p_1, ..., p_k, ..., p_n \rangle$, *(2)* $p_k = \langle +!g(\vec{t}), \chi, \chi^*, \pi \rangle$ *and (3) for any* $i < k$ $p_i = \langle \tau_i, \chi_i, \chi_i^*, \pi_i \rangle$ τ *does not unify with* $+!g(\vec{t})$, *then* ι *is cut to be* $\langle p_1, ..., p_{k-1} \rangle$ *(note that* ι *may become an empty intention).*

In case of adding a belief, the agent revises its agent belief theory with this belief and adopts an applicable plan from its plan library to react to this change of its beliefs (reactive characteristic).

Definition 11 *Let* $Val_E(\mathcal{S}_E(E)) = e$ *where* $e = \langle +b(\vec{t}), \iota \rangle$, *let* $\mathcal{S}_P(P) = p$ *where partially instantiated* p *is an applicable plan relative to triggering event* $+!g(\vec{t})$ *and current belief set* B. e *is said to be processed iff (1)* $\mathcal{B} = \mathcal{B} \circ_G b$ *and (2)* $\langle \iota, p \rangle \in I$

Finally, in case of removing a belief, the agent contracts that belief from its agent belief theory and adopts an applicable plan from its plan library to react to this change of its beliefs (reactive characteristic).

Definition 12 *Let* $Val_E(\mathcal{S}_E(E)) = e$ *where* $e = \langle -b(\vec{t}), \iota \rangle$, *let* $\mathcal{S}_P(P) = p$ *where partially instantiated* p *is an applicable plan relative to triggering event* $+!g(\vec{t})$ *and current belief set* B. e *is said to be processed iff (1)* $\mathcal{B} = \mathcal{B} -_G b$ *and (2)* $\langle \iota, p \rangle \in I$

We have following algorithm for *event processing*

```
1:  e = S_E(E)
2:  if e is not null then
3:      E = E \ {e}
4:      B = S_E(Δ)
5:      ⟨τ, ι⟩ = Val_E(e, B)
6:      if τ is of the form +!g(t⃗) then
7:          p = S_P(τ, B, P)
8:          if p is null then
9:              E = E ∪ {⟨τ, ι⟩}
10:         else
11:             I = I ∪ {⟨ι, p⟩}
12:     else if τ is of the form -!g(t⃗) then
13:         for all ι ∈ I do
14:             if ι = ⟨p₁, ..., pₖ, ⟨+!g(t⃗), ...⟩, ..., pₙ⟩
                then
15:                 ι = ⟨p₁, ..., pₖ⟩
16:             for all ⟨τ, ι⟩ ∈ E do
17:                 if ι = ⟨p₁, ..., pₖ, ⟨+!g(t⃗), ...⟩, ..., pₙ⟩
                    then
18:                     ι' = ⟨p₁, ..., pₖ₋₁⟩
19:                     E = E \ ⟨τ, ι⟩ ∪ ⟨trigger(pₖ), ι'⟩
20:     else if τ is of the form +b(t⃗) then
21:         Δ = Δ ∘ b(t⃗)
22:         p = S_P(τ, B, P)
23:         if p is null then
24:             I = I ∪ {ι}
25:         else
26:             I = I ∪ {⟨ι, p⟩}
27:     else if τ is of the form -b(t⃗) then
28:         Δ = Δ - b(t⃗)
29:         p = S_P(τ, B, P)
30:         if p is null then
31:             I = I ∪ {ι}
32:         else
33:             I = I ∪ {⟨ι, p⟩}
```

In our example, at node a there is only one external event for the robot to select, which is $+!rescue(P, F)$ to rescue P at node F. There is also only one plan intended with this event and selected belief set E_2,

which is p_3 instantiated by substitution $\{P/p, F/x\}$. Hence, an intention will be generated to put into set of intentions, which now is

$\langle +!rescue(P, F), (\{\emptyset\}, \{\emptyset\}), (\{\emptyset\}, \{trapped(P, F) \vee carry(p)\}), \langle !at(F), pick(P), !at(A), release(P) \rangle \rangle$

After this execution, the set of event is an empty set.

Intention Executing

Executing an intention is an important transition of AgentSpeak(I) agent program, it is the process when the agent acts pro-actively towards its environment to achieve some environmental stage. An intention will be executed based on the first formula in the body of the highest priority plan of the intention. This formula can be: an achievement goal, a test goal, or an action. In case of an achievement goal, an internal event will be generated. In case of a test goal, the agent will test if there exists a set of ground terms $\vec{c}$ that makes the test goal an element of the current belief set, and use this set for subsequential execution of the intention. Finally, in case of an action, the agent will perform that action, which may result in changing of environmental state. These executions are formalized below.

Definition 13 *Let* $\mathcal{S}_I(I) = \iota$, *where*

$$\iota = \langle \iota', \langle \tau, \chi, \chi^*, \langle !g(\vec{t}), h_2, ..., h_n \rangle \rangle \rangle$$

The intention ι *is said to be executed iff*

$$\langle +!g(\vec{t}), \langle \iota', \langle \tau, \chi, \chi^*, \langle h_2, ..., h_n \rangle \rangle \rangle \rangle \in E$$

Definition 14 *Let* $\mathcal{S}_I(I) = \iota$, *where*

$$\iota = \langle \iota', \langle \tau, \chi, \chi^*, \langle ?g(\vec{t}), h_2, ..., h_n \rangle \rangle \rangle$$

The intention ι *is said to be executed iff*

(1) there exists a substitution θ *such that* $g(\vec{t})\theta \in B$ *and*

(2) ι *is replaced by*

$$\iota = \langle \iota', \langle \tau, \chi, \chi^*, \langle h_2\theta, ..., h_n\theta \rangle \rangle \rangle$$

Definition 15 *Let* $\mathcal{S}_I(I) = \iota$, *where*

$$\iota = \langle \iota', \langle \tau, \chi, \chi^*, \langle a(\vec{t}), h_2, ..., h_n \rangle \rangle \rangle$$

The intention ι *is said to be executed iff (1)* ι *is replaced by*

$$\iota = \langle \iota', \langle \tau, \chi, \chi^*, \langle h_2, ..., h_n \rangle \rangle \rangle$$

and (2) $a(\vec{t})$ *is sent to agent action processor.*

Definition 16 *Let* $\mathcal{S}_I(I) = \iota$, *where*

$$\iota = \langle \iota', \langle \tau, \chi, \chi^*, \langle \rangle \rangle \rangle$$

The intention ι *is said to be executed iff* ι *is replaced by* ι'

Like processing an event, before executing any intention, the agent need to verify if the intention is still valid in its current belief set B, and repairs that intention if necessary.

We have following algorithm for *intention executing*

```
1:  ι = S_I(I)
2:  if ι is not null then
3:      I = I \ {ι}
4:      B = S_ε(Δ)
5:      if ι is invalid with respect to B then
6:          e = Rep_i(ι)
7:          E = E ∪ {e}
8:      else
9:          present ι as ⟨ι', p⟩
10:         if body(p) is empty then
11:             I = I ∪ {ι'}
12:         else
13:             present p as ⟨τ, χ, χ*, ⟨h, h_2, ..., h_n⟩⟩
14:             if h is an action then
15:                 perform h
16:                 p' = ⟨τ, χ, χ*, ⟨h_2, ..., h_n⟩⟩
17:                 I = I ∪ {⟨ι', p'⟩}
18:             else if h is of the form !g(t⃗) then
19:                 p' = ⟨τ, χ, χ*, ⟨h_2, ..., h_n⟩⟩
20:                 e = ⟨+h, ⟨ι', p'⟩⟩
21:                 E = E ∪ {e}
22:             else if h is of the form ?g(t⃗) then
23:                 find a substitution θ s.t. g(t⃗)θ ∈ B
24:                 if no substitution is found then
25:                     I = I ∪ {ι}
26:                 else
27:                     p' = ⟨τ, χ, χ*, ⟨h_2θ, ..., h_nθ⟩⟩
28:                     I = I ∪ {⟨ι', p'⟩}
```

Again, in RBot mind now, there is only one intention to execute. This intention is currently valid. The first element of the intention is a goal $!at(f)$. Hence, an internal event is generated, which is

$$\langle +!at(F), \langle p'_3 \rangle \rangle$$

where

$p'_3 = \langle +!rescue(P, F),\quad (\{\emptyset\},\quad \{\emptyset\}),\quad (\{\emptyset\},$
$trapped(P, F) \lor carry(p)\}),\quad \langle pick(P),\quad !at(A),$
$release(P) \rangle \rangle$

This event then is added into set of events. The original intention is removed from set of intentions.

5 COMPARISON WITH OTHER LANGUAGES

There have been several well known agent programming languages from very first language like Agent0 in 1993 (Shoham, 1993), to AgentSpeak(L) (Rao, 1996), Golog/ConGolog (Levesque et al., 1997; le Giacomo et al., 2000), 3APL (Hindriks et al.,

1999) in late 1990s. In this section, we will compare AgentSpeak(I) with three later agent programming languages (AgentSpeak(L) , ConGolog, and 3APL). The extensive advantage of AgentSpeak(I) in comparing with these languages is that AgentSpeak(I) allows agents to act with incomplete knowledge about environment. Furthermore, others agent programming languages leave a gap in how agents propagating their own beliefs during agents life, which is reasonably covered in AgentSpeak(I).

AgentSpeak(L): AgentSpeak(L) aims to implement of BDI agents in a logic programming style. It is an attempt to bridge the gap between logical theories of BDI and implementations. Syntactically, AgentSpeak(L) and AgentSpeak(I) are similar. However, the differences in plans, belief theory, and the semantics make AgentSpeak(I) programs extensively more capable than AgentSpeak(L) programs, especially when acting with incomplete knowledge about the environment.

3APL: 3APL is a rule-based language which is similar to AgentSpeak(I). A configuration of 3APL agent consists of a belief base, a goal base, and a set of practical reasoning (PR) rules, which are likely corresponding to belief theory, set of events and intentions, and plan library in AgentSpeak(I) respectively. The advantage that 3APL has over AgentSpeak(I) is the supporting of compound goals. Classification of PR rules in 3APL is only a special way of patition AgentSpeak(I) plan library, where we consider all plan with equal priority. Nevertheless, AgentSpeak(I) provides stronger support to agent abilities to perform in highly dynamic environment.

ConGolog: ConGolog is an extension of situation calculus. It is a concurrent language for high-level agent programming. ConGolog uses formal model semantics. ConGolog provides a logical perspective on agent programming in comparison with AgentSpeak(I) providing operational semantics that show how agent program propagates its internal states of beliefs, intentions, and events. Agent programs in ConGolog plan its actions from initial point of execution to achieve a goal. An assumption in ConGolog is that the environment changes only if a agent performs an action. This strong assumption is not required in AgentSpeak(I). Hence, ConGolog provides weeker supports to agent performance in comperation with AgentSpeak(I) when dealing with incomplete knowledge about the environment.

6 CONCLUSION & FUTURE RESEARCH

We have introduced a new agent programming language to deal with incomplete knowledge about environment. Syntax and operational semantics of the languages has been presented. Comparison of AgentSpeak(I) and current agent programming languages has been discussed. In short, agent programs in AgentSpeak(I) can effectively perform in a highly dynamic environment by making assumptions at two levels: when computing belief set and when planning or re-planning; detect planning problems raised by changes of the environment and re-plan when necessary at execution time; and finally propageting internal beliefs during execution time.

There are several directions that would be extended from this work. First, there would be an extension of background belief theory on belief change operators and temporal reasoning with beliefs and actions. Second, there would be an extension of this framework with multi-agent environment, where agent's intentions are influenced by its beliefs of others' beliefs and intentions. Third, there would be work on declarative goals on extension of AgentSpeak(I). And finally, there would be an extension which uses action theory to update agent beliefs during execution time.

REFERENCES

Alchourrón, C. E., Gärdenfors, P., and Makinson, D. (1985). On the logic of theory change: Partial meet contraction and revision functions. *Journal of Symbolic Logic*, 50:510–530.

Alferes, J. J., Pereira, L. M., and Przymusinski, T. C. (1996). Belief revision in non-monotonic reasoning and logic programming. *Fundamenta Informaticae*, 28(1-2):1–22.

Bratman, M. E. (1987). *Intentions, Plans, and Practical Reason*. Harvard University Press, Cambridge, MA.

Brewka, G. and Eiter, T. (2000). Prioritizing default logic. *Intellectics and Computational Logic, Papers in Honor of Wolfgang Bibel, Kluwer Academic Publishers, Applied Logic Series*, 19:27–45.

Darwiche, A. and Pearl, J. (1997). On the logic of iterated belief revision. *Artificial Intelligence*, 97(1-2):45–82.

Dastani, M., Boer, F., Dignum, F., and Meyer, J. (2003). Programming agent deliberation. In *Proceedings of the Autonomous Agents and Multi Agent Systems Conference 2003*, pages 97–104.

de Giacomo, G., , Y. L., and Levesque, H. (2000). Congolog, a concurrent programming language based on the situation calculus. *Artificial Intelligence*, 121:109–169.

Delgrande, J., Schaub, T., and Jackson, W. (1994). Alternative approaches to default logic. *Artificial Intelligence*, 70:167–237.

D'Inverno, M. and Luck, M. (1998). Engineering agentspeak(l): A formal computational model. *Journal of Logic and Computation*, 8(3):233–260.

Ghose, A. K. and Goebel, R. G. (1998). Belief states as default theories: Studies in non-prioritized belief change. In *proceedings of the 13th European Conference on Artificial Intelligence (ECAI98)*, Brighton, UK.

Ghose, A. K., Hadjinian, P. O., Sattar, A., You, J., and Goebel, R. G. (1998). Iterated belief change. *Computational Intelligence*. Conditionally accepted for publication.

Giordano, L. and Martelli, A. (1994). On cumulative default reasoning. *Artificial Intelligence Journal*, 66:161–180.

Hindriks, K., de Boer, F., van der Hoek, W., and Meyer, J.-J. (1999). Agent programming in 3apl. In *Proceedings of the Autonomous Agents and Multi-Agent Systems Conference 1999*, pages 357–401.

Levesque, H., R., R., Lesperance, Y., F., L., and R., S. (1997). Golog: A logic programming language for dynamic domains. *Journal of Logic Programming*, 31:59–84.

MaynardReidII, P. and Shoham, Y. (1998). From belief revision to belief fusion. In *Proceedings of the Third Conference on Logic and the Foundations of Game and Decision Theory (LOFT3)*.

Meyer, T., Ghose, A., and Chopra, S. (2001). Non-prioritized ranked belief change. In *Proceedings of the Eighth Conference on Theoretical Aspects of Rationality and Knowledge (TARK2001)*, Italy.

Poole, D. (1988). A logical framework for default reasoning. *Artificial Intelligence*, 36:27–47.

Rao, A. S. (1996). Agentspeak(l): Bdi agents speak out in a logical computable language. *Agents Breaking Away, Lecture Notes in Artificial Intelligence*.

Rao, A. S. and Georgeff, M. P. (1991). Modeling rational agents within a bdi-architecture. In *Proceedings of the Second International Conference on Principles of Knowledge Representation and Reasoning (KR'91)*, pages 473–484.

Rao, A. S. and Georgeff, M. P. (1995). Bdi agents: From theory to practice. In *Proceedings of the First International Conference on Multi-Agent Systems (ICMAS-95)*, San Francisco, USA.

Reiter, R. (1980). A logic for default reasoning. *Artificial Intelligence*, 13(1-2):81–132.

Riemsdijk, B., Hoek, W., and Meyer, J. (2003). Agent programming in dribble: from beliefs to goals using plans. In *Proceedings of the Autonomous Agents and Multi Agent Systems Conference 2003*, pages 393–400.

Shoham, Y. (1993). Agent-oriented programming. *Artificial Intelligence*, 60:51–93.

Wobcke, W. (2002). Intention and rationality for prs-like agents. In *Proceedings of the 15 Australian Joint Conference on Artificial Intelligence (AJAI02)*.

Wooldridge, M. (2000). *Reasoning about Rational Agent*. The MIT Press, London, England.

FEDERATED MEDIATORS FOR QUERY COMPOSITE ANSWERS

Dong Cheng and Nacer Boudjlida
LORIA-University Henri Poincaré Nancy 1
BP 239, 54506 Vandoeuvre Lès Nancy CEDEX(F)
Email: {cheng, nacer}@loria.fr

Keywords: Composite answer, Description Logics, Mediator, complementary.

Abstract: The capture, the structuring and the exploitation of the expertise or the capabilities of an "object" (like a business partner, an employee, a software component, a Web site, etc.) are crucial problems in various applications, like cooperative and distributed applications or e-business and e-commerce applications. The work we describe in this paper concerns the advertising of the capabilities or the know-how of an object. The capabilities are structured and organized in order to be used when searching for objects that satisfy a given objective or that meet a given need. One of the originality of our proposal is in the nature of the answers the intended system can return. Indeed, the answers are not Yes/No answers but they may be cooperative answers in that sense that when no single object meets the search criteria, the system attempts to find out what a set of "complementary" objects do satisfy the whole search criteria, every object in the resulting set satisfying part of the criteria. In this approach, Description Logics (DL) is used as a knowledge representation formalism and classification techniques are used as search mechanisms. The determination of the "complementary objects" is founded on the DL complement concept.

1 INTRODUCTION

In many situations and applications, one is faced to the problem of discovering "entities" that satisfy given requirements. On the other hand, most often, information retrieval in a distributed context, like the World Wide Web, usually lacks selectivity and provides large answer-sets due to the fact that the available information sources are not well structured nor well classified, as attested by the tremendous work about Semantic Web (W3C, 2003a). Moreover, most of the systems usually return yes/no answers (i.e. either they find out answers to a given query or they fail). The work we describe here concerns the publishing of the capabilities of given entities (i.e. what functionalities a given entity is offering, what expertise it has and so on). The capabilities are organized and structured in order to be exploited when searching for entities that satisfy an objective or that meet given needs (searching for Web services that offer given functions, searching for a component in the context of component-based design and component-based programming, searching for a business partner with a given expertise, looking for an employee whose records and expertise satisfy a given work po-

sition profile are application examples of our work). It is clear that these needs require the capture and the organization of the entities capabilities together with the classification of the entities and their capabilities. In this work, we adopted an object-oriented knowledge representation using description logics (DL-org, 2003). From the system architecture point of view, we opted for a model based on distributed and cooperative mediators (or traders). A significant originality of our approach resides in the type of answers we aim at providing. Indeed, when no single entity satisfies the search criteria, the systems attempts to determine a set of *complementary* entities who, when grouped together, satisfy the criteria.

The presentation is structured as follows. In section 2, we expose some motivations together with the architecture of the target system viewed as a Knowledge-Based Management System (KBMS). Section 3 briefly introduces elements of description logics and shows how description logics is used for entities capabilities management and retrieval. Concluding remarks are in section 4.

I. Seruca et al. (eds.), Enterprise Information Systems VI, 261–274.

2 MOTIVATION AND ARCHITECURE

The dynamic discovery of services or capabilities an "entity" offers, has different application domains. Component-based programming, electronic business (*e-business*) and even enterprise knowledge management (Nonaka and Takeuchi, 1995) are among the application domains in which there is a need for the discovery of services or capabilities an "entity" offers. The only syntactic description of an entity's capability (like the *signature* of a software component's service) is not satisfactory when using that description for answering a request: an additional semantic description is required. Moreover, the elicitation of possible relationships among services may contribute to find out "the best" service or the "the best complementary" services that satisfy a search query.

In *e-business*, this approach can be applied in the constitution of business alliances or when looking for business partners. For example, when trying to constitute a business alliance, the system we aim to develop services that may help in retrieving the most appropriate candidate partners. Furthermore, the work depicted hereafter may also serve for semantic-based discovery of Web services (W3C, 2003c) and it is in line with current activities on semantic and ontology for the Web (uddi.org, 2000; Dyck, 2002; W3C, 2003b; W3C, 2003a).

The purpose of this work requires formalizing and structuring the knowledge that concern the "entities" in a given application domain. We opted for Description Logics (DL) (DL-org, 2003; Horrocks, 2002b) as a knowledge representation formalism: it has the notable merit that a single mechanism (the classification mechanism) serves at the same time to build and to query extendible domain descriptions.

As a matter of comparison, in (Han et al., 1999), "entities" are design fragments that are described thanks to keywords, the relationships between the fragments are constituted by metrics that measures the similarity between fragments. In (Borgida and Devanhu, 1999), entities are object-oriented software components and description logics is used, notably, to describe their intended semantics together with possible constraints involving objects methods.

In (Bouchikhi and Boudjlida, 1998), "entities" are software objects and the capabilities of a software object are specified giving a syntactic part (signatures of the methods or operations the object offers) and a semantic part expressed as logical expressions (a pre-condition and a post-condition are associated with every object's method). The syntactic conformance of a method to a query is trivial and the semantic conformance uses theorem proving techniques.

One should notice that description logics has been used in the database domain (Borgida, 1995; Boudjlida, 1995)[1], not only for querying but also for database schema design and integration (Calvanese et al., 1998), for reasoning about queries (query containment, query refinement, query optimisation, ...) (Beeri et al., 1997). From our concern, description logics is used for query purposes with the special objective to produce more than "Yes or No" results.

From the system architecture point of view, we choose a trader (also called mediator) based architecture (OMG, 1992) very similar to the notion of *discovery agency* in the Web services architecture. In this architecture, an "entity", called *exporter*, publishes (*tells*) its capabilities at one or more mediators sites (see figure 1). Entities, called *importers*, send requests (*queries*) to the mediator asking for exporters fitted with a given set of capabilities.

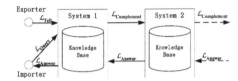

Figure 1: The Mediator-based Architecture

The mediator explores its knowledge base to try to satisfy the query. The capability search process is founded on the exported capabilities and on relationships between them, these relationships being transparently established by the mediator. When some exporters known from the mediator satisfy the query, the references of those exporters are sent back to the importer in $\mathcal{L}_{answer}$. Nevertheless, satisfying the query falls into different cases (Boudjlida, 2002) (see figure 2):

- Case1: There exist exporters that exactly satisfy the query;

- Case2: There exist exporters that fully satisfy the query, but their capabilities are wider than those requested;

- Case3: There exists no single exporters that fully satisfy the query, but when "combining" or composing capabilities from different exporter, one can fully satisfy the query;

- Case4: Neither a single exporter nor multiple exporters satisfy the query, but there exist some exporters that partly satisfy the query;

- Case5: No single exporter nor several exporters fully or partly satisfy the query.

---

[1]See also (DL-org, 2003) for the proceedings of the various "Knowledge Representation meets DataBase" (KRDB) Workshops.

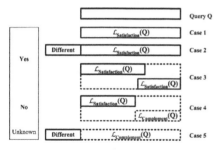

Figure 2: The cases of satisfaction

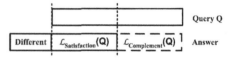

Figure 3: A model for composite answer

defined by $\mathcal{L}_{Query} \doteq \{$ DLs formulaes$\}$, and $\mathcal{L}_{Answer}$ is defined by two components the $\mathcal{L}_{Satisfaction}$ and $\mathcal{L}_{Complement}$. $\mathcal{L}_{Satisfaction}$ describes a satisfaction, that is a single entity or a set of entities satisfying a query Q. If Q is completely satisfied, its complement (noted $\mathcal{L}_{Complement}(Q)$) will be empty. In the contrary, the system will try to determine a complement for this answer. We define a function $Comp(-,-)$ to calculate the complement of an answer to a query: $\mathcal{L}_{Complement}(Q) = Comp(\mathcal{L}_{Satisfaction}(Q), Q)$. Intuitively this complement designates "the missing part" to an entity in order for that entity to satisfy the query.

The ultimate goal of this work is the design and the development of a set of services to export, import and mediate, as well as the study and the development of alternative strategies and mechanisms for mediators cooperation. The coming sections detail the adopted approach and its foundations, beginning with a short introduction to description logics.

One should notice that cases 4 and 5 would conduct to a failure of the query when only one mediator is implied. But, if we assume a grouping of mediators (into a federation of mediators), these cases are typical cases where cooperation among the mediators is required. In the case 5, the whole query is transmitted for evaluation to other mediators whereas in the case 4, we need to determine "what is missing" to the individuals to satisfy Q, that means to determine what part of the query is not satisfied by the found individuals. This part as well as the original query are transmitted then to a mediator of the federation. Conceptually, we can see the query as being addressed to "the union" of by the federated mediators' knowledge bases. Concretely, this union is explored from "near to near" within the federation, that means from a mediator to an other.

Let us now elaborate more on the conceptual framework and the underlying formal foundations. Given a query Q expressed as a sentence of a query language $\mathcal{L}_{Query}$, a simple result (noted $\mathcal{L}_{Answer}(Q)$) is generally returned in most of the systems and usually $\mathcal{L}_{Answer}(Q) \doteq \{$Yes, No, Unknown$\}$, the meaning of "Yes" is that one or several entities satisfy the $\mathcal{L}_{Query}$ and "No" is the opposite. In this work, we try to offer a $\mathcal{L}_{Answer}(Q)$ that may not be a single entity satisfying $\mathcal{L}_{Query}$, but that may possibly be a collection of entities where "the union" of the members of the collection of entities satisfies the search criteria of $\mathcal{L}_{Query}$. This collection can be found in a knowledge base or in a federation of knowledge bases (that means a set of knowledge bases).

In this work, we adopted a Description Logic language (DL) (DL-org, 2003), that were intensively developed and studied in the field of Knowledge Representation. So it is not surprising that they are particularly adapted for representing the semantics of real world situations including data semantics (Calvanese et al., 1998; Borgida, 1995). The query language is

3   COMPLEMENT AND COMPOSITE ANSWER

The determination of unsatisfied part of a query is founded on the concept of *complement* (Schmidt-Schauss and Smolka, 1991) in DLs and the test of the relation of subsumption between the concepts of the query and those in the mediator's base. The algorithm that we propose to test if this relation exists or not, presents the originality, in the case where the relation is not true, to identify the concepts of the query that are the reason of the non existence of the relation (concretely, it is about the concepts of the query that are not subsumed by the concepts in the mediator's base): these concepts describe "the part that is missing" to the individuals who partly satisfy the query. Let us now describe the proposal in a more formal way, beginning by defining the notion of complement to arrive progressively to the procedure of its calculation.

3.1   An Introduction to DLs

DLs (DL-org, 2003; Horrocks, 2002b; Napoli, 1997) is a family of knowledge representation languages where a description of a world is built using *concepts*, *roles* and *individuals*. The *concepts* model classes (sets of *concepts*, TBox)of individuals (sets of *individuals*, ABox) and they correspond to generic entities in an application domain. An *individual* is an instance of a concept. *Roles* model binary relationships among the individual classes. A concept is specified thanks to a structured description that is built giving *constructors* that introduce the roles associated with the concept and possible restrictions associated with some roles. Usually, the restrictions constrain the range of the binary relationship that is defined by a role and the role's cardinality.

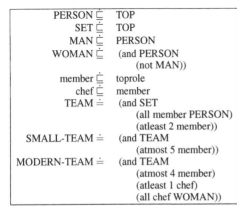

Figure 4: An exemple of LDs TBox

Concepts are of two types, primitive and defined concepts. *Primitive concepts* may be considered as atoms that may serve to build new concepts (the *defined concepts*). Similarly, *roles* may be primitive roles as well as defined roles. In the figure 4, PERSON and SET are primitive concepts: they are introduced using the symbol $\sqsubseteq$ and they are linked to a "TOP" concept ($\top$)[2]; TEAM SMALL-TEAM and MODERN-TEAM are defined concepts (they are introduced using the symbol $\doteq$. The *and* constructor enables defining concepts as a conjunction of concepts: these concepts are the immediate ascendants of the defined one. The *all* constructor constrains a role's range and the *at-least* and *at-most* constructors enable specifying the role's cardinals. Finally, the *not* constructor only applies to primitive concept.

Subsumption is the fundamental relationship that may hold among described concepts. Intuitively, a concept C subsumes a concept D, if the set of indi-

viduals represented by C contains the set of individuals represented by D. More formally, C subsumes D and it is denoted as $D \sqsubseteq C$ (or D is subsumed by C) if and only if $D^{\mathcal{I}}$ for every possible interpretation $\mathcal{I}$. C is called the subsuming concept and D is the subsumed. For example in figure 4, PERSON subsumes MAN, SMALL-TEAM is subsumed by TEAM.

The subsumption relationship organizes the concepts into a hierarchy of concepts. The classification process aims at determining the position of a new concept in a given hierarchy. In this framework, a query is represented as a concept Q to be classified in a given hierarchy. The result of the query is the set of instances of the concepts that are subsumed by Q. The classification is a process that enables discovering whether a subsumption relationship holds between a concept X, and those present in a hierarchy H. The classification process is decomposed into 3 steps:

- Retrieve the most specific subsuming concepts of X (denoted MSSC(X));

- Retrieve the most general concepts subsumed by X (denoted MGSC(X));

- (possibly) Update the links between X and its MSSC and its MGSC.

The result of MSSC and MGSC can determine the cases of satisfaction (see figure 5).

In DLs a classic definition of the complement[3]is: given two descriptions A and B in $\mathcal{ALCNR}$[3] as $A \sqsubseteq B$, the complementary of A relatively to B, noted $Comp(A, B)$, is defined as the description that is most general as $A \equiv B \sqcap C$. $Comp(A, B)$ corresponds to the minimal additional knowledge that is missing to a process of B to be an instance of A. For example, Comp(SMALL-TEAM, TEAM) = (at-most 5 member). The complementary of a concept relatively to another concept and smallest subsuming common of two concepts. This definition of the complement requires $(B \sqcap C) \equiv A$, where $(B \sqcap C) \equiv A \Leftrightarrow ((B \sqcap C) \sqsubseteq A) \wedge ((B \sqcap C) \sqsupseteq A)$. The determination of a complement is based on the subsumption relationship as explained in the next section where the test of the existence of the subsumption relationship is based on a Normalize-Compare process.

3.2 Determination of the Complement Concept

The aim of a normalization process is to put defined concepts to be compared, let say A and B, under a conjunctive form: $A = ($ and $A_1, A_2, A_3, \ldots, A_n)$ and $B = ($ and $B_1, B_2, B_3, \ldots, B_m)$. Once

---

[2]Intuitively the TOP concept is the "most general one" and it contains all the individuals while the BOTTOM concept ($\perp$) is the most specific one and is empty.

[3]$\mathcal{ALCNR}$ is a family of representation langage of DLs

normalized, two concepts can be easily compared to check wither the subsumption relationship holds between pairs of them or not: giving $A = ($ and $A_1, A_2, A_3, \ldots, A_n)$ and $B = ($ and $B_1, B_2, B_3, \ldots, B_m)$, the test "does the concept A subsume the concept B?" returns "true", if and only if $\forall A_i$ ($i \in 1, \ldots, n$) $\exists\ B_j$ ($j \in 1, \ldots, m$) such that $B_j \sqsubseteq A_i$.

The implementation of this process uses an array of Boolean (called "Table_Of_Test" further) to record the result of the subsumption relationship evaluation (see figure 5). In that figure, $C_1, C_2, C_3, \cdots, C_n$ denote the query concept under its normal form and $D_1, D_2, D_3, \ldots, D_m$ denotes the concepts "known from" the mediators, i.e. every D_j has to be viewed under its normal form $D_j^1, D_j^2, \cdots, D_j^{nj}$. Then $Table\_Of\_Test[D_j, C_i] = true$ means that $D_j^i \sqsubseteq C_i$. When the value returned by the function $Subsumes(C, D_j)$ is "false" (i.e. the concept D_j does not fully satisfy the concept C.), therefore we need to determine a possible complement of D_j relatively to C. Using the Table_Of_Test it is easy to get the complement of concept D_j relatively to the concept C. For example, "MODERN-TEAM subsumes SMALL-TEAM" is false, "(atmost 4 member), (atleast 1 chef) and (all chef WOMAN)" is false, then $Comp$(MODERN-TEAM,SMALL-TEAM)=(and (atmost 4 member) (atleast 1 chef) (all chef WOMAN)). Then using Table_Of_Test the definition of $Comp()$ is: $Comp(C, D) = \bigcap_{k=1}^{r} C_k, \forall k | TableofTest[k] = false$[4].

	C_1	C_2	$\ldots$	C_n
D_1	False	False	$\ldots$	True
D_2	False	True	$\ldots$	True
$\ldots$	$\ldots$	$\ldots$	$\ldots$	$\ldots$
D_m	False	False	$\ldots$	False
ORoD	False	True	$\ldots$	True
	ORoS	ANDoS		
	True	False		

Figure 5: Three parameters of "Table Of Test"

That means that the complement is given by the conjunction of all the atomic concepts for which the corresponding values in "Table Of Test" are "false".

The composition of the truth values will permit us to determine the cases of satisfaction. Let's consider a table $ORoD[1..n]$ as $ORoD[i] = \bigvee_{j=1}^{m} T[D_j, C_i]$. $ORoD[i] = true$ means that the concept C_i is satisfied by at least a D_k. If the conjunction of

MSSC	MGSC	ORoS	ANDoS	CASE
X	X	True	True	1
X	$\perp$	True	True	2
$\top$	$\perp$	True	True	3
$\top$	$\perp$	True	False	4
$\top$	$\perp$	False	False	5

Figure 6: The analyse of the satisfaction case

the values of $ORoD$, noted $ANDoS$, is true (i.e. $\bigwedge_{i=1}^{n} ORoD[i] = True$), it means that all the C_is are satisfied and therefore the query. When $ANDoS$ is false, the logical disjunction of the values of $ORoD$, noted $ORoS$, enables to determine a possible partial satisfaction. Indeed if $ORoS = \bigvee_{i=1}^{n} ORoD[i] = True$, it means that there exist some C_k that are satisfied. If both $ORoS$ and $ANDoS$ are false then no atomic concept D_j^k ($j \in 1..m$) satisfies a C_i.

The figure 6[5] summarizes this discussion (in this figure, the numbers in the CASE column refers to the satisfaction cases listed in section 2). By this analyse with the classification algorithm (Boudjlida, 2002), we can get a complete method to determine the satisfaction cases that were listed in section 2.

3.3   Status of The Implementation

Based on these algorithms, an experimental platform has been developed in *Java*. Some services, like testing the subsomption relationship, determining the complement of a concept and computing a composite answer, have been implemented on this platform. All these services can be accessed through a *Web Server* in a "classical" client/server architecture over the Web. The services accept the DL concepts written DAML+OIL (Horrocks, 2002a), an ontology language in *XML*. The DL concepts are encoded in *XML* and transmitted to the *Web Server* who in turn transmit them to the appropriate mediator service. Then a normalization class transforms them into *Java* objects and an experimental knowledge base, described in XML, is loaded and normalized into a *TBox* object when the service is started. All the algorithms of the mediator's services are implemented in the *TBox* class. The services' outputs are also encoded in *XML*. Furhermore, XML is also used to exchange information and concepts between the mediators when mediators' cooperation is needed. For example, in the service that computes a composite answer for a query concept, if the query concept is not satisfied in the local knowledge base, the complement concept is sent to next mediator as

---

[4]In the following, we will use T[x] instead of Table-OfTest[x]

[5]In this table, X is a concept, $\top$ is the concept TOP and $\perp$ is the concept BOTTOM.

an XML focument.

In the current status of the implementation, a mediator "discovers" an other mediator using a static mediator address list. More complex and dynamic discovery techniques will be supported in the coming versions. Moreover, we deliberately ignored the search of the actual *individuals* (*ABox*) that satisfy a query, i.e. in the current work, we only consider *TBoxes*.

4 CONCLUSION

In this paper, we presented a method and an algorithm for testing the subsumption relationship, determining concept complements and finding composite answers. Some service of subsumption test and determine *Complement* has been implemented in *Java*, that is based on a normalization-comparison algorithm and we can access these services by Web. One of the originality of this work is in the type of query answering we provide and also in the way we used and implemented the complement concept. Indeed, to the best of our knowledge, using the complement concept for query answers composition does not figure in the literature we had in hands nor in systems that implement DLs, like *RACER* (Haaslev and Moller, 2003) one of the most representative DL system.

Future work may consider the complexity of the algorithm, and the cooperation of mediators in heterogeneous environments, i.e. environments where mediators' knowledge bases are described in different languages.

REFERENCES

Beeri, C., Levy, A., and Rousset, M.-C. (1997). Rewriting Queries Using Views in Description Logics. In *ACM Symposium on Principles Of Database Systems*, pages 99–108, Tucson, Arizona.

Borgida, A. (1995). Description Logics in Data Management. *IEEE Transactions on Knowledge and Data Engineering*, 7(5):671–682.

Borgida, A. and Devanhu, P. (1999). Adding more "DL" to IDL: Towards more Knowledgeable Component Interoperability. In *21rst International Conference on Software Engineering, ICSE'99*, pages 378–387, Los Angeles, CA. ACM Press.

Bouchikhi, M. and Boudjlida, N. (1998). Using Larch to Specify the Behavior of Objects in Open Distributed Environments. In *Proceedings of the 1998 Maghrebian Conference on Software Engineering and Artificial Intelligence*, pages 275–287, Tunis, Tunisia. 98-R-300.

Boudjlida, N. (1995). Knowledge in Interoperable and Evolutionary Systems. In Dreschler-Fischer, L. and

Pribbenow, S., editors, *KRDB'95, Workshop on "Reasoning about Structured Objets: Knowledge Representation Meets Databases"*, pages 25–26, Bielefeld, Germany. (Position Paper).

Boudjlida, N. (2002). A Mediator-Based Architecture for Capability Management. In Hamza, M., editor, *Proceedings of the 6th International Conference on Software Engineering and Applications, SEA 2002*, pages 45–50, MIT, Cambridge, MA.

Calvanese, D., de Giacomo, D., Lenzerini, M., Nardi, D., and Rosati, R. (1998). Information Integration: Coceptual Modeling and Reasoning Support. In *6th International Conference on Cooperative Information Systems, CoopIS'98*, pages 280–291.

DL-org (2003). Description logics. http//dl.kr.org/.

Dyck, T. (2002). Uddi 2.0 provides ties that bind. (http://www.eweek.com/).

Haaslev, V. and Moller, R. (2003). Racer: Renamed abox and concept expression reasoner. http://www.fh-wedel.de/mo/racer/index.html.

Han, T.-D., Purao, S., and Storey, V. (1999). A Methodology for Building a Repository of Object-Oriented Design Fragments. In *18th International Conference on Conceptual Modelling, ER'99*, pages 203–217, Paris. Spriger Verlag. LNCS 1728.

Horrocks, I. (2002a). DAML+OIL: a description logic for the semantic web. *IEEE Data Engineering Bulletin*, 25(1):4–9.

Horrocks, I. (2002b). Description Logic: Axioms and Rules. Talk given at Dagstuhl "Rule Markup Technique" Workshop. http://www.cs.man.ac.uk/ horrocks/Slides/.

Napoli, A. (1997). Une introduction aux logiques de description. Technical Report RR No 3314, INRIA-LORIA, Nancy.

Nonaka, I. and Takeuchi, H. (1995). *The Knowledge Creating Company; How Japanese Companies Create the Dynamics of Innovation*. Oxford University Press.

OMG (1992). The Object Model Architecture Guide. Technical Report 91.11.1, Revision 2.0, Object Management Group.

Schmidt-Schauss, M. and Smolka, G. (1991). Attribute Concepts Description with Complements. *Artificial Intelligence Journal*, 48(1):1–26.

uddi.org (2000). UDDI: Universal Description, Discovery and Integration. Technical White Paper. (http://uddi.org).

W3C (2003a). Semantic Web. http://www.w3.org/2001/sw.

W3C (2003b). Web Ontology. http://www.w3.org/2001/sw/WebOnt.

W3C (2003c). Web Services. http://www.w3.org/2002/ws.

A WIRELESS APPLICATION THAT MONITORS ECG SIGNALS ON-LINE: ARCHITECTURE AND PERFORMANCE[1]

Jimena Rodríguez, Lacramioara Dranca, Alfredo Goñi and Arantza Illarramendi
University of the Basque Country (UPV/EHU).LSI Department. Donostia-San Sebastián. Spain
Web: http://siul02.si.ehu.es

Keywords: Wireless Application, Mobile Computing, Wireless Network, ECG Monitoring System

Abstract: In this paper, we present an innovating on-line monitoring system that has been developed by applying new advances in biosensors, mobile devices and wireless technologies. The aim of the system is to monitor people that suffer from heart arrhythmias without having to be hospitalized; and therefore, living a normal life while feeling safe at the same time. On the one hand, the architecture of the system is presented; and, on the other hand, some performance results and implementation details are explained showing how the previous solution can be effectively implemented and deployed into a system that makes use of PDAs, and wireless communications: Bluetooth and GPRS. Moreover, special attention is paid to two aspects: cost of the wireless communications and notification latency for the detected serious heart anomalies.

1 INTRODUCTION

Innovations in the fields of PDAs, wireless communications and vital parameter sensors enable the development of revolutionary medical monitoring systems, which strikingly improve the lifestyle of patients, offering them security even outside the hospital.

In this context we are developing a system that takes advantage of the latest advances in the technology in order to monitor on-line, people that suffer from heart arrhythmias. The system allows an anywhere and at any time monitoring and provides to its users the adequate medical assistance. So, the patient could have a normal life in his/her habitual environment without being constrained to a hospital room. The patient's tool, which replaces the traditional monitor (Holter) and supports Bluetooth technology, is reflected in a standard PDA that is a small, handheld computer that captures, processes, detects, analyzes and notifies possible abnormalities to a medical unit through the wireless network (GPRS) from anywhere and at any time. Moreover, the Bluetooth communication makes this tool even more comfortable for the user, replacing the cables of the sensors that pick up the cardiological signals.

Concerning related works, on the one hand, there are several commercial tools designed to monitor heart patients outside the hospital; from the traditional Holter (Despopoulos, 1994) that simply records heart signals named ECG (electrocardiogram), for 24 or 48 hours, which are later analyzed in the hospital, until the modern cellular phones e.g Vitaphone (Daja, 2001) that, in case of an emergency, can record the signals through the metal electrodes situated on its back and transmit them to the cardiac monitor center situated in the hospital. There are other commercial monitoring systems that use PDAs to store the ECG signals, e.g. Ventracor (Ventracor, 2003), Cardio Control (Cardio Control, 2003). For these systems additional features like GSM/GPRS transmission to an analyzing unit are also being developed.

On the other hand, in the research monitoring area, stand out several research projects like: @Home (Sachpazidis, 2002), TeleMediCare (Dimitri, 2003), or PhMon (Kunze, 2002), whose aims are to build platforms for real time remote monitoring.

All these systems are continuously sending ECGs to a medical center through a wireless communication network, where the signals are

[1] This work was mainly supported by the University of the Basque Country and the Diputación Foral de Gipuzkoa (co-supported by the European Social Fund)

J. Seruca et al. (eds.), Enterprise Information Systems VI, 267–274.
© *2006 Springer. Printed in the Netherlands.*

analyzed. In spite of the advantages these kinds of systems provide in relation to holters, they still present main problems related to the fact that the analysis is not performed in the place where the signal is acquired. Therefore, there is a *loss of efficiency* in the use of the wireless network because normal ECGs are also sent (and wireless communications imply a high cost); and, if the wireless network is not available at some moment (e.g. in a tunnel, in an elevator, etc.), there might be a loss of ECG signal with the corresponding risk of *not detecting some anomalies*.

Our proposal, the MOLEC system, is a PDA-based monitoring system that records user ECG signals and *locally* analyzes them in order to find arrhythmias. In case of detecting a high risk situation for the user, it sends an alarm with the corresponding ECG signal through the wireless network (GPRS) to a health center for further analysis and medical assistance.

The advantages of this approach are that provides 1) *local analysis:* even if wireless communication with the health center were unavailable, the signal could be analyzed locally at the PDA; 2) *low cost communication* since not the entire signal is sent; 3) *fast medical response* in risk situations for the user; 4) *accessibility*: data recorded in the system can always be queried whether locally or remotely; 5) *distributed computation:* the local analysis in each PDA implies a serious decrease of computational costs in the health center; 6) *openness*: it can be easy integrated in hospitals that manage clinical data through the XML and HL7 standard (HL7, 2003), a representation of clinical documents; 7) *adaptability*: possibility of working with different kinds of ECG sensors; 8) *simplicity*: making technical issues transparent to the users from the point of view of software and hardware components.

The goals of this paper are to present the global architecture of MOLEC, and more specifically the software modules needed in the PDA (in section 2); and to introduce some implementation details (in section 3) and performance results (in section 4), focusing on two important aspects: minimizing the cost of the wireless communications and obtaining a reasonable notification latency for the detection and notification of serious heart anomalies. Finally, in section 5, we present the conclusions.

2 GLOBAL ARCHITECTURE

Three main components form the global architecture of MOLEC (see figure 1, from left to right): 1) The *ECG Sensors* that pick up the electric impulses of

the heart. These sensors are the "intelligent" chips that communicate with the PDA through the bluetooth protocol. 2) The *PDA-Holter* that acquires the data signal in a PDA, records them, detects abnormalities and notifies them immediately in case they are considered serious. 3) The *Molec Hospital* receives the user alarm signals that are shown to the medical personal so that they can react promptly.

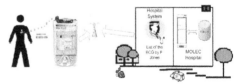

Figure 1: Architecture

2.1 ECG Sensors

The ECG sensors are carried by the user in order to register heart signals and send them to the PDA through the bluetooth protocol (Bluetooth, 2003). Bluetooth is a new standard for very low cost, short-range wireless communication. It enables different types of equipment to communicate wireless with each other and has been thought of as a cable replacement becoming the fastest growing communication standard ever.

Hence we consider that this technology has a promising future for the area of the ECG sensors and we developed the MOLEC project for the integration with bluetooth ECG sensors.

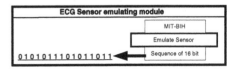

Figure 2: ECG sensor emulating module

Unfortunately, nowadays ECG sensor providers only sell their products with proprietary electrocardio analyzer software. That is why, in our case, the PDA communicates through bluetooth with an ECG sensor emulator placed in a computer device. The ECG signals are taken from a recognized freely distributed database, namely MIT-BIH Arrhythmia database (MIT-BIH, 2003), and sent in real-time as bit sequences to the PDA through the wireless network (see figure 2).

On the other hand, in the PDA-Holter, the Acquisition module receives the bit chains and translates them into a standard format that the whole system understands.

2.2 Molec Hospital

The other system that interacts with the PDA-Holter is the MOLEC Hospital whose main function is to customize the PDA-Holter for each user and to receive users' possible abnormalities. It maintains a large database with all the users registered, their historical and their progress. This could be very useful for the specialists when diagnosing or taking fast decisions in alarm cases.

Furthermore, MOLEC Hospital provides web services that allow querying user data stored in the PDA.

Those web services provide the same functionality that holters have associated in the specialized literature (Farreras, 2001) by a set of reports, which enables physicians to analyze the data easily and quickly and shows information about: 1) automatic arrhythmia detection and identification; 2) analysis of ST segments evolution; 3) ECG parameters. Therefore the data in the database can be queried, locally or remotely, to know different aspects that can be related to the anomalous situations.

In addition, the hospitals can easily incorporate the MOLEC Hospital system into their administration system since it does not interfere with existing applications.

2.3 PDA-Holter

The *PDA-Holter* is the user tool of MOLEC. It is responsible for acquiring the ECG data signal, recording it, detecting abnormalities and notifying them immediately in case they are considered serious. The PDA-Holter is formed by several modules that are explained in the next subsections.

ECG Signal Acquisition

The ECG signal acquisition module receives the digital signal and converts it into a format understandable by the whole system. It manages the Bluetooth communication among the ECG sensors and the PDA. Moreover it has to build signal packages (the "source packages") with a defined size from the bit chains received from the ECG sensors. In section 4, we present the experimental results that have leaded us to define the correct size of these packages.

Data Preprocessing Module

This module obtains the ECG signal in form of source packages and detects the typical part of the beat. An ECG signal consists of several beats that

succeeds with a frequency between 60 and 100 per minute. A normal beat contains a P wave, a QRS complex and one or two T waves. For the arrhythmia detection it is significant the identification of the presence or absence of these waves, the points where start, end and the peaks of them. We call these points 'wave events'.

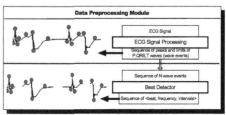

Figure 3: Data preprocessing module

The goal of the data processing module is to detect each beat from the original signal and the points that characterize it. This work is even more difficult if the signal has a high level of noise.

The task is realized in two steps (see Figure 3): Firstly, the ECG signal is processed in order to detect wave events (ECG Signal Processing). For the implementation of the ECG Signal Processing we have used, although slightly changed, a Fortran implementation (Jané, 1997) of an on-line detection algorithm developed by Pan & Tompkins (Pan, 1985) and provided by the recognized PhysioNet (PhysioNet, 1997). This tool was not specifically designed to be run in small computers like PDAs and usually has been used to process long ECG signals. However, we have been able to run it successfully in the PDA using as input small ECG signals (those corresponding to the "source packages" previously mentioned). Only minor changes related to memory management have been made in the "open source" of Ecgpuwave with the goal of increasing the processing speed.

Secondly, the sequence of wave events is transformed into a sequence of beats, it is computed the length of the relevant intervals and segments determined by two wave events (Beat Detector).

Decision Support Module

Once the beats with the corresponding wave events have been detected, the system can start the arrhythmia detection, task which is realized by the Decision Support Module (see Figure 4). Two main steps take place during this analysis: identification of the beat types and classification of the arrhythmias.

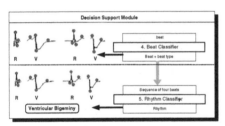

Figure 4: Decision Support Module

In order to *classify the beat* we have tested seventeen methods (Rodriguez, 2003) from the machine learning area and we have chosen the most appropriate one for this kind of data: the decision tree methods (Le Blanc, 1986) that approach discrete-valued target functions. The learned functions are represented by decision trees, but they can also be re-represented as a set of if-then rules to improve human readability. Those rules have been extracted, codified in a programming language and tested. The validation of the rules previously generated took place using the hold-out validation.

In order to *classify the rhythms*, we used a combination of rules: Cardiologic and Inferring rules. The Cardiologic rules were obtained through the translation of the arrhythmia descriptions found in the specialized cardiologic literature (Farreras, 2001) and in parallel, we obtained the Inferring rules by using techniques based on decision trees. Finally we combined them and chose the best rules to detect each rhythm. More details about the decision support module can be found in (Rodriguez, 2003).

Data Manager Module

The main goal of this module is to efficiently manage the restricted memory resources available in the PDA, at least when compared to the great capacity of ECG sensors to generate data.

It has knowledge about all the signals that are being acquired and the stage of its processing. For each packet, once the classification of the beats and rhythm is done, the Data Manager decides how to store each beat: in a regular file or in a database. Normal ECGs are stored in compress files and the anomalous ones are stored at the PDA database. More details about the data manager module can be found in (Rodriguez DOA, 2003).

Alarm Manager Module

This module receives the current heart rhythm and associated parameters and decides whether to generate an alarm. Not all the arrhythmias should be sent in real time to cardiologists so that they can confirm them and/or make their decisions: only those considered very dangerous by them.

With the help of some cardiologists, we have considered two groups, one for high-risk arrhythmias, that is, arrhythmias that should be notified to the hospital when they were detected by the system and the other one for the moderate-risk arrhythmias and normal rhythms that are stored but not immediately notified.

Moreover, we have defined a personalized alarm notification policy that allows deciding if an alarm is sent or not depending on the user parameters. For example: if the patient X presents a short ventricular tachycardia (a high-risk arrhythmia), that alarm would not be notified if the physician had previously defined that, for patient X, only tachycardias longer that thirty seconds should be notified. It has to be noticed that an on-line monitoring system like this would be useless if the cardiologists were bothered with not really relevant arrhythmias very often.

Sender Module

This module is in charge of the communication control between the PDA and the hospital. Hence, it establish and maintain the connection in order to send the alarm messages with the corresponding ECG signal fragments and to answer to the report or query solicitations that the hospital could make. A standard is used to transmit medical data: HL7 (HL7, 2003) that is contained into the XML message. An HL7 representation of clinical documents is called Clinical Document Architecture (CDA). The CDA is a document that specifies the structure and semantics of a clinical document. It can include text, image, sounds and other multimedia content. When the message is received by the hospital, the physician reads the report and confirms the result obtained by MOLEC. Notice that there are tools that can show the data represented in HL7 messages to physicians.

Interface Module

The interface module is responsible for data visualization and measurements display. The figure 5 shows a picture of the PDA-Holter. It provides a friendly interface that draws the ECG signal as soon as the current beat and rhythm types are obtained on-line by the Decision Support Module.

3 IMPLEMENTATION DETAILS

The platform used for the implementation of the PDA-Holter part of MOLEC has been the next PDA:

Figure 5: ECG visualization in MOLEC

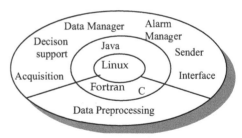

Figure 6: PDA platform

an iPaq 3970 which is a powerful device with a 400Mhz XScale processor, 64MB SDRAM and 48 MB Flash memory. Besides, it has a Linux support, the Familiar Linux distribution (Handhelds 2003), converting it in a complete embedded Linux system.

In figure 6, it can be observed that Linux has been the chosen operating system. The external layer of the figure shows the MOLEC modules that have been explained in the previous section and in the middle layer they can be seen the programming languages used for the implementation of them.

We chiefly have used Java because it is: 1) an object oriented language, 2) platform independent, 3) type safe; it provides 4) automatic memory management, 5) built in threads, 6) synchronized primitives and 7) exception handling, which makes it proper for the development of a critical time system like MOLEC is. Although many people agree that the Java performance is not as good as the one offered by other programming languages, this happens only with interpreted Java. In our prototype, we have compiled the Java source code with the GNU compiler for Java (GNU, 2003), what increased dramatically the processing performance.

For the signal preprocessing part, as this task supposes several mathematical calculus, we chose the Fortran and C languages.

For the implementation of the interface module, we have used the SWT libraries (Eclipse, 2003) because it has been possible to integrate them into our PDA platform (Xscale processor and Linux operating system), and to compile them with the GNU compiler. Moreover, they have provided a very acceptable processing performance (faster than graphical libraries that usually come with Java distributions like AWT and Swing). For the wireless communications, two technologies have been used: the Bluetooth technology and the General Packet Radio Server (GPRS). Bluetooth is a digital connection wireless standard that can transmit data up to a rate of 1

Mbps; and GPRS is a wireless network that allows sending and receiving data packages and its bandwidth is up to 56 Kbps. In section 2.1, we explain the difficulty to obtain the ECG sensors, so for the tests we have performed, the PDA communicates through Bluetooth with an ECG sensor emulator placed in a computer device. The ECG signals are taken from a recognized freely distributed database, namely MIT-BIH Arrhythmia database (MIT-BIH, 2003).

4 PERFORMANCE RESULTS

The main goal of our system is to monitor on-line the ECG signal from people suffering from heart arrhythmias. The technology proposed for the system, PDAs and wireless communications, imposes some restrictions that affect the design of MOLEC.

On the one hand, working with wireless communication technology is more expensive than using wired communication technology. Therefore, it is interesting to pay special attention to try to minimize the cost of the wireless communications and, at the same time, not to delay the notification of serious heart anomalies to the hospital.

On the other hand, it is known that the most powerful current PDAs, even with the latest technological advances, are environments with limited computing resources if compared to PCs.

Moreover, the processing tasks that a monitoring system implies require a high computation cost: the signal processing that obtains the sequence of beats, the classification process of those beats and the corresponding rhythms, and the visualization of the ECG signal. Note that the ECG sensors generate data very quickly. In our case, the data stored correspond to a signal with a frequency of 360 samples per second what is equivalent to 21,600 samples/minute.

Hence, we focus on efficiency in order to prove that a local processing of the ECG signal in a PDA would not introduce too much latency in detection of eventual alarms, compared with a system where the processing is made remotely.

The proposed architecture in section 3 is a functional solution for an ECG monitoring. However, it is also necessary a proper configuration of the processing threads of the system in order to obtain a system stable in time.

Therefore, it is essential to answer to the next question: how often does the analysis process have to be executed?, or, in other words, which is the proper size of the "source package" provided by the "ECG Signal Acquisition Module" that starts the processing in the PDA?

In this section, we are going to present the experiments that we have made with the goals of: calculating the rate of the processing cycle that the system can tolerate in order to not get overloaded, thus the smallest rhythm detection delay (finding the optimal processing rate); and of estimating the latency of the alarm notification and the communication costs with a medical monitoring center.

The test results are compared with the results obtained for the same parameters in a PC.

4.1 The Optimal Processing Rate

Each time the ECG Signal Acquisition receives ECG samples, the system must analyze them in order to find arrhythmias, performing in this way an *entire processing cycle*. The question we try to answer here is how frequently we should perform this processing, in other words, which is the processing rate for the system.

On the one hand, as we have mentioned in section 3, in order to identify arrhythmias, first we have to detect the beats from the ECG signal. The typical occurrence of the beats, in one minute, is between 60 and 100, therefore, the entire processing cycle (that means also the size of the ECG signal package analyzed) should not be less than one second since the probability to find a beat in such a short time interval is really tiny and besides, the algorithm of detecting the wave events is more accurate with longer signals.

On the other hand, the smaller the cycle duration is the faster the alarm detection could be. Unfortunately the computation cost for each cycle does not decrease proportionally to the cycle size and the system can get overloaded. Moreover, this cost differs from PDA to a normal PC since they have different computation power.

Hence, in order to establish the optimal processing rate we have tested the system performance for processing cycles of one and two

seconds respectively. Both types of test have been performed in the PDA and in the PC.

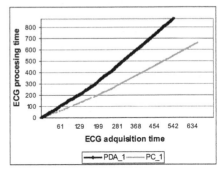

Figure 7: Processing rate of one second

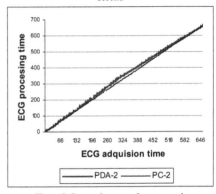

Figure 8: Processing rate of two seconds

The figures 7 and 8 show four functions: PC-1, PDA-1, PC-2 and PDA-2. Every point (x,y) of all those functions indicates that the signal package provided by the ECG Signal Acquisition at the second x is processed by the system at the second y. For PC-1 and PDA-1 functions, the entire processing cycle is of 1 second, and for PC-2 and PDA-2 functions it is of 2 seconds. In PC-1 and PC-2, entire processing cycle is performed in the PC, and, obviously PDA-1 and PDA-2 in the PDA.

As it can be observed in the figures, in both cases the system running in the PC achieves a stable state since the corresponding functions are very close to the diagonal function (that would mean that the signal packet received at second x is processed by the system at second x). The stability comes from the fact that the difference between the diagonal and the PC-x functions does not grow along the time. In other words, the system performs all the tasks before the next signal package has been arrived. In the PDA case, for processing cycles of one second, this property is not achieved. Nevertheless, good results are obtained for processing cycles of two seconds.

As we have explained before, the package size has a direct influence on the rhythm delay detection, and therefore, in the alarm detection. The average of the time necessary to detect the rhythm for this type of packages appears in figure 9.

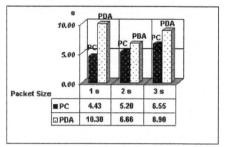

Figure 9: Rhythm detection delay

For packages of one second the PC achieves an average of 4.43 seconds in obtaining the rhythm, meanwhile the PDA needs 10.3 seconds, but, as the processing cannot be performed in real time, the rhythm detection delay would grow if the experiment duration were longer.

For packages of two seconds the PC obtains an average of 5.2s to detect the rhythm meanwhile the PDA needs approximate 6.66s to detect it.

Notice that we have also experimented with signal packages of 3 seconds and seen that real-time processing is also possible. But, as the rhythm delay time is greater than with signal packages of 2 seconds, so we conclude that the entire ECG analysis process should be performed in the PDA every 2 seconds.

Finally, an explanation of the rhythm detection delays obtained is because the detection algorithm used needs the previous beat types and the next three ones, in order to detect the rhythm for the current beat.

4.2 Alarm Notification: Cost and Latency

The aim of this subsection is to compare the MOLEC system, which only sends alarm signals to the medical center (according to the Alarm Manager Module policy described in section 3), with a system that continuously sends the ECG signals picked up from the sensors and detects the alarm in the medical

center. Supposing that a GPRS network is used for communication, we present further the communication costs for the alarm notification during 30 minutes of monitoring.

For this test we used three ECG records: the 100 record that does not contain any alarm, so there is no communication with the medical center; the 207 record that is from a patient with serious health problems and contains five minutes of alarms; and 124 record that is from a typical user, so it contains an average notifications amount. All the ECG signals used have the same sampling frequency (360 samples/second). For the system that sends all the signals we supposed that each sample has 2 bytes.

In the next figure it can be observed the amount of data that the system would send in each case.

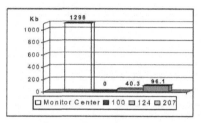

Figure 10: Communication costs

A system, that does not make any processing and compressing of the signal, would send approximately 1296Kb for each 30 minutes which means more than 2Mb/hour, meanwhile the MOLEC-PDA-Holter, in the worst case would send more than 100 times less. If no abnormalities are detected then there is no communication with the health center, as in the case of the record 100. Therefore the amount of communication with the health center is drastically reduced, and so the communication costs.

Another variable that should be taken into account is the delay between the time when the risk episode starts and the moment when the health center notices it.

The time needed for the MOLEC system to notify an alarm is

$$t_{notify} = t_{rhythm\ detection} + t_{alarm\ compression} + t_{communication\ latency}$$

In other words the notification delay depends on the time needed to detect the rhythm in the PDA, the time needed to compress the alarm message and the latency that the GPRS network involves in order to send it to the monitor center.

On the other hand, in the case of the systems that continuously send ECG signals to the medical center the notification delay would depend only on the communication delay over the GPRS network and the rhythm detection time in the medical center.

As it could be observed in the figure 9, the delay of the rhythm detection, with our algorithm, is greater in the PDA (around seven seconds) than in a normal PC with only one user (around four seconds). In a system with more users that continuously send ECG signals the costs to obtain the same results would be greater.

Moreover, a system that continuously sends ECG signals to a monitor center would send many, but small signal packages through the network, what means, if the connection is stable, a constant latency in the communication; meanwhile the MOLEC system sends compressed alarm messages from time to time but with a bigger amount which suppose a bigger latency to send it.

Therefore, the notification latency is a few seconds bigger in the MOLEC system but still remains in a reasonable threshold giving the possibility to the user to obtain medical assistance in time.

5 CONCLUSIONS

In this paper we have presented the global architecture of an innovative system called MOLEC that allows an on-line monitoring of people suffering from heart arrhythmias. Among the advantages of that system are the following ones: 1) Promptness: MOLEC detects anomalous rhythms, anywhere and anytime, as soon as they are produced, and sends the corresponding alarm to the hospital; and 2) Efficiency: MOLEC optimizes the use of wireless communications and PDA resources.

In order to achieve those advantages, we have designed and performed some experiments that consisted in calculating the rate of the processing cycle that the system can tolerate in order to be efficient, stable and the rhythm detection delay minimal. That time has been 2 seconds in the case of the PDAs. Special attention has also been paid in minimizing the cost of the wireless communications without increasing the delay time for the detected serious heart anomalies. That can be achieved by performing the ECG signal processing and rhythm classification locally in the PDA and by sending only alarms to the hospital.

REFERENCES

Bluetooth. 2003. www.bluetooth.com

Cardio Control.2003. www.cardiocontrol.com/cardio.htm

Daja, N., Relgin, I., Reljin B., 2001. Telemonitoring in Cardiology –ECG transmission by Mobile Phone. *Annals of the Academy of Studenica* 4, 2001.

Despopoulos, A.., Silbernagl, S. 1994, Texto y Atlas de fisiología. ISBN: 84-8174-040-3.

Dimitri Konstansas Val Jones, Rainer Hersog. 2003. MobiHealth- innovative 2.5/3G mobile services and applications for healthcare. *Workshop on Standardization in E-Health.* Geneva, Italy.

Eclipse 2003. http://www.eclipse.org/.

Farreras and Rozman, "Medicina interna". Decimatercera edición. Edición en CD-ROM. Sección 3. Cardiologia pag 395 – 523. October, 2001.

GNU 2003. http://gcc.gnu.org/java/

Handhelds 2003. http://www.handhelds.org/.

Health Level 7 (HL7). 2003. http://www.hl7.org/.

Jané, P., Blasi, A., García, J., Laguna, P. 1997. Evaluation of an Automatic Threshold Based Detector of Waveform Limits in Holter ECG with the QT database". Computers in Cardiology, vol. 24, pp. 295-298.

Kunze, C., Gromann, U., Stork, W., Müller-Glaser, K.D.,2002. Application of Ubiquitous Computing in Personal Health Monitoring Systems. *36. annual meeting of the German Society for Biomedical Engineering.*

Le Blanc, R., "Quantitative analysis of cardiac arrhythmias." CRC: Critical Review in Biomedical engineeering, 14(1):1-43, 1986

MIT-BIH Database Distribution. 2003. http://ecg.mit.edu/

Mitchell, T.M., "Machine Learning." ISBN 0-07-042807-7. Section 3: Decision tree learning. Pages 52-75.

Pan, J., Tompkin, W. J. 1985. A real-time QRS detection algorithm". *IEEE Trans. Biom. Eng.* BME-32: 230-236.

Rodríguez, J., Goñi A., Illarramendi, A. 2003. Classifying ECG in an On-Line Monitoring System. Submitted for Publication.

Rodríguez, J., Goñi A., Illarramendi, A. Capturing, Analyzing and Managing ECG Sensors Data in Handheld Devices. *DOA 2003.*

Sachpazidis 2002. @Home: A modular telemedicine system. Mobile Computing in Medicine, Proceedings of the 2. *Workshop on mobile computing. Heidelberg, Germany, 2002.*

Ventracor Limited. 2003 http://www.ventracor.com

PART 5

Human-Computer Interaction

CABA²L A BLISS PREDICTIVE COMPOSITION ASSISTANT FOR AAC COMMUNICATION SOFTWARE

Nicola Gatti

Dipartimento di Elettronica e Informazione, Politecnico di Milano
Piazza Leonardo da Vinci 32, I-20133, Milano, Italy
ngatti@elet.polimi.it

Matteo Matteucci

Dipartimento di Elettronica e Informazione, Politecnico di Milano
Piazza Leonardo da Vinci 32, I-20133, Milano, Italy
matteucci@elet.polimi.it

Keywords: AAC languages, accessibility to disabled users, hidden Markov model, intelligent user interface, symbolic prediction.

Abstract: In order to support the residual communication capabilities of verbal impaired peoples softwares allowing Augmentative and Alternative Communication (AAC) have been developed. AAC communication software aids provide verbal disables with an electronic table of AAC languages (i.e. Bliss, PCS, PIC, etc.) symbols in order to compose messages, exchange them via email, or vocally synthetize them, and so on. A current open issue, in thins kind of software, regards human-computer interaction in verbal impaired people suffering motor disorders. They can adopt only ad-hoc input device, such as buttons or switches, which require an intelligent automatic scansion of the AAC symbols table in order to compose messages. In such perspective we have developed CABA²L an innovative composition assistant exploiting an user linguistic behavior model adopting a semantic/probabilistic approach for predictive Bliss symbols scansion. CABA²L is based on an original discrete implementation of auto-regressive hidden Markov model called DAR-HMM and it is able to predict a list of symbols as the most probable ones according to both the previous selected symbol and the semantic categories associated to the symbols. We have implemented the composition assistant as a component of BLISS2003 an AAC communication software centered on Bliss language and experimentally validated it with both synthetic and real data.

1 INTRODUCTION

Nowadays, millions of verbal impaired people live in the world (Bloomberg and Johnson, 1990); their communication capabilities are permanently or temporarily corrupted and, for this reason, most of them suffer a condition of social exclusion. Verbal impaired people can not adopt canonic communicative media (Fodor, 1983), such as natural language, and, as the clinical experience evidences, their primary need is to try alternative ways, according to their residual capabilities, to communicate. In 1983 the International Society for Augmentative and Alternative Communication (ISAAC, 1983) has been established in USA with the aim to develop alternative instruments to allow verbal impaired people to communicate. ISAAC has been involved in developing both languages, namely, Augmentative and Alternative Communication languages (AAC) (Shane, 1981), and aids in order to support residual communicative capabilities in verbal disables. AAC languages are usually based on symbols and exploit peculiar com-

position rules simple enough to be learnt and used by verbal disables. Among the AAC languages we can cite: Bliss, PCS, PIC, PICSYMB, CORE, and Rebus.

Currently, disables adopt paper tables (see Figure 1) containing their most used AAC symbols and point in such tables the symbols related to what they want to communicate. In the AAC field other AAC aids exist, such as VOCAs (i.e. smart tablets that associate vocal inputs to specific symbols), but they evidence severe limitation with respect to effective verbal disables needs since they present a limited set di predefined sentences. Given this scenario, information technology plays a relevant role by providing the verbal disabled people with aids, such as AAC software applications, to support their communication. In fat, AAC software applications provide verbal impaired people with an electronic table of symbols where they can select AAC symbols to compose messages adopting canonical or ad-hoc AAC devices (e.g. joystick, tablet, switch, etc.). In addition, they offer other features, such as email message exchange and vocal synthesis.

I. Seruca et al. (eds.), Enterprise Information Systems VI, 277–284.
© *2006 Springer. Printed in the Netherlands.*

A current open issue concerning AAC communication software aids regards human-computer interaction in disables with motor disorders (Lee et al., 2001), that represent about the 60% of verbal impaired people. Motor disordered people are not able to use canonical input devices, such as keybord and mouse, but they can use only ad-hoc devices, such as buttons or switches according to their residual motor capabilities. Such devices operate providing the AAC software aid with an on/off input, so, in order to select AAC symbols from a table, it is required an automatic scansion of such table underlining the symbols they can select. The intelligent scansion mechanisms currently adopted in AAC software do not assure a relevant reduction of the time spent by verbal disables to compose messages: in fact person evidencing motor disorders can spend few minutes to compose a simple sentece. In such perspective we have developed CABA^{2}L (Composition Assistant for Bliss Augmentative Alternative Language) an innovative composition assistant that performs a predictive scansion of Bliss symbols and reduces up to 60% the time required to compose a message. CABA^{2}L is based on a discrete implementation of auto-regressive hidden Markov model (Rabiner, 1989) called DAR-HMM and it predicts a list of symbols as the most probable according to both the last selected symbol and the semantic categories associated to symbols. Moreover, the predictive model embedded in CABA^{2}L can be adapted to the specific disable user to better match his/her peculiar linguistic behavior.

The paper is structured as follows. In Section 2, we introduce current scansion mechanisms for verbal disables and underline prediction issues. Section 3 introduces Bliss symbolic prediction issues and probabilistic prediction techniques. Section 4 describes DAR-HMM and its implementation. Section 5 reports the experimental results we have obtained. Finally, Section 6 concludes the paper.

2 SENTENCE COMPOSITION IN PEOPLE WITH MOTOR DISORDERS

Currently some AAC software aids provide people suffering motor disorders with an automatic scansion of the symbol table (see Figure 1). A generic scansion mechanism can be described as follows: an highlight moves autonomously on an AAC symbol table according to a specific strategy, when the requested symbol is highlighted the user can select such symbol activating the device, then the highlight starts to move again. Each scansion mechanism is characterized by a specific ad-hoc input device and the scansion strategy.

Ad-hoc input devices allow the verbal disable to

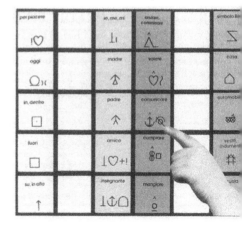

Figure 1: An AAC symbols table

start the scansion, select symbols, close the sentence, and activate features such as vocal synthesis. Each user adopts the device that best matches with his/her residual motor capabilities. The alternative/residual motor capabilities used are usually: blowing with the mouth, closing the eyes, pushing big buttons.

The scansion strategy determines what is the next symbol to highlight. In literature several automatic scansion strategies for AAC communication aids can be retrieved (Higginbotham et al., 1998) and each one of them exhibits advantages and drawbacks. Such strategies can be classified in (Swiffin et al., 1987):

- *linear scansion*: the symbols are presented sequentially from the first symbol of the table to the last one;

- *row-column scansion*: at first the rows are scanned, once the disable has selected a row, its columns are scanned (or vice versa) (Simpson and Koester, 1999);

- *scansion at subgroups*: the symbols are presented in groups fewer and fewer up to only one symbol;

- *predictive scansion*: it predicts the most probable symbols the user will use to continue the sentence according to a model of the user, and it presents the most probable ones.

The choice of the most adequate scansion strategy for the peculiar user depends on several factors, such as the mental and motor residual capabilities, the adopted AAC language and the size of the user symbols table. With respect to the user mental capabilities, both scansion at subgroups and row-column scansion require the user to remember exactly the place of the desired symbol, so they can not be used by disables evidencing severe mental impairments. With respect to the size of the symbol table linear scansion, row-column scansion and scansion at subgroups do not offer good performance if the number of symbols is elevate (50 symbols and more). Hence, current non predictive scansion strategies do not allow to verbal disables suffering motor disorders a relevant reduction in the time spent to compose sentences (Lee et al., 2001).

Although predictive scansion strategies could assure better performance (Koester and Levine, 1994), they are currently adopted in a small number of AAC assistitive technology aids. In particular *symbolic prediction* is currently adopted only in VOCAs, but it evidences severe limitations: it predicts symbols according to a strict set of sentences previously registered and do not exploit a linguistic behavior model of the user. In such a way such prediction system allows the user to compose a fixed number of messages and it is not able to generalize allowing the composition of new messages (Higginbotham et al., 1998). In literature numerous predictive techniques have been developed, but they have been applied mainly in alphabetical prediction. In such context the main prediction techniques (Aliprandi et al., 2003) employ a *statistical* approach (based on hidden Markov models and Bayesian networks), a *syntactic* and *strong syntactic* approach (based on linguistic models), a *semantic* approach (based on semantic networks), and hybrid approaches. To the best of our knowledge, currently symbolic predictive models do not exist.

The main issue with alphabetical predictive techniques, that prevents their use for symbolic prediction, is related to the size of the dictionary of items to be predicted and their composition rules. In fact, alphabetical prediction operates on a limited number (about 20) of items, the alphabetic signs, that can be organized in words known *a priori*. Conversely, symbolic prediction operates on a set of symbols variable in number that can be organized in different sequences according to the peculiar user linguistic capabilities. In addition alphabetical prediction techniques do not match with the symbolic prediction issue. On the other side, a pure statistical approach does not keep into account the peculiar AAC language structure, in fact each verbal impaired user adopts/develops an own syntactic model according to his/her residual mental capacities. This is also the reason for which the utilization of a pure syntactic approach for any user can not be achieved, and a pure semantic approach does not address the variability related to the residual user capacities.

We consider an ad-hoc hybrid approach as the right choice in this context; in the following sections of the paper we focus on the description of this prediction model since it represents the most original part of our work.

3 BLISS SYMBOLS PREDICTION AND GRAPHICAL MODELS

In our work we focus on the Bliss language (Bliss, 1966), since it is the most adopted and expressive among AAC languages. In the design of a composition assistant to predicts Bliss symbols, a set of peculiar requirements regarding both the *human-computer interface* and the *prediction model* can be established.

The composition assistant should suggest a limited number of symbols (around 4-5) not to confuse the disable user (Koester and Levine, 1994), the prediction must be accomplished in real time, and the scansion rate must be adaptable with the user needs (Cronk and Schubert, 1987). This last aspect addresses issues due to the high variability of residual mental and motor capabilities, in fact the composition assistant should be able to adapt the scansion rate according to the time required by the specific disable to read and select the highlighted symbol. With respect to the prediction model, a verbal impaired user can adopt all the Bliss symbols (about 2000), even if he/she usually adopts only a part of them (usually from 6-7 to 200), and it should be taken into account that the symbol to be predicted depends in some extents on the symbols selected previously.

We have adopted a semantic/probabilistic approach to model the user language behavior and we use this model in order to predict the most probable symbols to be suggested by an automatic scansion system. We have used the semantic approach to take advantage of a Bliss symbols categorization and the probabilistic approach both to take into account for uncertainties in the user language model and to give a reasonable estimate of the reliability of the proposed prediction.

In CABA^{2}L we have used a graphical model based on a variation of a classical Hidden Markov Models (HMM). Classical HMMs involve *states* and *symbols*, in particular they relate the probability that a particular symbol is emitted to the probability that the system is in particular state. Moreover they use a stochastic process to define the transition from a state to the other (see Figure 2).

In HMM a particular sequence of observation (i.e. observed symbols) is generated by choosing at time $t = 0$ the initial state $s_i \in S$ according to an initial probability distribution $\pi(0)$, a symbol v_k is generated from a multinomial probability distribution b_k^i associated to state s_i, and the system move from the present state s_i to the next state $s_{i'}$ of the sequence according to a transition probability $a_{ii'}$ to generate the next symbol. States in this model are not directly observable; symbols represent the only information that can be observed, and this is the reason for the term *hidden* in the model name. Notice that classical HMMs consider symbols as independent from each

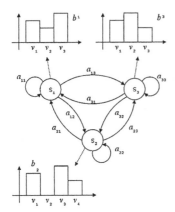

Figure 2: An example of Hidden Markov Model

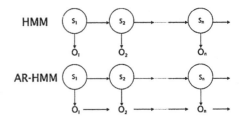

Figure 3: Comparison between HMM and AR-HMM

'food' because it connects the verb subcategory 'feeding', we have not a substantive subcategory 'animal' because it does not connect a specific category). We report such subcategories and the number of symbols assigned to each subcategory (note that a symbol can belong more than one category).

- *Verbs*: people movement (23), objects movement (15), body care (16), description (3), everyday (10), servile (7), emotional (7), feeding (33), other (180).

- *Adverbs*: time (67), exclamatory (12), place (28), quantity (17), holidays (12), color (23), other (20).

- *Adjectives*: opinion (29), character (18), physical description (33), food description (17), quantity (13), feeling (29), other (52).

- *Substantives*: food (141), cloth (38), body (47), everyday (26), people place (110), things place (22), other (600).

- *People*: possession (16), relation (47), job (38), other (51).

- *Punctuation*: question (13), other (36).

other given the present state; thus probability of observing symbol v_k at time t in a sequence of symbols does not depend on the symbol observed at time $t-1$, but it depends only on the present state s_i and, implicitly, the previous one $s_{i'}$ through the transition probability $a_{ii'}$ (Ghahramani, 2001).

HMMs could be adopted to implement a predictive models for Bliss symbols if we could assume that a symbol is predictable given the corresponding Bliss symbol category as the hidden state. However, this approach oversimplify the user language model described previously: it does not relate the emission of a symbol with the symbol previously emitted due to the independence assumption in HMMs. To face this issues we have adopted a particular extension of HMM, called AR-HMM (Auto-Regressive Hidden Markov Model) that relate the emitted symbol both to the actual state (as canonical HMM) and to the previous emitted symbol (Figure 3 illustrates the differences between canonical HMM and AR-HMM). In such a way we have a model that keeps into account the previous emission and it is still computationally tractable as described further on.

In order to identify the possible hidden states of an ad-hoc AR-HMM for the Bliss language, symbols have been divided into six categories according to their grammatic role, and, later, each category has been divided into a number of subcategories adopting the semantic networks formalism (Quillian, 1968) to keep into account the semantic of the symbols and the logic connection among two subcategories. This subcategories identification process has been accomplished in collaboration with experts in verbal rehabilitation to obtain subcategories not excessively specific that would have complicated the model without any reason (e.g., we have a substantive subcategory

4 DISCRETE AUTO-REGRESSIVE HIDDEN MARKOV MODEL

AR-HMMs are commonly used in literature for prediction in continuous systems and they usually describe the emission probability of an symbol/value according to a Gaussian distribution; the emission of Bliss symbol, however, is a discrete event that can be described adopting a multinomial probability distribution. In CABA²L, to overcome this problem, we have implemented a Discrete Auto-Regressive Hidden Markov Model (DAR-HMM) where the emission probability for a symbol is described using a bivariated multinomial distribution. In fact, we introduced the DAR-HMM as a first order extension of a

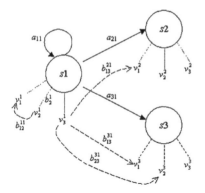

Figure 4: Symbols emission in DAR-HMM; s_i is the state (symbol subcategory), v_j are the observed symbol

classical HMM where the symbol emission probability depends on the present state and the last observed symbol as depicted in Figure 4.

DAR-HMM for symbolic prediction can be described using a parameter vector $\lambda = < \Pi^0, A, B >$, where $\Pi^0[N]$ is the vector of inital subcategory probability $\pi_i(0)$, $A[N][N]$ is the matrix with subcategory transition probabilities $a_{ii'}$, and $B[N][M][M+1]$ is the emission matrix[1] with symbol probabilities $b_{kk'}^{ii'}$ and b_k^i (see Appendix A for details). In CABA^{2}L, this λ vector has been estimated using a dataset of Bliss sentences. To do that, we have adopted a variation of the Baum-Welch algorithm, an iterative algorithm based on the Expectation-Maximization method (Bilmes, 1998; Dempster et al., 1977), adapting this technique to the specific case of DAR-HMM (see Figure 5).

Since the Baum-Welch algorithm is a greedy algorithm that can be trapped in local minima, the initialization estimate of λ parameter vector is a fundamental aspect. In literature a theoretical solution that addresses such issue does not exist; in practice, the adoption of a random or uniform distributed initialization for A and Π^0 has been verified to be adequate. In particular we adopt an uniform distribution as initial estimate for Π^0, and a distribution based on the knowledge about the phenomenon for A. Only

---

[1]From an implementation point of view matrix B could represent the main issue of this model (i.e., with $N = 30$ subcategories and $M \simeq 2000$ symbols the cells number amount is of the order of 10^8, about 400MBytes). However B can be considered a sparse matrix since from each subcategories only a part of symbols can be emitted, so the cells number is, approximately, lower than 10^4 and ad-hoc data structure such as *heap* or *priority queue* and optimized algorithms can be used to overcame memory occupancy and speed access issues.

arcs connecting subcategories in the semantic model of the language (see Section 3) should have a probability $a_{ii'} \neq 0$. However, we have assigned to the arcs between symbols and states that are not connected in the semantic network a very low probability, not to preclude the training algorithm to eventually discover unforeseen correlations.

The initial estimation for the B matrix is more critical so we have used the *Segmental k-Means* (Juang and Rabiner, 1990; Juang et al., 1986) technique to obtain a more confidential estimate. Such process considers a sub set of sentences composing the dataset, and, for each one, it looks for the best sequence of subcategories using the Viterbi algorithm to upgrades the symbols emission probabilities.

Given the initial values λ^0 for the model parameters, we use a modified Baum-Welch algorithm to estimate, from a real dataset, the model parameters through a sequence of temporary $\overline{\lambda}$ model parameters. As in any learning algorithm, the main issue is avoiding the *overfitting* phenomenon (Caruana et al., 2001), so we would like to stop the training phase according to the generalization error (i.e., the error on new samples) and not just observing the training error (i.e., the error on the training set). To do this, we have used the *K-fold cross-validation technique* (Amari et al., 1995); it consists in dividing the whole set of sentences into K similar subsets to use at each iteration $K - 1$ subsets for parameter estimation and the remaining validation set is used to valuate the convergence of model generalization error. In other words, we calculate the errors of the model in predicting the sentences of the validation set it has never seen, and we analyze the validation error function during training iterations of the Baum-Welch algorithm until it reaches its minimum.

In order to terminate the iteration at which the error function reaches its minimum, several practical techniques can be adopted, but none of them assures the achieving of the global minimum. We have chosen to adopt a termination criterion based on the *generalization loss* method (Prechelt, 1996). Given:

$$Err_{Opt}(t) = \min_{t' \leq t} Err_{Val}(t')$$

the minimum error is obtained at time t; consider

$$GL(t) \triangleq 100\left(\frac{Err_{Val}(t)}{Err_{Opt}(t)} - 1\right)$$

which represents the last increment in comparison with the minimum. The training phase is stopped whenever the generalization loss GL becomes bigger than a given threshold τ:

$$GL(t) > \tau.$$

In this approach, the error function could stabilize after a local minimum, without $GL(t)$ rising the threshold. In order to face such issue we have added to

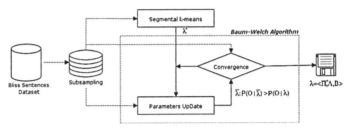

Figure 5: The training process

the stop criterion two condition relating the maximum number of iterations and the minimum improvement during learning.

5 EXPERIMENTAL RESULTS

DAR-HMM has been implemented in CABA^{2}L and, finally, integrated in BLISS2003, a communication software centered on Bliss language. CABA^{2}L receives from BLISS2003 the last selected symbol, calculates the most probable four symbols according to the established requirements, and scans them in an ad-hoc panel in the graphical interface before scanning the full table.

In order to validate DAR-HMM, we are interested in giving an estimated *training error* and *generalization error* in several user scenarios characterized by symbols, symbols subcategories, user residual linguistic capabilities, and user needs; we are also interested in evaluating the time required both for learning and prediction process. To accomplishing this validation, we have strictly collaborated with two Italian clinics for verbal impairments (PoloH and SNPI of Crema^2) evaluating the prediction performance in different scenarios; in this paper we report just two scenarios as the most significant ones:

1. a dataset of 20 sentences with 4 sub-categories and 7 symbols representing a verbal impaired person unskilled in Bliss utilization or suffering deep mental deficiency;

2. a dataset of 80 sentences with 18 sub-categories and 120 symbols representing a verbal impaired person skilled in Bliss use and without deep mental deficiency.

We have shuffled the sentences of each dataset in order to achieve a homogeneous dataset not affected by

---

^{2}PoloH is a information technology center that support AAC aids adoption. SNPI is the neuropsychiatric adolescent and infancy local service associated to the hospital of Crema, Italy.

Table 1: Training error: probability that the requested symbol is in the first four predicted symbols according to the datasets adopted to train the DAR-HMM

Predictions	Scenario 1		Scenario 2	
	Mean	Std. Dev.	Mean	Std. Dev.
1 symbol	0.343	0.055	0.250	0.017
2 symbols	0.563	0.074	0.299	0.028
3 symbols	0.778	0.067	0.319	0.033
4 symbols	0.908	0.056	0.345	0.042
not suggested	0.092	0.056	0.655	0.042

time correlation. In addition we have divided each dataset into two parts, respectively 80% of sentences in the first part and 20% of sentences in the second one. We have adopted the first part to training the model computing the training error. We have adopted the second one to evaluate the generalization error.

The training error expresses the effectiveness of the learning and it is obtained comparing the suggestion proposed by CABA^{2}L during the composition of sentences it has learnt. To estimate the correct prediction's probability, we have carried out over 800 simulations where we compare the suggested symbols and the one chosen by the user. In Table 1 mean and standard deviation for both the two scenarios are showed, they evidence a training error of about 9.2% for the first scenario and 65.5% for the second one taking into account a number of proposed symbols equals to 4 as suggested by therapist and according to the requirements from Section 3.

The generalization error expresses the effectiveness of the prediction system, and it is obtained comparing the suggestions proposed by CABA^{2}L during the composition of sentences that exhibit the same probability distribution with respect to the sentences it has learnt, but were not presented to the system during the training phase. To estimate the correct prediction's probability, we have carried out over 200 simulations where we compare the suggested symbols and the one chosen by the user. In Table 2 mean and standard deviation for both the two scenarios are showed, they evidence a generalization error of about 11.3% for the first scenario and 64.3% for the second one taking again into account a number of proposed symbols equals to 4 before. The values of mean and standard deviation evaluated in generalization error are very close to the values evaluated in training error, thus DAR-HMM evidences high generalization ability. Although the training and generalization errors are in the second scenario high we are confident to get better result just having a bigger dataset.

Time spent by verbal disables that collaborated with us in order to compose messages using BLISS2003 with respect to the time spent with adoption of a traditional scansion system has been reduced up to 60%. Tests have evidenced that the training phase requires few minutes depending on the size of the dataset and the number of symbols and subcategories, but this does not affect BLISS2003 performance, because it can be run on background. Conversely, these tests have proved that the symbols prediction is immediate (<1 second) and can be performed in real time.

6 CONCLUSIONS

In this paper we have analyzed the AAC symbols scansion issues for motor disordered persons establishing requirements according to literature and the experiences of several clinics for verbal disables that have collaborated with us. In particular we described prediction models currently adopted in AAC context and we designed an ad-hoc prediction model (DAR-HMM). We described DAR-HMM peculiarities: its formalism, ad-hoc emission rules, parameters initialization, training processes, stopping criterion, and implementation issues. We have applied DAR-HMM to the case of Bliss language introducing semantic categories for Bliss symbols. In addition, we integrated CABA^{2}L into BLISS2003 an AAC communication software based on Bliss, and experimentally validated it with real data in collaboration with two Italian clinical centers for verbal impaired people proving its effectiveness for reduction of the time spent to compose Bliss messages.

In future the performance of the prediction will be improved refining the prediction model. Moreover we would like to achieve on-line adaptation of the DAR-HMM to the linguistic behavior of the user and to take into account the evolution of the user linguistic capabilities, and to support other AAC languages with respect to Bliss, particularly PCS. Finally we will analyze the learnt semantic/probabilistic model of the linguistic behavior of the user in order to study relationships between disabilities and verbal impairments.

Table 2: Estimated generalization error: probability that the requested symbol is in the first four predicted symbols according to the datasets not adopted to train the DAR-HMM

Predictions	Scenario 1		Scenario 2	
	Mean	Std. Dev.	Mean	Std. Dev.
1 symbol	0.202	0.082	0.185	0.089
2 symbols	0.438	0.146	0.252	0.073
3 symbols	0.666	0.181	0.304	0.070
4 symbols	0.887	0.067	0.357	0.077
not suggested	0.113	0.067	0.643	0.077

REFERENCES

Aliprandi, C., Barsocchi, D., Fanciulli, F., Mancarella, P., Pupillo, D., Raffaelli, R., and Scudellari, C. (2003). AWE, an innovative writing prediction environment. In *Proc. of the Int. Human Computer Conf.*, Crete, Greece.

Amari, S., Finke, M., Muller, K. R., Murata, N., and Yang, H. (1995). Asymptotic statistical theory of overtraining and cross-validation. Technical Report METR 95-06, Dep. of Math. Eng. and Inf., Physics, Uni. of Tokyo, Tokyo.

Bilmes, J. (1998). A gentle tutorial of the EM Algorithm and its application to parameter estimation for Gaussian Mixture and Hidden Markov Models. Technical report, Dep. of Electrical Eng. and Comp. Sci. at Uni. of California, Berkeley.

Bliss, C. K. (1966). *Semantography*. Semantography Blissymbolic Communication, Sidney, Australia.

Bloomberg, K. and Johnson, H. (1990). A statewide demographic survey of people with severe communication impairments. *Augmentative and Alternative Communication*, 6:50–60.

Caruana, R., Lawrence, S., and Giles, C. L. (2001). Overfitting in neural networks: Backpropagation, conjugate gradient, and early stopping. In *Advances in Neural Information Processing Systems*, Denver, Colorado.

Cronk, S. and Schubert, R. (1987). Development of a real time expert system for automatic adaptation of scanning rates. In *Proc. of the Conf. on Rehabilitation Technology, RESNA*, volume 7, pages 109–111, Washington, DC, USA.

Dempster, A., Laird, N., and Rubin, D. (1977). Maximum likelihood from incomplete data via the EM algorithm. *Journal of Royal Statistical Society B*, 39:1–38.

Fodor, J. (1983). *The modularity of mind*. MIT Press, Cambridge, USA.

Ghahramani, Z. (2001). An introduction to hidden markov models and bayesian networks. *International Journal of Pattern Recognition and Artificial Intelligence*, 1:9–42.

Higginbotham, D. J., Lesher, G. W., and Moulton, B. J. (1998). Techniques for augmenting scanning communication. *Augmentative and Alternative Communication*, 14:81–101.

ISAAC (1983). Int. Soc. for Augmentative and Alternative Communication, Internet site. http://www.isaac-online.org. Last accessed October 1th, 2003.

Juang, B. and Rabiner, L. (1990). The segmental k-means algorithm for estimating parameters of hidden markov models. In *IEEE Trans. on Acoustics Speech and Signal processing*, ASSP-38, pages 1639–1641. IEEE Computer Society Press.

Juang, B., Rabiner, L., and Wilpon, G. (1986). A segmental k-means training procedure for connected word recognition. *AT&T Technical Journal*, 65:21–31.

Koester, H. and Levine, S. (1994). Learning and performance of ablebodied individuals using scanning systems with and without word prediction. *Assistive Technology*, page 42.

Lee, H.-Y., Yeh, C.-K., Wu, C.-M., and Tsuang, M.-F. (2001). Wireless communication for speech impaired subjects via portable augmentative and alternative system. In *Proc. of the Int. Conf. of the IEEE on Eng. in Med. and Bio. Soc.*, volume 4, pages 3777–3779, Washington, DC, USA.

Prechelt, L. (1996). Early stopping-but when? In *Neural Networks: Tricks of the Trade*, pages 55–69.

Quillian, M. (1968). Semantic memory. In *Minsky ed. Semantic Information Processing*. MIT Press, Cambridge.

Rabiner, L. (1989). A tutorial on hidden markov models and selected applications in speech recognition. In *Proc. of the IEEE*, 77, pages 257–286. IEEE Computer Society Press.

Shane, B. (1981). *Augmentative Communication: an introduction*. Blackstone, Toronto, Canada.

Simpson, R. C. and Koester, H. H. (1999). Adaptive one-switch row-column scanning. *IEEE Trans. on Rehabilitation Engineering*, 7:464–473.

Swiffin, A. L., Pickering, J. A., and Newell, A. F. (1987). Adaptive and predictive techniques in a cammunication prosthesis. *Augmentative and Alternative Communication*, 3:181–191.

APPENDIX A

In this appendix, we briefly describe the DAR-HMM according to the formalism adopted by Rabiner in (Rabiner, 1989) to specify classical hidden Markov models:

- $S \triangleq \{s_i\}$, subcategories set with $N = |S|$;

- $V \triangleq \{v_j\}$, predictable symbols set with $M = |V|$;

- $V^{(i)} = \{v_k^{(i)}\}$, set of symbols predictable in subcategory i with $M^{(i)} = |V^{(i)}|$ and $V = \bigcup_i V^{(i)}$;

- $O(t) \in V$, observed symbol at time t;

- $Q(t) \in S$, state at time t;

- $\pi_i(t) = P(Q(t) = s_i)$, probability that s_i is the actual subcategory at time t;

- $a_{ii'} = P(Q(t+1) = s_i | Q(t) = s_{i'})$, transition probability from $s_{i'}$ to s_i;

- $b_k^i = P(O(0) = v_k^{(i)} | Q(0) = s_i)$, probability of observing $v_k^{(i)}$ from subcategory s_i at $t = 0$;

- $b_{kk'}^{ii'} = P(O(t) = v_k^{(i)} | Q(t) = s_i, O(t-1) = v_{k'}^{(i')})$, probability of observing $v_k^{(i)}$ from the subcategory s_i having just observed $v_{k'}^{(i')}$.

DAR-HMM for symbolic prediction can thus be described using a parameter vector $\lambda =< \Pi^0, A, B >$, where $\Pi^0[N]$ is the vector of inital subcategory probability $\pi_i(0)$, $A[N][N]$ is the matrix with subcategory transition probabilities $a_{ii'}$, and $B[N][M][M+1]$ is the emission matrix with symbol probabilities $b_{kk'}^{ii'}$ and b_k^i. Given λ the vector of parameters describing a specific language behavior model, we can predict the first observed symbol as the most probable one at time $t = 0$:

$$
\begin{aligned}
\hat{O}(0) &= \underset{v_k^{(i)}}{\arg\max} \left(P(O(0) = v_k^{(i)} | \lambda) \right) \\
&= \underset{v_k^{(i)}}{\arg\max} \left(P(O(0) | Q(0), \lambda) P(Q(0)) \right) \\
&= \underset{v_k^{(i)}}{\arg\max} \left(b_k^i \cdot \pi_i(0) \right).
\end{aligned}
$$

Then mimicking the DAR-HMM generative model, to predict the tth symbol of a sentence we want to maximize the symbol probability in the present (hidden) state given the last observed symbol:

$$
P\left(O(t) = v_k^{(i)}, Q(t) = s_i | O(t-1) = v_{k'}^{(i')}, \lambda \right).
$$

Recalling that we can compute the probability of the current (hidden) state as:

$$
\begin{aligned}
P(Q(t)) &= \sum_{i'=1}^{N} P(Q(t)|Q(t-1)) P(Q(t-1)) = \\
&= \sum_{i'=1}^{N} \pi_{i'}(t-1) a_{ii'} = \pi_i(t),
\end{aligned}
$$

we obtain a recursive form for symbol prediction at time t:

$$
\hat{O}(t) = \underset{v_k^{(i)}}{\arg\max} \left(b_{kk'}^{ii'} \cdot \sum_{i'=1}^{N} \pi_{i'}(t-1) a_{ii'} \right).
$$

A METHODOLOGY FOR INTERFACE DESIGN FOR OLDER ADULTS

Mary Zajicek

Department of Computing, School of Technology, Oxford Brookes University, Wheatley Campus, Oxford OX33 1HX, UK, Email: mzajicek@brookes.ac.uk

Keywords: User models, interface design patterns, design methodology, universal accessibility, older adults, speech systems, memory support, strategies at the interface.

Abstract: This paper puts forward a new design method based upon Alexandrian patterns for interface design for particular user groups. The author has created a set of interface design patterns for speech systems for older adults with the aim of supporting the dynamic diversity in this group. The patterns themselves reflect a significant body of research work with this user group uncovering important information about how they interact with speech systems. The design knowledge embedded in these patterns is therefore closely linked to knowledge about the user and enables interface designers to clarify which users are excluded from their software.

1 INTRODUCTION

This paper is concerned with a new methodology for interface design for older adults using speech systems, where carefully describing the users for whom the system is defined will promote a better fit between user and system.

The paper outlines the characteristics of older adults as computer users and introduces the idea of patterns to encapsulate design recommendations for speech systems for this user group. Older adults to a greater or lesser degree experience memory impairment and a reduction in their ability to build strategies at the interface, characteristics which are modeled within the patterns.

The paper discusses the challenge of complying with legislation which promotes software accessibility for all user types and patterns is suggested as providing a useful framework within which software developers can analyse their prospective user group in this regard.

Eight interface design patterns are analyzed in terms of the user models they implicitly and explicitly encapsulate, and also in terms of the users they disadvantage.

2 WHY WOULD WE WANT TO MODEL USERS' ABILITIES?

Recently significant legislation has been introduced in the US and UK aimed at encouraging designers to ensure that software does not exclude certain user groups. Age related impairments older adults often exclude older adults from the use of standard software. For example the print may be to small or the multi-tasking interface may rely to heavily on good memory or their ability to build complex strategies in order to use the software.

A better understanding of older adults as users through modeling their attributes will enable interface designers to clarify which users are excluded by their software.

3 THE ORIGIN OF INTERFACE DESIGN PATTERNS

The idea for patterns and pattern language originated in the domain of architecture; with the publication more than twenty years ago of Christopher Alexander's book *The Timeless Way of Building* (Alexander, 1979). He proposed that one could achieve excellence in architecture by learning and using a carefully defined set of design rules, or

285

, Seruca et al. (eds.), Enterprise Information Systems VI, 285–292.
© 2006 Springer. Printed in the Netherlands.

patterns: and although the essence of a beautifully designed building is hard to define the application of patterns for room design etc can contribute to the design of the whole.

A pattern describes an element of design possibly together with how and why you would achieve it. For example Alexander created patterns which describe ways of placing windows in a room and designing a porch which achieves a successful transition between inside and outside a building. These include textual descriptions and diagrams or photos (Alexander, 1977).

Patterns for human-computer interface design were first discussed in the late nineties, and currently there exist a range of different pattern forms. Some pattern builders choose a purely narrative approach such as those found in the *Design of Sites* (Van Duyne et al., 2002) whereas others are more structured. Martin van Welie for example sets out patterns under the headings *Problem* and *Solution* Van Welie, 2002) A comprehensive list of pattern forms can be found at Sally Fincher's *Pattern Form Gallery* (Fincher, 2003).

The pattern form used in this paper, is based on Jennifer Tidwell's *UI Patterns and Techniques* (Tidwell, 2002) where the pattern has four sections, *Use When, Why, How*, and *Examples*. A fifth section entitled *Tradeoffs* has been included from the claims approach, as there are always tradeoffs when designing speech dialogues and these should be made explicit.

A full day workshop, 'Perspectives on HCI Patterns: Concepts and tools' at CHI 2003 was attended by several of the pattern developers referenced above, where they came up with the pattern Language Markup Language (PLML)(Fincher, 2003) which promises to provide a generic pattern format.

4 THE OLDER ADULT AS A USER

Adults as they get older experience a wide range of age related impairments including loss of vision, hearing, memory and mobility, the combined effects of which contribute to loss of confidence and difficulties in orientation and absorption of information. Significantly, age related impairments affect people at different rates and even any one individual from day to day. The need for Design for Dynamic Diversity to accommodate this dynamic diversity of ability in older adults was first proposed by Newell and Gregor (Newell & Gregor, 2000) and is demonstrated in interface design by Gregor Newell and Zajicek (Gregor et al., 2002).

Furthermore, gathering interface requirements from older adults requires considerable skill and understanding of the user group. Newell and Gregor also proposed (Newell & Gregor, 2000) that standard User Centered Design techniques, which rely on relatively homogeneous user groups for user testing, should be replaced by User Sensitive Inclusive Design, which seeks out diversity, in order to ensure that systems are truly usable by older adults result.

In summary then interface design for older adults is more complex than for standard groups, making optimum interface design more difficult to achieve. It is therefore particularly important that instances of design which work well for older adults should be carefully documented and passed on for other designers to use.

5 ADVANTAGES OF INTERFACE DESIGN PATTERNS FOR OLDER ADULTS

Guidelines provide a useful form of 'advice' for designers and are necessarily generalized for a range of applications. However the information embedded in the guideline has been distilled either from a form of craft knowledge, or theory or through experimentation. If the guideline comes with the 'reason' attached together with an example of the use of the guideline, the designer is a stronger position to utilize the information.

The W3C, Web Access Initiative Guidelines (Web Access Initiative Guidelines, 1999), which were developed for Web designers so that they could make their Web pages more accessible for non-standard users, are accompanied by the reasons for the guidelines, which enables the designer to be aware of who is or he is excluding if they do not follow the guidelines.

Designers therefore, especially those designing systems for older adults, would benefit from access to the information, experimental or otherwise, that gave rise to the guideline.

Academic papers of course exist which describe the experiments from which the guideline was distilled, but these contain more information than the designer requires. The argument here is that the information relevant to good design practice should be set out in a structured and informative way for easy access by the interface designer.

Interface designers are rarely older adults themselves and therefore have no concept of how it would feel to access a computer when you are experiencing the combined effects of memory, sight, and mobility loss coupled with reduced confidence that comes with slower processing of visual, spatial and verbal information. Furthermore, the dynamic diversity of ability in older adults poses particular challenges for interface designers.

A robust set of design patterns with a linking language is therefore a particularly important requirement for those designing systems for use by older adults. A set of clear and informative patterns together with information on how the patterns may be used together in a system i.e. the pattern language, would enable interface designers to access best practice and help them to create sympathetic and successful designs for older adults.

Importantly the patterns will reflect the experience of older adults through experimentation and observation, which the designers themselves are lacking. This in itself will nurture good design and provide a framework in which mistakes need not happen.

5 EXAMPLES OF INTERFACE DESIGN PATTERNS

Patterns for speech systems possess different properties compared with the more visually orientated graphical user interface patterns of Tidwell and van Welie (Tidwell, 2002),(Van Welie, 2002), and indeed the architectural patterns of Alexander (Alexander, 1977). Speech dialogues use two forms of input, speech and keypad, and output in the form of a speech message. The usability of the dialogue hinges on its structure and the quality of the output messages. Patterns relevant to speech systems therefore must include those concerned with the construction of output messages, and also those related to dialogue structure.

This section presents several patterns which deal with the quality of output messages in speech systems for older adults, and can be formed in either pre recorded or synthetic speech. They are categorized according to function, *Menu Choice Message, Confirmatory Message, Default Message, Context Sensitive Help Message, Talk Through Message*, and *Explanation Message* together with the dialogue structure patterns *Error Recovery Loop* and *Partition Input Message*. This is not a complete list of patterns for speech systems for older adults and can be developed further with additions and refinements.

6.1 Menu Choice Message

This pattern encapsulates design knowledge derived from experiments carried out with older adults using the voice Web browser BrookesTalk which offers a menu selection of functions in a Voice Help message which talks novice users through their interaction with the browser (Zajicek & Morrissey, 2003).

It was found that older adults were confused by long messages with many options and that they remembered more information from short messages. This phenomena was nor seen in younger people. Older adults also tend to remember the first and the last elements of a menu better.

Users were found to respond more favorably to key press menu selections expressed by mnemonic letter keys such as *A* for *address,* compared with function keys which caused much confusion. Finding letters on the keyboard was a major problem for older people using the voice Web browser.

Pattern name: Menu Choice Message

Use When: When the range of choices offered in the dialogue is small. Large numbers of choices should be broken up into sub menus. Keep the message as short as possible.

Why: Experiments show that older adults are confused by long messages and forget the possible options or remember only the first or last.

How: Short messages offering at most three selections should be used only with very well defined options where the user using pre-existing knowledge (not strategies that are worked out at the time) can see easily which of the selections will lead them to their goal. Example 1. demonstrates how this can be done. When there are three options, place the most commonly selected options last and first. Use mnemonic letters to identify menu items for key press entry, as in Example 2.

Example: 1.   "Would you like to deposit or withdraw money?", rather than 'Would you like to perform a credit or debit transfer?"
2.   "You have no page loaded.
Would you like to
Enter an address, press A
Perform a search, press S

Tradeoffs:	Menus usefully group end goals in a speech dialogue, and the smaller the menu the greater the number of interactions that will be needed to reach the end goal. The tradeoff is that reducing the number of options in the menu lengthens the interaction. Despite this drawback, experiments carried out with the VABS (Zajicek et al., 2003) showed that the short messages approach was most successful with older adults.

6.2 Confirmatory Message

The importance of confirmatory messages was demonstrated during experiments carried out with older adults using the voice Web browser BrookesTalk (Zajicek & Morrissey, 2001). Here confirmation was produced by a personal helper who answered *yes* or *no* to users' questions about their interaction. In the domain of speech dialogues the principle of confirmatory action is expressed in confirmatory messages that reassure the user that the interaction is going well.

Pattern name:	Confirmatory message
Use when:	After the user has input data, or made a choice or performed some other action that they might not be sure of.
Why:	To confirm that data has been input correctly or to draw the users attention to the progress of the dialogue. Research has shown that user confidence can be increased by confirmatory action and can aid the construction of conceptual models.
How:	After a data input event try to arrange for the output of a confirmatory message that contains the input data. In Example 1. the words in italic represent input data that has been embedded in a confirmatory sentence. The message confirms that the system still 'knows' that it is talking to Mary and mentions 7 pm so that the user can check the input. The words evening and appointment serve to frame the concept of the reminder. Confirmatory messages can also be used as in Example 2. to confirm that the dialogue is proceeding satisfactorily.
Example:	1. '*Mary* you have successfully booked a call reminder at *7 pm* on the evening before your appointment"

	2. "You have successfully logged on to the Voice Activated Booking System and have asked for a call reminder for your appointment on Wednesday the 8th November. What time would you like your call reminder?"
Tradeoffs:	Confirmatory messages increase the user's confidence in their interaction and aid the construction of conceptual models of the speech system. The tradeoff is between increasing confidence and adding to the length of the interaction. Confirmatory messages demand yet more attention of the user and can be irritating to confident users. Research has shown however, especially for systems designed primarily for first time users, that confirmatory messages should be used.

6.3 Default Input Message

Default input messages proved to be very useful in the VABS system where users' input reminder call times were not recognized. Users were usually happy with the default time of 7 pm for a reminder call as shown in Example 1.

Pattern name:	Default Input Message
Use when:	When a user is required to input data which has been misrecognised or when the user has failed to understand that data must be input. This can be used only when the input data is relatively imprecise and a default which would just about do is possible as in Example 1.
Why:	Because the system requires some input data in order to continue the interaction, or where the user has consistently avoided inputting the required data and is likely to terminate the interaction.
How:	The default input message should appear when an input has been misrecognised a certain number of times.
Example:	1. "Would 7 pm on the evening before your appointment be a good time for a reminder call?"

Tradeoff: The default input is possibly not the input that the user intended and they may or may not be satisfied with it. The possibility of not being satisfied is the tradeoff against the frustration of trying several times to enter the correct input or leaving the interaction with the task incomplete.

6.4 Context Sensitive Help Message

The VABS features several help areas within the dialogue. Users can say *Help* at any time during their interaction and a message, which is specifically relevant to the area of the dialogue they are currently using, will be output. Context sensitive help was invoked several times in the VABS [16] and was considered to be very useful.

Pattern name:	Context Sensitive Help Message
Use when:	When help in the context of the current task would be useful.
Why:	This message is a direct response to a user asking for help which maps closely to human-human dialogues when help is requested, and represents the most efficient way in which help can be provided. Context is important as it ensures that the message will be as short as possible as the message will contain only information relevant to the task in hand. Older adults experience difficulty in absorbing spoken information, and this type of message will provide only information which is necessary at the time.
How:	Identify areas in the interaction which relate to identifiable tasks and create explanatory messages for each task. Arrange for an input of *Help* to trigger the relevant context sensitive help message.
Example:	1. "This system uses voice recognition to understand your commands that should be spoken clearly. Giving your name helps the system to locate your current sessions and gives you access to more functions. You need to contact the center during office hours to register your name". 2. "This system is designed to offer users the ability to book or cancel a computer taster session. Speak your commands clearly and try

to use the words given in the question".

Tradeoffs:	There are no direct usability tradeoffs. This is the best way to provide help. Unfortunately some older adults forget that they have the option to ask for help so alternative methods which do not require the user to take the initiative, must be used as well. The only tradeoff is in the extra programming effort required to set up the help areas and messages.

6.5 Talk Through Message

showed that speech output that talks older adults through their interaction could enable people to use software where they hadn't been able to use it before (Zajicek & Morrissey, 2001).

Pattern name:	Talk Through Message
Use when:	When it would be helpful to be told where you are in the interaction and what you can do next.
Why:	Older adults find difficulty in building strategies at the interface, mainly because this activity relies on short-term memory. Memory loss means that it is difficult to remember what you did last time and to build up a model of how the interaction works.
How:	Where a new task is about to be tackled, talk through messages should be inserted to help with orientation to the new process. It is best to arrange for more competent users to switch off the messages when they are no longer needed.
Example:	1. 'You have arrived at the point where you tell us when you would like to come for your IT Taster Session. Sessions run from 10:30 to 15:30 every hour. Please say something like 'ten thirty' to see if the session is available".
Tradeoffs:	Talk through messages irritate confidant users and slow them down. They slow down even novice users and make for more speech output to listen to, but are considered to be most worthwhile for older adults.

6.6 Explanation Message

Older adults find speech interaction confusing. While younger people can adapt to the ways computers behave older people find it more difficult. Any explanation of what is happening can be useful.

Pattern name:	Explanation Message
Use when:	Use when the dialogue is behaving in a non-intuitive way or in a way that does not map onto usual human-human dialogue.
Why:	Interaction with a speech dialogue is often not intuitive to older adults, so it should explain itself as much as possible.
Example:	1. "There will be a short delay while your name is found on our database"
Tradeoff:	Extra messages make the dialogue longer. The tradeoff is between making the dialogue longer or making it clearer.

6.7 Error Recovery Loop

Errors and error recovery represent the main usability problem for speech systems.   Standard menu driven systems often start with a long set of instructions in a bid to avoid errors happening. Older users are not able to remember these messages, which also slow down the dialogue, rendering them useless. The pattern described here directs designers to embed instructions in an error recovery loop: in effect to wait for the error to happen and then try to recover it.

This approach is most useful in dialogues which are used mostly by experienced users who are unlikely to require any instruction and will if they use the dialogue successfully never have to listen to an error recovery message.

Pattern name:	Error Recovery Loop
Use when:	When errors in data input are likely to occur.
Why:	Because older adults cannot remember lengthy preliminary spoken instructions about data input. It is best to let them try to input data and if it goes wrong invoke an error recovery message.
How:	Count how many times a data input occurs and on each count invoke an increasingly detailed error recovery message. In the examples below Example 1. simply gives instructions

	for efficient input, but the more detailed Example 2. provides information about which might help the user work better with the system.
Example:	1. "Your name has not been recognized. Please speak slowly and clearly into the telephone.
	2. "The system is trying to match your name against the names it holds in the database. Please try to speak your name in the same way that you did when you registered for the Voice activated Booking System.
Tradeoffs:	This form of error recovery does not prepare the user in advance for possible errors, as they have to create the error before it is invoked. The tradeoff is against providing long instructions before the user embarks on a task.

6.8 Partitioned Input Message

The interaction paths taken through the VABS system by older adults was compared with the optimum path for each task (Zajicek et al., 2003) It was found that data input tasks showed the greatest deviation from the optimum route and this was because of misrecognition of utterances. Misrecognition of input causes considerable frustration in speech interaction and often leads to abandonment of the dialogue.

The Partitioned Input Messages in effect perform binary chops on the possible entry data (Brownsey et al., 1993) For example when a time for a reminder call is required instead of being asked to enter the time, the user would be asked 'Would you like your reminder call in the morning or afternoon?' as normally occurs when the session organizer sets up the reminder call. If the answer were morning the system would then respond 'Before eleven o'clock or after?' The dialogue would continue to halve the search area until a time is selected.

Pattern name:	Partitioned Input Message
Use when:	Use for any discrete input data which has up to sixteen possible values. Sixteen values requires four questions be asked to reach the correct value. More than sixteen values would require too many questions.
	This message type is particularly useful when the required input might be confusing. Example 1. tries to cope with IT Taster

Sessions on the VABS which are held on the half hour, while most users suggest a time on the hour if asked for input (they also ignore instructions asking them to use the half hour)

Why: This message replaces data input which is the most difficult part of speech dialogues. It is extremely error prone and older adults find difficulty in recovering from errors.

How: Set up messages that divide the number of possible input in two each time as shown in Example 1.

Example: 1.
(i) "Would you like to attend for taster sessions in the morning or afternoon of Wednesday 7th June?"
(ii) "Would you like to come before or after 11 in the morning?"
(iii) "Would you like to come at 11.30 or 12.30?"

Tradeoff: This method takes longer than direct data input but the tradeoff is that it reduces the frustration of misrecognition.

7 PATTERNS AND USER BEHAVIOUR

Eight interface design patterns are analyzed in terms of the user models they implicitly and explicitly encapsulate, and also in terms of the users they disadvantage.

Figure 1 sets out the patterns described above with reference to the user models they support and which users are disadvantaged by the pattern. With the following key:

A – Models dynamic diversity
B – Models memory impairment
C – Models strategy building impairment
D – Good HCI design for all users
E – Could slow down younger users

Pattern Name	A	B	C	D	E
Menu Choice Message		X	X	X	
Confirmatory Message			X	X	
Default Input Message			X	X	
Context Sensitive Help	X	X	X	X	
Talk Through Message		X	X		X
Explanation Message		X	X		X
Error Recovery Loop	X	X	X	X	
Partitioned Input		X	X		X

Figure 1: Properties of the patterns

With this categorization in place together with the patterns themselves inexperienced software designers can reference the patterns of the user groups they support.

Such designers will be able to see easily to what degree they are addressing concerns of universal accessibility and also be aware of the tradeoff in supporting one user model while at the same time disadvantaging another. For example we can see in Figure 1 that some interface design patterns that are useful for older adults lead to sub-optimal design for younger users.

Most importantly of all designers will be able to search out those design patterns which provide the optimal solution by supporting dynamic diversity and hence all users.

8 CONCLUSIONS

Explicit information about the accessibility of particular software design features by different sectors of society is able to support those who are required to make challenging design decisions concerning design for universal access, and who need to be aware of which users will be excluded from their software.

The legislative demand for interface design for a wider proportion of society will complicate the design decisions that software developers will have to make and in these cases the use of patterns categorized according to user model can be of great benefit.

ACKNOWLEDGMENTS

The author would like to thank Age Concern Oxfordshire for their valuable support for the work described above.

REFERENCES

Alexander, C., 1979, The Timeless Way of Building, Oxford University Press.

Alexander, C., Ishikawa, S., Silverstein, M., 1977, A Pattern Language: Towns, Buildings, Construction, Oxford University Press.

Brownsey K. Zajicek M. Hewitt J., 1994, A structure for user oriented dialogues in computer aided telephony, Interacting with Computers 6(4), 433 – 449.

Fincher, S., 2003, CHI 2003 Workshop Report, Interfaces No. 56, Journal of the BCS HCI Group.

Fincher, S., 2003, HCI Pattern-Form Gallery, http://www.cs.ukc.ac.uk/people/staff/saf/patterns/gallery.html, (last accessed 23.4.3).

Gregor, P., Newell, 2002, A., Zajicek, M., Designing for Dynamic Diversity – interfaces for older people, Proceedings of 5th ACM/SIGAPH Conf. on Assistive Technologies.

Newell A.F. & Gregor P., 2000, User Sensitive Inclusive Design – in search of a new paradigm, Proc A.C.M. Conference on Universal Usability, Washington, DC Nov. pp39-44.

Tidwell, J., 2002, UI Patterns and Techniques, http://time-tripper.com/uipatterns/about-patterns.html   (last accessed 22.4.3).

Van Duyne, D, Landay, J., Hong, J., 2002, The Design of Sites: Patterns, principles and processes for crafting a customer-centered web experience, Addison Weseley.

Van Welie, M., Interaction Design Patterns, http://www.welie.com/patterns/index.html, (last accessed 12.5.3), 2002.

Web Access Initiative Guidelines, 1999, http://www.w3.org/TR/WCAG10/, (last accessed 12.5.3).

Zajicek M. & Hall, S., 2000, Solutions for elderly visually impaired people using the Internet, In S. McDonald, Y. Waern, G. Cockton (eds) People and Computers XIV – Usability or Else!, Proceedings of HCI 2000, pp 299 – 307

Zajicek M., Morrissey W., 2001, Speech output for older visually impaired adults, Proceedings of IHM-HCI 503 - 513

Zajicek M., Morrissey, W., 2003, Multimodality and interactional differences in older adults, Special Issue "Multimodality: a Step Towards Universal Access' of Universal Access in the Information Society,(ed. N. Carbonell) Springer.

Zajicek M., Wales, R., Lee, A., 2003, Towards VoiceXML Dialogue Design for Older Adults, In Palanque P., Johnson P., O'Neill E (eds) Design for Society. Proceedings of HCI 2003

A CONTACT RECOMMENDER SYSTEM FOR A MEDIATED SOCIAL MEDIA

Michel Plu, Layda Agosto

France Telecom R&D; 2 avenue Pierre Marzin Lannion France
Email: michel.plu@rd.francetelecom.com; layda.agostofranco@rd.francetelecom.com

Laurence Vignollet; Jean-Charles Marty

Laboratoire SYSCOM, Unniversité de Savoie, Campus scientifique,Le Bourget Du lac Chambery France
Email:laurence.vignollet@univ-savoie.fr;jean-charles.marty@univ-savoie.fr

Keywords: Collaborative filtering, recommender systems, social network analysis, online communities, social media

Abstract: Within corporate intranet or on the WWW, a global search engine is the main service used to discover and sort information. Nevertheless, even the most "intelligent" ones have great difficulties to select those targeted to each user specific needs and preferences. We have built a mediated social media named SoMeONe, which helps people to control their information exchanges through trusted relationships. A key component of this system is a contact recommender, which helps people to open their relationship networks by exchanging targeted information with qualified new users. Instead of using only matching between interests of users, this "socially aware" recommender system also takes into account existing relationships in the social network of the system. In this paper, we describe the computations of those recommendations based on a social network analysis.

A NEW MEDIA FOR PERSONALIZED ACCESS TO INFORMATION

A large part of companies' knowledge is embedded in each employee's documents. Web technologies are now being used to make those numerous documents easily accessible through a decentralized intranet or extranet. The WWW also provides access to many interesting resources to any employees but they are lost through the huge quantity of available pages. Those information networks are becoming essential for being correctly informed. However, in such a web environment, information is distributed throughout the company or through the WWW. This makes it difficult to find information which is useful and relevant to each user's needs.

One of the great challenges of search engine tools, mainly based on an artificial (computer-based) centralized intelligence, is to be able to select relevant answers according to user's preferences, background, or current activity. In order to face this personalization challenge, we are developing a complementary approach based on users' distributed intelligence where the relevancy of a resource for a user is based on the existing references to this resource from other users and the trustworthiness of relationships between those users. This is based on our assumption that some users might prefer to trust other users than machine to obtain good advice about information resources. We are thus introducing a user-centric approach as opposed to a computer-centric one to develop a new intelligent interface for accessing the WWW.

This approach is supported by our collaborative system named SoMeONe (Social Media using Opinions through a trust Network) (Agosto, 2003). This system is particularly adapted to users preferring to access information which already has a certain approval, for instance, information coming from appreciated or skilled people in corresponding domains.

Key issues in this system are motivating users to exchange information and helping them to manage and optimise their relationship network. To deal with those problems we have integrated in SoMeOne a contact recommender system, which suggests that

Seruca et al. (eds.), Enterprise Information Systems VI, 293–300.
2006 Springer. Printed in the Netherlands.

some users exchange information with new users. We make the assumption that users will be motivated to produce and exchange good information in order to be recommended by the recommender. Those recommendations are not only based on the common interests of users but also on social qualities of each user. This "socially aware recommender system" is the focus of this paper.

2 SOCIAL MEDIA

The idea of using communication networks as a support tool to find "focused" people is not new. Newsgroups and mailing lists are the most famous examples of such collaborative systems. By using them, people are acquiring a new, social, cyber-behaviour that asks them to adopt new habits in working and even in thinking schemas. They form online communities in the sense of J. Preece (Preece, 2000). We call "social media" systems capable of relating persons to establish relationships. We call "mediated social network" the social network of a social media.

Using information technology can help to improve the flow of pertinent information between people and the global efficiency of the system by analysing the structure of a mediated social network. Such a mediated social network can be used to receive very personalized recommendations of information resources carefully selected by trusted users. By doing this, we develop a new vision where information navigates from users to users instead of having users navigating through information. We named this vision the "web of people" (Plu, 2003). The ultimate goal is to help people to get in contact with appropriate persons according to the diversity of their needs to find and filter suitable information.

Let's now look more deeply into one of the key issues presented before: the user motivation to share information. We assume this requirement to be true. Indeed, we believe that in our information society, and more particularly in a competitive and dynamic business environment, this collaborative behaviour is crucial for an awareness of new information and in order to receive support or credits from others. Bourdieu and others have also largely demonstrated the value of social capital not only as being the knowledge of individual workers but also the relations between them (Bourdieu, 1986). Consequently, it is sensible for companies that want to develop their social capital to develop and support cooperative behaviour in the everyday practice of their employees.

But even if this collaborative behaviour is supposed to be natural for our users, it has to be applied to our system. To deal with this requirement, one can imagine having a regulation component, which organizes the behaviour of users and applies a user management policy (Durand, 2003). An alternative approach is to integrate some components in the system to influence such users' behaviour in order to have them following the required behaviour rules. To illustrate how a technology can influence user's behaviour, one can look to how indexing technologies used by major Internet search engines have transformed the way web authors are designing their web pages.

The contact recommender system we are presenting is such a component. Within the SoMeONe system, a user has to be recommended to be able to receive information from new users. Thus, the recommender can recommend users with the required social behavior. However, having interesting information might not be sufficient for being recommended. The recommender has also to analyse the defined social qualities of the users' participation into the mediated social network. These social qualities of a user can depend for example on the credits s/he receives from others or the originality of his/her contribution (which means that no user could replace his/her contribution). One can imagine many other social qualities to qualify the user willingness to collaborate and the value or his/her participation to the community. Those social qualities can be computed using social network analysis techniques (Wasserman, 1994).

We call "**socially aware recommender system**" a recommender system that takes into account those social qualities to compute and rank its recommendations.

3 SOMEONE: A COOPERATIVE SYSTEM FOR PERSONALIZED INFORMATION EXCHANGE

To experiment those ideas, we have integrated such a recommender in our SoMeONE system (Agosto, 2003). The main goal of this system is to support the creation and management of mediated social networks. It helps users to exchange recommendations about good contents available through an information network like the WWW or corporate intranet. It is supposed to help people to improve and to optimise their mediated social network in order to discover and find information resources, which are adapted to their needs, taste, background, culture or any other personal features which make humans so different.

The way to share personal information in SoMeONe is described as follows:

- Each user manages a personal taxonomy, in order to annotate and to index their documents. Each element in that taxonomy is called a topic. A document could be for instance an email, an image, a video, or a report. In fact, it is anything that can be identified with an URL.
- When displayed, all information associated with a document (also called meta-information) is aggregated. For that, we introduce the concept of review. Reviews are created by associating topic(s) and other information (like a text annotation) on documents.
- The accessibility of reviewed information, and thus the exchange of information between users, depends on the accessibility of topics in the reviews. The accessibility of a topic is defined according to a list managed by the topic owner; this list is called a topic distribution list (TDL for short). It groups the users allowed to access all information having a review with the topic.
- We call a user's contacts, the set of users belonging to the distribution list of at least one of his/her topics. Those contacts could be friends, colleagues, family members, or any others.

Information is exchanged between users when they access the system using their personal home page. This page lets the user navigates through all information s/he is allowed to access, and let him/her to create new reviews for personal indexing purposes. However, creating a new review to a document discovered from a received review on that document makes it accessible to all the new users in the TDL of the topics associated to the new review. In consequence, personal indexing is automatically associated to information forwarding. As a result, information in the reviews, including document references, flow through the network of users according to the topic's TDL. We called "semantic addressing", this information routing process based on the indexing of information. This is the basic principle of the "web of people" where information navigates from users to users instead of having users navigating through information (Plu, 2003).

4 A "SOCIALLY AWARE" RECOMMENDER SYSTEM

The recommender we have developed and integrated in SoMeONe lets people have new contacts. It suggests to a user to add some users to the distribution list of some topics.

For this, the recommender needs first to identify topics which show the similar interests of two users. Like many others do, our recommender system is also using a collaborative filtering approach (Resnick, 1997). The originality of our work lies in the fact that we complement this approach with the computation of new ranking features based on social network analysis (Wasserman, 1994). The goal is to filter the recommendations obtained from the collaborative filtering process according to a personal information requirement and users social qualities corresponding to it. We qualify such a recommender as "socially aware".

In a **social network analysis**, people, groups or organizations that are members of social systems are treated as "sets of nodes" (linked by edges) –forming networks. They represent social structures. Given a set of nodes, there are several strategies for deciding how to collect measurements on the relations among them. Matrices or vectors can be used to represent information, and algebraic computations are done to identify specific patterns of ties among social nodes (Wasserman, 1994).

Differences in how users are connected can be a key indicator of the efficiency and "complexity" of the global social organization supported by the mediated social network. Individual users may have many or few ties. Individuals may be "sources" of ties, "sinks" (actors that receive ties, but don't send them), or both. The analysis of the relations between users can indicates a degree of "reciprocity" and "transitivity" which can be interpreted, for instance, as important indicators of stability.

The graph structure analysis of a mediated social network can be used for many purposes. It might be used to show users' roles, their position, their global appreciation, their dependency to communities to which they belong. It is also useful in order to qualify the exchanged information. Further in this paper, we present how we use these analysis techniques to propose new contacts.

Furthermore, social network analysis has also been largely used in a sub-field of classical information retrieval called biblio-metrics to analyse citations in scientific papers (Garfield, 1972). It has also led to the development of new algorithms for information retrieval algorithms for hypertext like PageRank (Brin, 1998). They are mainly based on the computation of a centrality measure of the nodes in a graph formed by web pages. The assumption is that a link provides some credit to the linked page

The **social network** we extract from the mediated social network supported by SoMeONe, is a directed graph consisting of a set of nodes with directed edges between pairs of nodes. Nodes are the topics of users and edges are their relations. Those relations between two topics are computed according to reviews being associated within those two topics. Thus, in this social network, there is an edge i from a topic v to a topic u, if the owner of topic u is receiving and taking information associated to topic v. In other words, the owner of topic u is in the distribution list of the topic v and takes at least one review containing the topic v and creates a new review on the same document with his/her topic u. Consequently, the graph representation will show the relation v → u.

The relation v → u indicates the flow of appreciated information through the network. It means that the owner of topic u is receiving and appreciates information from the owner of topic v.

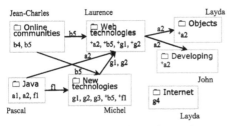

Figure 1: Mediated social network example

Figure 1 shows a graphical representation of a small part of such a network. In this example, there is six users. Each box shown as folders represents some of the topics of these users. Each relation v → u between topics is presented by a directed lattice. Reviewed information resources are noted with a lower case letter and a number. A label on a lattice means that a resource has been discovered from a review in the source topic.

Our **socially aware recommender system** first takes into account the interest of users and then takes into account the state of the users topics in the social networks.

In the first step, it finds the relationships of users with approximate interests (not only commons ones). This means that for instance, we avoid giving only recommendations directly obtained from intersections of appreciated items in the users' profiles, which is generally the strategy of existing systems. This first feature is obtained by our collaborative filtering techniques using repositories of already classified items (Plu, 2003). Second, the user can control the type of contact recommendations s/he is going to receive. This means that a user can define the strategy to rank computed recommendations. This last feature is accomplished by our SocialRank algorithm, which completes our collaborative filtering algorithm.

The SocialRank algorithm uses some social properties to filter topics which are candidates for recommendations (those topics initially computed with the collaborative filtering algorithm). The social properties used depend on the information strategy chosen by the users. They are computed by using the SoMeONe's social network described above.

By using those social properties as filters, two users with the same interest would not receive the same recommendations of contacts. Thus, this should avoid the traditional problem of "preferential attachment" in network based communication systems (Adar, 2000). The preferential attachment problem rises when most of users communicate with the same very small group of users. Recommending only experts to everyone could lead to this situation. We will see below (see section 5.3.4) how SoMeONe prevents such a situation by letting users choose another information strategy than the "Looking for Experts" strategy. More generally, different "social properties" computed from the social network analysis can be used to choose the contact recommendations in order to influence the way the social network will evolve! Thus, a socially aware recommender system can help to give the social network some interesting global properties depending on the global criteria the designer of a social media wants to optimise. Such interesting properties can be, for instance: a good clustering factor, a small diameter, a good global reciprocity or/and transitivity factor.

We assume that some users will be seeking to be recommended to others. Therefore, by using some specific social properties in the recommendation process, we think the recommender system can influence the motivation and participation of users. In other words, if users know the strategy used by the recommender system, we can assume that some users will try to adapt their behaviour according to it.

To be able to test this idea, we have first implemented the computation of some social properties and we have implemented some information strategies using those properties in order to select appropriate contact recommendations.

In order to let users to select one of the implemented strategies which best fit their needs we have ascribed "names" and descriptions to them. Here are the three we have already implemented and experimented:

- "**Looking for Experts**". The user only trust credited experts who filter information for him.
- "**Gathering all**". The user want to have the widest coverage of a topic, thus gathering as much information as possible,

- "**Going to the sources**". The user wants to obtain the newest information rapidly, avoiding users who are acting as intermediaries.

We have started with these three strategies but our goal is to look for new ones or improving the existing ones. By default, the "Going to the source" strategy is selected, but users can change it by editing her/his personal profile. This choice can be refined for each personal topic.

The formulae related to the computation of the social properties used by each "strategy" are explained in the SocialRank section.

5 COMPUTING CONTACT RECOMMENDATIONS

In this section we are going to present the three steps of our recommendation process. *Firstly*, we describe the collaborative filtering algorithm used to compute potential contact recommendations based on topic similarities using an existing classification of a large amount of URLs. *Secondly*, we specify the computation of social properties of each topic in the SoMeONe's social network. *Finally*, we show how we filter the potential contact recommendations obtained in the first step according to the topic similarities, the social properties of the recommended topics, and the information strategy chosen by users.

5.1 Collaborative Filtering

The bases of the collaborative filtering algorithm that we have built are presented in (Plu, 2003). It uses URL co-citations analysis. Co-citation is established when two users associate personal reviews to the same documents or to different documents referenced within the same category of a WWW directory. The recommendations of contacts are computed using one or more specialized directories. By directories, we mean repositories of web sites categorized by subject. For our tests we have started with the one provided by the Open Directory Project (http://www.dmoz.org).

The collaborative filtering algorithm (CFA) computes similarity between topics. It has to detect the case of two topics having reviews with URLs equal or similar to the URLs classified in the same ODP category. The CFA computes a similarity measure between each topic and each ODP category. Like others do, this similarity measure is based on URLs co-citation analysis. (the URLs to which the reviews inside topics make reference). This

similarity measure is computed according to the formula given in (Plu, 2003).

The CFA only computes the similarity between topics that do not belong to the same user. Pairs of similar topics noted (t1, t2) for topics labelled t1 and t2, are sorted according to the similarity measure S. Contact recommendations are then computed from those similar topics.

5.2 SocialRank

The SocialRank algorithm filters the topic recommendations according to some of their social properties.

Having the topics' taxonomy of users, and the distribution list of the topics defined, we are able to extract the social network explained above. We model this directed graph as an adjacent matrix. Each matrix element represents the relationship between two topics. As introduced above, a relationship is established when a user creates new reviews from other reviews received from other users. They thus establish relationships between their topics within the created reviews and the topics of others within the received reviews. To take into account the importance of each relation, each vertex is weighted with a measure W(e,f) representing the number of documents received from topic f and then reviewed with a topic e. We compute a matrix W with each element noted W(e, f), topic e being in the row and topic f in the column of the matrix, for the vertex from f . W(e,f) is computed with the formula:

$$W(e, f) = \frac{Card^*(e, f)}{card(e)} \quad (1) \qquad \text{or } W(e, f) = 0 \text{ if } card(e) = 0$$

Card*(e,f) counts all the documents having a review with the topic e and a review with the topic f, the review with topic f being older than the review with topic e; card (e) is the total number of reviews with topic e.

Using this W matrix, the SocialRank algorithm also computes one square matrix and two vectors of topics:
- A vector of experts E, in order to obtain the expert topics.
- A redundancy matrix R, in order to obtain redundant topics.
- A vector of originals O, in order to obtain original topics.

The computation of these matrix and vectors could be obtained by different methods, as clearly explained in (Wasserman, 1994).

To identify topics as "**experts**" we use a common centrality measure of a topic defined recursively according to the centrality of the topics receiving information from it. Each element E(e) of the expert vector is defined according to the recursive formula:

$$E(e)=\square_{h \in H} W(h,e)*E(h) \quad (2)$$

For the computation of vector E we use the algorithm named PageRank and used for WWW pages (Brin, 1998). But the matrix used has to reflect a reputation relation ("e is giving reputation to f", f←e). We consider that this relation is the invert of the relation modelled in our matrix W, which reflects the flow of information through the topics (f→e). Indeed, if a user reviews documents received with topic f with his topic e, then topic e is giving reputation (credit) to topic f. That is why we use the weight W(h, e) instead of W(e, h) to compute E(e).

The PageRank algorithm requires that the weights of the adjacent matrix W(e, f) have to be modified in W*(e, f) in order to have the following needed convergence properties (see (Brin, 1998) for more details). This is partly achieved because the new weights W*(e, f), once normalized, represent the probability for a document being reviewed with topic f to be reviewed with a topic e. Thus, our matrix W corresponds to a stochastic matrix. Following the PageRank algorithm, we also complete the graph with new connections in order to have all nodes connected.

To compute **redundancy and originality**, we first define vectors G(e) as the set of all topics g connected to topic e. Second, we define P(e, f) as the proportion of the relation between topic e and f among all the relations with topic e. P(e, f) is computed with the formula:

$$\text{If} \quad f \in G(e) \ P(e,f) = \frac{W(e,f)}{\square_{g \in G(e)} w(e,g)} \quad \text{else} \quad P(e,f)=0 \ (3)$$

The evaluation of redundancy between topics is computed in a matrix R. We define that a topic e is redundant with f if both are the same type of information sources because they have the same information obtained from the same sources. Explicitly, the redundancy between e and f depends on:
- If f is connected with e. This means that e is receiving information from f.
- If topics connected to e are also connected to f. This means that topics sending information to e are also sending it to f.

We compute R(e, f) according to the following formula:

$$R(e,f) = p(e,f) + \square_{g \in G(e)} p(e,g)p(f,g) \quad (4)$$

Finally we compute the vector O to represent original topics. The originality of a topic is measured according to

the novelty of URLs in the topic compared to the URLs received from connected topics. A topic e is original if it contains more URLs discovered by the owner of the topic than received from other topics. It also depends on the number of URLs in the topic. We compute the vector O according to the following formula:

$$O(e)=1- \square_{h \in G(e)} W(e,h) \quad (5)$$

5.3 Applying SocialRank

Now we illustrate these calculations with our social network example presented in figure 1 where there are six actors, seven topics shown as folders, and reviews noted with a lower case letter and a number. The URLs of the reviews belong to 4 ODP categories noted A,B,F,G. For example we note "a1" a review having an URL referenced in the category A of the ODP directory. A label on a lattice means that a URL has been discovered from a review in the source topic.

In this example, we suppose that the user Layda wants to obtain recommendations about her topic Internet. The CFA similarities computation produces the following recommendations: (Internet → New technologies) and (Internet → Web technologies) because those three topics have reviews on URLs referenced in the category G of the ODP category (even if their intersection is empty). A recommendation noted (t1→t2) means that owner of the topic t2 should be in the distribution list of the topic t1 if it is not the case.

Those initial recommendations are going to be analysed by our SocialRank algorithm. One issue of the analysis is which topic the system will recommend to Layda related to her topic Internet, Web technologies or New technologies (or both)? R is an important matrix because it helps to decide if two topics are redundant to each other. If so, which of them are more relevant to recommend according to the user specific needs? This decision is going to be applied to the topics Web technologies (noted WT) and New technologies (Noted NT).

Before the computation of R, we first have to compute W and P. From (1) we compute W(WT, NT). Then, we have:

$$W(WT, NT)=\frac{Card*(WT,NT)}{card(WT)}=\frac{3}{4}=0.75$$

(we assume that b5 were reviewed by WT before being reviewed by NT).

This means that the average of information received by Web technologies from New technologies is 0.75, which is high (meaning that their relation is important).

Here are the matrix W and P for our example:

P	NT	WT	Java	OC
NT			0.5	0.5
WT	0.6		0.2	0.2

W	NT	WT	Java	OC
NT			0.2	0.2
WT	0.75		0.25	0.25

With matrix P, we obtain the proportion of the relation between WT and NT among all the relations with WT. The value 0,6 indicates an important relation between both topics.

5.3.1 Evaluating redundant topics

As we explained above, matrix R helps to decide if two topics are redundant to each other. From (4), R(WT, NT) can be computed as

$$R(WT, NT) = \left[p(WT,NT) + \left(\frac{p(WT,OC)p(NT,OC)+}{p(WT,Java)p(NT,Java)+} \\ p(WT,NT)p(NT,NT) \right) \right] = 0.8$$

This value indicates a redundancy between WT and NT, which reveals that WT could be a similar information source to NT; therefore, it is relevant to recommend only one of them.

The same computation gives R(NT,WT) = 0,2. Notice that R(WT,NT) > R(NT,WT) ! This is an important result because it helps the system to decide which topics to recommend according to the user's strategy. We will develop this in a later section.

5.3.2 Evaluating experts

Let's now compute the expert property. If we follow (2), we will obtain E(WT) =0.095879; E(NT)= 0.080576 for topics WT and NT. This result is interpreted as follows:
- Web technologies is the more expert topic. We can notice (figure 1) that even if it does not have its own reviews, it has collected different reviews from two topics having a good level of expertise. Web technologies is supplying with its information two other topics, Objects and Developing, who are giving to it a kind of credibility or reputation.
- New technologies is at second level of expertise From figure 1, we can see that it has collected different reviews from two topics with a good level of expertise but it is supplying only one topic with its information! Remember that the computation of E is based on a centrality measure indicating a reputation degree (Brin,

1998). However, its level of expertise being higher than a defined threshold this topic is kept as candidate for being recommended.

5.3.3 Evaluating original topics

By applying (5), we obtain the next O vector values:

Topic	O(e)
Internet	1.0
Java	1.0
Online Communities	1.0
New technologies	0.6
Web technologies	-0.25
Developing	0.0
Objects	0.0

The result is interpreted as follows:
- Internet is the more original topic. The originality of Internet is evident because it is isolated, because it is not redundant with the others and because it can bring new information. Java and Online communities are also original topics because URLs have been reviewed with them before the other topics (see figure 1).
- However, comparing their place in the vector O, NT is more original than WT.

5.3.4 Applying users' strategies

Because WT and NT have been identified as redundant, only one will be chosen according to Layda's information strategy. If she has selected:
1. **Looking for experts**: This leads to the selection of a topic with the highest Expert property; the answer of the recommender would be WT.
2. **Gathering all**: The answer with this strategy is the topic having the highest value for R, therefore it would be WT because R(WT,NT) > R(NT,WT) (*reinforcing the global approval of WT over NT*).
3. **Going to the sources**: the selected topic would be NT, because the strategy gives priority to the most originals among topics with a sufficient level of expertise.
What happens if Layda does not define an initial strategy? We explained that one of the priorities of our mediated system is avoiding the preferential attachment problem (Jin, 2001). Therefore, the default strategy is "Going to the sources", because it should improve the reactivity of the social networks by minimizing intermediaries. Another important situation to encourage is the connection of independent components.
In order to protect user's information privacy, no user can add his identifier to the topic access list of any other user's private topics. Thus, recommendations displayed only suggest sending information to new users. In our example, the

system will recommend to Layda to add Michel owner of NT or Laurence, owner of WT to the distribution list of her topic Internet. But we assume that a user receiving new information will also send back new information. To encourage such reciprocal relationships the recommender needs also to check if the topic Internet satisfies Michel's or Laurence's information strategy for their topic NT or WT. Thus finally the recommender will try to choose the topic that will stratify the best the strategy of the two users involved in the suggested relationship.

6 CONCLUSION

In this paper, we've proposed to improve an original information exchange system, SoMeONe, which facilitates the creation of relationships between users, in order to cover each user's information need. We've included a contact recommendation module that helps users to open their closed relational network and thus discover new sources of information.

We had proposed in (Plu, 2003) to use a collaborative filtering algorithm. This algorithm suggests that a user exchanges reviews on information source that they have already evaluated or produced. But these recommendations have to be carefully chosen in order to not let him/her having a too big relational network and for the global efficiency of the social media. Thus, our SocialRank algorithm presented in this article filters those recommendations using the computation of one matrix and two vectors. This lets the system propose to users several information strategies to establish new relationships.

Many recommender systems have already been studied and some of them are operational like online bookshops (Resnick, 1997). However, our system recommends *users* instead of recommending *contents*. Thus it is more similar to McDonald's expertise recommender (McDonald, 1998). But as far as we know, none of the recommender systems integrate a traditional collaborative filtering algorithm with social properties resulting from social network analysis. The use of social network analysis to improve information retrieval in enterprise is also recommended in (Raghavan, 2002). But this paper does not present any recommender system in order to establish exchange relationships between users. Our work was partly inspired by the ReferalWeb system (Kautz, 1997) but in our system, we've introduced social properties and the social network is manually controlled by users, and evolves according to users accepting contact recommendations.

In order to test our ideas, we've introduced the system in the Intranet of France Telecom R&D and in the portal of the University of Savoie, inside the project called "Cartable Electronique"®. The usage of our system in these different contexts should allow us to validate our initial hypothesis: a recommendation process of carefully selected contacts should incite users to produce interesting information and develop collaborative behaviour.

REFERENCES

Agosto L., Plu M. Vignollet L, and Bellec P., 2003 SOMEONE: A cooperative system for personalized information exchange In *ICEIS'03,Volume 4, p. 71-78, Kluwer.*

Adar E. And Huberman B., 2000, Free Riding on Gnutella. First Monday, 5(10). (www.firstmonday.dk).

Bourdieu, P.,1986. The forms of capital. In *J. Richardson (Ed.), Handbook of theory and research for the sociology of education (pp. 241-258). New York: Greenwood.*

Brin S. and Page L, 1998, The anatomy of a large-scale hypertextual (Web) search engine. In *The Seventh International World Wide Web Conference.*

Durand G., Vignollet L., 2003, Améliorer l'engagement dans un collecticiel", *to be published IHM 2003, Caen, France, November 2003.*

Emily M. Jin, Michelle Girvan, and M. E. J. Newman, 2001, The structure of growing social networks, *Phys. Rev. E 64, 046132.*

Garfield E, 1972, Citation analysis as a tool In *journal evaluation. Science, 178.*

Kautz, H., Selman B., Shah M, 1997, Referral Web: Combining Social Networks and Collaborative Filtering. *CACM 40(3): 63-65.*

McDonald, D. and Ackerman, M.S., 1998. Just talk to me: A field study of expertise location. In *Proc. CSCW'98, pp. 315-324. New York: ACM.*

Plu M., Agosto L., Bellec P., Van De Velde W. 2003, The Web of People: A dual view on the WWW, In *Proc.of The Twelfth International World Wide Web Conference, Budapest, Best Alternate Track Paper.*

Raghavan, P., 2002, Social Networks: from the Web to the Enterprise. *IEEE Internet Computing, pp. 91-94, Jan/Feb 2002.*

Preece, J. 2000, Online Communities: Designing Usability, Supporting Sociability. *Chichester, UK: John Wiley & Sons, 439 pages.*

Resnick, P, and Varian, 1997, H.R. Recommender Systems. *Commun. ACM 40, 3 (56-58).*

Wasserman, S. and Faust K., 1994, Social Network Analysis: Methods and Applications. *Cambridge University Press.*

EMOTION SYNTHESIS IN VIRTUAL ENVIRONMENTS

Amaryllis Raouzaiou, Kostas Karpouzis and Stefanos Kollias
Image, Video and multimedia Systems Laboratory, National Technical University of Athens,
9, Heroon Politechniou street, 15773, Zographou, Athens, Greece
Email: {araouz, kkarpou}@image.ntua.gr, stefanos@cs.ntua.gr

Keywords: MPEG-4 facial animation, facial expressions, emotion synthesis

Abstract: Man-Machine Interaction (MMI) systems that utilize multimodal information about users' current emotional state are presently at the forefront of interest of the computer vision and artificial intelligence communities. Interfaces with human faces expressing emotions may help users feel at home when interacting with a computer because they are accepted as the most expressive means for communicating and recognizing emotions. Thus, emotion synthesis can enhance the atmosphere of a virtual environment and communicate messages far more vividly than any textual or speech information. In this paper, we present an abstract means of description of facial expressions, by utilizing concepts included in the MPEG-4 standard to synthesize expressions using a reduced representation, suitable for networked and lightweight applications.

1 INTRODUCTION

Current information processing and visualization systems are capable of offering advanced and intuitive means of receiving input and communicating output to their users. As a result, Man-Machine Interaction (MMI) systems that utilize multimodal information about their users' current emotional state are presently at the forefront of interest of the computer vision and artificial intelligence communities. Such interfaces give the opportunity to less technology-aware individuals, as well as handicapped people, to use computers more efficiently and thus overcome related fears and preconceptions.

Despite the progress in related research, our intuition of what a human expression or emotion actually represents is still based on trying to mimic the way the human mind works while making an effort to recognize such an emotion. This means that even though image or video input is necessary to this task, this process cannot come to robust results without taking into account features like speech, hand gestures or body pose. These features provide means to convey messages in a much more expressive and definite manner than wording, which can be misleading or ambiguous. While a lot of effort has been invested in examining individually these aspects of human expression, recent research (Cowie, Douglas-Cowie, Tsapatsoulis, Votsis, Kollias, Fellenz & Taylor, 2001) has shown that even this approach can benefit from taking into account multimodal information.

Multiuser environments are an obvious testbed of emotionally rich MMI systems that utilize results from both analysis and synthesis notions. Simple chat applications can be transformed into powerful chat rooms, where different users interact, with or without the presence of avatars that take part in this process, taking into account the perceived expressions of the users. The adoption of token-based animation in the MPEG-4 framework benefits such networked applications, since the communication of simple, symbolic parameters is, in this context, enough to analyze, as well as synthesize facial expression, hand gestures and body motion. While current applications take little advantage from this technology, research results show that its powerful features will reach the consumer level in a short period of time.

The real world actions of a human can be transferred into a virtual environment through a representative (avatar), while the virtual world perceives these actions and corresponds through respective system avatars who can express their emotions using human-like expressions and gestures.

In this paper we describe an approach to synthesize expressions via the tools provided in the MPEG-4 standard (Preda & Preteux, 2002) based on real measurements and on universally accepted assumptions of their meaning. These assumptions are

301

I. Seruca et al. (eds.), Enterprise Information Systems VI, 301–309.
© 2006 *Springer. Printed in the Netherlands.*

based on established psychological studies, as well as empirical analysis of actual video footage from human-computer interaction sessions and human-to-human dialogues. The results of the synthesis process can then be applied to avatars, so as to convey the communicated messages more vividly than plain textual information or simply to make interaction more lifelike.

2 MPEG-4 REPRESENTATION

In the framework of MPEG-4 standard, parameters have been specified for Face and Body Animation (FBA) by defining specific Face and Body nodes in the scene graph. The goal of FBA definition is the animation of both realistic and cartoonist characters. Thus, MPEG-4 has defined a large set of parameters and the user can select subsets of these parameters according to the application, especially for the body, for which the animation is much more complex. The FBA part can be also combined with multimodal input (e.g. linguistic and paralinguistic speech analysis).

2.1 Facial Animation

MPEG-4 specifies 84 feature points on the neutral face, which provide spatial reference for FAPs definition. The FAP set contains two high-level parameters, visemes and expressions. In particular, the Facial Definition Parameter (FDP) and the Facial Animation Parameter (FAP) set were designed in the MPEG-4 framework to allow the definition of a facial shape and texture, eliminating the need for specifying the topology of the underlying geometry, through FDPs, and the animation of faces reproducing expressions, emotions and speech pronunciation, through FAPs. By monitoring facial gestures corresponding to FDP and/or FAP movements over time, it is possible to derive cues about user's expressions and emotions. Various results have been presented regarding classification of archetypal expressions of faces, mainly based on features or points mainly extracted from the mouth and eyes areas of the faces. These results indicate that facial expressions, possibly combined with gestures and speech, when the latter is available, provide cues that can be used to perceive a person's emotional state.

The second version of the standard, following the same procedure with the facial definition and animation (through FDPs and FAPs), describes the anatomy of the human body with groups of distinct tokens, eliminating the need to specify the topology of the underlying geometry. These tokens can then be mapped to automatically detected measurements

and indications of motion on a video sequence, thus, they can help to estimate a real motion conveyed by the subject and, if required, approximate it by means of a synthetic one.

2.2 Body Animation

In general, an MPEG body is a collection of nodes. The Body Definition Parameter (BDP) set provides information about body surface, body dimensions and texture, while Body Animation Parameters (BAPs) transform the posture of the body. BAPs describe the topology of the human skeleton, taking into consideration joints' limitations and independent degrees of freedom in the skeleton model of the different body parts.

2.2.1 BBA (Bone Based Animation)

The MPEG-4 BBA offers a standardized interchange format extending the MPEG-4 FBA (Preda & Preteux, 2002). In BBA the skeleton is a hierarchical structure made of bones. In this hierarchy every bone has one parent and can have as children other bones, muscles or 3D objects. For the movement of every bone we have to define the influence of this movement to the skin of our model, the movement of its children and the related inverse kinematics.

3 EMOTION REPRESENTATION

The obvious goal for emotion analysis applications is to assign category labels that identify emotional states. However, labels as such are very poor descriptions, especially since humans use a daunting number of labels to describe emotion. Therefore we need to incorporate a more transparent, as well as continuous representation, that matches closely our conception of what emotions are or, at least, how they are expressed and perceived.

Activation-emotion space (Whissel, 1989) is a representation that is both simple and capable of capturing a wide range of significant issues in emotion. It rests on a simplified treatment of two key themes:

- *Valence*: The clearest common element of emotional states is that the person is materially influenced by feelings that are 'valenced', i.e. they are centrally concerned with positive or negative evaluations of people or things or events. The link between emotion and valencing is widely agreed
- *Activation level*: Research has recognised that emotional states involve dispositions to act in certain ways. A basic way of reflecting that

theme turns out to be surprisingly useful. States are simply rated in terms of the associated activation level, i.e. the strength of the person's disposition to take some action rather than none. The axes of the activation-evaluation space reflect those themes. The vertical axis shows activation level, the horizontal axis evaluation. A basic attraction of that arrangement is that it provides a way of describing emotional states which is more tractable than using words, but which can be translated into and out of verbal descriptions. Translation s possible because emotion-related words can be understood, at least to a first approximation, as referring to positions in activation-emotion space. Various techniques lead to that conclusion, including factor analysis, direct scaling, and others (Whissel, 1989).

A surprising amount of emotional discourse can be captured in terms of activation-emotion space. Perceived fullblown emotions are not evenly distributed in activation-emotion space; instead they tend to form a roughly circular pattern. From that and related evidence, (Plutchik, 1980) shows that there is a circular structure inherent in emotionality. In this framework, identifying the center as a natural origin has several implications. Emotional strength may be measured as the distance from the origin to a given point in activation-evaluation space. The concept of a full-blown emotion can then be translated roughly as a state where emotional strength has passed a certain limit. An interesting implication is that strong emotions are more sharply distinct from each other than weaker emotions with the same emotional orientation. A related extension is to think of primary or basic emotions as cardinal points on the periphery of an emotion circle. Plutchik has offered a useful formulation of that idea, the 'emotion wheel' (see Figure 1).

Activation-evaluation space is a surprisingly powerful device, and it has been increasingly used in computationally oriented research. However, it has to be emphasized that representations of that kind depend on collapsing the structured, high-dimensional space of possible emotional states into a homogeneous space of two dimensions. There is inevitably loss of information; and worse still, different ways of making the collapse lead to substantially different results. That is well illustrated in the fact that fear and anger are at opposite extremes in Plutchik's emotion wheel, but close together in Whissell's activation/emotion space. Extreme care is, thus, needed to ensure that collapsed representations are used consistently.

Figure 1: The Activation-emotion space

4 FACIAL EXPRESSIONS

There is a long history of interest in the problem of recognizing emotion from facial expressions (Ekman & Friesen, 1978), and extensive studies on face perception during the last twenty years (Davis & College, 1975). The salient issues in emotion recognition from faces are parallel in some respects to the issues associated with voices, but divergent in others.

As in speech, a long established tradition attempts to define the facial expression of emotion in terms of qualitative targets, i.e. static positions capable of being displayed in a still photograph. The still image usually captures the apex of the expression, i.e. the instant at which the indicators of emotion are most marked. More recently emphasis, has switched towards descriptions that emphasize gestures, i.e. significant movements of facial features.

In the context of faces, the task has almost always been to classify examples of archetypal emotions. That may well reflect the influence of Ekman and his colleagues, who have argued robustly that the facial expression of emotion is inherently categorical. More recently, morphing techniques have been used to probe states that are intermediate between archetypal expressions. They do reveal effects that are consistent with a degree of categorical structure in the domain of facial expression, but they are not particularly large, and there may be alternative ways of explaining them – notably by considering how category terms and facial parameters map onto activation-evaluation space (Karpouzis, Tsapatsoulis & Kollias, 2000).

Facial features can be viewed (Cowie et al., 2001) as either static (such as skin color), or slowly varying (such as permanent wrinkles), or rapidly varying (such as raising the eyebrows) with respect to time evolution. Detection of the position and shape of the mouth, eyes, particularly eyelids, wrinkles and extraction of features related to them are the targets of techniques applied to still images of humans. It has, however, been shown (Bassili, 1979), that facial expressions can be more accurately recognized from image sequences, than from a single still image. His experiments used point-light conditions, i.e. subjects viewed image sequences in which only white dots on a darkened surface of the face were visible. Expressions were recognized at above chance levels when based on image sequences, whereas only happiness and sadness were recognized at above chance levels when based on still images. Techniques which attempt to identify facial gestures for emotional expression characterization face the problems of locating or extracting the facial regions or features, computing the spatio-temporal motion of the face through optical flow estimation, and introducing geometric or physical muscle models describing the facial structure or gestures.

In general, facial expressions and emotions are described by a set of measurements and transformations that can be considered atomic with respect to the MPEG-4 standard; in this way, one can describe both the anatomy of a human face –basically through FDPs, as well as animation parameters, with groups of distinct tokens, eliminating the need for specifying the topology of the underlying geometry. These tokens can then be mapped to automatically detected measurements and indications of motion on a video sequence and, thus, help to approximate a real expression conveyed by the subject by means of a synthetic one.

5 GESTURES AND POSTURES

The detection and interpretation of hand gestures has become an important part of human computer interaction (MMI) in recent years (Wu & Huang, 2001). Sometimes, a simple hand action, such as placing one's hands over their ears, can pass on the message that he has had enough of what he is hearing; this is conveyed more expressively than with any other spoken phrase. To benefit from the use of gestures in MMI it is necessary to provide the means by which they can be interpreted by computers. The MMI interpretation of gestures requires that dynamic and/or static configurations of the human hand, arm, and even other parts of the human body, be measurable by the machine. First attempts to address this problem resulted in mechanical devices that directly measure hand and/or arm joint angles and spatial position. The so-called glove-based devices best represent this solutions' group.

Human hand motion is highly articulate, because the hand consists of many connected parts that lead to complex kinematics. At the same time, hand motion is also highly constrained, which makes it difficult to model. Usually, the hand can be modeled in several aspects such as shape (Kuch & Huang, 1995), kinematical structure (Lin, Wu & Huang, 200), dynamics (Quek, 1996), (Wilson & Bobick, 1998) and semantics.

Gesture analysis research follows two different approaches that work in parallel. The first approach treats a hand gesture as a two- or three dimensional signal that is communicated via hand movement from the part of the user; as a result, the whole analysis process merely tries to locate and track that movement, so as to recreate it on an avatar or translate it to specific, predefined input interface, e.g. raising hands to draw attention or indicate presence, in a virtual classroom.

The low level results of the approach can be extended, taking into account that hand gestures are a powerful expressive means. The expected result is to understand gestural interaction as a higher-level feature and encapsulate it into an original modal, complementing speech and image analysis in an affective MMI system (Wexelblat, 1995). This transformation of a gesture from a time-varying signal into a symbolic level helps overcome problems such as the proliferation of available gesture representations or failure to notice common features in them. In general, one can classify hand movements with respect to their function as:

- *Semiotic*: these gestures are used to communicate meaningful information or indications
- *Ergotic*: manipulative gestures that are usually associated with a particular instrument or job and
- *Epistemic*: again related to specific objects, but also to the reception of tactile feedback.

Semiotic hand gestures are considered to be connected, or even complementary, to speech in order to convey a concept or emotion. Especially two major subcategories, namely *deictic gestures* and *beats*, i.e. gestures that consist of two discrete phases, are usually semantically related to the spoken content and used to emphasize or clarify it. This relation is also taken into account in (Kendon, 1988) and provides a positioning of gestures along a continuous space.

6 FROM FEATURES TO SYMBOLS

6.1 Face

In order to estimate the users' emotional state in a MMI context, we must first describe the six archetypal expressions (joy, sadness, anger, fear, disgust, surprise) in a symbolic manner, using easily and robustly estimated tokens. FAPs and BAPs or BBA representations make good candidates for describing quantitative facial and hand motion features. The use of these parameters serves several purposes such as compatibility of created synthetic sequences with the MPEG-4 standard and increase of the range of the described emotions – archetypal expressions occur rather infrequently and in most cases emotions are expressed through variation of a few discrete facial features related with particular FAPs.

Based on elements from psychological studies (Ekman, 1993), (Parke, 1996), (Faigin, 1990), we have described the six archetypal expressions using MPEG-4 FAPs, which is illustrated in Table 1. In general, these expressions can be uniformly recognized across cultures and are therefore invaluable in trying to analyze the users' emotional state.

Table 1: FAPs vocabulary for archetypal expression description

Joy	open_jaw(F$_3$), lower_t_midlip(F$_4$), raise_b_midlip(F$_5$), stretch_l_cornerlip(F$_6$), stretch_r_cornerlip(F$_7$), raise_l_cornerlip(F$_{12}$), raise_r_cornerlip(F$_{13}$),close_t_l_eyelid(F$_{19}$), close_t_r_eyelid(F$_{20}$), close_b_l_eyelid(F$_{21}$), close_b_r_eyelid(F$_{22}$), raise_l_m_eyebrow (F$_{33}$), raise_r_m_eyebrow(F$_{34}$), lift_l_cheek (F$_{41}$), lift_r_cheek(F$_{42}$), stretch_l_cornerlip_o (F$_{53}$), stretch_r_cornerlip_o(F$_{54}$)
Sadness	close_t_l_eyelid(F$_{19}$), close_t_r_eyelid(F$_{20}$), close_b_l_eyelid(F$_{21}$), close_b_r_eyelid(F$_{22}$), raise_l_i_eyebrow(F$_{31}$), raise_r_i_eyebrow (F$_{32}$), raise_l_m_eyebrow(F$_{33}$), raise_r_m_eyebrow(F$_{34}$), raise_l_o_eyebrow (F$_{35}$), raise_r_o_eyebrow(F$_{36}$)
Anger	lower_t_midlip(F$_4$), raise_b_midlip(F$_5$), push_b_lip(F$_{16}$), depress_chin(F$_{18}$), close_t_l_eyelid(F$_{19}$), close_t_r_eyelid(F$_{20}$), close_b_l_eyelid(F$_{21}$),close_b_r_eyelid(F$_{22}$), raise_l_i_eyebrow(F$_{31}$), raise_r_i_eyebrow (F$_{32}$), raise_l_m_eyebrow(F$_{33}$), raise_r_m_eyebrow(F$_{34}$),raise_l_o_eyebrow (F$_{35}$), raise_r_o_eyebrow(F$_{36}$), squeeze_l_eyebrow(F$_{37}$), squeeze_r_eyebrow (F$_{38}$)

Fear	open_jaw(F$_3$), lower_t_midlip(F$_4$), raise_b_midlip(F$_5$), lower_t_lip_lm(F$_8$), lower_t_lip_rm(F$_9$), raise_b_lip_lm (F$_{10}$), raise_b_lip_rm(F$_{11}$), close_t_l_eyelid (F$_{19}$), close_t_r_eyelid(F$_{20}$), close_b_l_eyelid (F$_{21}$), close_b_r_eyelid(F$_{22}$), raise_l_i_eyebrow (F$_{31}$), raise_r_i_eyebrow(F$_{32}$), raise_l_m_eyebrow(F$_{33}$), raise_r_m_eyebrow (F$_{34}$), raise_l_o_eyebrow(F$_{35}$), raise_r_o_eyebrow (F$_{36}$), squeeze_l_eyebrow (F$_{37}$), squeeze_r_eyebrow (F$_{38}$)
Disgust	open_jaw (F$_3$), lower_t_midlip (F$_4$), raise_b_midlip (F$_5$), lower_t_lip_lm (F$_8$), lower_t_lip_rm (F$_9$), raise_b_lip_lm (F$_{10}$), raise_b_lip_rm (F$_{11}$), close_t_l_eyelid (F$_{19}$), close_t_r_eyelid (F$_{20}$), close_b_l_eyelid (F$_{21}$), close_b_r_eyelid(F$_{22}$), raise_l_m_eyebrow(F$_{33}$), raise_r_m_eyebrow(F$_{34}$), lower_t_lip_lm_o (F$_{55}$), lower_t_lip_rm_o (F$_{56}$), raise_b_lip_lm_o (F$_{57}$), raise_b_lip_rm_o (F$_{58}$), raise_l_cornerlip_o (F$_{59}$), raise_r_cornerlip_o (F$_{60}$)
Surprise	open_jaw (F$_3$), raise_b_midlip (F$_5$), stretch_l_cornerlip (F$_6$) , stretch_r_cornerlip (F$_7$), raise_b_lip_lm(F$_{10}$),raise_b_lip_rm(F$_{11}$), close_t_l_eyelid (F$_{19}$), close_t_r_eyelid(F$_{20}$), close_b_l_eyelid (F$_{21}$), close_b_r_eyelid (F$_{22}$), raise_l_i_eyebrow(F$_{31}$), raise_r_i_eyebrow (F$_{32}$), raise_l_m_eyebrow(F$_{33}$), raise_r_m_eyebrow (F$_{34}$), raise_l_o_eyebrow (F$_{35}$), raise_r_o_eyebrow (F$_{36}$), squeeze_l_eyebrow (F$_{37}$), squeeze_r_eyebrow (F$_{38}$), stretch_l_cornerlip_o (F$_{53}$), stretch_r_cornerlip_o (F$_{54}$)

Although FAPs provide all the necessary elements for MPEG-4 compatible animation, we cannot use them for the analysis of expressions from video scenes, due to the absence of a clear quantitative definition. In order to measure FAPs in real image sequences, we define a mapping between them and the movement of specific FDP feature points (FPs), which correspond to salient points on the human face. This quantitative description of FAPs provides the means of bridging the gap between expression analysis and synthesis. In the expression analysis case, the non-additive property of the FAPs can be addressed by a fuzzy rule system.

Quantitative modeling of FAPs is implemented using the features labeled as f_i ($i=1..15$) in Table 2 (Karpouzis, Tsapatsoulis & Kollias, 2000). The feature set employs feature points that lie in the facial area and, in the controlled environment of MMI applications, can be automatically detected and tracked. It consists of distances, noted as $s(x,y)$, where x and y correspond to Feature Points (Tekalp & Ostermann, 2000), between these protuberant points, some of which are constant during expressions and are used as reference points; distances between these reference points are used for normali zation purposes (Raouzaiou, Tsapatsoulis, Karpouzis & Kollias, 2002). The units for f_i are identical to those corresponding to FAPs, even in cases where no one-to-one relation exists.

Table 2: Quantitative FAPs modeling: (1) s(x,y) is the Euclidean distance between the FPs, (2) $D_{i\text{-NEUTRAL}}$ refers to the distance D_i when the face is its in neutral position.

FAP name	Feature for the description	Utilized feature
Squeeze_l_eyebrow (F_{37})	$D_1=s(4.5,3.11)$	$f_1=D_{1\text{-NEUTRAL}}-D_1$
Squeeze_r_eyebrow (F_{38})	$D_2=s(4.6,3.8)$	$f_2=D_{2\text{-NEUTRAL}}-D_2$
Lower_t_midlip (F_4)	$D_3=s(9.3,8.1)$	$f_3=D_3-D_{3\text{-NEUTRAL}}$
Raise_b_midlip (F_5)	$D_4=s(9.3,8.2)$	$f_4=D_{4\text{-NEUTRAL}}-D_4$
Raise_l_i_eyebrow (F_{31})	$D_5=s(4.1,3.11)$	$f_5=D_5-D_{5\text{-NEUTRAL}}$
Raise_r_i_eyebrow (F_{32})	$D_6=s(4.2,3.8)$	$f_6=D_6-D_{6\text{-NEUTRAL}}$
Raise_l_o_eyebrow (F_{35})	$D_7=s(4.5,3.7)$	$f_7=D_7-D_{7\text{-NEUTRAL}}$
Raise_r_o_eyebrow (F_{36})	$D_8=s(4.6,3.12)$	$f_8=D_8-D_{8\text{-NEUTRAL}}$
Raise_l_m_eyebrow (F_{33})	$D_9=s(4.3,3.7)$	$f_9=D_9-D_{9\text{-NEUTRAL}}$
Raise_r_m_eyebrow (F_{34})	$D_{10}=s(4.4,3.12)$	$f_{10}=D_{10}-D_{10\text{-NEUTRAL}}$
Open_jaw (F_3)	$D_{11}=s(8.1,8.2)$	$f_{11}=D_{11}-D_{11\text{-NEUTRAL}}$
close_t_l_eyelid (F_{19}) – close_b_l_eyelid (F_{21})	$D_{12}=s(3.1,3.3)$	$f_{12}=D_{12}-D_{12\text{-NEUTRAL}}$
close_t_r_eyelid (F_{20}) – close_b_r_eyelid (F_{22})	$D_{13}=s(3.2,3.4)$	$f_{13}=D_{13}-D_{13\text{-NEUTRAL}}$
stretch_l_cornerlip (F_6) (stretch_l_cornerlip_o)(F_{53}) – stretch_r_cornerlip (F_7) (stretch_r_cornerlip_o)(F_{54})	$D_{14}=s(8.4,8.3)$	$f_{14}=D_{14}-D_{14\text{-NEUTRAL}}$
squeeze_l_eyebrow (F_{37}) AND squeeze_r_eyebrow (F_{38})	$D_{15}=s(4.6,4.5)$	$f_{15}=D_{15\text{-NEUTRAL}}-D_{15}$

For our experiments on setting the archetypal expression profiles, we used the face model developed by the European Project *ACTS MoMuSys*, being freely available at the website http://www.iso.ch/ittf. Table 3 shows examples of profiles of the archetypal expression fear

(Raouzaiou, Tsapatsoulis, Karpouzis & Kollias, 2002).

Figure 2 shows some examples of animated profiles. Fig. 2(a) shows a particular profile for the archetypal expression *anger*, while Fig. 2(b) and (c) show alternative profiles of the same expression. The difference between them is due to FAP intensities. Difference in FAP intensities is also shown in Figures 2(d) and (e), both illustrating the same profile of expression *surprise*. Finally Figure 2(f) shows an example of a profile of the expression *joy*.

Table 3: Profiles for the Archetypal Expression Fear.

Profiles	FAPs and Range of Variation
Fear ($P_F^{(0)}$)	$F_3 \in [102,480], F_5 \in [83,353], F_{19} \in [118,370], F_{20} \in [121,377], F_{21} \in [118,370], F_{22} \in [121,377], F_{31} \in [35,173], F_{32} \in [39,183], F_{33} \in [14,130], F_{34} \in [15,135]$
$P_F^{(1)}$	$F_3 \in [400,560], F_5 \in [333,373], F_{19} \in [-400,-340], F_{20} \in [-407,-347], F_{21} \in [-400,-340], F_{22} \in [-407,-347]$
$P_F^{(2)}$	$F_3 \in [400,560], F_5 \in [-240,-160], F_{19} \in [-630,-570], F_{20} \in [-630,-570], F_{21} \in [-630,-570], F_{22} \in [-630,-570], F_{31} \in [260,340], F_{32} \in [260,340], F_{33} \in [160,240], F_{34} \in [160,240], F_{35} \in [60,140], F_{36} \in [60,140]$

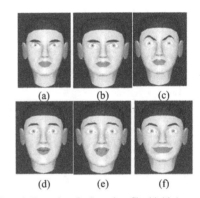

(a) (b) (c)

(d) (e) (f)

Figure 2: Examples of animated profile: (a)-(c) Anger, (d)-(e) Surprise, (f) Joy

6.1.1 Creating Profiles for Expressions Belonging to the Same Universal Emotion Category

As a general rule, one can define six general categories, each characterized by an archetypal emotion; within each of these categories, intermediate expres-

.ions are described by different emotional intensi-ies, as well as minor variation in expression details. From the synthetic point of view, emotions belong-ng to the same category can be rendered by animat-ng the same FAPs using different intensities. In the ase of expression profiles, this affect the range of variation of the corresponding FAPs which is appro-priately translated; the fuzziness introduced by the varying scale of FAP intensities provides mildly differentiated output in similar situations. This en-sures that the synthesis will not render "robot-like" animation, but drastically more realistic results. For example, the emotion group *fear* also contains *worry* and *terror* (Raouzaiou et al., 2002), synthe-ized by reducing or increasing the intensities of the employed FAPs, respectively.

We have created several profiles for the arche-typal expressions. Every *expression profile* has been created by the selection of a set of FAPs coupled with the appropriate ranges of variation and its ani-mation produces the selected emotion.

In order to define exact profiles for the arche-ypal expressions, we combine the following steps:
a) Definition of subsets of candidate FAPs for an archetypal expression, by translating the facial features formations proposed by psychological studies to FAPs,
b) Fortification of the above definition using varia-tions in real sequences and,
c) Animation of the produced profiles to verify appropriateness of derived representations.

The initial range of variation for the FAPs has been computed as follows: Let $m_{i,j}$ and $\sigma_{i,j}$ be the mean value and standard deviation of FAP F_j for the archetypal expression i (where $i=\{1 \rightarrow$ Anger, $2 \rightarrow$ Sadness, $3 \rightarrow$ Joy, $4 \rightarrow$ Disgust, $5 \rightarrow$ Fear, $6 \rightarrow$ Surprise$\}$), as estimated in (Raouzaiou et al., 2002) . The initial range of variation $X_{i,j}$ of FAP F_j for the expression i is defined as:
$$X_{i,j}=[m_{i,j}-\sigma_{i,j}, m_{i,j}+\sigma_{i,j}]. \quad (1)$$
for bi-directional, and
$$X_{i,j}=[max(0, m_{i,j}-\sigma_{i,j}), m_{i,j}+\sigma_{i,j}] \text{ or} \quad (2)$$
$$X_{i,j}=[m_{i,j}-\sigma_{i,j}, min(0, m_{i,j}+\sigma_{i,j})].$$
for unidirectional FAPs.

For example, the emotion group *fear* also con-ains *worry* and *terror* (Raouzaiou et al., 2002) which can be synthesized by reducing or increasing the intensities of the employed FAPs, respectively.

Table 4: Created profiles for the emotions terror and worry

Emotion term	Profile
Afraid	$F_3 \in [400,560]$, $F_5 \in [-240,-160]$, $F_{19} \in [-630,-570]$, $F_{20} \in [-630,-570]$, $F_{21} \in [-630,-570]$, $F_{22} \in [-630,-570]$, $F_{31} \in [260,340]$, $F_{32} \in [260,340]$, $F_{33} \in [160,240]$, $F_{34} \in [160,240]$, $F_{35} \in [60,140]$, $F_{36} \in [60,140]$
Terrified	$F_3 \in [520,730]$, $F_5 \in [-310,-210]$, $F_{19} \in [-820,-740]$, $F_{20} \in [-820,-740]$, $F_{21} \in [-820,-740]$, $F_{22} \in [-820,-740]$, $F_{31} \in [340,440]$, $F_{32} \in [340,440]$, $F_{33} \in [210,310]$, $F_{34} \in [210,310]$, $F_{35} \in [80,180]$, $F_{36} \in [80,180]$
Worried	$F_3 \in [320,450]$, $F_5 \in [-190,-130]$, $F_{19} \in [-500,-450]$, $F_{20} \in [-500,-450]$, $F_{21} \in [-500,-450]$, $F_{22} \in [-500,-450]$, $F_{31} \in [210,270]$, $F_{32} \in [210,270]$, $F_{33} \in [130,190]$, $F_{34} \in [130,190]$, $F_{35} \in [50,110]$, $F_{36} \in [50,110]$

   (a)   (b)   (c)

Figure 3: Animated profiles for (a) afraid, (b) terrified (c) worried

Table 4 and Figures 3(a)-(c) show the resulting pro-files for the terms *terrified* and *worried* emerged by the one of the profiles of *afraid*. The FAP values that we used are the median ones of the corresponding ranges of variation.

6.2 Gesture Classification

Gestures are utilized to support the outcome of the facial expression analysis subsystem, since in most cases they are too ambiguous to indicate a particular emotion. However, in a given context of interaction, some gestures are obviously associated with a par-ticular expression –e.g. *hand clapping* of high fre-quency expresses *joy, satisfaction-* while others can provide indications for the kind of the emotion ex-pressed by the user. In particular, quantitative fea-tures derived from hand tracking, like speed and amplitude of motion, fortify the position of an ob-served emotion; for example, *satisfaction* turns to *joy* or even to *exhilaration*, as the speed and ampli-tude of clapping increases.

Table 5 shows the correlation between some detectable gestures with the six archetypal expressions.

Table 5: Correlation between gestures and emotional states

Emotion	Gesture Class
Joy	hand clapping-high frequency
Sadness	hands over the head-posture
Anger	lift of the hand- high speed
	italianate gestures
Fear	hands over the head-gesture
	italianate gestures
Disgust	lift of the hand- low speed
	hand clapping-low frequency
Surprise	hands over the head-gesture

Given a particular context of interaction, gesture classes corresponding to the same emotional are combined in a "logical OR" form. Table 1 shows that a particular gesture may correspond to more than one gesture classes carrying different affective meaning. For example, if the examined gesture is *clapping*, detection of high frequency indicates *joy*, but a *clapping* of low frequency may express irony and can reinforce a possible detection of the facial expression *disgust*.

Animation of gestures is realized using the 3D model of the software package *Poser*, edition 4 of CuriousLabs Company. This model has separate parts for each moving part of the body. The Poser model interacts with the controls in Poser and has joints that move realistically, as in real person. Poser adds joint parameters to each body part. This allows us to manipulate the figure based on those parameters. We can control the arm, the head, the hand of the model by filling the appropriate parameters; to do this a mapping from BAPs to Poser parameters is necessary. We did this mapping mainly experimentally; the relationship between BAPs and Poser parameters is more or less straightforward.

Figure 4 shows some frames of the animation created using the Poser software package for the gesture "lift of the hand" in the variation which expresses *sadness*.

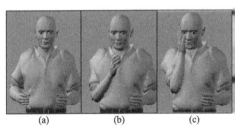

(a)	(b)	(c)

Figure 4: Frames from the animation of the gesture "lift of the hand"

7 CONCLUSIONS

Expression synthesis is a great means of improving HCI applications, since it provides a powerful and universal means of expression and interaction. In this paper we presented a method of synthesizing realistic expressions using lightweight representations. This method employs concepts included in established standards, such as MPEG-4, which are widely supported in modern computers and standalone devices.

REFERENCES

Kendon, A, 1988. How gestures can become like words. In *Crosscultural perspectives in nonverbal communication*. Potyatos, F. (ed.). Hogrefe, Toronto, Canada.

Wexelblat, A., 1995. An approach to natural gesture in virtual environments. In *ACM Transactions on Computer-Human Interaction*, Vol. 2, iss. 3.

Parke, F., Waters, K., 1996. *Computer Facial Animation*. A K Peters.

Quek, F., 1996. Unencumbered gesture interaction. In *IEEE Multimedia*, Vol. 3. no. 3.

Faigin, G., 1990. *The Artist's Complete Guide to Facial Expressions*. Watson-Guptill, New York.

Lin, J., Wu, Y., Huang, T.S., 2000. Modeling human hand constraints. In *Proc. Workshop on Human Motion*.

Bassili, J. N., 1979. Emotion recognition: The role of facial movement and the relative importance of upper and lower areas of the face. *Journal of Personality and Social Psychology, 37*.

Kuch, J. J., Huang, T. S., 1995. Vision-based hand modeling and tracking for virtual teleconferencing and telecollaboration. In *Proc. IEEE Int. Conf. Computer Vision*.

Karpouzis, K., Tsapatsoulis, N., Kollias, S., 2000. Moving to Continuous Facial Expression Space using the MPEG-4 Facial Definition Parameter (FDP) Set. In

Electronic Imaging 2000 Conference of SPIE. San Jose, CA, USA.

Davis, M., College, H., 1975. *Recognition of Facial Expressions.* Arno Press, New York.

Preda, M., Prêteux, F., 2002. Advanced animation framework for virtual characters within the MPEG-4 standard. In *Proc. of the International Conference on Image Processing.* Rochester, NY.

Tekalp, M., Ostermann, J., 2000. Face and 2-D mesh animation in MPEG-4.In *Image Communication Journal*, Vol.15, Nos. 4-5.

Ekman, P., Friesen, W., 1978. The Facial Action Coding System. In *Consulting Psychologists Press.* San Francisco, CA.

Ekman, P., 1993. Facial expression and Emotion. In *Am. Psychologist*, Vol. 48.

Cowie, R., Douglas-Cowie, E., Tsapatsoulis, N., Votsis, G., Kollias, S., Fellenz, W., Taylor, J., 2001. Emotion Recognition in Human-Computer Interaction. In *IEEE Signal Processing Magazine.*

Plutchik, R., 1980. *Emotion: A psychoevolutionary synthesis.* Harper and Row New York.

Whissel, C.M., 1989. The dictionary of affect in language. In *Emotion: Theory, research and experience: Vol 4, The measurement of emotions.* Plutchnik, R., Kellerman, H. (eds). Academic Press, New York.

Wilson, A., Bobick, A., 1998. Recognition and interpretation of parametric gesture. In *Proc. IEEE Int. Conf. Computer Vision.*

Wu, Y., Huang, T.S., 2001.Hand modeling, analysis, and recognition for vision-based human computer interaction. In *IEEE Signal Processing Magazine.* Vol. 18, iss. 3.

Raouzaiou, A., Tsapatsoulis, N., Karpouzis, K., Kollias, S., 2002. Parameterized facial expression synthesis based on MPEG-4. In *EURASIP Journal on Applied Signal Processing.* Vol. 2002, No. 10. Hindawi Publishing Corporation.

ACCESSIBILITY AND VISUALLY IMPAIRED USERS

António Ramires Fernandes, Jorge Ribeiro Pereira and José Creissac Campos
Departamento de Informática, Universidade do Minho
Portugal
{antonio.ramires,jrp,jose.campos}@di.uminho.pt

Keywords: Accessibility, Internet, Visually impaired users, talking browsers

Abstract: Internet accessibility for the visually impaired community is still an open issue. Guidelines have been issued by the W3C consortium to help web designers to improve web site accessibility. However several studies show that a significant percentage of web page creators are still ignoring the proposed guidelines. Several tools are now available, general purpose, or web specific, to help visually impaired readers. But is reading a web page enough? Regular sighted users are able to scan a web page for a particular piece of information at high speeds. Shouldn't visually impaired readers have the same chance? This paper discusses some features already implemented to improve accessibility and presents a user feedback report regarding the AudioBrowser, a talking browser. Based on the user feedback the paper also suggests some avenues for future work in order to make talking browsers and screen readers compatible.

1   INTRODUCTION

Internet accessibility is still an issue for people with disabilities, in particular for the visually impaired community. Web pages are designed based on the visual impact on the visitor with little or no concern for visually impaired people. HTML is commonly used as a design language and not as a content language.

Two types of complementary directions have emerged to help the visually impaired community:

* Raising the awareness of developers to accessibility issues and providing appropriate methods for web development and evaluation, see for example (Rowan et al., 2000);

* Developing tools that assist visually impaired users to navigate the web.

Sullivan and Matson (Sullivan and Matson, 2000) state that popular press typically reports that 95% or more of all Web sites are inaccessible to users with disabilities. The study in (Sullivan and Matson, 2000) shows a not so dark picture by performing a continuous accessibility classification. Nevertheless the paper still concludes that "...many Web designers either remain ignorant of, or fail to take advantage of, these guidelines" (Web Content Accessibility Guidelines by WC3).

Sanborn et. al. (Jackson-Sanborn et al., 2002) performed an evaluation of a large number of sites and concluded that 66.1% failed accessibility testing.

Developing strategies to make web pages more accessible is a solution proposed by many researchers. For instance Filepp et. al. (Filepp et al., 2002) propose an extension for HTML tables. Adding specific tags to HTML tables would allow web page designers to add contextual information.

However these extensions are still a long way from becoming a standard. Furthermore, even when they do become a standard, there is still the issue of getting web designers to follow them. The W3C Guidelines have been around for quite some time and the results from (Jackson-Sanborn et al., 2002) and (Sullivan and Matson, 2000) show that a large percentage of web designers do not follow the proposed guidelines.

Based on these studies we can conclude that accessibility for the visually impaired community remains an issue. Some solutions have emerged to help this particular community of disabled people providing tools that assist users to navigate the web. These solutions can be categorized regarding their scope:

General Purpose Screen readers

Web Specific Talking Web browsers and Transcoding

Screen readers provide a general purpose solution

I. Seruca et al. (eds.), Enterprise Information Systems VI, 310–315.
© 2006 Springer. Printed in the Netherlands.

o the accessibility problem for the visually impaired community. Their main advantage is being able to ingle handedly deal with most software. However his lack of specificity also implies that screen read-rs are not optimized to deal with any application in articular.

IBM(IBM, 2000) proposes a transcoding system to improve web accessibility which explores similarities between a web page and its neighboring. Common layout structure is then removed, hopefully retaining he important parts of the page.

Talking browsers such as IBM's Homepage Reader[1], Brookes Talk[2] (Zajicek et al., 2000) and the AudioBrowser[3] (Fernandes et al., 2001), on the other hand offer a solution to specific tasks: web browsing and e-mail. Being specific solutions they are unable to deal with other tasks besides web surfing. Never-heless a specific solution can represent a significant advantage to the user.

Talking browsers and transcoding approaches can ake advantage of the underlying structure of the doc-ument, and present different views of the same docu-ment to the user.

In this paper we shall explore the avenue of solu-ions based on talking browsers. In section 2 we shall ocus mainly on features offered by these applications hat improve real accessibility. Section 3 reports on he feedback provided by users of a particular solu-ion, the Audiobrowser. Conclusions and some av-nues for future work are proposed in section 4.

2 TALKING BROWSERS

n this section some features and issues related to talk-ng browsers web solutions are presented. The focus s mainly on features that provide an added value to he user and not on basic features such as basic navi-gation.

2.1 Integration

An important issue in these solutions is to allow the visually impaired user to share its web experience with regular and near sighted users. All the solutions presented in the first section deal with this issue. The BM approach is to allow users to resize the window, onts, and colors. An alternative solution is used both by the Brookes Talk and the AudioBrowser: a distinct area where the text which is being read is dis-played in a extra large font. These areas can be resized

to a very large font making it easier for even seriously near-sighted users to read the text.

All solutions also provide a standard view of the page therefore allowing the visually impaired and near-sighted users to share their experience with reg-ular sighted users. This feature is essential to allow for full inclusion of users with disabilities in the In-formation Society.

2.2 Document Views

The Brookes Talk solution provides an abstract of the web page comprising key sentences. This approach, reduces the amount of text to about 25% and therefore gives the user an ability to quickly scan the contents of the page.

The AudioBrowser includes a feature that attempts to get the user as quickly as possible to the page's contents. A significant number of web pages has a graphical layout based on two or three columns. The first column usually contains a large set of links, and the main contents is on the second column. Normal reading of one of such pages implies that the user must first hear the set of links before the application reaches the main content itself. In order to get the user as quickly as possible to the main contents of the web page the links are removed. This eliminates most of the content of the first column, therefore the user reaches the main content with just a few key strokes. Figure 1[4] shows the text which will be read using this feature, and figure 2 show the full text of the page as understood by the browser.

It is clear from the figures that using this feature provides a much faster access to the real contents of the web page. In figure 2 the first news item "O pres-idente do Banco Central..." is not even visible on the window, whereas in figure 1 it appears very near to the top. Another clue is the size of the dragging bar which gives a hint regarding the amount of the text in both views.

Note that table navigation doesn't provide the same functionality since web pages tend to use tables as a design feature and not a content feature. Therefore navigating on a table can be cumbersome.

Based on the same assumption the AudioBrowser allows for the linearization of tables. The reading is currently row based. In this way the artifacts caused by tables tend to be eliminated.

The AudioBrowser also provides a third mode where all the document's hierarchy is presented. In this mode the user is presented with a hierarchical tree where tables, cells and headings are parent nodes of the tree. The text, links and images are the leaf nodes

---

[1] Available at http://www-3.ibm.com/able/solution_offerings/hpr.html

[2] Available at http://www.brookes.ac.uk/schools/cms/research/speech/btalk.htm

[3] Available at http://sim.di.uminho.pt/audiobrowser

---

[4] The text in the images is in Portuguese since the Au-dioBrowser is currently being developed for a Portuguese audience only.

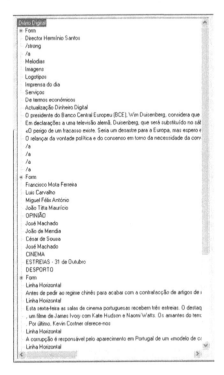

Figure 1: Document View with links removed

Figure 2: Normal View of the Document

of the tree. This mode gives the user an insight on the structure of the page, see figure 3.

The AudioBrowser presents any of these views while at the same time presenting a view of the page as seen on Internet Explorer, see figure 4[5]. The ability to present simultaneously multiple views of the page is useful not only for a visitor of the page, but also for the web designer as we will point out in section 4.

2.3 Links

In all talking browsers, as well as in screen readers quick access to links is provided. The AudioBrowser goes one step further by classifying the links. Links are classified as:

- external;
- internal;
- anchor;
- an e-mail;

---
[5]The images of individuals and commercial brands were deliberately blurred.

- internal files;
- external files.

The notion of an external link is not as clear as one might think. The semantics of external imply that the link will lead to a web page outside the group of related pages under the same base address. The base address can be the domain itself, a subdomain, or even a folder.

For instance in geocities, each user is granted an area that has as the base address www.geocities.com/userName. Pages outside this base address, although in the same domain are external to the site from a semantic point of view.

Nevertheless, this classification, even if based only on domains as base addresses, is extremely useful in some circumstances. Consider a web searching engine such as Google. The internal links represent the options of the search engine. Once the search has been performed the external links provide the user with a quick access to the results.

Long documents with anchors are another example. In this case the anchors can provide a sort of table of contents.

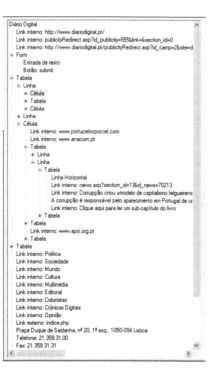

Figure 3: Hierarchical View of the Document

Figure 4: The AudioBrowser

2.4   Bookmarks

Bookmarking a web page is a common procedure amongst internet users. However the default bookmarking offered in Internet Explorer is not powerful enough to satisfy fully the visually impaired user, or as a matter of fact for any kind of user.

The idea behind bookmarking is to allow a user to save the address of a web page in order to get back to it latter. This serves a purpose when we consider small web pages, with little volume of text. When we consider large pages, with considerable amounts of text, it may be of use to specify a particular piece of text.

It may be the case that the user wants to bookmark not the page itself, but a specific location in the page, for instance a paragraph. This would allow the user to stop reading a web page at a particular location, and then get back to that location latter without having to start from the beginning of the document again.

Another example where the benefits of bookmarking a specific location of a web page would be of great use is to allow users to skip text in the beginning of the document. A significant number of pages have

a fixed structure, where only content varies. As mentioned before, it is common to have a left column with links to sections of the site and other sites. Bookmarking the beginning of the main content area, would allow the user to skip the links section when the page is loaded.

Currently the AudioBrowser seems to be the only talking browser that has this feature, including compatibility with Internet Explorer's favorites. Jaws[6], a popular screen reader, also offers a similar feature called PlaceMarkers.

2.5   E-mail

E-mail is no longer restricted to text messages: messages can be composed as a web page. Hence using the same tools as those used for web browsing makes perfect sense. The AudioBrowser is capable of handling e-mail at a basic level, providing the same set of features that are used for web browsing. The AudioBrowser attempts to integrate visually impaired users with regular sighted users, and therefore it uses the same mailbox as Outlook, hence has access to the same received messages. The navigation on the messages is identical to the navigation on a web page, therefore the interface is already familiar to the user.

3   USER FEEDBACK

In this section we discuss the feedback we got from users during the project as well as some problems that arose when attempting to perform usability evaluation.

---

[6]Available at http://www.freedomscientific.com/ fs_products/software_jaws.asp

Visually impaired users were involved in the project from its early design stages, and helped in defining the initial requirements for the tool. They were also involved in analyzing early prototypes of AudioBrowser.

To evaluate AudioBrowser's current version we planned a number of usability tests with its users. This process turned out more problematic than what we had initially envisaged. This was partly due to the typical problem of convincing software developers to perform usability evaluation, but mainly due to difficulties in setting up the testing sessions.

Performing usability tests with users is always a difficult and expensive process. We found this even more so when we are considering visually impaired users. As point out in (Stevens and Edwards, 1996), when trying to evaluate assistive technologies difficulties may arise due to a number of factors:

- Variability in the user population — besides the fact that they will all be visually impaired users, there is not much more that can be said to characterize the target audience of the tool (and even that assumption has turned out to be wrong, as it will be discussed later in this section).

  One related problem that we faced had to do with the variability of use that different users will have for navigating the web. Due to this, identifying representative tasks for analysis turned out to be a problem.

- Absence of alternatives against which to compare results — in our case this was not a problem since there are other tools that attempt to help users in performing similar tasks.

- Absence of a large enough number of test subjects to attain statistical reliability — this was a major issue in our case. In fact, we had some difficulty in finding users willing to participate in the process. We had access to a reduced number of users and some reluctance was noticed in participating due to (self-perceived) lack of technical skills (a "I don't know much about computers, so I can't possibly help you" kind of attitude). We were, nevertheless, able to carry out a few interviews, and it is fair to state that the users that participated did so enthusiastically.

One further problem that we faced related to identifying exactly what was being analyzed in a given context. The AudioBrowser enables its users to access pages on the web. Suppose that, when visiting some specific page, some usability problem is identified. How should we decided whether the problem relates to the tool or whether it relates to the page that is being accessed? For simple (static) pages this might be easy to decide. For more complex sites, such as web based applications (where navigation in the site

becomes an issue), it becomes less clear whether the problem lies with the tool or whether it lies with the site itself.

Due to these issues, we decided to perform informal interviews with the available users, in order to assess their level satisfaction with the tool. More formal usability analysis being left for latter stages.

Even if the reduced number of interviews carried out does not enable us to reach statistically valid conclusions, it enabled us to address some interesting questions regarding the usability of the AudioBrowser tool. The analysis addressed two key issues:

- the core concept of the AudioBrowser — a tool tailored specifically to web page reading;

- the implementation of such concept in the current version of the tool.

Regarding the first issue, the focus on the structure of the text (as represented by the HTML code), instead of focusing on the graphical representation of such text, was clearly validated as an advantage of the AudioBrowser when compared with traditional screen readers. Such focus on the structure of the text enables a reading process more oriented towards the semantic content of the page (instead of its graphical representation), and a better navigation over the information contents of the page.

Regarding the second issue, the tool was found satisfactory in terms of web navigation. However, its implementation as a stand-alone tool (i.e., a tool that is not integrated with the remainder assistive technologies present in the work environment) was found to be an obstacle to its widespread use by the visually impaired community. Aspects such as the use of a separate speech synthesizer from the one used for interaction with the operating systems, create integration problems of the tool regarding the remaining computational environment, and can become difficult barriers for users which are less proficient at the technological level. This is an issue that had not been previously considered, and that clearly deserves further consideration.

Besides the planned usability testing, we have also received reports from regular sighted users who employ the AudioBrowser to check their own web pages regarding structure and accessibility. The hierarchical view of the page provided by the AudioBrowser allows these users to spot potential accessibility and syntax problems that would otherwise be hard to discover. This was a somewhat unexpected application of the tool, and it stresses the difficulties with identifying the end user population of a software artifact.

4 CONCLUSIONS AND FUTURE WORK

On this paper we have presented AudioBrowser, a talking browser that aims at enabling visually impaired users to efficiently navigate the web. AudioBrowser takes advantage of the underlying structure of the document in order to better present its content, and is able to present different views of the same document enabling the user to choose the view that better fits its navigational needs at each moment. This feature is useful not only to visually impaired users, but also for web designers since it allows them to have a broader perspective of the construction of the page. We have received reports of several web designers that are using the AudioBrowser to this effect.

Features and issues related to talking browsers were introduced. In this context some of the main features of the AudioBrowser were described. Focus was on features that provide increased accessibility.

From a usability point of view the main objection, as mentioned previously, is the need to switch back and forth from using the browser to a screen reader, which is still needed for all the other tasks. This is one usability problem that was not foreseen neither by the developers nor the visually impaired people that participated on the AudioBrowser project from the very beginning.

A talking browser and a screen reader are incompatible because they both produce speech, and therefore they can not be working simultaneously.

However talking browsers have several advantages over screen readers and should not be put aside. Talking browsers make it easy to manipulate the web page and present different views, therefore minimizing the scanning time for visually impaired users.

Can talking browsers and screen readers be compatible? A possible solution for this problem could be to have the browser not producing any speech at all. Instead the browser would produce text that would then be read by the screen reader. It may seem absurd to have a talking browser not talking at all, but under this approach there is in fact "talking" to the screen reader. In order for this solution to be successful the process would have to be completely transparent to the user. To the user the application would be an enhanced web browser.

A totally different approach would be to have a web service that provides a subset of the functionality of a talking browser solution. This requires a proxy based approach where a web address would be provided. The page would be transcoded in several views in a web server, and all those views would be supplied to a regular browser, for instance using frames. The user would be able to specify which views would be of interest, and each view, plus the original page, would be

supplied in a separate frame properly identified. Although this approach requires extra bandwidth we believe that with the advent of broadband, and considering that the different views have only text, i.e. no images, the overhead would be bearable considering the extra functionality.

Combining a proxy based approach and a talking browser can provide an enhanced web experience, as the transcoded web pages may contain special tags recognized by the talking browser.

ACKNOWLEDGEMENTS

The research reported in here was supported by SNRIP (The Portuguese National Secretariat of Rehabilitation and Integration for the Disabled) under program CITE 2001, and also FCT (Portuguese Foundation for Science and Technology) and POSI/2001 (Operational Program for the Information Society) with funds partly awarded by FEDER.

REFERENCES

Fernandes, A. R., Martins, F. M., Paredes, H., and Pereira, J. (2001). A different approach to real web accessibility. In Stephanidis, C., editor, *Universal Access in H.C.I.*, *Proceedings of HCI International 2001*, volume 3, pages 723–727. Lawrence Erlbaum Associates.

Filepp, R., Challenger, J., and Rosu, D. (2002). Improving the accessibility of aurally rendered html tables. In *Proceedings of the fifth international ACM conference on Assistive technologies*, pages 9–16. ACM Press.

IBM (2000). Web accessibility transcoding system. http://www.trl.ibm.com/projects/acc_tech/attrans_e.htm.

Jackson-Sanborn, E., Odess-Harnish, K., and Warren, N. (2002). Website accessibility: A study of ada compliance. Technical Report Technical Reports TR-2001-05, University of North CarolinaŨChapel Hill, School of Information and Library Science, http://ils.unc.edu/ils/research/reports/accessibility.pdf.

Rowan, M., Gregor, P., Sloan, D., and Booth, P. (2000). Evaluating web resources for disability access. In *Proceedings of ASSETS 2000*, pages 13–15. ACM, ACM Press.

Stevens, R. D. and Edwards, A. D. N. (1996). An approach to the evaluation of assistive technology. In *Proceedings of ASSETS '96*, pages 64–71. ACM, ACM Press.

Sullivan, T. and Matson, R. (2000). Barriers to use: Usability andcontent accessibility on the webŚs most popular sites. In *Proceedings on the conference on universal usability, 2000*, pages 139–144. ACM Press.

Zajicek, M., Venetsanopoulos, I., and Morrissey, W. (2000). Web access for visually impaired people using active accessibility. In *Proc International Ergonomics Association 2000/HFES 2000*.

PERSONALISED RESOURCE DISCOVERY SEARCHING OVER MULTIPLE REPOSITORY TYPES
Using user and information provider profiling

Boris Rousseau, Parisch Browne, Paul Malone, Mícheál ÓFoghlú
Telecommunications Software Systems Group (TSSG), Waterford Institute of Technology, Waterford, IRELAND
Email: brousseau@tssg.org, pbrowne@tssg.org, pmalone@tssg.org, mofoghlu@tssg.org

Paul Foster, Venura Mendis
BTexact Technologies, Orion Building, Adastral Park, Martlesham Heath, Suffolk, IP5 3RE, United Kingdom
Email: paul.w.foster@bt.com, venura.2.mendis@bt.com

Keywords: E-Learning, personalisation, profiling, user profile, information provider profile, resource discovery, multiple repository types.

Abstract: The success of the Information Society, with the overabundance of online multimedia information, has become an obstacle for users to discover pertinent resources. For those users, the key is the refinement of resource discovery as the choice and complexity of available online content continues to grow. The work presented in this paper will address this issue by representing complex extensible user and information provider profiles and content metadata using XML and the provision of a middle canonical language to aid in learner-to-content matching, independent of the underlying metadata format. This approach can provide a federated search solution leading to personalise resource discovery based on user requirements and preferences, seamlessly searching over multiple repository types. The novelty of the work includes the complex extensible user profiles, information provider profiles, the canonical language and the federated search strategy. Although, the work presented is focused on E-Learning, the general ideas could be applied to any resource discovery or information retrieval system.

1 INTRODUCTION

Most current E-Learning resource discovery systems (GESTALT, 1998) employ relatively simple algorithms when searching for content. The more complex of these resource discovery services (RDS) may use a thesaurus to find similar words and build a set of related pages. This allows the user to be provided with a 'Find Similar Pages' option. Although early research in the area of Artificial Intelligence (Spark, 1978) provided some solutions, a successful Information Retrieval system should take into account the identity of the end user performing the search. Such identity incorporates their needs, what type of content they prefer or indeed whether they have available resources to access the content found. Future successful RDSs must consider these factors when executing search queries. This can be best achieved through the use of

metadata. Metadata (Day, 2000) is traditionally defined as information on the resources, not only to indicate the nature of the content, but also to provide information about the user as well as the provider of the content.

In this work, models for describing this metadata are explored and new ones developed where necessary. This paper will also demonstrate how this metadata can be used to provide personalised resource discovery, thus facilitating the user's requirement for pertinent information, and the provider's requirement for maintaining multiple, diverse, repository types, while at the same time facilitating the business model that can support this.

The Information Society Technologies (IST) project GUARDIANS (GUARDIANS, 2000) has undertaken this approach and this paper describes a large part of the work. This paper will present and address the issues faced during the project regarding

316

I. Seruca et al. (eds.), Enterprise Information Systems VI, 316–324.

.ser and information provider profiling as well as he search strategies to enable customisable resource discovery. The first section will cover the user and nformation provider profiling, in addition to content netadata extensions for preferences weighting acilitating the ranking of results found. The main ection will present the work carried out on the anonical language and the federated search strategy andling multiple repository types to provide ersonalised resource discovery.

? PROFILING

?.1 User Profile

Vith the growth of e-commerce and the Internet, the athering of information on preferences, activities nd characteristics of clients and customers has ecome quite important, as this information can acilitate personalised content delivery. The idea of ser profiling can be summarised as "one that enders the user with an experience that is tailored to is/her current situation" (Suryanarayana, Hjelm 002). The issue of user profiling is quite complex s such profile should be as generic as possible with compromise between storing too little and too nuch information. A starting point is to use XML eXtensible Markup Language, 2000), in order to be xportable to other system components and to ncorporate information about the user's preferred anguage and the technological platform for ommunication.

As described in (Rousseau et al., 2003), nvestigation of the existing profiling standards evealed that while each of the standards nvestigated had its own merits it was felt that none ally addressed the profiling needs of the project. pecifications researched include the IMS Learner nformation Package (IMS LIP, 2001) specification, he IEEE Public and Private Information (IEEE API, 2002) Learner standard, and the TV Anytime TV Anytime, 1999) and vCard (vCard, 1996) pecifications. Based on this research, a complex, xtensible, generic user profile model is developed nainly based on the IMS LIP specification, the jeneric User Profile (GUP). The profile contains nformation on the user stored in 'sections' as shown n Table 1.

Table 1: Sections within the GUARDIANS Generic User Profile

GUP Section	Description
Accessibility	User platform, applications, disabilities, languages etc.
Affiliation	Organisations with which the learner has associations or membership.
Usage History	What the learner has previously searched and/or accessed.
Relationship	Relationships between GUP elements.
Interest	Interests of the learner, classified by domain.
Contact Details	The learner's contact details.
Qualifications	Formal qualifications that the learner has previously acquired.
Goals	Learning objectives of the learner.

Although the IMS LIP specification is quite complete, it was felt that extensions where needed to facilitate the search process.

A first extension is the usage history building on the TV Anytime forum specification. Such extension allows to record previous searches information and to reuse it in future ones. A usage history instance fragment follows:

```
<history>
  <InstanceId>history_01</InstanceId>
  <actionhistory>
    <datetime>2002-07-23T20:00</datetime>
    <action>
      <defaulttype>Select</defaulttype>
      <item itemused="INSP">
        <value>NASA</value>
      </item>
      <url>http://www.nasa.com</url>
    </action>
  </actionhistory>
</history>
```

The 'action' subsection depicts whether the user has selected some content (itemused="Content") or an INSP (itemused="INSP"). In the case above, if the user decides to do his next search using "astronomy" as a keyword, "NASA" related content is more likely to come up on his search results.

A second extension allows the user to further refine his/her preferences indicating greater or lesser importance with weightings. These weightings help at the query-building phase to refine further the search and at the rating of results found stages. A weighted fragment follows:

```
<language weighting="10">it</language>
<language weighting="2">en</language>
```

With this in place, the user gets resources preferably in Italian. English content is also suitable but with a lesser importance.

2.2 Information Service Provider Profile

In the standards development community, much of the profiling work seems excessively devoted to user profiles and how they might be used for resource discovery personalisation and communication with a single Service Provider. However, in GUARDIANS this process is seen as only half of the story, the user should choose which service provider he/she wants to enrol with or use. This section details the requirements for storing information on service providers. It will determine what information must be stored in order to adequately describe a service provider and its content and how it may be represented.

The Information Service Provider (INSP) Profile data-model can be used to store information on a service provider on a per-repository basis. It stores both domain specific metadata and generic metadata and defines an aggregated view of the information stored in its repository. As the INSP Profile is essentially an aggregation or summary of the content and services hosted or offered by the INSP, one of its functions must be to act as a collection level description such as those defined by Research Support Library Programme (RSLP, 1999) and UKOLN (UKOLN). In addition it must also function as a searchable resource and be able to operate across multiple domains.

IMS Learning Resource Metadata Information Model Version 1.2 (IMS, 2001) is a specification derived from Version 3.5 Learning Object Metadata Scheme working document of the IEEE LTSC LOM Working Group (IEEE LTSC LOM, 2002). The differences lie in the redefinition of some of the elements, some of which have a new type and/or a new description and/or a new multiplicity. Although both specifications are suitable for the INSP profile, IMS seems to have scope according to up-to-date work coming from IMS and IEEE.

The key information held in the INSP profile is shown in Table 2.

Table 2: Sections within the GUARDIANS INSP profile

INSP Section	Description
Service Name	The common name of the service.
Description	Description of the service.
Contact Details	Information service contact details.
Metametadata	Detail about the metadata contained in the profile.
Legal Constraints	Legal Issues surrounding the use of the content held by the INSP.
Payment information	Details of payment methods accepted by the INSP.
Security Information	Level of security required to access the various elements in this profile.
Relationships	Relationships between instance metadata stored locally or in other INSP profiles.
Classifications	Classification system.
Taxonpaths	A taxonomic path in a specific classification system. Each succeeding level is a refinement in the definition of the higher level.
Keywords	Selected keywords from multiple keyword lists. Keywords can be weighted.

One important element in the INSP profile is the classification. Similarly to a library it represents the categories covered by the service provider. An instance fragment follows:

```
<classification>
  <purpose>
    <choice>Educational content in
    Science</choice>
  </purpose>
  <taxonpath>
    <source>www.cosmos.com</source>
    <taxon>
      <identifier>Stars</identifier>
      <entry>004.41</entry>
    </taxon>
    ...
  </taxonpath>
</classification>
```

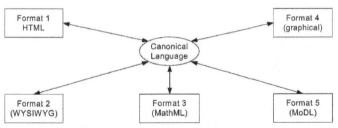

Figure 1: Canonical data model solution

From this extract, the 'identifier' section indicates that the service provider offers some resources on the subject of Software Engineering.

There is a requirement in the INSP data model to allow INSPs to offer hosting to content providers in multiple domains or application areas. In addition, some information service providers may wish to extend their profile with other information outside of the standard structure defined above.

The obvious solution is to use a two-category structure: one generic category (for contact details, legal constraints, payment information, etc) and an unbound number of domain specific categories (for keywords and classifications) to handle multiple repository types.

2.3 Storage and Retrieval of Profile Information

The overall system is based upon profiles. The success of the query depends largely on how those profiles are mapped and on the profile retrieval performance. For storage and retrieval of user and service provider profiles information, different solutions were investigated:

- Local client file system storage.
- Central RDBMS Database storage.
- Central LDAP Directory Service.

Although, storing profile information on a local drive is convenient, the issue of storing space would arise, as the number of profiles gets larger. Such solution would require investigating and implementing compression mechanisms, which would ultimately slow down the profile information retrieval process.

The second solution is to store the data in a relational database system such as Oracle (Chang et al., 2000). The general principles are discussed in (Kanne and Moerkotte, 2000) and (Florescu and Kossmann, 1999). However, at the time of the implementation, no mature, reliable XML database management solution could solve this problem. Also, such a deployment is heavyweight and

consequently would affect the systems' performance.

The final and chosen option is to store the data in a Directory Service such as the Lightweight Directory Access Protocol, a simple variant of the X.500 ISO standard (Howes et al., 1995). Some basic classes for persons in an organisation are directly derived from the X500 Directory Services standards. A directory is a specialised database optimised for storage, manipulation and retrieval of information in a globally scalable system, supporting sophisticated filtering capabilities and high volume search request.

However, unlike database management systems, directory services do not support complicated transactions or rollbacks. A profile in a directory service refers to a person or an organisation having one or more relationships with the organisation responsible for the maintenance of the directory. For instance, an Internet Service Provider that stores personal details and access rights. For an LDAP Directory Service to implement a profile, the information should be stored as classes ranging from abstract to more specific ones. For instance, abstract classes could be general information such as contact details and description.

3 CANONICAL LANGUAGE

An underlying concept of the GUARDIANS is that it has no knowledge of the metadata formats on which the repositories are based. Hence, some mechanism is needed to transform the metadata from one format to another. For example, the water molecule ($H2O$) can be written in HTML as something like:

<FONT CLASS="molecule">H₂0</FONT>

Mathematicians will represent this molecule in MathML (MathML, 2001) as:

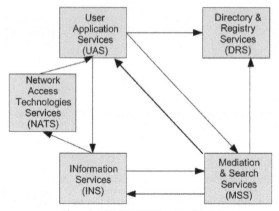

Figure 2: GUARDIANS Functional Architecture

```
<math>
  <msub>
    <mi>H</mi>
    <mn>2</mn>
  </msub>
  <mi>O</mi>
</math>
```

Whereas chemists might use the MoDL (Molecular Dynamics Language) (MoDL, 1999)

```
<DEFINE type='molecule' name='Water' >
<atom type='O' id='o1' position='0 0 0' />
<atom type='H' id='h1' position='-2 1 0.5'/>
<atom type='H' id='h2' position='2 1 0.5'/>
<bond from='h1' to='o1'/>
<bond from='h2' to='o1'/>
</DEFINE>
```

After investigation, the most suitable model for transforming structured metadata was determined to be a canonical data model rather than providing the transformations between all those formats. This model requires that as a new metadata format be added it is only necessary to create a mapping between the new metadata format and the canonical middle language. This is shown in Figure 1.

The Basic Semantic Registry (ISO/IEC 11179 Part 6, 1997) makes use of this canonical language (CL) to translate from one metadata format into one or more other(s). Most significantly, the BSR is used to map user preferences to content metadata representing the information provider's content, regardless of the content metadata format. It is the job of the BSR to provide mappings between the user profile and each of these target metadata types.

As the BSR is responsible for all XML metadata conversions, it uses XSLT (XSL Transformations, 1999). Of course because XSLT is quite a specific language, it is sometimes necessary to re-format the data to enable its successful processing and translation.

4 FEDERATED SEARCH STRATEGY

The personalised resource discovery strategy is performed by a software component set called Mediation and Search Services (MSS, figure 2), which comprises a Mediator and a Search Service. For the purpose of the federated search strategy we will only concentrate on the components of interest for the search: the Mediation and Search Services.

The resource discovery strategy works on a three-phase basis. The initial pass, performed by the Mediator, is to select INSPs who can provide content suitable for the learner initiating the search. The second phase of the search is performed by the Search Service component of the MSS, which searches on the user selected INSPs for the relevant content. The third phase is the results collection and ranking, delivering the pool of results back to the user.

4.1 Finding the Relevant INSP

This is achieved through the Mediator component matching the user's profile (GUP) with the INSP profiles stored in the Directory and Registry Service (DRS). The underlying technology used in this matching is XSLT (XSL Transformations, 1999).

The Mediator serves as the middle tier interacting with the INSP profile, the graphical user interface (UAS in figure 2) and the actual Search Service. From the UAS, in interaction with the user profile, the user defines his current preferences and keywords to formulate a search request. Those user preferences are then mapped to the canonical language. A sample extract is as follows:

Table 3: GUP preferences mapping to the canonical language

GUP	CL
//accessibility/language='en'	//general/description/language='en'
//accessibility/preference/refinement='video/quicktime'	//general/technical/preference='video/quicktime'
//accessibility/preferences/preference/type='Operating System'	//general/technical/title='Operating System'

Those types of mappings are expressed in XSLT (Bradley, 2000) as simple 'select-match' expressions, which are used to select the current element to match it to a particular target element.

Once this mapping is achieved, an XPath query (Clark and DeRose, 1999) can be formulated in the canonical language with the relevant user information. This query formulation process is similar to the second phase's, hence will be described in the next section.

4.2 Finding the Relevant Resources

For each of the INSPs selected by the Mediator, a subset of the INSP profile is retrieved from the DRS. Through this mechanism the location, type (query type) and format (metadata schema) of each INSP's metadata repository is discovered.

In the next step, preferences are processed using an XSLT document similar to the one defined in Table 3 but this time with the INSP information. Once the previous step is performed a general query is formulated, based on the canonical language (CL). However, this query cannot be executed against any repository since it is schema "unaware". To obtain a schema specific query, the Search Service has to call the BSR. A query is built according to the type and format of the repository. An example of such query for an English-speaking user requesting a search with 'universe' as a keyword and 'quicktime' as his preferred format could be:

```
<search>
 <repositoryname>rep 1</repositoryname>
 <querystring>[!CDATA
  /lom/general/language[text()="en"] |
  /lom/general//lom [(/lom/general/title/
langstring[contains(text(),"universe") or
  /lom/general/description/langstring[
```

```
  contains(text(),"universe")]]
  /lom/technical/format[text()="video/
quicktime"]
 </querystring>
 <querylanguage>XPATH</querylanguage>
</search>
```

In this example, 'universe' is the only input from the user, language and format are derived from the user's profile. This query is then delivered to the location specified and results added to the overall pool of results.

4.3 Results Handling

A result manager component of the MSS is in charge of collecting, ranking and re-formatting the results before they are sent back to the user. The idea is to create a result collection, which is parsed and used for ranking. This result collection is ranked according to the preferences, keywords, etc. This was developed in such a way to allow extension of the rating algorithm, for instance to use other fields from the User Profile. Once accomplished, the results are stored into the following structure:

```
<resourceResult id="r.1">
<title>The Sun</title>
<description>The movie describe some of the
different satellites studying the Sun: The
hubble telescope, Solar max, and the very
large array in new Mexico; and information
about the solar system.</description>
<location>http://www.ist-guardians.org/
astronomy/Sun.mov</location>
<ranking>0.68</ranking>
<format>application/quicktime movie</format>
<inspName>INSP 1</inspName>
</resourceResult>
```

This example represents the XML structure of the results, which are returned by the Search Service. Basically, results are represented the same way as a normal web search engine with the following features describing the XML document above:

- A title to identify the result found.
- A description, to briefly identify what the resource is about.
- A location, to provide a link to the resource found.
- A ranking, as a degree of relevance of this result that will be displayed to the user later on.

- A format representing the resource format for display purposes. For instance, the type of movie, audio, text to know the platform and requirement for displaying it to the user.
- An INSP name, in case the user wants to come back to this particular INSP later on. (Part of the action history in the user profile)

The results discovered are rated using a simplistic mechanism as follows:
1: an arbitrary base score (30%) is given for all results (since it has been found, matching a minimum of one keyword).
2: a score is given for each keyword found in the title (20%).
3: a score is given for each keyword found in the description (6%).
4: a bonus score is given if the title or description contains more than one keyword (10 and 5%).
5: a score is given for the preference level at which the result was found (3%).
A greater number of preferences matched, means a better, more personalised result for the user.

5 CONCLUSION AND FUTURE WORK

As the number of resources on the Internet continues to grow, user faces the issue of information overload. In this situation, reliable search tools that enable personalisation of resource discovery and information retrieval becomes crucial. This is specifically true in the E-Learning domain, where users (students or researchers) have a clear need to retrieve information relevant to their preferences (language, interest, platforms, etc). Simple text-based search engines are not sufficient anymore. Several improvements have been made in the past few years showing a better search accuracy. For instance, Google (Page, 1998) now provides a new improved HTML based search engine with regard to quicker delivery and better search accuracy. Although such tools are successful, it is only a partial solution, it only delays the problem as more and more information (educational, recreational, etc) becomes available and as the number users still increases.

A complete solution to this problem is the combination of current and emerging technologies and standards to offer better interaction between the user and federated search strategies. This solution, presented in this paper, has been researched and implemented by the author in the E-Learning context of the GUARDIANS European project as part of its Mediation Service component. It offers a very efficient search facility that enhances the user's learning experience through the usage of smart functionalities (components and resources) for discovery and retrieval of educational resources. Although this work is based on E-Learning resources, one could easily fit it into the overall context of information retrieval on the Internet.

Although the search strategy using XPath performed successfully, it was felt that the queries were limited with regards to performance and flexibility. Indeed, to incorporate most of the user preferences, the XPath was complicated and major results reformatting had to be performed. For this reason this initial work was extended and an XML querying solution using XQuery (Boag et al., 2002) was proposed in (Rousseau, Leray, 2003).

Another important point to consider is that the matching between user profile and metadata was limited but it would be possible to include more information about the user. For example, the search could use the affiliation to only search for INSPs with which the user is affiliated. It could also use qualification details to only retrieve information relevant to the user's previous qualification, diplomas and other licenses or certifications. However, the user profile might still be extended with new features according to future development in the E-Learning community.

The ranking algorithm implementation was an interesting part of the work. However, with time constraints and the lack of information about how to actually develop a precise ranking mechanism. It was first developed as a basic algorithm, only taking care of the keywords. For a possible commercialisation purpose, it should have taken into account a few more feature from the user profile, specifically provide a complex algorithm using weighting attributes. It is expected that the authors will be involved into future research in the area of stopwords, tf.ifd, coordination level, etc (Baeza-Yates, 1999).

Nowadays, there is a lot of hype around agents. In the context of this work, an agent would enable automatic discovery of the user's platform capabilities. This issue was encountered while populating the user profile with some device information. Hence, a typical user would be unaware of its device(s) capabilities and will require an automatic detection mechanism. Also, a good balance between static and dynamic profile information should be researched further to present the user with a reliable profile that requires the minimum efforts to fill in. A form of interaction between the profiling mechanism and the user is therefore crucial to get some feedbacks to the system.

The abstract representation of data on the World Wide Web, also known as the Semantic Web

(Berners et al., 2001), is gradually taking over the current HTML based Web. In the near future, the development in the area will lead in significant new possibilities to enhance and process the data that they merely display at present. Hence, programs will be able to exchange information with others and automate services. Such functionalities together with the flexibility of XML will be promoted using agents, that will help users tracking down resources and match them against their criteria and preferences.

REFERENCES

Baeza-Yates, R. and Ribeiro-Neto, B. Modern Information Retrieval, *Addison-Wesley, ACM Press, 1st edition (May 1999)*. ISBN: 020139829X

Berners-Lee T., Hendler J. and Lassila O. The Semantic Web. A new form of Web content that is meaningful to computers will unleash a revolution of new possibilities. *Scientific American, May 17, 2001*.

Boag, S., Chamberlin, D., Fernandez, M.F., Florescu, D., Robie, J., Simeon, J., and Stefanescu, M., eds 2002. XQuery 1.0: An XML Query Language. *W3C Working Draft*, http://www.w3.org/TR/2002/WD-xquery-20020430/

Bradley, N., September 7, 2000. The XSL Companion. *Addison-Wesley Pub Co; 1st edition*. ISBN: 0201674874

Chang, B., Scardina, M., Karun, K., Kiritzov, S., Macky, I., Novoselsky, A. and Ramakrishnan, N., 2000. ORACLE XML Handbook. *Oracle Press*. ASIN: 007212489X

Clark, J., and DeRose, S. eds 1999. XML Path Language (XPath) version 1.0. *W3C Recommendation*. http://www.w3.org/TR/xpath

Day, M., Summer 2001. Metadata in a nutshell. *Article published in Information Europe, p. 11. Information Europe quarterly magazine of EBLIDA*.

Florescu, D., and Kossmann, D., 1999. A Performance Evaluation of Alternative Mapping Schemes for Storing XML Data in a Relational Database. *Technical report no. 3680, INRIA, Le Chesnay Cedex, France*.

GESTALT, Getting Educational Systems Talking Across Leading-Edge Technologies, EU project (started in October 1998) Web Site: http://www.fdgroup.com/gestalt/

GUARDIANS project, 2000. *Gateway for User Access to Remote Distributed Information and Network Services, started in October 2000*. Web site: http://www.ist-guardians.tv/

Howes, T., Yeong, W. and Kille, S, 1995. Lightweight Directory Access Protocol (LDAP). *The Internet Society, RFC 1770*.

IEEE Learning Technology Standards Committee WG12: Learning Object Model, 6 March 2002. http://ltsc.ieee.org/wg12/

IEEE PAPI, 01 February 2002. *IEEE Public and Private Information draft 8 specifications*. Available at: http://www.edutool.com/papi/

IMS LIP version 1.00, 18 March 2001. *Learner Information Package Specification*. Available at: http://www.imsglobal.org/profiles/index.cfm

IMS Learning Resource Metadata Specification, 01 October 2001. http://www.imsglobal.org/metadata/index.cfm

ISO/IEC 11179 Part 6, 1997. *Information technology - Specification and standardization of data elements - Part 6: Registration of data elements*. Available online at: http://www.iso.ch/

Kanne, C.-C., and Moerkotte, G., 2000. Efficient Storage of XML Data. *Proceeding of the International Conference on Data Engineering*. San Diego, California, p. 198.

MathML, W3C math specification, 21 February 2001, http://www.w3.org/Math

MoDL - Molecular Dynamics Language project, 29 July 1999, http://xml.coverpages.org/modl.html

Page, L., Brin, S. The anatomy of a large-scale hypertextual Web search engine, *Computer Networks and ISDN Systems, Volume 30, Issues 1-7, April 1998, Pages 107-117*.

RDS. Distributed Systems Technology Centre: Research Data Unit. *Resource Discovery – A Definition*. Available from http://www.dstc.edu.au/RDU/rd_define.html

Rousseau, B., Browne, P., Malone, P., ÓFoghlú, M., 2003. User Profiling for Content Personalisation in Information Retrieval. *In the ACM Symposium on Applied Computing, special track on Information Access and Retrieval*. ACM Press

Rousseau, B., Leray, E., ÓFoghlú, M., 2003. Metadata & Information Management issues in XML-based Mediation. *In ICEIS'03 Fifth International Conference on Enterprise Information Systems, Angers, FRANCE, pages 375-379*. ICEIS Press.

RSLP. Research Support Libraries Programme British initiative, September 1999, http://www.rslp.ac.uk/

Spark, K. Jones, Artificial Intelligence: What can it offer to Information Retrieval. *In Proceedings of the Informatics 3, Aslib, ed., London, 1978*.

Suryanarayana, L., Hjelm, J., May 7-11, 2002. Profiles for Situated Web. Johan. *In WWW 2002, Honolulu, Hawaii, USA*. ACM Press 1-58113-449-5/02/0005.

TV Anytime forum, formed in 1999. Web site, available at: http://www.tv-anytime.org/

UKOLN, centre of expertise in digital information management, University of Bath, England. http://www.ukoln.ac.uk/

vCard, December 1996. The Internet Mail Consortium (IMC), available at: http://www.imc.org/pdi/vcardoverview.html

XML, the eXtensible Markup Language 1.0 second Edition. *W3C Recommendation 6 October 2000*, http://www.w3.org/TR/REC-xml

XSL Transformations (XSLT), version 1, *W3C Recommendations, 16 November 1999*, http://www.w3.org/TR/xslt

AUTHOR INDEX